DATE			

BAKER & TAYLOR

Introduction

to

RABBINIC
LITERATURE

THE ANCHOR BIBLE REFERENCE LIBRARY is designed to be a third major component of the Anchor Bible group, which includes the Anchor Bible commentaries on the books of the Old Testament, the New Testament, and the Apocrypha and the Anchor Bible Dictionary. While the Anchor Bible commentaries and the Anchor Bible Dictionary are structurally defined by their subject matter, the Anchor Bible Reference Library serves as a supplement on the cutting edge of the most recent scholarship. The series is open-ended; its scope and reach are nothing less than the biblical world in its totality, and its methods and techniques the most up-to-date available or devisable. Separate volumes will deal with one or more of the following topics relating to the Bible: anthropology, archaeology, ecology, economy, geography, history, languages and literatures, philosophy, religion(s), theology.

As with the Anchor Bible commentaries and the Anchor Bible Dictionary, the philosophy underlying the Anchor Bible Reference Library finds expression in the following: the approach is scholarly, the perspective is balanced and fair-minded, the methods are scientific, and the goal is to inform and enlighten. Contributors are chosen on the basis of their scholarly skills and achievements, and they come from a variety of religious backgrounds and communities. The books in the Anchor Bible Reference Library are intended for the broadest possible readership, ranging from world-class scholars, whose qualifications match those of the authors, to general readers, who may not have special training or skill in studying the Bible but are as enthusiastic as any dedicated professional in expanding their knowledge of the Bible and its world.

David Noel Freedman
GENERAL EDITOR

THE ANCHOR BIBLE REFERENCE LIBRARY

Introduction

to

RABBINIC
LITERATURE

Jacob Neusner

ABRL

DOUBLEDAY

New York   London   Toronto   Sydney   Auckland

IN MEMORY OF PAMELA VERMES

ohevet yisrael

THE ANCHOR BIBLE REFERENCE LIBRARY
PUBLISHED BY DOUBLEDAY
a division of Bantam Doubleday Dell Publishing Group, Inc.,
1540 Broadway, New York, New York 10036

THE ANCHOR BIBLE REFERENCE LIBRARY, DOUBLEDAY, and the portrayal of an anchor with the
letters ABRL are trademarks of Doubleday, a division of Bantam Doubleday Dell
Publishing Group, Inc.

Library of Congress Cataloging-in-Publication Data

Neusner, Jacob, 1932–
    Introduction to rabbinic literature / Jacob Neusner.—1st ed.
      p. cm.—(The Anchor Bible reference library)
    Includes index.
    ISBN 0-385-47093-2
    1. Rabbinical literature—History and criticism.   2. Judaism—History—Talmudic period,
10–425. I. Title. II. Series.
BM496.5.N48   1994
296.1—dc20   93-28109
                                                             CIP

CONTENTS

PREFACE

THIS BOOK INTRODUCES RABBINIC LITERATURE AS THAT CANON REACHED CLO-
sure at the end of late antiquity, in the seventh century c.e. (= a.d.[1]). The Judaic
canon is presented both as a whole (in Part One) and document by document (in
Parts Two through Five). In each case we pay close attention to the identification
of the respective documents' distinctive traits of rhetoric, logic of coherent discourse, and topical, even propositional, program. In this way we differentiate each
document from all others, doing so in a manner consistent for all documents
equally, by appeal to objective criteria of readily identified characteristics.

The audience for this introduction is English-speaking readers with an interest
in rabbinic Judaism who wish to know the character of each of that Judaism's
normative and canonical writings, beyond the Hebrew Scriptures of ancient Israel.
In all cases, I provide a sufficient sample so that readers enjoy a direct encounter,
in my form-analytical translation, with the writing itself. Since rabbinic literature
took shape during the nascent and formative age of Christianity, I address at appropriate points the particular interests of those engaged by the other great religion
aborning in the Land of Israel in the earliest centuries c.e. and provide a measure
of perspective through remarks of comparison and contrast.

[1] c.e. stands for Common Era, often used as a more neutral reference point than a.d. All dates to follow
refer to the Common Era unless otherwise noted by b.c.e. = Before the Common Era = b.c.

My goal is that readers may be able to open English translations of the documents introduced here and immediately find themselves at home, quite familiar with the territory. That explains why I have given generous samples of each of the documents, in the theory that once readers have worked their way through the specified passages, they will have a model for further study on their own. Admittedly, I have a second goal, which should be exposed. I place a very high value on the documents set forth here, which I conceive to take their place at the heights of humanity's intellectual achievement and heritage. Sheer love of the writing made me want to share with the readers a small sample of a vast treasury of wisdom, learning, beauty, but, above all, intellectual incandescence. Here is Israel's light, beyond Scripture Israel's treasury, for all to see. This introduction does not pretend to objectivity on the intellectual excellence and spiritual quality of what is introduced. I cannot imagine any reader of these pages who would want things any other way.

The selection of documents accords with the present scholarly consensus. That consensus assigns to the formative age of the Judaism portrayed in rabbinic literature the Mishnah, Tosefta, and two Talmuds, on the one side, and the Tannaite Midrash compilations focused upon the Pentateuch, Mekhilta, Sifra, and the two Sifrés, Numbers and Deuteronomy, as well as those produced by the authorities of the Talmuds, called Amoraim: Genesis Rabbah, Leviticus Rabbah, Lamentations Rabbah, Pesiqta deRab Kahana (and its imitation, Pesiqta Rabbati), Esther Rabbah I, Song of Songs Rabbah, Ruth Rabbah, on the other. In addition tractate Abot, the Fathers, and its talmud, Abot deRabbi Natan, the Fathers According to Rabbi Nathan, belong to the rabbinic literature of this period.[2] Rabbinic literature, of course, extends from late antiquity through medieval and modern times and continues to flourish in our own day. We deal only with its formative age.

A word of explanation on the translations given here is required. All translations are my own. They follow a single, consistent reference system. I use a Roman numeral to identify a completed unit of thought ("chapter"), one that can be fully understood within the limits of its own materials, an Arabic numeral for a cogent but contingent propositional unit (a "paragraph" of a larger composition) that is both comprehensible in its own terms but also contingent for full meaning on a larger structure, and a letter for the smallest whole unit of thought (a "sentence").

In this way, readers immediately see how I conceive discourse to be constructed, being able to compare the formal traits of one whole unit of thought with another, one cogent but contingent proposed unit with another, and so on upward. The entire analytical discussion of rhetoric, logic of coherent discourse, and even topical and propositional program, document by document, begins in this form-analytical translation of mine. No other translations into English or any

---

[2] I follow the catalog of Moses D. Herr, "Midrash," *Encyclopaedia Judaica* 11:1512.

other language provide any reference system at all, beyond (in some few cases) page and line numbers, alongside chapter numbers; the translations of the Talmud of Babylonia give page number, with obverse/reverse signs (i.e., 18A, 18B); those of the Talmud of the Land of Israel give page number or Mishnah-paragraph number, and in neither case are we told what the translator conceives constitute the completed units of thought or the components thereof. In the translation of the Midrash compilations matters are still more chaotic. The reason that I found it necessary to make my own translations of all of the documents was that no existing editions in the original Hebrew or translations made possible any analytical work whatsoever, and none had been done.

This is the book that I have always wanted to write. But it has taken me a long time to do it—nearly forty years, from the day, in 1954, that I first met a page of the Talmud of Babylonia and, at the age of twenty-two, found my intellectual home: the first genuinely interesting set of intellectual problems I had encountered, the most consistently compelling ones I ever addressed. Utterly engaged by the document and then the literature that reached its climax in that writing, I determined then to spend my life finding out precisely what it was and where it fit into the life of the humanity's intellect. From then to now, I have walked an absolutely straight path, and every single day has marked a step forward for me. Here I summarize in a systematic way what I have thought important to learn about rabbinic literature as a whole, and each of its components in the formative age of Judaism.

I owe the idea of writing this book to Professor Morna Hooker, Cambridge University. To others the idea for this book must seem obvious: systematically lay out in one place results covering so many documents, in monographs published in so many volumes, as to be inaccessible to everybody but me. I took for granted everyone knew what I knew. But in fact the idea of writing a systematic introduction to rabbinic literature came to me from a dear friend, and when she first offered it, I did not see her point.

In the summer semester of 1992 when I was Fellow at Clare Hall, Cambridge, I had the good fortune to get to know Professor Hooker, and her husband, Professor David Stacey, neighbors of mine in Robinson Hall, across the street from my college. When we first met, she asked me what I was doing in Cambridge. I told her I was completing my final monographic exercise on the complete, systematic description of the entirety of rabbinic literature. This last task was the large-scale characterization of the relationships between the two Talmuds, the Talmud of the Land of Israel and the Talmud of Babylonia. Things were not coming out as I had expected, and I was finding the results, shading over as they were into hermeneutics and theology, fascinating and puzzling. But when I had solved that problem, I should have completed a quarter-century of work, I told her.

Courteously forestalling the anticipated disquisition on Yerushalmi-Bavli comparisons with which I was preoccupied, she asked me very simply, "Well, what in general do I have to know about rabbinic literature?" She meant, herself and her students of the New Testament, and the same question covered her husband and his students of the Old Testament. And both clearly had in mind, as well, anyone with an interest in antiquity. People in general knew that rabbinic literature formed a massive set of sources relevant to a wide variety of questions; but a systematic guide to that literature, providing guidance into the reading of the documents one by one, was lacking.

I was puzzled, thinking I'd already spelled out the answer to that question. After all, I had nearly finished the work of translating, and writing an introduction to, each of the documents. Her question rested; we went on to other things. But by her, in her tactful manner, I was made to realize that while I knew what I had learned about each of the documents of rabbinic literature, no one else did or probably ever would. I had produced too large a corpus of writing to expect that to find out what I wished to say about the documents overall, someone would work through the hundreds of volumes of translations, introductions, and studies. I thought I knew precisely what she meant. Absorbed in my own thought, I did not; I was obtuse.

In response to what I thought was the answer to her question, I wrote *What We Cannot Show, We Do Not Know. Rabbinic Literature and the New Testament* (Philadelphia, 1994: Trinity Press International). In correspondence I showed her the plan of the book I had written thinking to answer her question. Very promptly, and with impeccable tact, she wrote back, "No, that's not quite what I meant. I meant, tell me about the different documents." Only then did I realize that Professor Hooker was unlikely to collect and work through all of my translations and introductions to all of the rabbinic literature; nor would anybody else. The many colleagues who wished to know what that literature offers also might find useful a complete picture in a single book.

So, she made it clear, it was time to put everything together in a reasonably accessible and wholly systematic way. Since no one was likely to go looking up what I had had to say about each of the documents that I had translated and introduced, what was needed from me was a complete précis—method and result—document by document. I brought the idea to my main publishers, and, among them, Doubleday immediately agreed. This I present here, in this one place summarizing the main findings of half a lifetime of everyday work.

The editor of this series, Professor David Noel Freedman, generously devoted his best energies to my manuscript and made thousands of valuable suggestions, all of which I adopted. He also made of me a lifelong friend and admirer, because of his wit, learning, critical acumen, and sheer devotion to the work of others. I gladly acknowledge a formidable debt to him for his work on this book and on its sequel and express my thanks to one of the academy's truly splendid citizens. He teaches us all what it means to be a colleague.

While I have enjoyed the work required for every one of the five hundred books I have published, among them all, accomplishing this work of summary and conclusion and closure has given me the greatest satisfaction. First, it marks a definitive closure; I have accomplished my goals. More important, it allows me, after all, to go off in completely new directions—new to me, utterly untouched by anyone else—concerning the historical description of the theology of rabbinic Judaism. From the day I first saw a page of the Talmud of Babylonia, which was just after the end of the Festival of Sukkot in 1954, to the present day, I have asked myself the questions that now, with the rabbinic literature in hand, I can address; nearly forty years of work come to a conclusion here and permit me now to begin to ask a further set of questions about Judaism.

I call attention also to my *Classics of Judaism* (Louisville, 1995: Westminster/ John Knox Press), which is a presentation for the purpose of a college textbook of some of the results that are given here. There are numerous topical intersections, but little overlap.

In the bibliographical footnotes that head each chapter, I refer to the other works of mine, the results of which are set forth in a very concise way in this book.

Since the work on the Bavli set into perspective all my prior findings, this book most immediately sets forth viewpoints formed in the past three years. In connection with the completion of my research in its final phase, on the Talmud of Babylonia, I acknowledge with thanks also the overseas universities that have afforded to me research opportunities during the summer semesters since coming to Florida, when that work came to its fruition. These are the University of Frankfurt for the Martin Buber Professorship; Clare Hall, Cambridge University, for the position of Visiting Fellow, later converted to Life Member; and Åbo Akademi, the Swedish-language university of Åbo, Finland, for a Research Professorship awarded by the Research Institute of the Åbo Academy Foundation.

No work of mine can omit reference to the exceptionally favorable circumstances in which I conduct my research. I wrote this book at the University of South Florida, which has afforded me an ideal situation in which to conduct a scholarly life. I express my thanks for not only the advantage of a Distinguished Research Professorship, which must be the best job in the world for a scholar, but also of a substantial research expense fund, ample research time, and some stimulating and cordial colleagues. In the prior chapters of my career, I never knew a university that prized professors' scholarship and publication and treated with respect the professors who actively pursue research. The University of South Florida, and nine universities that comprise the Florida State University System as a whole, exemplify the high standards of professionalism that prevail in publicly sponsored higher education in the United States and provide the model that privately sponsored universities would do well to emulate. Here there are rules, achievement counts, and presidents, provosts, and deans honor and respect the university's principal mission: scholarship, scholarship alone—both in the classroom and in publication.

My beloved colleague James Strange read several of the chapters to advise me on whether I was following a model that would accomplish my goals, and I appreciate his goodwill and wise counsel.

Jacob Neusner
Distinguished Research Professor of Religious Studies
University of South Florida
Tampa

INTRODUCTION

RABBINIC LITERATURE FORMS THE PRINCIPAL EVIDENCE CONCERNING THE particular Judaism that predominated from ancient times to our own day, the one that appeals to the myth of divine revelation to Moses at Sinai of the Torah in two media, oral and written, hence "the Judaism of the dual Torah." That Judaic system came to full expression in the writings produced from the second to the seventh century C.E. (Common Era = A.D.) by the sages of the Land of Israel ("the Holy Land," "Palestine") and Babylonia. This book meets the need for a comprehensive introduction, for readers with little prior acquaintance with Judaism, to the entire literature, as a whole and by its several documents. Such readers will find in these pages the basic information needed to consult, understand, and appreciate a vast corpus of religious writing in Judaism. To that end, the documents of rabbinic literature as the canon had taken shape by the closure of the definitive writing, the Talmud of Babylonia, in the seventh century,[1] are systematically introduced in this book, first as a whole, then item by item in sequence, and finally in the context of a reconstruction of the history of Judaism that documentary analysis yields.

---

[1] For a survey of other Midrash compilations, besides those introduced here, see Stemberger-Strack, pp. 329–41, 347–49, 350–93. These items either clearly are medieval, or the dates are so uncertain that we have no basis for assigning them to the formative age.

1.
THE JUDAISM REPRESENTED
BY RABBINIC LITERATURE

Rabbinic literature forms the canon of the Judaism of the dual Torah as that corpus reached conclusion by the end of late antiquity. "The dual Torah" refers to revelation through two media: writing, on the one side; oral formulation and oral transmission through memory, on the other. The myth of the dual Torah maintains that when God revealed the Torah at Sinai, God transmitted the Torah in two media. The one in writing is now contained in the written Torah (which the Christian world calls "the Old Testament").[2] The other medium by which the Torah reached Israel was through memory, that is, the other Torah was transmitted orally and memorized by great prophets, then sages, down to the time of the masters who appear in the Mishnah.

This conception of another, orally formulated and orally transmitted Torah— this memorized Torah—characterizes this Judaism and no other. In accord with the myth that accounts for rabbinic literature, we find the substance of the memorized Torah, that is to say, the oral Torah, in the writings of the ancient rabbis of late antiquity. While placing themselves into an oral tradition that began at Sinai, these rabbis wrote their books from ca. 200 to 600. It follows that a generative, indeed defining, theological and hermeneutical problem of this Judaism derives from the task of showing the relationship between the two parts of the one whole Torah of Sinai.

The specific documents' character vastly complicates that hermeneutical task, since none of the writings of the rabbinic canon copies traits of Scripture or otherwise pretends to belong to the written part of the Torah, e.g., in form, style, topic, or program; all of them define themselves in terms wholly independent of Scripture. The first act of writing down a document of this oral Torah produced the Mishnah, a philosophical law code that reached closure at about 200, but contains materials representing views held for the prior two centuries. The Mishnah is written in a Hebrew different from that of Scripture, cites authorities entirely different from those of Scripture, attributes a negligible portion of its statements to origin at Sinai, and by rarely even citing the written Torah, hardly pretends to relate to, let alone form part of, a single Torah with the written Torah.

Further writings that fall into the classification of (oral) Torah follow suit. These include the Tosefta, a collection of supplements to the Mishnah's laws. Then came a commentary to the Mishnah accomplished in the Land of Israel called the

---

[2] "Written Torah" to begin with refers to the Pentateuch, but encompasses, in fact, the entirety of the Hebrew Scriptures of ancient Israel. The Protestant Christian world knows the same as the Old Testament. The Roman Catholic world includes in the Old Testament the Apocryphal books as well, which the Judaism of the dual Torah does not acknowledge as canonical at all.

Talmud of the Land of Israel, of about the year 400, and this was followed by a second such commentary, done in the Jewish communities of Babylonia and called the Talmud of Babylonia, of about the year 600. These documents all form exegetical exercises for the Mishnah.

Along with the Mishnah, Scripture of course provided the other foundation writing. But here too, a clear line always is drawn between Scripture and its interpretation, so that the claim that Scripture exegesis forms part of one whole Torah revealed to Moses finds no support, formal or otherwise, in the rabbinic writings. Taking the form of commentaries and amplifications of various kinds, these invariably stand as distinct from Scripture as the Mishnah does. Rabbinic literature encompasses commentaries to the written Torah by the sages of the age, such as Sifra to Leviticus; Sifré to Numbers; another Sifré, this one to Deuteronomy; Genesis Rabbah; Leviticus Rabbah; and the like. All of these voluminous documents—more than a score in all—contain the teachings of sages in late antiquity, from the first through the sixth centuries of the Common Era, and all together they form that other, that oral Torah, that God revealed to Moses at Sinai. When we examine them in sequence and systematically trace their formulary and propositional programs, we gain access to the history of the formation of the Judaism set forth by rabbinic literature.

That history is spun out in the tension between the autonomy of the rabbinic documents and their connection to Scripture. The first exegetical task of those who received the Mishnah invariably was to show whether, and how, the Mishnah's statements form part of the one whole Torah of Sinai. In the two Talmuds this was commonly accomplished by providing pentateuchal proof texts for Mishnah passages that omitted them. The Midrash compilations, for their part, initially found order and structure, as well as irreducible facts, in Scripture, forming themselves into phase-by-phase commentaries. In later times they framed propositions by appeal to Scripture, closing the gap between conceptions held by sages and those put forth in Scripture. But, beginning to end, the Midrash compilations carefully observed the boundaries between commentary and text.

Documentary analysis of the rabbinic literature shows that three stages mark the development of the Judaism of the dual Torah. The first is defined by the traits of the Mishnah; the second, those of the Talmud of the Land of Israel; and the third, those of the Talmud of Babylonia. In each case the Midrash compilations associated with those principal documents, Sifra and the two Sifrés for the Mishnah, Genesis Rabbah and Leviticus Rabbah for the Talmud of the Land of Israel, and Song of Songs Rabbah, Ruth Rabbah, Lamentations Rabbati, and Esther Rabbah Part One for the Talmud of Babylonia, exhibit the same traits that mark the counterpart writings.

2.

Judaism without Christianity, Judaism despite Christianity

Since these same centuries marked the formative age of Christianity, it is natural to ask whether and how the rabbinic literature exhibits responses to the formation of another scriptural religion beside the Judaism of the dual Torah. The first phase of rabbinic literature, the Mishnaic one, in no way responds to issues important to Christianity at that same time and only rarely and elliptically appears to acknowledge the existence of the new scriptural religion within Israel. The second phase, that set forth in the Talmud of the Land of Israel, by contrast, shows systematic attention, in rabbinic literature, to issues prominent in the confrontation between the two scriptural religions then in competition. While the Judaism that reached its first formulation in writing began in 200 with the Mishnah (itself drawing upon statements of conceptions formulated over the preceding centuries), it is only in the Talmud of the Land of Israel, ca. 400, and its closely allied documents, Genesis Rabbah and Leviticus Rabbah, that that Judaism's principal and indicative doctrines, symbols, and beliefs came to full and complete expression.

The Mishnah shows us, therefore, a version of the Judaism of the dual Torah that reached writing before Christianity made an impact on the Judaic sages, while the Talmud of the Land of Israel and its associates show us the changes that were made in the encounter with Christianity as the triumphant religion of the Roman state. The first full statement of that Judaism of the dual Torah is contained in the Talmud of the Land of Israel, with complementary materials in other documents of the same age, namely, the end of that critical century which began with Constantine's declaring Christianity licit, then the favored religion, and which ended with the Roman Empire's declaring Christianity the religion of the state. The Judaism that took shape in the Land of Israel in the fourth century, attested by documents brought to closure in the fifth, responded to that Christianity and in particular to its challenge to the Israel of that place and time and flourished in Israel, the Jewish people, so long as the West was Christian. In the Christian and Muslim worlds, the Judaism of the dual Torah met no serious competition from other Judaisms so long as Christianity and the later Islam defined the context in which Judaism addressed Israel, the Jewish people, because the challenges of the one, and consequently, later on, of the other as well, defined the system and structure set forth by that Judaism.

3.

THE PERSPECTIVE OF COMPARISON: IF THE LITERATURE OF CHRISTIANITY WERE COMPARABLE IN CHARACTER TO RABBINIC LITERATURE

Perspective on the writings we shall consider is afforded by comparison with the writings that earliest Christianity produced at the same time and in many of the same places. For this purpose a simple contrast will serve. Let me set forth a simple mental experiment. Let us try to imagine the task of an introduction to Christian literature, if Christianity were written down in the way in which Judaism is. What should we expect as the Christian counterpart to rabbinic literature? That is to say, what should we know, and how should we know it, if the records of early Christianity were like the rabbinic literature of late antiquity that we shall consider in this introduction?

(1) What could we know, if all the literature of early Christianity had reached us in a fully homogenized and intellectually seamless form? Not only the New Testament, but all the works of the church fathers, from Justin to Augustine, now would be represented as expressions of one communal mind, dismembered and built into a single harmonious logical structure on various themes. True, they would be shown constantly to disagree with one another. But the range of permissible disagreement would define a vast area of consensus on all basic matters, so that a superficial contentiousness would convey something quite different: one mind on most things, beginning to end. The names of the fathers would be attached to some of their utterances. But all would have gone through a second medium of tradents and redactors—the editors of the compendium (the Patristic Talmud), so to speak—and these editors picked and chose what they wanted of Justin, and what of Origen, what of Tertullian, and what of Augustine, in line with what the editors themselves found interesting. In the end, the picture of the first six centuries of early Christianity would be the creation of people of the sixth century, out of the sherds and remnants of people of the first five. Our work then would be to uncover what happened before the end through studying a document which portrays a timeless world.

Not only would the document be so framed as implicitly to deny historical development of ideas, but the framers also would gloss over diverse and contradictory sources of thought. I do not mean only that Justin, Irenaeus, and Tertullian would be presented as individual authors in a single, timeless continuum. I mean that all Gnostic and Catholic sources would be broken up into sense units and their fragments rearranged in a structure presented as representative of a single Christianity, with a single, unitary theology. This synthesized ecumenical body of Christian thought would be constructed so as to set out judgments on the principal theological topics of the day, and these judgments would have been accepted as normative from that day to this. So the first thing we must try to imagine is a Christianity which reaches us fully harmonized and whole—a Christianity of Nicaea and Chalcedon, but not of Arians, Nestorians, monophysites, and the rest, so there is no distinctive Justin nor Augustine, no Irenaeus and no Gnostics, and surely no Nag Hammadi, but all are one "in Christ Jesus," so to speak.

(2) Let me emphasize that this would be not merely a matter of early Christian literature's reaching us without the names of the authors of its individual documents. The thing we must try to imagine is that there would be no individual documents at all. Everything would have gone through a process of formation and redaction that obliterated the marks of individuality. Just as the theology would be one, so would the form and style of the documents that preserved it. Indeed, what would be striking about this picture of Christianity would be not that the tractate of Mark lacks the name of Mark, but that all of the tractates of the Gospels would be written in precisely the same style and resort to exactly the same rhetorical and redactional devices. Stylistic unity so pervasive as to eliminate all traces of individual authorship, even of most preserved sayings, would now characterize the writings of the first Christians. The sarcasm of Irenaeus, the majesty of Augustine, the exegetical ingenuity of Origen, the lucid historicism of Aphrahat—all are homogenized. Everyone talks in the same way about the same things.

(3) And now to come to a principal task of the study of early Christianity: what should we know about Jesus, and how should we know it, if sayings assigned to Jesus in one book were given to Paul in a second, to John in a third, and to "They said" or "He said to them" in a fourth? Can we imagine trying to discover the historical Jesus on this turf? If even the provenance of a saying could not be established on the basis of all those to whom it is attributed, if, often, even a single *Vorlage* and *Ur-text* could not be postulated? Then what sort of work on the biography and thought of any of the early figures of Christianity would be credible?

Rabbinic literature, as we shall see in this introduction, document by document presents us with rabbinic Judaism in homogenized, seamless form. Its documents are anonymous and carefully obliterate all marks of individual authorship. No writing we now examine may reliably be assigned to a named author, and numerous sayings given to one figure in one document find their way into the mouth of another authority in a different document. Rabbinic literature accomplishes its goals, forming of itself a canon and representing that "one whole Torah of Moses, our Rabbi" that the sages who produced the literature claimed to transmit to Israel, the holy people. In these pages we consider the rabbinic literature as a whole and in all of its parts: both the documents we have, and also the documents we do not have. Then we turn, finally, to a picture of the history of the Judaism that that literature sets forth. Here is an introduction to the whole and to the parts: literature, history, religion. Omitted in this introduction to rabbinic literature is only the dimension of the theology of rabbinic Judaism that sustains that literature.

The perspective just now offered gains depth when we realize that rabbinic literature encompasses yet a third kind of writing, a biographical kind, which generates only two documents. These writings concern the sage, his sayings and exemplary actions. Yet even here, individuation and personality are deliberately homogenized and therefore obliterated—traits contrary to the paramount ones of Christian literature of the same time and importance. The possibility of an Augustine had no counterpart in rabbinic literature, and where that literature does focus upon sages, its character underlines that fact. Among the components of rabbinic literature was no entire document, now extant, organized around the life and teachings of a particular sage. None bears the marks of an individual author's style or preferences. All are governed by objective and public conventions of style and protocols of expression.

Not only so, but where events in the lives of sages do occur, they are thematic and not biographical in organization, e.g., stories about the origins, as to Torah study, of diverse sages; death scenes of various sages. The sage as such, whether Aqiba or Yohanan ben Zakkai or Eliezer b. Hyrcanus, never in any rabbinic document defines the appropriate organizing principle for sequences of stories or sayings. And there is no other in which the sage forms an organizing category for any material purpose. A considerable volume of ambitious compositions, e.g., collections of sayings assigned to a named authority or stories told about him, sequential stories about a given authority, never took shape.

Contrast, therefore, the vast and ambitious compilations devoted to the Mishnah and Scripture, with the only two counterparts that draw together the torah of sages. The first is Abot, "The Fathers," or as I should prefer, "The Founders," and the second is that talmud to that document, which is The Fathers According to Rabbi Nathan. In comparison with the numerous and huge compilations devoted to the Mishnah and Scripture, in proportion to rabbinic literature as a whole, tractate Abot and its talmud scarcely register. By contrast, most of Patristic literature comprises the individual writings of named authorities. That simple fact shows us how different are the documents of rabbinic literature from those of formative Christianity, and underlines the importance of providing access to rabbinic literature through a systematic introduction to the literature as a whole and of its individual documents as well. Those interested in earliest Christianity will find in the pages of this book the way not taken, just as rabbinic literature must find in the writings of Christianity a source of comparison and contrast.

But these contrasts should only highlight the definitive trait shared by both Christianity's and Judaism's foundation documents. In these documents, the two respective sets of writers put down what it means to know God in God's self-manifestation—but also to preserve and hand on that knowledge of God in the distinctive medium of knowledge set forth in writing. Both groups undertook the same goal. For Christianity, it was to put down in written form (and in tradition) the record of God incarnate in Jesus Christ. For Judaism, it was to set down in writing the oral part of the record of the Torah that God gives in two media, written and oral, to Moses, our rabbi, at Sinai, and, through the masters and disciples in the chain of tradition to Sinai, every day since then.

As everyone knows, from the perspective of Christianity, in the Gospels and the writings beyond, Christians wrote down the record of God's self-revelation in Jesus Christ. And, along these same lines, since the generative theological principle of the Judaism of the dual Torah maintains that holy Israel meets God in the Torah, the stakes in rabbinic literature prove equally transcending and surpassing. In these books, "our sages of blessed memory" wrote down the record of God's self-revelation in the Torah. That is what is at stake in the writing of these books: finding a way appropriately to record what God has let humanity know through the gift ("revelation") of the Torah.

4.

INTRODUCING RABBINIC LITERATURE

Now briefly to explain the plan and specific program of this introduction: Part One addresses the literature seen whole. After an overview of rabbinic literature, in Chapter 1, we begin with a general account of analytical procedures pertaining to all documents. A systematic introduction asks the same questions of all writings. In the case of this introduction, after a characterization of the document as a whole, I systematically make reference to the three differentiating characteristics that distinguish one document from another, or species of documents from other species. These indicative traits are those of rhetoric and topic or even propositional program, defined in Chapter 2, and the logic of coherent discourse characteristic of each writing, spelled out in Chapter 3. The dialectics of rabbinic literature is described in Chapter 4. These then characterize the respective documents and permit us to differentiate each from the others.

We proceed in the shank of the book, Parts Two, Three, and Four, to a systematic examination of the three types of writing in rabbinic literature:

[1] Mishnah and its exegesis,
[2] Scripture and its amplification,
[3] stories about and sayings attributed to sages.

Each of the documents that amplify and extend the Mishnah and Scripture respectively are set forth in Parts Two and Three, with the description systematically following the analytical program set forth in Part One.

Providing perspective on the kind of writing we do have, Part Four explains the documents we do not have—gospels—and then addresses the two documents of rabbinic literature that are devoted to sages and their sayings and exemplary doings. Part Five, by Professor Paul V. McCracken Flesher, introduces the Aramaic translations of Scripture, both those demonstrably deriving from rabbinic sages and those of indeterminate origin or sponsorship.

THE INTRODUCTIONS TO THE VARIOUS DOCUMENTS, VIEWED ONE BY ONE: The thesis that governs this introduction is that rabbinic literature is to be differentiated by its writing. Therefore the task is to characterize not only the whole, as is accomplished in Part One, but also the parts, one by one. It follows that each of the documents in the shank of the book, Parts Two and Three, Chapters 5–24, is set forth in accord with a single pattern. I identify the document and set forth the facts of how we have access to this particular piece of writing, that is, the available translations into English. Then I present an analysis of the differentiating traits of the document, its rhetoric, logic of coherent discourse, and topical or propositional program. Finally, for each writing, I give a sample passage, with a few comments to point up the distinctive traits of the representative selection. In this way I aim at introducing the reader to each component of rabbinic literature so that the several documents are accessible and useful for the study of religion in late antiquity. At a few points the character of the document subject to representation requires some modifications of this basic plan.

BIBLIOGRAPHY: Most of the chapters open with a bibliographical footnote, drawing attention to other approaches to the problem of introducing the document at hand, besides the one given here. Several important bibliographical resources in that connection are used throughout. The first and most important is H. L. Strack and Günter Stemberger, *Introduction to the Talmud and Midrash* (Minneapolis, 1992: Fortress Press), translated by Markus Bockmuehl. For rabbinic literature Stemberger has given us the sole comprehensive and up-to-date bibliographical study known to me in any language. For a great many problems, he gives first-class state-of-the-question studies, providing a thorough and reliable account of many problems on which received scholarship has worked. Throughout the bibliographical notes, I refer readers to Stemberger for an account of the several documents' textual history, editions, and translations into languages other than English, as well as an account of prior scholarship.

State-of-the-question studies on many important problems on which rabbinic literature sheds light are provided by Lester L. Grabbe, *Judaism from Cyrus to Hadrian* (Minneapolis, 1992: Fortress Press). II. *The Roman Period,* Grabbe does not focus upon rabbinic literature and history, but at many points he addresses issues where that literature figures, and his guidance is judicious and astute. Comparable state-of-the-question accounts for the later period are provided by Stemberger. His work makes it superfluous to summarize in these pages the history of scholarship on each of our documents, since the work is now fully realized by him.

5.

OTHER INTRODUCTIONS
TO RABBINIC LITERATURE

Readers will find interesting the comparison between the theory of introduction worked out in detail here and that followed by alternative approaches to the same problem of systematic and coherent description, analysis, and interpretation of rabbinic literature, as a whole and in its components. That comparison will show that each introduction identifies a particular set of questions of special interest; those that predominate here are rarely raised elsewhere. Not only so, but information deemed important elsewhere, concerning matters of establishing the correct Hebrew text, text criticism, manuscript evidence, and the like, is not the focus of interest here. Having chosen my audience, I also have framed an introduction that addresses the questions attracting these readers to this set of writings; the issues I raise are those of general intelligibility and the shared intellectual sensibility of Western scholarship. I further have taken account, and not repeated the findings, of prior approaches to the same literature.

That is why I have not gone back over questions that in general are settled and satisfactorily treated in other introductions. Rather, I have systematically referred readers to where they can find the information that others highlight and I set aside in favor of the program followed in these pages. Not counting the mainly bibliographic and state-of-the-question work of Stemberger, cited above, this is the fifth systematic introduction to rabbinic literature to appear in the recent past. I hope that readers will compare and contrast my methods and results with those of others writing in English who have set forth their views on how the work should be done and what it is meant to yield. These are as follows:

1. John Bowker, *The Targums and Rabbinic Literature. An Introduction to Jewish Interpretations of Scripture* (Cambridge, 1969: Cambridge University Press).

2. Hyam Maccoby, *Early Rabbinic Writings* (Cambridge, 1988: Cambridge University Press). III. *Cambridge Commentaries on Writings of the Jewish and Christian World, 200 BC to AD 200,* edited by P. R. Ackroyd, A. R. C. Leaney, and J. W. Packer.

3. Shmuel Safrai, editor; Peter J. Tomson, executive editor, *The Literature of the Sages.* First Part. *Oral Tora, Halakha, Mishna, Tosefta, Talmud, External Tractates* in the series *Compendia Rerum Iudaicarum ad Novum Testamentum.* Section Two. *The Literature of the Jewish People in the Period of the Second Temple and the Talmud* (Assen/ Maastricht and Philadelphia, 1987: Van Gorcum and Fortress Press). These articles are briefly summarized at the chapters that deal with their topics.

Note also the announced continuation, Shmuel Safrai, editor; Peter J. Tomson, executive editor, *The Literature of the Sages.* Second Part. *Midrash, Aggada, Midrash Collections, Targum, Prayer,* which as of the date of the publication of this book has ·not yet appeared.

4. The entries on each document in *Encyclopaedia Judaica* (New York and Jerusalem, 1971: MacMillan and Keter). These are cited under the names of the various authors and cover every document treated here. The entries by M. D. Herr are noteworthy for their consistent plan; the others are haphazard and not always illuminating.

The opening footnotes of each chapter in the shank of the book identify the relevant pages and rapidly review what is to be found in them. Each of these colleagues and the respective authors of the entries in *Encyclopaedia Judaica* have set forth theories, whether fully worked out or pertinent to only a single piece of writing, on how to introduce rabbinic literature, as well as what it is important that we know about the various documents.

I do not survey the state of various questions. That is not only because Stemberger does so in an admirable and responsible way. It is also because I have devoted a number of other books to the systematic reading of, and commentary upon, the available scholarship on rabbinic literature. Three of the state-of-the-question studies that I have edited are *The Formation of the Babylonian Talmud. Studies on the Achievements of Late Nineteenth and Twentieth Century Historical and Literary-Critical Research.* Leiden, 1970: Brill; *The Modern Study of the Mishnah.* Leiden, 1973: Brill; and *The Study of Ancient Judaism.* New York, 1981: Ktav. Second printing: Atlanta, 1992: Scholars Press for South Florida Studies in the History of Judaism. This is in two volumes: I. *Mishnah, Midrash, Siddur,* and II. *The Palestinian and Babylonian Talmuds.* The bibliographical essays on Midrash and the two Talmuds are directly relevant to this book, and in them much valuable bibliographical data will be found. These sustained examinations of the received scholarly tradition provide perspective on the methods used in this introduction.

Clearly, I have made choices among the alternative approaches that I have studied and so wish to explain the reasons. The methods that guide this introduction to the documents are explained both in detail and in academic context in the following works: *Studying Classical Judaism: A Primer.* Louisville, 1991: Westminster/John Knox Press; *The Ecology of Religion: From Writing to Religion in the Study of Judaism.* Nashville, 1989: Abingdon; *Paradigms in Passage: Patterns of Change in the Contemporary Study of Judaism.* Lanham, Maryland, 1988: University Press of America. Studies in Judaism Series; and *Wrong Ways and Right Ways in the Study of Formative Judaism. Critical Method and Literature, History, and the History of Religion.* Atlanta, 1988: Scholars Press for Brown Judaic Studies. Finally, the context in which this work is carried on is described in my *The Public Side of Learning. The Political Consequences of Scholarship in the Context of Judaism.* Chico, 1985: Scholars Press for the American Academy of Religion *Studies in Religion* Series.

6.

The Documentary Approach
to Rabbinic Literature

Let me briefly place this introduction into the context of scholarship that has taken place in the last quarter of this century. The results presented here reach back over thirty years of work of mine. In 1972, at the end of ten years of historical work on *A Life of Yohanan ben Zakkai, A History of the Jews in Babylonia, The Rabbinic*

Traditions about the Pharisees, and *Eliezer ben Hyrcanus: The Tradition and the Man,* I reached the conclusion, expressed in *Development of a Legend: Studies on the Traditions Concerning Yohanan ben Zakkai,* that everything I had done was uncritical and therefore worthless as rigorous learning. The reason was that everything began with the attribution of a saying to a named authority or the narration of a story about the named authority, and while adding layers of supposedly critical rhetoric, I had in fact taken for granted the facticity of these attributions: what the document said a sage said, he really said; what it said he did, he really did. On the strength of that unexamined premise, I had formed my entire scholarly program, beginning to end. For I could not claim to write the history of Yohanan ben Zakkai or the Jews in Babylonia, the ideas and teachings of the Pharisees or of Eliezer b. Hyrcanus, unless I knew for sure that everything that all documents assigned to those names or subjects was reliably attributed to them; that the stories were accurate accounts of how things really were.

That premise is not wrong, merely beyond all verification; therefore a different set of questions had to be framed—questions congruent to the character of our evidence. If attributions do not form the irreducible fact for the analysis of rabbinic writing, then the character of the respective documents presented itself as the obvious alternative. In focusing upon the systematic analysis of the writings, rather than the substance of what was written in the names of specific authorities, I discovered a new road to be taken into the description, analysis, and interpretation of the history of Judaism in late antiquity. It was represented by the documents on which I had chosen to work. Why so radical a turning?

A simple fact clearly had constituted an insuperable obstacle in the road that I—in the tradition of my entire field of study—had taken for more than a decade. It may be simply stated. I could not either validate or falsify the attributions of sayings to named authorities, upon which my, and all other, historical work rested. I reached the conclusion that the foundations, in irrefutable fact, of the utilization of all evidence were irreparably flawed, and that nothing I had done, or anyone else for that matter, met the simple test: how do you know that what you say, on the basis of the sources in hand and the way you read them, is so? What we cannot show, we do not know. Then, I asked myself, what are the facts we really do have in hand? The simplest is, the facticity of the documents, one by one. While the wordings may vary from one textual witness to the next, while the repertoire of materials may shift from one manuscript to another, the various documents viewed one by one do exhibit distinctive and differentiating traits; these awaited discovery and elucidation, and that is what, I determined, I had to do. That decision explains how and why this introduction forms the culmination of so many years of work.

For on the basis of the simple fact that the document forms an irreducible fact, but the facticity of the attribution of sayings in a given document or in all of them together to a single named authority was subject to serious doubt, I concluded the work resting on attributions—which is to say, historical work of one kind. Now began historical work of another kind, for I required a different starting point for all future work, besides the one provided by the attribution of a saying to a named authority, on the one side, or the telling of a story about him, on the other. Since everything I had done, and the entire scholarly literature and tradition within which I worked, presupposed the facticity of what in fact lay beyond all rigorous testing, I went off in search of some other way of studying the rabbinic literature, besides the uncritical one that I knew and followed.

As is clear, by way of a working hypothesis I determined that the irrefutable fact, the uncontingent, independent variable, was the document. I could think of no governing facts besides the attribution, on the one side, or the documentary locus, on the other. It is the simple fact that everything we have received from rabbinic Judaism in late antiquity comes to us in the documents of rabbinic literature. So all future study depended upon the systematic characterization of those documents.

In 1972 I started with the first of these, which is the Mishnah, and two decades later concluded with the last, which is the Talmud of Babylonia. In the interim, I translated for the first time approximately a third of the volume of that literature— the Tosefta, the Talmud of the Land of Israel, Sifra, and some other documents— and retranslated, but for the first time providing a form-analytical presentation, all of the other documents, including the Mishnah, the Talmud of Babylonia, and the Midrash compilations in their entirety. That explains why I have now translated and introduced every document that with confidence is assigned to late antiquity's rabbis (as distinct from other than rabbinic sources, on the one side, or writings that came to closure after the Muslim conquest marked the end of antiquity and the beginning of the Middle Ages, on the other). Each, furthermore, has now been systematically translated and fully analyzed as to rhetoric, logic of coherent discourse, and topical and propositional program, by me.[3] That is the considerable *oeuvre* that is summarized here in a systematic and succinct way in the pages of this book.

[3] I collected and printed as a single volume all of the important negative reviews, down to 1990, of various volumes of this *oeuvre* in *The Origins of Judaism. Religion, History, and Literature in Late Antiquity* (New York, 1991: Garland Press). XX. *The Literature of Formative Judaism: Controversies on the Literature of Formative Judaism*. I collected some of my reviews of the results of others, past and present, in my *Ancient Judaism. Debates and Disputes*. Chico, 1984: Scholars Press for Brown Judaic Studies; *Ancient Judaism. Debates and Disputes. Second Series*. Atlanta, 1990: Scholars Press for South Florida Studies in the History of Judaism; and *Ancient Judaism. Debates and Disputes. Third Series. Essays on the Formation of Judaism, Dating Sayings, Method in the History of Judaism, the Historical Jesus, Publishing Too Much, and Other Current Issues*. Atlanta, 1993: Scholars Press for South Florida Studies in the History of Judaism; and also *Judaic Law from Jesus to the Mishnah. A Systematic Reply to Professor E. P. Sanders*. Atlanta, 1993: Scholars Press for South Florida Studies in the History of Judaism, and *Are There Really Tannaitic Parallels to the Gospels? A Refutation of Morton Smith*. Atlanta, 1993: Scholars Press for South Florida Studies in the History of Judaism.

PART ONE

RABBINIC LITERATURE
AS A WHOLE

I

DEFINING RABBINIC LITERATURE

AND ITS PRINCIPAL PARTS

THE JUDAISM OF THE DUAL TORAH, WHICH TOOK SHAPE IN THE FIRST SEVEN centuries C.E.,[1] rests upon the conception of Torah, meaning revelation. Rabbinic literature forms part of that Torah and is valued because of that conviction; that is why, in its Judaism, rabbinic literature is important. What God reveals ("gives") in the Torah is God's self-manifestation in one aspect: God's will, expressed in partic-

[1] For further discussion of the definition of rabbinic literature, see the following:

Stemberger-Strack, General Introduction, pp. 1–118; on oral and written tradition, pp. 35–50.

Bowker, pp. 40–93: a brief introduction to rabbinic literature; halakhah and aggadah, Midrash and Mishnah, pp. 40–48; the transmission of oral Torah, pp. 48–53; rabbinic literature in general, pp. 53ff. Bowker also treats medieval Midrash compilations; Megillat Ta'anit; Seder 'Olam; Tanna debe Eliyyahu; etc.

Y. Gafni, "The Historical Background" (defining the rabbinic period, second Temple institutions and the sages, the Pharisaic movement, Hillel and the House of Hillel, Hasidim and Zealots, destruction and the Yavne Period, Bar Kokhba and the later Tannaitic period, the Amoraic period in the Land of Israel, the Amoraic period in Babylonia), in Safrai, *Literature of the Sages*, pp. 1–34. On the dates of the rabbinic period: "While rabbinic literature may have taken on a literary format in the first five centuries of the Common Era, the contents of this material may at times reflect ideas, practices, and even statements handed down from earlier phases of Jewish development, most particularly the days of the second Jewish commonwealth, which commenced with the return to Zion (548 B.C.E.) and building of the second Temple (c. 516 B.C.E.), and concluded with the destruction of Jerusalem by Titus (70 C.E.) . . . by the first century C.E. there already existed within the Jewish community a significant body of oral

ular in an account of the covenant between God and Israel. That refers to the identification of the contracting parties, on the one side, and what the covenant entails for the life of Israel with God, on the other. That is the religious context defined by the Judaism of the dual Torah in which the literature of rabbinic Judaism is written, valued, and studied.

While one among several Judaic systems of antiquity, in fact the Judaism of the dual Torah set forth the most important canon of a Judaism to emerge from ancient times. That is because it is the Judaism that proved normative from its formative

---

tradition, both in the form of biblical commentary as well as 'regulations handed down by former generations and not recorded in the Laws of Moses.' Rabbinic literature thus frequently serves as a conduit for the transmission of ideas and statements whose genesis preceded the rabbinic era by decades or even hundreds of years. For the student of rabbinic history the fact that a statement issuing—in literature—from the mouth of R. Aqiba may have its roots in the teachings of an anonymous sage hundreds of years earlier is indeed inhibiting, but it is only after we accept this basic premise that rabbinic literary development can be placed in its proper perspective." The same applies to his view to Midrash compilations as well: "Midrashim redacted at a later date frequently preserve much earlier material, the antiquity of which may be established through a comparison with early non-rabbinic Jewish or Christian literature."

Maccoby, pp. 1–30: "a corporate literary effort, in which a large number of experts . . . is engaged in a common enterprise: the clarification of Scripture and the application of it to everyday life;" the oral Torah, pp. 3–5; canonicity, pp. 5–7; the style of rabbinic writings, pp. 8–9; Pharisees and Sadducees, pp. 9–11; Pharisees and rabbis, pp. 11–16; historical background; halakhah and aggadah, pp. 16–22; aggadah and Midrash, pp. 22–25; Mishnah and Midrash, pp. 25–29; the targums, pp. 29–30. Note also under "miscellaneous works," Maccoby discusses Seder Olam and "the mystical literature," pp. 38–39; the main rabbinic figures, pp. 39–46; "the main ideas of the early rabbinic literature," e.g., the nature of God, the covenant people, the Land, the promise of a transformed world, pp. 46–48. General characterization (p. 48): "Thus the rabbinical literature, though wholly subordinating itself to Scripture, which it endeavors to 'search' and explicate, in fact contains great originality arising from the struggle to make biblical values actual in the times in which the rabbis found themselves." Maccoby treats in the rubric of rabbinic literature the synagogue liturgy as well, pp. 204–17; "history," pp. 218–29, gives samples of Megillat Ta'anit and Seder 'Olam Rabbah.

S. Safrai, "Halakhah" (general characteristics, origins of the halakhah, the origin of independent halakhah, sources of the halakhah of the sages, stages in the history of Tannaitic halakhah), in Safrai, *Literature of the Sages*, pp. 121–210.

S. Safrai, "Oral Tora" (the scope of oral Torah, origin and nature of oral Torah, ways of literary creation, oral Torah and rabbinic literature, terminology of oral Torah, central religious concepts developed in oral Torah), in Safrai, *Literature of the Sages*, pp. 35–120.

On the topic of Judaism as a scriptural religion, see William Scott Green, "Writing with Scripture," in my *Writing with Scripture: The Authority and Uses of the Hebrew Bible in the Torah of Formative Judaism*. Philadelphia, 1989: Fortress Press, pp. 7–23. On the formation of the rabbinic literature out of the compilation of available compositions, see this writer's *Making the Classics in Judaism: The Three Stages of Literary Formation*. Atlanta, 1990: Scholars Press for Brown Judaic Studies; and for the distinction between the composition and the composite, see *The Rules of Composition of the Talmud of Babylonia. The Cogency of the Bavli's Composite*. Atlanta, 1991: Scholars Press for South Florida Studies in the History of Judaism.

centuries to our own day and produced most of the Judaic systems that now flourish. That Judaism, drawing upon older materials of course, beginning with the Old Testament itself, finds its definitive symbol in the Torah, written and oral. Its distinctive myth appeals to the story that at Sinai God revealed revelation, or "Torah," to Moses in two media. One medium for revelation was in writing, hence "the written Torah," *Torah shebikhtab,* corresponding to the Old Testament of Christianity.[2] The other medium for revelation was through oral formulation and oral transmission, hence through memorization, hence "the oral Torah," *Torah she be'al peh,* the memorized Torah. The Judaism of the dual Torah bestows upon its authorities, or sages, the title of "rabbi," hence is called rabbinic Judaism; it appeals for its ultimate authority to the Talmud of Babylonia, or Bavli, hence is called talmudic Judaism; it enjoys the status of orthodoxy, hence is called "normative" or "classical" Judaism. Today, the rabbinic literature valued as canonical by the Judaism of the dual Torah forms the court of final appeal to all Judaisms, from Orthodoxy both integrationist and segregationist, to Reform, Conservative, Reconstructionist, and all other known Judaic systems of a religious character. Each invokes in its own way and for its own purposes the received writings of the Judaism of the dual Torah.

1.
THE CONCEPT OF A HOLY BOOK
IN THE JUDAISM OF THE DUAL TORAH

The literature of rabbinic Judaism therefore takes its place as a component of that Torah: part of God's revelation to Israel. But it is only one of the three parts that comprise the Torah. In the Judaism of the dual Torah, the Torah is set forth and preserved in three media, (1) a book, the Hebrew Scriptures or Old Testament, (2) a memorized oral tradition, first written down in the Mishnah, ca. A.D. 200, and other ancient documents, and (3) the model of a sage who embodies in the here and now the paradigm of Moses, called a rabbi. Other Judaic systems identified other holy books, in addition to Scripture, for their canon. The canon of rabbinic Judaism is only one, distinct and autonomous corpus of writings; other Judaisms defined their own canons in accord with their systems' requirements. Each canon then recapitulated its system and no other.

That is to say, since in antiquity, as in modern times, diverse sets of books have been defined as the canon of one Judaism or another, we recognize at the outset a simple fact. No single, unitary, linear "Judaism" ever existed, from the beginnings

---

[2] Note the qualification of this matter given in note 2 of the Introduction.

to the present, defining an "orthodoxy." Quite to the contrary, a variety of Judaisms—Judaic systems, comprising a way of life, worldview, and definition of a social entity, an "Israel"—have flourished. Comparison of one Judaic system with another shows that each is autonomous and freestanding. Each Judaic system appeals to its distinctive symbolic structure, explains itself by invoking its particular myth, sets forth its indicative way of life, accounts for its way of life by appealing to its own worldview. The Judaic system revealed by Philo side by side with the one preserved in the Essene library found at the Dead Sea, or with the Judaic system presented by the ancient rabbis with the Judaic system defined by the Pentateuchal editors in the fifth century B.C.E., makes the point quite clear. Harmonizing all of the diverse Judaisms into a single Judaism imposes a theological construct upon diverse and discrete historical facts. Since (except in the theological context) there never has been a single, "orthodox," unitary and harmonious "Judaism," against which all "heterodox" or "heretical" Judaisms have to be judged, we recognize that each Judaism is to be described in its own terms, meaning, in the context of its literature or other enduring evidences.

The concept of a sacred text in the Judaism of the dual Torah therefore finds definition in the myth of the dual Torah. In fact, all components of that Torah are secondary. What comes first is the myth of the memorized Torah, what follows is the identification of the documents that enjoy the status of components of that memorized Torah. The Judaism of the dual Torah by definition does not find its definition in a book—e.g., the Old Testament. Its generative principle is quite the opposite: God did not resort solely to a book to convey and preserve the divine message. It was through teachings, which could be transmitted in more than a single form. Consequently, a way lay open to encompass more than the Old Testament as Torah, and, indeed, in late antiquity, Torah found ample room not only for truth formulated in words—whether written down or memorized—but also for gestures, indeed, also for persons. Consequently the sage could be received as a Torah and treated as such.

An important and simple statement of that fact will prove the point. A sage himself was equivalent to a scroll of the Torah—a material, legal comparison, not merely a symbolic metaphor.

A.   He who sees a disciple of a sage who has died is as if he sees a scroll of the Torah that has been burned.

Y. Moed Qatan 3:7.X

I.   R. Jacob bar Abayye in the name of R. Aha: "An elder who forgot his learning because of some accident which happened to him—they treat him with the sanctity owed to an ark [of the Torah]."

Y. Moed Qatan 3:1.XI

The sage therefore is represented as equivalent to the scroll of the Torah, and, turning the statement around, the scroll of the Torah is realized in the person of the sage. The conception is not merely figurative or metaphorical, for, in both instances, actual behavior was affected. Still more to the point, what the sage *did* had the status of law; the sage was the model of the law, thus once again he enjoyed the standing of the human embodiment of the Torah. Since the sage exercised supernatural power as a kind of living Torah, his very deeds served to reveal law, as much as his word expressed revelation. That is a formidable component of the argument that the sage embodied the Torah, another way of saying that the Torah was incarnated in the person of the sage.

The capacity of the sage himself to participate in the process of revelation is illustrated in two types of materials. First of all, tales told about rabbis' behavior on specific occasions immediately are translated into rules for the entire community to keep. Accordingly, he was a source not merely of good example but of prescriptive law.

> X.   R. Aha went to Emmaus, and he ate dumpling [prepared by Samaritans].
> Y.   R. Jeremiah ate leavened bread prepared by them.
> Z.   R. Hezekiah ate their locusts prepared by them.
> AA. R. Abbahu prohibited Israelite use of wine prepared by them.

> Y. Abodah Zarah 5:4:III

Along with hundreds of parallels in the rabbinic literature, these reports of what rabbis had said and done enjoyed the same authority, as statements of the law on eating what Samaritans cooked, as did citations of traditions in the names of the great authorities of old or of the day. What someone did served as a norm, if the person was a sage of sufficient standing. The precedent entered the Torah, and what a sage said became part of the oral component of the one whole Torah that God gave to Moses at Sinai. That is the mythic premise on which these and similar stories are told and preserved.

It follows that the Judaism of the dual Torah is not a religion of a book, though that Judaism does venerate books as well as orally formulated and orally transmitted teachings. The reason is that this Judaism does not take form solely through sacred texts. It is not a religion that appeals to a book for its authority and definition of truth. It appeals to truth that is preserved in diverse media, books, words preserved not in books but in memorized formulas, and, finally, the lives, gestures, and deeds of holy persons. It follows that the Judaism of the dual Torah appeals not solely to texts, oral or written, and it is assuredly not a religion that derives from a book in particular. It is a religion that receives its revelation in a variety of media, and, by definition, it is therefore not a religion of a book. But it does refer to a canon, which serves to recapitulate the system just now adumbrated. Let us rapidly survey the canonical writings that comprise rabbinic literature.

2.

DEFINING RABBINIC LITERATURE

A simple definition follows from what has been said. Rabbinic literature is the corpus of writing produced in the first seven centuries C.E. by sages who claimed to stand in the chain of tradition from Sinai and uniquely to possess the oral part of the Torah, revealed by God to Moses at Sinai for oral formulation and oral transmission, in addition to the written part of the Torah possessed by all Israel. Among the many diverse documents produced by Jews in late antiquity, the first seven centuries of the Common Era (C.E. = A.D.), only a small group cohere and form a distinctive corpus, called "rabbinic literature." Three traits together suffice to distinguish rabbinic literature from all other Jewish (ethnic) and Judaic (religious) writing of that age.

[1] These writings of law and exegesis, revered as holy books, copiously cite the Hebrew Scriptures of ancient Israel ("written Torah").

[2] They acknowledge the authority, and even the existence, of no other Judaic (or gentile) books but the ancient Israelite Scriptures.

[3] These writings promiscuously and ubiquitously cite sayings attributed to named authorities, unique to those books themselves, most of them bearing the title "rabbi."

Other writings of Jews, e.g., Josephus, to begin with do not claim to set forth religious systems or to form holy books. Other Judaic writings ordinarily qualify under the first plank of the definition, and the same is to be said for Christian counterparts. The second element in the definition excludes all Christian documents. The third dismisses all writings of all Judaisms other than the one of the dual Torah. Other Judaisms' writings cite scriptural heroes or refer to a particular authority; none except those of this Judaism sets forth, as does every rabbinic document,[3] extensive accounts of what a large number of diverse authorities say, let alone disputes among them. "Rabbinic" is therefore an appropriate qualifier for this Judaism, since what distinguishes it from all others is the character of its authorities (the matter of title being a mere detail) and the myth that accounts for its distinctive character.

Any book out of Judaic antiquity that exhibits these three traits—focus upon law and exegesis of the Hebrew Scriptures, exclusion of all prior tradition except for Scripture, and appealing to named sages called rabbis, falls into the category of rabbinic literature. All other Jewish writings in varying proportions exhibit the first trait, and some the second as well, but none all three. It goes without saying that no named authority in any rabbinic writing, except for scriptural ones, occurs in any other Judaic document in antiquity (excluding Gamaliel in Acts), or in another Jewish one either (excluding Simeon b. Gamaliel in Josephus's histories).

---

[3] With the possible exception of those Targumim that exhibit the definitive traits of origin in rabbinic circles, e.g., Onqelos; see Chapter 25.

Rabbinic literature is divided into two large parts, each part formed as a commentary to a received part of the Torah, one oral, the other written. The written part requires no attention here: it is simply Scripture (Hebrew: "the written Torah," TaNaKH, Torah, Nebi'im, Ketubim, a.k.a. "the Old Testament" part of the Bible). The oral part begins with the Mishnah, a philosophical law code that reached closure at the end of the second century; the written part, of course, comprises the Pentateuch and other books of ancient Israelite Scripture. Promulgated under the sponsorship of the Roman-appointed Jewish authority of the Land of Israel ("Palestine"), Judah the Patriarch, the Mishnah formed the first document of rabbinic literature and therefore of the Judaic system, "rabbinic Judaism," or "the Judaism of the dual Torah," that took shape in this period. The attributed statements of its authorities, named sages or rabbis called Tannaites ("repeaters," "memorizers," for the form in which the sayings were formulated and transmitted), enjoyed the standing of traditions beginning at Sinai. Numerous anonymous sayings, alongside the attributed ones and bearing upon the same controverted questions, appear as well.

THE MISHNAH AND THE EXEGETICAL TRADITION OF THE ORAL TORAH: Comprising six divisions, dealing with agriculture, holy seasons, women and family affairs, civil law and politics, everyday offerings, and cultic purity, the Mishnah served as the written code of the Patriarch's administration in the Land of Israel, and of that of his counterpart, the Exilarch, in Iranian-ruled Babylonia as well. Alongside the Mishnah's compilation of sages' sayings into well-crafted divisions, tractates, and chapters, other sayings of the same authorities circulated, some of them finding their way, marked as deriving from Tannaite authority, into the Tosefta and the two Talmuds.

Three exegetical documents formed around parts of the Mishnah. These were, specifically,

[1] the Tosefta, a compilation of supplementary sayings organized around nearly the whole of the Mishnah as citation and gloss, secondary paraphrase, and freestanding complement thereto, of no determinate date but probably concluded about a century after the closure of the Mishnah, hence ca. 300; and two Talmuds, or sustained and systematic commentaries to the Mishnah,

[2] the Talmud of the Land of Israel, which reached closure in ca. 400, a commentary to most of the tractates of the Mishnah's first four divisions,

[3] the Talmud of Babylonia, concluded in ca. 600, providing a sustained exegesis to most of the tractates of the Mishnah's second through fifth divisions.

The Tosefta's materials occasionally form the basis for exegetical compositions in the two Talmuds, but the second Talmud's framers know nothing about the compositions, let alone composites, of the prior Talmud, even though they frequently do cite sayings attributed to authorities of the Land of Israel as much as of Babylonia. So the line of the exegesis and extension of the Mishnah extends in an inverted Y, through the Tosefta to the two, autonomous Talmuds.

Mishnah

Tosefta

Talmud of the Land of Israel (Yerushalmi)   Talmud of Babylonia (Bavli)

SCRIPTURE AND THE EXEGETICAL TRADITION OF THE WRITTEN TO-RAH: Parts of the written Torah attracted sustained commentary as well, and altogether, these commentaries, called Midrash compilations, form the counterpart to the writings of Mishnah exegesis. It should be noted that both Talmuds, in addition, contain large composites of Midrash exegesis, but they are not organized around books or large selections of Scripture. The part of rabbinic literature that takes Scripture, rather than the Mishnah, as its organizing structure covers the Pentateuchal books of Exodus, Leviticus, Numbers, and Deuteronomy, and some of the writings important in synagogue liturgy, particularly Ruth, Esther, Lamentations, and Song of Songs, all read on special occasions in the sacred calendar. Numbering for late antiquity twelve compilations in all, the earliest compilations of exegesis, called Midrash, were produced in the third century, the latest in the sixth or seventh.

SAGES AND THE EXEMPLARY TORAH: There is a third, small type of writing in rabbinic literature, which concerns teachings of sages on theological and moral questions. This comprises a very small, freestanding corpus, tractate Abot ("The Fathers," or founders) and Abot deRabbi Nathan ("The Fathers According to Rabbi Nathan"). The former collects sayings of sages, and the latter contributes in addition stories about them. But the bulk of rabbinic literature consists of works of exegesis of the Mishnah and Scripture, which is to say, the principal documents of the Torah, oral and written respectively. But throughout the documents of the oral Torah also are collected compositions and large compilations that are devoted to the sayings and exemplary deeds of named sages. No documents took shape to be made up out of that kind of writing, which, nonetheless, was abundant.

MISHNAH AND MIDRASH, *HALAKHAH* AND *AGGADAH:* Viewed as a whole, therefore, we see that the stream of exegesis of the Mishnah and exploration of its themes of law and philosophy flowed side by side with exegesis of Scripture. Since the Mishnah concerns itself with normative rules of behavior, it and the documents of exegesis flowing from it ordinarily are comprised of discussion of matters of law, or, in Hebrew, *halakhah*. Much of the exegesis of Scripture in the Midrash compilations concerns itself with norms of belief, right attitude, virtue, and proper motivation. Encased in narrative form, these teachings of an ethical and moral character are called *aggadah*, or lore.

Midrash exegesis of Israelite Scripture in no way was particular to the rabbinic literature. To the contrary, the exegesis of the Hebrew Scriptures had defined a convention of all systems of Judaism from before the conclusion of Scripture itself; no one, including the sages who stand behind rabbinic literature, began anywhere but in the encounter with the written Torah. But collecting and organizing documents of exegeses of Scripture in a systematic way developed in a quite distinct circumstance.

For rabbinic literature, the circumstance was defined by the requirement of Mishnah exegesis. The Mishnah's character itself defined a principal task of Scripture exegesis. Standing by itself, providing few proof texts to Scripture to back up its rules, the Mishnah bore no explanation of why Israel should obey its rules. Brought into relationship to Scripture, by contrast, the Mishnah gained access to the source of authority by definition operative in Israel, the Jewish people. Accordingly, the work of relating the Mishnah's rules to those of Scripture got under way alongside the formation of the Mishnah's rules themselves. It follows that explanations of the sense of the document, including its authority and sources, would draw attention to the written part of the Torah.

We may classify the Midrash compilations in three successive groups: exegetical, propositional, and exegetical-propositional (theological).

[1] EXEGETICAL DISCOURSE AND THE PENTATEUCH: One important dimension, therefore, of the earliest documents of Scripture exegesis, the Midrash compilations that deal with Leviticus, Numbers, and Deuteronomy, measures the distance between the Mishnah and Scripture and aims to close it. The question is persistently addressed in analyzing Scripture: precisely how does a rule of the Mishnah relate to, or rest upon, a rule of Scripture? That question demanded an answer, so that the status of the Mishnah's rules, and, right alongside, of the Mishnah itself, could find a clear definition. Collecting and arranging exegeses of Scripture as these related to passages of the Mishnah first reached literary form in Sifra, to Leviticus, and in two books, both called Sifré, one to Numbers, the other Deuteronomy. All three compositions accomplished much else. For, even at that early stage, exegeses of passages of Scripture in their own context and not only for the sake of Mishnah exegesis attracted attention. But a principal motif in all three books concerned the issue of Mishnah-Scripture relationships.

A second, still more fruitful path in formulating Midrash clarifications of Scripture also emerged from the labor of Mishnah exegesis. As the work of Mishnah exegesis got under way, in the third century, exegetes of the Mishnah and others alongside undertook a parallel labor. They took an interest in reading Scripture in the way in which they were reading the Mishnah itself. That is to say, they began to work through verses of Scripture in exactly the same way—word for word, phrase for phrase, line for line—in which, to begin with, the exegetes of the Mishnah pursued the interpretation and explanation of the Mishnah. Precisely the types of exegesis that dictated the way in which sages read the Mishnah now guided their reading of Scripture as well. And, as people began to collect and organize comments in accord with the order of sentences and paragraphs of the Mishnah, they found the stimulation to collect and organize comments on clauses and verses of Scripture. This kind of verse-by-verse exegetical work got under way in the Sifra and the two Sifrés, but reached fulfillment in Genesis Rabbah, which presents a line-for-line reading of the book of Genesis. Characteristic of the narrowly exegetical phase of Midrash compilation is the absence of a single, governing proposition, running through the details. It is not possible, for example, to state the main point, expressed through countless cases, in Sifra or Sifré to Deuteronomy.[4]

[2] FROM EXEGESIS TO PROPOSITION: A further group of Midrash compilations altogether transcends the limits of formal exegesis. Beyond these two modes of exegesis—search for the sources of the Mishnah in Scripture, line-by-line reading of Scripture as of the Mishnah—lies yet a third, an approach we may call "writing with Scripture," meaning, using verses of Scripture in a context established by a propositional program independent of Scripture itself. To understand it, we have to know how the first of the two Talmuds read the Mishnah. The Yerushalmi's authors not only explained phrases or sentences of the Mishnah in the manner of Mishnah and Scripture exegetes. They also investigated the principles and large-scale conceptual problems of the document and of the law given only in cases in the Mishnah itself. That is to say, they dealt not alone with a given topic, a subject and its rule, and the cases that yield the rule, but with an encompassing problem or a principle and its implications for a number of topics and rules.

This far more discursive and philosophical mode of thought produced for Mishnah exegesis sustained essays on principles cutting across specific rules. Predictably, this same intellectual work extended from the Mishnah to Scripture. Exegesis of Scripture beyond that focused on words, phrases, and sentences produced discursive essays on great principles or problems of theology and morality. Discursive exegesis is represented, to begin with, in Leviticus Rabbah, a document that reached closure, people generally suppose, sometime after Genesis Rabbah, thus ca. 450 and that marked the shift from verse-by-verse to syllogistic reading of verses of Scripture. It was continued in Pesiqta deRab Kahana, organized around themes pertinent to various holy days through the liturgical year, and Pesiqta Rabbati, a derivative and imitative work.

Typical of discursive exegesis of Scripture, Leviticus Rabbah presents not phrase-by-phrase systematic exegeses of verses in the book of Leviticus, but a set of thirty-seven topical essays. These essays, syllogistic in purpose, take the form of citations and comments on verses of Scripture, to be sure. But the compositions range widely over the far reaches of the Hebrew Scriptures while focusing narrowly upon a given theme. They moreover make quite distinctive points about that theme. Their essays constitute compositions, not merely composites. Whether devoted to God's favor to the poor and humble or to the dangers of drunkenness, the essays, exegetical in form, discursive in character, correspond to the equivalent, legal essays, amply represented in the Yerushalmi. The framers of Pesiqta deRab Kahana carried forward a still more abstract and discursive mode of discourse, one in which verses of Scripture play a subordinated role to the framing of an implicit syllogism, which predominates throughout, both formally and in argument.

---

[4] But that does not characterize Sifré to Numbers.

[3] SAYING ONE THING THROUGH MANY THINGS: Writing with Scripture reached its climax in the theological Midrash compilations formed at the end of the development of rabbinic literature. A fusion of the two approaches to Midrash exegesis, the verse-by-verse amplification of successive chapters of Scripture and the syllogistic presentation of propositions, arguments, and proofs deriving from the facts of Scripture, was accomplished in the third body of Midrash compilations: Ruth Rabbah, Esther Rabbah Part One, Lamentations Rabbah, and Song of Songs Rabbah. Here we find the verse-by-verse reading of scriptural books. But at the same time, a highly propositional program governs the exegesis, each of the compilations meaning to prove a single, fundamental theological point through the accumulation of detailed comments.

HALAKHAH AND AGGADAH, MISHNAH AND MIDRASH IN A SINGLE DE-FINITIVE DOCUMENT: The Talmud of Babylonia, or Bavli, which was the final document of rabbinic literature, also formed the climax and conclusion of the entire canon and defined this Judaism from its time to the present. The Talmud of Babylonia forms the conclusion and the summary of rabbinic literature, the most important document of the entire collection. One of its principal traits is the fusion of Mishnah and Scripture exegesis in a single compilation. The authors of units of discourse collected in the Talmud of Babylonia or Bavli drew together the two, up-to-then distinct, modes of organizing thought, either around the Mishnah or around Scripture. They treated both Torahs, oral and written, as equally available in the work of organizing large-scale exercises of sustained inquiry. So we find in the Bavli a systematic treatment of some tractates of the Mishnah. And within the same aggregates of discourse, we also find (in somewhat smaller proportion to be sure, roughly 60 percent to roughly 40 percent in a sample made of three tractates) a second principle of organizing and redaction. That principle dictates that ideas be laid out in line with verses of Scripture, themselves dealt with in cogent sequence, one by one, just as the Mishnah's sentences and paragraphs come under analysis, in cogent order and one by one.

DATING RABBINIC DOCUMENTS: While we have no exact dates for the closure of any of the documents of rabbinic literature—all the dates we have are mere guesses—we have solid grounds on setting them forth in the sequence (1) Mishnah, Tosefta, (2) Yerushalmi, (3) Bavli for the exegetical writings on the Mishnah; and (1) Sifra and the two Sifrés, (2) Leviticus Rabbah, Pesiqta deRab Kahana, Pesiqta Rabbati, (3) Ruth Rabbah, Esther Rabbah Part One, Lamentations Rabbah, and Song of Songs Rabbah for the exegetical writings on Scripture. The basis in the case of the sequence from the Mishnah is citation by one compilation of another, in which case the cited document is to be dated prior to the document that does the citing. The basis in the case of the sequence from Scripture is less certain; we assign a post-Mishnah date to Sifra and the two Sifrés because of the large-scale citation of the former in the latter. The rest of the sequence given here rests upon presently accepted and conventional dates and therefore cannot be regarded as final.

Study of the history of rabbinic Judaism through the literature just now set forth must proceed document by document, in the sequence presently established for their respective dates of closure. In such a study of documentary sequences, e.g., how a given topic or theme is set forth in one writing after another, we learn the order in which ideas came to expression in the canon. We therefore commence at the Mishnah, the starting point of the originally oral part of the canon. We proceed systematically to work our way through tractate Abot, the Mishnah's first apologetic, then the Tosefta, the Yerushalmi, and the Bavli at the end. Along the same lines, the sequence of Midrash compilations is to be examined and the results, if possible, correlated with those of the Mishnah and its companions. In tracing the order in which ideas make their appearance, we ask about the components in sequence so far as we can trace the sequence. The traits of documents govern, and the boundaries that separate one from another also distinguish sayings from one another. The upshot is the study of the documents one by one, with emphasis on their distinguishing traits. When properly analyzed data are in hand, the work of forming of the facts a coherent, historical account of the whole may get under way. A further, theological task, within Judaism, is to form of the facts a cogent system and structure.

3.

ATTRIBUTIONS OF SAYINGS TO SAGES
AND THEIR PLACE IN RABBINIC LITERATURE

The documentary examination of the rabbinic literature is not the only way taken to describe the writings. Another approach to the examination of rabbinic literature takes as the units of study not the successive documents and their definitive qualities, but rather, the sayings attributed to named authorities. This approach to the examination of rabbinic literature treats as inconsequential the task of describing the documents in their own terms, one by one. It deals with the themes of the literature read as a single corpus, rather than the traits of documents inclusive of their topical programs. The topical-biographical reading of rabbinic literature rests on the (definitive) fact that nearly every composition in rabbinic literature will contain an attributed statement, as well as anonymous ones. Some therefore suppose that instead of reading rabbinic literature document by document, we should collect all the sayings assigned to a given authority and provide an account of the literature solely in terms of its contents. These sayings found in diverse documents then are to be classified as to time and place by the names associated with given compositions, rather than classified as to sequence by the presently assumed order of closure of the writings themselves. The result is that a principal mode of describing rabbinic literature alternative to the one followed here is biographical.[5]

It would follow that contrary to the principles of organization followed in this introduction, the traits of documents might take subordinate position, attributions of sayings defining the correct modes of categorization and ordering of the literature. Without regard to the documentary origin of those assigned sayings, such an approach to the study of rabbinic literature then would work out the intellectual-biographical sequences, e.g., all the sayings given to a given authority, or topical ones, assuming the validity of the attribution of a saying to a sage who lived at a given time and therefore assigning that opinion to the age in which that sage lived. This approach ignores the lines of structure and order set forth by the documents themselves and takes for granted that the compilers of documents played no role in the shaping of the compositions that they collected. Documents then are taken to represent random points of compilation, not purposive and deliberate statements.

Examining attributions of sayings to named authorities and ignoring the documentary traits of individual writings presents problems. The decisive one is that we cannot demonstrate, and therefore cannot take as fact, that what is attributed to a given sage really was said by him. The facticity of the documents is beyond question; the reliability of attributions is not. The reason is simple. No tests of validation or falsification of attributions have yet been devised to indicate which attributions are reliable, which not. The kind of internal evidence that would suffice—authenticated writings of said authority in his own style and on his own account—such as we have for earliest figures in Christianity, such as Paul or Justin, Origen or Augustine—does not exist. The rabbinic documents rarely assign to named authorities sayings that exhibit traits of an individual character; most sayings exhibit the stylistic traits that predominate in the document that contains them. That means traits of individual style and form are obliterated, and that fact raises the question of how reliable what is attributed to that name is going to be.

Tests of falsification of the entire body of attributions, by contrast, yield positive results. When we seek evidence that attributions served a purpose other than factually assigning a given saying to a given name, we find ample indication that that was the case. What is attributed to a given name is not consistently assigned to that name; or we may find attributed to a given name both a statement and its very opposite. A saying assigned to a given authority in one document is assigned to someone else in another; a saying that is assigned to a given authority in one document occurs in different form altogether in his name in some other; and it is routine in the two Talmuds to revise attributions, reversing the sponsorship of a given position, for instance, so that Rabbi X, originally thought to have said A, is

---

[5] This is the way taken by Stemberger-Strack, which devotes to "the rabbis" half of the general introduction (56 out of 118 pages), pp. 62–118. By contrast, in this introduction to exactly the same literature, we entirely bypass the matter of named authorities, for reasons explained presently.

given opinion B, and Rabbi Y, who is supposed to have said B, is given opinion A. It follows that whatever the semiotic meaning of attributing sayings to named authorities, considerations of historical accuracy in the contemporary sense figured only in a limited way. While the writings before us are characterized by the attribution of numerous sayings to named authorities, those attributions do not provide secure evidence that the named authority really said what was attributed to him.

Sayings of individual sages come down to us in collective compositions, so we cannot demonstrate that Rabbi X wrote a book in which his views are given, preserved by his immediate disciples for instance. We do not know that a given rabbi really said what is imputed to him at all, since there are no external witnesses to any attribution. All we have in hand is that the framers of document A have assigned diverse sayings to various names. Some facts make us wonder whether those assignments rest on the facts of a given figure's actual statements. First, the same saying may occur in more than a single name. What document A gives to Rabbi X, document B gives to Rabbi Y. Second, the actual wording of sayings assigned to individuals rarely bears distinctive traits and most commonly conforms to an overall pattern, imposed, in a given document, upon all sayings. These specific negative factors join a general one. In the picture we have of the formation of the documents and of the sayings in them, we cannot point to evidence of processes of individual writing, e.g., Rabbi X wrote book Y, or even to a program of preserving the very words of Rabbi X on the part of his disciples. The collective character of the writings before us testifies to a different purpose altogether from one which would preserve the particular views of a given individual. In rabbinic literature we have in hand something other than minutes of meetings, actual words spoken by particular authorities, that is, something other than the results, for conditions pertaining in antiquity, of the counterpart of careful observations by trained reporters, with tape recorders or TV cameras.

Not only so, but the documents formalize whatever they use and impose their own distinctive, documentary-rhetorical preferences on nearly everything in hand. Some maintain that while we do not have in hand the actual words, we do have the gist of what someone said. They suppose that while we do not know exactly what he said, we do know what he was thinking. But that carries us onto still more dubious ground. For attributions even of the gist of what is said by themselves cannot be shown to be reliable. We have no way of demonstrating that a given authority really maintained the views assigned to him—even if not in the actual words attributed to him. There are no sources in which we can check what is attributed, e.g., a given authority's own writings, preserved by his disciples; diaries, notes, personal reflections of any kind. We have only the judgment and record provided by the collectivity of sages represented by a given authorship: that is, the document and that alone. What we cannot show we do not know.

Since the various compositions of the canon of formative Judaism derive not from named, individual authors but from collective decisions of schools or academies, we cannot take for granted that attributions of sayings to individuals provide facts. We cannot show that if a given rabbi is alleged to have made a statement, he really did say what is assigned to him. We do not have a book or a letter he wrote such as we have, for example, for Paul or Augustine or other important Christian counterparts to the great rabbis of late antiquity. We also do not know that if a story was told, things really happened in the way the storyteller says, in some other way, or not at all.

Accordingly, we cannot identify as historical in a narrow and exact sense sayings or stories that come down to us in the canon of Judaism. Attributions of sayings, narratives of stories—these tell us only what those who assigned the sayings approved, on the one side, or what they believed ought to have happened, on the other. Sayings and stories therefore attest to the viewpoint of the framers of the documents who collected the sayings and stories and gave them a position of authority in the compilations they produced. What is absolutely firm and factual, therefore, is that these books represent views held by the authorship behind them. At the point at which a document reached conclusion and redaction, views of a given group of people reached the form at that moment of closure in which we now have them (taking account of variations of wording). That is why we do not know with any certainty what people were thinking prior to the point at which, it is generally assumed, a given document was redacted. Accordingly, if we wish to know the sequence in which views reached their current expression, we have recourse to the conventional order and rough dating assigned by modern scholarship to the several documents, from the Mishnah through the Bavli. All of the rabbinic compilations are collective, official writings of their institutional sponsors, and none of them speaks for an individual authority. We examine rabbinic literature document by document because the documents alone form solid facts, starting points for further study of history, religion, and the literature of Judaism itself.

4.
THE RELATIONSHIPS AMONG THE
DOCUMENTS OF RABBINIC LITERATURE

If, however, we read documents one by one, as autonomous of one another, we have also to know how they interrelate. Describing the documents one by one therefore marks only the first step in the analysis of rabbinic literature. Only when we know to what degree a document speaks for its authorship and to what degree it carries forward a received position can we come to an estimate of the character of that document's testimony to the unfolding of the system of rabbinic Judaism as a whole:

[1] essentially its own and representative of the authorship of its stage in the unfolding of the canon—or

[2] essentially continuous with what has gone before—or

[3] somewhere in the middle.

Seen one by one, moreover, documents stand in three relationships to one another and to the system of which they form part, that is, to Judaism as a whole. Three stages, therefore, mark the analysis of documents, corresponding to the three possible relationships that can characterize the canonical writings as a whole.

[1] Each document is to be seen all by itself, that is, as autonomous of all others (though all documents may well concur on some basic, commonly inert facts, e.g., the unity of God).

[2] Each document is to be examined for its connections or relationships with other documents universally regarded as falling into the same classification, as Torah.

[3] And, finally, in the theology of Judaism each document is to be allowed to take its place as part of the undifferentiated aggregation of documents that all together constitute the canon of, in the case of Judaism, the "one whole Torah revealed by God to Moses at Mount Sinai."

These several relationships that situate the documents of rabbinic literature may now be described in terms of (1) autonomy, the stage of description; (2) connection, the stage of analysis, comparison, and contrast; and (3) continuity, the stage of interpretation (whether historical or theological). That is to say, each of the writings is to be read as an autonomous statement on its own terms, with close attention to its distinctive, definitive traits of rhetoric, logic, and topic. Each further has to be brought into relationship with other writings of its species, e.g., exposition of the Mishnah or of Scripture, and sayings found in more than a single document are to be compared and contrasted as well. Finally, all writings are to be seen as part of a single coherent literature, a canon, meant to make a statement, elements of which derive from all of the documents equally. The first stage is descriptive, defining each writing; the second is analytical, comparing one writing with another; the third is synthetic, joining all the documents into a whole statement. In the final chapter of this introduction we shall examine a theory of how the various documents cohere into a single, continuous history, that is, how they all together set forth the formative history of rabbinic Judaism. The three stages of documentary study may be characterized as follows:

[1] AUTONOMY: If a document comes down to us within its own framework, exhibiting its own distinctive traits of rhetoric, topic, and logic, as a complete book with a beginning, middle, and end, in preserving that book, the canon presents us with a document on its own and not solely as part of a larger composition or construct. So we too see the document as it reaches us, that is, as autonomous.

[2] CONNECTION: If, second, a document contains materials shared verbatim or in substantial content with other documents of its classification, or if one document refers to the contents of other documents, then the several documents that clearly wish to engage in conversation with one another have to address one another. That is to say, we have to seek for the marks of connectedness, asking for the meaning of those connections.

[3] CONTINUITY: Finally, since the community of the faithful of Judaism, in all of the contemporary expressions of Judaism, concur that documents held to be authoritative constitute one whole, seamless "Torah," that is, a complete and exhaustive statement of God's will for Israel and humanity, we take as a further appropriate task, if one not to be done here, the description of the whole out of the undifferentiated testimony of all of its parts. These components in the theological context are viewed, as is clear, as equally authoritative for the composition of the whole: one, continuous system. In taking up such a question, we address a problem not of theology alone, though it is a correct theological conviction, but one of description, analysis, and interpretation of an entirely historical order.

The several documents that make up rabbinic literature relate to one another in yet three other important ways.

[1] All of them refer to the same basic writing, the Hebrew Scriptures. Many of them draw upon the Mishnah and quote it. So the components of the canon join at their foundations.

[2] As the documents reached closure in sequence, the later authorship can be shown to have drawn upon earlier, completed documents. So the writings of the rabbis of the talmudic corpus accumulate and build from layer to layer.

[3] Among two or more documents some completed units of discourse, and many brief, discrete sayings, circulated, for instance, sentences or episodic homilies or fixed sayings (e.g., moral maxims) of various kinds.

So in some (indeterminate) measure the several documents draw not only upon one another, as we can show, but also upon a common corpus of materials that might serve diverse editorial and redactional purposes. The extent of this common corpus of floating sayings can never be fully known. We know only what we have, not what we do not have. So we cannot say what has been omitted, or whether sayings that occur in only one document derive from materials available to the editors or compilers of some or all other documents. That is something we never can know.

5.

INTERTEXTUALITY OR INTRATEXTUALITY:
RABBINIC LITERATURE AS A COMMUNITY
OF TEXTS

Since the several rabbinic documents stand distinct from one another, each with its own rhetorical, logical, and topical program, they relate not "intertextually" but "intratextually." That is to say, when the framers of a composition wish to allude to another document, e.g., Scripture, they say so in so many words. They ordinarily give a clear signal that that document is cited, ordinarily using such citation language as "as it is said" or "as it is written." The accepted definitions of intertextuality, which emphasize the implicit bonds that form an invisible web holding together all writings, therefore do not apply. Rabbinic literature forms a library, in which a common collection unites discrete items, rather than an un-differentiated body of writing.

To clarify this perspective, consider the analogy of a library. Books brought together form a library. Each title addresses its own program and makes its own points. But books produced by a cogent community constitute not merely a library but a canon: a set of compositions each of which contributes to a statement that transcends its own pages. The books exhibit intrinsic traits that make of them all *a community of texts*. We should know on the basis of those characteristics that the texts form a community even if we knew nothing more than the texts themselves. In the Judaic writings, moreover, the documents at hand are held by Judaism to form a canon.

Seeing the whole as continuous, which is quite natural, later theology main-tains that all of the documents of rabbinic literature find a place in "the Torah." But that is an imputed and theological, not an inductive and intrinsic, fact. It is something we know only on the basis of information—theological convictions about the one whole Torah God gave to Moses in two media—deriving from sources other than the texts at hand, which, on their own, do not link each to all and all to every line of each. Extrinsic traits, that is, imputed ones, make of the discrete writings a single and continuous, uniform statement: one whole Torah in the mythic language of Judaism. The community of Judaism imputes those traits, sees commonalities, uniformities, deep harmonies: one Torah of one God. In secu-lar language, that community expresses its system—its worldview, its way of life, its sense of itself as a society—by these choices, and finds its definition in them. Hence, in the nature of things, the community of Judaism forms a *textual commu-nity*. That cogent community that forms a canon out of a selection of books there-fore participates in the process of authorship, just as the books exist in at least two dimensions.

Let us turn to the problem of the community of texts, utilizing the dimensions just now defined in our description of the canon. We take the measure of two of the three dimensions just now introduced, *autonomy*, on the one side, and *connec-tion*, on the second. (Continuity among all documents introduces theological, not literary, problems for analysis.) That is to say, a book enjoys its own autonomous standing, but it also situates itself in relationship to other books of the same classi-fication. Each book bears its own statement and purpose, and each relates to others of the same classification. The community of texts therefore encompasses individ-uals who (singly or collectively) comprise (for the authorships: compose) books. But there is a set of facts that indicates how a book does not stand in isolation. These facts fall into several categories. Books may go over the same ground or make use in some measure of the same materials. The linkages between and among them therefore connect them. Traits of rhetoric, logic, and topic may place into a single classification a number of diverse writings. Then there is the larger consensus of members who see relationships between one book and another and so join them together on a list of authoritative writings. So, as is clear, a book exists in the dimensions formed of its own contents and covers, but it also takes its place in the second and third dimensions of relationship to other books.

Then the relationships in which a given document stands may be expressed in the prepositions *between* and *among*. That is to say, in its intellectual traits a document bears relationship, to begin with, to some other, hence we describe relationships between two documents. These constitute formal and intrinsic matters: traits of grammar, arrangements of words and resonances as to their local meaning, structures of syntax of expression and thought. But in its social setting a document finds bonds among three or more documents, with all of which it is joined in the imagination and mind of a community. These range widely and freely, bound by limits not of form and language, but of public policy in behavior and belief. Documents because of their traits of rhetoric, logic, and topic form a community of texts. Documents because of their audience and authority express the intellect of a textual community.

The principal issue worked out in establishing a community of texts is hermeneutical, the chief outcome of defining a textual community, social and cultural. The former teaches us how to read the texts on their own. The latter tells us how to interpret texts in context. When we define and classify the relationships between texts, we learn how to read the components—words, cogent thoughts formed of phrases, sentences, paragraphs—of those texts in the broader context defined by shared conventions of intellect: rhetoric, logic, topic. More concretely, hermeneutical principles tell how, in light of like documents we have seen many times, to approach a document we have never before seen. Hermeneutics teaches the grammar and syntax of thought. Memorizing a passage of a complex text will teach the rhythms of expression and thought that make of the sounds of some other document an intelligible music. Not only so, but documents joined into a common classification may share specific contents, not only definitive traits of expression—meaning and not solely method.

6.

COMPOSITIONS AND COMPOSITES:
THE PREHISTORY OF RABBINIC DOCUMENTS

Any introduction to rabbinic literature must answer the question, what about the materials upon which the various documents draw? The question concerns sources or traditions utilized by framers of rabbinic documents but not made up by those compilers. The documents give ample evidence that before the work of compilation got under way, a process of composition had gone forward and in some passages had reached conclusion. That is not by reason of the citations, of indeterminate reliability, of sayings to named figures, even though these have to be addressed, if not treated as irreducible historical facts. It is because the literary traits of the documents themselves ordinarily permit us to identify compositions that are quite distinct in indicative traits from the larger composite of which they now form a component.

For example, a given document defines for us its definitive structure—the paramount literary forms, the rhetorical preferences of the editors, the modes of logical coherence, even the topical program. Then materials clearly not put together in conformity with the document's protocol present themselves as candidates for inclusion in a list of compositions utilized, but not made up, by the document's own framers. Most of the rabbinic writings exhibit the character of compilations, and only a few of them appear to conform to a single convention of thought and expression, beginning to end. The Mishnah and Sifra typify the latter kind of document; Tosefta, the two Talmuds, and most of the Midrash compilations, the former. In the composite documents, as we shall see at some length, one principle of coherent discourse, that of propositional logic, serves in compositions, while another, that of fixed association to a set of statements (e.g., verses of Scripture or clauses of the Mishnah), molds compositions into composites. It follows that rabbinic documents on the very surface implicitly attest to the availability of statements—whether writings or oral traditions—made up prior to inclusion in the documents in which they now occur.

Internal evidence within the documents themselves guides us toward an answer to the question of the prehistory of rabbinic documents. Specifically, we may categorize the completed units of thought that comprise each of the documents by appeal to external, redactional traits. Some of those completed units of thought, which we may call compositions, clearly serve the purposes of the framers of the document in which they occur; others accomplish the goals of compilers of a kind of document we do have, but not the document in which we now find them. And still others present the anomaly of writings composed for a kind of compilation that we simply do not have at all.

It is a fact that the rabbinic writings make occasional use of freestanding individual sayings that circulated in ways we cannot now define. But, to a much more considerable extent, they all utilize for the formation of their composites sizable numbers of previously completed compositions and even composites of such compositions, and any account of the rabbinic literature requires attention to the materials that contribute to the formation of those books. We know that that is a fact, because, while each of the documents that make up the canon of Judaism exhibits distinctive traits in logic, rhetoric, and topic, so that we may identify the purposes and traits of form and intellect of the authorship of that document, they also use compositions and even composites that do not exhibit those distinctive traits at all.

Most rabbinic documents in various proportion contain some completed units of thought—propositional arguments, sayings, and stories for instance. A few of these may travel from one document to another. It follows that the several documents intersect through shared materials. Furthermore, these completed compositions compiled in two or more documents by definition do not carry out the rhetorical, logical, and topical program of a particular document. So while documents are autonomous but also connected through such shared materials, therefore, we must account for the history of not only the documents in hand but also the completed pieces of writing that move from here to there.

Three stages mark the formation of rabbinic documents, viewed individually. We work from the finished writing backward to the freestanding compositions that framers or compilers or authors of those documents utilized.

[1] Moving from the latest to the earliest, one stage is marked by the definition of a document, *its* topical program, *its* rhetorical medium, *its* logical message. These are definitive traits we have now explained, and some of the compositions compiled in a document exhibit the traits of the document as a whole. The document as we know it in its basic structure and main lines therefore comes at the end of the process. It follows that writings that clearly serve the program of that document and carry out the purposes of its authorship were made up in connection with the formation of *that* document.

[2] Another, prior stage is marked by the preparation of writings that do not serve the needs of a particular document now in our hands, but could have carried out the purposes of an authorship working on a document of a *type* we now have. The existing documents then form a model for defining other kinds of writings worked out to meet the program of a documentary authorship.

[3] But—and now we come to the heart of the matter—there are other types of writings that in no way serve the needs or plans of any document we now have, and that furthermore, also cannot find a place in any document of a type that we now have. These writings, as a matter of fact, very commonly prove peripatetic, traveling from one writing to another, equally at home in, or alien to, the program of the documents in which they end up. These writings therefore were carried out without regard to a documentary program of any kind, the program exemplified by the canonical books of the Judaism of the dual Torah. They form the earliest in the three stages of the writing of the units of completed thought that in the aggregate form the canonical literature of the Judaism of the dual Torah of late antiquity.

As a matter of fact, therefore, a given canonical document of the Judaism of the dual Torah draws upon three classes of materials, and these were framed in temporal order. Last comes the final class, the one that the redactors themselves defined and wrote; prior is the penultimate class that could have served other redactors but did not serve these in particular; and earliest of all in the order of composition (at least, from the perspective of the ultimate redaction of the documents we now have) is the writing that circulated autonomously and served no redactional purpose we can now identify within the canonical documents. Let us consider a concrete example of the distinction between writings that conform to the purposes of a document we now have and those that do not, with the Mishnah and the Talmud of Babylonia as our illustrative cases.

[1] THE MISHNAH: A document that is written down essentially in its penultimate and ultimate stages, taking shape within the redactional process and principally there, is the Mishnah. In that writing, the patterns of language, e.g., syntactic structures, of the apodosis and protasis of the Mishnah's smallest whole units of discourse are framed in formal, mnemonic patterns. They follow a few simple rules. These rules, once known, apply nearly everywhere and form stunning evidence for the document's cogency. They permit anyone to reconstruct, out of a few key phrases, an entire cognitive unit, and even complete intermediate units of discourse. Working downward from the surface, therefore, anyone can penetrate into the deeper layers of meaning of the Mishnah. Then and at the same time, while discovering the principle behind the cases, one can easily memorize the whole by mastering the recurrent rhetorical pattern dictating the expression of the cogent set of cases. For it is easy to note the shift from one rhetorical pattern to another and to follow the repeated cases, articulated in the new pattern downward to its logical substrate. So syllogistic propositions, in the Mishnah's authors' hands, come to full expression not only in *what* people wish to state but also in *how* they choose to say it. The limits of rhetoric define the arena of topical articulation.

The Mishnah's formal traits of rhetoric—to which we return in Chapter 2—indicate that the bulk of the document has been formulated all at once, and not in an incremental, linear process extending into a remote past. These traits, common to a series of distinct cognitive units, are redactional, because they are imposed at that point at which someone intended to join together discrete (finished) units on a given theme. The varieties of traits particular to the discrete units and the diversity of authorities cited therein make it highly improbable that the several units were formulated in a common pattern and then preserved until later on, still further units, on the same theme and in the same pattern, were worked out and added. The entire indifference, moreover, to historical order of authorities and the concentration on the logical unfolding of a given theme or problem without reference to the sequence of authorities confirm the supposition that the work of formulation and that of redaction go forward together.

The principal framework of formulation and formalization in the Mishnah is the intermediate division rather than the cognitive unit. The least formalized formulary pattern, the simple declarative sentence, turns out to yield many examples of acute formalization, in which a single distinctive pattern is imposed upon two or more (very commonly, groups of three or groups of five) cognitive units. While an intermediate division of a tractate may be composed of several such conglomerates of cognitive units, it is rare indeed for cognitive units formally to stand wholly by themselves. Normally, cognitive units share formal or formulary traits with others to which they are juxtaposed and the theme of which they share. It follows that the principal unit of formulary formalization is the intermediate division and not the cognitive unit. And what that means for our inquiry is simple: we can tell when it is that the ultimate or penultimate redactors of a document do the writing.

Now let us see that vast collection of writings that exhibits precisely the opposite trait: a literature in which, while doing some writing of their own, the redactors collected and arranged available materials.

[2] THE TALMUD OF BABYLONIA: In the pages of this document, a kind of writing that in no way defines a document now in our hands or even a type of document we can now imagine, that is, one that in its particulars we do not have but that conforms in its definitive traits to those that we do have, may also be identified. The final organizers of the Talmud of Babylonia had in hand a tripartite corpus of inherited materials awaiting composition into a final, closed document.

First, in the initial type of material, in various states and stages of completion, sages addressed the Mishnah or took up the principles of laws that the Mishnah had originally brought to articulation. These compositions the framers of the Bavli organized in accord with the order of those Mishnah tractates that they selected for sustained attention.

Second, they had in hand received materials, again in various conditions, pertinent to Scripture, both as Scripture related to the Mishnah and also as Scripture laid forth its own narratives. These they set forth as Scripture commentary. In this way, the penultimate and ultimate redactors of the Bavli laid out a systematic presentation of the two Torahs, the oral, represented by the Mishnah, and the written, represented by Scripture.

And, third, the framers of the Bavli also had in hand materials focused on sages. These in the received form, attested in the Bavli's pages, were framed around twin biographical principles, either as strings of stories about great sages of the past or as collections of sayings and comments drawn together solely because the same name stands behind all the collected sayings. These can easily have been composed into biographies. This is writing that is utterly outside of the documentary framework in which it is now preserved; nearly all narratives in the rabbinic literature, not only the biographical ones, indeed prove remote from any documentary program exhibited by the canonical documents in which they now occur.

The Bavli as a whole lays itself out as a commentary to the Mishnah. So the framers wished us to think that whatever they wanted to tell us would take the form of Mishnah commentary. But a second glance indicates that the Bavli is made up of enormous composites, themselves closed prior to inclusion in the Bavli. Some of these composites—around 40 percent of Bavli's whole—were selected and arranged along lines dictated by a logic other than that deriving from the requirements of Mishnah commentary. The components of the canon of the Judaism of the dual Torah prior to the Bavli had encompassed amplifications of the Mishnah, in the Tosefta and in the Yerushalmi, as well as the same for Scripture. As we have already noted, these are found in such documents as Sifra to Leviticus, Sifré to Numbers, another Sifré, to Deuteronomy, Genesis Rabbah, Leviticus Rabbah, and the like. But there was no entire document, now extant, organized around the life and teachings of a particular sage. Even the Fathers According to Rabbi Nathan, which contains a good sample of stories about sages, is not so organized as to yield a life of a sage, or even a systematic biography of any kind.

Where events in the lives of sages do occur, they are thematic and not biographical in organization, e.g., stories about the origins, as to Torah study, of diverse sages; death scenes of various sages. The sage as such, whether Aqiba or Yohanan ben Zakkai or Eliezer b. Hyrcanus, never in that document defines the appropriate organizing principle for sequences of stories or sayings. And there is no other in which the sage forms an organizing category for any material purpose.

Accordingly, the decision that the framers of the Bavli reached was to adopt the two redactional principles inherited from the antecedent century or so and to reject the one already rejected by their predecessors, even while honoring it.

[1] They organized the Bavli around the Mishnah.

[2] They adapted and included vast tracts of antecedent materials organized as scriptural commentary. These they inserted whole and complete, not at all in response to the Mishnah's program.

[3] While making provision for small-scale compositions built upon biographical principles, preserving both strings of sayings from a given master (and often a given tradent—a disciple responsible to memorize sayings of a given master) as well as tales about authorities of the preceding half millennium, they never created redactional compositions, of a sizable order, that focused upon given authorities. But sufficient materials certainly lay at hand to allow doing so.

While we cannot date these freestanding writings, we may come to a theory on their place in the unfolding of the rabbinic literature. We ask in particular about the compositions and even large-scale composites that stand autonomous of any redactional program we have in an existing compilation or of any we can even imagine on the foundations of said writings. Compositions of this kind, as a matter of hypothesis, are to be assigned to a stage in the formation of classics prior to the framing of the now-available documents. For, as a matter of fact, all of our now extant writings adhere to a single program of conglomeration and agglutination, and all are served by composites of one sort, rather than some other. Hence we may suppose that at some point prior to the decision to make writings in the model that we now have but in some other model people also made up completed units of thought to serve these other kinds of writings. These persist, now, in documents that they do not serve at all well. And we can fairly easily identify the kinds of documents that they can and should have served quite nicely indeed. These then are the three stages of literary formation in the making of the classics of Judaism.

Of the relative temporal or ordinal position of writings that stand autonomous of any redactional program we have in an existing compilation or of any we can even imagine on the foundations of said writings we can say nothing. These writings prove episodic; they are commonly singletons. They serve equally well everywhere, because they demand no traits of form and redaction in order to endow them with sense and meaning. We can understand these compositions entirely within the information their authors have given us; no context in some larger document or even composite is required to make sense of what is before us. So these kinds of compositions are essentially freestanding and episodic, not referential and allusive. They are stories that contain their own point and do not invoke, in the making of that point, a given verse of Scripture. They are sayings that are utterly ad hoc. A variety of materials fall into this—from a redactional perspective—unassigned, and unassignable, type of writing. They do not belong in books at all. Whoever made up these pieces of writing did not imagine that what he was forming required a setting beyond the limits of his own piece of writing; the story is not only complete in itself but could stand entirely on its own; the saying spoke for itself and required no nurturing context; the proposition and its associated proofs in no way were meant to draw nourishment from roots-penetrating nutriments outside of its own literary limits.

Where we have utterly hermetic writing, able to define its own limits and sustain its point without regard to anything outside itself, we know that here we are in the presence of authorships that had no larger redactional plan in mind, no intent on the making of books out of their little pieces of writing. We may note that among the "unimaginable" compilations is not a collection of parables, since parables rarely stand free and never are inserted for their own sake. Whenever in the rabbinic canon we find a parable, it is meant to serve the purpose of an authorship engaged in making its own point; and the point of a parable is rarely, if ever, left unarticulated. Normally it is put into words, but occasionally the point is made simply by redactional setting. It must follow that in this canon, the parable cannot have constituted the generative or agglutinative principle of a large-scale compilation.

The three stages in the formation of materials ultimately compiled in the rabbinic documents in our hand correspond, as a matter of fact, to a taxonomic structure, that is, three types of writing.

[1] The first type—and last in assumed temporal order—is writing carried out in the context of the making, or compilation, of a classic. That writing responds to the redactional program and plan of the authorship of a classic.

[2] The second type—penultimate in order—is writing that can appear in a given document but better serves a document other than the one in which it (singularly) occurs. This kind of writing does not likely fall within the same period of redaction as the first. For while it is a type of writing under the identical conditions, it also is writing that presupposes redactional programs in no way in play in the ultimate, and definitive, period of the formation of the canon: when people did things this way, and not in some other. That is why it is a kind of writing that was done prior to the period in which people limited their redactional work and associated labor of composition to the program that yielded the books we now have.

[3] The third kind of writing originates in an indeterminate period, probably prior to the other two—before the documentary norms had reached definition. It is carried on in a manner independent of all redactional considerations such as are known to us. Then it should derive from a time when redactional considerations played no paramount role in the making of compositions. A brief essay, rather than

a sustained composition, was then the dominant mode of writing. People could have written both long and short compositions—compositions and composites— at one and the same time. But writing that does not presuppose a secondary labor of redaction, e.g., in a composite, probably originated when authors or authorships did not anticipate any fate for their writing beyond their labor of composition itself.

Along these same lines of argument, this writing may or may not travel from one document to another. What that means is that the author or authorship does not imagine a future for his writing. What fits anywhere is composed to go no-where in particular. Accordingly, what matters is not whether a writing fits one document or another, but whether, as the author or authorship has composed a piece of writing, that writing meets the requirements of any document we now have or can even imagine. If it does not, then we deal with a literary period in which the main kind of writing was ad hoc and episodic, not sustained and docu-mentary.

The upshot is simple: whether the classification of writing be given a temporal or merely taxonomic valence, the issue is the same: have these writers done their work with documentary considerations in mind? In these cases it is clear that they have not. Then where did they expect their work to make its way? Anywhere it might, because, so they assumed, fitting in nowhere in particular, it found a suitable locus everywhere it turned up. But I think temporal, not merely taxonomic, con-siderations pertain.

Now extra- and non-documentary kinds of writing derive from either (1) a period prior to the work of the making of Midrash compilations and the two Talmuds alike; or (2) a labor of composition not subject to the rules and considera-tions that operated in the work of the making of Midrash compilations and the two Talmuds. As a matter of hypothesis, non-documentary writing is more likely to come prior to making any kind of documents of consequence, and extra-documentary writing comes prior to the period in which the specificities of the documents we now have were defined. That is to say, writing that can fit anywhere or nowhere is to be situated at a time prior to writing that can fit somewhere but does not fit anywhere now accessible to us, and both kinds of writing are prior to the kind that fits only in the documents in which it is now located.

And given the documentary propositions and theses that we can locate in all of our compilations, we can only assume that the non-documentary writings enjoyed, and were assumed to enjoy, ecumenical acceptance. That means, very simply, when we wish to know the consensus of the entire textual (or canonical) community, we turn not to the distinctive perspective of documents, but the (ap-parently universally acceptable) perspective of the extra-documentary composi-tions.

Non-documentary compositions took shape not only separated from, but in time before, the documentary ones. Non-documentary writings in general focus on matters of very general interest. These matters may be assembled into two very large rubrics: virtue, on the one side, reason, on the other. Stories about sages fall into the former category; all of them set forth in concrete form the right living that sages exemplify. Essays on right thinking, the role of reason, the taxonomic priority of Scripture, the power of analogy, the exemplary character of cases and precedents in the expression of general and encompassing rules—all of these intellectually coercive writings set forth rules of thought as universally applicable, in their way, as are the rules of conduct contained in stories about sages, in theirs. A great labor of generalization is contained in both kinds of non-documentary and extra-documentary writing. And the results of that labor are then given concrete expression in the documentary writings in hand; for these, after all, do say in the setting of specific passages or problems precisely what, in a highly general way, emerges from the writing that moves hither and yon, never with a home, always finding a suitable resting place.

Now, admittedly, that rather general characterization of the non-documentary writing is subject to considerable qualification and clarification. But it does provide a reason to assign temporal priority, not solely taxonomic distinction, to the non-documentary compositions. We can have had commentaries of a sustained and systematic sort on Psalms or Chronicles, which we do not in fact have from late antiquity, on the one side, or treatises on virtue, such as Torah study or the master-disciple relationship, which we also do not have, on the second, or biographies ("gospels") on the third—to complete the triangle. The materials that could have comprised such documents are abundant in the rabbinic literature. But we do not have these kinds of books.

The books we do have not only preserve the evidences of the possibility of commentaries and biographies. More than that, they also bring to rich expression the messages that such books will have set forth. And most important, they also express in fresh and unanticipated contexts those virtues and values that commentaries and biographies ("gospels") meant to bring to realization, and they do so in accord with the modes of thought that sophisticated reflection on right thinking has exemplified in its way as well. So when people went about the work of making documents, they did something fresh with something familiar. They made cogent compositions, documents, texts enjoying integrity and autonomy. But they did so in such a way as to form of their distinct documents a coherent body of writing, of books a canon, of documents a system. And this they did in such a way as to say, in distinctive and specific ways, things that in former times people had expressed in general and broadly applicable ways. Now that we have examined the canon as a whole and identified its principal parts, let us turn to the differentiation of those parts: the criteria that distinguish one document from all others.

II

DISTINGUISHING DOCUMENTS
BY DISTINCTIVE CHARACTERISTICS:
RHETORIC AND TOPIC

1.
RHETORIC, LOGIC, TOPIC:
THE DIFFERENTIATING TRAITS
OF RABBINIC DOCUMENTS

THREE DEFINITIVE TRAITS PERMIT DIFFERENTIATING ONE DOCUMENT FROM AN-
other in rabbinic literature, and correct translation of a rabbinic document makes
possible the identification of these traits:[1]

[1] the rhetoric or formal preferences of a piece of writing, which dictate,
without respect to meaning, how sentences will be composed;

---

[1] The other introductions to rabbinic literature do not address the matters of rhetoric, logic, and topic.
For further reading and bibliography on the form analysis of rabbinic literature, see my *A History of the
Mishnaic Law of Purities*. Leiden, 1977: Brill. XXI. *The Redaction and Formulation of the Order of Purities in
the Mishnah and Tosefta*. That is where I lay out the basic definitions and inquiries pursued throughout.
The explanation of the necessity of form-analytical translation is given in *Translating the Classics of
Judaism. In Theory and in Practice*. Atlanta, 1989: Scholars Press for Brown Judaic Studies. The matter of
form criticism and the problem of appropriate translation are not treated in the other introductions to
rabbinic literature.

[2] the logic of coherent discourse, which determines how one sentence will be joined to others in context; how groups of sentences will cohere and form completed units of thought; and, finally, how said units of thought agglutinate or are otherwise held together in large-scale components of complete documents;

[3] the topical program of the writing, which indicates the subject and may also indicate the problematic—what we wish to know about the subject—of that same writing.

By invoking these three criteria, which are entirely familiar in the analysis of literature in antiquity, we may distinguish each document from all others and establish a clear definition for every piece of writing in the literature. The reason is simple: a received discipline of thought and expression governed all writing that has survived in rabbinic literature.

[1] RHETORIC: Writers in this literature followed formal conventions, making choices never particular to a given author but always set forth, to begin with, by a repertoire of commonly understood fixed arrangements of words. These fixed arrangements, transcending particular meanings, signaled the purpose and even the context of a given set of sentences; following one form, rather than another, therefore dictated to the reader of a passage the character and intent of that passage: its classification. Correct translation will underscore the regularities of form and formulation.

[2] LOGIC OF COHERENT DISCOURSE: Since the rabbinic writings ordinarily set forth not discrete sentences—aphorisms that stand alone, each in lapidary splendor—but cogent sets of sentences forming whole units of coherent thought ("paragraphs" in our language), we also have to identify the principles of logic that connect one sentence to another. That logic of coherent discourse has the power to make of a group of sentences a whole that is greater than the sum of the parts. Proper translation will point up the distinct small whole units of thought ("sentences") and further show how these units of thought coalesce in completed units of thought (paragraphs) and how sets of paragraphs hold together to make coherent statements ("chapters" or major parts thereof).

[3] TOPIC, PROPOSITION: Every document treats a specific topic. Moreover, many documents set forth sustained exercises in the analysis of a concrete problem pertinent to a given topic. Some entire documents, early and late in the formation of the literature, are so set forth as to demonstrate propositions we are able to identify and define. Few books in rabbinic literature aim merely at collecting and arranging information. Nearly all documents, to the contrary, work on not a topic in general but a specific problem concerning that topic, that is, a problematic; most of the documents set forth propositions that emerge out of masses of detail and may come to concrete expression through diverse details.

The governing protocols served because no document in rabbinic literature ever accommodated idiosyncratic preference. Not a single one comes to us from an individual writer or author (e.g., Paul, Josephus, Philo); none collects the sayings or composites formulated in a single school (e.g., Matthew). All documents enjoy the sponsorship of sages as a group, whether we call the group an authorship or redactors or compilers or editors. Not only so, but the compositions of which the composites are comprised themselves follow rigid rules of formulation and expression. When, therefore, we identify those rules, we can classify documents by differentiating among a limited repertoire of available choices.

Each document requires close analysis within its own limits, then comparison with other documents: first, those of its species; then, those not of its species. When compared as to rhetoric, topic, and logic of coherent discourse, nearly all of the documents will yield ample evidence that a restricted formal repertoire dictated to writers how they were to formulate their ideas if those ideas were to find a place in this particular document. Some forms appear in more than one document, others are unique to the writings in which they appear. Two examples of the former are the exegetical form and the dispute.

[1] EXEGETICAL FORM: The exegetical form requires two elements only: citation of a phrase of Scripture or a clause of the Mishnah, followed by a few words of paraphrase or other explanation.

[2] THE DISPUTE: The dispute form requires the presentation in a single syntactic pattern of two or more conflicting opinions on a given problem. The form will commonly have a topic sentence that implicitly conveys a problem and two or more elliptical solutions to the problem, each bearing attribution to a named authority. An alternative will have a problem and solution assigned to one authority, or given anonymously, followed by, And Rabbi X says . . . , in a contrary opinion.

Dominant in the Midrash compilations but paramount also in the two Talmuds' treatment of the Mishnah, the exegetical form commonly defines the smallest whole unit of thought ("sentence") in a larger composition or composite ("paragraph," "chapter," respectively). No Midrash compilation relies solely on the exegetical form for the formulation of its materials; every one of them uses that form as a building block. The dispute form serves both legal and exegetical writers, the Mishnah and Talmuds and Midrash compilations as well. It proves definitive in some documents, the Mishnah and Tosefta in particular; subordinate in others, including Midrash compilations and the two Talmuds.

These two forms exemplify the character of rhetoric of rabbinic literature as a whole, showing us how a limited repertoire of syntactical conventions governed throughout. Fixed patterns of rhetoric, for example, the arrangement of words in recurrent syntactic patterns chosen out of a much larger repertoire of possibilities, provide the clues for distinguishing one document from another, since preferences of one set of writers and compositors differed from those of another, and explaining the basis for choices leads us deep into the definition of the respective documents as a whole.

All of these statements will be fully illustrated in the chapters that introduce the documents of rabbinic literature. Here and in the following chapter, our task is only a theoretical introduction to the principles of analysis that serve throughout. For that purpose, here we examine specific writings and identify two matters. First is the issue of rhetoric. We identify a document's formal preferences and also define the function served by those preferences, that is to say, the role that they serve in the presentation of the message of the document overall. For this purpose we consider one Midrash compilation, Sifré to Deuteronomy, and the Mishnah. Second is the matter of topical program. We shall ask at the concluding unit of this chapter what it means to differentiate one document from another by reference to its topic or problematic: differentiating criteria, objectively defined, systematically (not subjectively) applied.

2.
The Rhetoric of Sifré to Deuteronomy

For our sample of a Midrash compilation's forms, we briefly turn to Sifré to Deuteronomy. For its building blocks of formal expression, this document's authorship, overall, utilizes two distinct kinds of rhetorical forms or modes of patterned language.[2] One establishes a syllogism, makes a point, and the other serves only to amplify a cited formula, e.g., a verse or a clause of a verse. The latter, which we may call the exegetical form, is formally simple and indeed serves also as a building block for varieties of the form.

The exegetical form yields a single fact, commonly a half-sentence, not fully articulated as a proposition at all (though standing by itself, it constitutes a proposition), a thought out of all relationship to other thoughts in the same context. It consists only of "clause + phrase," that is, a cited formula from a document other than the one subject to composition by the present authorship, followed by a statement, ordinarily a phrase of a sentence or at most a whole sentence, by the authorship of the document at hand. The whole then adds up to a sentence, explicit or merely implied. Syllogistic form of composing sentences joins a number of exegeses into a common list, all items of which yield the same conclusion. The framer may wish to maintain that "spoke" always bears the sense of "admonish," and to do so, he will then catalog numerous verses of clauses of verses or whole verses in which "spoke" bears the clear sense, established in context (not always cited verbatim but commonly merely subject to allusion), of "admonish." The upshot of this arrangement of connected sentences that yield a conclusion is that we have a proposition, argued in the (to us in the West) entirely normal philosophical way. That of course represents only one among many possible propositional forms of discourse. (Later in this chapter we shall see the counterpart, in logic, of "exegetical

[2] In Chapter 13, we shall further differentiate among these forms; here it suffices to identify the simplest ones, which provide the building blocks for the more complex forms that, in due course, we shall examine.

form" and "propositional form.") Let me forthwith present the repertoire of rhetorical forms in our document.

Exegetical form always is single and atomistic. It invariably makes possible only ad hoc amplification of a verse or a phrase. It yields one fact, not many; its context—e.g., two or more exegetically formed sentences—generates no conclusion beyond any one statement (sentence/fact) and establishes no connection between one sentence and the next. (Showing the logic that unites such sentences within a larger composition will require considerable attention and forms the centerpiece of this chapter.) What we have in the propositional forms, however varied, always is two or more sentences formed into a proposition and an argument. So exegetical form leaves facts to stand by themselves, and all propositional forms join two or more facts together to make of them something that transcends their sum. Exegetical form, by contrast, comprises singleton sentences, rather than components of a more sustained discourse. I cannot overstress that these singletons invariably deal with a detail and in their context as part of a sequential composition of sentences bear no explicit implications for any phrase or issue beyond themselves.

In the propositional form, yielding a syllogistic argument, all paragraphs or sustained and complex units of thought made up of simple sentences, in one way or another, set forth propositions and demonstrate them by amassing probative facts, e.g., examples. The patterning of the individual sentences of course varies. But the large-scale rhetoric, involving the presentation of a proposition, in general terms, and then the amassing of probative facts (however the sentences are worded), is essentially uniform. All propositional forms unite two or more sentences/facts and draw conclusions from the union perceived between them. These two forms yield a number of variations, which are spelled out in detail in Chapter 13. For our present purpose, it suffices to register the fact that recurrent rhetorical patterns dominate nearly the whole of the document.

The upshot is that we may classify the entire document within a handful of rhetorical forms, of which for the present purpose there are only two that matter. The same is so of most other documents of rabbinic literature. If the same forms governed throughout, however, then the upshot would be that we deal with rhetorically undifferentiable documents. The opposite is the case, as we shall now see when we take up the language and program of the Mishnah.

3.

THE MISHNAH'S TOPICAL ORGANIZATION
AND ITS PATTERNED LANGUAGE AND FORMS

Our task is to work inductively from the regularities of form to the rules that govern. Since rhetoric governs not only the formulation of sentences, but the definition of the document overall, we work from the outermost surface inward.

That means we start with the topical organization of the document, which is to be discerned simply by outlining the subjects that are treated, one by one.

THE TOPICAL ORGANIZATION OF THE MISHNAH: We commence with the simple question of how the document is organized. The answer is that the preferred mode of layout is through themes, spelled out along the lines of the logic embedded in those themes. The Mishnah is divided up into six principal divisions, each expounding a single, immense topic. The tractates of each division take up subtopics of the principal theme. The chapters then unfold along the lines of the (to the framers) logic of the necessary dissection of the division. That the themes unfold in accord with an inner logic we can identify is proved very simply. Once we identify the topical units of a tractate, we may ask why one unit comes before or after some other; in nearly all cases, we can answer that question in a simple way: any other ordering of the units of the tractate will have yielded an unintelligible document, e.g., one question has to be taken up before another can be asked at all. That trait marks tractates, not the divisions, which are ordered in size.

While that mode of organization may appear to be necessary or "self-evident" (it is how we should have written a law code, is it not?), we should notice that there are three others found within the document, but not utilized extensively or systematically. These therefore represent rejected options. One way is to collect diverse sayings around the name of a given authority. The whole of tractate Eduyyot is organized in that way. A second way is to express a given basic principle through diverse topics, e.g., a fundamental rule cutting across many areas of law, stated in one place through all of the diverse types of law through which the rule or principle may be expressed. No tractate is set up in that way, but a chapter or two may find its principle of coherence in a principle of law covering diverse topics, e.g., things done by reason of maintaining the social order (Mishnah tractate Gittin 5:8–9). A third way is to take a striking language pattern and collect sayings on diverse topics which conform to the given language pattern (e.g., M. Kelim 13:2, M. Parah 8:2–7, among many). Faced with these possible ways of organizing materials, the framers of the Mishnah chose to adhere to a highly disciplined thematic-logical principle of organization.

THE INTERNAL EVIDENCE OF THE TOPICAL DIVISION OF THE MISHNAH: In antiquity paragraphing and punctuation were not commonly used. Long columns of words would contain a text—as in the Torah today—and the student of the text had the task of breaking up those columns into tractates, chapters, sentences, large and small sense units. Now, if we had the entire Mishnah in a single immense scroll and spread the scroll out on the ground—perhaps the length of a football field!—we should have no difficulty at all discovering the point, on the five-yard line, at which the first tractate ends and the second begins, and so on down the field to the opposite goal. For from Berakhot at the beginning to Uqsin at the end, the breaking points practically jump up from the ground like white lines of lime: change of principal topic. So, the criterion of division, internal to the document and not merely imposed by copyists and printers, is thematic. That is, the tractates are readily distinguishable from one another since each treats a distinct topic. So if the Mishnah were to be copied out in a long scroll without the significance of lines of demarcation among the several tractates, the opening pericope of each tractate would leave no doubt that one topic had been completed and a new one undertaken.

The same is so within the tractates. Intermediate divisions of these same principal divisions are to be discerned on the basis of internal evidence, through the confluence of theme and form. That is to say, a given intermediate division of a principal one (a chapter of a tractate) will be marked by a particular, recurrent, formal pattern in accord with which sentences are constructed, and also by a particular and distinct theme, to which these sentences are addressed. When a new theme commences, a fresh formal pattern will be used. Within the intermediate divisions, we are able to recognize the components, or smallest whole units of thought (hereinafter, cognitive units), because there will be a recurrent pattern of sentence structure repeated time and again within the unit and a shifting at the commencement of the next theme. Each point at which the recurrent pattern commences marks the beginning of a new cognitive unit. In general, an intermediate division will contain a carefully enumerated sequence of exempla of cognitive units, in the established formal pattern, commonly in groups of three or five or multiples of three or five (pairs for the first division).

THE RHETORICAL REPERTOIRE OF THE MISHNAH: This brings us to the matter of rhetorical forms. The cognitive units—"paragraphs" or "completed statements of thought"—resort to a remarkably limited repertoire of formulary patterns. Mishnah manages to say whatever it wants in one of the following ways:

1. the simple declarative sentence, in which the subject, verb, and predicate are syntactically tightly joined to one another, e.g., He who does so and so is such and such;

2. the duplicated subject, in which the subject of the sentence is stated twice, e.g., He who does so and so, lo, he is such and such;

3. mild apocopation, in which the subject of the sentence is cut off from the verb, which refers to its own subject, and not the one with which the sentence commences, e.g., He who does so and so . . . , it [the thing he has done] is such and such;

4. extreme apocopation, in which a series of clauses is presented, none of them tightly joined to what precedes or follows, and all of them cut off from the predicate of the sentence, e.g., He who does so and so . . . , it [the thing he has done] is such and such . . . , it is a matter of doubt whether . . . or whether . . . lo, it [referring to nothing in the antecedent, apocopated clauses of the subject of the sentence] is so and so. . . .

5. In addition to these formulary patterns, in which the distinctive formulary traits are effected through variations in the relationship between the subject and the predicate of the sentence, or in which the subject itself is given a distinctive development, there is yet a fifth. In this last one we have a contrastive complex predicate, in which case we may have two sentences, independent of one another, yet clearly formulated so as to stand in acute balance with one another in the predicate, thus, He who does . . . is unclean, and he who does not . . . is clean.

It naturally will be objected: is it possible that a simple declarative sentence may be described as a formulary pattern, alongside the rather distinctive and unusual constructions which follow? True, by itself, a tightly constructed sentence consisting of subject, verb, and complement, in which the verb refers to the subject, and the complement to the verb, hardly exhibits traits of particular formal interest. Yet a sequence of such sentences, built along the same gross grammatical lines, may well exhibit a clear-cut and distinctive pattern. When we see that three or five "simple declarative sentences" take up one principle or problem, and then, when the principle or problem shifts, a quite distinctive formal pattern will be utilized, we realize that the "simple declarative sentence" has served the formulator of the unit of thought as aptly as did apocopation, a dispute, or another more obviously distinctive form or formal pattern. The contrastive predicate is one example; the Mishnah contains many more, types of "simple declarative sentences."

The important point of differentiation, particularly for the simple declarative sentence, therefore appears in the intermediate unit, as I just said, and thus in the interplay between theme and form. It is there that we see a single pattern recurring in a long sequence of sentences, e.g., the X which has lost its Y is unclean because of its Z. The Z which has lost its Y is unclean because of its X. Another example will be a long sequence of highly developed sentences, laden with relative clauses and other explanatory matter, in which a single syntactical pattern will govern the articulation of three or six or nine exempla. That sequence will be followed by one repeated terse sentence pattern, e.g., X is so and so, Y is such and such, Z is thus and so. The former group will treat one principle or theme, the latter some other. There can be no doubt, therefore, that the declarative sentence in recurrent patterns is, in its way, just as carefully formalized as a sequence of severely apocopated sentences or of contrastive predicates or duplicated subjects.

The dominant stylistic traits of the Mishnah is the acute formalization of its syntactical structure, and its carefully framed sequences of formalized language, specifically, its intermediate divisions, so organized that the limits of a theme correspond to those of a formulary pattern. The balance and order of the Mishnah are particular to the Mishnah. There is no reason to doubt that if we asked the authorities behind the Mishnah the immediate purpose of their systematic use of formalized language, their answer would be to facilitate memorization. For that is the

proximate effect of the acute formalization of their document. Much in its character can be seen as mnemonic.

WHAT WE LEARN ABOUT A DOCUMENT FROM ITS RHETORICAL
RULES: The formal aspects of Mishnaic rhetoric are empty of content. This is
proved by the fact that pretty much all themes and conceptions can be reduced to
the same few formal patterns. These patterns are established by syntactical recur-
rences, as distinct from recurrence of sounds. The same words do not recur. Long
sequences of patterned and disciplined sentences fail to repeat the same words—
that is, use syllabic balance, rhythm, or sound—yet they do establish a powerful
claim to order and formulary sophistication and perfection. That is why we could
name a pattern "he who . . . it is . . ." apocopation: the arrangement of the words
as a grammatical pattern, not their substance, is indicative of pattern. Accordingly,
while we have a document composed along what clearly are mnemonic lines, the
Mishnah's susceptibility to memorization rests principally upon the utter abstraction of recurrent syntactical patterns, rather than on the concrete repetition of
particular words, rhythms, syllabic counts, or sounds. A sense for the deep, inner
logic of word patterns, of grammar and syntax, rather than for their external similarities, governs the Mishnaic mnemonic.

This fact—the creation of pattern through grammatical relationship of syntactical elements, more than through concrete sounds—tells us that the people who
memorized conceptions reduced to these particular forms were capable of extraor-
dinarily abstract cognition and perception. Hearing peculiarities of word order in
diverse cognitive contexts, their ears and minds perceived regularities of grammatical arrangement, repeated functional variations of utilization of diverse words.
They grasped from such subtleties syntactical patterns not expressed by recurrent
external phenomena such as sounds, rhythms, or key words, and autonomous of
particular meanings. What they heard, it is clear, were not only abstract relationships but also principles conveyed along with and through these relationships. For
what was memorized was a recurrent and fundamental notion, expressed in diverse
examples but also in recurrent rhetorical-syntactical patterns. Accordingly, what
the memorizing student of a sage could and did hear was what lay far beneath the
surface of the rule: the unstated principle, the unsounded pattern. This means that
the prevalent mode of thought was attuned to what lay beneath the surface; minds
and ears perceived what was not said behind what was said and how it was said.

4.

THE MATTER OF MNEMONICS

What has been said about the dispute form and about the layout and rhetoric of
the Mishnah raises the question, "what about the orality of the literature, meaning,

how it exhibits traits of rhetoric meant to facilitate memorization?" For the formalization of language clearly facilitates remembering what is said, e.g., rhymes and rhythms. While all of the rabbinic literature claims to emerge from a long tradition of oral formulation and oral transmission, only some documents exhibit pronounced mnemonic patterns, others do not. One of them was published not in writing but through a process of oral formulation and oral transmission, the Mishnah. The same traits that characterize the Mishnah—a high degree of formalization of compositions, not only the organization of composites—do not mark other documents. But mnemonic traits may be discerned also in compositions utilized by the compilers of most of the other documents of rabbinic literature.

To identify mnemonic qualities, we focus upon the Mishnah in particular, because it is, as noted, the one document that is consistently written to facilitate ready memorization. What is of interest here is that the principles by which the apodosis and protasis of the Mishnah's smallest whole units of discourse are framed follow formal, mnemonic patterns. The patterns of language, e.g., syntactic structures, follow a few simple rules. These rules, once known, apply nearly everywhere. They permit anyone to reconstruct, out of a few key phrases, an entire cognitive unit, and, more important, as we shall see, complete intermediate units of discourse.

As we have now noted, an intermediate unit of discourse serves to make a single point, that is, to present a given logical proposition. The logical proposition (for example, a general or encompassing rule) rarely comes to articulate expression. Rather, it will be given a set of concrete exemplifications. Three or five or more cases will make the point in detail. Put together, they turn out to express, through examples, a logical proposition. That is what I mean in referring to logic and topic. The underlying logic ordinarily is expressed only in topical form, through concrete instances of what only seldom is stated in so many words. What is the place of rhetoric? A single rhetorical pattern will govern the whole set of topical instances of a logical proposition. When the logical-topical program changes, the rhetorical pattern will change too.

The mnemonics of the Mishnah therefore rests on the confluence of three elements: (1) deep logic, (2) articulated topic, and (3) manifest rhetoric. Working downward from the surface, anyone can penetrate into the deeper layers of meaning of the Mishnah. Then and at the same time, while discovering the principle behind the cases, one can easily memorize the whole by mastering the recurrent rhetorical pattern dictating the expression of the cogent set of cases. For it is easy to note the shift from one rhetorical pattern to another and to follow the repeated cases articulated in the new pattern downward to its logical substrate. So syllogistic propositions, in the Mishnah's authors' hands, come to full expression not only in what people wish to state but also in how they choose to say it. The limits of rhetoric define the arena of topical articulation. Once we ask what three or five joined topical propositions have in common, we state the logic shared among them all.

This brings us to the apodosis and its mnemonic traits. The smallest whole unit of discourse is made up of fixed, recurrent formulas, clichés, patterns, or little phrases, out of which whole pericopae, or large elements in pericopese, e.g., complete sayings, are constructed. Small units of tradition, while constitutive of pericopese, do not generate new sayings or legal problems, as do apophthegmatic formulas. An example of part of a pericope composed primarily of recurrent formulas is as follows:

> *A basket of fruit intended for the Sabbath*
> House of Shammai declare exempt
> And the House of Hillel declare liable.

The italicized words are not fixed formulas. *And* is redactional; the formulation of the statement of the problem does not follow a pattern. The "Houses" sentences, by contrast, are formed of fixed, recurrent phrases, which occur in numerous pericopese. Similarly:

> House of Shammai say . . . House of Hillel say . . .

are fixed small units, whether or not the predicate matches; when it balances, we have a larger unit of tradition composed of two small units:

1. House of Shammai say,	2. it is subject to the provision, when water be put (Lev. 11:34)
3. House of Hillel say,	4. it is not subject to the provision, when water be put (Lev. 11:34)

In this pericope, only the statement of the problem or protasis, not given, would constitute other than a fixed unit; House of Shammai/Hillel + say are complete units, and the opinions in the apodosis are others—thus, as I said, a pericope, the apodosis of which is composed entirely of fixed, small units of tradition. By definition these small formulas cannot be random, or they would not constitute formulas. Such small units are whole words, not syntactical or grammatical particles.

Another example of the power of mnemonics to govern formulation of rules in the Mishnah derives from Mishnah tractate Berakhot 8:7. First we examine the pericope as a whole:

> *[As for] one who ate but forgot and did not recite the grace [after meals]*—
> The House of Shammai say, "He should return to his place and recite the grace."
> But the House of Hillel say, "He should recite the grace in the place in which he remembered [that he had not recited]."

If we eliminate the attributives, we find each statement composed of three elements, which correspond in ascending, then descending order:

(1) He should return (2) to his place and (3) recite the grace.
He should (3) recite the grace (2) in the place in which (1) he remembered

The two statements, in fact, only differ at (1), "return" vs. "remember"; the Hebrew words are HZR vs. ZKR, so that once we know what is at issue and the governing formula, all we need to remember is that one house gets the H, the other the K; the H comes first in the alphabet, so goes to the House of Shammai, which nearly always gives its opinion first, and the K then follows for the House of Hillel. I cannot imagine a more thoroughgoing effort to formulate a penetrating mnemonics than that. And it is routine in the Mishnah, and in disputes throughout the rabbinic literature, to find counterparts in formalization in mnemonic patterns to this remarkably simple, skillful formulation.

So much for the apodosis, X says/Y says, where the memorization-repertoire (even merely a matched count of syllables) very commonly defines how things may be said. What about the protasis? We consider the protasis and its mnemonic characteristics in two parts. Internal evidence proves that the arrangement by topical divisions and their subdivisions ("tractates," "chapters") is fundamental to the redaction of the Mishnah. Once a primary theme shifts, we know that the redactors have completed their treatment of one subject and commenced that of another. We shall now ask whether the dissection, into intermediate divisions, of these same principal divisions is shown by internal evidence to be equivalently fundamental to the redaction of the document.

Since we seek to discern the boundary lines within the principal divisions of the Mishnah for which the redactors of the Mishnah bear responsibility, we revert to our examination of the internal evidence about the aggregation of materials into intermediate divisions. What internal evidence permits us to differentiate the intermediate divisions, or sizable aggregations, of completed cognitive units? What criteria, specifically, will emerge out of the fundamental character itself? Answers to these questions solve the problem of the mnemonics of the protasis in mnemonically formulated rabbinic documents.

[1] TOPIC: The first of two criteria derives from the nature of the principal divisions themselves: theme. We know that it is along thematic lines that the redactors organized vast corpora of materials into principal divisions, tractates. These fundamental themes themselves were subdivided into smaller conceptual units. The principal divisions treat their themes in units indicated by the sequential unfolding of their inner logical structure. Accordingly, one established criterion for distinguishing one aggregate of materials from some other, fore or aft, will be a shift in the theme, or the predominant and characteristic concern, of a sequence of materials.

[2] RHETORIC: Normally, when the topic changes, the mode of expression—the formal or formulary character, the patterning of language—will change as well.

These two matters, theme and form, therefore must be asked to delineate for us the main lines of the intermediate segments or subdivisions of the Mishnah's principal divisions, the "chapters." There are therefore four logical possibilities for the application of the two stated criteria, $+A +B$, $+A-B$, $-A+B$, $-A-B$:

1.   coherent themes expressed through coherent formulary patterns;
2.   coherent themes lacking coherent formulary patterns;
3.   coherent formulary patterns lacking coherent themes;
4.   incoherent themes and incoherent formulary patterns.

In this case the only reason to imagine that we deal with a subdivision is that before and after a set of materials that lacks coherence of theme and form are sets which do exhibit traits of coherent theme and/or form, that is, subdivisions demarcated by one of the first three possible combinations.

We distinguish to begin with between two kinds of formulary patterns. First is the pattern that is internal to the idea, which is expressed and which predominates in the formulation of that idea, its linguistic formalization. If this pattern recurs for two or more cognitive units, then we have a formulary trait internal to the pattern of language of each element in a subdivision. Each and every cognitive unit within said subdivision will express its particular concept or thought in conformity with this common pattern, which therefore is to be designated as internal to the whole. The recurrent pattern of syntax or language is equally tradental and redactional, in that what is to be expressed is the work of those responsible for the formulary and formalized character and the cognitive substance of the subdivision in all of its parts and as a whole. Second is the pattern which is superficial and external to the idea which is expressed, and which occurs chiefly at the outset of a cognitive unit. The arrangement of words of said unit will ignore this external formulary trait. What is to be said can be, and is, stated without regard to the superficial trait shared by several cognitive units.

Indeed, we may readily discern that the formulary trait of a series of cognitive units is external to the formulation of all of them, simply because each cognitive unit goes its own way, stating its ideas in its own form or formulary pattern, without any regard whatsoever for the formal traits of other units to which it is joined. The joining—the shared language or formulary or formal pattern—is therefore external to the several units. The present distinction, between internally unitary formulary traits characteristic of a sequence of cognitive units and externally unitary formulary traits shared by a sequence of cognitive units, explains why the first of our four logical possibilities, $+A+B$ (coherent themes, coherent forms), yields two analytical categories. The second logical possibility, $+A-B$, requires no refinement. We observe that some clear-cut sequences of cognitive units talk about the same distinctive subject, but make no effort to conform to a discernible pattern of language. Occasionally we discern subdivisions which are differentiated by formulary patterns but which go over many legal themes, that is, $-A+B$.

What about the simple declarative sentence—once again? This brings us to the question of whether in fact the omnipresent declarative sentences are as a whole differentiable in terms of recurrent syntactical patterns. In order to spell out the character and distribution of declarative sentences of various sorts, I have taken each stich of the apodosis of a dispute and treated it as if it were a complete sentence. I thus add the protasis to one of the two (or more) stichs of the apodosis. Since we already know that the attributive, X says, is a form independent of what is expressed and external to the formulary pattern in which it appears, I delete the attributive:

> *A chicken which is cooked for two hours*
> */the House of Shammai say/*
> *is uncooked.*

This procedure allows us to see the traits of the several cognitive units that, in theory, serve as primary components of the dispute. It further shows us how the dispute's composite character preserves the syntactical traits of its (prior) units and how such traits conform to their tradental-redactional setting.

The decisive formulary traits occur in the protasis, that is, the opening element of a cognitive unit. They may or may not continue throughout the unit. In apocopation, for example, we find the striking disjunctures of components of the subject in particular at the inaugural sentence of a cognitive unit, while declarative sentences may follow until the problem and solution of the unit have been expressed. The differentiating formulary characteristics are thus to be discovered in the commencement of the unit. These traits will be revealed, in that opening sentence, either in the subject or in the predicate. The decisive differentiation is exhibited in the connection—the interface—between the subject and the predicate.

One sort of sentence flows smoothly from subject to verb to complement or predicate. The verb refers to the subject and is completed at the complement or predicate. This sort of sentence is characterized as the simple declarative sentence. In another sort, the subject of the sentence is duplicated, but then leads directly into the predicate. Sometimes this is effected through a shift in word order, e.g., *chickens—when are they fully cooked in the pot?* That is, the topic, "chickens," is placed before the interrogative, "when." This pattern would not seem peculiar at all, were it not for the numerous instances in which the word order yields nothing like the duplicated protasis, e.g., *A chicken which is cooked for three hours is fully boiled.* There is only one construction in which the formulary peculiarity is exhibited in the apodosis, and this is the contrastive complex, in which we have a clear-cut balance between the predicate of one sentence, normally a brief one, and that which follows, e.g., *X/unclean, Y/clean.*

Two further complex constructions complete our taxonomy, both of them exhibiting apocopation, the one mild, the other severe, and both affecting the subject of the sentence or its protasis (in the case of the latter). What is cut off, or apocopated, is the subject of the sentence, which is disconnected from the verb of the same sentence. When we have a complete disjuncture between the opening unit(s) and the predicate, so that the latter refers to, and depends upon, nothing in the former, then we have the extreme apocopation which is so striking a formulary pattern in our order. Mild apocopation, by contrast, normally begins "he who" (or "that which"), and the predicate, while not referring to the subject of "he who"/"that which," does join up to an element of the inaugural clause, e.g., to the implied or stated object of "he who" or "that which," or to the consequence of what "he who does" has done. The extreme apocopation, as I said, is made extreme because none of the stichs that form the subject of the sentence in fact is joined to the predicate. They may be many or few, but invariably, none is the subject of, or even refers to, the predicate at all. These definitions of formulary patterns exhaust the large-scale categories of syntactical-grammatical types among which all declarative sentences may be divided.

Coherent formulary patterns do characterize sizable sequences of cognitive units on a single theme. These traits, common to a series of distinct cognitive units, are redactional, because they are imposed at that point at which someone intended to join together discrete (finished) units on a given theme. The varieties of traits particular to the discrete units and the diversity of authorities cited therein, including masters of two or three or even four strata from the turn of the first century C.E. to the end of the second, make it highly improbable that the several units were formulated in a common pattern and then preserved until later on, still further units, on the same theme and in the same pattern, were worked out and added. The entire indifference, moreover, to historical order of authorities and concentration on the logical unfolding of a given theme or problem without reference to the sequence of authorities confirm the supposition that the work of formulation and that of redaction went forward together.

When we have sizable constructions of cognitive units, all of them conforming to a single, highly distinctive formulary pattern, which itself is internal to the expression of the ideas stated therein, we have no reason whatsoever to doubt that the whole was both made up and put together by one and the same hand. In such constructions the tradental and redactional work is coincident. The other, and principal, sort of intermediate division, that in which an externally unitary formulary pattern is applied to a single theme or problem, has now to be reconsidered. Having a clear notion of the gross formulary pattern that characterizes all of those many intermediate divisions distinguished by a common theme and a common formulary pattern consisting of "simple declarative sentences," we now refine our earlier results.

The bulk of the work of giving expression to the cognitive units therefore is carried out in the processes of redaction, which resulted in the formation—patterning and aggregation—of the intermediate divisions of the several tractates—in their formulation, and, it is obvious, in their organization and thematic arrangement. I state with heavy emphasis: The Mishnah is the work of tradent-redactors. The mnemonic consists of the confluence of topic and rhetoric at the level of deep logic. Other documents have to be dealt with on their own terms; it suffices to state, as a matter of generalization, that documents also are to be differentiated by their mnemonic traits, if any.

5.

TOPICAL CRITERIA
OF DOCUMENTARY DIFFERENTIATION

Bypassing the definition and explanation of the logic of coherent discourse, to which we shall devote the next chapter, we come at the end to the very simple matter of the topical program of a document. We already have noticed that the Mishnah is laid out in accord with a well-articulated topical program. That is not the only document in rabbinic literature that is distinguished from others by the subjects that it treats and even the propositions that, throughout, its framers wish to set forth. Topical considerations differentiate nearly every document from all others; only a few documents, such as the Tosefta, are not immediately distinguished by their subject matter.

It is simple fact that each Midrash compilation differs from all others by reason of its choice of a book of Scripture for close reading and analysis. Only one book, Leviticus, is the subject of two distinct Midrash compilations, Sifra and Leviticus Rabbah, and these compilations intersect only in their choice of subject. In rhetoric, topic, and logic, they have nothing in common, each writing raising its own questions, neither addressing a single issue important to the other, even on the rare occasion that both documents examine the same verse of Leviticus.

Not only so, but, as we have already noted, the various Midrash compilations may be divided into groups, early, middle, and late, distinguished by their definition of the tasks of exegesis: close reading of verses, syllogistic constructions made up of facts provided by verses, and large-scale demonstration of a few simple propositions, respectively. Distinguishing the successive documents of Mishnah exegesis, Tosefta and the two Talmuds, by contrast, is not so simple, since, as a matter of simple fact, all of them address the Mishnah. But any careful reading allows us to distinguish the Tosefta's interests in the Mishnah from those of the Yerushalmi, and the differentiation of the Yerushalmi from the Bavli is readily undertaken. In the latter case, a clearly defined problematic, definitive in the Bavli and absent in the Yerushalmi, validates the notion that we may differentiate documents by appeal to topic or problematic.

Classifying topical traits of a document involves recourse to a variety of extrinsic distinctions of a purely formal and therefore objective character. One is between law and norms of behavior as against lore and norms of belief, a distinction to which we have already resorted. Another is between Scripture and the Mishnah. Let us begin with these simple points of differentiation and comparison, referring only to a selection of the documents to be considered later in this book.

Law, Norms of Behavior	*Lore, Norms of Belief*
Mishnah	Abot
Tosefta	Genesis Rabbah
Sifra	Leviticus Rabbah
Sifré to Numbers	(Yerushalmi)
Yerushalmi	(Bavli)
Bavli	

The point of distinction does not seem to me to make much of a difference. We cannot classify the two Talmuds either as principally devoted to law or as mainly focused upon lore; certainly the Bavli exhibits nearly equal interest in each. Genesis Rabbah, for its part, lays forth a theology of history, with important dimensions affecting behavior, and Leviticus Rabbah provides an equivalent topical program, with further interest in ethical rules governing not only belief but also behavior. So the distinction between behavior and belief bears no promise for criteria of differentiation by topic. Let us proceed to another set of criteria: Scripture and its topical program.

Here we compare two or more documents that focus on Scripture and ask whether the authorships have chosen the same themes or different ones. By "theme" I mean not so much the concrete narrative of Scripture at a given passage as a broader frame of interest. For example, while the Mishnah does not introduce themes of history and its interpretation, Scripture does, so two or more documents may fall into the same classification, in regard to Scripture and its topical program, if they take up issues of the meaning of history. More to the point, both Sifra and Leviticus Rabbah treat the book of Leviticus, so they share a common text. Yet it would be difficult to imagine two more different compositions. The topical plan of the one bears nothing in common with the topical plan of the other—to which, in fact, the book of Leviticus serves at best as an ancillary matter: pretext, not even proof text.

So if we take up the differentiation of those compilations that focus on Scripture, we realize that a labor of comparison and contrast is at hand: topical as much as rhetorical (or, as we see in Chapter 3, logical). But when we do so, we find ourselves comparing incomparables. Topical connections based on shared interest in Scripture do not emerge. Each document makes the points its authorship wished to make, and these have no bearing on those another authorship, in a different document—even one based on the same book of Scripture—planned to establish.

The Mishnah presents a rather sizable and cogent set of topics, and here also two or more authorships may intersect in their choices of what, within that set, they choose to take up and amplify and explain. Our brief excursion into taxonomy of topics and propositions requires us to move beyond the limits of our sample. But the facts on which our taxonomy rests are self-evidently and broadly available. What we wish to know is how the documents subsequent to the Mishnah treat the topical program of the Mishnah. Three classifications must serve, all in relationship to that program. In the first type of document, the Mishnah's program of topics is completely ignored. In the second, the entire plan of topics is systematically covered, beginning to end. In the third, the framers pick and choose the topics they wish to treat.

I	*II*	*III*
All Ignored	*All Covered*	*Selected Passages Treated*
Abot	Tosefta	Sifra
Genesis Rabbah		Sifré to Numbers
		Leviticus Rabbah
		Yerushalmi
		Bavli

The third division alone attracts our attention. We may forthwith explain why for the two scriptural-exegetical compilations, on Leviticus and Numbers, respectively, one thing—one passage of the Mishnah—is included and not another. The polemic of the framers accounts for the passages of the Mishnah that will be selected. Both documents deal with verses on the theme or program of which the Mishnah contains no law whatsoever, and this is blatant in Sifré to Numbers in particular. There are simply no Mishnah tractates on the subjects paramount in a number of important legal passages in the book of Numbers. So the intent of the authorship of both scriptural-exegetical compilations is systematically and sequentially to cover all of the verses of *their* chosen scriptural passages, and therefore, as a matter of fact, it is only incidental to that purpose that their compositions intersect with passages of the Mishnah. The criterion of topical connections yields relationships only between the two Talmuds.

Since the two Talmuds formulate their compositions as commentaries to the Mishnah, on the surface both of them fall into a single classification as to topic. That is to say, the topical program of each is the Mishnah. But as a matter of fact, a topical criterion distinguishes the one from the other, and that is for a simple and well-known reason. Only partially intersecting at three of the Mishnah's six divisions—Appointed Times, Women, and Damages, one Talmud covers one set of Mishnah topics, the other a different set. The Yerushalmi treats Agriculture, ignoring Holy Things; the Bavli comments on Holy Things, omitting Agriculture; neither treats Purities. There are also tractates within the various divisions treated in one Talmud and not the other, for instance, all of Niddah is supplied with Talmud in the Bavli, but only a few chapters in the Yerushalmi, but that fact may testify only to the vagaries of survival of manuscript evidence. For its part, as we see, Tosefta covers all six divisions. So, in all, there is no formal topic that joins the eight post-Mishnaic writings. Let us now survey some specific documents and show how topic permits us to differentiate one from the next.

TRACTATE ABOT

1. **Scripture and Its Topical Program**
   Verses of Scripture serve as proof texts. There is no pretense of opening Scripture to discover appropriate topics for discussion. The order of verses of Scripture is ignored throughout.
2. **The Mishnah and Its Topical Program**
   Abot does not recognize a single topic that occurs in the Mishnah.

THE TOSEFTA

1. **Scripture and Its Topical Program**
   Where the Tosefta takes up scriptural topics, they have reached the Tosefta via the Mishnah. Not only does the Tosefta cover nearly everything in the Mishnah, it also addresses scriptural themes only when the Mishnah directly or implicitly introduces those themes. So the dependence on the topical program of the Mishnah is complete.
2. **The Mishnah and Its Topical Program**
   The Tosefta's topical program derives directly from the Mishnah's, pure and simple.

THE YERUSHALMI

1. **Scripture and Its Topical Program**
   Scripture occasionally provides an organizing structure, e.g., a sequence of verses that will be systematically expounded. Scripture commonly provides proof texts for Mishnah rules. The topical program of Scripture is reorganized in accord with the topical program of the Mishnah and then brought into juxtaposition therewith.
2. **The Mishnah and Its Topical Program**
   The topical program of the Mishnah predominates, beginning, middle, and end.

SIFRA

1. **Scripture and Its Topical Program**
   Sifra works its way through Scripture's program and introduces passages of the Mishnah as Scripture invites our attention to them. So we deal

with the opposite of the foregoing. Here the topical program of Scripture predominates and defines both structure and program.

2. **The Mishnah and Its Topical Program**

    The introduction of a passage of the Mishnah is on account of the interests of Scripture, which, at that point, intersect with the Mishnah's discussion. I see no pretense at an interest in the Mishnah on its own terms. The contrary is the case. The Mishnah contributes proof texts to the authorship of Sifra, much as Scripture provides proof texts to the authorship of the Mishnah.

SIFRÉ TO NUMBERS

1. **Scripture and Its Topical Program**

    A verse of Scripture will be systematically expounded, clause by clause. So it is Scripture's program that defines the topical plan.

2. **The Mishnah and Its Topical Program**

    The introduction of a Mishnah passage will serve the polemic identified earlier: exegesis, not reason, provides reliable guidance to the law. The Mishnah plays a substantially smaller part in the topical program of our sample of Sifré to Numbers than it does in Sifra.

GENESIS RABBAH

1. **Scripture and Its Topical Program**

    The topical program of Scripture predominates, beginning, middle, and end. But we should not miss the highly selective character of the choice of passages requiring exegesis. In fact the topics of Scripture are shaped to broader agenda, specifically, propositions concerning the character of the creator and creation. Only in a rather general sense can we say that the exegetical program of Genesis Rabbah corresponds to the topical program of Scripture. Once we move from topic to proposition, we see the appropriate classification.

2. **The Mishnah and Its Topical Program**

    The Mishnah plays no role whatsoever.

LEVITICUS RABBAH

1. **Scripture and Its Topical Program**

    Here I see little evidence that Scripture's topical program has predominated, even though on the surface, what we have is a systematic play on various verses of Scripture. The fundamental proposition guides us to the topic of Scripture, and that proposition is distinct from Scripture. The fresh and independent topical program of Leviticus Rabbah, not the dependence upon Scripture of the framers of the topical program, is what emerges.

2. **The Mishnah and Its Topical Program**
    I see no interest whatsoever in the topical program of the Mishnah, with
    which Leviticus Rabbah never intersects. In a general way we may say that
    while the Mishnah is interested in giving the laws of everyday life, Leviti-
    cus Rabbah contributes the laws of history and society. In theological
    terms, the one speaks of sanctification, the other of salvation.

THE BAVLI

1. **Scripture and Its Topical Program**
    The framers of the Bavli included systematic treatments of scriptural
    themes even when the requirements of Mishnah exegesis did not dictate it.
2. **The Mishnah and Its Topical Program**
    The topical program of the Mishnah dictates to the framers of the Bavli
    the subjects they will treat.

The result of our detailed sorting out of the classifications of our samples of the
eight documents (excluding the Mishnah) corresponds to our original hypothesis.

The topical program of Scripture proves less paramount than we should have
expected. It plays no independent role in some of the documents and only a limited one in others, predominating in only a few.

Topical Identity	Topical Selectivity	Topical Indifference
Sifra	Bavli	Abot
Sifré to Numbers	Genesis Rabbah	Tosefta
	Yerushalmi	
	Leviticus Rabbah	

The documents that form strong connections on one basis form equally strong ties
on another. That we see in particular with the first of the three entries.

Since my claim is only that we may classify documents by topic or even proposition, let us conclude with the taxonomy afforded by diverse approaches to the
Mishnah's topical program. The documents fall into these possible classifications:
wholly dominated by the Mishnah's themes, wholly dominated by Scripture's topics, dominated by neither, dominated by both. Abot ignores the Mishnah's program, so too do Genesis Rabbah and Leviticus Rabbah. Tosefta adheres to the
Mishnah's program. Sifra, Sifré to Numbers, the Yerushalmi, and the Bavli select
passages to be treated. So we find taxonomic connections among the Tosefta, Yerushalmi, and Bavli. We find taxonomic ties also between Sifra and Sifré to Numbers, in their shared polemic concerning the Mishnah's appropriate foundations,
and between Genesis Rabbah and Leviticus Rabbah in their shared indifference to
the Mishnah. The eight documents then break into these divisions:

Topical Identity	Topical Selectivity	Topical Indifference
Tosefta	Sifra	Abot
	Sifré to Numbers	Genesis Rabbah
	Bavli	Leviticus Rabbah
	Yerushalmi	

Once more we see that Sifra and Sifré to Numbers form a tightly connected corpus, as do Genesis Rabbah and Leviticus Rabbah. The relationships among Tosefta, Yerushalmi, and Bavli are somewhat more complex. The upshot of our taxonomic distinction is to find in the topical criterion grounds for identifying connections among some of our documents, but discerning substantial points of disconnectedness among others.

It follows that when we describe documents, we shall pay considerable attention to the topical and (where pertinent) propositional program that in part distinguishes that document from all others. But clearly, while we have succeeded in demonstrating that documents require differentiation, the points of differentiation thus far—rhetoric, topic—do not carry us deep into the inner dynamics of a piece of writing. It is when we can identify the governing logic that we find our way into the very processes of thought—analysis and argument—that produce a document and also, when joined to rhetoric and topic, distinguish one document from all others. So our picture of how to analyze any given rabbinic document is only two-thirds complete.

III

DOCUMENTARY COHERENCE AND DIFFERENTIATION: THE FOUR LOGICS OF COHERENT DISCOURSE IN RABBINIC LITERATURE

1.
DEFINING LOGICS OF COHERENT DISCOURSE

THE WORD "LOGIC" HERE STANDS FOR THE DETERMINATIVE PRINCIPLE OF INTELligibility of discourse and cogency of thought.[1] Logic is what tells people that one thing connects, or intersects, with another, while something else does not, hence, making connections between this and that, but not this and the other thing. And logic further tells people what follows from the connections that they make, generating the conclusions that they are to draw. Governing logic tells us what is thinkable and what is not, what can be said intelligibly and what cannot. Accordingly, the first thing we want to know about any piece of writing is its logic of cogent discourse. Logic is what joins one sentence to the next and forms the whole into paragraphs of meaning, into intelligible propositions, each with its place and sense

---

[1] The question of how documents' compositions and composites cohere is not raised in the other introductions. On the analysis of logics of coherent discourse, see my *The Making of the Mind of Judaism.* Atlanta, 1987: Scholars Press for Brown Judaic Studies and *The Formation of the Jewish Intellect. Making Connections and Drawing Conclusions in the Traditional System of Judaism.* Atlanta, 1988: Scholars Press for Brown Judaic Studies. The other introductions to rabbinic literature do not discuss this question.

in a still larger, accessible system. And logic as a matter of fact makes possible the sharing of propositions of general intelligibility and therefore forms the cement of a whole literature, such as the one under examination in this book.

The matter of defining the governing logic bears more than formal consequence. It also introduces the social side of a literature. Specifically, because of shared logic, one mind connects to another, yielding self-evidence, so that in writing or in orally formulated and orally transmitted teaching, public discourse becomes possible. Because of logic debate on issues of general interest takes place. Still more to the point, because of logic a mere anthology of statements about a single subject becomes a composition of theorems about that subject, so that facts serve to demonstrate and convey propositions. Through logic the parts, bits and pieces of information, add up to a sum greater than themselves, generate information or insight beyond what they contain. What people think—exegesis of discrete facts in accord with a fixed hermeneutic of the intellect—knows no limit. How they think makes all the difference. Since, as we shall see in the shank of this book, each of the documents of rabbinic literature sets forth a cogent statement, a clear picture of the conventions of logic that permit cogent discourse is required.

Modes of patterned thought form propositions out of facts, turning information into knowledge, knowledge into a system of sense and explanation and therefore composing a shared structure of sensibility and meaning for the social order. The logic of coherent discourse exhibited by the writer of a given document is what tells people about how to make interesting connections between one thing, one fact for instance, and some other, therefore instructing them on what deserves notice and what can be ignored. Every document in the rabbinic literature selects a particular means of holding together two or more sentences and forming of them a coherent thought, that is to say, of making the whole more than the sum of the parts. There are, in fact, four such logics, three of them entirely familiar, one of them not.

First, let us consider a concrete example of how a logic of coherent discourse turns facts into propositions, information into truth. The simple sequence moves us from two unrelated facts to two connected facts and thence to a proposition. Here is one example of a possible logic of coherent discourse:

[1]   I threw a rock at a dog. It rained.
[2]   I threw a rock at a dog, then it rained.
[3]   If I throw a rock at a dog, it will rain.

The first set of sentences contains no link, so no conclusions are to be drawn. No unstated premise tells me how the two sentences relate, or whether they relate at all. I am mute. The second set presents a temporal, narrative link; this happened, then that happened. Conclusions may or may not be drawn. Two events are juxtaposed, but the "then" carries with it no judgment on causation or other modes of explanation, that is, of coherence between sentences. A narrative line extends from the former to the latter sentence. The third formulation of course establishes a conditional link between two facts, forming of them an allegation as to what will happen if one does such and so. The "if" of course may be replaced with a "since," and a variety of other joining language will establish a connection between the two sentences (or clauses of one sentence). The third case shows us how the sum of the whole exceeds the parts.

This simple set of sentences shows what I mean when I point out that some facts are inert, others bear consequence. Facts that fail to intersect with others in general gain slight notice; those that form structures and convey sense gain systematic consequence and ultimately form an encompassing account of how things are and should be, why we do things one way and not another: an ethos, an ethics, an account of a "we," altogether, a system. The convention of a shared logic of coherent discourse moreover explains to people about the consequences of the connections that they are taught to perceive, yielding conclusions of one sort rather than another, based on one mode of drawing conclusions from the connections that are made, rather than some other.

Making connections and drawing conclusions represent abstractions. Let me give a concrete example of what is under discussion. It is, very simply, what constitutes the "and" and the "equals" of thought, e.g., in the sentence, "two and two equal four." The way in which people add up two and two to make four always requires the appeal to the *and,* and that is what endures, that *and* of the two and two equal four, and, too, the *equal,* which is to say, the conclusion yielded by the *and.* The logic lasts: the *and* of making connections, the *equal* of reaching conclusions. This endures: the certainty that—to shift the symbols that serve to clarify this simple point—X + Y are connected and generate conclusion Z, but that (for purposes of discussion here) the symbol # and the number 4 are not connected and therefore, set side by side, produce a mere nonsense-statement, e.g., # and 4 equal ★. The conventions that govern thought and discourse permit us to make one such statement but not the other.

2.

THE PROPOSITIONAL LOGIC
OF PHILOSOPHICAL DISCOURSE

Propositional and syllogistic logic is the most familiar to us in the West and it also is the most commonplace in the rabbinic literature, though the forms that convey the proposition or syllogism are unfamiliar to us. Philosophical discourse is built out of propositions and arguments from facts and reason. The cogency of discourse—the *and* that joins two sentences together into a cogent statement—derives from the argument we wish to make, the fact we wish to establish, the proposition we wish to prove. The tension in this mode of thought arises from the trait of mind that derives from two facts a third, one that transcends the givens. The resolution, then, comes from the satisfying demonstration, out of what we know, of something we did not know but wish to find out, or of something we think we know and wish to prove.

The syllogistic character of philosophical discourse is familiar to us all. That is why commonplaces such as "(1) All Greeks are liars, (2) Demosthenes is a Greek, (3) (Therefore) Demosthenes is a liar," need not detain us. In that sequence, fact (1) and fact (2) come together to prove a fact that is not contained within either (1) or (2). Syllogistic logic yields a sum greater than the parts. From our perspective, we want to identify the connection between two facts. And what matters in the famous syllogism at hand is that the proposition, (3), is what joins fact (1) to fact (2) into joined and cogent sentences, that is, in the language of the preceding section, the *equal* generates the *and*. In the document before us, the idiom is exceedingly odd, which makes all the more valuable the exemplification of what is, in fact, a perfectly routine mode of thought. For the issue at hand is one of connection, the *and* of the *two and two,* that is, not of fact (such as is conveyed by the statement of the meaning of a verse or a clause of a verse) but of the relationship between one fact and another. And at stake in the connection is the proposition, the *equal* of the *two and two* equal *four.*

The critical point is in the *equals,* since it is at that result that the point of the connection is both realized and established. We see a connection between one item and the next because of the third item that the first two generate. In the logic at hand connection rests upon conclusion. And let me with emphasis state the central point: *that relationship, connection, is shown in a conclusion different from the established facts of two or more sentences that we propose to draw when we set up as a sequence two or more facts and claim out of that sequence to propose a proposition different from, transcending, the facts at hand.*

We demonstrate propositions in a variety of ways, appealing to both a repertoire of probative facts and a set of accepted modes of argument. In this way we engage in a kind of discourse that gains its logic from what, in general, we may call philosophy: the rigorous analysis and testing of propositions against the canons of an accepted reason. The connection produced by the cogent discourse of philosophy therefore accomplishes the miracle of making the whole more—or less— than the sum of the parts, that is, in the simple language we have used up to now, showing the connections between fact 1 and fact 2, in such wise as to yield proposition A.

Before we move to our concrete example, let me introduce a secondary, but in our context, important, alternative way of conducting philosophical argument—a way at the foundation of all scientific inquiry. It is the demonstration we know, in general, as comparison and contrast, the search for the rules that express the order and sense of diverse facts. We seek to identify what discrete facts have in common and thereby to state the rule common to them all, e.g., to identify a genus, then its species, and on downward. The fundamental logic of cogency here is simple: something is like something else, therefore it follows the rule of that something else; or it is unlike that something else, therefore it follows the opposite of the rule governing that something else. The way in which the result is presented tells us the principle of cogency. When we classify, we identify a genus and its species and lay them forth in their nomothetic system. The layout often takes the form of a list. The logic before us on that account is called the science of making lists, that is, *Listenwissenschaft,* a way to classify and so establish a set of probative facts, which compel us to reach a given conclusion.

These probative facts may derive from the classification of data, all of which point in one direction and not in another. A catalog of facts, for example, may be so composed that through the regularities and indicative traits of the entries, the catalog yields a proposition. A list of parallel items all together point to a simple conclusion; the conclusion may or may not be given at the end of the catalog, but the catalog—by definition—is pointed. All of the cataloged facts are taken to bear self-evident connections to one another, established by those pertinent shared traits implicit in the composition of the list, therefore also bearing meaning and pointing through the weight of evidence to an inescapable conclusion. The discrete facts then join together because of some trait common to them all. This is a mode of classification of facts to lead to an identification of what the facts have in common and—it goes without saying—an explanation of their meaning. These and other modes of philosophical argument are entirely familiar to us all. In calling all of them "philosophical," I mean only to distinguish them from the other three logics we shall presently examine.

The first document to yield a concrete example for our purposes is not in a readily accessible form, e.g., a propositional argument or a list; it is not an essay or a well-composed philosophical argument, but rather a document in the form of a commentary. The choice of this rather odd way of setting forth a proposition, of joining two facts into a cogent statement or linking two sentences into a paragraph (in literary terms), is critical to my argument. For I maintain that the form, commentary, bears no implications for the logic of discourse contained within that form. Arrangements of words by themselves tell us little about the logic that operates therein. To demonstrate the irrelevance of mere form in the analysis of logic, I choose a commentary. In general, a commentary works its way through discrete entries and does not necessarily propose to prove large-scale propositions. On formal grounds, therefore, we should not anticipate a fine example of propositional argument to emerge from writing in such a form. But we now see that a commentary can put together facts into arguments and propositions, sentences into paragraphs, as much as an essay.

We turn to Sifré to Deuteronomy, a systematic commentary on much of the book of Deuteronomy. The pertinent verse is the following: "For the Lord will vindicate his people and repents himself [Jewish Publication Society version: take revenge] for his servants, when he sees that their might is gone, and neither bond

nor free is left" (Dt. 32:36). The proposition is not explicitly stated but it is repeatedly implied: when the Israelites are at the point of despair, then God will vindicate
them. We shall now see a systematic demonstration of the proposition that when
things are at their worst and the full punishment impends, God relents and saves
Israel. And what is critical is at the pivots and the joinings of sentences.

SIFRÉ TO DEUTERONOMY

CCCXXVI:II
1. A.   ". . . when he sees that their might is gone, and neither bond nor
         free is left":
    B.   When he sees their destruction, on account of the captivity.
    C.   For all of them went off.

Let me make explicit, in terms of the first case, how I conceive the connections to
be established, the conclusion to be drawn. A represents the conclusion, that is,
the proposition to be proved. B, C present the facts that are connected. C is the
first fact, namely, all of them went off into exile. B then is the second fact, that (1)
God saw that they had gone into captivity, and (2) they were without arrogance
or power, yielding the unstated conclusion, (3) he had mercy on them, and that
then validates the proposition, A. Turned around, the second and third of the
three sentences work together so as to make a point that neither one of them by
itself establishes, and that is how such a syllogism works in general. Then a sequence of syllogisms of the same kind, not all of them fully spelled out and most
of them as truncated as the first, make the same point, establishing the besought
theorem by setting forth numerous demonstrations of that theorem: "When he
sees. . . ."

2. A.   Another teaching concerning the phrase, ". . . when he sees":
    B.   When they despaired of redemption.
3. A.   Another teaching concerning the phrase, ". . . when he sees [that
         their might is gone, and neither bond nor free is left]":
    B.   When he sees that the last penny is gone from the purse,
    C.   in line with this verse: "And when they have made an end of breaking
         in pieces the power of the holy people, all these things shall be fin-
         ished" (Dan. 12:7) [Hammer's translation, Sifré to Deuteronomy, *ad
         loc.*].
4. A.   Another teaching concerning the phrase, ". . . when he sees that
         their might is gone, and neither bond nor free is left":
    B.   When he sees that among them there are no men who seek mercy
         for them as Moses had,
    C.   in line with this verse: "Therefore he said that he would destroy

them, had not Moses his chosen one stood before him in the breach"
(Ps. 106:23). . . .

5. A. Another teaching concerning the phrase, ". . . when he sees that
        their might is gone, and neither bond nor free is left":
    B. When he sees that among them there are no men who seek mercy
        for them as Aaron had,
    C. in line with this verse: "And he stood between the dead and the living
        and the plague was stayed" (Num. 17:13).
6. A. Another teaching concerning the phrase, ". . . when he sees that
        their might is gone, and neither bond nor free is left":
    B. When he sees that there are no men who seek mercy for them as
        Phineas had,
    C. in line with this verse: "Then stood up Phineas and wrought judg-
        ment and so the plague was stayed" (Ps. 106:30).

Despite the form of a commentary on a verse of Scripture, we assuredly can identify the regnant proposition, which, as a matter of fact, joins the individual facts
into a cogent exercise of syllogistic proof.

Among the available means of linking sentence to sentence in paragraphs, the
first, now amply exemplified, is to establish propositions that rest upon philosophical bases, e.g., through the proposal of a thesis and the composition of a list of facts
that prove the thesis. This is to us an entirely familiar, Western mode of scientific
expression, that is, through the classification of data that, in a simple way, as we
noted, is called the science of making lists (*Listenwissenschaft*). No philosopher in
antiquity will have found unintelligible these types of units of thought, even
though the source of facts in the present instance, Scripture, not established
social norms or observations of nature, and the mode of appealing to facts,
citations of Scripture, rather than allusions to generally prevailing patterns and
norms, would have proved alien to such a philosopher. The connection, the process of thought—these seem to me entirely commonplace in the intellectual world
at large.

3.

THE TELEOLOGICAL LOGIC OF NARRATIVE

In the teleological logic of connection-making and conclusion-drawing, the logic
of coherence invokes a fictive tension and its resolution. It appeals for cogency to
the purpose and direction of an arrangement of facts, ordinarily in the form of
narrative. Teleological or narrative logic further serves quite effectively as a mode
of making connections between two facts, that is, linking two otherwise unrelated

sentences, and presenting conclusions based on the linkage. In this mode of thought, we link fact to fact and also prove (ordinarily implicit) propositions by appeal to teleology, that is, the end or purpose of discussion that makes sense of all detail. The tension of narrative derives from the open-endedness of discourse. We are told a series of facts, or a problem is set forth, such that only when we see in the sequence of the series of facts the logical, inevitable outcome do we find a resolution: that sense, that fittingness of connection, which makes of the parts a cogent whole. Accordingly, a proposition (whether or not it is stated explicitly) may be set forth and demonstrated by showing through the telling of a tale (of a variety of kinds, e.g., historical, fictional, parabolic, and the like) that a sequence of events, real or imagined, shows the ineluctable truth of a given proposition. Whence the connection? The logic of connection demonstrated through narrative, rather than philosophy, is simply stated. It is connection attained and explained by invoking some mode of narrative in which a sequence of events, first this, then that, is understood to yield a proposition, first this, then that—*because of this*. That manufactured sequence both states *and also establishes* a proposition in a way different from the philosophical and argumentative mode of propositional discourse.

Whether or not the generalization is stated in so many words rarely matters, because the power of well-crafted narrative is to make unnecessary an author's explicitly drawing the moral. Narrative sees cogency in the purpose and direction and of course outcome, appealing for its *therefore* to the necessary order of events understood as causative. That is then a logic or intelligibility of connection attained through teleology: the claim of goal or direction or purpose, *therefore* cause, commonly joining facts through the fabric of a tale, presenting the *telos* in the garb of a story of what happened because it had to happen. Narrative logic thus makes connections and draws conclusions and conveys a proposition through the setting forth of happenings in a framework of inevitability, in a sequence that makes a point, e.g., establishes not merely the facts of what happens, but the teleology that explains those facts. Then we speak not only of events—our naked facts—but of their relationship. We claim to account for that relationship teleologically, in the purposive sequence and necessary order of happenings. In due course we shall see how various kinds of narratives serve to convey highly intelligible and persuasive propositions.

For an example of narrative, I turn to another rabbinic document, The Fathers according to Rabbi Nathan. Here we have a parable that supplies a simple example of how narrative links fact to fact in cogent discourse and further conveys with powerful logic a clear proposition:

THE FATHERS ACCORDING TO RABBI NATHAN

I:XIII. 2. A. R. Simeon b. Yohai says, "I shall draw a parable for you. To what may the first man be compared? He was like a man who had a wife at home. What did that man do? He went and brought a jug and put in it a certain number of dates and nuts. He caught a scorpion and put it at the mouth of the jug and sealed it tightly. He left it in the corner of his house.

B. "He said to her, 'My daughter [for husbands referred to wives as daughters], whatever I have in the house is entrusted to you, except for this jar, which under no circumstances should you touch.' What did the woman do? When her husband went off to market, she went and opened the jug and put her hand in it, and the scorpion bit her, and she went and fell into bed. When her husband came home from the market, he said to her, 'What's going on?'

C. "She said to him, 'I put my hand into the jug, and a scorpion bit me, and now I'm dying.'

D. "He said to her, 'Didn't I tell you to begin with, "Whatever I have in the house is entrusted to you, except for this jar, which under no circumstances should you touch?"' He got mad at her and divorced her.

E. "So it was with the first man.

F. "When the Holy One, blessed be He, said to him, *Of all the trees of the garden you certainly may eat, but from the tree of knowledge of good and evil you may not eat, for on the day on which you eat of it, you will surely die* (Gen. 2:17),

G. "on that day he was driven out, thereby illustrating the verse, *Man does not lodge overnight in honor* (Ps. 49:24)."

Simeon's point is that by giving man the commandment, God aroused his interest in that tree and led man to do what he did. The explicit proposition is the first point, we sin on account of our obsession. The implicit proposition is that God bears a measure of guilt for the fall of man. The issue of connection should be made explicit. Let us consider the sequence of sentences of the opening unit:

1. A man had a wife at home

2. He went and brought a jug

3. . . . put in it a certain number of dates and nuts.

4. He caught a scorpion

5. . . . put it at the mouth of the jug

6. . . . sealed it tightly.

7. . . . He left it in the corner of his house.

Nos. 1, 2, 3, and 4 bear no connection whatsoever. Nos. 4–7, of course, form a single sentence, but that sentence on its own stands utterly unrelated to the earlier of the two sentences, Nos. 1–3. However, we realize, the sequence of clauses and sentences, all of them discrete, in fact form a tight fit, since they bear the burden of the narrative. At the end, then, the narrative reaches its point and, retrospectively, establishes a very close connection between clause and clause, sentence and sentence. It is the goal, the teleology, of the composition, that joins the components of the composition to one another, and that happens only at the end. Our trust in the narrator's purpose is what allows us to suspend our suspicion that we are linking things that stand out of all relationship with one another. The linkage imparted at the end then makes sense of everything from the outset, and that is what I mean by a logic of teleology, as distinct from propositional logic, which results in the making of connections and the drawing of conclusions.

4.
The Non-Propositional Logic of Fixed Association

This brings us to an unfamiliar mode of establishing connections between sentences, which I call the logic of fixed association. Though difficult to define in familiar terms, it forms the critical and indicative logic of discourse of a variety of rabbinic documents. It is a logic that to begin with bears a negative trait, in that in this logic we find connection *without* conclusion, that is, the *and* but not the *equals* or the "therefore." In this logic, the two *and* the two do not *equal* anything. Then on what basis do we impute or introduce the *and* at all? The cogency of two or more facts is imputed and extrinsic. The *and* is not sensible, intrinsic, propositional, or purposive. But in rabbinic literature document after document appeals to precisely this logic of fixed association. Not only so, but even highly propositional compositions, of considerable dimensions, are linked together not syllogistically but solely through extrinsic, fixed association. It follows that writers of documents of rabbinic literature do perceive cogency through fixed association without either syllogistic or even teleological proposition. That cogency, the connection lacking all proposition, derives from a sense of the order and proportion of data extrinsic to those at hand.

What is it that effects connection in the logic of fixed association? Fixed associations derive from an extrinsic and conventional list of items deemed joined for reasons pertinent to those items. Then each fact or sentence joined together fore and aft with others finds its own relationship to that extrinsic connection, without the slightest connection to other facts or sentences that stand, in writing or in mental sequence, in the same context, fore and aft. Discrete facts, propositions, or sentences hang together because they refer equally to an available protocol of associations. Hence it is a logic that rests upon conventional connections. It ap-

peals, rather, to protocols—e.g., lists of things, a given text, a sequence of facts—
that are known and familiar, rather than on logico-propositional connections that
are unknown and subject to discovery. It is meaning imputed, not discovered. The
contrast to the logic most familiar to us in the West is readily grasped. In philosophical logic we set up a sequence of two or more facts and claim out of that
sequence to propose a proposition different from, transcending, the facts at hand.
Here, by contrast, we join two or more facts or sentences without pretending that
any proposition whatsoever is to be demonstrated. That is why the sequence that
links in one composition sentence 1, then sentence 2, then sentence 3, though
there is no propositional connection between 1 and 2 or 2 and 3, rests upon principles of intelligibility practically unknown to us. It is easy to find appropriate illustrations.

For an illustration, we return to an already familiar compilation. I give a sustained passage, a sequence of freestanding sentences, bearing no relationship, sequential let alone propositional, to one another. What makes me insist that the
sentences are discrete? A simple test suffices. Were the following items given in
some other order, viewed in that other sequence, they would make precisely as
much, or as little, sense as they do in the order in which we see them. But in
syllogistic logic, all the more so in teleological logic (though not in *Listenwissenschaft*), the order of facts bears consequence. Indeed, reversing the order of sentences yields either a proposition exactly contrary to the one that is argued, or
mere gibberish. In what follows, by contrast, the order of sentences has no bearing
upon any proposition, and given the power of the correct ordering of facts/sen-
tences in both syllogistic argument and teleological logic alike, the utter incapacity
of order to impart meaning shows us that we have in hand a logic other than the
philosophical-syllogistic or the teleological. Now to our passage:

SIFRÉ TO DEUTERONOMY

XXV:I.   1.   A.   "What kind of place are we going to? Our kinsmen have
taken the heart out of us, saying, ['We saw there a people
stronger and taller than we, large cities with walls sky-
high, and even Anakites']" (Dt. 1:25–28):

B.   They said to him, "Moses, our lord, had we heard these
things from ordinary people, we should have never believed it.

C.   "But we have heard it from people whose sons are ours
and whose daughters are ours."

XXV:II.   1.   A.   "We saw there a people . . . taller than we":

B.   This teaches that they were tall.

2.   A.   ". . . and greater . . .":

B.   This teaches that they were numerous.

XXV:III.   1.   A.   ". . . large cities with walls sky-high, and even Anakites":

        B.   Rabban Simeon b. Gamaliel says, "In the present passage, Scriptures speak in exaggerated language: 'Hear, O Israel, you are going to pass over the Jordan this day to go in to dispossess nations greater and mightier than yourself, cities great and fortified up to heaven' (Dt. 9:1).

        C.   "But when God spoke to Abraham, Scripture did not use exaggerated language: 'And we will multiply your seed as the stars of the heaven' (Gen. 26:4), 'And we will make your seed as the dust of the earth' (Gen. 13:16)."

XXV:IV.   1.   A.   ". . . and even Anakites did we see there":

        B.   This teaches that they saw giants on top of giants, in line with this verse: "Therefore pride is as a chain about their neck" (Ps. 73:6).

XXV:V.   1.   A.   "And we said to you":

        B   He stressed to them, "It is not on our own authority that we speak to you, but it is on the authority of the Holy One that we speak to you."

XXV:VI.   1.   A.   "Do not be frightened and do not be afraid of them":

        B.   On what account?

        C.   "For the Lord your God is the one who goes before you."

        D.   He said to them, "The one who did miracles for you in Egypt and all these miracles is going to do miracles for you when you enter the land:

        E.   "'According to all that he did for you in Egypt before your eyes' (Dt. 1:30).

        F.   "If you do not believe concerning what is coming, at least believe concerning what has already taken place."

That each unit of thought, signified by a Roman numeral, stands by itself hardly needs proof, since it is a self-evident fact. Were we to present the several items in a different order, that shift would have no effect whatsoever upon the meaning of the passage. That proves that the individual sentences bear no relationship to one another. Then it follows that there is no *equals*. All we have is a sequence of unrelated sentences, not a cogent paragraph; the sentences do not appeal to their neighbors, fore or aft, to prove a proposition beyond themselves; and each one, standing by itself, makes a point that bears no connection to any other in context—*except* for the verse of Deuteronomy, the base verse, that all of them cite and claim to elucidate in one way or another. I cannot imagine how, apart from the mere statement of the facts, I can show more vividly that a sequence of utterly unrelated sentences has been laid forth before us. They occur in context of sequences of highly propositional units of thought.

    The third logic therefore rests upon the premise that an established sequence of facts, e.g., holy days, holy persons, holy words, in a manner extrinsic to the sense of what is said joins whatever is attached to those words into a set of cogent statements, even though said sequence does not form of those statements propositions of any kind, implicit or explicit. The protocol of associated items, that is, the established sequence of words, may be made up of names always associated with one another. It may be made up of a received text, with deep meanings of its own, e.g., a verse or a clause of Scripture. It may be made up of the sequence of holy days or synagogue lections, which are assumed to be known by everyone and so to connect on their own.

The fixed association of these words, whether names, whether formulas such as verses of Scripture, whether lists of facts, serves to link otherwise unrelated statements to one another and to form of them all not a proposition but, nonetheless, an entirely intelligible sequence of connected or related sentences. Fixed association forms the antonym of free association. There is no case in rabbinic literature, among the documents translated by me, in which the contents of one sentence stimulate a compositor to put down the next sentence only because one thing happens to remind the compositor of something else, that is, without any reference to a principle of association external to both sentences (our "fixed association"), and also without any reference to a shared proposition that connects the two (our "propositional cogency").

To show the full power of the logic of fixed association, quite independent of the fixed associations defined by sequences of verses of Scripture and hence in no way serving as a commentary of any kind, I turn to a few lines of Mishnah-tractate Abot, The Fathers, Chapter One. That chapter is made up of three units, first, three names, then five paired names, finally, three more names. The first three names are Moses (and the following), then Simeon the Righteous, then Antigonos. The groups of pairs are the two Yosés, Joshua b. Perahiah and Nittai the Arbelite, Judah b. Tabbai and Simeon b. Shatah, Shemaiah and Abtalion, and finally, Hillel and Shammai. Then at the end come Gamaliel, Simeon his son, and (repetitiously) Simeon b. Gamaliel. That the names are not random but meaningful, that the fixed association of name A with name B, name C with name D, name E with name F, and so on, is deemed cogent—these are the premises of all discourse in Chapter One of The Fathers. The premise rests on the simple fact that these names are announced as sequential, set by set—e.g., the first holds office M, the second, office N—and then in their unfolding, the first group is prior in time to the second, and on down. The order matters and conveys the information, therefore, that the compositor or author wishes to emphasize or rehearse. So when we claim that the logic of fixed association links sentences into meaningful compositions, even though it does not find cogency in the proposition at hand, we believe that claim rests upon the givens of reading the chapter at hand that universally prevail among all interpreters. I present in italics the apodosis—the propositions, the things that people say, which would correspond to the propositions of a syllogistic, philosophical discourse. In plain type is the attributive, or, in the less precise usage introduced earlier, the protasis.

THE FATHERS CHAPTER ONE

1:1.   MOSES received the Torah at Sinai and handed it on to Joshua, Joshua to elders, and elders to prophets. And prophets handed it on to the men of the great assembly. They said three things: *Be prudent in judgment. Raise up many disciples. Make a fence for the Torah.*

1:2.   SIMEON THE RIGHTEOUS was one of the last survivors of the great assembly. He would say: *On three things does the world stand: On the Torah, and on the Temple service, and on deeds of loving-kindness.*

1:3.   ANTIGONUS OF SOKHO received [the Torah] from Simeon the Righteous. He would say: *Do not be like servants who serve the master on condition of receiving a reward, but [be] like servants who serve the master not on condition of receiving a reward. And let the fear of Heaven be upon you.*

That the names are intended signals is shown, of course, by the reference of No. 2 to No. 1 and No. 3 to No. 2. The rest of the chapter proceeds along these same lines. No unfolding proposition emerges from what is attributed to the named sages, and, indeed, most of the assigned statements stand autonomous of one another.

Now if we ask ourselves what the italicized words have in common, how they form a cogent discourse, the answer is clear. They have nothing in common, and they certainly do not so make connections as to draw a conclusion (though some may claim they are joined in overall theme), and, standing by themselves, they do not establish a proposition in common. As propositions in sequence, they do not form an intelligible discourse. But—and this must stand as a premise of all argument—in the mind of the authorship of The Fathers, which has set matters forth as we see them, those same words serve intelligible discourse. But the principle of cogency, upon which intelligibility rests, does not derive from what is said. A shared topic by itself does not in our view constitute an adequate logic of connection between two otherwise discrete sentences, though, admittedly, a shared topic is better than none at all.

To recapitulate: the principle is that things are deemed to form a fixed sequence, specifically, the list of named authorities. The premise that because Rabbi X is linked on a common list—a text, a canon of names—with Rabbi Y, and linked in that order, first X, then Y, accounts (for the authorship at hand) for the intelligibility of the writing before us: this is connected to that. That is to say, the logic joining one sentence to another in The Fathers derives from the premise of fixed associations, or, stated in more general terms, an established or classic text. This formulation of fixed associations, this received text—in this case, a list of names—joins together otherwise unrelated statements. What makes two or more sequential sentences into an intelligible statement overall (or in its principal parts) is not *what* is said but (in this context) *who* does the saying. The list of those canonical names, in proper order, imparts cogency to an otherwise unintelligible sequence of statements (any one of which, to be sure, is as intelligible as the statement, "All Greeks are philosophers").

The upshot is a statement that relies for intelligibility upon the premise of fixed associations, e.g., an established text. The text does not have to be a holy book and it need not even be in writing. It may consist of a list of names, a passage of Scripture, a known sequence of events, as in the Pesher writings, or even the well-known sequence of events in the life of a holy man. But the *and* of this connection—hence also the mode of drawing conclusions if any—differs in its fundamental logic of cogency from one that relies for intelligibility upon either narrative, on the one side, or philosophical and syllogistic thought, on the other. What holds the whole together is knowledge shared among those to whom the writing is addressed, hence the "fixed" part of "fixed association," as distinct from (mere) free association.

5.

METAPROPOSITIONAL DISCOURSE

Despite its formidable name, this kind of logic is not difficult to grasp; essentially it amounts to making a point of an abstract character by exemplifying the same concrete fact over and over again. Then the reader can identify out of the cases the proposition that is intended. Metapropositional discourse forms a subspecies of propositional; the former is not articulated, the latter is. That is to say, propositional discourse involves setting forth facts to prove a point, such as the authorship of the Mishnah accomplished, or laying out facts to point to a conclusion, as in the case of narrative.

This sort of discourse characterizes philosophy, including of course natural philosophy. Metapropositional discourse proves the unity of diverse cases by imposing a single program of analytical questions—hence "methodical-analytical"—upon a virtually unlimited range of problems. This demonstration of the proposition, within the deep structure of argument, that all things fit into a single pattern is accomplished through sorting out many and diverse cases, and the discourse repeatedly invokes a fixed set of questions. And that kind of inquiry marks science, natural and social, as we know it today. It is the supreme effort to put two and two together and therefore to explain four.

I call this classification of logic in discourse metapropositional because the effect is to present two propositions, one immediate and at the surface, the other within the subterranean layers of thought, with the latter the more encompassing of the two, of course. The former—propositions concerning the case at hand—may derive from familiar modes of argument, making connections between two facts and drawing a conclusion from them. Or the superficial discourse may present what appears to be merely a simple assertion of fact, with no further conclusion to be drawn or even intended. But the latter—the metapropositional level—always sets forth a fundamental proposition and proves it.

For this higher level of discourse manages time and again to make a single point even while examining many points, and it is that capacity to conduct discourse at two levels, the one near at hand, the other at the level of recurrent polemic, that I find remarkable. Metapropositional discourse does not repeat itself; there is no recourse to only one proposition in every instance. But the propositions indeed prove few, and a survey of the canonical writings underlines the limited program of thought encompassed by this mode of discourse: the propositions are few, but they recur everywhere. That is why the upshot is to prove the unities of diverse things, and to do so in such a way that, time and again, one is able to articulate the proposition that is demonstrated through recurrent proofs of little things.

Metapropositional discourse of course forms a subdivision of propositional discourse. What distinguishes this species from its genus is not only that in these cases, the compositors make two points, one on the surface, another underneath. This mode of thought, seeking unity in diversity in a highly particular way, affects a broad range of documents; it is an instance of that process that, in the aggregate, defines traits indicative not of particular documents but of large sectors of the canon as a whole. Indeed, the intellectually highly structured character of the Mishnah, with its systematic and orderly exposition of the extension or restriction of rules, its rigorous exercise in comparison and contrast, sets the style and defines the task for later authorships, to the end of the formation of the canon in late antiquity. Not only so, but the mind trained in seeking unity in diversity, and unity susceptible of statement in proposition, works systematically through an amazingly broad program of topical inquiry and repeatedly produces that single, besought result. Out of this kind of mind, capable of making connections among wildly diverse data, science can have arisen, so far as science seeks connections and draws conclusions to explain connections. But in so stating, I have once more moved too far ahead of my argument. What of the propositional character or metapropositional discourse?

The propositions that are proven in each instance are in one case minor and in the other encompassing. The minor proposition is on the surface, the rule prevailing in a detail of law. The encompassing generalization bears global consequence, that is, for example, reason alone bears reliable results, and the like. Commonly, the surface generalization forms little more than a clause or a verse followed by a phrase in amplification thereof. Yet the unit of thought may be enormous, relative to the size—number of words—of the completed units of thought in our document. Reading the cases of Scripture and transforming them into general rules suitable for restatement in, and as, the Mishnah, the authorship of Sifré to Deuteronomy, for example, accomplished an amazing feat of sheer brilliance: holding many things together within a single theoretical framework. What is critical in holding together discourse in these items therefore is the imposition of a fixed analytical method, rather than the search for a generalization and its demonstration or proof. These items are topically discrete but time and again present the application of a fixed analytical system or structure or produce, in an episodic instance, a recurrent proposition of an analytical character (e.g., extension or restriction of a rule, demonstration that solely through Scripture are firm conclusions to be established).

One recurring exercise, which fills up much of the discussion of the legal passages of Deuteronomy in Sifré to Deuteronomy, for example, systematically proposes to generalize the case discourse of the book of Deuteronomy and to reframe the case into the example of a general law. The "if a person does such and so" or the details of a case as spelled out in Scripture will be subjected to a sustained exercise of generalization. In this exercise the author does two things. Either—in the process of generalization—he will restrict the rule or he will extend it. If Scripture contains a detail, such as the statement of a case always demands, one should ask whether that detail restricts the rule to a kind of case defined by the detail, or whether that detail represents a more general category of cases and is to be subjected, therefore, to generalization. (In the word choice of contemporary philosophy, the fixed analytical method at hand investigates issues of *generalizability*.) Here is an example of many instances in which the authorship of a sustained discourse proposes to turn a case into a law.

SIFRÉ TO DEUTERONOMY

CLXVI:I.   1.   A.   "[You shall also give him] the first fruits of your new grain and wine and oil, [and the first shearing of your sheep. For the Lord your God has chosen him and his descendants, out of all your tribes, to be in attendance for service in the name of the Lord for all time]"(Dt. 18:1–6):

B.   This teaches that offerings are taken up for the priestly rations only from produce of the finest quality.

The point applies to more than the case at hand. At issue is whether we extend or restrict the applicability of the rule. Here we restrict it.

2.   A.   Just as we find that as to two varieties of produce of fruit-bearing trees, priestly rations are not taken from the one to provide the requisite gift for the other as well,

B.   so in the case of two varieties of produce of grain and vegetables, priestly rations are not taken from the one to provide the requisite gift for the other as well.

No. 2 is parachuted down and has no bearing upon anything in the cited verse. But the importance is to derive a general rule, as stated at B, which applies to a broad variety of categories of priestly gifts, just as at No. 1.

> CLXVI:II. 1. A. "... the first shearing of your sheep:"
> B. not the fleece that falls off when the sheep is dipped.
> 2. A. "... the first shearing of your sheep:"
> B. excluding a sheep that suffers from a potentially fatal ailment.
> 3. A. "... the first shearing of your sheep:"
> B. whether in the land or abroad.

No. 1 is particular to our verse, Nos. 2, 3 are general rules invoked case by case. These items are not coherent, one by one, and the three sentences in no way state a single proposition, explicit or otherwise. And yet the exercise of analysis is uniform—I could give many dozens of cases in which precisely the same distinctions are made—and the purpose is clear. It is to impose upon the case a set of generalizing issues, which yield either restrictive or expansive definitions. This is a fine instance of what I mean by attaining cogent discourse—linking one sentence to another—through an established methodical analysis of one sort or another.

> CLXVI:IV. 1. A. "You shall also give him:"
> B. This indicates that there should be sufficient fleece to constitute a gift.
> C. On this basis sages have ruled:
> D. How much does one give to the priest?
> E. Five selas' weight in Judah, equivalent to ten in Galilee, bleached but not spun,
> F. sufficient to make a small garment from it,
> G. as it is said, "You shall also give him:"
> H. This indicates that there should be sufficient fleece to constitute a gift.

The same pattern recurs as before, and the interest is in an autonomous program. This represents a different kind of methodical analysis. The framer wishes to relate a verse of Scripture to a rule in the Mishnah and so asks how C–F are founded on Scripture. G–H go over the ground of A–B. The work of restriction or expansion of the rule is now implicit, of course. Metapropositional discourse takes a central place in some documents, e.g., Sifra and the two Talmuds, none at all in many others.

To conclude: metapropositional discourse brings to expression a range of logic that shows unity in diversity, demonstrates that many things follow a single rule, and demonstrates how a few simple propositions underlie many complex statements of fact. That mode of thought seeks connections at the deepest structure of thought and proposes to explain by reference to a single rule a various and vast universe of fact. Metapropositional logic makes a single fabric out of the threads of propositional logic that fill up the loom comprised by one document after another. Sifra and the two Sifrés stood for that large sector of the canonical writings that all together serve to make a few fundamental points, applicable to many cases indeed. The two Talmuds present us with the same phenomenon: systemic and generalizing thinking about the discrete propositional statements presented by the Mishnah. And yet, while the two Sifrés and Sifra (among other writings) prove essentially metapropositional in their overall structure, attaining cogency by doing one thing many times and showing the inner simplicity of the outwardly complex propositions at hand, the Yerushalmi—and by extension, the Bavli—does not follow suit. Quite to the contrary, if we had to characterize the paramount logic of cogent discourse of the Yerushalmi, we should have to identify the prevailing principle of joining one statement to another, that is, of making connection, not with propositional, let alone metapropositional, discourse, but with the connection imposed by fixed association, that alone. For while the several units of completed thought in the two Talmuds systematically connect fact to fact, sentence to sentence, through the shared proposition generated by what is reasoned and syllogistic argument, those units of thought themselves find connection only in their common reference point, the Mishnah. The two Talmuds, as we shall see, succeed in making enormous statements because they join syllogistic logic, which stands behind the bulk of their compositions, to fixed associative logic, which holds the compositions together in huge composites.

The prevailing logics in some documents work in both the parts and the whole, in one and the same way, connecting sentence to sentence, and also paragraph to paragraph. In the Mishnah, Genesis Rabbah, and Leviticus Rabbah, the same logic of propositional discourse that links sentence to sentence also links paragraph to paragraph. That is to say, propositions join one fact or sentence to another and make of the whole a single cogent statement. Still broader propositions join one large-scale cogent statement ("paragraph" in the language of the opening sentence) to another cogent statement. The logic of the whole also defines the logic of the parts. And the same is so of the metapropositional discourse that makes the accomplishment of the authorship of Sifra so remarkable and imparts noteworthy force and sustained argument to the discrete statements of the two Sifrés as well.

In all three documents, the metapropositional program of the parts imparts its character to large stretches of the whole as well. We may therefore conclude that some documents hold together as a whole and also in part in one and the same way. They will find connections between their sentences and among the compositions of sentences by systematically setting forth propositions, argued along the lines of syllogism and worked out through the analysis accomplished by classification, comparison and contrast, of genus and species, for instance, and this they will do throughout. Or authorships will impose a single subterranean program upon data of unlimited diversity and show, point by point and overall as well, the unities within diverse facts—documents that persistently make metapropositional points and all together find cogency through those recurrent exercises of deep and methodical analysis.

But the Yerushalmi and the Bavli differ in their basic logical structure from all the other documents. For the authorships of these writings compose their completed units of thought principally as propositional or metapropositional statements. The logic, then, connects one fact to another, one sentence to another, in such a way as to form a proposition. But the joining of one completed unit of thought ("paragraph," "propositional statement") to another finds connection not in a still larger exercise of propositional discourse but rather by appeal to the connection imposed through the fixed association accomplished by the framers of the Mishnah or by the author of Scripture. That mixing of two logics, the propositional for medium-range discourse, the fixed associative for large-scale composition, differentiates the two Talmuds from all other canonical writings.

6.

TRADITION, COMMENTARY, AND LOGIC

The logic of fixed association clearly serves the purpose of composing in some sort of cogent way the discrete observations about this and that of which a commentary to a fixed text is made up. But, as our survey of the documents of rabbinic literature will show us, the prevailing logic is not exegetical for the sentences or fixed associative for the logic of coherent discourse, but highly propositional. Most large-scale and sustained units of cogent discourse, except for the Bavli, appeal for cogency to propositions, not to fixed associations, such as characterize commentaries of a certain sort and other compilations of exegeses of verses of Scripture.

Strictly speaking, commentary has no need for propositions in order to establish coherence among discrete sentences, though through commentary an authorship may propose to prove propositions (as is the case with methodical-analytical demonstrations via metapropositional logic). A document formed in order to convey exegesis attains cogency and imparts connections to two or more sentences by appeal to fixed associations. It makes no call upon narrative, does not demand recurrent methodical analyses. The text that is subjected to commentary accomplishes the joining of sentence to sentence, and to that cogency, everything else proves secondary. For, by definition, a commentary appeals for cogency to the text that the commentators propose to illuminate.

True, they may frame their commentary in diverse, appropriate ways. For example, they may comment by translating. They may comment by tacking paragraphs—stories, expositions of ideas, and the like—onto constituent structures of the base-verse. But, overall, the genre, commentary, dictates its own rhetoric, such as we have noticed, and its own logic. The logic of commentary, narrowly viewed, is that of fixed-associative compositions.

But, as a matter of fact, most of the rabbinic commentaries to Scripture proved highly propositional, not only in general, but also in detail, not only in proposition, but also in process and in rhetorical pattern. What holds things together in large-scale, sustained discourse does not rely upon the verse at hand to impose order and cogency upon discourse. Writers, as in the middle and late Midrash compilations we shall examine, ordinarily appeal to propositions to hold two or more sentences together. If, by definition, a commentary appeals for cogency to the text that the commentators propose to illuminate, then far more common is a document that is in no essential way a commentary. The logic is not that of a commentary, and the formal repertoires show strong preference for other than commentary form. So far as commentary dictates both its own rhetoric and its own logic, the documents have to be described in the aggregate as highly argumentative, profoundly well-crafted, and cogent sets of propositions. Authors found a need for propositions to attain cogency or impart connections to two or more sentences, called upon narrative, demanded recurrent analyses of a single sort.

IV

THE DIALECTICAL ARGUMENT

IN RABBINIC LITERATURE

1.
DEFINING THE DIALECTICAL ARGUMENT

DIALECTICAL ARGUMENT—THE MOVEMENT OF THOUGHT THROUGH CONTEN-
tious challenge and passionate response, initiative and counterploy—characterizes
the Talmud of Babylonia in particular, but finds a limited place, also, in other
rabbinic documents.[1] A definition of that trait of important writings therefore is
called for. The dialectical, or moving, argument is important because, in the sus-

[1] I find no discussion of the dialectics of rabbinic literature in the other introductions. For further
reading on dialectics in rabbinic literature, see my comparison of the two Talmuds in the seven volumes
of *The Bavli's Unique Voice. A Systematic Comparison of the Talmud of Babylonia and the Talmud of the Land
of Israel*. Atlanta, 1993: Scholars Press for South Florida Studies in the History of Judaism. Of special
relevance is Volume VII. *What Is Unique about the Bavli in Context? An Answer Based on Inductive Description, Analysis, and Comparison*. Note also my *Invitation to the Talmud. A Teaching Book*. Second edition,
completely revised, San Francisco, 1984: Harper & Row; and, especially, the pair of theological works
that identify dialectics as the key to the hermeneutics that forms the theological medium of the Judaism
set forth in rabbinic literature: *Judaism States Its Theology: The Talmudic Re-Presentation* (Atlanta, 1993.
Scholars Press for South Florida Studies in the History of Judaism), and *Judaism's Theological Voice: The
Talmudic Melody* (on press at the University of Chicago Press for 1994). I find it significant that in the

tained conflict provoked by the testing of propositions in contention, argument turns fact into truth. Making a point forms of data important propositions. The exchanges of propositions and arguments, objects and ripostes, hold together, however protracted. While the Talmud of Babylonia forms the principal arena for dialectics in rabbinic literature, the same mode of thinking and writing occurs elsewhere in the halakhic literature, from the Mishnah onward to the Talmud of the Land of Israel. But all of our cases will derive from the Bavli.

"Dialectical" means moving or developing an idea through questions and answers, sometimes implicit, but commonly explicit. What "moves" is the flow of argument and thought, from problem to problem. The movement is generated specifically by the raising of contrary questions and theses. What characterizes the dialectical argument in rabbinic literature is its meandering, its moving hither and yon. It is not a direct or straight-line movement, e.g., thesis, antithesis, synthesis. Rather, the rabbinic dialectical argument—the protracted, sometimes meandering, always moving flow of contentious thought—raises a question and answers it, then raises a question about the answer, and, having raised another question, then gives an answer to that question, and it continues in the same fashion. So it moves hither and yon; it is always one, but it is never the same, and it flows across the surface of the document at hand.

Those second and third and fourth turnings differentiate a dialectical from a static argument, much as the bubbles tell the difference between still and sparkling wine. The always-sparkling dialectical argument is one principal means by which the Talmud or some other rabbinic writing accomplishes its goal of showing the connections between this and that, ultimately demonstrating the unity of many "thises and thats." These efforts at describing the argument serve precisely as well as program notes to a piece of music: they tell us what we are going to hear; they cannot play the music.

The dialectical argument opens the possibility of reaching out from one thing to something else, not because people have lost sight of their starting point or their goal in the end, but because they want to encompass, in the analytical argument as it gets under way, as broad and comprehensive a range of cases and rules as they possibly can. The movement from point to point in reference to a single point that accurately describes the dialectical argument reaches upward toward a goal of proximate abstraction, leaving behind the specificities of not only cases but laws, carrying us upward to the law that governs many cases, the premises that undergird many rules, and still higher to the principles that infuse diverse premises; then the principles that generate other, unrelated premises, which, in turn, come to expression in other, still-less-intersecting cases. The meandering course of argument comes to an end when we have shown how things cohere.

---

index to Stemberger-Strack, there is no entry for "dialectic," and the topic does not occur in the other introductions surveyed here. Stemberger discusses "rabbinical hermeneutics," pp. 17–34, but this pertains to the "middot," or exegetical principles.

2.

AN EXAMPLE OF A DIALECTICAL ARGUMENT

The passage that we consider occurs at the Babylonian Talmud Baba Mesia 5B–6A, which is to say, Talmud to Mishnah Baba Mesia 1:1–2. Boldface type signifies origin in the Mishnah or the Tosefta; italics stand for Aramaic; plain type for Hebrew. Our interest is in the twists and turns of the argument and what is at stake in the formation of a continuous and unfolding composition:

[5B] IV. 1. A. **This one takes an oath that he possesses no less a share of it than half, [and that one takes an oath that he possesses no less a share of it than half, and they divide it up]:**

The rule of the Mishnah, which is cited at the head of the sustained discussion, concerns the case of two persons who find a garment. We settle their conflicting claim by requiring each to take an oath that he or she owns title to no less than half of the garment, and then we split the garment between them.

Our first question is one of text criticism: analysis of the Mishnah paragraph's word choice. We say that the oath concerns the portion that the claimant alleges he possesses. But the oath really affects the portion that he does not have in hand at all:

    B. *Is it concerning the portion that he claims he possesses that he takes the oath, or concerning the portion that he does not claim to possess?* [S. Daiches, Baba Mesia (London, 1948: Soncino) *ad loc.*: "The implication is that the terms of the oath are ambiguous. By swearing that his share in it is not 'less than half,' the claimant might mean that it is not even a third or a fourth (which is 'less than half'), and the negative way of putting it would justify such an interpretation. He could therefore take this oath even if he knew that he had no share in the garment at all, while he would be swearing falsely if he really had a share in the garment that is less than half, however small that share might be"].

    C. *Said R. Huna, "It is that he says, 'By an oath! I possess in it a portion, and I possess in it a portion that is no more than half a share of it.'"* [The claimant swears that his share is at least half (Daiches).]

Having asked and answered the question, we now find ourselves in an extension of the argument; the principal trait of the dialectical argument is now before us:

(1) but (2) maybe the contrary is the case, so (3) what about—that is, the setting aside of a proposition in favor of its opposite. Here we come to the definitive trait of the dialectic argument: its insistence on challenging every proposal with the claim, "maybe it's the opposite?" This pestering question forces us back upon our sense of self-evidence; it makes us consider the contrary of each position we propose to set forth. It makes thought happen. True, the Talmud's voice's "but"—the whole of the dialectic in one word!—presents a formidable nuisance. But so does all criticism, and only the mature mind will welcome criticism. Dialectics is not for children, politicians, propagandists, or egoists. Genuine curiosity about the truth shown by rigorous logic forms the counterpart to musical virtuosity. So the objection proceeds:

> D. *Then let him say,* "By an oath! The whole of it is mine!"

Why claim half when the alleged finder may as well demand the whole cloak?

> E. *But are we going to give him the whole of it?* [Obviously not, there is another claimant, also taking an oath.]

The question contradicts the facts of the case: two parties claim the cloak, so the outcome can never be that one will get the whole thing.

> F. *Then let him say,* "By an oath! Half of it is mine!"

Then—by the same reasoning—why claim "no less than half," rather than simply half?

> G. *That would damage his own claim* [which was that he owned the whole of the cloak, not only half of it].

The claimant does claim the whole cloak, so the proposed language does not serve to replicate his actual claim. That accounts for the language that is specified.

> H. *But here too is it not the fact that, in the oath that he is taking, he impairs his own claim?* [After all, he here makes explicit the fact that he owns at least half of it. What happened to the other half?]

The solution merely compounds the problem.

> I. *[Not at all.] For he has said,* "The whole of it is mine!" [And, he further proceeds,] "And as to your contrary view, By an oath, I do have a share in it, and that share is no less than half!"

We solve the problem by positing a different solution from the one we suggested at the outset. Why not start where we have concluded? Because if we had done so, we should have ignored a variety of intervening considerations and so should have expounded less than the entire range of possibilities. The power of the dialectical argument now is clear: it forces us to address not the problem and the solution alone, but the problem and the various ways by which a solution may be reached; then, when we do come to a final solution to the question at hand, we have reviewed all of the possibilities. We have seen how everything flows together, nothing is left unattended.

The dialectical argument in the Talmud and in other rabbinic writings therefore undertakes a different task from the philosophical counterpart. What we have here is not a set piece of two positions, with an analysis of each, such as the staid philosophical dialogue exposes with such elegance; it is, rather, an analytical argument, explaining why this, not that, then why not that but rather this; and onward. When we speak of a moving argument, this is what we mean: what is not static and merely expository, but what is dynamic and always contentious. It is not an endless argument, an argument for the sake of arguing, or evidence that important to the Talmud and other writings that use the dialectics as a principal mode of dynamic argument is process but not position. To the contrary, the passage is resolved with a decisive conclusion, not permitted to run on.

But the dialectical composition proceeds—continuous and coherent from point to point, even as it zigs and zags. We proceed to the second cogent proposition in the analysis of the cited Mishnah passage, which asks a fresh question: why an oath at all?

> 2. A. [It is envisioned that each party is holding on to a corner of the cloak, so the question is raised:] Now, since this one is possessed of the cloak and standing right there, and that one is possessed of the cloak and is standing right there, why in the world do I require this oath?

Until now we have assumed as fact the premise of the Mishnah's rule, which is that an oath is there to be taken. But why assume so? Surely each party now has what he is going to get. So what defines the point and effect of the oath?

> B. Said R. Yohanan, "This oath [to which our Mishnah passage refers] happens to be an ordinance imposed only by rabbis,
> C. "so that people should not go around grabbing the cloaks of other people and saying, 'It's mine!'" [But, as a matter of fact, the oath that is imposed in our Mishnah passage is not legitimate by the law of the Torah. It is an act taken by sages to maintain the social order.]

We do not administer oaths to liars; we do not impose an oath in a case in which we may end up with a case in which one of the claimants takes an oath for something he knew to be untrue, since one party really does own the cloak, the other really has grabbed it. The proposition solves the problem—but hardly is going to settle the question. On the contrary, Yohanan raises more problems than he solves. So, we ask, how can we agree to an oath in this case at all?

> D. *But why then not advance the following argument: since such a one is suspect as to fraud in a property claim, he also should be suspect as to fraud in oath-taking?*

Yohanan places himself into the position of believing in respect to the oath what we will not believe in respect to the claim on the cloak, for, after all, one of the parties before us must be lying! Why sustain such a contradiction: gullible and suspicious at one and the same time?

> E. *In point of fact, we do not advance the argument: since such a one is suspect as to fraud in a property claim, he also should be suspect as to fraud in oath-taking, for if you do not concede that fact, then how is it possible that the All-Merciful has ruled, "One who has conceded part of a claim against himself must take an oath as to the remainder of what is subject to claim"?*

If someone claims that another party holds property belonging to him or her, and the one to whom the bailment has been handed over for safekeeping, called the bailee, concedes part of the claim, the bailee must then take an oath in respect to the rest of the claimed property, that is, the part that the bailee maintains does not belong to the claimant at all. So the law itself—the Torah, in fact—has sustained the same contradiction. That fine solution, of course, is going to be challenged:

> F. *Why not simply maintain, since such a one is suspect as to fraud in a property claim, he also should be suspect as to fraud in oath-taking?*
> G. *In that other case, [the reason for the denial of part of the claim and the admission of part is not the intent to commit fraud, but rather,] the defendant is just trying to put off the claim for a spell.*

We could stop at this point without losing a single important point of interest; everything is before us. One of the striking traits of the large-scale dialectical composition is its composite character. Starting at the beginning, without any loss of meaning or sense, we may well stop at the end of any given paragraph of thought. But the dialectics insists on moving forward, exploring, pursuing, insisting; and were we to remove a paragraph in the middle of a dialectical composite, then all that follows would become incomprehensible. That is a mark of the dialectical argument: sustained, continuous, and coherent—yet perpetually in control and capable of resolving matters at any single point.

Now, having fully exposed the topic, its problem, and its principles, we take a tangent indicated by the character of the principle before us: when a person will or will not lie or take a false oath. We have a theory on the matter; what we now do is expound the theory, with special reference to the formulation of that theory in explicit terms by a named authority:

> H. This concurs with the position of Rabbah. [For Rabbah has said, "On what account has the Torah imposed the requirement of an oath on one who confesses to only part of a claim against him? It is by reason of the presumption that a person will not insolently deny the truth about the whole of a loan in the very presence of the creditor and so entirely deny the debt. He will admit to part of the debt and deny part of it. Hence we invoke an oath in a case in which one does so, to coax out the truth of the matter."]
>
> I. For you may know, [in support of the foregoing], that R. Idi bar Abin said R. Hisda [said]: "He who [falsely] denies owing money on a loan nonetheless is suitable to give testimony, but he who denies that he holds a bailment for another party cannot give testimony."

The proposition is now fully exposed. A named authority is introduced, who will concur in the proposed theoretical distinction. He sets forth an extralogical consideration, which of course the law always will welcome: the rational goal of finding the truth overrides the technicalities of the law governing the oath.

Predictably, we cannot allow matters to stand without challenge, and the challenge comes at a fundamental level, with the predictable give-and-take to follow:

> J. But what about that which R. Ammi bar. Hama repeated on Tannaite authority: "[If they are to be subjected to an oath,] four sorts of bailees have to have denied part of the bailment and conceded part of the bailment, namely, the unpaid bailee, the borrower, the paid bailee, and the one who rents."
>
> K. *Why not simply maintain, since such a one is suspect as to fraud in a property claim, he also should be suspect as to fraud in oath-taking?*
>
> L. *In that case as well, [the reason for the denial of part of the claim and the admission of part is not the intent to commit fraud, but rather,] the defendant is just trying to put off the claim for a spell.*
>
> M. *He reasons as follows: "I'm going to find the thief and arrest him." Or: "I'll find [the beast] in the field and return it to the owner."*

Once more, "if that is the case" provokes yet another analysis; we introduce a different reading of the basic case before us, another reason that we should not impose an oath:

>   N. *If that is the case, then why should one who denies holding a bail-ment ever be unsuitable to give testimony? Why don't we just main-tain that the defendant is just trying to put off the claim for a spell? He reasons as follows: "I'm going to look for the thing and find it."*
>
>   O. *When in point of fact we do rule,* He who denies holding a bailment is unfit to give testimony, *it is in a case in which witnesses come and give testimony against him that at that very moment, the bailment is located in the bailee's domain, and he is fully informed of that fact, or, alternatively, he has the object in his possession at that very moment.*

The solution to the problem at hand also provides the starting point for yet another step in the unfolding exposition. Huna has given us a different resolution of mat-ters. That accounts for No. 3, and No. 4 is also predictable:

> 3. A. *But as to that which R. Huna has said* [when we have a bailee who offers to pay compensation for a lost bailment rather than swear it has been lost, since he wishes to appropriate the article by paying for it, (Daiches)], "They impose upon him the oath that the bailment is not in his possession at all,"
>
>   B. *why not in that case invoke the principle, since such a one is suspect as to fraud in a property claim, he also should be suspect as to fraud in oath-taking?*
>
>   C. *In that case also, he may rule in his own behalf, I'll give him the money.*
>
> 4. A. *Said R. Aha of Difti to Rabina, "But then the man clearly trans-gresses the negative commandment:* 'You shall not covet.'"
>
>   B. "You shall not covet" *is generally understood by people to pertain to something for which one is not ready to pay.*

Yet another authority's position now is invoked, and it draws us back to our starting point: the issue of why we think an oath is suitable in a case in which we ought to assume lying is going on; so we are returned to our starting point, but via a circuitous route:

> 5. A. [6A] *But as to that which R. Nahman said,* "They impose upon him [who denies the whole of a claim] an oath of inducement," *why not in that case invoke the principle, since such*

> *a one is suspect as to fraud in a property claim, he also should be suspect as to fraud in oath-taking?*
>
> B. *And furthermore, there is that which R. Hiyya taught on Tannaite authority:* "Both parties [employee, supposed to have been paid out of an account set up by the employer at a local store, and storekeeper] take an oath and collect what each claims from the employer," *why not in that case invoke the principle, since such a one is suspect as to fraud in a property claim, he also should be suspect as to fraud in oath-taking?*
>
> C. *And furthermore, there is that which R. Sheshet said,* "We impose upon an unpaid bailee [who claims that the animal has been lost] three distinct oaths: first, an oath that I have not deliberately caused the loss, that I did not put a hand on it, and that it is not in my domain at all," *why not in that case invoke the principle, since such a one is suspect as to fraud in a property claim, he also should be suspect as to fraud in oath-taking?*

We now settle the matter:

> D. *It must follow that we do not invoke the principle at all, since such a one is suspect as to fraud in a property claim, he also should be suspect as to fraud in oath-taking.*

What is interesting is why walk so far to end up where we started: do we invoke said principle? No, we do not. What we have accomplished on our wanderings is a survey of opinion on a theme, to be sure, but opinion that intersects at our particular problem as well. The moving argument serves to carry us hither and yon; its power is to demonstrate that all considerations are raised, all challenges met, all possibilities explored. This is not, as I said, merely a set-piece argument, where we have proposition, evidence, analysis, conclusion; it is a different sort of thinking altogether, purposive and coherent, but also comprehensive and compelling for its admission of possibilities and attention to alternatives.

3.

THE IMPORTANCE OF THE DIALECTICAL ARGUMENT IN RABBINIC LITERATURE

What then is at stake in the dialectical argument? I see three complementary results. All of them, in my view, prove commensurate to the effort required to follow these protracted, sometimes tedious disquisitions.

First, we test every allegation by a counterproposition, so serving the cause of truth through challenge and constant checking for flaws in an argument.

Second, we survey the entire range of possibilities, which leaves no doubts about the cogency of our conclusion.

Third, quite to the point, by the give-and-take of argument, we ourselves are enabled to go through the thought processes set forth in the subtle markings that yield our reconstruction of the argument. We not only review what people say, but how they think: the processes of reasoning that have yielded a given conclusion. Sages and disciples become party to the modes of thought; in the dialectical argument, they are required to replicate the thought processes themselves.

Let me give a single example of the power of the dialectical argument to expose the steps in thinking that lead from one end to another: principle to ruling, or ruling to principle. In the present instance, the only one we require to see a perfectly routine and obvious procedure, we mean to prove the point that if people are permitted to obstruct the public way, if damage was done by them, they are liable to pay compensation. First, we are going to prove that general point on the basis of a single case. Then we shall proceed to show how a variety of authorities, dealing with diverse cases, sustain the same principle.

TALMUD BABA MESIA 10:5 / O-X

O. **He who brings out his manure to the public domain—**

P. **while one party pitches it out, the other party must be bringing it in to manure his field.**

Q. **They do not soak clay in the public domain,**

R. **and they do not make bricks.**

S. **And they knead clay in the public way,**

T. **but not bricks.**

U. **He who builds in the public way—**

V. **while one party brings stones, the builder must make use of them in the public way.**

W. **And if one has inflicted injury, he must pay for the damages he has caused.**

X. **Rabban Simeon b. Gamaliel says, "Also: He may prepare for doing his work [on site in the public way] for thirty days [before the actual work of building]."**

We begin with the comparison of the rule before us with another Tannaite position on the same issue, asking whether an unattributed, therefore authoritative, rule stands for or opposes the position of a given authority; we should hope to prove that the named authority concurs. So one fundamental initiative in showing how many cases express a single principle—the concrete demonstration of the unity of the law—is to find out whether diverse, important authorities concur on the principle, each ruling in a distinctive case; or whether a single authority is consistent in ruling in accord with the principle at hand, as in what follows:

I. 1. A. *May we say that our Mishnah paragraph does not accord with the view of R. Judah? For it has been taught on Tannaite authority:*

    B. **R. Judah says, "At the time of fertilizing the fields, a man may take out his manure and pile it up at the door of his house in the public way so that it will be pulverized by the feet of man and beast, for a period of thirty days. For it was on that very stipulation that Joshua caused the Israelites to inherit the land" [T. B.M. 11:8E–H].**

    C. You may even maintain that he concurs with the Mishnah's rule [that **while one party pitches it out, the other party must be bringing it in to manure his field**]. R. Judah concedes that if one has caused damage, he is liable to pay compensation.

In line with the position just now proposed, then Judah will turn out to rule every which way on the same matter. And that is not an acceptable upshot.

    D. *But has it not been taught in the Mishnah:* **If the storekeeper had left his lamp outside the storekeeper is liable [if the flame caused a fire]. R. Judah said, "In the case of a lamp for Hanukkah, he is exempt" [M. B.Q. 6:6E–F],** because he has acted under authority. *Now surely that must mean,* under the authority of the court [and that shows that one is not responsible for damage caused by his property in the public domain if it was there under the authority of the court]!

The dialectic now intervenes. We have made a proposal. Isn't it a good one? Of course not; were we to give up so quickly, we should gain nothing:

    E. *No, what it means is, on the authority of carrying out one's religious obligations.*

By now, the reader is able to predict the next step: "but isn't the contrary more reasonable?" Here is how we raise the objection.

    F. *But has it not been taught on Tannaite authority:*

    G. in the case of all those concerning whom they have said, "They are permitted to obstruct the public way," if there was damage done, one is liable to pay compensation. But R. Judah declares one exempt from having to pay compensation.

> H. *So it is better to take the view that our Mishnah paragraph does not concur with the position of R. Judah.*

The point of interest has been introduced: whether those permitted to obstruct the public way must pay compensation for damages they may cause in so doing. Here is where we find a variety of cases that yield a single principle:

> 2. A. *Said Abayye, "R. Judah, Rabban Simeon b. Gamaliel, and R. Simeon all take the position that* in the case of all those concerning whom they have said, 'They are permitted to obstruct the public way,' if there was damage done, one is liable to pay compensation.
>
>   B. *"As to R. Judah, the matter is just as we have now stated it."*

Simeon b. Gamaliel and Simeon now draw us to unrelated cases:

> C. *"As to Rabban Simeon b. Gamaliel, we have learned in the Mishnah:* **Rabban Simeon b. Gamaliel says, 'Also: He may prepare for doing his work [on site in the public way] for thirty days [before the actual work of building].'**
>
> D. *"As to R. Simeon, we have learned in the Mishnah:* **A person should not set up an oven in a room unless there is a space of four cubits above it. If he was setting it up in the upper story, there has to be a layer of plaster under it three handbreadths thick, and in the case of a stove, a handbreadth thick. And if it did damage, the owner of the oven has to pay for the damage. R. Simeon says, 'All of these measures have been stated only so that if the object did damage, the owner is exempt from paying compensation if the stated measures have been observed'"** [M. B.B. 2:2A–F].

We see then that the demonstration of the unity of the law and the issue of who stands, or does not stand, behind a given rule, go together. When we ask about who does or does not stand behind a rule, we ask about the principle of a case, which leads us downward to a premise, and we forthwith point to how that same premise underlies a different principle yielding a case—so how can X hold the view he does, if that is his premise, since at a different case he makes a point with a principle that rests on a contradictory premise. The Mishnah and the Talmud are comparable to the moraine left by the last ice age, fields studded with boulders. For the Talmud, reference is made to those many disputes that litter the pages and impede progress. That explains why much of the Talmud is taken up with not only sorting out disputes, but also showing their rationality, meaning, reasonable people have perfectly valid reasons for disagreeing about a given point, since both parties share the same premises but apply them differently; or they really do not differ at all, since one party deals with one set of circumstances, the other with a different set of circumstances.

4.
THE LAW BEHIND THE LAWS

The dialectical argument proves the ideal medium for the assertion, through sustained demonstration alone, of the union of laws in law. Specifically, if all we know is laws, then we want to find out what is at stake in them. Accordingly, the true issues of the law emerge from the detailed rulings of the laws. Generalization takes a variety of forms, some yielding a broader framework into which to locate a case, others a proposition of consequence. Let me give an obvious and familiar instance of what is to be done. Here is an example of a case that yields a principle:

TALMUD BABA MESIA TO 9:11

A. **(1) A day worker collects his wage any time of the night.**

B. **(2) And a night worker collects his wage any time of the day.**

C. **(3) A worker by the hour collects his wage any time of the night or day.**

I. 1. A. *Our rabbis have taught on Tannaite authority:*

B. How on the basis of Scripture do we know, **A day worker collects his wage any time of the night?**

C. "[You shall not oppress your neighbor or rob him.] The wages of a hired servant shall not remain with you all night until the morning" (Lev. 19:13).

D. And how on the basis of Scripture do we know, **and a night worker collects his wage any time of the day?**

E. "[You shall not oppress a hired servant who is poor and needy] . . . you shall give him his hire on the day on which he earns it, before the sun goes down" (Dt. 23:14–15).

F. *Might I say that the reverse is the case [the night worker must be paid during the night that he does the work, in line with Lev. 19:13, and the day worker by day, in line with Dt. 23:15]?*

G. Wages are to be paid only at the end of the work [so the fee is not payable until the work has been done].

What do we learn from this passage? Specifically, two points.

[1] Scripture yields the rule at hand;

[2] Scripture also imposes limits on the formation of the law; but one generalization, that the law of the Mishnah derives from the source of Scripture.

And, if we take a small step beyond, of course, we learn that the two parts of the Torah are one. The hermeneutics instructs us to ask, how on the basis of Scripture do we know . . . ? Its premise then is that Scripture forms the basis for rules not expressed with verses of the written Torah. The theological principle conveyed in the hermeneutics expressed in the case is that the Torah is one and encompasses both the oral and the written parts; the oral part derives its truths from the written part.

Now, if I had to identify the single most important theological point that the Talmud and other writings that use dialectics set forth, it is that the laws yield law, the truth exhibits integrity, all of the parts—the details, principles, and premises—holding together in a coherent manner. To understand how generalizations are attained, however, we cannot deal only with generalizations. So we turn to a specific problem of category formation, namely, in the transfer of property, whether or not we distinguish between a sale and a gift. That is, in both instances property is transferred. But the conditions of transfer clearly differ; in the one case there is a quid pro quo, in the other, not. Now, does that distinction make a difference? The answer to that question will have implications for a variety of concrete cases, e.g., transfers of property in a dowry, divisions of inheritances and estates, the required documents and procedures for effecting transfer of title, and the like. If, then, we know the correct category formation—the same or not the same category—we form a generalization that will draw together numerous otherwise unrelated cases and (more to the point) rules.

One way to accomplish the goal is to identify the issue behind a dispute, which leads us from the dispute to the principle that is established and confirmed by a dispute on details, e.g., whether or not the principle applies, and, if it does, how it does. In this way we affirm the unity of the law by establishing that all parties to a dispute really agree on the same point; then the dispute itself underlines the law's coherence:

TALMUD BABA BATRA 1:3

A. **He whose [land] surrounds that of his fellow on three sides,**
B. **and who made a fence on the first, second, and third sides—**
C. **they do not require [the other party to share in the expense of building the walls].**
D. **R. Yosé says, "If he built a fence on the fourth side, they assign to him [his share in the case of] all [three other fences]."**

In the following dispute, we ask what is subject to dispute between the two named authorities, B–C.

2. A. *It has been stated:*
    B. R. Huna said, "All is proportional to the actual cost of building the

fence [Simon: which will vary according to the materials used by the one who builds the fence]."

C.   Hiyya bar Rab said, "All is proportionate to the cost of a cheap fence made of sticks [since that is all that is absolutely necessary]."

To find the issue, we revert to our Mishnah rule. The opinions therein guide the disputing parties. Each then has to account for what is subject to dispute in the Mishnah paragraph. Then the point is, the Mishnah's dispute is not only rational, but it also rests upon a shared premise, affirmed by all parties. That is the power of D.

D.   *We have learned in the Mishnah:* **He whose [land] surrounds that of his fellow on three sides, and who made a fence on the first, second, and third sides—they do not require [the other party to share in the expense of building the walls].** Lo, if he fences the fourth side too, he must contribute to the cost of the entire fence. *But then note what follows:* **R. Yosé says, "If he built a fence on the fourth side, they assign to him [his share in the case of] all [three other fences]."** *Now there is no problem from the perspective of R. Huna, who has said,* "All is proportional to the actual cost of building the fence [Simon: which will vary according to the materials used by the one who builds the fence]." *Then we can identify what is at issue between the first authority and R. Yosé. Specifically, the initial authority takes the view that we proportion the costs to what they would be if a cheap fence of sticks was built, but not to what the fence-builder actually spent, and R. Yosé maintains that under all circumstances, the division is proportional to actual costs. But from the perspective of Hiyya bar Rab, who has said,* "All is proportionate to the cost of a cheap fence made of sticks [since that is all that is absolutely necessary]," *what can be the difference between the ruling of the initial Tannaite authority and that of R. Yosé? If, after all, he does not pay him even the cost of building a cheap fence, what in the world is he supposed to pay off as his share?*

We now revert to the dialectics, but a different kind. Here we raise a variety of possibilities, not as challenges and responses in a sequence, but as freestanding choices; the same goal is at hand, the opportunity to examine every possibility. But the result is different: not a final solution but four suitable ones, yielding the notion that a single principle governs a variety of cases. That explains why we now have a set of four answers, all of them converging on the same principle:

E.   *If you want, I shall say that what is at issue between them is the fee to be paid for a watchman. The initial authority holds that he pays the cost of a watchman, not the charge of building a cheap fence, and R. Yosé says that he has to pay the cost of building a cheap fence.*

F.   *But if you prefer, I may say that at issue between them is the first, second, and third sides, in which instance the initial Tannaite authority has the other pay only the cost of fencing the fourth side, not the first three, and R. Yosé maintains he has to pay his share of the cost of fencing the first three sides too.*

G.   *And if you prefer, I shall maintain that at issue between them is whether the fence has to be built by the owner of the surrounding fields or the owner of the enclosed field if the latter pays the cost of the whole. The initial Tannaite authority says that the consideration that leads the owner of the enclosed field to have to contribute at all is that he went ahead and built the fourth fence, so he has to pay his share of the cost of the whole; but if the owner of the surrounding fields is the one who went ahead and did it, the other has to pay only the share of the fourth fence. For his part, R. Yosé takes the position that there is no distinction between who took the initiative in building the fourth fence, whether the owner of the enclosed field or the owner of the surrounding field. In either case the former has to pay the latter his share of the whole.*

H.   *There are those who say, in respect to this last statement, that at issue between them is whether the fourth fence has to be built by the owner of the enclosed field or the surrounding fields so that the former has to contribute his share. The initial Tannaite authority holds that even if the owner of the surrounding fields makes the fourth fence, the other has to contribute to the cost, and R. Yosé maintains that if the owner of the enclosed field takes it on himself to build the fourth fence, he has to pay his share of the cost of the whole, because through his action he has shown that he wants the fence, but if the owner of the surrounding fields builds the fourth side, the other pays not a penny [since he can say he never wanted a fence to begin with].*

The premise of E is that the owner of the land on the inside has a choice as to the means of guarding his field; but he of course bears responsibility for the matter. F agrees that he bears responsibility for his side, but adds that he also is responsible for the sides from which he enjoys benefit. And of course G concurs that the owner of the inner field is responsible to protect his own property. H takes the same view. What we have accomplished is, first, to lay a foundation in rationality for the dispute of the Mishnah paragraph, and, further, to demonstrate that all parties to the dispute affirm the responsibility to pay one's share of that from which one benefits. Justice means no free lunch.

5.

THE UNITY OF THE LAW

In what follows, the unity of the law extends from agreements behind disputes to a more fundamental matter: identifying the single principle behind many diverse cases. What do diverse cases have in common? Along these same lines, that same hermeneutics wants us to show how diverse authorities concur on the same principle, dealing with diverse cases; how where there is a dispute, the dispute represents schism vs. consensus, with the weight of argument and evidence favoring consensus; where we have a choice between interpreting an opinion as schismatic and as coherent with established rule, we try to show it is not schismatic; and so on and so forth. All of these commonplace activities pursue a single goal, which is to limit the range of schism and expand the range of consensus, both in political, personal terms of authority, and, more to the point, in the framework of case and principle. If I had to identify a single hermeneutical principle—that is, a defining melody—that governs throughout, it is the quest for harmony, consensus, unity, and above all, the rationality of dispute: reasonable disagreement about the pertinence or relevance of established, universally affirmed principles.

Here is a fine instance of the working of the hermeneutics that tells us to read the texts as a single coherent statement, episodic and unrelated cases as statements of a single principle. The principle is: it is forbidden for someone to derive uncompensated benefit from somebody else's property. That self-evidently valid principle of equity—"thou shalt not steal" writ small—then emerges from a variety of cases; the cases are read as illustrative. The upshot of demonstrating that fact is to prove a much-desired goal. The law of the Torah—here, the written Torah, one of the ten commandments no less!—contains within itself the laws of everyday life. So one thing yields many things; the law is coherent in God's mind, and retains that coherence as it expands to encompass the here and now of the social order. The details as always are picayune, the logic practical, the reasoning concrete and applied; but the stakes prove cosmic in a very exact sense of the word. The problem involves a two-story house, owned by the resident of the lower story. The house has fallen down. The tenant, upstairs, has nowhere to live. The landlord, downstairs, does not rebuild the house. The tenant has the right to rebuild the downstairs part of the house and to live there as long as the landlord does not complete the rebuilding of the house and also refund to the tenant the cost of rebuilding the part that the tenant has reconstructed for himself. Judah rejects this ruling, and, in doing so, invokes a general principle, by no means limited to the case at hand. Then the Bavli will wish to show how this governing principle pertains elsewhere.

MISHNAH-TRACTATE BABA MESIA 10:3 AND TALMUD BABA MESIA 117A–B

A. **A house and an upper story belonging to two people which fell down—**

B. **[if] the resident of the upper story told the householder [of the lower story] to rebuild,**

C. **but he does not want to rebuild,**

D. **lo, the resident of the upper story rebuilds the lower story and lives there,**

> E. until the other party compensates him for what he has spent.
>
> F. R. Judah says, "Also: [if so,] this one is [then] living in his fellow's [housing]. [So in the end] he will have to pay him rent.
>
> G. "But the resident of the upper story builds both the house and the upper room,
>
> H. "and he puts a roof on the upper story,
>
> I. "and he lives in the lower story,
>
> J. "until the other party compensates him for what he has spent."

At issue is a principle, which settles the case at hand. It is whether or not one may gratuitously derive benefit from someone else's property. We shall now show that Judah repeatedly takes that position in a variety of diverse cases:

> I. 1. A. [117B] Said R. Yohanan, "In three passages R. Judah has repeated for us the rule that it is forbidden for someone to derive benefit from somebody else's property. *The first is in the Mishnah passage at hand. The next is in that which we have learned in the Mishnah.*"

The case that is now introduced involves an error in dyeing wool. The premise of the rulings is that dyeing always enhances the value of the wool, whether it is dyed of one color or some other. On that basis, the following is quite clear:

> B. He who gave wool to a dyer to dye it red, and he dyed it black, or to dye it black, and he dyed it red—
>
> C. R. Meir says, "The dyer pays him back the value of his wool."
>
> D. And R. Judah says, "If the increase in value is greater than the outlay for the process of dyeing, the owner pays him back for the outlay for the process of dyeing. And if the outlay for the process of dyeing is greater than the increase in the value of the wool, the owner pays him [the dyer] only the increase in the value of the wool" [M. B.Q. 9:4G–K].
>
> E. *And what is the third? It is as we have learned in the Mishnah:*
>
> F. He who paid part of a debt that he owed and deposited the bond that has been written as evidence covering the remaining sum with a third party, and said to him, "If I have not given you what I still owe the lender between

      now and such-and-such a date, give the creditor his bond of indebtedness," if the time came and he has not paid,

G.   **R. Yosé says, "He should hand it over."**

H.   **And R. Judah says, "He should not hand it over" [M. B.B. 10:5A–E].**

I.   *Why [does it follow that Judah holds that it is forbidden for someone to derive benefit from somebody else's property]? Perhaps when R. Judah takes the position that he does here, it is only because there is blackening of the walls.*

J.   [Freedman: the new house loses its newness because the tenant is living there, so the house owner is sustaining a loss, and that is why the tenant has to pay rent];

K.   as to the case of the dyer who was supposed to dye the wool red but dyed it black, *the reason is that he has violated his instructions, and we have learned in the Mishnah:*

L.   **Whoever changes [the original terms of the agreement]— his hand is on the bottom [M. B.M. 6:2E–F].** [That is to say, the decision must favor the other party, the claim of the one who has changed the original terms being subordinated.]

M.   *And as to the third case,* **the one who has paid part of his debt,** *here we deal with an enticement, and we infer from this case that R. Judah takes the position that in the case of a come-on, there is no transfer of title.*

Yohanan's observation serves the purpose of showing how several unrelated cases of the Mishnah really make the same point: you shall not steal. The voice of the Talmud—that is to say, the dialectics itself—then contributes an objection and its resolution, making Yohanan's statement plausible and compelling, not merely an observation that may or may not be so.

An ideal way of demonstrating the unity of the law is to expose the abstract premise of a concrete rule, and that without regard to the number of discrete cases that establish the same rule. Here is a case in which the theological principle, a stipulation may not be made contrary to what is written in the Torah, is shown to form the premise of a concrete case; then the case once more merely illustrates the principle of the Torah, which delivers its messages in just this way, through exemplary cases. 2.A commences with a common attributive formula, said x . . . said y. . . . This bears the meaning, said x in the name of y (and on his authority). Judah is then the tradent of the opinion or ruling, and Samuel the original source. Such an attributive formula may encompass three or more names and is common in both Talmuds.

Talmud to Makkot 1:1L–N, 1:2, 1:3/I.2

2.   A.   And said R. Judah said Samuel, "He who says to his fellow, '. . . on the stipulation that the advent of the Seventh Year will not abrogate the debts'—the Seventh Year nonetheless abrogates those debts."

      B.   *May one then propose that Samuel takes the view that* that stipulation represents an agreement made contrary to what is written in the Torah, and, as we know, any stipulation contrary to what is written in the Torah is a null stipulation? *But lo, it has been stated:*

      C.   He who says to his fellow, "[I make this sale to you] on the stipulation that you may not lay claim of fraud [by reason of variation from true value] against me"—

      D.   Rab said, "He nonetheless may lay claim of fraud [by reason of variation from true value] against him."

      E.   Samuel said, "He may not lay claim of fraud [by reason of variation from true value] against him."

      F.   *Lo, it has been stated in that connection: said R. Anan, "The matter has been explained to me such that Samuel said, 'He who says to his fellow, "[I make this sale to you] on the stipulation that you may not lay claim of fraud [by reason of variation from true value] against me"—he has no claim of fraud against him. [If he said,] ". . . on the stipulation that in the transaction itself, there is no aspect of fraud," lo, he has a claim of fraud against him.'"*

      G.   Here too, the same distinction pertains. If the stipulation was, "on condition that you do not abrogate the debt to me in the Sabbatical Year," then the Sabbatical Year does not abrogate the debt. But if the language was, "on condition that the Sabbatical Year itself does not abrogate the debt," the Sabbatical Year does abrogate the debt.

What is at stake in this issue is of course not only jurisprudential principles but theological truth, concerning the power of language. In the Torah, language is enchanted; it serves, after all, for the principal medium of the divine self-manifestation: in words, sentences, paragraphs, a book: the Torah. So what one says forms the foundation of effective reality: it makes things happen, not only records what has happened.

But what happens if one makes a statement that ordinarily would prove effective, but the contents of the statement contradict the law of the Torah? Then such a stipulation is null. Why? Because the Torah is what makes language work, and if the Torah is contradicted, then the language is no more effective— changing the world to which it refers, the rules or conditions or order of existence—than it would be if the rules of grammar were violated. Just as, in such a case, the sentence would be gibberish and not convey meaning, so in the case at hand, the sentence is senseless and null.

6.
DIALECTICS AND THE INTELLECTUAL DYNAMICS OF RABBINIC LITERATURE

The main consequence for the rabbinic literature of formation through dialectical arguments more than through any other mode of thought and writing is simply stated. It is the power of that mode of the representation of thought to show us—as no other mode of writing can show—not only the result but the workings of the logical mind. By following dialectical arguments, we ourselves enter into those same thought processes, and our minds then are formed in the model of rigorous and sustained, systematic argument. The reason is simply stated. When we follow a proposal and its refutation, the consequence thereof, and the result of that, we ourselves form partners to the logical tensions and their resolutions; we are given an opening into the discourse that lies before us. As soon as matters turn not upon tradition, to which we may or may not have access, but reason, specifically, challenge and response, proposal and counterproposal ("maybe matters are just the opposite?"), we find an open door before us.

For these are not matters of fact but of reasoned judgment, and the answer, "well, that's my opinion," in its "traditional form," namely, that is what Rabbi X has said so that must be so, finds no hearing. Moving from facts to reasoning, propositions to the process of counterargument, the challenge resting on the mind's own movement, its power of manipulating facts one way rather than some other and of identifying the governing logic of a fact—that process invites the reader's or the listener's participation. The author of a dialectical composite presents a problem with its internal tensions in logic and offers a solution to the problem and a resolution of the logical conflicts.

What is at stake in the capacity of the framer of a composite, or even the author of a composition, to move this way and that, always in a continuous path, but often in a crooked one? The dialectical argument opens the possibility of reaching out from one thing to something else, and the path's wandering is part of the reason. It is not because people have lost sight of their starting point or their goal in the end, but because they want to encompass, in the analytical argument as it gets under way, as broad and comprehensive a range of cases and rules as they can. The movement from point to point in reference to a single point that accurately describes the dialectical argument reaches a goal of abstraction. At the point at which we leave behind the specificities of not only cases but laws, sages carry the argument upward to the law that governs many cases, the premises that undergird many rules, and still higher to the principles that infuse diverse premises; then the principles that generate other, unrelated premises, which, in turn, come to expression in other, still-less-intersecting cases. The meandering course of argument comes to an end when we have shown how things cohere that we did not even imagine were contiguous at all.

The dialectical argument forms the means to an end. The distinctive character of the Talmuds' and other documents' particular kind of dialectical argument is dictated by the purpose for which dialectics is invoked. Specifically, the goal of all argument is to show in discrete detail the ultimate unity of the law. The hermeneutics of dialectics aims at making manifest how to read the laws in such a way as to discern that many things really say one thing. The variations on the theme then take the form of detailed expositions of this and that. Then our task is to move backward from result to the reasoning process that has yielded said result: through regression from stage to stage to identify within the case not only the principles of law that produce that result, but the processes of reasoning that link the principles to the case at hand. And when we accomplish our infinite regression, we move from the workings of literature to its religious character and theological goal: it is to know God in heaven, represented, on earth, by the unity of the law, the integrity of the Torah. Now let us turn to the specific documents that comprise rabbinic literature, starting with the Mishnah and its successor writings.

PART TWO

The Mishnah and
Its Exegesis

V

THE MISHNAH

1.

IDENTIFYING THE DOCUMENT

THE MISHNAH IS A PHILOSOPHICAL LAW CODE, COVERING TOPICS OF BOTH A theoretical and practical character.[1] It was produced at about 200 C.E. under the sponsorship of Judah, Patriarch (*nasi*) or ethnic ruler of the Jews of the Land of

---

[1] For further reading and bibliography on the topic of this chapter, see the following:

Baruch M. Bokser, Joel Gereboff, William Scott Green, Gary G. Porton, and Charles Primus, "Bibliography on the Mishnah," in *Study of Ancient Judaism,* I, pp. 37–54.

Bowker, pp. 46–48: the Mishnah's origin in exegesis; pp. 53–61.

Abraham Goldberg, "The Mishna—a Study Book of Halakha" (origins and development, R. Aqiba and his pupils, the four layers, principles of editing, arrangement, the more important teachers, language, text, reduction to writing, authority, bibliography, manuscripts [by Michael Krupp]), in Safrai, *Literature of the Sages,* pp. 211–62.

Maccoby, pp. 30–35; selected passage, pp. 49–133.

Neusner, "The Modern Study of the Mishnah," in *Study of Ancient Judaism,* I, pp. 3–26

Stemberger-Strack, pp. 119–66: bibliography in general and by tractates; explanation of terms; survey of contents; is the structure of the Mishnah original; origin of the Mishnah; biblical interpretation as the origin of the Mishnah; prehistory of the Mishnah; redaction of the Mishnah; text: manuscripts, editions, translations; the interpretation of the Mishnah.

Israel. It comprises sixty-two tractates, divided by topics[2] among six divisions, as follows:

1. AGRICULTURE (Zera'im): Berakhot (blessings); Peah (the corner of the field); Demai (doubtfully tithed produce); Kilayim (mixed seeds); Shebi'it (the seventh year); Terumot (heave offering or priestly rations); Ma'aserot (tithes) Ma'aser Sheni (second tithe); Hallah (dough offering); Orlah (produce of trees in the first three years after planting, which is prohibited); and Bikkurim (firstfruits).

2. APPOINTED TIMES (Mo'ed): Shabbat (the Sabbath); erubin (the fictive fusion meal or boundary); Pesahim (Passover); Sheqalim (the Temple tax); Yoma (the Day of Atonement); Sukkah (the festival of Tabernacles); Besah (the preparation of food on the festivals and Sabbath); Rosh Hashshanah (the New Year); Taanit (fast days); Megillah (Purim): Mo'ed Qatan (the intermediate days of the festivals of Passover and Tabernacles); Hagigah (the festal offering).

3. WOMEN (Nashim): Yebamot (the levirate widow); Ketubot (the marriage contract); Nedarim (vows); Nazir (the special vow of the Nazirite); Sotah (the wife accused of adultery); Gittin (writs of divorce); Qiddushin (betrothal).

4. DAMAGES or civil law (Neziqin): Baba Qamma, Baba Mesia, Baba Batra (civil law, covering damages and torts, then correct conduct of business, labor, and real estate transactions); Sanhedrin (institutions of government; criminal penalties); Makkot (flogging); Shabuot (oaths); Eduyyot (a collection arranged on other than topical lines); Horayot (rules governing improper conduct of civil authorities);

5. HOLY THINGS (Qodoshim): Zebahim (everyday animal offerings); Menahot (meal offerings); Hullin (animals slaughtered for secular purposes); Bekhorot (firstlings); Arakhin (vows of valuation); Temurah (vows of exchange of a beast for an already consecrated beast); Keritot (penalty of extirpation of premature death); Me'ilah (sacrilege); Tamid (the daily whole offering); Middot (the layout of the Temple building); Qinnim (how to deal with bird offerings designated for a given purpose and then mixed up);

Ephraim E. Urbach, "Mishnah," in *Encyclopaedia Judaica* 12:93–109: the sources of the Mishnah, how the Mishnah was produced and arranged, how the Mishnah was published (orally or in writing), the division of the Mishnah, the text of the Mishnah, editions, commentaries, and translations.

Among this writer's studies, the following are the most important: *Judaism. The Evidence of the Mishnah.* Chicago, 1981: University of Chicago Press. Second edition, augmented: Atlanta, 1987: Scholars Press for Brown Judaic Studies; *The Economics of the Mishnah.* Chicago, 1989: University of Chicago Press, *Rabbinic Political Theory: Religion and Politics in the Mishnah.* Chicago, 1991: University of Chicago Press; and *Judaism as Philosophy. The Method and Message of the Mishnah.* Columbia, 1991: University of South Carolina Press. *A History of the Mishnaic Law of Purities; of Holy Things; of Appointed Times; of Women; and of Damages* (Leiden, 1975–1984: E. J. Brill), in forty-three volumes, provides a systematic translation of the Mishnah and the Tosefta, side by side, showing the relationships of the two documents, and descriptions of the history and system of the Mishnah pertaining to its principal categories.

[2] As noted in Chapter 2, topical considerations govern the arrangement of all tractates and most of their contents.

6. PURITY (Tohorot): Kelim (susceptibility of utensils to uncleanness); Ohalot (transmission of corpse uncleanness in the tent of a corpse); Negaim (the uncleanness described at Lev. 13–14); Parah (the preparation of purification water); Tohorot (problems of doubt in connection with matters of cleanness); Miqvaot (immersion pools); Niddah (menstrual uncleanness); Makhsirin (rendering susceptible to uncleanness produce that is dry and so not susceptible); Zabim (the uncleanness covered at Lev. 15); Tebul-Yom (the uncleanness of one who has immersed on that self-same day and awaits sunset for completion of the purification rites); Yadayim (the uncleanness of hands); Uqsin (the uncleanness transmitted through what is connected to unclean produce).

In volume, the sixth division covers approximately a quarter of the entire document. Topics of interest to the priesthood and the Temple, such as priestly fees, conduct of the cult on holy days, conduct of the cult on ordinary days, management and upkeep of the Temple, and the rules of cultic cleanness, predominate in the first, second, fifth, and sixth divisions. Rules governing the social order form the bulk of the third and fourth. Of these tractates, only Eduyyot is organized along other than topical lines, rather collecting sayings on diverse subjects attributed to particular authorities. The Mishnah as printed today always includes Abot (sayings of the sages), but that document reached closure about a generation later than the Mishnah. While it serves as its initial apologetic, it does not conform to the formal, rhetorical, or logical traits characteristic of the Mishnah overall.

The stress of the Mishnah throughout on the priestly caste and the Temple cult point to the document's principal concern, which centered upon sanctification, understood as the correct arrangement of all things, each in its proper category, each called by its rightful name, just as at the creation as portrayed in the Priestly document, and just as with the cult itself as set forth in Leviticus. Further, the thousands of rules and cases (with sages' disputes thereon) that comprise the document upon close reading turn out to express in concrete language abstract principles of hierarchical classification. These define the document's method and mark it as a work of a philosophical character. Not only so, but a variety of specific, recurrent concerns, for example, the relationship of being to becoming, actual to potential, the principles of economics, the politics, correspond point by point to comparable ones in Graeco-Roman philosophy, particularly Aristotle's tradition. This stress on proper order and right rule and the formulation of a philosophy, politics, and economics, within the principles of natural history set forth by Aristotle, explain why the Mishnah makes a statement to be classified as philosophy, concerning the order of the natural world in its correspondence with the supernatural world.

The system of philosophy expressed through concrete and detailed law presented by the Mishnah consists of a coherent logic and topic, a cogent worldview and comprehensive way of living. It is a worldview which speaks of transcendent things, a way of life in response to the supernatural meaning of what is done, a heightened and deepened perception of the sanctification of Israel in deed and in deliberation. Sanctification thus means two things: first, distinguishing Israel in all its dimensions from the world in all its ways; second, establishing the stability, order, regularity, predictability, and reliability of Israel in the world of nature and supernature, in particular at moments and in contexts of danger. Danger means instability, disorder, irregularity, uncertainty, and betrayal. Each topic of the system as a whole takes up a critical and indispensable moment or context of social being. Through what is said in regard to each of the Mishnah's principal topics, what the system expressed through normative rules as a whole is fully stated. Yet if the parts severally and jointly give the message of the whole, the whole cannot exist without all the parts, so well joined and carefully crafted are they all. The details become clear in our survey of the document's topical program.

2.
TRANSLATIONS INTO ENGLISH

All translations of the Talmud of Babylonia include translations of the Mishnah tractates to which that Talmud provides a commentary. In addition, two systematic, complete translations of the Mishnah into English are H. Danby, *The Mishnah* (Oxford, 1933, Oxford University Press), and this writer's *The Mishnah. A New Translation* (New Haven, 1987: Yale University Press). The Hebrew text most commonly consulted is H. Albeck, *Shisha Sidré Mishnah* (Tel Aviv and Jerusalem, 1954–58), in six volumes. The definitive study of the text of the Mishnah is J. N. Epstein, *Introduction to the Text of the Mishnah* (Jerusalem, 1948, 1964: Magnes Press of the Hebrew University), in Hebrew.

3.
RHETORIC

The rhetorical characteristics of the Mishnah are set forth in Chapter 2, sections 3 and 4.

4.
LOGIC OF COHERENT DISCOURSE

The Mishnah's sole logic of coherent discourse is philosophical, indeed, most commonly syllogistic. It is a logic that rests on the coherence yielded by the classification of things by their intrinsic traits and the formulation of the rule governing things of a given class; one classification is then compared and contrasted to others of a like character, with the object of setting forth the hierarchy of the classifications. This method of scientific inquiry is called *Listenwissenschaft,* that is, natural history: classification of things in accord with their intrinsic taxonomic traits, and (concomitantly) the hierarchization of the classes of things, that is, species of the same genus.

How this logic of coherent discourse forms quantities of facts into coherent propositions is illustrated by Mishnah tractate Sanhedrin 2:2–3, where the authorship wishes to say that Israel has two heads, one of state, the other of cult, the king and the high priest, respectively, and that these two offices are nearly wholly congruent with one another, with a few differences based on the particular traits of each. Broadly speaking, therefore, our exercise is one of setting forth the genus and the species. The genus is head of holy Israel. The species are king and high priest. Here are the traits in common and those not shared, and the exercise is fully exposed for what it is, an inquiry into the rules that govern, the points of regularity and order, in this minor matter, of political structure. My outline, imposed in boldface type, makes the point important in this setting.

MISHNAH TRACTATE SANHEDRIN CHAPTER TWO

1. **The rules of the high priest: subject to the law, marital rites, conduct in bereavement**

Mishnah Tractate Sanhedrin 2:1

A. A high priest judges, and [others] judge him;

B. gives testimony, and [others] give testimony about him;

C. performs the rite of removing the shoe (Deut. 25:7–9) and [others] perform the rite of removing the shoe with his wife.

D. [Others] enter levirate marriage with his wife, but he does not enter into levirate marriage,

E. because he is prohibited to marry a widow.

F. [If] he suffers a death [in his family], he does not follow the bier.

G. "But when [the bearers of the bier] are not visible, he is visible; when they are visible, he is not.

H. "And he goes with them to the city gate," the words of R. Meir.

I. R. Judah says, "He never leaves the sanctuary,

J. "since it says, 'Nor shall he go out of the sanctuary' (Lev. 21:12)."

K. And when he gives comfort to others

L. the accepted practice is for all the people to pass one after another, and the appointed [prefect of the priests] stands between him and the people.

M. And when he receives consolation from others,

N.   all the people say to him, "Let us be your atonement."

O.   And he says to them, "May you be blessed by Heaven."

P.   And when they provide him with the funeral meal,

Q.   all the people sit on the ground, while he sits on a stool.

2.   **The rules of the king: not subject to the law, marital rites, conduct in bereavement**

Mishnah Tractate Sanhedrin 2:2

A.   The king does not judge, and [others] do not judge him;

B.   does not give testimony, and [others] do not give testimony about him;

C.   does not perform the rite of removing the shoe, and others do not perform the rite of removing the shoe with his wife;

D.   does not enter into levirate marriage, nor [do his brothers] enter levirate marriage with his wife.

E.   R. Judah says, "If he wanted to perform the rite of removing the shoe or to enter into levirate marriage, his memory is a blessing."

F.   They said to him, "They pay no attention to him [if he expressed the wish to do so.]"

G.   [Others] do not marry his widow.

H.   R. Judah says, "A king may marry the widow of a king.

I.   "For so we find in the case of David, that he married the widow of Saul,

J.   "For it is said, 'And I gave you your master's house and your master's wives into your embrace' (2 Sam. 12:8)."

Mishnah Tractate Sanhedrin 2:3

A.   [If] [the king] suffers a death in his family, he does not leave the gate of his palace.

B.   R. Judah says, "If he wants to go out after the bier, he goes out,

C.   "for thus we find in the case of David, that he went out after the bier of Abner,

D.   "since it is said, 'And King David followed the bier' (2 Sam. 3:31)."

E.   They said to him, "This action was only to appease the people."

F.   And when they provide him with the funeral meal, all the people sit on the ground, while he sits on the couch.

3.   **Special rules pertinent to the king because of his calling**

Mishnah Tractate Sanhedrin 2:4

A.   [The king] calls out [the army to wage] a war fought by choice on the instructions of a court of seventy-one.

B.   He [may exercise the right to] open a road for himself, and [others] may not stop him.

C.   The royal road has no required measure.

D.   All the people plunder and lay before him [what they have seized], and he takes the first portion.

E.   "He should not multiply wives to himself" (Deut. 17:17)—only eighteen.

F.   R. Judah says, "He may have as many as he wants, so long as they do not entice him [to abandon the Lord (Deut. 7:4)]."

G.   R. Simeon says, "Even if there is only one who entices him [to abandon the Lord]—lo, this one should not marry her."

H.   If so, why is it said, "He should not multiply wives to himself"?

I.   Even though they should be like Abigail [(1 Sam. 25:3)].

J.   "He should not multiply horses to himself" (Deut. 17:16)—only enough for his chariot.

K.   "Neither shall he greatly multiply to himself silver and gold" (Deut. 17:16)—only enough to pay his army.

L.   "And he writes out a scroll of the Torah for himself" (Deut. 17:17)

M.   When he goes to war, he takes it out with him; when he comes back, he brings it back with him; when he is in session in court, it is with him; when he is reclining, it is before him,

N.   as it is said, "And it shall be with him, and he shall read in it all the days of his life" (Deut. 17:19).

Mishnah Tractate Sanhedrin 2:5

A.   [Others may] not ride on his horse, sit on his throne, handle his scepter.

B.   And [others may] not watch him while he is getting a haircut, or while he is nude, or in the bathhouse,

C.   since it is said, "You shall surely set him as king over you" (Deut. 17:15)—that reverence for him will be upon you.

The philosophical cast of mind is amply revealed in this well-formed and highly formalized essay, which in concrete terms effects a taxonomy through the matching of data of an identical class, a study of the genus, national leader, and its two species, (1) king, (2) high priest: how are they alike, how are they not alike, and what accounts for the differences. The premise is that national leaders are alike and follow the same rule, except where they differ and follow the opposite rule from one another. But that premise also is subject to the proof effected by the survey of the data consisting of concrete rules, those systemically inert facts that here come to life for the purpose of establishing a proposition. By itself, the fact that, e.g., others may not ride on his horse bears the burden of systemic proposition. In the context of an argument constructed for nomothetic, taxonomic purposes, the same fact is active and weighty. The logic of coherence undertakes the search for points in common and therefore also points of contrast. We seek connection between fact and fact, sentence and sentence in the subtle and balanced rhetoric of the Mishnah, by comparing and contrasting two things that are like and not alike.

At the logical level, too, the Mishnah falls into the category of familiar philosophical thought. Once we seek regularities, we propose rules. What is like another things falls under its rule, and what is not like the other falls under the opposite rule. Accordingly, as to the species of the genus, so far as they are alike, they share the same rule. So far as they are not alike, each follows a rule contrary to that governing the other. So the work of analysis is what produces connection, and therefore the drawing of conclusions derives from comparison and contrast: the *and,* the *equal.* The proposition, then, that forms the conclusion concerns the essential likeness of the two offices, except where they are different, but the subterranean premise is that we can explain both likeness and difference by appeal to a principle of fundamental order and unity. The high priest and king fall into a single genus, but speciation, based on traits particular to the king, then distinguishes the one from the other.

5.

TOPICAL PROGRAM

To understand the complete system set forth by the Mishnah, we review the six divisions as they were finally spelled out.

THE DIVISION OF AGRICULTURE   treats two topics: first, producing crops in accord with the scriptural rules on the subject; second, paying the required offerings and tithes to the priests, Levites, and poor. The principal point of the division is that the Land is holy, because God has a claim both on it and upon what it produces. God's claim must be honored by setting aside a portion of the produce for those for whom God has designated it. God's ownership must be acknowledged by observing the rules God has laid down for the use of the Land. In the temporal context in which the Mishnah was produced, some generations after the disastrous defeat by the Romans of Bar Kokhba and the permanent closure of Jerusalem to Jews' access, the stress of the division brought assurance that those aspects of the sanctification of Israel—the Land of Israel, Israel itself and its social order, the holy cycle of time—that survived also remained holy and subject to the rules of heaven.

THE DIVISION OF APPOINTED TIMES   carried forward the same emphasis upon sanctification, now of the high points of the lunar-solar calendar of Israel.

The second division forms a system in which the advent of a holy day, like the Sabbath of creation, sanctifies the life of the Israelite village through imposing on the village rules on the model of those of the Temple. The purpose of the system, therefore, is to bring into alignment the moment of sanctification of the village and the life of the home with the moment of sanctification of the Temple on those same occasions of appointed times. The underlying and generative logic of the system comes to expression in a concrete way here. We recall the rule of like and opposite, comparison and contrast. What is not like something follows the rule opposite to that pertaining to that something. Here, therefore, since the village is the mirror image of the Temple, the upshot is dictated by the analogical-contrastive logic of the system as a whole. If—speaking in an eternal present tense—things are done in one way in the Temple, they will be done in the opposite way in the village. Together the village and the Temple on the occasion of the holy day therefore form a single continuum, a completed creation, thus awaiting sanctification. The village is made like the Temple in that on appointed times one may not freely cross the lines distinguishing the village from the rest of the world, just as one may not freely cross the lines distinguishing the Temple from the world. But the village is a mirror image of the Temple. The boundary lines prevent free entry into the Temple, so they restrict free egress from the village. On the holy day what one may do in the Temple is precisely what one may not do in the village.

So the advent of the holy day affects the village by brining it into sacred symmetry in such wise as to effect a system of opposites; each is holy, in a way precisely the opposite of the other. Because of the underlying conception of perfection attained through the union of opposites, the village is not represented as conforming to the model of the cult, but of constituting its antithesis. The world thus regains perfection when on the holy day heaven and earth are united, the whole completed and done: the heaven, the earth, and all their hosts. This moment of perfection renders the events of ordinary time, of "history," essentially irrelevant. For what really matters in time is that moment in which sacred time intervenes and effects the perfection formed of the union of heaven and earth, of Temple, in the model of the former, and Israel, its complement. It is not a return to a perfect time but a recovery of perfect being, a fulfillment of creation, which explains the essentially ahistorical character of the Mishnah's Division of Appointed Times. Sanctification constitutes an ontological category and is effected by the creator.

This explains why the division in its rich detail is composed of two quite distinct sets of materials. First, it addresses what one does in the sacred space of the Temple on the occasion of sacred time, as distinct from what one does in that same sacred space on ordinary, undifferentiated days, which is a subject worked out in Holy Things. Second, the division defines how for the occasion of the holy day one creates a corresponding space in one's own circumstance, and what one does, within that space, during sacred time. The division as a whole holds together through a shared, generative metaphor. It is, as I said, the comparison, in the context of sacred time, of the spatial life of the Temple to the spatial life of the village, with activities and restrictions to be specified for each, upon the common occasion of the Sabbath or festival. The Mishnah's purpose therefore is to correlate the sanctity of the Temple, as defined by the holy day, with the restrictions of space and of action which make the life of the village different and holy, as defined by the holy day.

THE DIVISION OF WOMEN   defines women in the social economy of Israel's supernatural and natural reality. Women acquire definition wholly in relationship to men, who impart form to the Israelite social economy. The status of women is effected through both supernatural and natural, this-worldly action. Women formed a critical systemic component, because the proper regulation of women—subject to the father, then the husband—was deemed a central concern of Heaven, so that a betrothal would be subject to heaven's supervision (Qiddushin, sanctification, being the pertinent tractate); documents, such as the marriage contract or the writ of divorce, drawn up on earth, stand also for heaven's concern with the sanctity of women in their marital relationship; so too, Heaven may through levirate marriage dictate whom a woman marries. What man and woman do on earth accordingly provokes a response in heaven, and the correspondences are perfect. So women are defined and secured both in heaven and here on earth, and that position is always and invariably relative to men.

The principal interest for the Mishnah is interstitial, just as, in general, sanctification comes into play at interstitial relationships, those that require decisive classification. Here it is the point at which a woman becomes, and ceases to be, holy to a particular man, that is, enters and leaves the marital union. These transfers of women are the dangerous and disorderly points in the relationship of woman to man, therefore, the Mishnah states, to society as well. The division's systemic statement stresses the preservation or order in transactions involving women and (other) property. Within this orderly world of documentary and procedural concerns a place is made for the disorderly conception of the marriage not formed by human volition but decreed in heaven, the levirate connection. Mishnah tractate Yebamot states that supernature sanctifies a woman to a man (under the conditions of the levirate connection). What it says by indirection is that man sanctifies too: man, like God, can sanctify that relationship between a man and a woman, and can also effect the cessation of the sanctity of that same relationship.

Five of the seven tractates of the Division of Women are devoted to the formation and dissolution of the marital bond. Of them, three treat what is done by man here on earth, that is, formation of a marital bond through betrothal and marriage contract and dissolution through divorce and its consequences. The division and its system therefore delineate the natural and supernatural character of the woman's role in the social economy framed by man: the beginning, end, and middle of the relationship. The whole constitutes a significant part of the Mishnah's encompassing system of sanctification, for the reason that heaven confirms what men do on earth. A correctly prepared writ of divorce on earth changes the status of the woman to whom it is given, so that in heaven she is available for sanctification to some other man, while without that same writ, in heaven's view, should she go to some other man, she would be liable to be put to death. The earthly deed and the heavenly perspective correlate. That is indeed very much part of the larger system, which says the same thing over and over again.

THE DIVISION OF DAMAGES   comprises two subsystems, which fit together in a logical way. One part presents rules for the normal conduct of civil society. These cover commerce, trade, real estate, and other matters of everyday intercourse, as well as mishaps, such as damages by chattels and persons, fraud, overcharge, interest, and the like, in that same context of everyday social life. The other part describes the institutions governing the normal conduct of civil society, that is, courts of administration, and the penalties at the disposal of the government for the enforcement of the law. The two subjects form a single tight and systematic dissertation on the nature of Israelite society and its economic, social, and political relationships, as the Mishnah envisages them. The main point of the first of the two parts of the division is that the task of society is to maintain perfect stasis, to preserve the prevailing situation, and to secure the stability of all relationships. To this end, in the interchanges of buying and selling, giving and taking, borrowing and lending, it is important that there be an essential equality of interchange. No party in the end should have more than what he had at the outset, and none should be the victim of a sizable shift in fortune and circumstance. All parties' rights to, and in, this stable and unchanging economy of society are to be preserved. When the condition of a person is violated, so far as possible the law will secure the restoration of the antecedent status.

The goal of the system of civil law is the recovery of the prevailing order and balance, and preservation of the established wholeness of the social economy This idea is powerfully expressed in the organization of the three tractates that comprise the civil law, which treat first abnormal and then normal transactions. The framers deal with damages done by chattels and by human beings, thefts and other sorts of malfeasance against the property of others. The civil law in both aspects pays closest attention to how the property and person of the injured party so far as possible are restored to their prior condition, that is, a state of normality. So attention to torts focuses upon penalties paid by the malefactor to the victim, rather than upon penalties inflicted by the court on the malefactor for what he has done. When speaking of damages, the Mishnah thus takes as its principal concern the restoration of the fortune of victims of assault or robbery. Then the framers take up the complementary and corresponding set of topics, the regulation of normal transactions. When we rapidly survey the kinds of transactions of special interest, we see from the topics selected for discussion what we have already uncovered in the deepest structure of organization and articulation of the basic theme.

The other half of this same unit of three tractates presents laws governing normal and routine transactions, many of them of the same sort of those dealt with in the first half. At issue, for example, are deposits of goods or possessions that one person leaves in safekeeping with another. Called bailments, cases of such transactions occur in both wings of the triple tractate, first, bailments subjected to misappropriation, or accusation thereof, by the bailiff, then, bailments transacted under normal circumstances. Under the rubric of routine transactions are those of workers and householders, that is, the purchase and sale of labor; rentals and bailments; real estate transactions; and inheritances and estates. Of the lot, the one involving real estate transactions is the most fully articulated and covers the widest range of problems and topics. The three tractates of the civil law all together thus provide a complete account of the orderly governance of balanced transactions and unchanging civil relationships within Israelite society under ordinary conditions.

The character and interests of the Division of Damages present probative evidence of the larger program of the philosophers of the Mishnah. Their intention is to create nothing less than a full-scale Israelite government, subject to the administration of sages. This government is fully supplied with a constitution and bylaws. It makes provision for a court system and procedures, as well as a full set of laws governing civil society and criminal justice. This government, moreover, mediates between its own community and the outside ("pagan") world. Through its system of laws it expresses its judgment of the others and at the same time defines, protects, and defends its own society and social frontiers. It even makes provision for procedures of remission, to expiate its own errors. The (then nonexistent) Israelite government imagined by the second-century philosophers centers upon the (then nonexistent) Temple and the (then forbidden) city, Jerusalem. For the Temple is one principal focus. There the highest court is in session; there the high priest reigns.

The penalties for law infringement are of three kinds, one of which involves sacrifice in the Temple. (The others are compensation, physical punishment, and death.) The basic conception of punishment, moreover, is that unintentional infringement of the rules of society, whether "religious" or otherwise, is not penalized but rather expiated through an offering in the Temple. If a member of the people of Israel intentionally infringes against the law, to be sure, that one must be removed from society and is put to death. And if there is a claim of one member of the people against another, that must be righted, so that the prior, prevailing status may be restored. So offerings in the Temple are given up to appease heaven and restore a whole bond between heaven and Israel, specifically on those occasions on which without malice or ill will an Israelite has disturbed the relationship. Israelite civil society without a Temple is not stable or normal, and not to be imagined. And the Mishnah is above all an act of imagination in defiance of reality.

The plan for the government involves a clear-cut philosophy of society, a philosophy that defines the purpose of the government and ensures that its task is not merely to perpetuate its own power. What the Israelite government, within the Mishnaic fantasy, is supposed to do is to preserve a perfect, steady-state society. That state of perfection which, within the same fantasy, the society to begin with everywhere attains and expresses forms the goal of the system throughout: no change anywhere from a perfect balance, proportion, and arrangement of the social order, its goods and services, responsibilities and benefits. This is in at least five aspects:

First of all, one of the ongoing principles of the law, expressed in one tractate after another, is that people are to follow and maintain the prevailing practice of their locale.

Second, the purpose of civil penalties, as we have noted, is to restore the injured party to his prior condition, so far as this is possible, rather than merely to penalize the aggressor.

Third, there is the conception of true value, meaning that a given object has an intrinsic worth, which, in the course of a transaction, must be paid. In this way the seller does not leave the transaction any richer than when he entered it, or the buyer any poorer (parallel to penalties for damages).

Fourth, there can be no usury, a biblical prohibition adopted and vastly enriched in the Mishnaic thought, for money ("coins") is what it is. Any pretense that it has become more than what it was violates, in its way, the conception of true value.

Fifth, when real estate is divided, it must be done with full attention to the rights of all concerned, so that once more, one party does not gain at the expense of the other.

In these and many other aspects the law expresses its obsession with the perfect stasis of Israelite society. Its paramount purpose is in preserving and ensuring that that perfection of the division of this world is kept inviolate or restored to its true status when violated.

THE DIVISION OF HOLY THINGS   presents a system of sacrifice and sanctuary. The division centers upon the everyday and rules always applicable to the cult: the daily whole offering, the sin offering and guilt offering which one may bring any time under ordinary circumstances; the right sequence of diverse offerings; the way in which the rites of the whole, sin, and guilt offerings are carried out; what sorts of animals are acceptable; the accompanying cereal offerings; the support and provision of animals for the cult and of meat for the priesthood; the support and material maintenance of the cult and its building. We have a system before us: the system of the cult of the Jerusalem Temple, seen as an ordinary and everyday affair, a continuing and routine operation. That is why special rules for the cult, both in respect to the altar and in regard to the maintenance of the buildings, personnel, and even the whole city, will be elsewhere—in Appointed Times and Agriculture. But from the perspective of Holy Things, those divisions intersect by supplying special rules and raising extraordinary (Agriculture: land-bound; Appointed Times: time-bound) considerations for that theme which Holy Things claims to set forth in its most general and unexceptional way: the cult as something permanent and everyday.

THE DIVISION OF PURITIES   presents a very simple system of three principal parts: sources of uncleanness, objects and substances susceptible to uncleanness, and modes of purification from uncleanness. So it tells the story of what makes a given sort of object unclean and what makes it clean. Viewed as a whole, the Division of Purities treats the interplay of persons, food, and liquids. Dry inanimate objects or food are not susceptible to uncleanness. What is wet is susceptible. So liquids activate the system. What is unclean, moreover, emerges from uncleanness through the operation of liquids, specifically, through immersion in fit water of requisite volume and in natural condition. Liquids thus deactivate the system. Thus, water in its natural condition is what concludes the process by removing uncleanness. Water in its unnatural condition, that is, deliberately affected by human agency, is what imparts susceptibility to uncleanness to begin with. The uncleanness of persons, furthermore, is signified by body liquids or flux in the case of the menstruating woman and the *zab* (the person suffering from the form of uncleanness described at Lev. 15:1ff.). Corpse uncleanness is conceived to be a kind of effluent, a viscous gas, which flows like liquid. Utensils for their part receive uncleanness when they form receptacles able to contain liquid.

In sum, we have a system in which the invisible flow of fluidlike substances or powers serves to put food, drink, and receptacles into the status of uncleanness and to remove those things from that status. Whether or not we call the system "metaphysical," it certainly has no material base but is conditioned upon highly abstract notions. Thus in material terms, the effect of liquid is upon food, drink, utensils, and man. The consequence has to do with who may eat and drink what food and liquid, and what food and drink may be consumed in which pots and pans. These loci are specified by tractates on utensils and on food and drink.

The human being is ambivalent. Persons fall in the middle, between sources and loci of uncleanness, because they are both. They serve as sources of uncleanness. They also become unclean. The *zab*, suffering the uncleanness described in Leviticus 15, the menstruating woman, the woman after childbirth, and the person afflicted with the skin ailment described in Leviticus Chapters 13 and 14—all are sources of uncleanness. But being unclean, they fall within the system's loci, its program of consequences. So they make other things unclean and are subject to penalties because they are unclean. Unambiguous sources of uncleanness never constitute loci affected by uncleanness. They always are unclean and never can become clean: the corpse, the dead creeping thing, and things like them. Inanimate sources of uncleanness and inanimate objects convey uncleanness *ex opere operato;* their status of being unclean never changes; they present no ambiguity. Systemically unique, man and liquids have the capacity to inaugurate the processes of uncleanness (as sources) and also are subject to those same processes (as objects of uncleanness).

OMITTED TOPICS: When we listen to the silences of the system of the Mishnah, as much as to its points of stress, we hear a single message. It is a message of a system that answered a single encompassing question, and the question formed a stunning counterpart to that of the sixth century B.C.E. The Pentateuchal system addressed one reading of the events of the sixth century, highlighted by the destruction of the Jerusalem Temple in 586 B.C.E. At stake was how Israel as defined by that system related to its land, represented by its Temple, and the message may be simply stated: what appears to be the given is in fact a gift, subject to stipulations. The precipitating event for the Mishnaic system was the destruction of the Jerusalem Temple in A.D. 70; the question turned obsession with the defeat of Bar Kokhba and the closure of Jerusalem to Jews. The urgent issue taken up by the Mishnah was, specifically, what, in the aftermath of the destruction of the holy place and holy cult, remained of the sanctity of the holy caste, the priesthood, the holy land, and, above all, the holy people and its holy way of life? The answer was that sanctity persists, indelibly, in Israel, the people, in its way of life, in its land, in its priesthood, in its food, in its mode of sustaining life, in its manner of procreating and so sustaining the nation.

The Mishnah's system therefore focused upon the holiness of the life of Israel, the people, a holiness that had formerly centered on the Temple. The logically consequent question was, what is the meaning of sanctity, and how shall Israel attain, or give evidence of, sanctification. The answer to the question derived from the original creation, the end of the Temple directing attention to the beginning of the natural world that the Temple had embodied. For the meaning of sanctity the framers therefore turned to that first act of sanctification, the one in creation. It came about when, all things in array, in place, each with its proper names, God blessed and sanctified the seventh day on the eve of the first Sabbath. Creation was made ready for the blessing and the sanctification when all things were very good, that is to say, in their rightful order, called by their rightful name. An orderly nature was a sanctified and blessed nature, so dictated Scripture in the name of the supernatural. So to receive the blessing and to be made holy, all things in nature and society were to be set in right array. Given the condition of Israel, the people, in its land, in the aftermath of the catastrophic war against Rome led by Bar Kokhba in 132–135, putting things in order was no easy task. But that is why, after all, the question pressed, the answer proving inexorable and obvious. The condition of society corresponded to the critical question that obsessed the system builders.

6.

A SAMPLE PASSAGE

The reference to omitted divisions requires attention to how the Mishnah's system encompasses important subjects which are not defined as principal components of the document's entire structure. For our sample passage, therefore, we ask how the Mishnah treats the matter of history, and that passage further permits us to consider the role of history in rabbinic literature. Since Rabbinic literature contains not a single sustained history book, comparable for example to Joshua, Judges, Samuel, and Kings, on the one side, or to Josephus's narratives, on the other, our sample will provide a picture of how the Mishnah treats questions that writings of other Judaisms, including Scripture, take up in narrative, teleological form. Rabbinic literature starting with the Mishnah addresses historical questions in its own way. (How Midrash compilations treat history will be examined in context.) Since every Judaism takes up the past ("history") and uses the formulation of the past in the presentation of its systemic message, the inquiry into rabbinic literature requires us to find out how writers write the counterpart to history.

The (superficially) ahistorical system set forth by the framers of the Mishnah identifies as a sample passage of the document examples of how the framers of the system deal with history and the laws of history. Because of the critical importance of the Mishnah in rabbinic literature, we give a generous sample of its treatment of a single topic across the surface of the document, three of the six divisions, specifically: paragraphs of Rosh Hashshanah Chapter Four, Taanit Chapter Four, and, of primary interest, Zebahim Chapter Fourteen. To understand what is at issue, we must recall that the framers of the Mishnah present us with a kind of historical thinking quite different from the one that they, along with all Israel, had inherited in Scripture. The legacy of prophecy, apocalypse, and mythic history handed on by the writers of the books of the Hebrew Scriptures of ancient Israel, for instance, Jeremiah, Daniel, and Genesis, Exodus, and Deuteronomy, respectively, exhibits a single and quite familiar conception of history. First of all, history refers to events seen whole. Events bear meaning, form a pattern, and, therefore, deliver God's message and judgment.

The upshot is that every event, each one seen on its own, must be interpreted in its own terms, not as part of a pattern but as significant in itself. What happens is singular, therefore an event to be noted, and points toward lessons to be drawn for where things are heading and why. If things do not happen at random, they also do not form indifferent patterns of merely secular, social facts. What happens is important because of the meaning contained therein. That meaning is to be discovered and revealed through the narrative of what has happened. So for all Judaisms until the Mishnah, the writing of history serves as a form or medium of prophecy. Just as prophecy takes up the interpretation of historical events, so historians retell these events in the frame of prophetic theses. And out of the two—historiography as a mode of mythic reflection, prophecy as a means of mythic construction—emerges a picture of future history, that is, what is going to happen. That picture, framed in terms of visions and supernatural symbols, in the end focuses, as much as do prophecy and history writing, upon the here and now.

History consists of a sequence of one-time events, each of them singular, all of them meaningful. These events move from a beginning somewhere to an end at a foreordained goal. History moves toward eschatology, the end of history. The teleology of Israel's life finds its definition in eschatological fulfillment. Eschatology therefore constitutes not a choice *within* teleology, but the definition *of* teleology. That is to say, a theory of the goal and purpose of things (teleology) is shaped solely by appeal to the account of the end of times (eschatology). History done in this way then sits enthroned as the queen of theological science. Events do not conform to patterns. They form patterns. What happens matters because events bear meaning, constitute history. Now, as is clear, such a conception of mythic and apocalyptic history comes to realization in the writing of history in the prophetic pattern or in the apocalyptic framework, both of them mythic modes of organizing events. We have every right to expect such a view of matters to lead people to write books of a certain sort, rather than of some other. In the case of Judaism, obviously, we should expect people to write history books that teach lessons or apocalyptic books that through pregnant imagery predict the future and record the direction and end of time. And in antiquity that kind of writing proves commonplace among all kinds of groups and characteristic of all sorts of Judaisms but one. And that is the Judaism of the Mishnah. Here we have a Judaism that does not appeal to history as a sequence of one-time events, each of which bears meaning on its own. What the Mishnah has to say about history is quite different, and, consequently, the Mishnah does not conform in any way to the scriptural pattern of representing, and sorting out, events: history, myth, apocalypse.

The first difference appears right at the surface. The Mishnah contains no sustained narrative whatsoever, very few tales, and no large-scale conception of history. It organizes its system in nonhistorical and socially unspecific terms. That is to say, there is no effort at setting into a historical context, e.g., a particular time, a place, a circumstance defined by important events, any of the laws of the Mishnah. The Mishnah's system is set forth out of all historical framework, as we observed in Chapter 1. That is a medium for the presentation of a system that has no precedent in prior systems of Judaism or in prior kinds of Judaic literature. The law codes of Exodus and Deuteronomy, for example, are set forth in a narrative framework, and the priestly code of Leviticus, for its part, appeals to God's revelation to Moses and Aaron, at specific times and places. In the Mishnah we have neither narrative nor setting for the representation of law.

Instead of narrative which, as in Exodus, spills over into case law, the Mishnah gives description of how things are done in general and universally, that is, descriptive laws. Instead of reflection on the meaning and end of history, it constructs a world in which history plays little part. Instead of narratives full of didactic meaning, the Mishnah's authorship, as we shall see in a moment, provides lists of events so as to expose the traits that they share and thus the rules to which they conform. The definitive components of a historical-eschatological system of Judaism—description of events as one-time happenings, analysis of the meaning and end of events, and interpretation of singular happenings (not in patterns)—none of these commonplace constituents of all other systems of Judaism (including nascent

Christianity) of ancient times finds a place in the Mishnah's system of Judaism. So the Mishnah finds no precedent in prior Israelite writings for its mode of dealing with things that happen. The Mishnah's way of identifying happenings as consequential and describing them, its way of analyzing those events it chooses as bearing meaning, its interpretation of the future to which significant events point—all those in context were unique. In form the Mishnah represents its system outside of all historical framework.

Yet to say that the Mishnah's system is ahistorical could not be more wrong. The Mishnah presents a different kind of history. Its authorship revises the inherited conception of history and reshapes that conception to fit into its own system. When we consider the power of the biblical myth, the force of its eschatological and messianic interpretation of history, the effect of apocalypse, we must find astonishing the capacity of the Mishnah's framers to think in a different way about the same things. As teleology, the system of the Mishnah was constructed outside the eschatological mode of thought in the setting of the biblical world of ancient Israel. This formation of a systemic teleology without resort to eschatology, in a world in which statements of goals and ends of things otherwise ordinarily took the form of the story of the end of the world as people knew it and the beginning of a messianic, perfect age, thus proves amazing. By "history," as the opening discussion makes clear, I mean not merely events, but how events are so organized and narrated as to teach lessons, reveal patterns, tell us what we must do and why, what will happen to us tomorrow. In that context, some events contain richer lessons than others; the destruction of the Temple of Jerusalem teaches more than a crop failure, being kidnapped into slavery more than stubbing one's toe. Furthermore, lessons taught by events—"history" in the didactic sense—follow a progression from trivial and private to consequential and public.

The framers of the Mishnah explicitly refer to very few events, treating those they do mention within a focus quite separate from what happened—the unfolding of the events themselves. They rarely create or use narratives. More probative still, historical events do not supply organizing categories or taxonomic classifications. We find no tractate devoted to the destruction of the Temple, no complete chapter detailing the events of Bar Kokhba, nor even a sustained celebration of the events of the sages' own historical life. When things that have happened are mentioned, it is neither in order to narrate, nor to interpret and draw lessons from, the event. It is either to illustrate a point of law or to pose problem of the law—always *en passant,* never in a pointed way. So when sages refer to what has happened, this is casual and tangential to the main thrust of discourse. Famous events of enduring meaning, such as the return to Zion from Babylonia in the time of Ezra and Nehemiah, gain entry into the Mishnah's discourse only because of the genealogical divisions of Israelite society into castes among the immigrants (M. Qiddushin 4:1). Where the Mishnah provides little tales or narratives, moreover, they more often treat how things in the cult are done in general than what, in particular, happened on some one day. It is sufficient to refer casually to well-known incidents. Narrative, in the Mishnah's limited rhetorical repertoire, is reserved for the narrow framework of what priests and others do on recurrent occasions and around the Temple. In all, that staple of history, stories about dramatic events and important deeds, in the minds of the Mishnah's jurisprudents provide little nourishment. Events, if they appear at all, are treated as trivial. They may be well-known, but are consequential in some way other than is revealed in the detailed account of what actually happened. Let me now show some of the principal texts that contain and convey this other conception of how events become history and how history teaches lessons.

Sages' treatment of events determines what in the Mishnah is important about what happens. Since the greatest event in the century and a half, from ca. 50 to ca. 200, in which the Mishnah's materials came into being was the destruction of the Temple in 70, we must expect the Mishnah's treatment of that incident to illustrate the document's larger theory of history: what is important and unimportant about what happens. The treatment of the destruction occurs in two ways. First, the destruction of the Temple constitutes a noteworthy fact in the history of the law. Why? Because various laws about rite and cult had to undergo revision on account of the destruction. The following provides a stunningly apt example of how the Mishnah's philosophers regard what actually happened as being simply changes in the law. We begin with Mishnah tractate Rosh Hashshanah Chapter Four.

ROSH HASHSHANAH CHAPTER FOUR
4:1–3

A.   The festival day of the New Year which coincided with the Sabbath—

B.   in the Temple they would sound the *shofar.*

C.   But not in the provinces.

D.   When the Temple was destroyed, Rabban Yohanan ben Zakkai made the rule that they should sound the *shofar* in every locale in which there was a court.

E.   Said R. Eleazar, "Rabban Yohanan b. Zakkai made that rule only in the case of Yabneh alone."

F.   They said to him, "All the same are Yabneh and every locale in which there is a court."

M. Rosh Hashshanah 4:1

A.   And in this regard also was Jerusalem ahead of Yabneh:

B.   in every town which is within sight and sound [of Jerusalem], and nearby and able to come up to Jerusalem, they sound the *shofar.*

C.   But as to Yabneh, they sound the *shofar* only in the court alone.

M. Rosh Hashshanah 4:2

A.   In olden times the *lulab* was taken up in the Temple for seven days, and
     in the provinces, for one day.
B.   When the Temple was destroyed, Rabban Yohanan ben Zakkai made the
     rule that in the provinces the *lulab* should be taken up for seven days, as a
     memorial to the Temple;
C.   and that the day [the sixteenth of Nisan] on which the *omer* is waved
     should be wholly prohibited [in regard to the eating of new produce]
     [M. Suk. 3:12].

M. Rosh Hashshanah 4:3

First, let us examine the passage in its own terms, and then point to its consequence for the argument about history. The rules of sounding the *shofar* run to the
special case of the New Year which coincides with the Sabbath, M. 4:1A–C.
Clearly, we have some diverse materials here since M. 4:1A–D (+ E–F), are formally different from M. 4:3. The point of difference, however, is clear, since
M. 4:3A has no counterpart at M. 4:1A–C, and this is for redactional reasons. That
is, to connect his materials with what has gone before, the redactor could not
introduce the issue of M. 4:1A–C with the formulary, *In olden times . . . When
the Temple was destroyed. . . .* Consequently, he has used the more common, mild
apocopation to announce his topic, and then reverted to the expected formulary
pattern, which, I think, characterized M. 4:1A–C as much as M. 4:3. M. 4:2A
assumes a different antecedent construction from the one we have, a formulary
which lists points in which Jerusalem is ahead of Yabneh, and, perhaps, points in
which Yabneh is ahead of Jerusalem. But M. 4:2 clearly responds to M. 4:1E's
view. The meaning of the several entries is clear and requires no comment.

But the point as to the use and meaning of history does. What we see is that
the destruction of the Temple is recognized and treated as consequential—but
only for the organization of rules. The event forms division between one time and
some other, and, in consequence, we sort out rules pertaining to the Temple and
synagogue in one way rather than in another. That, sum and substance, is the
conclusion drawn from the destruction of the Temple, which is to say, the use that
is made of that catastrophe: an indicator in the organization of rules. What we see
is the opposite of an interest in focusing upon the one-time meaning of events.
Now it is the all-time significance of events in the making of rules. Events are now
treated not as irregular and intrinsically consequential but as regular and merely
instrumental.

The passages before us leave no doubt about what sages selected as important
about the destruction: it produced changes in synagogue rites. Although the sages
surely mourned the destruction and the loss of Israel's principal mode of worship,
and certainly recorded the event of the ninth of Ab in the year 70, they did so in
their characteristic way: they listed the event as an item in a catalog of things that
are like one another and so demand the same response. But then the destruction

no longer appears as a unique event. It is absorbed into a pattern of like disasters, all exhibiting similar taxonomic traits, events to which the people, now well-schooled in tragedy, know full well the appropriate response. So it is in demonstrating regularity that sages reveal their way of coping. Then the uniqueness of the event fades away, its mundane character is emphasized. The power of taxonomy in imposing order upon chaos once more does its healing work. The consequence was reassurance that historical events obeyed discoverable laws. Israel's ongoing life would override disruptive, one-time happenings. So catalogs of events, as much as lists of species of melons, served as brilliant apologetic by providing reassurance that nothing lies beyond the range and power of ordering system and stabilizing pattern. Here is yet another way in which the irregular was made regular and orderly, subject to rules:

MISHNAH TRACTATE TAANIT 4:6–7

4:6. A. Five events took place for our fathers on the seventeenth of Tammuz, and five on the ninth of Ab.

  B. On the seventeenth of Tammuz
    (1) the tablets [of the Torah] were broken,
    (2) the daily whole offering was canceled,
    (3) the city wall was breached,
    (4) Apostemos burned the Torah, and (5) he set up an idol in the Temple.

  C. On the ninth of Ab
    (1) the decree was made against our forefathers that they should not enter the land,
    (2) the first Temple,
    (3) the second [Temple] were destroyed,
    (4) Betar was taken,
    (5) the city was plowed up [after the war of Hadrian].

  D. When Ab comes, rejoicing diminishes.

4:7. A. In the week in which the ninth of Ab occurs it is prohibited to get a haircut and to wash one's clothes.

  B. But on Thursday of that week these are permitted,

  C. because of the honor due to the Sabbath.

  D. On the eve of the ninth of Ab a person should not eat two prepared dishes, nor should one eat meat or drink wine.

  E. Rabban Simeon b. Gamaliel says, "He should make some change from ordinary procedures."

  F. R. Judah declares people obligated to turn over beds.

  G. But sages did not concur with him.

I include M. Taanit 4:7 to show the context in which the list of M. 4:6 stands. The stunning calamities cataloged at M. 4:6 form groups, reveal common traits, so are subject to classification. Then the laws of M. 4:7 provide regular rules for responding to, coping with, these untimely catastrophes, all (fortuitously) in a single classification. So the raw materials of history are absorbed into the ahistorical, supernatural system of the Mishnah. The process of absorption and regularization of the unique and one-time moment is illustrated in the passage at hand.

A still more striking example of the reordering of one-time events into all-time patterns derives from the effort to put together in a coherent way the rather haphazard history of the cult inherited from Scripture, with sacrifices made here and there and finally in Jerusalem. Now the entire history of the cult, so critical in the larger system created by the Mishnah's lawyers, produced a patterned, therefore sensible and intelligible, picture. As is clear, everything that happened turned out to be susceptible of classification, once the taxonomic traits were specified. A monothetic exercise, sorting out periods and their characteristics, took the place of narrative, to explain things in its own way: first this, and then that, and, in consequence, the other. So in the neutral turf of holy ground, as much as in the trembling earth of the Temple mount, everything was absorbed into one thing, all classified in its proper place and by its appropriate rule. Indeed, so far as the lawyers proposed to write history at all, they wrote it into their picture of the long tale of the way in which Israel served God: the places in which the sacrificial labor was carried on, the people who did it, the places in which the priests ate the meat left over for their portion after God's portion was set aside and burned up. This "historical" account forthwith generated precisely that problem of locating the regular and orderly, which the philosophers loved to investigate: what happens when a given set of cases is governed by two distinct rules, so that we do not know how to classify the cases? We see the intersection of conflicting, but equally correct, taxonomic rules at M. Zebahim 14:9, below. The passage that follows therefore is history, so far as the Mishnah's creators proposed to write history: the reduction of events to rules forming compositions of regularity, therefore meaning. We follow Mishnah-tractate Zebahim Chapter Fourteen.

MISHNAH TRACTATE ZEBAHIM 14:4-8

I.   A.   Before the tabernacle was set up, (1) the high places were permitted, and (2) [the sacrificial] service [was done by] the firstborn (Num. 3:12-12, 8:16-18).

      B.   When the tabernacle was set up, (1) the high places were prohibited, and (2) the [sacrificial] service [was done by] priests.

      C.   Most Holy Things were eaten within the veils, Lesser Holy Things [were eaten] throughout the camp of Israel.

M. Zebahim 14:4

II.   A.   They came to Gilgal.

      B.   The high places were prohibited.

C.   Most Holy Things were eaten within the veils, Lesser Holy
     Things, anywhere.

M. Zebahim 14:5

III. A.   They came to Shiloh.
      B.   The high places were prohibited.
      C.   (1) There was no roof-beam there, but below was a house of stone,
           and hangings above it, and (2) it was "the resting place" (Deut.
           12:9).
      D.   Most Holy Things were eaten within the veils, Lesser Holy Things
           and second tithe [were eaten] in any place within sight [of Shiloh].

M. Zebahim 14:6

IV.   A.   They came to Nob and Gibeon.
      B.   The high places were permitted.
      C.   Most Holy Things were eaten within the veils, Lesser Holy Things,
           in all the towns of Israel.

M. Zebahim 14:7

V.   A.   They came to Jerusalem.
      B.   The high places were prohibited.
      C.   And they never again were permitted.
      D.   And it was "the inheritance" (Deut. 12:9).
      E.   Most Holy Things were eaten within the veils, Lesser Holy Things
           and second tithe within the wall.

M. Zebahim 14:8

Let us rapidly review the formal traits of this lovely composition, because those
traits justify my insistence that we are dealing with a patterning of events. This set
of five formally balanced items bears remarkably few glosses. The form is best
revealed at M. 14:5, 7. M. 14:6C is the only significant gloss. M. 14:4 sets up a
fine introduction, integral to the whole despite its interpolated and extraneous
information at A2, B2. M. 14:8C is essential; D is a gloss, parallel to M. 14:6C2.
The unitary construction is self-explanatory. At some points it was permitted to
sacrifice on high places, at others, it was not, a neat way of harmonizing Scripture's
numerous contradictions on the subject. M. 14:4B depends upon Lev. 17:5. M.
14:5 refers to Joshua 4:19ff.; M. 14:6, to Joshua 18:1. The "resting place" of Deut.
12:9 is identified with Shiloh. At this point the obligation to separate second tithe
is incurred, which accounts for the conclusion of M. 14:4D. M. 14:7 refers to 1
Samuel 21:2, 7, after the destruction of Shiloh, and to I Kings 3:4. M. 14:8 then
identifies the "inheritance" of Deut. 12:9 with Jerusalem.

1 4 : 9

A.   All the Holy Things which one sanctified at the time of the prohibi-
     tion of the high places and offered at the time of the prohibition of
     high places outside—

B.   lo, these are subject to the transgression of a positive commandment
     and a negative commandment, and they are liable on their account
     to extirpation [for sacrificing outside the designated place, Lev.
     17:8–9, M. 13:1A].

C.   [If] one sanctified them at the time of the permission of high places
     and offered them up at the time of the prohibition of high places,

D.   lo, these are subject to transgression of a positive commandment
     and to a negative commandment, but they are not liable on their
     account to extirpation [since if the offerings had been sacrificed
     when they were sanctified, there should have been no violation].

E.   [If] one sanctified them at the time of the prohibition of high places
     and offered them up at the time of the permission of high places,

F.   lo, these are subject to transgression of a positive commandment,
     but they are not subject to a negative commandment at all.

M. Zebahim 14:9

Now we see how the Mishnah's sages turn events into rules and show the
orderly nature of history. The secondary expansion of M. 14:4–8 is in three parts,
A–B, C–D, and E–F, all in close verbal balance. The upshot is to cover all sorts of
circumstances within a single well-composed pattern. This is easy to represent by
simple symbols. We deal with two circumstances and two sets of actions: The
circumstance of the prohibition of high places, (−), and that of their permission
(+), and the act of sanctification of a sacrifice (A) and offering it up, (B), thus:

A: −A −B = negative, positive, extirpation

C: +A +B = negative, positive

E: −A +B = positive only.

We cannot have +A +B, since there is no reason to prohibit or to punish the
one who sanctifies and offers up a sacrifice on a high place when it is permitted to
do so (!). Accordingly, all possible cases are dealt with. In the first case, both sanctification and offering up take place at the time that prohibition of high places applies. There is transgression of a positive commandment and a negative commandment. The negative is Deut. 12:13, the positive, Deut. 12:14. *Take heed that you do
not offer your burnt-offerings at every place that you see; but at the place which the Lord will
choose in one of your tribes, there you shall offer your burnt-offerings.* The mixtures, C and
E, then go over the same ground. If sanctification takes place when it is permitted
to sanctify animals for use in high places, but the offering up takes place when it
is not allowed to do so (e.g., the former for M. 14:4, the latter, M. 14:6), extirpa-

tion does not apply (Lev. 17:5–7). When we then reverse the order (e.g., M. 14:6, M. 14:7), there is no negative (Deut. 12:13), but the positive commandment (Deut. 12:14) has been transgressed. But matters do not stop here. The rule-making out of the raw materials of disorderly history continues unabated.

14:10

A. These are the Holy Things offered in the tabernacle [of Gilgal, Nob, and Gibeon]:

B. Holy Things which were sanctified for the tabernacle.

C. Offerings of the congregation are offered in the tabernacle.

D. Offerings of the individual [are offered] on a high place.

E. Offerings of the individual which were sanctified for the tabernacle are to be offered in the tabernacle.

F. And if one offered them up on a high place, he is free.

G. What is the difference between the high place of an individual and the high place of the community?

H. (1) Laying on of hands, and (2) slaughtering at the north [of the altar], and (3) placing [of the blood] round about [the altar], and (4) waving, and (5) bringing near.

I. R. Judah says, "there is no meal-offering on a high place [but there is in the tabernacle]"—

J. and (1) the priestly service, and (2) the wearing of garments of ministry, and (3) the use of utensils of ministry, and (4) the sweet-smelling savor, and (5) the dividing line for the [tossing of various kinds of] blood, and (6) the rule concerning the washing of hands and feet.

K. But the matters of time, and remnant, and uncleanness are applicable both here and there [by contrast to M. 14:3F–I].

M. Zebahim 14:10

When M. 14:4–8 refer to a high place that was permitted, and refer also to the presence of veils, it is assumed that there were both a tabernacle (hence the veils) and also high places. This must mean Gilgal, M. 14:5, and Nob and Gibeon, M. 14:7. Now the issue is, if there are both a tabernacle and a high place, which sorts of offerings belong to which kind of altar? It follows that the pericope treats the situations specified at M. 14:5, 7, a secondary expansion. A is answered by B. C–F go on to work out their own interests, and cannot be constructed to answer A, because they specify *are offered in the tabernacle* as a complete apodosis, which A does not require and B clearly does not want. B tells us that even though it is permitted to offer a sacrifice on a high place, a sacrifice which is set aside for the tabernacle (obviously) is to be offered there. Then C–F work the matter out. C and D are clear as stated. Holy Things that are sanctified for the tabernacle are offerings of the congregation (C). It is taken for granted that they are meant for the tabernacle, even when not so designated as specified by B. Individuals' sacrifices are assumed to be for high places unless specified otherwise (D). Obviously, if they are sanctified for the tabernacle, E, they are sacrificed there. But there is no reason to inflict liability if they are offered on a high place, F. The whole is carefully worked out, leaving no unanswered questions.

G then asks what difference there is between the high place which serves an individual, and "the high place"—the tabernacle—which serves the congregation, that is, the ones at Gilgal, Nob, and Gibeon. H specifies five items; J, six more; and Judah brings the list up to twelve. K completes the matter. The reference to *time* requires explanation, since it is shorthand. The word refers to the priest's improper intention to eat the flesh or burn the sacrificial parts after the appropriate time, and the priest's doing so imparts to the meat or sacrificial parts the status of refuse. The word choice—*time*—is unexpected. It conveys an attitude as to the time of disposing of the sacrificial parts of meat at a time other than the right time, e.g., too soon or, as here, too late. The inclusion of M. Zeb. 14:9, structurally matching M. Taanit 4:7, shows us the goal of the historical composition. It is to set forth rules that intersect and produce confusion, so that we may sort out confusion and make sense of all the data. The upshot may now be stated briefly: the authorship at hand had the option of narrative, but chose the way of philosophy: generalization through classification, comparison, and contrast.

The Mishnah absorbs into its encompassing system all events, small and large. With what happens the sages accomplish what they do with everything else: a vast labor of taxonomy, an immense construction of the order and rules governing the classification of everything on earth and in heaven. The disruptive character of history—one-time events of ineluctable significance—scarcely impresses the philosophers. They find no difficulty in showing that what appears unique and beyond classification has in fact happened before and so falls within the range of trustworthy rules and known procedures. Once history's components, one-time events, lose their distinctiveness, then history as a didactic intellectual construct, as a source of lessons and rules, also loses all pertinence. So lessons and rules come from sorting things out and classifying them, that is, from the procedures and modes of thought of the philosopher seeking regularity. To this labor of taxonomy, the historian's way of selecting data and arranging them into patterns of meaning to teach lessons proves inconsequential. One-time events are not what matters. The world is composed of nature and supernature. The repetitious laws that count are those to be discovered in heaven and, in heaven's creation and counterpart, on earth. Keep those laws and things will work out. Break them, and the result is predictable: calamity of whatever sort will supervene in accordance with the rules. But just because it is predictable, a catastrophic happening testifies to what has always been and must always be, in accordance with reliable rules and within categories already discovered and well explained. That is why the lawyer-philosophers of the mid-second century produced the Mishnah—to explain how things are. Within the framework of well-classified rules, there could be messiahs, but no single Messiah.

Up to now I have contrasted "history" with "philosophy," that is, disorderly and unique events as against rules governing all events and emerging inductively from them. I therefore have framed matters in such a way that the Mishnah's system appears to have been ahistorical and antihistorical. Yet in fact the framers of the Mishnah recognized the past-ness of the past and hence, by definition, laid out a conception of the past that constitutes a historical doctrine. Theirs was not an antihistorical conception of reality but a deeply historical one, even though it is a conception of the meaning of history different from the familiar one. It was, in two words, social scientific, not historical in the traditional sense of history-writing. Let me explain this difference, since it is fundamental to understanding the Mishnah's system as essentially philosophical and, in our terms, scientific.

For modern history-writing, what is important is to describe what is unique and individual, not what is ongoing and unremarkable. History is the story of change, development, movement, not of what does not change, develop, or move. For the thinkers of the Mishnah, historical patterning emerges as today scientific knowledge does, through taxonomy, the classification of the unique and individual, the organization of change and movement within unchanging categories. That is why the dichotomy between history and eternity, change and permanence, signals an unnuanced exegesis of what was, in fact, a subtle and reflective doctrine of history. That doctrine proves entirely consistent with the large perspectives of scribes, from the ones who made omen series in ancient Babylonia to the ones who made the Mishnah.

How, then, in the Mishnah does history come to full conceptual expression? History as an account of a meaningful pattern of events, making sense of the past and giving guidance about the future, begins with the necessary conviction that events matter because they form series, one after another. And when we put a series together, we have a rule, just as when we put cases together, we can demonstrate the rule that governs them all. The Mishnah's authorship therefore disposes of historical events just as it sorts out anything else of interest: correct composition of contracts, appropriate disposition of property, proper conduct on a holy day— all things imputed through specific events, formed so that we can derive out of the concrete the abstract and encompassing rule. What we see, therefore, is the congruence of language and thought, detail and main point, subject matter and sheltering system.

That is why we may not find surprising the Mishnah's framers' reluctance to present us with an elaborate theory of events, a fact fully consonant with their systematic points of insistence and encompassing concern. Events do not matter, one by one. The philosopher-lawyers exhibited no theory of history either. Their conception of Israel's destiny in no way called upon historical categories of either narrative or didactic explanation to describe and account for the future. The small importance attributed to the figure of the Messiah as a historical-eschatological figure, therefore, fully accords with the larger traits of the system as a whole. Let me speak with emphasis: if what is important in Israel's existence is sanctification, an ongoing process, and not salvation, understood as a one-time event at the end, then no one will find reason to narrate history.

The theology of the Mishnah encompasses history and its meaning, but, we now realize, history and the interpretation of history do not occupy a central position on the stage of Israel's life portrayed by the Mishnah. The critical categories derive from the modalities of holiness. What can become holy or what is holy? These tell us what will attract the close scrutiny of our authorship and precipitate sustained thought, expressed through very concrete and picayune cases. If I had to identify the two most important foci of holiness in the Mishnah, they would be, in the natural world, the land, but only the Holy Land, the Land of Israel, and, in the social world, the people, but only the People of Israel. In the interplay among Land, People, and God, we see the inner workings of the theological vision of the sages of the Mishnah. So much for the Mishnah. Now we turn to the exposition, elaboration, and extension of its rules in the reformation of its system by its heirs and exegetes.

7.

THE CRITICAL PLACE OF THE MISHNAH IN RABBINIC LITERATURE

When, in ca. 200, the Mishnah reached closure and was received and adopted as law by the state-sanctioned Jewish governments in both the Roman Empire, in the Land of Israel, and in Babylonia, in Iran, the function and character of the document precipitated a considerable crisis. Politically and theologically presented as the foundation for the everyday administration of the affairs of Jewry, the Mishnah ignored the politics of the sponsoring regimes. Essentially ahistorical, the code hardly identified as authoritative any known political institution, let alone the patriarchate in the Land of Israel, the exilarchate in Babylonia.

True, that political-institutional flaw (from the viewpoint of the sponsoring authorities) scarcely can have proved critical. But silence of the authorship of the Mishnah on the theological call for their document presented not a chronic but an acute problem. Since Jews generally accepted the authority of Moses at Sinai, failure to claim for the document a clear and explicit relationship to the Torah of Moses defined that acute issue. Why should people accept as authoritative the rulings of this piece of writing? Omitting reference to a theological, as much as to a political, myth, the authorship of the Mishnah also failed to signal the relationship between their document and Scripture. Since, for all Judaisms, Hebrew Scriptures in general, and the Pentateuch in particular, represented God's will for Israel, silence on that matter provoked considerable response. Let me now spell out in some ✓ detail the political, theological, and literary difficulties presented by the Mishnah to any theory that the Mishnah formed part of God's revelation to Moses at Sinai.

Laws issued to define what people were supposed to do could not stand by themselves; they had to receive the imprimatur of heaven, that is, they had to be given the status of revelation. Accordingly, to make its way in Israelite life, the Mishnah as a constitution and code demanded for itself a theory of beginnings at (or in relation to) Sinai, with Moses, from God. The character of the Mishnah itself hardly won confidence that, on the face of it, the document formed part of, or derived from, the revelation at Sinai. It was originally published through oral formulation and oral transmission, that is, in the medium of memorization. But it had been in the medium of writing that, in the view of all of Israel until about A.D. 200, God had been understood to reveal the divine word and will. The Torah was a written book. People who claimed to receive further messages from God usually wrote them down. They had three choices in securing acceptance of their account. All three involved linking the new to the old.

In claiming to hand on revelation, they could, first, sign their books with the names of biblical heroes. Second, they could imitate the style of biblical Hebrew. Third, they could present an exegesis of existing written verses, validating their ideas by supplying proof texts for them. From the closure of the Torah literature in the time of Ezra, circa 450 B.C., to the time of the Mishnah, nearly seven hundred years later, we do not have a single book alleged to be holy and at the same time standing wholly out of relationship to the Holy Scriptures of ancient Israel. The Pseudepigraphic writings fall into the first category, the Essene writings at Qumran into the second and third. We may point also to the Gospels, which take as a principal problem demonstrating how Jesus had fulfilled the prophetic promises of the Old Testament and in other ways carried forward and even embodied Israel's Scripture.

Insofar as a piece of Jewish writing did not find a place in relationship to Scripture, its author laid no claim to present a holy book. The contrast between Jubilees and the Testaments of the Patriarchs, with their constant and close harping on biblical matters, and the several books of Maccabees, shows the differences. The former claim to present God's revealed truth; the latter, history. So a book was holy because in style, in authorship, or in (alleged) origin it continued Scripture, finding a place therefore (at least in the author's mind) within the canon, or because it provided an exposition of Scripture's meaning. But the Mishnah made no such claim. It entirely ignored the style of biblical Hebrew, speaking in a quite different kind of Hebrew altogether. It is silent on its authorship through sixty-two of the sixty-three tractates (the claims of Abot are post facto).

In any event, nowhere does the Mishnah contain the claim that God had inspired the authors of the document. These are not given biblical names and certainly are not alleged to have been biblical saints. Most of the book's named authorities flourished within the same century as its anonymous arrangers and redactors, not in remote antiquity. Above all, the Mishnah contains scarcely a handful of exegeses of Scripture. These, where they occur, play a trivial and tangential role. So here is the problem of the Mishnah: different from Scripture in language and style, indifferent to the claim of authorship by a biblical hero or divine inspiration, stunningly aloof from allusion to verses of Scripture for nearly the whole of its discourse—yet authoritative for Israel.

So the Mishnah was not a statement of theory alone, telling only how matters will be in the eschaton. Nor was it a wholly sectarian document, reporting the view of a group without standing or influence in the larger life of Israel. True, in some measure it bears both of these traits of eschatology and sectarian provenance. But the Mishnah was (and is) law for Israel. It entered the government and courts of the Jewish people, both in the motherland and also overseas, as the authoritative constitution of the courts of Judaism. The advent of the Mishnah therefore marked a turning in the life of the nation-religion. The document demanded explanation and apology. And the one choice one did not face, as a Jew in third-century Tiberias, Sepphoris, Caesarea, or Beth Shearim, in Galilee, was to ignore the Mishnah and the issues inherent in its character as a piece of writing given political standing by the ethnarch.

True, one might refer solely to ancient Scripture and tradition and live life out within the inherited patterns of the familiar Israelite religion-culture. But as soon as one dealt with the Jewish government in charge of everyday life—went to court over the damages done to a crop by a neighbor's ox, for instance—one came up against a law in addition to the law of Scripture, a document the principles of which governed and settled all matters. So the Mishnah rapidly came to confront the life of Israel. The people who knew the Mishnah, the rabbis or sages, came to dominate that life. And their claim, in accord with the Mishnah, to exercise authority and the right to impose heavenly sanction came to perplex. There were two solutions to the problem set forth by the character of the Mishnah.

[1] THE MISHNAH AS AN AUTONOMOUS, FREESTANDING COMPONENT OF THE TORAH OF SINAI: One response was represented by the claim that the authorities of the Mishnah stood in a chain of tradition that extended back to Sinai; stated explicitly in the Mishnah's first apologetic, tractate Abot, that circulated from approximately a generation beyond the promulgation of the Mishnah itself, that view required amplification and concrete demonstration. This approach treated the word *torah* as a common noun, as the word that spoke of a status or classification of sayings. A saying was *torah,* that is, enjoyed the status of *torah* or fell into the classification of *torah,* if it stood in the line of tradition from Sinai.

[2] THE MISHNAH IS SUBORDINATE TO THE WRITTEN PART OF THE TORAH BUT CAN BE SHOWN TO STAND ON THE WRITTEN TORAH'S AUTHORITY: A second response took the same view of *torah* as a common noun. This response was to treat the Mishnah as subordinate to, and dependent upon, Scripture. Then *torah* was what fell into the classification of the revelation of *Torah* by God to Moses at Sinai. The way of providing what was needed within that theory was to link state-

ments of the Mishnah to statements ("proof texts") of Scripture. The Tosefta, ca. 300, a compilation of citations of and comments upon the Mishnah, together with some autonomous materials that may have reached closure in the period in which the work of redaction of the Mishnah was going on, as well as the Talmud of the Land of Israel, ca. 400, fairly systematically did just that.

The former solution treated Torah with a small *t,* that is to say, as a generic classification, and identified the Mishnah with the Torah revealed to Moses at Sinai by claiming a place for the Mishnah's authorities in the process of tradition and transmission that brought torah—no longer, the Torah, the specific writing comprising the Five Books of Moses—to contemporary Israel, the Jewish people. It was a theological solution, expressed through ideas, attitudes, and implicit claims, but not through sustained rewriting of either Scripture or the Mishnah.

The latter solution, by contrast, concerned the specific and concrete statements of the Mishnah and required literary, not merely theological, statements, precise and specific to passages of the Mishnah, one after the other. What was demanded by the claim that the Mishnah depended upon, but therefore enjoyed the standing of, Scripture, was a line-by-line commentary upon the Mishnah in light of Scripture. But this too, I stress, treated *torah* as a common noun.

[3] The Redefinition of the Torah: The third way emerged in Sifra, a sustained and profound philosophical reading of the book of Leviticus, to be considered in detail in Chapter 11. Sifra's solution would set aside the two solutions, the theological and the literary, and explore the much more profound issues of the fundamental and generative structure of right thought, yielding, as a matter of fact, both Scripture and the Mishnah. This approach insisted that *Torah* always was a proper noun. There was, and is, only the Torah. But this—the Torah—demanded expansion and vast amplification. When we know the principles of logical structure and especially those of hierarchical classification that animate the Torah, we can undertake part of the task of expansion and amplification, that is, join in the processes of thought that in the mind of God yielded the Torah. For when we know how God thought in giving the Torah to Moses at Sinai and so accounting for the classifications and their ordering in the very creation of the world, we can ourselves enter into the Torah and participate in its processes.

Presenting the two Torahs in a single statement constituted an experiment in logic, that logic, in particular, that made cogent thought possible and that transformed facts into propositions, and propositions into judgments of the more, or the less, consequential. While the Mishnah's other apologists wrote the written Torah into the Mishnah, Sifra's authorship wrote the oral Torah into Scripture. That is to say, the other of the two approaches to the problem of the Mishnah, the one of Sifra, to begin with claimed to demonstrate that the Mishnah found its correct place within the written Torah itself. Instead of citing verses of Scripture in the context of the Mishnah, the authorship of Sifra cited passages of the Mishnah in the context of Scripture, Leviticus in particular. Exactly how they did so will be set forth in Chapter 11.

What the three accounts of the Mishnah's relationship to the Torah achieved, each in its own way, cohered to yield a single consequence. All three insisted on a privileged position for the Mishnah within, or at least in intimate relationship to, the Torah of Sinai. That explains two facts that together demonstrate the absolute uniqueness of the Mishnah in rabbinic literature. First, the Mishnah as a document acknowledged no prior writing, except—and then only episodically—Scripture itself. Second, the Mishnah alone among rabbinic documents itself received sustained and systematic commentaries in the model of those accorded to Scripture. Every document that followed the Mishnah, that is to say, the entirety of rabbinic literature except for the Mishnah, took shape as a commentary to a prior document, either Scripture or the Mishnah itself. So the entirety of rabbinic literature testifies to the unique standing of the Mishnah, acknowledging its special status, without parallel or peer, as the oral part of the Torah.

VI

THE TOSEFTA

1.

IDENTIFYING THE DOCUMENT

A huge supplement to the Mishnah, four times larger than the document it amplifies, the Tosefta, ca. 300,[1] exhibits none of the documentary traits that mark as autonomous the other rabbinic writings. Wholly depending upon the Mishnah for its rhetoric, topical program, and logic of coherent discourse, the Tosefta is like a vine on a trellis. It has no structure of its own but most commonly cites and glosses

---

[1] For further reading and bibliography on the topic of this chapter, see the following:

Bowker, pp. 61–64.

Abraham Goldberg, "The Tosefta—Companion to the Mishna" (character and date, arrangement and contents, structural layers, commentary and supplement to the Mishna, the Tosefta and the baraitot in the Talmudim, editing, Tannait prominent in the Tosefta, bibliography: editions, commentaries and translations, introductions and research, Tosefta manuscripts [by Michael Krupp]), in Safrai, *Literature of the Sages*, pp. 283–302.

Moses David Herr, "Tosefta," in *Encyclopaedia Judaica* 15:1283–1285: structure, editions, and commentaries; the Tosefta was not edited before the end of the fourth century; "the compiler did not add, omit, or change his material in any way, but collected the material that was at his disposal. . . . The aim of this anonymous compiler and redactor was obviously to produce a collection that would serve as a supplement to the Mishnah."

a passage of the Mishnah, not differentiating its forms and wording of sentences from those of the cited passage. Only seldom—for somewhat under a sixth of the whole of its volume—does the Tosefta present a statement that may be interpreted entirely independent of the Mishnah's counterpart (if any). The Tosefta covers nearly the whole of the Mishnah's program but has none of its own.

What marks the document as dependent, further, is that its sentences by themselves do not hold together at all. Their order consistently refers to that of the Mishnah's statements. The logic of consistent discourse, affecting more than two or three sentences at a time, is wholly fixed-associative. The dependent status of the Tosefta derives from the simple fact that for most of the document we simply cannot understand a line without first consulting the Mishnah's counterpart statement. Once a text derives from some other document not only its coherence, but even the first level of meaning of its sentences one by one, we no longer can maintain that we have a freestanding statement, let alone a systemic one. The document contains three kinds of writings.

[1] The first consists of verbatim citations and glosses of sentences of the Mishnah.

[2] The second is made up of freestanding statements that complement the sense of the Mishnah but do not cite a Mishnah paragraph verbatim. These statements can be fully understood only in dialogue with the Mishnah's counterpart.

[3] The third comprises freestanding, autonomous statements, formulated in the manner of the Mishnah but fully comprehensible on their own.

The editors or compilers of the Tosefta arranged their materials in accord with two principles, and these govern the order of the Tosefta's statements in correspondence to the Mishnah's. First will come statements that cite what the Mishnah's sentences say, and this ordinarily will occur in the order of the Mishnah's statements. Second, in general Mishnah citation and gloss will be succeeded by Mishnah amplification, which is to say, sentences that do not cite the Mishnah's corresponding ones, but that cannot be understood without reference to the Mishnah's rule or sense. The first two kinds of statements are the ones that cannot be fully understood without knowledge of the Mishnah, which defines their context. Third in sequence, commonly, will be the small number of freestanding statements which can be wholly understood on their own and without appeal to the sense

Maccoby, pp. 35–36; selected passages, pp. 133–47.

Stemberger-Strack, pp. 167–81: general bibliography; the relationship of Tosefta to the Mishnah and the Talmuds; name, structure, contents, origin; the text of the Tosefta; printed editions; translations; commentaries.

This writer's *History of the Mishnaic Law* (in forty-three volumes) presents the Tosefta unit by unit in relationship to the corresponding Mishnah passages and comments on the whole. The results are briefly summarized in *The Tosefta: Its Structure and Its Sources*. Atlanta, 1986: Scholars Press for Brown Judaic Studies. Reprise of pertinent results in *Purities* I–XXI, and *The Tosefta. An Introduction*. Atlanta, 1992: Scholars Press for South Florida Studies in the History of Judaism, which provide a systematic account of the document.

or principle of the corresponding Mishnah passage; and in some few cases, these compositions and even composites will have no parallel in the Mishnah at all.

Autonomous statements require attention in their own right. These comprise paragraphs that make their own point and can be fully understood in their own terms. These freestanding materials are of two kinds. First, some autonomous materials work on topics important to a passage in the Mishnah and are placed by the Tosefta's framers in a position corresponding to the thematic parallel in the Mishnah. What marks these materials as autonomous is that while they intersect with the Mishnah's topic, their interest in that topic bears no point in common with the Mishnah's treatment of the same topic. A second criterion, which is complementary, is that we can understand what follows without referring to the Mishnah for any purpose. The second type of autonomous materials addresses topics omitted in the Mishnah, and that type is included in the Tosefta only because in the Mishnah there may be a tangential reference to the topic treated by Tosefta's compositors. The criterion of classification, then, is even simpler than that governing the first type. The Tosefta's authorship has collected this kind of material from we know not where. It could have been composed in the same period as the writing of the Mishnah.

While these freestanding statements that could as well have stood in the Mishnah as in the Tosefta itself may have reached final formulation prior to the closure of the Mishnah, most of the document either cites the Mishnah verbatim and comments upon it, or can be understood only in light of the Mishnah even though the Mishnah is not cited verbatim, and that is sound reason for assigning the formulation of most of the document and the compilation of the whole to the time after the Mishnah was concluded. The first two types of materials certainly were written after the closure of the Mishnah. The Tosefta as a whole, covering all three types, was compiled sometime after the conclusion of the Mishnah in ca. 200 but before the formation of the Talmud of the Land of Israel, ca. 400, which frequently cites materials found in the Tosefta and interprets the Mishnah in light of the Tosefta's complements. The compilation therefore is a work of the third century, 200–300.

But in substance the document's claim proves still stronger. The Tosefta's materials, coherent and cogent not among themselves but only in relationship to the Mishnah, serve as the Mishnah's first commentary, first amplification, and first extension. If by a talmud, we mean a sustained, systematic commentary to the Mishnah, following a program of exegesis and analysis, then the Tosefta must be called the first talmud, prior to the ones done in the Land of Israel by ca. 400 or completed in Babylonia by ca. 600. Since both Talmuds read Mishnah passages through Tosefta complements to the Mishnah, the Tosefta forms the bridge between the Talmuds and much of the Mishnah.

But that does not mean the Tosefta is a very accessible document. The opposite is the case. And the reason derives from the Tosefta's very character as a document of mediation, expansion, and extension of another piece of writing. The Tosefta, as is now clear, makes sense only in relationship to the Mishnah. That is so not only for its program and order, which are defined by the Mishnah, but also for its individual compositions. Each completed unit of thought of the Tosefta is to be understood, to begin with, in relationship with the Mishnah: is it a citation of and commentary to the Mishnah passage that forms its counterpart? Is the passage fully to be comprehended on its own or only in relationship to a counterpart passage of the Mishnah? Or is the passage freestanding? The answers to these three questions define the first step in making any sense at all of a passage of the Tosefta, as our sample passage will indicate.

2.
TRANSLATIONS INTO ENGLISH

The only complete translation in any language is that of this writer: *The Tosefta: Translated from the Hebrew.* New York, 1977–80: Ktav. I–VI.[2] Volume I is made up of the writer's students' translations of tractates of the first division and was edited by him along with Richard S. Sarason.

3.
RHETORIC

Replicating the forms of the Mishnah, the Tosefta exhibits no rhetorical program distinctive to itself. The close adherence to the Mishnah's formal protocol is shown by a simple fact. Except for passages in which the Mishnah is briefly cited, so the character of what follows as a gloss is clear, differentiating a passage that occurs only in the Tosefta from a corresponding one in the Mishnah is not readily accomplished.

4.
LOGIC OF COHERENT DISCOURSE

The Tosefta depends upon the Mishnah in yet another way. Its whole redactional framework, tractates and subdivisions alike, depends upon the Mishnah's. None-

---

[2] The translation of Volume VI, covering the sixth division, has appeared in a second printing: Atlanta, 1990: Scholars Press for South Florida Studies in the History of Judaism. With a new preface.

theless, the Tosefta's compilers do introduce a second principle of organization, which, in conversation with the Mishnah, yields a coherent pattern that governs the sequence of statements. As noted earlier, first they follow the general outline of the Mishnah's treatment of a topic. Accordingly, if we set up a block of materials in the Tosefta side-by-side with a corresponding block of those of the Mishnah, we should discern roughly the same order of discourse. But, second, the Tosefta's arrangers also lay out their materials in accord with their own types. That is to say, they will tend (1) to keep as a group passages that cite and then comment upon the actual words of the Mishnah's base passage, then (2) to present passages that amplify in the Tosefta's own words opinions fully spelled out only in response to the Mishnah's statements, and, finally, (3) to give at the end, and as a group, wholly independent and autonomous sayings and constructions of such sayings.

That redactional pattern may be shown only to be a tendency, a set of not-uncommon policies and preferences, not a fixed rule. But when we ask how the Tosefta's editors arranged their materials, it is not wholly accurate to answer that they follow the plan of the Mishnah's counterparts. There will be some attention, also, to the taxonomic traits of the units of discourse of which the Tosefta itself is constructed. That is why two distinct editorial principles come into play in explaining the arrangement of the whole.

5.

TOPICAL PROGRAM

The Tosefta, as is already clear, stands nearly entirely within the circle of the Mishnah's interests, rarely asking questions about topics omitted altogether by the Mishnah's authors, always following the topical decisions on what to discuss as laid down by the founders of the whole. One cannot write about the Tosefta's theology or law as though these constituted a system susceptible of description and interpretation independent of the Mishnah's system. At the same time, the exegetes of the Mishnah, in the Tosefta and in the two Talmuds, stand apart from, and later than, the authors of the Mishnah itself. Accordingly, the exegetes systematically say whatever they wish to say by attaching their ideas to a document earlier than their own, and by making the principal document say what they wish to contribute.

The system of expressing ideas through reframing those of predecessors preserves the continuity of tradition and imposes a deep stability and order upon the culture framed by that tradition. The Tosefta not only depends for structure, order, and sense upon the Mishnah, but in general, the materials assembled in the Tosefta set forth no viewpoint other than that of the Mishnah's counterpart materials, clarified, refined, and improved. No study has as yet shown a sustained tendency in the Tosefta to execute a distinct exegesis of the Mishnah in such wise as to recast the sense or character of the Mishnah's program, though in numerous passages, the work of commentary shades over into a fresh reading of a specific problem.

6.

A SAMPLE PASSAGE

If the readers were to take up this writer's English translation of the Tosefta and begin reading on page one, by page three they would close the book and declare it unintelligible, a complete mishmash with no order, sense, proportion, or meaning. They would be justified in concluding that the document served as a mere scrapbook of this and that, lacking all focus, sense, and purpose, a kind of *genizah* within the covers of a book. But when they realize—by reading the Tosefta side by side with the corresponding Mishnah paragraphs and chapters—that the framers did follow a principle of organization, which we can define and demonstrate to have applied throughout, then they can no longer dismiss the Tosefta as a mere scrapbook, essentially unintelligible in its own terms. Once we recognize that the authorship has carefully and thoughtfully organized matters, we understand that it was accomplishing a highly sophisticated literary purpose.

That conclusion should hardly be surprising, since even the most superficial traits of the document—its organization in close correspondence with the Mishnah, by the Mishnah's tractates, by the Mishnah's tractates' chapter divisions, by the Mishnah's tractates' chapter divisions' subdivisions—demonstrate the same fact. Indeed, the authorship of the Tosefta was made up of literary craftsmen of the highest order, with remarkable skills of organization. Theirs, after all, was not a (mere) commentary, since without printing, arranging a commentary around a text in the middle of the page is not very easy; and, more to the point, the Mishnah was published orally, not in writing but through processes of memorization, so that by definition, printing or no, the commentary form of literary formulation and expression was simply not available. They solved their problem in the very odd way that we now discern.

But the character of the Tosefta governs the possibilities of presenting here a sample in such a way that the traits of the document, not merely a few lucid sentences, may be set forth. To see how the Tosefta fits into the sweep of the rabbinic literature extending from the Mishnah, ca. 200, through the Tosefta, ca. 200–300, to the Talmud of the Land of Israel or Yerushalmi, ca. 400, we follow a single passage. This allows us to place the Tosefta into its larger context. What is important, we shall observe, is how the Tosefta receives the Mishnah and transmits it forward; in the passage before us, the first of the two Talmuds addresses not so much the Mishnah as the Mishnah as transmitted by the Tosefta. (The second Talmud follows suit but will not detain us.) We shall now see in great detail precisely how the Tosefta adds its amplification and explanation to the Mishnah. But that is only part of the picture of the place of the Tosefta in rabbinic literature. We have further to examine how the Yerushalmi and the Bavli in sequence take up the Tosefta's reading of the Mishnah. Then we shall grasp how profoundly the whole of rabbinic literature in its formative age focuses upon the Tosefta. For the Tosefta, not the Mishnah, forms the hub: the hinge on which the door swings open (or shut).

The following pages present a chapter of the Mishnah, Mishnah tractate Berakhot Chapter Eight, in relationship to the Tosefta to that chapter. There follows the Yerushalmi's and finally the Bavli's treatment of the same chapter. We shall see how the Tosefta precipitates discourse, which then proceeds in quite unanticipated directions. In this way we get a good sense of proportion and balance: where the Tosefta matters, where it is left behind as the later authorities develop new interests altogether. The main point we shall observe is the position of the Tosefta in relationship to the Mishnah before and the first of the two Talmuds afterward. That we see when we follow the words of the Mishnah as these are augmented and revised in the Tosefta, then the words of the Tosefta as these are explained and made the starting point for further discussion in the two Talmuds. From a certain point in each case, the exposition of the Mishnah as the Tosefta reads the Mishnah falls away and other interests come to the fore; I give only the passages in which the Tosefta figures prominently as the Mishnah's first, and authoritative, exposition.

I. MISHNAH TRACTATE BERAKHOT CHAPTER EIGHT

I

8:1. A. These are the things that are between the House of Shammai and the House of Hillel in [regard to] the meal:

B. The House of Shammai say, "One blesses over the day, and afterward one blesses over the wine."

And the House of Hillel say, "One blesses over the wine, and afterward one blesses over the day."

8:2. A. The House of Shammai say, "They wash the hands and afterward mix the cup."

And the House of Hillel say, "They mix the cup and afterward wash the hands."

8:3. A. The House of Shammai say, "He dries his hands on the cloth and lays it on the table."

And the House of Hillel say, "On the pillow."

8:4. A. The House of Shammai say, "They clean the house, and afterward they wash the hands."

And the House of Hillel say, "They wash the hands, and afterward they clean the house."

8:5. A. The House of Shammai say, "Light, and food, and spices, and *Hab-dalah.*"

And the House of Hillel say, "Light, and spices, and food, and *Hab-dalah.*"

B. The House of Shammai say, "'Who created the light of the fire.'"

And the House of Hillel say, "'Who creates the lights of the fire.'"

8:6. A. They do not bless over the light or the spices of gentiles, or the light or the spices of the dead, nor the light or the spices which are before an idol.

B. And they do not bless over the light until they make use of its illumination.

8:7. A. He who ate and forgot and did not bless [say Grace]—

B. The House of Shammai say, "He should go back to his place and bless."

And the House of Hillel say, "He should bless in the place in which he remembered."

C. Until when does he bless? Until the food has been digested in his bowels.

8:8. A. Wine came to them after the meal, and there is there only that cup—

B. The House of Shammai say, "He blesses the wine, and afterward he blesses the food."

And the House of Hillel say, "He blesses the food, and afterward he blesses the wine."

C. They respond *Amen* after an Israelite who blesses, and they do not respond *Amen* after a Samaritan who blesses, until hearing the entire blessing.

The Mishnah chapter goes over rules on the conduct of meals, first for Sabbaths and festivals, then in general, with special concern for preserving the cultic purity of the meal. That means the people at the meal keep the laws of cultic cleanness set forth in the book of Leviticus, as these are interpreted by the sages of the Torah. The details are explained in the Tosefta, Yerushalmi, and Bavli, and we do well to allow the course of rabbinic thought and writing to carry us into the matter. Here is how the Tosefta confronts the same themes and also cites some of the passages verbatim.

TOSEFTA TO MISHNAH BERAKHOT CHAPTER EIGHT
5:21 (EDITION S. LIEBERMAN, P. 28, IS. 41–2)

They answer *Amen* after a gentile who says a blessing with the divine name. They do not answer *Amen* after a Samaritan who says a blessing with the divine name until they have heard the entire blessing.

5.25 (Lieberman, P. 29, IS. 53–57).

A.   [The] things which are between the House of Shammai and the House of Hillel in [regard to] the meal:

B.   The House of Shammai say, "One blesses over the day, and afterward he blesses over the wine, for the day causes the wine to come, and the day is already sanctified, but the wine has not yet come."

C.   And the House of Hillel say, "One blesses over the wine, and afterward he blesses over the day, for the wine causes the Sanctification of the day to be said.

"Another explanation: The blessing over the wine is regular [= always required when wine is used], and the blessing over the day is not continual [but is said only on certain days]."

D.   And the law is according to the words of the House of Hillel.

5:26 (Lieberman, PP. 29–30, IS. 57–61)

A.   The House of Shammai say, "They wash the hands and afterward mix the cup, lest the liquids which are on the outer surface of the cup be made unclean on account of the hands, and in turn make the cup unclean."

B.   The House of Hillel say, "The outer surfaces of the cup are always deemed unclean.

"Another explanation: The washing of the hands must always take place immediately before the meal.

C.   "They mix the cup and afterward wash the hands."

5:27 (Lieberman, P. 30, IS. 61–65)

A.   The House of Shammai say, "He dries his hands on the napkin and leaves it on the table, lest the liquids which are in the napkin be made unclean on account of the cushion, and then go and make the hands unclean."

B.   And the House of Hillel say, "A doubt in regard to the condition of liquids so far as the hands are concerned is resolved as clean."

C.   "Another explanation: Washing the hands does not pertain to unconsecrated food.

D.   "But he dries his hands on the napkin and leaves it on the cushion, lest the liquids which are in the napkin be made unclean on account of the table, and they go and render the food unclean."

5:28 (Lieberman, p. 30, Is. 65–68)

A.   The House of Shammai say, "They clean the house, on account of the waste of food, and afterward they wash the hands."

B.   The House of Hillel say, "If the waiter was a disciple of a sage, he gathers the scraps which contain as much as an olive's bulk.

C.   "And they wash the hands and afterward clean the house."

5:29 (Lieberman, P. 30, IS. 68–72)

A.   The House of Shammai say, "He holds the cup of wine in his right hand and spiced oil in his left hand."
He blesses over the wine and afterward blesses over the oil.

B.   And the House of Hillel say, "He holds the sweet oil in his right hand and the cup of wine in his left hand."

C.   He blesses over the oil and smears it on the head of the waiter. If the waiter was a disciple of a sage, he [the diner] smears it on the wall, because it is not praiseworthy for a disciple of a sage to go forth perfumed.

5:30 (Lieberman, PP. 30–31, IS. 72–75)

A.   R. Judah said, "The House of Shammai and the House of Hillel did not dispute concerning the blessing of the food, that it is first, or concerning the *Habdalah,* that it is at the end.
"Concerning what did they dispute?"
"Concerning the light and the spices, for—
"The House of Shammai say, 'Light and afterward spices.'
"And the House of Hillel say, 'Spices and afterward light.'"

5:30 (Lieberman, P. 31, IS. 75–77)

B.   He who enters his home at the end of the Sabbath blesses the wine, the light, the spices, and then says *Habdalah.*

C.   And if he has only one cup [of wine] he leaves it for after the meal and then says all [the liturgies] in order after [reciting the blessing for] it.

5:31 (Lieberman, P. 31, IS. 81–85)

A.   If a person has a light covered in the folds of his garment or in a lamp, and sees the flame but does not use its light, or uses its light but does not see its flame, he does not bless [that light]. [He says a blessing over the light only] when he both sees the flame and uses its light.
As to a lantern—even though he had not extinguished it (that is, it has been burning throughout the Sabbath), he recites a blessing over it.

B.   They do not bless over the light of gentiles. One may bless over [the flame of] an Israelite kindled from a gentile, or a gentile who kindled from an Israelite.

5:32 (Lieberman, P. 31, IS. 80–81)

In the house of study—
The House of Shammai say, "One [person] blesses for all of them."
And the House of Hillel say, "Each one blesses for himself."

Clearly, the Tosefta has a variety of materials. Some of the materials are freestanding, but some simply cite and gloss the Mishnah. We see in the following comparison just how these things come to the surface. I add in italics the amplificatory language of the Tosefta. That is where the Tosefta's character as a set of glosses to, and an elaborate, secondary development of, the Mishnah emerges.

THE TOSEFTA AND THE MISHNAH
TO MISHNAH TRACTATE BERAKHOT
CHAPTER EIGHT COMPARED

Mishnah	*Tosefta*
M. 8:1. A. These are the things which are between the House of Shammai and the House of Hillel in [regard to] the meal:	Tos. 5:25. [The] things which are between the House of Shammai and the House of Hillel [as regards] the meal:
B. The House of Shammai say, "One blesses the day, and afterward one blesses over the wine."	The House of Shammai say, "One blesses the day, and afterward one blesses over the wine, *for the day causes the wine to come, and the day is already sanctified, but the wine has not yet come.*"
And the House of Hillel say, "One blesses the wine, and afterward one blesses over the day."	And the House of Hillel say, "One blesses over the wine, and afterward one blesses the day, *for the wine causes the Sanctification of the day to be said.* "*Another matter: The blessing of the wine is continual, and the blessing of the day is not continual.*" *And the law is according to the words of the House of Hillel.*
M. 8:2.A. The House of Shammai say, "They wash the hands and afterward mix the cup."	Tos. 5:26. The House of Shammai say, "They wash the hands and afterward mix the cup, *lest the liquids which are on the outer surfaces of the cup may be made unclean on account of the hands, and they may go back and make the cup unclean.*"
And the House of Hillel say, "They mix the cup and afterward wash the hands."	The House of Hillel say, "*The outer surfaces of the cup are perpetually unclean.* "*Another matter: The washing of the hands is only [done] near [at the outset of] the meal.* "They mix the cup and afterward wash the hands."

8:3.A. The House of Shammai say, "He dries his hands on the napkin and lays it on the table." And the House of Hillel say, "On the cushion."

5:27. The House of Shammai say, "He dries his hands on the napkin and lays it on the table, *lest the liquids which are in the napkin may be made unclean on account of the pillow, and they may go and make the hands unclean.*"

The House of Hillel say, *"A case of doubt in regard to the condition of liquids so far as the hands are concerned is resolved as clean.*

"Another matter: Washing the hands does not pertain to unconsecrated food. But he dries his hands on the napkin and leaves it on the cushion lest the liquids which are in the pillow may be made unclean on account of the table, and they may go and render the food unclean."

M. 8:4.A. The House of Shammai say, "They clean the house and afterward wash the hands."

And the House of Hillel say, "They wash the hands and afterward clean the house."

Tos. 5:28. The House of Shammai say, "They clean the house *on account of the waste of food* and afterward wash the hands."

The House of Hillel say, *"If the waiter was a disciple of a sage, he gathers the scraps which contain as much as on olive's bulk.*

"They wash the hands and afterward clean the house."

8:5.A. The House of Shammai say, "Light, and food, and spices, and *Habdalah.*"

And the House of Hillel say, "Light, and spices, and food, and *Habdalah.*"

5:30. R. Judah said, *"The House of Shammai and the House of Hillel did not dispute concerning the blessing of the food, that it is first, and concerning the* Habdalah *that it is the end. Concerning what did they dispute? Concerning the light and the spices, for* the House of Shammai say, 'Light and *afterward* spices,' and the House of Hillel say, 'Spices and *afterward* light.'"

[NO EQUIVALENT.]

B. The House of Shammai say, "'Who created the light of the fire.'"

And the House of Hillel say, "'Who creates the lights of the fire.'"

M. 8:8.A. Wine came to them after the meal, and there is there only that cup—

B. The House of Shammai say, "He blesses over the wine and

Tos. 5:30 (Lieberman, p. 31, ls. 75–77). *He who enters his home at the end of the Sabbath blesses over the wine, the light, the spices, and then says* Habdalah.

afterward he blesses over the food."

And the House of Hillel say, "He blesses over the food and afterward he blesses over the wine."

[If wine came to them after the meal and] there is there only that cup the House of Shammai say, "He blesses the wine and then the food."

(The House of Hillel say, "He blesses the food and then the wine.")

M. 8:6.A. They do not bless the light or the spices of gentiles, nor the light or the spices of the dead, nor the light or the spices which are before an idol.

B. And they do not bless the light until they make use of its illumination.

M. 8:8.C. They respond *Amen* after an Israelite who blesses, and they do not respond *Amen* after a Samaritan who blesses, until one hears the entire blessing.

And if he has only one cup [of wine], he leaves it for after the meal and then says them all in order after [blessing] it.

If he has only one cup [of wine] [he leaves it for after the meal and then says them all in order, thus:] Wine, then food.

Tos. 5:31 B. They do not bless the light of gentiles. *An Israelite who kindled [a flame] from a gentile, or a gentile who kindled from an Israelite—one may bless [such a flame].*
Tos. 5:31 (Lieberman, p. 31, ls. 81–85). A. *If a person has a light covered in the folds of his garment or in a lamp, and he sees the flame but does not use its light, or uses its light but does not see its flame, he does not bless. [He blesses only] when he both sees the flame and uses its light.*
Tos. 5:21 (Lieberman, p. 28, ls. 41–2). *They answer "Amen" after a blessing with the divine name recited by a gentile.*
They do not answer *Amen* after a Samaritan who blesses *with the divine name* until they hear the entire blessing.

The pattern is clear. We simply cannot understand a line of the Tosefta without turning to the Mishnah. That means that the Tosefta passage before us must have been composed after the Mishnah was in hand, that is, after 200, and that the authorship of the Tosefta had in mind the clarification of the received document, the Mishnah.

THE TOSEFTA AND THE TWO TALMUDS: When we examine the two Talmuds' reading of the Mishnah, we shall see how both Talmuds' compositions' authors have cited the Tosefta passage and formed a commentary to that. So without access to the indicated passages, we cannot grasp what the Talmuds want to know about the Mishnah—which in this case is the sense of the Tosefta's wording in the Tosefta's commentary to the Mishnah. In this context the Talmuds form secondary expansions of the Tosefta, rather than commentaries directly upon the Mishnah. But, of course, we shall presently see that the two Talmuds accomplish their own goals, not only serving the purposes of the compilers of the Tosefta.

We come now to the first of the two Talmuds, the Talmud of the Land of Israel, a.k.a. the Yerushalmi. To understand what follows we must know that the Yerushalmi will address a chapter of the Mishnah by citing the Mishnah in small blocks, not reading it whole but only in phrases and clauses. Our special interest is in the place of the Tosefta in the Yerushalmi's structure. What we shall see is that the Yerushalmi is consecutive upon not the Mishnah but the Tosefta's reading of the Mishnah. I abbreviate the parts of the Yerushalmi's chapter that do not pertain to our problem, indicating cuts by an addition of three dots. What is important in what follows is the form of the document, and we shall not be detained with an elaborate explanation of the details. What we want to see is the sequence from the Mishnah through the Tosefta to the Talmud. Since that is the purpose of this abbreviated abstract, I facilitate matters by underlining the passages of the Yerushalmi at which the Tosefta defines discourse.

IV. YERUSHALMI TO MISHNAH BERAKHOT
CHAPTER EIGHT

8:1.   **The House of Shammai say, "One blesses the day and afterward one blesses over the wine."**
And the House of Hillel say, "One blesses over the wine and afterward one blesses the day."

I.   A.   *What is the reason of the House of Shammai?*
The Sanctification of the day causes the wine to be brought, and the man is already liable for the Sanctification of the day before the wine comes.
What is the reason of the House of Hillel?
The wine causes the Sanctification of the day to be said.
Another matter: Wine is perpetual, and the Sanctification is not perpetual. [What is always required takes precedence over what is required only occasionally.]

B.   R. Yosé said, "[It follows] from the opinions of them both that with respect to wine and *Habdalah,* wine comes first.
"Is it not the reason of the House of Shammai that the Sanctification of the day causes the wine to be brought, and here, since *Habdalah* does not cause wine to be brought, the wine takes precedence?
"Is it not the reason of the House of Hillel that the wine is perpetual and the Sanctification is not perpetual, and since the wine is perpetual, and the *Habdalah* is not perpetual, the wine comes first?"

C. R. Mana said, "From the opinions of both of them [it follows] that with respect to wine and Habdalah, *Habdalah* comes first.

"*Is it not the reason of the House of Shammai that* one is already obligated [to say] the Sanctification of the day before the wine comes, and here, since he is already obligated for *Habdalah* before the wine comes, *Habdalah* comes first?

"*Is it not the reason of the House of Hillel that* the wine causes the Sanctification of the Day to be said, and here, since the wine does not cause the *Habdalah* to be said, *Habdalah* comes first?"

D. R. Zeira said, "From the opinions of both of them [it follows] that they say *Habdalah* without wine, but they say the Sanctification only with wine."

E. *This is the opinion of R. Zeira, for* R. Zeira said, "They may say *Habdalah* over beer, *but they go from place to place* [in search of wine] *for the Sanctification.*"

II. A. R. Yosé b. Rabbi said, "They are accustomed there [in Babylonia], where there is no wine, for the prayer leader to go before the ark and say one blessing which is a summary of the seven, and complete it with, 'Who sanctifies Israel and the Sabbath Day.'"

B. *And thus the following poses a difficulty for the opinion of the House of Shammai: How should one act on the evenings of the Sabbath?* He *who was sitting and eating on the evening of the Sabbath,* and it grew dark and became Sabbath evening, and there was there only that one cup—[The House of Shammai say, "Wine, then food," and the House of Hillel say, "Food, then wine," so Mishnah 8:8].

Do you say he should leave it for the end of the meal and say all of them [the blessings] on it?

What do you prefer?

Should he [first] bless the day? The food takes precedence.

Should he bless the food? The wine takes precedence.

Should he bless the wine? The day takes precedence.

C. *We may infer* [the answer] *from this:*

If wine came to them after the meal, and there is there only that cup—

R. Ba said, "Because it [the wine's] is a brief blessing, [he says it first, for] perhaps he may forget and drink [the wine]. But here, since he says them all over the cup, he will not forget [to say a blessing over the wine in the cup]."

D. What, then, should he do according to the opinion of the House of Shammai?

Let him bless the food first, then bless the day, and then bless the wine.

E.   *And this poses difficulty for the opinion of the House of Hillel: How should one act at the end of the Sabbath?*

If he was sitting and eating on the Sabbath and it grew dark and the Sabbath came to an end, and there is there only that cup—

Do you say he should leave it [the wine] for after the meal and say them all on it?

What do you prefer?

Should he bless the wine? The food comes first.

Should he bless the food? The light comes first.

Should he bless the light? The *Habdalah* comes first.

F.   *We may infer* [the solution to the impasse] *from this:* R. Judah said, "The House of Shammai and the House of Hillel did not differ concerning the blessing of the food, that it comes first, nor concerning *Habdalah,* that it comes at the end.

"Concerning what did they differ?"

"Concerning the light and the spices, for:

"The House of Shammai say, 'The spices and afterward the light.'

"And the House of Hillel say, 'The light and afterward the spices.'"

[G.   R. Ba and R. Judah in the name of Rab (said), "The law is according to him who says, 'Spices and afterward light.'"]

H.   What should he do according to the opinion of the House of Hillel?

Let him bless the food, afterward bless the wine, and afterward bless the light.

III.   A.   As to [the beginning of the] festival day which coincides with the end of the Sabbath—

R. Yohanan said, "[The order of prayer is] wine, Sanctification, light, *Habdalah*."

Hanin bar Ba said in the name of Rab, "Wine, Sanctification, light, *Habdalah, Sukkah,* and season."

And did not Samuel rule according to this teaching of R. Hanina?

B.   R. Aha said in the name of R. Joshua b. Levi, "When a king goes out and the governor comes in, they accompany the king and afterward bring in the governor."

C.   Levi said, "Wine, *Habdalah,* light, Sanctification." . . .

8:2.   **The House of Shammai say, "They wash the hands and afterward mix the cup." And the House of Hillel say, "They mix the cup first and afterward wash the hands."**

I. A. *What is the reason of the House of Shammai?*
So that the liquids which are on the outer side of the cup may not be made unclean by his hands and go and make the cup unclean.
What is the reason of the House of Hillel?
The outer side of the cup is always unclean [so there is no reason to protect it from the hands' uncleanness].
Another matter: One should wash the hands immediately before saying the blessing.

B. *R. Biban in the name of R. Yohanan* [said], *"The opinion of the House of Shammai is in accord with R. Yosé and that of the House of Hillel with R. Meir, as we have learned there* [Mishnah Kelim 25:7–8]:
"[In all vessels an outer part and an inner part are distinguished, and also a part by which they are held.]
"R. Meir says, 'For hands which are unclean and clean.'
"R. Yosé said, 'This applies only to clean hands.'"

C. R. Yosé in the name of R. Shabbetai, and R. Hiyya in the name of R. Simeon b. Laqish [said], "For *Hallah* [dough-offering] and for washing the hands, a man goes four miles [to find water]."
R. Abbahu in the name of R. Yosé b. R. Hanina said, "This is what he said, '[If the water is] before him [that is, on his way, in his vicinity, or near at hand, he must proceed to it and wash]. But if it is behind him [that is, not on his way], they do not trouble him [to obtain it and wash].'" . . .

8:3. **The House of Shammai say, "He dries his hands on the napkin and puts it on the table."**
And the House of Hillel say, "On the cushion."

I. A. The Mishnah deals with either a table of marble [which is not susceptible to uncleanness] or a table that can be taken apart and is not susceptible to becoming unclean.

B. *What is the reason of the House of Shammai?*
So that the liquids which are on the napkin may not become unclean from the cushion and go and render his hands unclean.
And what is the reason of the House of Hillel?
The condition of doubt[ful uncleanness] with respect to the hands is always resolved as clean. [That is, when there is a condition of doubtful uncleanness, the decision with respect to the hands is always that the hands are clean.]
Another reason: The [question of the cleanness of] hands

does not apply to unconsecrated food [which in any case is not made unclean by unclean hands which are unclean in the second remove].

C. *And according to the House of Shammai, does* [the question of the cleanness of] hands [indeed] apply to unconsecrated food? . . .

8:4. **The House of Shammai say, "They clean the house and afterward wash the hands." And the House of Hillel say, "They wash the hands and afterward clean the house."**

I. A. *What is the reason of the House of Shammai?*

    B. Because of the waste of food.

    C. *And what is the reason of the House of Hillel?*

    D. If the servant is clever, he removes the crumbs which are less than an olive's bulk, and they wash their hands and afterward they clean the house.

8:5. **The House of Shammai say, "Light, and food, and spices, and *Habdalah.*" And the House of Hillel say, "Light, and spices, and food, and *Habdalah.*" The House of Shammai say, "'Who created the light of the fire.'" And the House of Hillel say, "'Who creates the lights of the fire.'"**

I. A. It was taught:

    B. R. Judah said, "The House of Shammai and the House of Hillel did not differ concerning the [blessing for] the meal, that it comes at the beginning, or concerning *Habdalah,* that it comes at the end. And concerning what did they differ? Concerning the light and spices, for the House of Shammai say, 'Spices and light.' And the House of Hillel say, 'Light and spices.'"

    C. R. Ba and R. Judah in the name of Rab [said], "The law is in accord with him who says, 'Spices and afterward light.' [That is, Judah's House of Shammai.]"

    D. The House of Shammai say, "The cup [should be] in his right hand, and the sweet oil in his left hand. He says [the blessing for] the cup and afterward says the blessing for the sweet oil."

    E. The House of Hillel say, "The sweet oil [should be] in his right hand and the cup in his left hand, and he says [the blessing for] the sweet oil and rubs it in the head of the servant. If the servant is a disciple of a sage, the sage rubs it on the wall, for it is not fitting for a disciple of a sage to go forth scented in public." . . .

    L. **[The House of Shammai say, "'Who created . . .'"]**

    M. According to the opinion of the House of Shammai, [one should say as the blessing for wine], "Who created the fruit of the vine" [instead of "who creates . . . ," as actually is said.]

N.   According to the opinion of the House of Hillel, [one should say,] "Who creates the fruit of the vine" [as is indeed the case].

O.   [The Shammaite reply:]

P.   The wine is newly created every year, but the fire is not newly created every hour. . . .

This truncated passage serves to show how heavily the Yerushalmi's compositions' authors have relied upon the Tosefta's reading of the Mishnah. Stated simply: without the Tosefta, there would have been no Talmud—at least, at the present passage of the Mishnah.

The same characterizes the second Talmud's approach to the same Mishnah paragraphs. We see immediately the simple fact that the Bavli's authorship appeals directly to the Tosefta, without addressing the program of the Yerushalmi. While, therefore, both Talmuds are organized as commentaries to the Mishnah, they are entirely autonomous of one another. The Babylonian Talmud does not expand upon the earlier one but forms its own discussions in accord with its own program. While the Bavli treats the Mishnah in the same way as does the Yerushalmi, in addition, the authorship of the second Talmud moved in a direction all its own, systematically commenting in large and cogent compositions upon not only the Mishnah but also Scripture, that is, on both the oral and the written Torahs. Once more, the sample abbreviates the text, giving only the parts relevant to an understanding of the character of the Tosefta. I again underline the Talmud's own contribution, as distinct from that of the Tosefta, and we shall see very clearly that that contribution consists of a close, analytical reading of the Tosefta, not the Mishnah.

V. BAVLI BERAKHOT TO MISHNAH TRACTATE BERAKHOT CHAPTER EIGHT THE HOUSES' DISPUTES

I.   [A]   [51b] *Gemara: Our rabbis have taught:*

[B]   **The things that are between the House of Shammai and the House of Hillel in** [regard to] **a meal:**

[C]   **The House of Shammai say, "One blesses over the day and afterward blesses over the wine, for the day causes the wine to come, and the day has already been sanctified, while the wine has not yet come."**

[D]   **And the House of Hillel say, "He blesses over the wine and afterward blesses over the day, for the wine causes the Sanctification to be said.**

[E]   **"Another matter: The blessing over the wine is perpetual, and the blessing over the day is not perpetual. Between that which is perpetual and that which is not perpetual, that which is perpetual takes precedence."**

[F]   And the law is in accordance with the words of the House of Hillel.

[G]   *What is the purpose of* "another matter"?

[H]   *If you should say that there* [in regard to the opinion of the House of Shammai] *two* [reasons are given] *and here* [in regard to the opinion of the House of Hillel] *one, here too* [in respect to the House of Hillel], *there are two* [reasons, the second being]: "The blessing of the wine is perpetual and the blessing of the day is not perpetual. That which is perpetual takes precedence over that which is not perpetual."

[I]   And the law is in accord with the opinion of the House of Hillel.

[J]   *This is obvious* [that the law is in accord with the House of Hillel], *for the echo has gone forth* [and pronounced from heaven the decision that the law follows the opinion of the House of Hillel].

[K]   *If you like, I can argue that* [this was stated] before the echo.

[L]   *And if you like, I can argue that* it was after the echo, and [the passage is formulated in accord with the [opinion of] [52a] R. Joshua, who stated, "They do not pay attention to an echo [from heaven]."

[M]   *And is it the reasoning of the House of Shammai that the blessing of the day is more important?*

[N]   *But has a Tanna* [an authority of the time of the Mishnah] *not taught:* "He who enters his house at the close of the Sabbath blesses over the wine and the light and the spices and afterward he says *Habdalah*. And if he has only one cup, he leaves it for after the food and then says the other blessings in order after it." [*Habdalah* is the blessing of the day, yet comes last!]

[O]   *But lo, on what account* [do you say] *this is the view of the House of Shammai? Perhaps it is the House of Hillel*['s opinion]?

[P]   *Let* [such a thought] *not enter your mind, for the Tanna teaches:* "Light and afterward spices." *And of whom have you heard who holds this opinion? The House of Shammai, as a Tanna has taught:*

[Q]   Judah said, "The House of Shammai and the House of Hillel did not differ concerning the [blessing of the] food, that it is at first, and the *Habdalah,* that it is at the end.

[R]   "Concerning what did they dispute? Concerning the light and the spices.

[S]   **"For the House of Shammai say, 'Light and afterward spices.'**

[T]   **"And the House of Hillel say, 'Spices and afterward the light.'"**

[U]   *And on what account* [do you suppose that] *it is the House of Shammai as* [interpreted by] *R. Judah? Perhaps it is [a teaching in accord with] the House of Hillel [as interpreted by] R. Meir?*

[V]   *Do not let such a thing enter your mind, for lo, a Tanna teaches here in our Mishnah:* The House of Shammai say, "Light and food and spices and *Habdalah.*"

[W]   And the House of Hillel say, "Light and spices, food and *Habdalah.*"

[X]   *But there, in the* "baraita," *lo he has taught:* "If he has only one cup, he leaves it for after the food and then says the other blessings in order after it."

[Y]   *From this it is to be inferred that it is the House of Shammai's teaching, according to the* [interpretation] *of R. Judah.*

[Z]   *In any event there is a problem* [for the House of Shammai now give precedence to reciting a blessing for the wine over blessing the day].

[AA]   *The House of Shammai suppose that the coming of the holy day is to be distinguished from its leaving. As to the coming of the* [holy] *day, the earlier one may bring it in, the better. As to the leaving of the festival day, the later one may take leave of it, the better, so that it should not seem to us as a burden.*

[BB]   *And do the House of Shammai hold the opinion that* Grace requires a cup [of wine]? *And lo, we have learned:* [If] wine came to them after the food, and there is there only that cup, the House of Shammai say, "He blesses over the wine and afterward blesses over the food." [So Grace is said *without* the cup.]

[CC]   *Does this not mean that he blesses it and drinks* [it]?

[DD]   *No. He blesses it and leaves it.*

[EE]   But has not a master said, "He that blesses must [also] taste [it]."

[FF]   *He does taste it.*

[GG]   And has not a master said, "Tasting it is spoiling it."

[HH]   *He tastes it with his hand* [finger].

[II]   And has not a master said, "The cup of blessing requires a [fixed] measure." *And lo, he diminishes it from its fixed measure.*

[JJ]   [We speak of a situation in which] *he has more than the fixed measure.*

[KK]   *But lo, has it not been taught:* If there is there *only* that cup . . . [so he has not more].

[LL]   *There is not enough for two, but more than enough for one.*

[MM]   *And has not R. Hiyya taught:* House of Shammai say, "He blesses over the wine and drinks it, and afterward he says Grace."

[NN]   Then we have two Tannas [traditions] in respect to the opinion of the House of Shammai.

II.   [A]   **The House of Shammai say,** ["They wash the hands and afterward mix the cup]. . . .

[B]   *Our Rabbis have taught:*

[C]   **The House of Shammai say, "They wash the hands and**

afterward mix the cup, for if you say they mix the cup first, [against this view is] **a** [precautionary] **decree to prevent the liquids on the outer sides of the cup, which are unclean by reason of his hands'** [touching them], **from going back and making the cup unclean."**

[D]   *But will not the hands make the cup itself unclean* [without reference to the liquids]?

[E]   The hands are in the second remove of uncleanness, and the [object unclean in] the second remove of uncleanness cannot [then] render [another object unclean] in the third [remove] in respect to profane foods, [but only to Heave-offering]. But [this happens] only by means of liquids [unclean in the first remove].

III.   [A]   **And the House of Hillel say, "They mix the cup and afterward wash the hands, for if you say they wash the hands first,** [against this view is] **a** [precautionary] **decree lest the liquids which are** [already] **on the hands become unclean on account of the cup and go and render the hands unclean."**

[B]   *But will not the cup* [itself] *make the hands unclean?*

[C]   A vessel cannot render a man unclean.

[D]   *But will they* [the hands] *not render the liquids which are in it* [the cup] *unclean?*

[E]   *Here we are dealing* with a vessel the outer part of which has been made unclean by liquid. The inner part is clean but the outer part is unclean. *Thus we have learned:*

[F]   [If] a vessel is made unclean on the outside by liquid, the outside is unclean, [52b] but its inside and its rim, handle, and haft are clean. If, however, the inside is unclean, the whole [cup] is unclean.

[G]   *What, then, do they* [the Houses] *dispute?*

[H]   *The House of Shammai hold that* it is prohibited to make use of a vessel whose outer parts are unclean by liquids, as a decree on account of the drippings. [There is] *no* [reason] *to decree* lest the liquids on the hands be made unclean by the cup.

[I]   *And the House of Hillel reckon that* it is permitted to make use of a vessel whose outer part is made unclean by liquids, *for drippings are unusual. But there is reason to take care* lest the liquids which are on the hands may be made unclean by the cup.

[J]   **Another matter:** [So that] **immediately upon the washing of the hands** [may come] **the meal** [itself].

[K]   *What is the reason for this additional explanation?*

[L]   *This is what the House of Hillel said to the House of Shammai: "According to your reasoning, in saying that* it is prohibited to make use of a cup whose outer parts are unclean, *we decree on account of the drippings. But even so,* [our opinion] *is better,* for **immediately upon the washing of the hands** [should come] **the meal."**

IV. [A] **The House of Shammai say, "He dries his hand on the napkin. . . ."**

[B] *Our rabbis have taught:*

[C] **The House of Shammai say, "He wipes his hands with the napkin and lays it on the table, for if you say, 'on the cushion,'** [that view is wrong, for it is a precautionary] **decree lest the liquids which are on the napkin become unclean on account of the cushion and go back and render the hands unclean."**

[D] *And will not the cushion* [itself] *render the napkin unclean?*

[E] A vessel cannot make a vessel unclean.

[F] *And will not the cushion* [itself] *make the man unclean?*

[G] A vessel cannot make a man unclean.

[H] **And the House of Hillel say, "'On the cushion,' for if you say, 'on the table,'** [that opinion is wrong, for it is a] **decree lest the liquids become unclean on account of the table and go and render the food unclean."**

[I] *But will not the table render the food which is on it unclean?*

[J] *We here deal with a table which is unclean in the second remove,* and something unclean in the second remove does not render something unclean in the third remove in respect to unconsecrated food, except by means of liquids [which are always unclean in the first remove].

[K] *What* [principle] *do they dispute?*

[L] *The House of Shammai reckon that* it is prohibited to make use of a table unclean in the second remove, as a decree on account of those who eat Heave-offering [which is rendered unfit by an object unclean in the second remove].

[M] *And the House of Hillel reckon that* it is permitted to make use of a table unclean in the second remove, for those who eat Heave-offering [the priests] are careful.

[N] Another matter: There is no scriptural requirement to wash the hands before eating unconsecrated food.

[O] *What is the purpose of* "another explanation"?

[P] *This is what the House of Hillel said to the House of Shammai: If you ask what is the difference in respect to food, concerning which we take care, and in respect to the hands, concerning which we do not take care—even in this regard* [our opinion] *is preferable,* for there is no scriptural requirement concerning the washing of the hands before eating unconsecrated food.

[Q]   It is better that the hands should be made unclean, *for there is no scriptural basis for* [washing] *them,* and let not the food be made unclean, *concerning which there is a scriptural basis* [for concern about its uncleanness]. . . .

We now see what it means to state that the Tosefta is the first talmud, that is to say, the first sustained and systematic commentary to the Mishnah. In the two Talmuds' reading of the Mishnah, the sequence is the same: (1) the Mishnah paragraph; (2) the Tosefta's amplification of the reasons for the Mishnah's rule; (3) the Talmuds' clarification of the wording and reasoning of the Tosefta's amplification of the reasons for the Mishnah's rule. The passage places the Tosefta into a different light from the one that at the outset seemed to illuminate matters.

True, the Tosefta is not a freestanding document, presenting its own viewpoint, propositions, and even system. It is secondary, derivative, dependent. Were the whole of rabbinic literature beyond Scripture, on the one side, and the Mishnah, on the other, to conform to the traits of the Tosefta, that literature would hardly attract much attention. It would strike later generations as dull, derivative, and merely traditional. But the Tosefta's characteristics—referential, dependent, episodic—and its authors' failure to endow their writing with intrinsically attractive traits of form and interesting aspects of logic and proposition should not obscure the importance of the document in context. And it is in context that the Tosefta gains its critical importance.

For the Tosefta may be compared to a hinge, on which a door swings; the Tosefta forms the hinge for many doors—otherwise closed before us—in both Talmuds. And it is of course the Mishnah's first talmud. Not only so, but as a talmud, the Tosefta succeeds in ways in which the later Talmuds do not. That is simply because the Tosefta covers nearly the whole of the Mishnah, nearly all lines of all tractates, while the two Talmuds take up only a restricted selection of the Mishnah tractates. The Talmuds' arbitrary selectivity—thirty-nine in the Yerushalmi of the Mishnah's sixty-two tractates, and the Bavli thirty-seven of the Mishnah's tractates—mark both documents as deceptive: picking and choosing, they form of the Mishnah a statement to their own tastes, the act of choice representing a powerful judgment indeed.

So while the Tosefta remains a strange, inaccessible piece of writing, and while the Tosefta in no way forms a document in the ways in which the other writings of rabbinic literature constitutes documents, still, the Tosefta stands firm as one of the most important compilations in that entire canon. It is the sole document in rabbinic literature to set forth an authentically traditional statement. Its compilers received the Mishnah and systematically, in an orderly way, clarified or amplified nearly every line. The Tosefta—and not the two Talmuds—provides the key to the Mishnah, both Talmuds frequently acknowledge that fact, and those later commentators to the Mishnah who understood that fact made of the Mishnah the profound document that its original authors intended it to be.

VII

The Talmud of the Land of Israel

1.

Identifying the Document

WE COME NOW TO THE TWO TALMUDS, THE TALMUD OF THE LAND OF ISRAEL, ca. 400 C.E., and the Talmud of Babylonia, ca. 600 C.E. Since the second of the two forms the definitive statement of the Judaism of the dual Torah and defines the curriculum of Torah study in the very centers in which the Torah is studied as God's word and will for Israel, we do well to begin by considering the purpose that these documents were meant to serve. The Talmuds propose to state in writing the basic rules of the social order, and to show us how to discover the right rule, based on the principles God has made known in the Torah, for the affairs of every-day life. The Talmuds are documents full of debates on erudite and esoteric questions. But in the debates about fine points of law, ritual, and theology, "our sages of blessed memory" formulated through concrete examples the rules of right thinking and accurate formulation in words of God's will for the here and now. For they held that the Torah is given to purify the hearts of humanity, and that what God really wants is the heart. But there, in the center of life, in the streets and homes of the holy community, Israel, what does that mean? It is through close and careful thinking about little things that "our sages" brought the Torah's great principles into the everyday world of ordinary people. The media of language, logic, and law express the message of the Torah of Sinai. The Talmuds show us how, for the purposes of portraying the entirety of the social order, its culture and its politics alike, people write in signals an account of their modes of thought and how these are to be replicated anytime and anywhere.

The Talmuds demand attention because they constitute the foundation documents of a social order, writings that were formed by political-intellectual figures who proposed to say in a single place how they thought Israel under God's rule through the Torah as they taught it should form a political entity and a cogent, albeit composite, society. At stake in protracted and sometimes hard-to-follow arguments is the demonstration that the way people formulated their thought responded to the manner in which they perceived the social world they proposed to set forth. The issue of general intelligibility therefore pertains to the interplay between writing and the social order. For the documents under study here set forth a detailed account of intellectuals' fabrication; the community life of an entire society: its politics, economics, philosophy; its culture, mode of thought, manner of appreciation; its place in the here and now and under the aspect of eternity: the Godly society as God would have it.

These Talmuds are not unique in humanity's efforts to put down in words the social world people are meant to form. They may be compared to such visions as those of More's *Utopia* or Plato's *Republic* or Aristotle's *Politics,* though More, Plato, and Aristotle might have had difficulty with the comparison of their books with the book produced by "our sages of blessed memory." Unlike *Utopia*, the *Republic,* and the *Politics,* our sages of blessed memory wrote a book that really did form the constitution and bylaws, the prescription for thought and action, reasoning and criticism, of an enduring social order.

The second of the two documents, the Bavli, enjoys a prime place among writings that really did accomplish their authors' purposes. More, Plato, and Aristotle by the same measure failed. None wrote for an "Israel," a specific group in the here and now, and none was read by an "Israel" in quest of answers to the question, how shall we in all our particularity form the Godly society, the holy community revealed from heaven. So More left literature, Plato a masterpiece of political fantasy, yielding catastrophe when fully realized in Fascism, and Aristotle a fructifying theory of merely intellectual consequence, ignored by the prince whom he meant to serve as pedagogue. Only when taken over by medieval Christian philosophy did Aristotle find a hearing for his *Politics* and for his economics. But our sages of blessed memory left as their monument not a book but the enduring social world that read their book and found in society and its relationships the medium for realizing the Torah's message: an amazing result of merely writing a book. Our problem is, when we actually read the book, we find it picayune and nit-picking, full of dry debates on matters of no practical consequence. When we respond in that way, we face the kind of writing that these sages intentionally set forth: God lives in the details, so we have to learn to think about the details—but to think in accord with large and encompassing principles. The challenge is to discover the patience to follow an extended, sometimes meandering argument about matters of no practical consequence. The reward, when we do so, is to see how intellectuals used their best powers to make sense of the endless details of ordinary life that each of us knows as the social world, where we live. Now to the examination of the documents in all their splendor.

First, to define matters: a talmud—generically defined—is a sustained, systematic amplification and analysis of passages of the Mishnah and other teachings alongside the Mishnah, inclusive of the Tosefta, that are accorded the status of Tannaite authority. Of the genus talmud there are two species, the Tosefta on the one side, the two Talmuds on the other. These further subspeciate into the Talmud of the Land of Israel (a.k.a. the Yerushalmi), ca. 400,[1] and the Talmud of Babylonia (a.k.a. the Bavli), ca. 600. The former treats the first four divisions of the Mishnah; the latter, the second through the fifth; each is independent of the other, the two meeting only at parts of the Mishnah and sharing, further, some sayings attributed to authorities after the Mishnah; but these the documents' respective authorships read each in its own way.

The genus talmud as a source of information in clarification of the Mishnah was established by the Tosefta; but there, as we have seen in our review of that document, information was left inert, the Tosefta's framers, knowing nothing of dialectics (other than what they found on rare occasion in the Mishnah itself).

---

[1] For further reading and bibliography on the topic of this chapter, see the following:

Baruch M. Bokser, "An Annotated Bibliographical Guide to the Study of the Palestinian Talmud," in Neusner, *Study of Ancient Judaism,* II, pp. 1–120.

Bowker, pp. 64–65.

Abraham Goldberg, "The Palestinian Talmud" (Tannaim and Amoraim; Palestinian and Babylonian Talmud; importance of the Palestinian Talmud; the Palestinian Amoraim and the Mishna; relationship to Mishna, Tosefta, and Baraitot; editing; authority; bibliography; manuscripts of the Palestinian Talmud [by Michael Krupp]), in Safrai, *Literature of the Sages,* pp. 303–22.

Maccoby's introduction does not make reference to this document at all, though he does treat documents of its period.

Louis I. Rabinowitz, "Talmud, Jerusalem," in *Encyclopaedia Judaica* 15:772–779: contents; characteristics; acceptance of the two Talmuds; editions; commentaries.

Stemberger-Strack, pp. 182–207: terms; the name; contents and structure; the absence of many tractates; repetitions within the Palestinian Talmud (numerous, literal repetitions of long sections); origin of the Yerushalmi; redaction, probably ca. 410–420, in Tiberias; nature of the redaction; sources; the Mishnah of the Yerushalmi; Midrashic material in the Yerushalmi; Babylonian traditions in the Yerushalmi; the text; manuscripts; printed editions; translation.

This writer's introduction to the Yerushalmi is in *The Talmud of the Land of Israel. A Preliminary Translation and Explanation.* Chicago: University of Chicago Press: 1985. XXXV. *Introduction. Taxonomy.* On the place of the Yerushalmi in the history of Judaism, see *Judaism in Society: The Evidence of the Yerushalmi. Toward the Natural History of a Religion.* Chicago, 1983: University of Chicago Press. Second printing, with a new preface: Atlanta, 1991: Scholars Press for South Florida Studies in the History of Judaism; and *Judaism and Christianity in the Age of Constantine. Issues of the Initial Confrontation.* Chicago, 1987: University of Chicago Press. Further discussion is in *The Yerushalmi. The Talmud of the Land of Israel. An Introduction.* Northvale, N.J., 1993: Jason Aronson, Inc.

What characterizes the other species of talmud, the one that encompasses the two Talmuds, is the translation of information into principle, the systematic formation of argument, the translation of facts, the raw materials of analytical inquiry, through the modes of thought of applied reason and practical logic, into systemic truth.

The subspecies of the species formed of the two Talmuds must be differentiated. What the first Talmud contributed was the definition of a talmud in which received facts ("traditions") were treated as active and consequential, requiring analysis and deep thought. The second Talmud transformed thought into argument, subordinating fact to the fully realized processes of dialectical argument and reasoning. So the three talmuds, the Tosefta, the Talmud of the Land of Israel, and the Talmud of Babylonia, in sequence expanded the definition of the genus talmud, each adding an important component of that definition.

Both Talmuds—Yerushalmi, Bavli—are formed into commentaries to some of the same passages of the Mishnah. Both are laid out in the same way, that is, as ad hoc treatments of phrases or even whole paragraphs of the Mishnah, the two Talmuds are identical in form, species of a genus. The two Talmuds defined Mishnah commentary in a distinctive way, through their active program of supplying not merely information but guidance on its meaning: a program of inquiry, a set of consequential issues, in place of mere information. That program would be fully realized only in the second, and last, of the two Talmuds.

But both Talmuds in common exhibit definitive traits as well. Specifically they share the program of harmonizing one rule or principle with another. Both, furthermore, propose to uncover the scriptural foundation of the Mishnah's rules. In common, therefore, they undertake the sustained demonstration of the theology of the Torah: its perfection, on the one side; its unity (oral and written), on the other. Because of that fact, we may properly speak of "the Talmuds," since both do one thing, though the second does another in addition. In this chapter we shall examine what the two Talmuds have in common; in the next, we shall differentiate the second from the first.

To begin with, the two Talmuds look alike. That is because both comment on the same prior text, the Mishnah. Both take up a few sentences of that prior text and paraphrase and analyze them. Both ask the same questions, e.g., clarifying the language of the Mishnah, identifying the scriptural foundations of the Mishnah's rules, comparing the Mishnah's rules with those of the Tosefta or other texts of Tannaite status. They furthermore are comparable because they organize their materials in the same way. They moreover take up pretty much the same topical agenda, in common selecting some divisions of the Mishnah and ignoring others, agreeing in particular to treat the matters of everyday practice, as distinct from theory, covered by the Mishnah's divisions of Appointed Times, Women, and Damages. Both documents are made up of already available compositions and composites, which we may identify, in each document, by reference to the same literary traits or indications of completion prior to inclusion in the Talmuds. So they exhibit traits of shared literary policy.

In both, moreover, we find not only the same received document, the Mishnah, but—as we saw in Chapter 6—occasionally also citations of, and allusions to, the same supplementary collection to the Mishnah, the Tosefta, and also a further kind of saying, one bearing the marks of formalization and memorization that serve to classify it as authoritative ("Tannaite") but external to the composition of the Mishnah and the compilation of the Tosefta. The points of coincidence are more than formal, therefore, since both Talmuds cite the same Mishnah tractates, at some points the same Tosefta passages, and also, from time to time, the same external Tannaite formulations.

Not only are the two Talmuds alike, but in their canonical context, the two Talmuds also are different from all other documents of the Judaism of the dual Torah in the formative age. First of all, among Mishnah-centered writings in the canon—the Tosefta, Sifra, the two Sifrés, the Bavli, and the Yerushalmi—only the two Talmuds conduct sustained analytical inquiries over a broad range of problems. The Tosefta is not an analytical document; we have to supply the missing analytical program (as the authors of the two Talmuds, but particularly the Bavli, themselves discovered early on). Sifra treats the Mishnah in only a single aspect, while the two Talmuds cover that aspect generously, along with a far more elaborate program. They pursue no encompassing exegetical program. So the two Talmuds are unique in context.

While set forth in a manner that implicitly bears the attributes of a commentary, that is, a mere amplification of received truth, as commentaries to the Mishnah, the two Talmuds express, in a cogent and coherent way, the topical, rhetorical, and logical choices, forming well-crafted statements and viewpoints, of their respective authorships, as we shall now see. The two Talmuds therefore comprise a genus, talmud, made up of two species, the Talmud of the Land of Israel and the Talmud of Babylonia. But—as we shall see in Chapter 8—what speciates vastly overrides what unites the species into a genus; the form is common, and we shall see, much of the burden of thought. Where the Talmuds differ, it is in the deepest layers of discourse, but not on the surface of the medium or in the messages they set forth.

2.

TRANSLATIONS INTO ENGLISH

The only complete translation into any European language is this writer's *Talmud of the Land of Israel. A Preliminary Translation and Explanation* (Chicago, 1984–93: University of Chicago Press) I–XXXV. Tractates in that translation were contributed in addition by Tzvee Zahavy, Roger Brooks, Richard S. Sarason, Alan J. Avery-Peck, Martin Jaffee, B. Barry Levi, and Edward Goldman.

3.

RHETORIC AND LANGUAGES

The distinctive rhetorical patterns of interest here concern the formation of composites and of large-scale compositions, not of individual paragraphs as in the case of the Mishnah. We consider the rhetoric and languages of both documents together.

Both Talmuds invariably do to the Mishnah one of these four things, and each of these procedures will ordinarily be expressed in patterned language. It suffices here to classify the types of patterns:

[1] text criticism;

[2] exegesis of the meaning of the Mishnah, including glosses and amplifications;

[3] addition of scriptural proof texts of the Mishnah's central propositions; and

[4] harmonization of one Mishnah passage with another such passage or with a statement of the Tosefta.

Each of these types of compositions follows a well-defined form, so that if we were given only an account in abstract terms of the arrangement of subject and predicate or a simple account of the selection of citation language (e.g., "as it is said," "our rabbis have taught,") we could readily predict the purpose of the composition or composite. So formal traits accompany the purpose of the commentary compositions and other compositions and composites and permit differentiation of one type from another.

The first two of these four procedures remain wholly within the narrow frame of the Mishnah passage subject to discussion. Therefore, in the natural order of things, what the two Talmuds will find interesting in a given Mishnah passage will respond to the same facts and commonly will do so in much the same way. The second pair take an essentially independent stance vis-à-vis the Mishnah pericope at hand. Part of the rhetorical convention of the Talmuds governs the order in which types of compositions—Mishnah text criticism, exegesis, scriptural proof texts, and the like—are set forth. Ordinarily, the order for both Talmuds is the same as given above. While both Talmuds conform to complex and distinctive rhetorical programs, what makes them different from all other documents of rabbinic literature is not only rhetoric but logic, to which we turn forthwith.

THE BILINGUAL CHARACTER OF THE TALMUDS AND ITS TAXONOMIC IMPLICATIONS: Both Talmuds utilize both Hebrew and Aramaic, and an aspect of the rhetorical program that guides their writers and compilers therefore involves their use of two languages in a single piece of writing. Documents that utilize two or more languages but are addressed to a single audience convey information not only through what is said but also through the language in which a message is set forth. In the Talmuds the choice of language carried in particular a message, one of classification. A reader or listener who read or heard Aramaic immediately knew what kind of discourse was under way, and when Hebrew was used, the reader or listener forthwith understood the status and purpose of the discourse that was then subject to representation. The selection of one language over another gave the signal that sayings, and, more to the point, whole paragraphs and even long and sustained passages in one language were to be classified in one way, sayings or entire compositions in another, in a different way. And that taxonomic function served by the choice of language bore no relationship to the circumstance of time, place, personality, let alone the original words that were said; the same named speakers are given statements in two languages, depending upon the purpose served by a given statement within the unfolding of discourse.

"Language"—Hebrew or Aramaic—here refers to the basic sentences and paragraphs in which a whole thought is expressed. These invariably obey the rules of syntax and grammar, follow the rhetorical rules, of one language and not some other. If Aramaic is the paramount language, then even though Hebrew occurs, it will always bear marks that it is being quoted for a purpose dictated by the discourse that is in Aramaic: Hebrew will be illustrative; Aramaic, determinative. If the language of a passage is Hebrew, then the occurrence of an Aramaic phrase, e.g., a sentence that is represented as a quotation of what someone says in everyday parlance, will not affect the grammar and syntax (not to mention the word choices) of the whole. Ordinarily, therefore, the smallest rhetorical signals will wholly conform to the conventions of one language, and when the other language occurs, it is by way of quotation, on the one side, or utilization of technical terms, on the other. For example, a sentence wholly written in Aramaic may quote a verse of Scripture in biblical Hebrew, or a sentence of the Mishnah in Middle Hebrew. But the structure of that sentence will be in Aramaic. That is not an example of bi- or multilingual writing at all, any more than using *terminus technicus,* rather than "technical term," would have made the penultimate sentence a mixture of Latin and English. It is a sentence in English, using two Latin words.

In the Talmuds what is said in Hebrew is represented as authoritative and formulates a normative thought or rule. What is said in Aramaic is analytical and commonly signals an argument and formulates a process of inquiry and criticism. That is how language serves a taxonomic purpose: Hebrew is the language of the result; Aramaic, of the way by which the result is achieved; Hebrew is the formulation of the decision; Aramaic, of the work of deliberation. Each language serves to classify what is said in that language, and we always know where we stand, in a given process of thought and the exposition of thought, by reference to the language that is used at that particular place in the sustained discourse to which we are witness. That fixed rule, utilizing language for the purpose of classifying what is said in that language, characterizes only the Talmuds. All other documents treated here as canonical, except Daniel, Ezra, and Nehemiah, are monolingual, ordinarily in Hebrew, so that where Aramaic occurs, it is generally a brief allusion to something deemed external to what the author wishes to say in his own behalf, e.g., a citation of everyday speech, invariably assumed to be in Aramaic.

Where Hebrew is used, it is ordinarily for the purpose of setting forth facts, deriving from authoritative writings, on the one side, or authoritative figures, on the other. Where Aramaic is used, it is ordinarily for the purpose of analyzing facts, though it may serve also to set forth cases that invariably are subordinated to the analytical task. And the choice of language has no bearing upon the identity of the speaker. The simple fact that in the pages of the Talmuds the same figures "speak" in both Hebrew and Aramaic proves that at stake is not merely "how people said things," let alone ipsissima verba; if for instance Yohanan in the Land of Israel or Samuel and Rab in Babylonia are sometimes represented as speaking in Hebrew and other times in Aramaic, the function served by using the two languages, respectively, must form the point of inquiry into how and why these languages are used where and when they make their appearance. The choice of language clearly conveys part of the message that the authorship means to set forth, signaling to the reader precisely what is happening at any given point. Along these same lines, a story told in Aramaic yields a formulation of a general rule or conclusion, presented in (Middle) Hebrew. Once more, the function of the language that is chosen, within the same sustained unit of thought, clearly is to make one thought in one way, another thought in a different way.

Where we find Hebrew, the language of quotation, it will commonly signal one of three facts which, through the very choice of language, our author wishes to tell us:

[1] a passage is from the Hebrew Scriptures;

[2] a passage is from the Mishnah or the Tosefta (or from a corpus of sayings out of which the Tosefta as we have it was selected; for our purposes that is a distinction that makes no difference);

[3] a statement that is authoritative and forms a normative formulation, a rule to be generalized and obeyed even where not from the Mishnah or Scripture, but from a named or anonymous authority of the time of the document itself.

While biblical Hebrew differs from Middle or Mishnaic Hebrew, the use, in the Talmuds, of either kind of Hebrew invariably is the same. It is to set forth a normative statement. The fact that sayings of sages will be (re)formulated into the same Hebrew as the Mishnah's conveys the further claim, of course, that those sayings enjoy the same standing and authority as what is in Scripture or Mishnah, and that allegation clearly is signaled by the choice of Hebrew for, e.g., something said by Samuel, Rab, or Yohanan. That the issue is one of authority and standing of what is said is furthermore demonstrated by a rhetorical signal, which assigns to the authority of a professional memorizer of traditions, or Tannaite master, a given formulation. Whenever we find that signal in any of its variations, all of them formed out of the same Hebrew letters, T and N, with a Y or an A (aleph), what follows invariably is in (Middle) Hebrew. The voice of the document is in

Aramaic, and that is where the authors of compositions and framers of composite speak.

4.
LOGIC OF COHERENT DISCOURSE

The two Talmuds are made up of sizable systematic statements of propositions, syllogistic arguments fully worked out and elegantly exposed. But these are joined together not into a sustained essay on a given subject, like a dialogue of Plato or tractate of Aristotle, but as commentaries to the Mishnah or to Scripture and the Mishnah. It follows that two principles of logical discourse are at play. For the statement of propositions, sizable arguments, and proofs, the usual philosophical logic dictates the joining of sentence to sentences and the composition of paragraphs, that is, completed thoughts. For the presentation of the whole, the other logic, the one deriving from imputed, fixed associations, external to the propositions at hand, serves equally well. The framers of the Talmuds drew together the results of work that people prior to their own labors already had completed. Available as both completed documents and also sizable components, statements awaiting agglutination or conglomeration in finished documents, these ready-made materials were sewn together with only one kind of thread. Whatever the place and role of the diverse types of logics that formed the compositions, through their fusion of distinct logics, the framers of the two Talmuds made whatever they chose of their inheritance serve the distinctive purpose of their documents.

The two Talmuds therefore are made up of compositions, complete in themselves, which have been formed into composites. The framers of the Talmuds then resort to two distinct logics of coherent discourse to form of their materials whole and cogent documents. Philosophical logic ordinarily holds together into cogent paragraphs the discrete sentences of a given composition. The logic of fixed association then connects into protracted statements of a cogent character otherwise unrelated sequential sentences, and also joins into sizable compositions entire paragraphs that on their own, through their own propositions, in no way coalesce. The authorship of the Talmuds in the making of medium- and large-scale logical connections, thus resorted to two distinct principles of cogent discourse: the one of propositional connection within completed units of thought, a connection discovered through the pursuit of reasoned speculative inquiry; and the second, of fixed associative connection between and among those same completed units of thought, producing large-scale compositions.

Sizable numbers of the completed units of thought of the Talmuds find inner cogency through the development of a proposition concerning a given theme. Overall, these units of completed thought are linked to one another through the connections supplied for the Talmuds extrinsically by both the Mishnah and Scripture. As we noted in Chapter 1, the framers of the Talmuds had in hand a tripartite corpus of inherited materials awaiting composition into a final, closed document. First, they took up materials, in various states and stages of completion, pertinent to the Mishnah or to the principles of laws that the Mishnah had originally brought to articulation. Second, they had in hand received materials, again in various conditions, pertinent to the Scripture, both as the Scripture related to the Mishnah and also as the Scripture laid forth its own narratives. Third, they possessed freestanding compositions and composites, which did not address the Mishnah or Scripture but were organized topically. And that fact points to the way in which the logic of fixed association governed their work.

Here is an example, drawn from the Bavli, of the way in which the Talmuds' framers made use of the logic of fixed association in that dual way that involved appeal for cogency to both the Mishnah and Scripture. We revert to Mishnah tractate Sanhedrin Chapter Two, now as the Bavli's authorship presents the matter, since that passage has already shown us the working of the propositional logic that governs throughout the Mishnah. Since our interest is in identifying passages in which both the Mishnah and Scripture serve to hold together discrete compositions, ordinarily of a propositional character, I give only highlights. These will then illustrate the workings of the logic of fixed association in the two Talmuds. Where numbers appear in square brackets, they refer to the Bavli's pagination. Verses of Scripture are given in italics, Mishnah and Tosefta citations in boldface type.

BAVLI TRACTATE SANHEDRIN TO MISHNAH TRACTATE SANHEDRIN 2:3

A. **[If] [the king] suffers a death in his family, he does not leave the gate of his palace.**

B. **R. Judah says, "If he wants to go out after the bier, he goes out,**

C. **"for thus we find in the case of David, that he went out after the bier of Abner,**

D. **"since it is said, 'And King David followed the bier' (2 Sam. 3:31)."**

E. **They said to him, "This action was only to appease the people."**

F. **And when they provide him with the funeral meal, all the people sit on the ground, while he sits on a couch.**

I. A. Our rabbis have taught on Tannaite authority:

B. In a place in which women are accustomed to go forth after the bier, they go forth in that way. If they are accustomed to go forth before the bier, they go forth in that manner.

C. R. Judah says, "Women always go forth in front of the bier.

D. "For so we find in the case of David that he went forth after the bier of Abner.

E. "For it is said, *'And King David followed the bier'* (2 Sam. 3:31)."

F. **They said to him, "That was only to appease the people [M. 2:3D–E].**

G. "They were appeased, for David would go forth among the men and come in among the women, go forth among the women and come in among the men,

H. "as it is said, *'So all the people and all Israel understood that it was not of the king to slay Abner'* (2 Sam. 3:37)."

The Bavli's authorship now inserts a sizable exposition on David's relationship with Abner, and this goes its own way, without regard to the amplification of M. Sanhedrin 2:3 D–E, cited just now. The following not-very-cogent unit of discourse makes no single point but holds together because of the systematic amplification of the cited verses. No. II stands by itself and sets the stage for what is to follow.

II. A. Raba expounded, "What is the meaning of that which is written, *'And all the people came to cause David to eat bread'* (2 Sam. 3:35)?

B. "It was written, 'to pierce David' [with a K], but we read, 'to cause him to eat bread' [with a B].

C. "To begin with they came to pierce him but in the end to cause him to eat bread."

III. A. Said R. Judah said Rab [that is, "R. Judah said that Rab said"], "On what account was Abner punished? Because he could have prevented Saul but did not prevent him [from killing the priests of Nob, (1 Sam. 22:18)]."

B. R. Isaac said, "He did try to prevent him, but he got no response."

C. And both of them interpret the same verse of Scripture: *"And the king lamented for Abner and said, Should Abner die as a churl dies, your hands were not bound or your feet put into fetters"* (2 Sam. 2:33).

D. He who maintains that he did not try to stop Saul interprets the verse in this way: "Your hands were not bound nor were your feet put into fetters"—so why did you not try to stop him? *"As a man falls before the children of iniquity so did you fall"* (2 Sam. 3:33).

E. He who maintains that he did try to stop Saul but got no response interprets the verse as an expression of amazement: "Should he have died as a churl dies? Your hands were not bound and your feet were not put into fetters."

F. Since he [Abner] did protest, why [is the quotation from the lament of David valid, namely:] "As a man falls before the children of iniquity, so did you fall"?

G. In the view of him who has said that he did protest, why was he punished?

H. Said R. Nahman bar Isaac, "Because he held up the coming of the house of David by two and a half years."

The framer reverts to the Mishnah passage and proceeds. What we have now is the familiar program of Mishnah exegesis: amplification of words and phrases in the instance of No. IV, of which I present only a few of the components:

IV. A. **And when they provide him with the funeral meal, [all the people sit on the ground, while he sits on a couch] [M. 2:3F]:**

B. What is the couch?

C. Said Ulla, "It is a small couch."

D. Said [some] rabbis to Ulla, "Now is there something on which, up to that time, he had never sat, and now we seat him on that object?"

E. Raba objected to this argument, "What sort of problem is this? Perhaps it may be compared to the matter of eating and drinking, for up to this point we gave him nothing to eat or drink, while now we bring him food and drink. . . ."

The ongoing discussion of the matter provides a secondary development of the rules pertaining to the couch under discussion and need not detain us. Yet another example of a sizable composition appealing for cogency to Scripture is tacked on to M. 2:4 A–D. Here is another composition that holds together solely because of reference to verses of Scripture. Specifically, 2 Sam. 13 forms the center, and the various sentences then are joined to that center, but not to one another:

III. A. Said R. said Rab, "David had four hundred sons, all of them born of beautiful captive women. All grew long locks plaited down the back. All of them seated in golden chariots.

B. "And they went forth at the head of troops, and they were the powerful figures in the house of David."

C. And R. Judah said Rab said, "Tamar was the daughter of a beautiful captive woman.

D. "For it is said, *'Now, therefore, I pray you, speak to the king, for he will not withhold me from you'* (2 Sam. 13:13).

E. "Now if you hold that she was the daughter of a valid marriage, would the king ever have permitted [Amnon] to marry his sister?

F. "But, it follows, she was the daughter of a beautiful captive woman."

G. *"And Amnon had a friend, whose name was Jonadab, son of Shimeah, Da-*

vid's brother, and Jonadab was a very subtle man" (2 Sam. 13:3): Said R. Judah said Rab, "He was subtle about doing evil."

H. *"And he said to him, Why, son of the king, are you thus becoming leaner. . . . And Jonadab said to him, Lie down on your bed and pretend to be sick . . . and she will prepare the food . . . and she took the pan and poured [the cakes] out before him"* (2 Sam. 13:4ff.): Said R. Judah said Rab, "They were some sort of pancakes."

I. *"Then Amnon hated her with a very great hatred"* (2 Sam. 13:15): What was the reason?

J. Said R. Isaac, "One of his hairs got caught [around his penis and cut it off] making him one whose penis had been cut off."

K. But was she the one who had tied the hair around his penis? What had she done?

L. Rather, I should say, she had tied a hair around his penis and made him into one whose penis had been cut off.

M. Is this true? And did not Raba explain, "What is the sense of the verse, *'And your renown went forth among the nations for your beauty'* (Ex. 16:14)? It is that Israelite women do not have armpit or pubic hair."

N. Tamar was different, because she was the daughter of a beautiful captive woman.

O. *"And Tamar put ashes on her head and tore her garment of many colors"* (2 Sam. 13:19):

P. It was taught on Tannaite authority in the name of R. Joshua b. Qorhah, "Tamar established a high wall at that time [protecting chastity]. People said, 'If such could happen to princesses, all the more so can it happen to ordinary women.' If such could happen to virtuous women, all the more so can it happen to wanton ones!"

Q. Said R. Judah said Rab, "At that time they made a decree [21B] against a man's being alone with any woman [married or] unmarried."

R. But the rule against a man's being alone with [a married woman] derives from the authority of the Torah [and not from the authority of rabbis later on].

S. For R. Yohanan said in the name of R. Simeon b. Yehosedeq, "Whence in the Torah do we find an indication against a man's being alone [with a married woman]? As it is said, *'If your brother, son of your mother, entice you'* (Deut. 13:7).

T. "And it is the fact that the son of one's mother can entice, but the son of the father cannot entice? Rather, it is to tell you that a son may be alone with his mother, and no one else may be alone with any of the consanguineous female relations listed in the Torah."

U. Rather, they made a decree against a man's being alone with an unmarried woman.

V.   *"And Adonijah, son of Haggith, exalts himself, saying, I will be king"*
     (1 Kgs. 1:5):

W.   Said R. Judah said Rab, "This teaches that he tried to fit [the crown
     on his head], but it would not fit."

X.   *"And he prepares chariots and horses and fifty men to run before him"*
     (1 Kgs. 1:5):

Y.   So what was new [about princes' having retinues]?

Z.   Said R. Judah said Rab, "All of them had had their spleen removed
     [believed to make them faster runners] and the flesh of the soles of
     their feet cut off."

The final example of how Scripture serves to connect one sentence to another
shows us, from the citation of the Mishnah onward, a systematic interest not in
the Mishnah but in Scripture and its exposition.

BAVLI TRACTATE SANHEDRIN TO MISHNAH TRACTATE SANHEDRIN 2:5

A.   **[Others may] not ride on his horse, sit on his throne, handle
     his scepter.**

B.   **And [others may] not watch him while he is getting a hair-
     cut, or while he is nude, or in the bathhouse,**

C.   **since it is said, *"You shall surely set him as king over you"* (Deut.
     17:15)—that reverence for him will be upon you.**

I.   A.   Said R. Jacob said R. Yohanan [R. Jacob said that R. Yohanan said],
          "Abishag would have been permitted to be married to Solomon, but
          was forbidden to be married to Adonijah.

     B.   "She would have been permitted to Solomon, because he was king,
          and the king is permitted to make use of the scepter of [a former]
          king.

     C.   "But she was forbidden to Adonijah, for he was an ordinary person."

II. A.   And what is the story of Abishag?

     B.   It is written, *"King David was old, stricken in years. . . . His servants said
          to him, Let there be sought . . ." And it is written, "They sought for him a
          pretty girl . . ." and it is written, "And the girl was very fair, and she became
          a companion to the king and ministered to him"* (1 Kgs. 1:1–5).

     C.   She said to him, "Let's get married."

     D.   He said to her, "You are forbidden to me."

     E.   She said to him, "When the thief fears for his life, he seizes virtue."

     F.   He said to them, "Call Bath Sheba to me."

     G.   And it is written, *"And Bath Sheba went into the king to the chamber"*
          (1 Kgs. 1:15).

     H.   Said R. Judah said Rab, "At that time [having had sexual relations

with David] Bath Sheba wiped herself with thirteen cloths [to show
that he was hardly impotent, contrary to Abishag's accusation]."

I. Said R. Shemen bar Abba, "Come and take note of how difficult is
an act of divorce.

J. "For lo, they permitted King David to be alone [with the woman],
but they did not permit him to divorce [one of his other wives]. . . ."

The exposition of the Mishnah hardly requires insertion of these materials, the
cogency of which derives rather from Scripture.

One difference in the utilization of fixed associative logic between the two
Talmuds may be noted. While for the Yerushalmi, the Mishnah provides the principal means of holding together discrete compositions, in the Bavli, two principal
sources of fixed associations served, the Mishnah and Scripture. The authorships
of the tractates of the Bavli first of all organized the Bavli around the Mishnah, just
as the framers of the Yerushalmi had done. Second, they also adapted and included
vast tracts of antecedent materials, which they organized as scriptural commentary.
These they inserted whole and complete, not at all in response to the Mishnah's
program. That second medium of fixed association through Scripture is uncommon in the Yerushalmi.

The Bavli's compositors, by contrast, joined the Mishnah to Scripture in such
a way as to give final form and fixed expression, through their categories of the
organization of all knowledge, to the Torah as it had been known, sifted, searched,
approved, and handed down, even from the remote past to their own day. Accordingly, the Bavli's ultimate framers made the decision to present large-scale discussions along lines of order and sequence dictated not by topics and propositional
arguments concerning them. Rather they selected the two components of 'the one
whole Torah, oral and written, of Moses, our Rabbi, at Sinai," and these they set
forth as the connections that held together and ordered all discourse. That is how
they organized what they knew, on the one side, and made their choices in laying
out the main lines of the structure of knowledge, on the other.

5.

TOPICAL PROGRAM

Little of what the Talmuds' authorships present in a propositional form derives
cogency and force from a received statement, and most of it does not. True, many
of the propositions of the two Talmuds, in the nature of things, address the meaning of paragraphs of the Mishnah, and most of the documents are laid out as a
commentary to either the Mishnah or Scripture. But the authorship of each of the
compositions and the framer of the respective composites has selected out of Scrip-

ture and the Mishnah the passages or topics it wishes to amplify. At stake is the re-formation of the (oral part of the) Torah in a way not envisaged by its writers. The Talmuds do not merely clarify the Mishnah; both of them in point of fact re-present the Torah—a very different thing.

The writers of the Mishnah created a coherent document, with a topical program formed in accord with the logical order dictated by the characteristics of a given topic, and with a set of highly distinctive formulary and formal traits as well. But these are obscured when the document is taken apart into bits and pieces and reconstituted in the way in which the Talmuds do. The redefinition of the Torah accomplished by the Talmuds therefore represented a vast revision of the initial writing down of the oral component of the Torah—a point at which the hermeneutics shaded over into a profoundly theological activity.

For now the Mishnah is read by the Talmuds as a composite of discrete and essentially autonomous rules, a set of atoms, not an integrated molecule, so to speak. In so doing, the most striking formal traits of the Mishnah are obliterated. More important, the Mishnah as a whole and complete statement of a viewpoint no longer exists. Its propositions are reduced to details. But what is offered instead? The answer is, a statement that on occasion recasts details in generalizations encompassing a wide variety of other details across the gaps between one tractate and another. This immensely creative and imaginative approach to the Mishnah vastly expands the range of discourse. But the consequence is to deny to the Mishnah both its own mode of speech and its distinctive and coherent message. So, as I said at the outset, the two Talmuds formulate their own hermeneutics, to convey their theological system:

[1] defining the Torah and

[2] demonstrating its perfection and comprehensive character: unit, harmony, lineal origin from Sinai.

What the second Talmud would later on add to that first stage in theological re-presentation of the Torah is instantiation through modes of analysis of the unity, lineal formation, and harmony of the Torah. But the framers of the first Talmud assuredly affirmed the same points.

Both authorships take an independent stance when facing the Mishnah, making choices, reaching decisions of their own. Both Talmuds' framers deal with Mishnah tractates of their own choice, and neither provides a Talmud to the entirety of the Mishnah. What the Mishnah therefore contributed to the Talmuds was not received in a spirit of humble acceptance by the sages who produced either of the two Talmuds. Important choices were made about what to treat, hence what to ignore. The exegetical mode of reception did not have to obscure the main lines of the Mishnah's system. But it surely did so. The discrete reading of sentences, or, at most, paragraphs, denying all context, avoiding all larger generalizations except for those transcending the specific lines of tractates—this approach need not have involved the utter reversal of the paramount and definitive elements of the Mishnah's whole and integrated worldview (its "Judaism"). But doing these things did facilitate the revision of the whole into a quite different pattern. That represents a re-presentation of the Torah, one of considerable originality indeed.

A second trait, already familiar to us, joins with the foregoing. The Mishnah rarely finds it necessary to adduce proof texts from the written Torah in support of its statements. The Talmuds, by contrast, find it appropriate whenever possible to cite scriptural proof texts for the propositions of the Mishnah. While the various tractates of the Mishnah relate in different ways to Scripture, the view of the framers of the Talmud on the same matter is not differentiated. So far as they are concerned, proof texts for Mishnaic rules are required. These will be supplied in substantial numbers. And that is the main point. The Mishnah now is systematically represented as not standing free and separate from Scripture, but dependent upon it. The authority of the Mishnah's laws then is reinforced. But the autonomy of the Mishnah as a whole is severely compromised. Just as the Mishnah is represented in the Talmud as a set of rules, rather than as a philosophical essay, so it is presented, rule by rule, as a secondary and derivative development of Scripture. It would be difficult to imagine a more decisive effort to reformulate the Torah than is accomplished by this work.

The undifferentiated effort to associate diverse Mishnah laws with Scripture is to be viewed together with the systematic breakup of the Mishnah into its diverse laws. The two quite separate activities produce a single effect in both Talmuds. They permit the Talmuds to represent the state of affairs pretty much as the framers of the Talmuds wish to do. Theology as a creative venture here determines to (re)define the Torah. And how is this done? Everything is shown to be continuous: Scripture, Mishnah, the Tosefta where cited, the authoritative sayings labeled Tannaite where used, ending in—the Talmud itself (whichever Talmud we examine, the effect being the same)! Then all things, as now shaped by the rabbis of the Talmud(s), have the standing of Scripture and represent the authority of Moses (now called "our Rabbi"). Accordingly, once the Mishnah enters either of the two Talmuds it nowhere emerges intact. It is wholly preserved, but in bits and pieces, shaped and twisted in whatever ways the Talmuds wish. The Torah now forms a single, continuous statement. And that is the work of the first Talmud, not only of the second.

The question has now to be asked, when do the Talmuds speak for themselves, not for the Mishnah? Second, what sorts of units of discourse contain such passages that bear what is "Talmudic" in the two Talmuds? These two questions produce the same answers for both Talmuds, allowing us to characterize the topical or propositional program of the two Talmuds.

[1] THEORETICAL QUESTIONS OF LAW NOT ASSOCIATED WITH A PARTICULAR PASSAGE OF THE MISHNAH. In the first of the two Talmuds there is some tendency, and in the second, a very marked tendency, to move beyond the legal boundaries set by the Mishnah's rules themselves. More general inquiries are taken up. These of course remain within the framework of the topic of one tractate or another,

although there are some larger modes of thought characteristic of more than a single tractate.

[2] EXEGESIS OF SCRIPTURE SEPARATE FROM THE MISHNAH. It is under this rubric that we find the most important instances in which the Talmuds present materials essentially independent of the Mishnah.

[3] HISTORICAL STATEMENTS. The Talmud contains a fair number of statements that something happened, or narratives about how something happened. While many of these are replete with biblical quotations, in general they do not provide exegesis of Scripture, which serves merely as illustration or reference point.

[4] STORIES ABOUT, AND RULES FOR, SAGES AND DISCIPLES, SEPARATE FROM DISCUSSION OF A PASSAGE OF THE MISHNAH. The Mishnah contains a tiny number of tales about rabbis. These serve principally as precedents for, or illustrations of, rules. The Talmuds by contrast contain a sizable number of stories about sages and their relationships to other people.

When the Talmuds present us with ideas or expressions of a world related to, but fundamentally separate from, that of the Mishnah, that is, when the Talmuds wish to say something other than what the Mishnah says and means, they will take up one of two modes of discourse. Either we find exegesis of biblical passages, with the value system of the rabbis read into the scriptural tales; or we are told stories about holy men and paradigmatic events, once again through tales told in such a way that a didactic and paranetic purpose is served. It follows that the Talmuds are composites of three kinds of materials:

[1] exegeses of the Mishnah (and other materials classified as authoritative, that is, Tannaite),

[2] exegeses of Scripture, and

[3] accounts of the men who provide both.

Both Talmuds then constitute elaborate reworkings of the two antecedent documents: the Mishnah, lacking much reference to Scripture, and the Scripture itself. The Talmuds bring the two together into a synthesis of their compilers' own making, both in reading Scripture into Mishnah, and in reading Scripture alongside of, and separate from, Mishnah.

If, therefore, we want to point to what is Talmudic in either of the two Talmuds it is the exegesis of Scripture, on the one side, and the narration of historical or biographical tales about holy men, on the other. Since much of the biblical exegesis turns upon holy men of biblical times, we may say that the Talmuds speak for themselves alone, as distinct from addressing the problems of the Mishnah, when they tell about holy men now and then. But what is genuinely new in the Talmuds, in comparison and contrast to the Mishnah, is the inclusion of extensive discourse on the meaning imputed to Scripture.

It follows that the two Talmuds stand essentially secondary to two prior documents: Mishnah (encompassing for this purpose the whole corpus labeled Tannaite, whenever and wherever produced, much being later than the Mishnah and some being Babylonian), on the one side, and Scripture, on the other. The Mishnah is read in the Talmuds pretty much within the framework of meaning established by the Mishnah itself. Scripture is read as an account of a world remarkably like that of the rabbis of the Talmuds. When the rabbis speak for themselves, as distinct from the Mishnah, it is through exegesis of Scripture. (But any other mode of reading Scripture, to them, would have been unthinkable. They took for granted that they and Scripture's heroes and sages lived in a single timeless plane.)

Let us now turn to three more questions, the answers to which equally characterize both Talmuds' programs of exegesis, the counterpart to the topical program of the Mishnah:

[1] What do rabbis in the two Talmuds do in common when they read the Mishnah?

[2] What are their modes of thought, their characteristic ways of analysis?

[3] What do we learn about their worldview from the ways in which they receive and interpret the worldview they have inherited in the Mishnah?

These are the very questions, we now realize, that the Talmuds answer on their own account, not only the Mishnah's. The Talmudic exegetes of the Mishnah brought to the document no distinctive program of their own. The exegetes did not know in advance of their approach to a law of the Mishnah facts about the passage not contained within the boundaries of the language of the Mishnah passage itself (except only for facts contained within other units of the same document). Rejecting propositions that were essentially *a priori,* they proposed to explain and expand precisely the wording and the conceptions supplied by the document under study.

In not a single instance did the Mishnah exegetes in either Talmud appear to twist and turn the language and message of a passage, attempting to make the words mean something other than what they appear to say anyhow. The framers of both Talmuds' reading of the Mishnah take as the measure of truth the clear and present sense of the Mishnah's own language and formulations, rarely asking the Mishnah's rule to confirm a judgment extrinsic to the Mishnah's message. While the Talmuds follow a coherent hermeneutics that is very much their own, there is no exegetical program revealed in the Talmuds' reading of the Mishnah other than that defined, to begin with, by the language and conceptions of one Mishnah passage or another. Seen whole, the Talmuds appear to be nothing more than secondary developments of the Mishnah. If there is nothing *in particular* that is Talmudic, nonetheless, there is much *in general* that in both Talmuds is Talmudic. This is in entirely familiar respects.

First, the Mishnah was set forth by Judah the Patriarch, who sponsored the document, whole and complete, a profoundly unified, harmonious document. The Talmud insists upon obliterating the marks of coherence. It treats in bits and pieces what was originally meant to speak whole. That simple fact constitutes what is original, stunningly new, and, by definition, Talmudic. Second, the Mishnah, also by definition, delivered its message in the way chosen by Judah the Patriarch. That is to say, by producing the document as he did, the Patriarch left no space for the very enterprises of episodic exegesis undertaken so brilliantly by his immediate continuators and heirs.

True, a rather limited process of explanation and gloss of words and phrases, accompanied by a systematic inquiry into the wording of one passage or another, got under way, probably at the very moment, and within the very process, of the Mishnah's closure. But Judah the Patriarch did not precipitate the work of commentary. Insofar as the larger messages and meanings of the document are conveyed in the ways Judah the Patriarch chose, for instance, through formalization of language, through contrasts, through successive instances of the same normally unspecified, general proposition, the messages emerge with clarity. The need for exegesis was surely not generated by his own program for the Mishnah. Quite to the contrary, Judah chose for his Mishnah a mode of expression and defined for the document a large-scale structure and organization, which, by definition, were meant to stand firm and autonomous. Rabbi Judah the Patriarch's Mishnah speaks clearly and for itself. It contains the wherewithal of its own exegesis.

The true power of the two Talmuds emerges when we realize that the Mishnah did not merely come to closure. At the very moment at which it was completed, the Mishnah also formed a closed system, that is, a whole, complete statement that did not require facts outside of its language and formulation, so made no provision for commentary and amplification of brief allusions, as the Talmuds' style assuredly does. The Mishnah refers to nothing beyond itself except, episodically, Scripture. It promises no information other than what is provided within its limits. It raises no questions for ongoing discussion beyond its decisive, final, descriptive statements of enduring realities and fixed relationships.

The Talmuds' single irrevocable judgment is precisely opposite: this text needs a commentary. The Talmuds' first initiative is to reopen the Mishnah's closed system, almost at the moment of its completion and perfection. That at the foundations is what is Talmudic about the Talmuds: their daring assertion that the concluded and completed demanded clarification and continuation. Once that assertion was made to stick, nothing else mattered very much. The two Talmuds' message was conveyed in the very medium of the Talmud: a new language, focused upon a new grid of discourse to review a received writing.

In the two Talmuds in common we address a program of criticism of the Mishnah framed by independent and original minds. How is this made manifest? Let us quickly bypass the obvious points of independent judgment, the matter of insistence that the very word choices of the Mishnah require clarification, therefore prove faulty. The meanings and amplification of phrases represent the judgment that Judah's formulation, while stimulating and provocative, left much to be desired. These indications of independence of judgment among people disposed not merely to memorize but to improve upon the text provided by Judah the Patriarch hardly represent judgments of substance. Rather, let us turn to the two most striking:

[1] the provision of scriptural proof texts for the propositions of various passages of the Mishnah;

[2] the rewriting, in the Mishnah's own idiom, if not in its redactional and disciplinary patterns, of much of the law.

As to the former, of course, the message is familiar and clear. The propositions of the Mishnah cannot stand by themselves but must be located within the larger realm of scriptural authority. As to the latter, the Tosefta's compositions and other Tannaite passages, serving as an exegetical complement to the Mishnah's corresponding passages, imitate the Mishnah. For they are phrased in the way in which the Mishnah's sentences are written (as distinct from the utterly different way in which the Talmuds' own sentences are framed, e.g., in Hebrew rather than in the Talmuds' Aramaic). And yet they show equivalent independence of mind. They indicate that where sages of the time of the Talmuds took up Mishnaic passages, they were not at all limited to the work of gloss and secondary expansion. They recognized and exercised a quite remarkable freedom of initiative. They undertook to restate in their own words, but imitating the Mishnah's style, the propositions of the Mishnah passage at hand.

That is, they both cite what the Mishnah had said and also continue, in imitation of the Mishnah's language, the discourse of the Mishnah passage itself. These Toseftan or other Tannaite complements to the Mishnah—a vast number of them demonstrably written after the closure of the Mishnah—are Talmudic in two senses. First, they come to expression in the period after the Mishnah had reached closure, as is clear from the fact that the exact language of the Mishnah is cited prior to the labor of extension, expansion, and revision. So they are the work of the Talmuds' age and authority. Second, they derive from precisely the same authorities responsible for the formation of the Talmuds as a whole.

Accordingly, both the insistence upon adducing proof texts for passages the Patriarch judged not to need them and the persistent revision and expansion of the Mishnah, even in clumsy imitation of the Mishnah's syntax, rhetoric, and word choices, tell us once more this simple truth: the Talmuds are distinctively Talmudic precisely when the Mishnah itself defines the Talmuds' labor, dictates their ideas, directs their rhetoric, determines their results.

The very shift in usable language, from "the Mishnah" (as a whole) to "the Mishnah passage" or "the Mishnaic law at hand" indicates the true state of affairs. On the surface, in all manner of details, the two Talmuds are little more than secondary and derivative documents, explaining the Mishnah itself in trivial ways, or expanding it in a casuistic and logic-chopping manner. But viewing that same surface from a different, more distant perspective and angle, we see things quite differently. In detail the Talmuds changed nothing. Overall, the Talmuds left nothing the same. And, it follows, in general, the two Talmuds stand close together, not only in form, but in program and much else.

In the two Talmuds we find little to deem Talmudic in particular. But in them both, equally, there is much that is Talmudic in general. The particular bits and pieces are Mishnaic. But—as I have stressed in pointing to the theological character of both Talmuds—the Talmuds leave nothing of the Mishnah whole and intact. Their work upon the whole presents an essentially new construction. Through the

Mishnah, Judah contributed to the Talmuds most of the bricks, but little of the mortar, and none of the joists and beams. The design of the whole bore no relationship to the Patriarch's plan for the Mishnah. The sages of the Talmud did the rest. They alone imagined, then built, the building. They are the architects, theirs is the vision. The building is a monument to the authority of the sage above all.

What is most definitively indicative of the Talmudic sages' freedom of imagination is the exercise—by each set of authors—of free choice even among the Mishnah's tractates awaiting exegesis. We do not know why some tractates were chosen for Talmudic expansion and others left fallow. We may speculate that the Yerushalmi's omission of all reference to the entire division of Holy Things, on the everyday conduct of the Temple, and to most of the division of Purities, on the sources of uncleanness, objects subject to uncleanness, and modes of removing contamination, constitutes a radical revision of the law of Judaism. What for Judah the Patriarch was close to 50 percent of the whole story in volume, forming two of his six divisions in structure, for that Talmud's designers (I assume early as much as late), was of no importance. That is an amazing fact, attesting on its own to the Talmuds' formulation of their own program and statement, independent of that of the Mishnah even while expressed wholly in the form of a commentary to the Mishnah. Here too, we find the Torah once more subject to (re)definition; nothing of course would be omitted; but choices clearly were made about what is to be brought to the fore.

Both Talmuds in common address the tractates of Appointed Times, Women, and Damages, the second, third, and fourth divisions of the Mishnah. That is, then, where the comparisons and contrasts have to take place. Interest in the division of Appointed Times involved extensive discussion of the conduct of the cult on extraordinary days. Perhaps at issue here was not what had to be omitted (the cult on appointed times) but what people wanted to discuss, the home and village on those same holy occasions. So the former came in the wake of the latter. Inclusion of the divisions of Women, on the family and the transfer of women from father to husband and back, and Damages, on civil law and institutions, is not hard to explain. The sages fully expected to govern the life of Israel, the Jewish people, in its material and concrete aspects. These divisions, as well as some of the tractates of the division on Appointed Times, demanded and received attention. Ample treatment of the laws in the first division, governing the priests' rations and other sacred segments of the agricultural produce of the Holy Land, is to be expected among authorities living not only in, but also off, the Holy Land.

If we stand back and reflect on the Mishnah's program, we recognize how different is that of the respective Talmuds. The Mishnah covers a broad variety of topics. The Talmuds contribute none of their own, but trawl across the entire surface of the Mishnah. The Mishnah is organized topically. The Talmuds may be broken down into discrete compositions and neatly joined composites, none of them framed as freestanding, topical formations, all of them in one way or another depending upon the Mishnah for order and coherence. The Mishnah lays out rules and facts about a world beyond itself. The Talmuds negotiate rules and recast facts into propositions that concern the Mishnah—a different focus of discourse and perspective altogether. Continuous with the Mishnah, the two Talmuds in point of fact redirect the Mishnah not only by destroying its integrity and picking and choosing with its topical (and propositional) program, but also by forming of the detritus of the received writing a statement of their own. But it was not a statement that in the end concerned the Mishnah at all, rather, a statement about the Torah, and a statement of the Torah.

In accepting authority, in centering discourse upon the ideas of other men, in patiently listing even the names behind authoritative laws from olden times to their own day, the sages and framers of the Talmud accomplished exactly the opposite of what we might have supposed they wanted to do. They made a commentary. On the surface, that suggests they wanted merely to continue and strengthen the received tradition. But they obliterated the text. They loyally explained the Mishnah. But they turned the Mishnah into something else than what it had been. They patiently hammered out chains of tradition, binding themselves to the authority of the remote and holy past. But it was, in the end, a tradition of their own design and choosing. That is, it was not tradition but a new creation. And so these Talmuds of ours, so loyal and subservient to the Mishnah of Judah the Patriarch, turn out to be less reworkings of received materials than works—each one of them—of remarkably independent judgment. The Talmuds speak humbly and subserviently about received truth, always in the name only of Moses and of sages of times past. But in the end it is truth not discovered and demonstrated, but determined and invented and declared.

The redactional program of the men responsible for laying out the materials of Talmuds may now be described. There is a pronounced tendency in both Talmuds to move from close reading of the Mishnah and then the Tosefta outward to more general inquiry into the principles of a Mishnah passage and their interplay with those of some other, superficially unrelated passage, and, finally, to more general reflections on law not self-evidently related to the Mishnah passage at hand or to anthologies intersecting only at a general topic. Unlike the Mishnah, the Talmuds reveal no effort to systematize sayings in larger constructions, or to impose a pattern upon all individual sayings. If the Mishnah is framed to facilitate memorization, then we must say that the Talmuds' materials are not framed with mnemonics in mind. If the Mishnah focuses upon subsurface relationships in syntax, the Talmud in the main looks like notes of a discussion. These notes may serve to recreate the larger patterns of argument and reasoning, a summary of what was thought and perhaps also said. The Talmud preserves and expresses concrete ideas, reducing them to brief but usually accessible and obvious statements. The Mishnah speaks of concrete things in order to hint at abstract relationships, which rarely are brought to the surface and fully exposed.

The Mishnah hides. The Talmuds spell out. The Mishnah hints. The Talmuds repeat *ad nauseam*. The Mishnah is subtle, the Talmuds are obvious; the one restrained and tentative, the others aimed at full and exhaustive expression of what is already clear. The sages of the Mishnah rarely represent themselves as deciding cases. Only on unusual occasions do they declare the decided law, at best reticently spelling out what underlies their positions. The rabbis of the Talmuds harp on who holds which opinion and how a case is actually decided, presenting a rich corpus of precedents. They seek to make explicit what is implicit in the law. The Mishnah is immaterial and spiritual, the Talmud earthy and social. The Mishnah deals in the gossamer threads of philosophical principle, the Talmud in the coarse rope that binds this one and that one into a social construction. The Mishnah speaks of a world in stasis, an unchanging, eternal present tense where all the tensions of chaos are resolved. The Talmuds address the real Israel in the here and now of ever-changing times, the gross matter of disorder and history. Clearly, the central traits of the Mishnah, revealed in the document at its time of closure in ca. A.D. 200, were revised and transformed into those definitive of the Talmud at its time of closure in ca. A.D. 400 for the earlier Talmud, 600 for the later. We know only that when we compare the Mishnah to the Talmuds we find in each case two intertwined documents, quite different from one another both in style and in values. Yet they are so tightly joined that the Talmud appears in the main to provide mere commentary and amplification for the Mishnah. So in important, superficial traits the two Talmuds are indistinguishable.

6.

A SAMPLE PASSAGE

The illustration derives from both Talmuds' reading of a brief passage of Mishnah tractate Makkot. The unity of purpose—Mishnah commentary—and the identity of proposition—the unity of the Torah, its perfection—should not obscure the simple fact that the two Talmuds do not intersect except at the Mishnah and at Scripture. The Talmuds bear each its own message, but both ask the same questions. Mishnah and Tosefta passages in both Talmuds are in boldface, Bavli's use of Aramaic in italics, Hebrew in regular type. We begin with the Yerushalmi:

YERUSHALMI TO MAKKOT 1:8
= BAVLI TO MAKKOT 1:10

[A] **He whose trial ended and who fled and was brought back before the same court—**

[B] **they do not reverse the judgment concerning him [and re-try him].**

[C] **In any situation in which two gerim [proselytes] up and say, "We testify concerning Mr. So-and-so that his trial ended in the court of such-and-such, with Mr. So-and-so and Mr. So-and-so as the witnesses against him,"**

[D] lo, this one is put to death.

[E] **[Trial before] a sanhedrin applies both in the Land and abroad.**

[F] **A sanhedrin which imposes the death penalty once in seven years is called murderous.**

[G] **R. Eleazar b. Azariah says, "Once in seventy years."**

[H] **R. Tarfon and R. Aqiba say, "If we were on a sanhedrin, no one would ever be put to death."**

[I] **Rabban Simeon b. Gamaliel says, "So they would multiply the number of murderers in Israel."**

[I. A] **[Trial before a] sanhedrin applies both in the Land and abroad [M. 1:8E],**

[B] as it is written, "And these things shall be for a statute and ordinance to you throughout your generations in all your dwellings" (Num. 35:29).

[C] And why does Scripture say, "You shall appoint judges and officers in all your towns [which the Lord your God gives you]" (Deut. 16:18) In the towns of the Land of Israel.

[D] The meaning is that in the towns of Israel they set up judges in every town, but abroad they do so only by districts.

[E] It was taught: R. Dosetai b. R. Yannai says, "It is a religious require-ment for each tribe to judge its own tribe, as it is said, 'You shall appoint *judges* and officers in all your towns which the Lord your God gives you, according to your tribes'" (Deut. 16:18).

[II. A] Rabban Simeon b. Gamaliel taught, "Those declared liable to the death penalty who fled from the Land abroad—they put them to death forthwith [upon recapture].

[B] "If they fled from abroad to the Land, they do not put them to death forthwith, but they undertake a trial *de novo*."

The Yerushalmi wants the scriptural proof for the Mishnah's allegation. The Mish-nah has set forth a variety of rules. The framers of the Yerushalmi's composition therefore go in search of the scriptural foundations for those rules. The task then is to harmonize the implications at hand. Since the proof text, I.B., yields results contrary to the assumed implications of that at C, D must indicate otherwise. Unit II is an independent saying, generally relevant to M. 1:8E. It is a simple paraphrase and clarification.

The Bavli does the same thing, but makes its own points. The comparison, then, is based on the shared program; the contrast, the different results.

BAVLI TO MISHNAH TRACTATE MAKKOT 1:10

A. **He whose trial ended and who fled and was brought back before the same court—**

B. **they do not reverse the judgment concerning him [and retry him].**

C. **In any situation in which two get up and say, "We testify concerning Mr. So-and-so that his trial ended in the court of such-and-such, with Mr. So-and-so and Mr. So-and-so as the witnesses against him,"**

D. **lo, this one is put to death.**

E. **[Trial before] a sanhedrin applies both in the land and abroad.**

F. **A sanhedrin which imposes the death penalty once in seven years is called murderous.**

G. **R. Eleazar b. Azariah says, "Once in seventy years."**

H. **R. Tarfon and R. Aqiba say, "If we were on a sanhedrin, no one would ever be put to death."**

I. **Rabban Simeon b. Gamaliel says, "So they would multiply the number of murderers in Israel."**

I. 1. A. **He whose trial ended and who fled and was brought back before the same court—they do not reverse the judgment concerning him [and retry him]:**

B. Before that court in particular the judgment is not reversed, but it may be reversed before some other court! *But then it is taught further on:* **In any situation in which two get up and say, "We testify concerning Mr. So-and-so that his trial ended in the court of such-and-such, with Mr. So-and-so and Mr. So-and-so as the witnesses against him," lo, this one is put to death**!

C. Said Abbayye, "This is no contradiction. The one statement refers to a court in the Land of Israel, the other, to a court abroad."

D. *For it has been taught on Tannaite authority:*

E. **R. Judah b. Dostai says in the name of R. Simeon b. Shatah, "If one fled from the Land to abroad, they do not reverse the verdict pertaining to him. If he fled from abroad to the Land, they do reverse the verdict concerning him, because of the higher priority enjoyed by the Land of Israel" [T. San. 3:11A–B)].**

II. 1. A. **[Trial before] a sanhedrin applies both in the Land and abroad:**

B. *What is the source of this rule?*

C. *It is in line with that which our rabbis have taught on Tannaite authority:*

D. "And these things shall be for a statute of judgment to you throughout your generations in all your dwellings" (Num. 35:29)—

E. we learn from that statement that the sanhedrin operates both in the Land and abroad.

F. If that is so, then why does Scripture state, "Judges and offices you shall make for yourself in all your gates that the Lord God gives you tribe by tribe" (Deut. 16:18) [meaning only in the tribal land, in the Land of Israel]?

G. "In your own gates you set up courts in every district and every town, but outside of the Land of Israel you set up courts in every district but not in every town."

III. 1. A. **A sanhedrin which imposes the death penalty once in seven years is called murderous. R. Eleazar b. Azariah says, "Once in seventy years":**

B. *The question was raised: does the statement,* **A sanhedrin which imposes the death penalty once in seven years is called murderous** *mean that even one death sentence was enough to mark the sanhedrin as murderous, or is this merely a description of how things are?*

C. *The question stands.*

IV. 1. A. **R. Tarfon and R. Aqiba say, "If we were on a sanhedrin, no one would ever be put to death." Rabban Simeon b. Gamaliel says, "So they would multiply the number of murderers in Israel":**

B. *So what would they actually do?*

C. R. Yohanan and R. Eleazar both say, 'Did you see whether or not the victim was already dying from something, or was he whole when he was killed?'" [Such a question would provide grounds for dismissing the charge of murder, if the witnesses could not answer properly.]

D. *Said R. Ashi, "If they said that he was whole, then, 'Maybe the sword only cut an internal lesion?'"*

E. *And in the case of a charge of consanguineous sexual relations, what would they actually do?*

F. *Both Abbayye and Raba said, "Did you see the probe in the kohl-flask [actually engaged in sexual relations]?"*

G. *And as to rabbis, what would suffice for conviction?*

H. *The answer accords with Samuel, for said Samuel, "In the case of a charge of adultery, if the couple appeared to be committing adultery [that would be sufficient evidence]."*

Standard Mishnah exegesis in both Talmuds is represented by this brief passage from Bavli Makkot. The counterpart Talmud presents numerous exercises that follow the same program. We start, I, with a challenge to the implications of the stated rule, I.B, yielding a dissonance, which is ironed out by a suitable distinction. We proceed, II, to a scriptural source for the passage at hand. Item III raises a theoretical question meant to clarify the sense of the language before us. Entry IV reverts to the systematic glossing of the language and sense of the Mishnah. There is no kind of comment in this passage that the Yerushalmi does not provide as well; each of these types of inquiry is standard for both Talmuds.

Finally, we conclude with some observations concerning the Yerushalmi in particular. When we speak of "the Yerushalmi," it is because the document while drawing on a variety of voices presents a single melody. To appreciate what that means, we must remember that the Yerushalmi is broken up into multiple brief discourses, discussions of the meaning and sense of the phrases and sentences of the Mishnah. Nearly every discourse—perhaps 90 percent of the whole—of the Yerushalmi addresses one main point: the meaning of the Mishnah. For the Yerushalmi, the life of Israel reaches the level of analysis within the integument of the Mishnah. That is to say, the Mishnah is about life, while the Yerushalmi is about the Mishnah. Accordingly, the traits of the Mishnah defined the problematic, of both intellect and politics, confronting the heirs of the Mishnah, the disciples of the final generation of the Mishnah's redaction and formulation onward. They, for their part, set the patterns that followed, treating the Mishnah as Torah, proposing to receive and realize its revelation. But then how can people make a statement of their own, when their focus is upon statements of others, prior to themselves?

The reason is simple. The Yerushalmi speaks about the Mishnah in essentially a single voice, about fundamentally few things. Its mode of speech as much as of thought is uniform throughout. Diverse topics produce slight differentiation in modes of analysis. The same sorts of questions phrased in the same rhetoric—a moving, or dialectical, argument, composed of questions and answers—turn out to pertain equally well to every passage of the Mishnah; it generally takes up a single, not very complex or diverse, program of inquiry. The Yerushalmi also utilizes a single, rather limited repertoire of exegetical initiatives and rhetorical choices for whatever discourse about the Mishnah the framers of the Yerushalmi propose to undertake. Accordingly, as is clear, the Yerushalmi presents us with both a uniformity of discourse and a monotony of tone. The Yerushalmi speaks in a single voice. That voice by definition is collective, not greatly differentiated by traits of individuals. Individuals in the Yerushalmi, unlike in the Mishnah, do not speak uniformly, but the differences are not marked. Let me spell this out, because its consequences for the history of the ideas contained within Yerushalmi will prove definitive.

The Yerushalmi identifies no author or collegium of authors. When I say that the Yerushalmi speaks in a single voice, I mean to say that it everywhere speaks uniformly, consistently, and predictably. The voice is the voice of a book, the voice of an author, the voice we hear when we read: one voice. The message is one deriving from a community, the collectivity of sages or textual community for whom and to whom the book speaks. The document seems, in the main, to intend to provide notes, an abbreviated script which anyone may use to reconstruct and reenact formal discussions of problems: about this, one says that. Curt and often arcane, these notes can be translated only with immense bodies of inserted explanation. All of this script of information is public and undifferentiated, not individual and idiosyncratic. We must assume people took for granted that out of the signs of speech, it would be possible for anyone to reconstruct speech, doing so in accurate and fully conventional ways. So the literary traits of the document presuppose a uniform code of communication: a single voice, such as we have now considered. To define the Yerushalmi's voice in greater detail, however, we have to consider the other Talmud and specify how it differs. For each of the two Talmuds exhibits highly distinctive and characteristic qualities of discourse, and they can best be differentiated only in the comparison and contrast of the one with the other.

VIII

The Talmud of Babylonia

1.

Identifying the Document

WE COME TO THE SINGLE MOST IMPORTANT DOCUMENT IN RABBINIC LITERATURE, the Talmud of Babylonia or Bavli. We do well to stand back and examine the document first of all in the context of the study of religion. In this Talmud, holy Israel, assembled in academies formed for the study of the Talmud and its codes and commentaries and for the formation of a holy community defined by that writing, meets God. Here is where holy Israel (a theological, not a secular category, therefore not to be confused with the State of Israel) studies the Torah that God reveals at Sinai—every day.

Let us consider that simple, factual statement in context. All religions may be divided into two kinds, those that focus upon immediate experience and the ones that mediate the everyday through the prism of a long past. Believers in the former expect to, and do, enjoy an immediate encounter with God. Believers in the latter meet God in books as well. What happens in the here and now is shaped by what, to begin with, those books teach them to expect to find. All religions, furthermore, may be divided into two kinds, those that address a select group, identified out of a larger society, and those that set forth an account of the social order that encompasses an entire society. Believers in the former in general attend to the concerns of their group in particular, and issues of consequence in the end derive from a rather private agenda. Believers in the latter treat as critical matters of public policy that concern the ordering of the well-ordered society that their religion proposes to set forth. Within the limitations of literacy, the former kind of religion may or may not meet God in holy books. But the latter type always does, since, as a matter of fact, the representation of the entirety of the social order by its nature will impose the duty of putting everything together and writing everything down in some coherent manner, whether as a law code, a prophecy that in messages from God on political subjects or economic attitudes addresses the here and now, or in some other kind of writing, of general intelligibility, upon the social order.

Every Judaism, past to present, appeals to not only immediate experience but also received and authoritative writings that set forth, and make accessible, inherited religious experience as well. Beginning with the Judaism of the Pentateuch composite, some Judaisms, by no means all of them, have moreover formulated their Judaisms in terms of the politics of the social order. These Judaisms set forth their worldview, defined their way of life, and delineated their "Israel," the name, in every Judaism, of the social entity that understands itself by appeal to the worldview and that realizes the way of life, in documents of broad social vision and concern. That is to say, many Judaisms understood "Israel" to be a political entity, fully empowered; delineated the way of life of their "Israel" as an economic unit, responsible for the proper interchange, within a specified rationality, of scarce resources (however these may have been identified); and portrayed their "Israel" as the embodiment of a philosophical or a theological imperative. Those Judaisms then set forth systems that concerned themselves with the entire order of things: Israel in relationship to all the nations, the castes of Israel in relationship to one another; the proper definition and conduct of the social unit, the household, which also formed the economic unit; the uses of legitimate power, sanctions to preserve order, rewards for sustaining it. These Judaisms in writing therefore put forth prescriptions for the affairs of that "Israel" understood, wherever it was located, as a freestanding political entity, in our language, a nation-society-culture-church.

One of those Judaisms of the latter classification, by far the most important one, the Judaism of the dual Torah, moreover produced a book, the Talmud of Babylonia or Bavli, that was meant to set forth together and all at once that way of life, worldview, theory of "Israel"—that account of not only Israel's, but the world's, social order and purpose under God's rule. The Talmud served as the constitution and bylaws of the Israel of whom that Judaism spoke. It portrayed the way of life and it set forth the worldview of that Judaism. As a matter of fact, the Talmud from the time of its closure in ca. 600 A.D., just before the Muslim conquest of the Middle East, North Africa, and much of southern and western Europe, until the nineteenth century, accomplished the goals of its writers. It did define the social order for nearly the whole of its "Israel."

That remarkable record of success—the envy of any writer interested in issues of politics in relationship to culture and religion—finds few counterparts. Among political writings of surpassing theoretical interest, Plato's *Republic* and Aristotle's *Politics,* to name two important documents, influenced many thinkers, but no constitution copied Plato's *Republic,* and no politics responded to Aristotle's wonderful theory of the whole. Nor did More's *Utopia* provide for anyone a model of how to write up the rules of a state. Among law codes, few single documents—Justinian's is one, Napoleon's another—compete with the Talmud as an enduring and ubiquitously influential statement of the law through the specification of the laws. Since the Talmud set forth not only decisions in right array but also portrayed in intimate exemplary detail the compelling model of correct modes of thought, a further comparison is in order. Among theories of human behavior, properly construed, formulations of ethics and, even more, the modes of thought and analysis by which right decisions are reached, we ask for counterparts but find none. Accounts of right thinking about right action in the formation of public policy and private behavior of the scope and dimensions of the Talmud's account—Plato's *Dialogues,* for instance—do not measure up to the Talmud's in three indicative matters.

First, the Talmud shows how practical reason does its work to make diverse issues and actions conform to a single principle. Second, the Talmud shows how applied logic discerns the regular and the orderly in the confusion and disorder of everyday conflict. Third, the Talmud portrays the right way of thinking about problems that may be worked out in many different analytical modes. Where are we to find massive displays of applied logic and practical reasoning in the analysis of the minutiae of the workaday world, showing in the everyday the intimations of regularity, order, compelling purpose, that, all together, point to the governance of a reasonable Creator of an orderly and sensible creation—nature and social order alike? In the Talmud, but not in many other writings.

That fact draws our attention to the importance of writing. The generative question here is this: precisely how do authors who set forth to write a document bearing so grave a responsibility, so lofty an ambition, as the Talmud, actually write? If we wonder how practical visionaries, men of learning but also of affairs, propose to say everything in one place in the way in which the authors of the Talmud said everything about the politics of the social order in a single document, here is one of the few occasions for finding an answer. To define the challenge to writing, we should ask for a solution to the following problem. A hundred years after the founding of the American nation, roughly at the turn of the twentieth century, we are asked to take the Constitution of the United States of America and the first ten amendments, the Federalist Papers, the decisions of the Supreme Court down to *Marbury vs. Madison,* the judges' notes as well, the *Congressional Record* of that age, and the United States Code; to collect, as well, the corresponding documents of the Presbyterian Church and its synods; to add to the task a respectable selection of the writings of Benjamin Franklin, Washington Irving, Henry David Thoreau, and Ralph Waldo Emerson; and having mastered the whole, write in a single document everything that we have learned—in such a way as to show future readers how we have reached our conclusions and why these conclusions are compelling and ineluctable.

That formidable task must then begin with a solution to the problem of writing: precisely how do we propose to take over and reshape in discourse that compels assent so varied a legacy? How are we going to give purpose and structure and order to materials that share a common theme—the creation of the United States of America—but little else? This bare-bones account of what I conceive, in their terms and context, the authors of the Bavli to have accomplished defines the problem of this book. The data are technical and detailed. But for the culture and politics of writing, what is at stake is weighty and broadly intelligible.

What makes possible the analysis of the document as a whole is a simple fact. It is that the Talmud in its thirty-seven tractates is entirely uniform, and the stylistic preferences exhibited on any given page characterize every other page of the document. That same fact justifies my insistence that the document's author's or authors' indicative traits of mind, as conveyed in the rules of communication, attest to a vision of a shared realm of discourse, a shared existence, the social order imagined but also portrayed. When people everywhere, whatever the subject or problem, turn out to speak in the same way, and, as we shall see, even to say the same thing about many things, they certainly attract attention to the distinctive traits of expression that they deem correct throughout. What we find on one page we find on every other page, the same rhetoric, the same logic, the same law underlying laws. When, therefore, we examine a single page or a single chapter, we see the entirety of the writing. Given its massive dimensions, then, we are on firm ground in asking about that textual community that has in such a uniform way communicated its message through its method.

When we realize that that community's writing ultimately imposed its method, as much as its message, upon the social world to which its authors proposed to speak, we understand how full and rich is that resource of culture contained within the writing before us. Reaching closure in ca. 600 A.D., the Bavli, with its ongoing discourse of continuous, intimate commentary, magisterial code, and concrete, niggling application through centuries afterward, defined the world order of Judaism. From the end of late antiquity at the rise of Islam to nearly the present day, that one writing predominated. The intellectual foundations of social action, the beliefs and values of culture, the national consensus that defined ways of forming family and conduct of the everyday life—the ethos and ethics of the diverse people of Israel, wherever they lived, to begin with responded to—and aimed to realize in concrete ways—the religious system set forth in that vast document. If, therefore, we wish to understand the relationship between the ideas that people hold and the world that they make for themselves, we find in that Talmud an example rich in promise.

For writing, as people now appreciate, not only sets forth messages through the statement of propositions. Writing also bears signification through how things are said, indeed, perhaps in a more effective and profound way than through what is said. If, therefore, we wish to move from writing to the world that that writing is meant to adumbrate, formulate, portray and even—in word and sound, then in deed and fact—realize, we can do well to pay close attention to a document that made the world that its authors intended to make. Not only so, but that world came to realization to begin with within the intellectual life of the very readers that the authors to begin with proposed to influence and shape. Few documents in the entire history of the West—the Bible created by Christianity is one, the writings of Aristotle another—have so informed and shaped society in the way in which, within the community of Israel, the Jewish people, the Bavli did. So in the study of the relationship of ideas and society, writing and the message that is communicated and realized through writing, this document bears special interest.

That is why the manner of writing may instruct us on matters of general intelligibility and public consequence. And when we deal with a document that itself is intended as a plan for the conduct of life of an entire society, one the plan of which in time was realized, we realize that what is at stake are considerable concerns of culture. So while we pay close attention to some rather arcane and technical problems in a remote and unfamiliar piece of writing, in these pages we see how modes of thought themselves convey—and effect—social, indeed even public, policy. Language, the logical representation of coherent thought, the representation of one important thing through many unimportant ones—these traits of a literary culture instruct us on the formation of the social order of the foundation document that exhibits them. Through them the textual community frames the social order.

We deal in particular with a document remarkable for its power to define the social order of an entire people, living under diverse rules of politics, culture, economy, and society. Wherever Jews lived from the seventh century to nearly our own time, they found in the Talmud of Babylonia the rules that would govern their social order. What makes the modes of thought of the Talmud important, therefore, is that, through thinking in this way, rather than in some other, people formulated a public policy in the grandest dimensions of their shared lives. What makes those modes of thought accessible is the uniformity of discourse characteristic of the Talmud of Babylonia or Bavli. That uniform discourse produces the recurrence of a few fixed forms and formulas. The rather monotonous, even tedious, character of the writing at hand attests to its authorship's adherence to a few rules that prove determinative beginning to end. The document exhibits remarkable integrity; the limits of the document clearly are delineated, and when other documents are introduced in evidence, they too are marked in the manner in which, in this period and within the technical limitations operative then, people were able to cite or place in quotations or footnote materials borrowed from other sources. This is a writing that does not (merely) allude or hint at something found somewhere else, it articulately cites, it explicitly quotes. Within the limits of the Bavli, the document defines its own infrastructure in both rhetoric and logic. And, as we see, beyond the limits of the writing, the world beyond responded, thinking in some way as one and so ordering the affairs of families and communities in the way in which they did, rather than in some other. We now take up one of the most successful documents of all time, one that, like Scripture ("the Bible," "the Old Testament") defines how entire communities live out their lives and define their social order.

Stated very simply, the Talmud of Babylonia is the single most important document of rabbinic literature—and, as a matter of fact, of Judaism.[1] When we know

[1] For further reading and bibliography of the topic of this chapter, see the following:

Eliezer Berkovits, "Talmud, Babylonian," in *Encyclopaedia Judaica* 15:755–768: methods of study; scope of the Babylonian Talmud; Mishnah and Gemara; interpretation and application; development and conclusion of the Babylonian Talmud; style; text; minor tractates; commentaries, manuscripts; authority, influence; translations.

Bowker, pp. 65–67.

David Goodblatt, "The Babylonian Talmud," in Neusner, *Study of Ancient Judaism*, II, pp. 120–99.

Abraham Goldberg, "The Babylonian Talmud" (the Halakhic tradition in Babylonia; the Babylonian academies and generations of sages; the Babylonian approach to the Mishnah; "The Mishna is lacking and thus the Tanna teaches"; relationship to Tosefta, baraitot, and Palestinian Talmud; the Aggada in the Babylonian Talmud; the sugya; the Savoraim; redaction; authority; bibliography; manuscripts of the Babylonian Talmud [by Michael Krupp]) in Safrai, *Literature of the Sages*, pp. 323–66.

M. B. Lerner, "The External Tractates," covering Derekh Erets, Semahot, Kalla, Sofrim, and the Seven Minor Tracts, in Safrai, *Literature of the Sages*, pp. 367–403.

Maccoby's introduction ignores this document entirely. But see "Tannaitic Passages in the Talmud [= Talmud of Babylonia only] (Baraitas)," pp. 182–85.

Zeev, Safrai, "Post-Talmudic Halakhic Literature in the Land of Israel," in Safrai, *Literature of the Sages*, pp. 404–10.

Stemberger-Strack, pp. 208–44: structure and contents; origin, redaction; sources; baraitot; Midrashim; Palestinian sources from the Amoraic period; amalgamation of the Tradition; the contribution of the Saboraim; Geonic additions; the text; manuscripts; printed editions; translations; the authority of the Babylonian Talmud; commentaries; introductions to the Talmud; the Talmud in controversy.

This writer's monographic studies include the following: *The Bavli and Its Sources: The Question of Tradition in the Case of Tractate Sukkah*. Atlanta, 1987: Scholars Press for Brown Judaic Studies; *The Talmud: Close Encounters*. Minneapolis, 1991: Fortress Press; *Tradition as Selectivity: Scripture, Mishnah, Tosefta, and Midrash in the Talmud of Babylonia. The Case of Tractate Arakhin*. Atlanta, 1990: Scholars Press for South Florida Studies in the History of Judaism; *Language as Taxonomy. The Rules for Using Hebrew and Aramaic in the Babylonian Talmud*. Atlanta, 1990: Scholars Press for South Florida Studies in the History of Judaism; *The Bavli That Might Have Been: The Tosefta's Theory of Mishnah-Commentary Compared with that of the Babylonian Talmud*. Atlanta, 1990: Scholars Press for South Florida Studies in the History of Judaism; *The Rules of Composition of the Talmud of Babylonia. The Cogency of the Bavli's Composite*. Atlanta, 1991: Scholars Press for South Florida Studies in the History of Judaism; *The Bavli's One Voice: Types and Forms of Analytical Discourse and Their Fixed Order of Appearance*. Atlanta, 1991: Scholars Press for South Florida Studies in the History of Judaism; *The Bavli's One Statement. The Metapropositional Program of Babylonian Talmud Tractate Zebahim Chapters One and Five*. Atlanta, 1991: Scholars Press for South Florida Studies in the History of Judaism; *How the Bavli Shaped Rabbinic Discourse*. Atlanta, 1991: Scholars Press for South Florida Studies in the History of Judaism; *The Bavli's Massive Miscellanies. The Problem of Agglutinative Discourse in the Talmud of Babylonia*. Atlanta, 1992: Scholars Press for South Florida Studies in The History of Judaism; *Sources and Traditions. Types of Composition in the Talmud of Babylonia*. Atlanta, 1992: Scholars Press for South Florida Studies in the History of Judaism; *The Law Behind the*

what marks the Bavli in particular, meaning, how it differs from the prior Talmud, we shall understand why. While the Talmud of the Land of Israel sticks close to its primary document, the Mishnah, and amplifies it, the Talmud of Babylonia takes its own path. The Bavli vastly transcends the Mishnah and, utterly autonomous of the first Talmud as well, forms an eloquent statement of its own. Identifying the Talmud of Babylonia suffices with two points.

First comes the simple definition that the Bavli is a commentary to the Mishnah, which in basic formal and programmatic traits is just like the Yerushalmi. These shared superficial, definitive traits were defined in Chapter 7.

The second point of definition is to distinguish the second from the first Talmud. Both Talmuds do appeal to some sources in common: Scripture, Mishnah, episodic passages that we find also in the Tosefta, and a few sayings attributed to authorities who flourished after the closure of the Mishnah, e.g., earlier masters in the Talmudic process that yielded the Talmuds of each country, Yohanan and Simeon b. Laqish, for the Land of Israel, Rab and Samuel, for Babylonia. But the common use of received sayings rarely permits us to predict the direction and purpose of the compositions of the two Talmuds; each will go its own way, guided by its own concerns, pursuing its own interests. For the framers of the Bavli drew upon their distinctive, local sources for compositions and composites, and the framers of the Yerushalmi drew upon their equivalently distinctive, local sources for compositions and composites.

As a matter of fact, the framers of the compositions, all the more so for the composites of the second Talmud, do precisely what they wish with such shared sayings or stories, and the Bavli's compositors did not respond to or build upon compositions, still less composites, shared with the earlier Talmud. The compositions and composites that comprise the Bavli occasionally use imported parts, that

---

Laws. *The Bavli's Essential Discourse*. Atlanta, 1992: Scholars Press for South Florida Studies in the History of Judaism; *The Bavli's Primary Discourse. Mishnah Commentary, Its Rhetorical Paradigms and Their Theological Implications in the Talmud of Babylonia Tractate Moed Qatan*. Atlanta, 1992: Scholars Press for South Florida Studies in the History of Judaism; *The Discourse of the Bavli: Language, Literature, and Symbolism. Five Recent Findings*. Atlanta, 1991: Scholars Press for South Florida Studies in the History of Judaism; *The Bavli's Intellectual Character. The Generative Problematic in Bavli Baba Qamma Chapter One and Bavli Shabbat Chapter One*. Atlanta, 1992: Scholars Press for South Florida Studies in the History of Judaism; *Decoding the Talmud's Exegetical Program: From Detail to Principle in the Bavli's Quest for Generalization. Tractate Shabbat*. Atlanta, 1992: Scholars Press for South Florida Studies in the History of Judaism; *The Principal Parts of the Bavli's Discourse: A Final Taxonomy. Mishnah-Commentary, Sources, Traditions, and Agglutinative Miscellanies*. Atlanta, 1992: Scholars Press for South Florida Studies in the History of Judaism; *The Torah in the Talmud. A Taxonomy of the Uses of Scripture in the Talmuds. Tractate Qiddushin in the Talmud of Babylonia and the Talmud of the Land of Israel. I. Bavli Qiddushin Chapter One*. Atlanta, 1992: Scholars Press for South Florida Studies in the History of Judaism; *The Torah in the Talmud. A Taxonomy of the Uses of Scripture in the Talmuds. Tractate Qiddushin in the Talmud of Babylonia and the Talmud of the Land of Israel. II. Yerushalmi Qiddushin Chapter One. And a Comparison of the Uses of Scripture by the Two Talmuds*. Atlanta, 1992: Scholars Press for South Florida Studies in the History of Judaism; *The Bavli's Unique Voice. A Systemic Comparison of the Talmud of Babylonia and the Talmud of the Land of Israel*, in seven volumes, Scholars Press for South Florida Studies in the History of Judaism; and *Talmudic Thinking: Language, Logic, and Law*. Columbia, 1992: University of South Carolina Press.

is, sayings from the other locale, but in any event are taken apart and then remanufactured at home. "The one whole Torah of Moses, our Rabbi"—written in Scripture, oral in the Mishnah and related sayings classified as Tannaite—therefore divides by place. The rabbinic traditions are bound by place. The rabbis' re-presentation of the Torah is profoundly localized and particularized by the Talmud of Babylonia. Standing for Judaism outside of the Land of Israel, that localized representation of the Torah went in, for centuries to come, to define Judaism.

2.
TRANSLATIONS INTO ENGLISH

The first and best complete translation of the Talmud of Babylonia is Israel Epstein, ed., *The Babylonian Talmud* (London, 1948: Soncino Press), printed in eighteen volumes. The second complete translation—the only one based on the principles of form analysis—now in print is this writer's *The Talmud of Babylonia. An American Translation* (Missoula, Chico, then Atlanta, 1984–93: Scholars Press for Brown Judaic Studies), in seventy-five volumes. Further translations into English are presently under way, but none has as yet come close to completion.

3.
RHETORIC

The second Talmud's formal repertoire falls into the same classifications as that of the first, and the taxonomic character of the use of Aramaic and Hebrew, set forth in Chapter 7, is identical. Differences in word choice and redactional signals that have no bearing on the appreciation of the documents in context need not detain us; these are fully spelled out, for those familiar with the documents in their original languages, in the introductions cited in note 1.

4.
LOGIC OF COHERENT DISCOURSE

The mixture of propositional logic for most compositions and the logic of fixed association for nearly all composites that characterizes the Yerushalmi pertains to the Bavli as well.

5.

TOPICAL PROGRAM

What has been said about the two Talmuds' topical program requires no repetition. The sole point of difference is in detail. That is, the Bavli treats the second through the fifth divisions of the Mishnah, in contrast to the Yerushalmi's examination of the first through fourth. The difference in how the two Talmuds treat the same Mishnah passage is spelled out presently. It is in the Bavli's distinctive hermeneutics that the principal difference between the two Talmuds emerges.

6.

A SAMPLE PASSAGE

A sample passage has already been given in Chapter 4. Other large samples are given below, in sections 7 through 9.

7.

THE COMPARISON AND CONTRAST OF THE TWO TALMUDS: HOW THE BAVLI DIFFERS FROM THE YERUSHALMI

Both Talmuds say the same thing in pretty much the same way, but the second Talmud radically differs from the first. That is so because, first, as noted, all of its compositions and composites were prepared locally and not imported from the Holy Land, and, second, its hermeneutics of the Mishnah is original. The two Talmuds routinely treat the same Mishnah but only very rarely intersect other than at a given Mishnah paragraph or Tosefta selection. Ordinarily, each Talmud pursues its own interests when reading a passage shared with the other.

WAS THERE A Q?   In this context readers familiar with New Testament Gospels research will wonder whether a common source—a "Q"—was drawn upon by writers of compositions that occur in the respective Talmuds, asking, do the Bavli and Yerushalmi draw on (a) "Q"? At some points, they do draw on available materials, ordinarily, sayings floating hither and yon. It is very common that these finished materials occur also in the Tosefta, in the way in which we noted in Chapter

6. So in theory there could have been a "Q." But if there was, analysis of the shared sayings proves that it was not like a "Q" of the size and importance of the one that is attested by Matthew and Mark and used by Luke.

WAS THERE A SHARED EXEGETICAL PROTOCOL? If there is no shared corpus of sayings, then does a topical protocol define both Talmuds' Mishnah exegesis, that is, a protocol of topics or problems associated with a given Mishnah pericope but not articulated therein? Such a protocol would have told the exegetes of that pericope, or the compilers of compositions deemed pertinent to that pericope, what subject they should treat (over and above the subject of the pericope); or what problem they should investigate (over and above the problem explicit in the pericope). If such a protocol were in play, then when discussing a given Mishnah paragraph, compilers of both Talmuds will have introduced the same themes, not mentioned in the Mishnah (whether in the paragraph at hand or in some other paragraph) but held in common to belong to the clarification of that Mishnah paragraph.

Here again, an analogy may clarify for New Testament scholars what is at stake here. It is clear that for the authors of the four canonical Gospels as well as all of the extracanonical ones, a shared protocol, not spelled out, dictated the subjects that should be treated and the order in which they should occur. That is to say, if we propose to talk about Jesus Christ, his life and teachings, we follow an established program. We are going to discuss, e.g., the Passion, and, moreover, the Passion is going to appear at the end of the narrative. A biographical narrative will intrude throughout. That protocol governs in all four Gospels, without regard to the character of the Passion Narrative, on the one side, or the program of sayings and stories to be utilized in the articulation of the various Gospels, respectively, on the other: a fine example of a blatant topical (narrative) protocol.

In fact, no substantial, shared exegetical protocol or tradition, either in fully spelled-out statements in so many words, or in the gist of ideas, or in topical conventions, or in intellectual characteristics, governed the two Talmuds' reading of the same Mishnah paragraph. The Bavli presents an utterly autonomous statement, speaking in its own behalf and in its own way about its own interests. The shared traits are imposed, extrinsic, and formal, that is, documents cited by one set of writers and by another. The differentiating characteristics are intrinsic and substantive: what is to be done with the shared formal statements taken from prior writings? The framers of the Bavli in no way found guidance in the processes by which the Yerushalmi's compositions and composites took shape, either in the dim past of the document, or, it goes without saying, in the results of those processes as well. The Talmuds differ not in general only, but in detail; not in how they make their statements or in what they say but, at a more profound level, they part company in their very generative layers, in the intellectual morphology characteristic of each.

COMPARING THE TWO TALMUDS' READING OF THE SAME MISHNAH
PARAGRAPH: If we compare the way in which the two Talmuds read the same
Mishnah, we discern consistent differences between them. The principal difference
between the Talmuds is that difference that distinguishes jurisprudence from philosophy. The Yerushalmi talks in details, the Bavli in large truths; the Yerushalmi
tells us what the Mishnah says, the Bavli, what it means. The Bavli demonstrates
how the Mishnah's laws form law, the way in which its rules attest to the ontological unity of truth. (We have already touched on that point in Chapter 4.) The Bavli
thinks more deeply about deep things, and, in the end, its authors also think about
different things from those that occupy the writers of the Yerushalmi. How do the
Talmuds compare? The formidable example we shall now examine in some detail
yields these generalizations:

[1] the first Talmud analyzes evidence, the second investigates premises;

[2] the first remains wholly within the limits of its case, the second vastly transcends the bounds of the case altogether;

[3] the first wants to know the rule, the second asks about the principle and its
implications for other cases.

The one Talmud provides an exegesis and amplification of the Mishnah; the
other, a theoretical study of the law in all its magnificent abstraction—transforming
the Mishnah into testimony to a deeper reality altogether: to the law behind the
laws. And it is that to which the Bavli itself attests—a hermeneutics that insists
upon inquiry into premises, implications, and principles behind cases and how they
coalesce—that forms the theological re-presentation of the Torah accomplished by
the Bavli itself. So the contrast between the two Talmuds affords access to more
than merely literary data on how two commentaries to the same text differ—much
more. To make these points stick, we turn to Mishnah tractate Gittin 1:1 as read
by both Talmuds. Let us first look at the passage and the way that the Yerushalmi
reads it. As usual, passages of the Mishnah or Tosefta are given in boldface type.

YERUSHALMI TO GITTIN 1:1

[A] **[43a] He who delivers a writ of divorce from overseas must
state, "In my presence it was written, and in my presence it
was signed."**

[B] **Rabban Gamaliel says, "Also: He who delivers [a writ of di-
vorce] from Reqem or from Heger [must make a similar decla-
ration]."**

[C] **R. Eliezer says, "Even from Kefar Ludim to Lud."**

[D] **And sages say, "He must state, 'In my presence it was written,
and in my presence it was signed,' only in the case of him who
delivers a writ of divorce from overseas,**

[E] **"and him who takes [one abroad]."**

[F] **And he who delivers [a writ of divorce] from one overseas**

province to another must state, "In my presence it was written, and in my presence it was signed."

[G] **Rabban Simeon b. Gamaliel says, "Even [if he brings one] from one jurisdiction to another [in the same town.]"**

[I.A] Now here is a problem. In the case of one who brings a deed of gift from overseas, does he have to state, "Before me it was written and before me it was signed"? [Why is the rule more strict for writs of divorce?]

[B] R. Joshua b. Levi said, "The case [of writs of divorce] is different, for [overseas] they are not expert in the details of preparing writs of divorce [properly]."

[C] Said R. Yohanan, "It is a lenient ruling which [sages] have provided for her, that she should not sit an abandoned wife [unable to remarry]."

[D] And is this a lenient ruling? It is only a stringent one, for if the messenger did not testify, "In my presence it was written, and in my presence it was signed," you are not indeed going to permit the woman to remarry [at all], [so what sort of a lenient ruling do we have here]?

[E] Said R. Yosé, "The strict requirement which you have imposed on the matter at the outset, requiring the messenger to testify, 'Before me it was written and before me it was signed,' turns out to be a lenient ruling which you have set for the case at the end. For if the husband later on should come and call into question the validity of the document, his cavil will be null."

[F] [As to the denial of credibility to the husband's challenge to the validity of the writ of divorce,] R. Mana contemplated ruling, "That applies to a complaint dealing with matters external to the body of the document itself."

[G] But as to a complaint as to the body of the document itself [do we believe him]? [Surely we take seriously his claim that the document is a forgery.]

[H] And as to a complaint [against the writ] which has no substance [one may not take the husband's cavil seriously].

[I] And even in the case of a cavil which has substance [should he not be believed]? [Surely he should be believed.]

[J] Said R. Yosé b. R. Bun, "[No, the original statement stands in all these cases]. [That is to say,] since you have said that the same reason you have applied in the case for a more stringent requirement at the outset, that the messenger must declare, 'Before me it was [written, and before me it was] signed,—for that same reason you have imposed a lenient ruling at the end, for if the husband later on should come and call into question the validity of the document, his cavil will be null. So we must conclude that there is no difference at all whether the complaint against the validity of the document pertains to matters external to the body of

the document or to matters internal to the body of the document, nor is there any difference whether the complaint deals with matters of no substance or matters of substance. [Once the necessary formula is recited by the messenger, the document has been validated against all future doubts.]"

[K]   And yet should one take into account that invalid witnesses may have signed the document?

[L]   Said R. Abun, "The husband is not suspect of disrupting [the wife's future marriage] in a matter which is in the hands of heaven, [but is suspect of doing so only in a matter which lies before a court]. [Hence we do not take account of the husband's issuing such a complaint as is entered at G.]

[M]   "In a court proceeding he is suspect of disrupting the wife's [future marriage]. For since he knows full well that if he should come and register a complaint against the validity of the document, his complaint will be deemed null, even he sees to it [when he prepares the writ] that it is signed by valid witnesses."

Unit I clarifies the force of the required declaration. Once the messenger so states, the husband cannot later on invalidate the document. Since, in the meantime, it is assumed that the wife will remarry, the importance of limiting the original husband's power is self-evident. That, sum and substance, is what interests the Yerushalmi.

Now let us see how the Bavli reads the same paragraph. I give only part of the discussion, the first nine units of a score that comprise one of the Talmud's great, sustained composites—enough so that the point is abundantly clear. Use of italics here indicates Aramaic, regular type, Hebrew.

BAVLI TO GITTIN 1:1

A.   **He who delivers a writ of divorce from overseas must state, "In my presence it was written, and in my presence it was signed."**

B.   **Rabban Gamaliel says, "Also: He who delivers [a writ of divorce] from Reqem or from Heger [must make a similar declaration]."**

[C]   **R. Eliezer says, "Even from Kefar Ludim to Lud."**

[D]   **And sages say, "He must state, 'In my presence it was written, and in my presence it was signed,' only in the case of him who delivers a writ of divorce from overseas,**

I. 1. A.   What is the operative consideration here?

        B.   Said Rabbah, [2B] "Because [Israelites overseas] are inexpert in

the requirement that the writ be prepared for the particular person for whom it is intended."

C. Raba said, "Because valid witnesses are not readily found to confirm the signatures [and the declaration of the agent serves to authenticate the signatures of the witnesses]."

D. *So what is at issue between these two explanations?*

E. *At issue between them is a case in which two persons brought the writ of divorce [in which case Raba's consideration is null], or a case in which a writ of divorce was brought from one province to another in the Land of Israel [in which case the consideration of Rabbah is null], or from one place to another in the same overseas province.*

I. 2. A. *And from the perspective of Rabbah, who has said, "Because [Israelites overseas] are inexpert in the requirement that the writ be prepared for the particular person for whom it is intended," there should still be a requirement that the writ of divorce be brought by two persons, such as is the requirement in respect to all acts of testimony that are spelled out in the Torah [in line with Deut. 19:15]!*

B. An individual witness is believed where the question has to do with a prohibition [for example, as to personal status, but not monetary matters].

C. *Well, I might well concede that we do hold,* an individual witness is believed where the question has to do with a prohibition, *for example, in the case of a piece of fat, which may be forbidden fat or may be permitted fat, in which instance the status of a prohibition has not yet been assumed. But here, with regard to the case at hand, where the presence of a prohibition is assumed, namely, that the woman is married, it amounts to a matter involving prohibited sexual relations,* and a matter involving sexual relations is settled by no fewer than two witnesses.

D. Most overseas Israelites are expert in the rule that the document has to be written for the expressed purpose of divorcing this particular woman.

E. *And even R. Meir, who takes account of not only the condition of the majority but even that of the minority [in this case, people not expert in that rule], concedes the ordinary scribe of a court knows the law full well, and it was rabbis who imposed the requirement. But here [3A] so as to prevent the woman from entering the status of a deserted wife [unable to remarry], they made the rule lenient.*

F. *Is this really a lenient ruling? It is in fact a strict ruling, since, if you require that the writ of divorce be brought by two messengers, there is no possibility of the husband's coming and challenging its validity and having it invalidated, but if only one person brings the document, he can still do so!*

G. Since the master has said, "As to how many persons must be present when the messenger hands over the writ of divorce to the wife, there is a dispute between R. Yohanan and R. Hanina. One party maintains it must be at least two, the other three." *Now, since that is the fact, the messenger will clarify the husband's intentions to begin with, and the husband under such circumstances is not going to come and try to invalidate the writ and so get himself into trouble later on.*

I. 3. A. *Now from the perspective of Raba, who said that the operative consideration is,* "Because valid witnesses are not readily found to confirm the signatures [and the declaration of the agent serves to authenticate the signatures of the witnesses]," *there should still be a requirement that the writ of divorce is brought by two persons, such as is the requirement in respect to all acts of confirming the validity of documents in general!*

    B. An individual witness is believed where the question has to do with a prohibition [for example, as to personal status, but not monetary matters].

    C. *Well, I might well concede that we do hold,* an individual witness is believed where the question has to do with a prohibition, *for example, in the case of a piece of fat, which may be forbidden fat or may be permitted fat, in which instance the status of a prohibition has not yet been assumed. But here, with regard to the case at hand, where the presence of a prohibition is assumed, namely, that the woman is married, it amounts to a matter involving prohibited sexual relations,* and a matter involving sexual relations is settled by no fewer than two witnesses.

    D. *Well, in strict law, there should be no requirement that witnesses confirm the signature on other documents either, in line with what R. Simeon b. Laqish said, for said* R. Simeon b. Laqish, "Witnesses who have signed a document are treated as equivalent to those who have been cross-examined in court." *It was rabbis who imposed the requirement. But here so as to prevent the woman from entering the status of a deserted wife [unable to marry], they made the rule lenient.*

    E. *Is this really a lenient ruling? It is in fact a strict ruling, since, if you require that the writ of divorce be brought by two messengers, there is no possibility of the husband's coming and challenging its validity and having it invalidated, but if only one person brings the document, he can still do so!*

    F. Since the master has said, "As to how many persons must be present when the messenger hands over the writ of divorce to the wife, there is a dispute between R. Yohanan and R. Hanina. One party maintains it must be at least two, the other three." *Now, since that is the fact, the messenger will clarify the husband's intentions to begin with, and the husband under such circumstances is not going to come and try to invalidate the writ and so get himself into trouble later on.*

I. 4. A. *So how come Raba didn't give the operative consideration that Rabbah did?*

B. *He will say to you, "Does the Tannaite rule state,* **In my presence it was written** *for the purpose of divorcing this woman in particular,* **and in my presence it was signed** *for the purpose of divorcing this woman in particular?"*

C. And Rabbah?

D. *Strictly speaking, it should have been formulated for Tannaite purposes in that way. But if you get verbose, the bearer may omit something that is required.*

E. *So, well, even as it is, the bearer may omit something that is required!*

F. *One out of three phrases he may leave out, but one out of two phrases he's not going to leave out.*

G. *So how come Rabbah didn't give the operative consideration that Raba did?*

H. *He will say to you, "If so, the Tannaite formulate should be,* **In my presence it was signed**—*and nothing more! What need do I have for the language,* **In my presence it was written***? That is to indicate that we require that the writ be prepared for the sole purpose of divorcing this particular woman.*

I. And Raba?

J. *Strictly speaking, it should have been formulated for Tannaite purposes in that way. But if it were done that way, people might come to confuse the matter of the confirmation of documents in general and hold that only a single witness is required for that purpose.*

K. And Rabbah?

L. *But is the parallel all that close? There the required language is, "We know that this is Mr. So-and-so's signature," while here it is, 'In my presence. . . .'" In that case, a woman is not believed to testify, in this case, a woman is believed to testify. In that case, an interested party cannot testify, here an interested party can testify.*

M. And Raba?

N. *He will say to you, "Here, too, if the agent says, 'I know . . . ,' he is believed, and since that is the fact, there really is the consideration [if he says only, 'In my presence it was signed' (Simon)], people might come to confuse the matter of the confirmation of documents in general and hold that only a single witness is required for that purpose."*

I. 5. A. *From the perspective of Rabbah, who has said,* "Because [Israelites overseas] are inexpert in the requirement that the writ be prepared for the particular person for whom it is intended," *who is the authority that requires that* the writ of divorce be both written for the particular person for whom it is intended *and also requires* [3B] that it be signed for the particular person for whom it is intended? *It obviously isn't R. Meir, for he requires the correct declaration as to the signing of the document, but not as to the writing of the document, for we have learned in the Mishnah:* **They do not write [a writ of divorce] on something which is attached to the ground. [If] one wrote it on something attached to the ground, then plucked it up, signed it, and gave it to her, it is legitimate [M. 2:4A–B].** [The anonymous rule, assumed to stand for Meir, holds that what matters is the signing, not the writing, of the document.] *It also cannot be R. Eleazar, who maintains that the writing be done properly* [with correct intentionality as to the preparation of the document for the particular woman to whom it is to be given as a writ of divorce], *but as to the signing, he imposes no such requirement.*

And, further, should you say that, in point of fact, it really is R. Eleazar, and as to his not requiring correct procedure as to the signing of the document with proper specificity [with correct intentionality as to the preparation of the document for the particular woman to whom it is to be given as a writ of divorce], *that is on the strength of the authority of the Torah, but as to the position of rabbis, he would concur that that requirement must be met—if that is your claim, lo, there are three kinds of writs of divorce that rabbis have declared invalid [but the Torah has not invalidated], and among them, R. Eleazar does not include one that has not been signed with appropriate intentionality for that particular woman, as we see in the following Mishnah:* **There are three writs of divorce which are invalid, but if the wife [subsequently] remarried [on the strength of those documents], the offspring [nonetheless] is legitimate: [if] he wrote it in his own handwriting, but there are no witnesses on it; there are witnesses on it, but it is not dated; it is dated, but there is only a single witness—lo, these are three kinds of invalid writs of divorce, but if the wife [subsequently] remarried, the offspring is valid. R. Eleazar says, "Even though there are no witnesses on it [the document itself], but he handed it over to her in the presence of witnesses, it is valid. And she collects [her marriage contract] from mortgaged property. For witnesses sign the writ of divorce only for the good order of the world" [M. Git. 9:4].**

B.   *Well, then, it must be R. Meir, and so far as he is concerned, as to his not requiring correct procedure as to the signing of the document with proper specificity* [with correct intentionality as to the preparation of the document for the particular woman to whom it is to be given as a writ of divorce], *that is on the strength of the authority of the Torah, but as to the position of rabbis, he would concur that that requirement must be met.*

C.   Yes, but said R. Nahman, "R. Meir would rule, 'Even if one found it in the garbage [4A] and had it properly signed and handed it over to her, it is a valid writ of divorce'"! *And, as a matter of fact, this ruling is to say, "valid so far as the Torah is concerned," then the language that R. Nahman should have used is not, R. Meir would rule, but rather, The rule of the Torah is. . . .*

D. *Rather, the position before us represents the view of R. Eleazar, and the case in which R. Eleazar does not require a signature incised for the sake of the particular woman for whom the document is prepared, that is a case in which there are no witnesses at all. But in a case in which there are witnesses, he does impose that requirement. For said R. Abba, "R. Eleazar concurs in the case of a writ disqualified on the base of its own character that it is invalid [and here we have invalid witnesses]."*

E. *R. Ashi said, "Lo, who is the authority at hand? It is R. Judah, for we have learned in the Mishnah:* **R. Judah declares it invalid, so long as writing it and signing it are [not] on something which is plucked up from the ground."**

F. *So to begin with why didn't we assign the passage to R. Judah?*

G. *We first of all reverted to R. Meir, for an otherwise unattributed statement in the Mishnah belongs to R. Meir. We reverted to R. Eleazar, because it is an established fact for us that in matters of writs of divorce, the decided law is in accord with his position.*

I. 6. A. *We have learned in the Mishnah:* **Rabban Gamaliel says, "Also: He who delivers [a writ of divorce] from Reqem or from Heger [must make a similar declaration]." R. Eliezer says, "Even from Kefar Ludim to Lud":**

B. *And said Abbayye, "We deal with towns that are near the Land of Israel and those that are entirely surrounded by the Land of Israel."*

C. *And said Rabbah bar bar Hannah, "I myself have seen that place, and the distance is the same as that between Be Kube and Pumbedita."*

I. 7. A. *Does it then follow that the initial Tannaite authority before us takes the view that when bringing a writ of divorce from the places named here, one need not make the stated declaration? Then is not this what is under dispute between the two authorities: The one authority takes the view that the operative consideration is,* because [Israelites overseas] are inexpert in the requirement that the writ be prepared for the particular person for whom it is intended, *and the residents of these areas have learned what to do; and the other authority holds that the operative consideration is,* because valid witnesses are not readily found to confirm the signatures [and the declaration of the agent serves to authenticate the signatures of the witnesses], *and in these places, too, witnesses are not readily found.*

B. *Not at all. Rabbah can work matters out in accord with his theory, and Raba can work matters out in accord with his theory.*

C. *Rabbah can work matters out in accord with his theory: All parties concur that the reason for the required declaration is that* [Israelites overseas] are inexpert in the requirement that the writ be prepared for the particular person for whom it is intended, *and here, what is at issue is, the initial authority holds that since these are located near the Land of Israel, they learn what is required; then Rabban Gamaliel comes along to say that those located in areas surrounded by the Land of Israel have learned the rules, while those nearby have not; then R. Eliezer comes along to indicate that those located in areas surrounded by the Land of Israel also are not exempt,* so as not to make a distinction among territories all assigned to the category of "overseas."

D. *Raba can work matters out in accord with his theory: All parties concur that the reason for the required declaration is that* valid witnesses are not readily found to confirm the signatures. *The initial Tannaite authority takes the view that these locales, since they are located near the border, will produce witnesses; Rabban Gamaliel comes along to say that in the areas surrounded by the Land of Israel, witnesses are going to be readily turned up, while in the areas near the Land, that is not the case; then R. Eliezer comes along to say that also in the areas surrounded by the Land of Israel, that is not the case,* so as to make a distinction among territories all assigned to the category of "overseas."

I. 8. A. *We have learned in the Mishnah:* **And sages say, "He must state, 'In my presence it was written, and in my presence it was signed,' only in the case of him who delivers a writ of divorce from overseas, and him who takes [one abroad]":**

B. *Does it then follow that the initial Tannaite authority before us takes the view that one who takes a writ of divorce overseas is not required to make the stated declaration? Then is not this what is at issue? The one authority maintains that the operative consideration is,* because [Israelites overseas] are inexpert in the requirement that the writ be prepared for the particular person for whom it is intended, [4B] *and the residents of these areas have learned what to do; and the other authority holds that the operative consideration is,* because valid witnesses are not readily found to confirm the signatures [and the declaration of the agent serves to authenticate the signatures of the witnesses], *and in these places, too, witnesses are not readily found.*

C. *Rabbah can work matters out in accord with his theory, and Raba can work matters out in accord with his theory.*

D. Rabbah can work matters out in accord with his theory: All parties concur that the reason for the required declaration is that

[Israelites overseas] are inexpert in the requirement that the writ be prepared for the particular person for whom it is intended, *and here, what is at issue is, whether we make a decree extending the obligation that applies to one who brings a writ from overseas to the Land of Israel to the person who takes a writ from the Land of Israel overseas, and the rabbis cited below maintain that we do make a decree covering one who takes such a writ overseas on account of the decree covering bringing such a decree to the Land of Israel.*

E. *Raba can work matters out in accord with his theory: All parties concur that the reason for the required declaration is that* valid witnesses are not readily found to confirm the signature.

I. 9. A. *We have learned in the Mishnah:* **And he who delivers [a writ of divorce] from one overseas province to another must state, "In my presence it was written, and in my presence it was signed."**

B. Lo, if he takes it from one place to another in the same overseas province, he does not have to make the required declaration. *Now that poses no problem to Raba [who can explain why], but it does present a conflict with the position of Rabbah!*

C. *Do not draw the conclusion that* if he takes it from one place to another in the same overseas province, he does not have to make the required declaration. *Rather, draw the conclusion that* if he brings it from one province to another in the Land of Israel, he does not have to make that declaration.

D. *But that position is spelled out explicitly in the Mishnah paragraph itself:* **He who delivers a writ of divorce in the Land of Israel does not have to state, "In my presence it was written, and in my presence it was signed"!**

E. *If I had only that statement to go by, I should have concluded that that is the case only after the fact, but to begin with, that is not the rule. So we are informed to the contrary.*

F. *There are those who set up the objection in the following language:* **[And he who delivers [a writ of divorce] from one overseas province to another must state: "In my presence it was written, and in my presence it was signed":]** Lo, if he takes it from one place to another in the same overseas province, he does not have to make the required declaration. *Now that poses no problem to Rabbah [who can explain why], but it does present a conflict with the position of Raba!*

G. *Do not draw the conclusion that* if he takes it from one province to another in the Land of Israel he does not have to make the declaration, *but say:* Lo, if it is written the same province overseas, he does not have to make that declaration, but if it is from one province to another in the Land of Israel, *what is the law?* He has to make the declaration.

H.   *Then the Tannaite formulation ought to be:* **And he who delivers [a writ of divorce]** without further articulation.

I.   In point of fact, even if one brings a writ of divorce from one province to another in the Land of Israel, *he also does not have to make the declaration, for, since there are pilgrims, witnesses will always be available.*

J.   *That poses no problem for the period at which the house of the sanctuary is standing, but for the period in which the house of the sanctuary is not standing, what is to be said?*

K.   *Since courts are well established, there still will be plenty of witnesses.*

I should gladly present the remainder of this monumental composition (not a mere composite but a cogent and continuous statement), which runs on for twenty ambitious units, but enough has been given to establish the character of the whole. Readers may stipulate that Bavli proceeds in the same fair and balanced manner to expose the dispute of Yohanan and Joshua b. Levi: if this, then what about that; if that, then what about this; how does this deal with that, how does that deal with this—and so on through a movement, a minuet really, of perfect classical order, proportion, balance. But enough has been given to provide a full grasp of the Bavli's intellectual morphology. Here the Yerushalmi, as much as the Bavli, presents a sustained argument, not just a snippet of self-evidently useful information, as at its reading of Mishnah Baba Mesia 1:1.

The contrast between the two Talmuds scarcely requires spelling out. At their reading of M. Gittin 1:1, where the Talmuds intersect but diverge in the reading of the Mishnah paragraph, we are able to identify what is at issue. The Yerushalmi presents two theses, A–C, then challenges the second of the two, D–E. This produces a secondary inspection of the facts of the matter, F–I, and a resolution of the issues raised, J; then another secondary issue, K–M. Is there an *Auseinandersetzung* between the two conflicting parties, Joshua b. Levi and Yohanan? Not at all. There is, in fact, no exchange. Instead of a dialogue, formed into an ongoing set of challenges, we have the voice of the Talmud intervening, "and is this a lenient ruling at all?" There is no pretense that Joshua asks a question of Yohanan, or Yohanan to Joshua. The controlling voice is that of the Talmud itself, which sets up pieces of information and manipulates them.

Bavli at I.5, by contrast, presents us with one of the Bavli's many superb representations of issues, and we see that the goal of contention is not argument for its own sake, nor is the medium the message, as some have imagined. Starting at the beginning, the Bavli at I.1 states the contrary explanations and identifies the issues between them. Then one position is examined, challenged, defended—fully exposed. The second position is given equal attention, also challenged, also defended, in all, fully exposed. The two positions having been fairly stated and amply argued, we proceed to the nub of the matter: if X is so right, then why has Y not adopted his position? And if Y, then why not X? This second level of exchange allows each position to be re-defended, re-explained, re-exposed—all on fresh grounds. Now at this point, we have identified two or more principles that have been combined to yield a position before us, so the question arises, what authority, among those who stand behind the law, holds these positions, which, while not contradictory, also are not commonly combined in a single theory of the law? I.5 then exposes the several possibilities—three major authorities, each with his several positions to be spelled out and tested against the allegations at hand.

Here is an occasion on which we can see the differences between the Yerushalmi's and the Bavli's representation of a conflict of principles contained within a Mishnah ruling. The Yerushalmi maintains that at issue is the inexpertness of overseas courts vs. a lenient ruling to avoid the situation of the abandoned wife; the Bavli, inexpertness of overseas courts vs. paucity of witnesses. How these diverse accounts differ in intellectual character and also program is hardly revealed by that brief précis. When we see how the two Talmuds respond to the same question, just now set forth, we realize that the Bavli is different from the Yerushalmi not in detail but in its very character. Despite commonalities of form, which validate comparison, the two Talmuds in fact are utterly unlike pieces of writing. The Bavli makes its own statement not merely because it very often says different things from the Yerushalmi or because it says different things in different ways (though both are the case).

The reason that the Bavli does commonly what the Yerushalmi does seldom and then rather clumsily—the balancing of arguments, the careful formation of a counterpoint of reasons, the excessively fair representation of contradictory positions (Why doesn't X take the position of Y? Why doesn't Y take the position of X? Indeed!)—is not that the Bavli's framers are uninterested in conclusions and outcome. It is that for the second Talmud, the deep structure of reason is the goal, and the only way to penetrate into how things are at their foundations is to investigate how conflicting positions rest on principles to be exposed and juxtaposed, balanced, and, if possible, negotiated, or if necessary, left in the balance.

WHAT MARKS THE BAVLI AS UNIQUE: What characterizes the Bavli and not the Yerushalmi is the search for the unitary foundations of the diverse laws, through an inquiry into the premises of discrete rules, the comparison and contrast of those premises, the statement of the emergent principles, and the comparison and contrast of those principles with the ones that derive from other cases and their premises—a process, an inquiry, without end into the law behind the laws. What the Yerushalmi ignores but the Bavli urgently seeks, beyond its presentation of the positions at hand, is to draw attention to the premises of those positions, the reasoning behind them, the evidence that supports them, the argument that transforms evidence into demonstration, and even the authority, among those who settle questions by expressing opinions, who can hold the combination of principles or premises that underpin a given position.

When we observe that one Talmud is longer than the other, or one Talmud gives a fuller account than the other, we realize that such an observation is trivial. The real difference between the Talmuds emerges from a different trait. It is the Bavli's completely different theory of what it wishes to investigate. And that difference derives from the reason that the framers of the Bavli's compositions and composites did the work to begin with. The outlines of the intellectual character of the work flow from the purpose of the project, not the reverse; and thence, the modes of thought, the specifics of analytical initiative—all these are secondary to intellectual morphology. So first comes the motivation for thought, then the morphology of thought, then the media of thought, in that order.

That explains why the difference between the Yerushalmi and the Bavli is the difference between jurisprudence and philosophy: the one is a work of exegesis in search of clarity of rules and, at its best, in quest of the jurisprudential system; the other, an exercise of sustained, critical, and dialectical argument and analysis in quest of philosophical truth. To state matters simply, the Yerushalmi presents and explains the laws, the rule for this, the rule for that—pure and simple; "law" bears its conventional meaning of jurisprudence. The Bavli presents the law, now in the philosophical sense of the abstract issues, the matters of theory, the principles at play far beneath the surface of detailed discussion, the law behind the laws. And that, we see, is not really "law," in any ordinary sense of jurisprudence; it is law in a deeply philosophical sense: the rules that govern the way things are, that define what is proportionate and orderly and properly composed.

What is interesting therefore is that even when the facts are the same, the issues identical, and the arguments matched, the Bavli's author manages to lay matters out in a very distinctive way. And that way yields as a sustained, somewhat intricate argument (requiring us to keep in the balance both names and positions of authorities and also the objective issues and facts) what the Yerushalmi's method of representation gives us as a rather simple sequence of arguments. The Bavli's presentation is one of thrust and parry, challenge and response, assertion and counterassertion, theoretical possibility and its exposure to practical facts ("if I had to rely . . . I might have supposed . . ."); and, of course, the authorities of the Bavli (not only the framers) are even prepared to rewrite the received Tannaite formulation. That initiative can come, I should think, only from someone totally in command of the abstractions and able to say, the details have to be this way; so the rule of mind requires; and so it shall be.

TO SUMMARIZE: The Yerushalmi's message is that the Mishnah yields clear and present rules; its medium is the patient exegesis of Mishnah passages, the provision and analysis of facts required in the understanding of the Mishnah. That medium conveys its message about not the Mishnah alone, but about the laws. The Bavli, for its part, conveys its message in a coherent and persistent manner through its ever-recurring medium of analysis and thought. We miss the point of the message if we misconstrue the medium: it is not the dialectical argument, and a mere reportage of questions and answers, thrust and parry, proposal and counterproposal—that does not accurately convey the unique medium of the Bavli, not at all. Dialectical arguments occur, if not commonly, in other rabbinic writings. Where we ask for authority behind an unstated rule and find out whether the same authority is consistent as to principle in other cases altogether, where we show that authorities are consistent with positions taken elsewhere—here above all we stand in the very heart of the Bavli's message, but only if we know what is at stake in the medium of inquiry.

8.

The Bavli's Unique Hermeneutics

The medium for the expression of the Bavli's statement of its own was dictated by the form and assignment of the document. Since the Talmud was a commentary in form, hermeneutics served as the mode of expression for whatever, within or beyond the commentary, the framers wished to say. When we understand how the Bavli's own statement is made, its principles for the reading of the received writing, then we can identify the hermeneutics. What makes the second Talmud unique is contained in the ways in which its hermeneutics differed from that of the first,. By showing people how to think, then, in the context of the revealed Torah, the Bavli's framers maintained that one could also guide them to what to think: through right reasoning formed into right attitudes, right thoughts led to right deeds. In the "how" of thought, the "what" found form and substance.

The Bavli speaks about the Mishnah in essentially a single voice, about fundamentally few things. Its mode of speech as much as of thought is uniform throughout. Diverse topics produce slight differentiation in modes of analysis. The same sorts of questions phrased in the same rhetoric—a moving, or dialectical, argument, composed of questions and answers—turn out to pertain equally well to every subject and problem. The Babylonian Talmud's discourse forms a closed system, in which people say the same thing about everything. To state in a single phrase the governing hermeneutic of the Talmud: the task of interpretation is to uncover the integrity of the truth that God has manifested in the one and unique revelation, the Torah (oral and written). By "integrity" is meant not merely the result of facile harmonization but the rigorous demonstration that the Torah, at its foundations, makes a single statement, whole, complete, cogent, and coherent; harmonious; unified and beyond all division. The message of the first document of the oral Torah, the Mishnah, was the hierarchical unity of all being in the One on high. Then the right medium for that message is the Bavli on account of the character of its hermeneutics, best summarized as its quest for abstraction. Since the Mishnah's authorship undertook precisely the same inquiry, how the Mishnah and the Bavli deal with the problem of showing the integrity of truth shows us the center and soul of the rabbinic literature as the two dominant documents of Judaism set matters forth.

The Mishnah's version of the integrity of truth focuses upon the unity of all being in hierarchical ontology. A single metaproposition encompasses the multitude of the Mishnah's proposition, which is, all classes of things stand in a hierarchical relationship to one another and in that encompassing hierarchy, there is a place for everything. The theological proposition that is implicit but never spelled out, of course, is that one God occupies the pinnacle of the hierarchy of all being; to that one God, all things turn upward, from complexity to simplicity; from that one God, all things flow downward, from singularity to multiplicity. Showing that all things can be ordered, and that all orders can be set into relationship with one another, we of course transform method into message. The message of hierarchical classification is that many things really form a single thing, the many species a single genus, the many genera an encompassing and well-crafted, cogent whole. Every time we speciate, we affirm that position. Each successful labor of forming relationships among species, e.g., making them into a genus, or identifying the hierarchy of the species, proves it again. Not only so, but when we can show that many things are really one, or that one thing yields many (the reverse and confirmation of the former), we say in a fresh way a single immutable truth, the one of this philosophy concerning the unity of all being in an orderly composition of all things within a single taxon. Exegesis always is repetitive—and a sound exegesis of the systemic exegesis must then be equally so, everywhere explaining the same thing in the same way. To state with emphasis that one large argument—the metaproposition—that the Mishnah's authorship sets forth in countless small ways: the very artifacts that appear multiple in fact form classes of things, and, moreover, these classes themselves are subject to a reasoned ordering, by appeal to this-worldly characteristics signified by properties and indicative traits.

Monotheism hence is to be demonstrated by appeal to those very same data that for paganism prove the opposite. The way to one God, ground of being and ontological unity of the world, lies through "rational reflection on oneself and on the world," this world, which yields a living unity encompassing the whole. That claim, conducted in an argument covering overwhelming detail in the Mishnah, emerges quite directly. The whole composition of thought is set forth, in the correct intellectual manner, through the patient classification of things by appeal to the traits that they share, with comparison and contrast among points of difference then yielding the governing rule for a given classification. And the goal was through proper classification of things to demonstrate the hierarchical order of being, culminating in the proposition that all things derive from and join within (in secular language) one thing or (in the language of philosophy of religion) the One, or (in the language of Judaism) God.

How does the Talmud of Babylonia join in the work of forming a monotheist canon? Matching the Mishnah's ontology of hierarchical unity of all being is the

Bavli's principle that many principles express a single one, many laws embody one governing law, which is the law behind the laws. The Mishnah establishes a world in stasis: lists of like things, subject to like rules. The Bavli portrays a world in motion: lists of like things form series; but series too conform to rules. The Mishnah sets forth lists; the Bavli, series. Demonstrating in conclusion and in message that the truth is one, whole, comprehensive, cogent, coherent, and harmonious— these sustained points of insistence on the character of mind and the result of thought form the goal of the Bavli's framers. The Bavli's paramount intellectual trait is its quest through abstraction for the unity of the law, the integrity of truth. The Bavli's quest for unity leads to the inquiry into the named authorities behind an unassigned rule, showing that a variety of figures can concur, meaning, names that stand for a variety of distinct principles can form a single proposition of integrity. That same quest insists on the fair and balanced representation of conflicting principles behind discrete laws, not to serve the cause of academic harmony, but to set forth how, at their foundations, the complicated and diverse laws may be explained by appeal to simple and few principles; the conflict of principles, then, is less consequential than the demonstration that diverse cases may be reduced to only a few principles.

The Bavli's version of the integrity of truth aims to show in countless cases the cogency of (jurisprudential) laws in (philosophical) law. And it is through the right hermeneutics that that is demonstrated, the message conveyed in a rational manner. Having shown that diverse topics of the Mishnah are so represented as to make a single set of cogent points about hierarchical classification, I turn directly to the problem of the Bavli: can the same claim be made of the Mishnah's greatest single commentary, that it too says one thing about many things? The answer to the "can" lies in rhetoric: do the people talk in the same way about many subjects? The answer—by this point obvious, after seven parts of a monograph on the uniqueness of discourse in the Bavli—is that they do. Then what is it that "our sages of blessed memory" say time and again? A single case will answer that question, again in the contrast between the two Talmuds. It is the two Talmuds' reading of Mishnah-tractate Qiddushin 2:2. The suitor declares an act of betrothal, but only on a condition. If the condition is not met, the betrothal is null. But if the condition is disadvantageous to the woman and she accepts it, and the condition is not met, then the woman is better off than before: do we still regard failure to meet the condition as a cause of nullifying the betrothal? That is the issue of the Mishnah rule. The two positions are A–G vs. H. Then we see how the Talmuds find it fitting to discuss that dispute.

YERUSHALMI TO MISHNAH TRACTATE QIDDUSHIN 2:2

[A] **"Be betrothed to me for this cup of wine," and it turns out to be honey—**

[B] **"of honey," and it turns out to be wine,**

[C]   "with this silver denar," and it turns out to be gold,

[D]   "with this gold one," and it turns out to be silver—

[E]   "on condition that I am rich," and he turns out to be poor,

[F]   "on condition that I am poor," and he turns out to be rich—

[G]   she is not betrothed.

[H]   R. Simeon says, "If he deceived her to [her] advantage, she is betrothed."

[I]   "On condition that I am a priest," and he turns out to be a Levite,

[J]   "on condition that I am a Levite," and he turns out to be a priest,

[K]   "a Netin [a descendant of the Gibeonites assigned to the Temple service in the time of Joshua]," and he turns out to be a mamzer,

[L]   "a mamzer [the offspring of parents who are not permitted by the law of the Torah ever to marry, e.g., brother and sister]," and he turns out to be a Netin,

[M]   "a town-dweller," and he turns out to be a villager,

[N]   "a villager," and he turns out to be a town-dweller,

[O]   "on condition that my house is near the bath," and it turns out to be far away,

[P]   "far," and it turns out to be near;

[Q]   "on condition that I have a daughter or a slave girl who is a hairdresser," and he has none,

[R]   "on condition that I have none," and he has one;

[S]   "on condition that I have no children," and he has;

[T]   "on condition that he has," and he has none—

[U]   in the case of all of them, even though she says, "In my heart I wanted to become betrothed to him despite that fact," she is not betrothed.

[V]   And so is the rule if she deceived him.

The Yerushalmi treats the issue before us in the following passage:

[II. A]   R. Simeon says, "If he deceived her to her advantage, she is betrothed" [M. 2:2H].

[B]   R. Yohanan said, "R. Simeon concurs that if he deceived her about an advantage as to genealogy, she is not betrothed."

[C]   Said R. Yosé, "The Mishnah itself has made the same point: 'On condition that I am a priest,' and he turns out to be a Levite [etc.] [M. 2:2I]."

[D]   Now there is no problem in the case in which he claimed to be
      **a priest and turns out to be a Levite, [that she is not be-
      trothed].**

[E]   [But if he claimed to be] a Levite and he turned out to be a
      priest, [there too she is not betrothed, for] she has the right to
      say, "I do not want his superior airs to lord it over me."

That, sum and substance of the matter, completes the Yerushalmi's treatment. Here
is the Bavli's counterpart; I do not repeat the Mishnah paragraph.

II. 1. A.   **R. Simeon says, "If he deceived her to [her] advantage,
              she is betrothed":**

         B.   *But doesn't R. Simeon accept the following:* **wine, and it turned
              out to be vinegar; vinegar, and it turned out to be wine—
              both parties have the power to retract [M. Baba Batra
              5:6K–L]***? Therefore, there are people who are perfectly happy with
              wine, others with vinegar; so here too, some are happy with silver and
              not with gold at all.*

We immediately find a different case, but one in which the same premise operates
as the premise of the rule here: people accept a deception that leaves them better
off; why should Simeon exact the full measure of truth?

         C.   *Said R. Shimi bar Ashi, "I bumped into Abbayye, who was in session
              and explaining this matter to his son: here with what case do we deal? It
              is one in which* a man said to his agent, Go, lend me a silver denar,
              and with it betroth Miss So-and-so in my behalf,' and the agent
              went and lent him a gold denar. *One authority maintains that the
              man was meticulous about the instructions, and the other, that* all he
              was doing was giving him good advice on how to proceed
              ['showing him the place'].*"*

The solution is to redefine the case at hand, showing how the issue is different
from what it seemed to be when we asked our question. But then we submit the
redefinition to the test of the actual language before us: does the claim conform
to the facts?

         D.   *If it is true that the Mishnah speaks of an agent, then the language should
              be not,* **Be betrothed to me,** *but rather,* **Be betrothed to** *him!
              And so too, not* **If he deceived her to [her] advantage,** *but
              rather,* **If he deceived** *him to [his]* **advantage***!*

         E.   *But to begin with it was of gold* [Freedman, *Baba Batra* (London,

> 1948: Soncino) *ad loc.*: the agent knew full well that he was
> giving a gold denar].

Now there is a second effort to clarify the matter in such a way as to leave both parties with good arguments. Here we see the real goal: it is to make sure that both contending masters' opinions are equally defensible. And that means, they must form their dispute around two valid, but conflicting principles, as F now accomplishes:

> F.   *Rather, said Raba, "I and the lion of the group explain it—and who might that lion of the group be? It is R. Hiyya bar Abin: here with what case do we deal? One in which* she said to her agent, go and receive for my token of betrothal from Mr. So-and-so, who said to me, 'be betrothed to me with a denar of silver,' and he went and the other gave him a denar of gold. *One authority maintains that the woman was meticulous about the instructions, and the other, that* all she was doing was giving him good advice on how to proceed ['showing him the place'].*"*
>
> G.   *And what is the meaning of the language,* **and it turns out to be***?*
>
> H.   *It was wrapped up in a cloth [and only when the women got it did she know what it was].*

We have accomplished our first goal: showing that both sides in the Mishnah operate in the same range of rationality; each has a valid view; principles are at stake, and harmonies consist of equally valid principles, which apply to specific cases in diverse, sometimes conflicting, ways. But we move outward from our case and its principles to a broadening of the issue to its deeper premise: the character of a stipulation given to an agent. If I hire someone to do something for me, and I tell him or her, go do it in such and such place, is that specification of the place part of the instruction, or is it just good advice as to a suitable location for the mission? How, in other words, do we explain the meaning and use of language?

> 2.   A.   *Said Abbaye, "R. Simeon, Rabban Simeon b. Gamaliel, and R. Eleazar, all take the view that in a case such as this, in giving these instructions, all he was doing was giving him good advice on how to proceed ['showing him the place'].*"*
>
>   B.   *R. Simeon: as we have just now said.*

We now survey a variety of unrelated cases, which rest on distinct principles of law but turn out to share common premises as to language and its meaning.

Now my remarks at the beginning of Chapter 7 and again at the start of this chapter come to mind. I claimed that the Talmuds, and the Bavli in particular, show us how abstract thought is brought to bear on the nitty-gritty of everyday life. Here we have seen a substantial example of what this means. What have we learned about how intellect in God's service sanctifies the everyday? The answer is, we try to form links between commonplace situations and the great principles of equity and justice, good order and right action, that the Torah reveals. And we form those links by finding the right language for things.

The upshot is, it is in language that we find the deepest unities of being; the words people use form the bridge from mind to mind; and from their minds to God's mind, to which humanity gains access because the Torah tells how God speaks and what God says. The premise of discourse is simply stated: the Torah is the one reliable account of who God is and what God does, how God thinks and the rules that govern God's, and humanity's, rationality. That is what is at stake, when sages investigate the meaning of language in the concrete details of laws and cases. So the sages who wrote the Talmud move on to this inquiry into how a variety of cases turn out to concern the profound premise: what do people mean by what they say?

C. *R. Simeon, Rabban Simeon b. Gamaliel: as we have learned in the Mishnah:* [49A] **An unfolded document [has] the signatures within [at the bottom of a single page of writing]. And one which is folded has the signatures behind [each fold]. An unfolded document, on which its witnesses signed at the back, or a folded document, on which its witnesses signed on the inside—both of them are invalid. R. Hananiah b. Gamaliel says, "One which is folded, on the inside of which its witnesses signed their names, is valid, because one can unfold it." Rabban Simeon b. Gamaliel says, "Everything is in accord with local custom"** [M.B.B. 10:1]. *Now in reflecting on this matter [we said], well, doesn't the first authority concur,* **Everything is in accord with local custom?** *And said R. Ashi, "This refers to a place in which a plain one [one that is flat, not folded and witnessed leaf by leaf but only at the top or bottom] was customary, and a folded one was made, or a place in which a folded one was customary, and a plain one was made. All parties concur that the one who gave instructions was meticulous about the matter. Where is the point of dispute? Where both forms are acceptable, and the husband said to the scribe, 'Make a plain one,' but the scribe went and made a folded one. One authority maintains that the husband was meticulous about the instructions, and the other, that all he was doing was giving him good advice on how to proceed ['showing him the place']."*

D. *R. Eleazar: as we have learned in the Mishnah:*

E. **The woman who said, "Receive my writ of divorce for me in such-and-such a place," and he [the messenger] received it for her in some other place—**

F. **it is invalid.**

G. **R. Eliezer declares it valid [M. Git. 6:3K-M].**

H. *Therefore* all he was doing was giving him good advice on how to proceed ["showing him the place"].

3. A. Said Ulla, "The Mishnah's controversy concerns only a monetary advantage, but as to a genealogical advantage, all parties concur that she is not betrothed. *How come? 'I really don't want a shoe that is bigger than my foot.'*"

   B. *So too it has been taught on Tannaite authority:* **R. Simeon concedes that if he deceived her to her advantage in a matter of genealogy, she is not betrothed [T. Qid. 2:5I].**

   C. *Said R. Ashi, "A close reading of our Mishnah paragraph yields the same conclusion, for the Tannaite formulation is as follows:*

   D. **"'. . . on condition that I am a priest,' and he turns out to be a Levite,**

   E. **"'. . . on condition that I am a Levite,' and he turns out to be a priest,**

   F. **"'. . . a Netin,' and he turns out to be a mamzer,**

   G. **"'. . . a mamzer,' and he turns out to be a Netin [M. 2:3A–D].**

   H. *"And in these matters, R. Simeon does not take issue."*

   I. *Objected Mar bar R. Ashi, "Well, note the further Tannaite formulation:*

   J. **"'. . . on condition that I have a daughter or a slave girl who is an adult [alt.: a hairdresser],' and he has none,**

   K. **"'. . . on condition that I have none,' and he has one—**

   L. *"and these represent monetary advantages, and yet here too R. Simeon does not take issue! Rather, he differs in the first clause, and likewise in the second, and here too, he differs in the first clause, and here too!"*

   M. *But how are the matters comparable? In that case, both items represent a monetary advantage, so he differs in the first clause, and the same in the second. But here, where it is a matter of a genealogical advantages, if he did differ, it should have been made explicit in the Tannaite formulation.*

Now when we compare the two Talmuds, we see in the way in which the Bavli differs from the Yerushalmi the reason for the Bavli's remarkable power over the mind and heart of Judaism.

When we review the two Talmuds' reading of the same Mishnah paragraph, the contrast shows us what is at stake in the second Talmud's hermeneutics. The Yerushalmi's composition wants to make the point that Simeon will go along with an advantageous claim as to genealogy, a point that the Mishnah rule itself is shown to register. And that concludes the Yerushalmi's message. It is important because it shows us how a perfectly competent commentator does the job: clarify, define, conclude. The contrast between the Yerushalmi's and the Bavli's reading of the same passage shows us the difference between competence and genius. The Bavli covers the same ground, but much more, and in a more complex manner. On the surface, the difference is that the Bavli is intellectually active; the Yerushalmi, virtually inert. But the difference at the foundations is not merely one of ability or vitality but fundamental program: the Bavli has a different issue in mind, a different task in hand; the stakes are much higher, not merely clarification of laws but discovery of abstract truth.

First, we address the generalization, not a particular detail. And to make the analysis abstract at the very outset, we frame the issue in another context altogether, that of a transaction in wine. What has wine to do with a betrothal? Nothing, of course, in fact—but everything if the truth is shown to possess integrity. So the Bavli accomplishes its principal purpose of moving always toward the general, transcending the details of a case in favor of its principle, moving beneath the surface of a particular toward its abstract premise. And that is accomplished not in so many words but implicitly, in the simple statement before us. Not only so, but if this did not accomplish the purpose, II.2 states matters in general terms all over again—but the terms now shift to another matter altogether. How do we interpret instructions that a person gives an agent? Now, it is clear, that issue inheres in a variety of cases, which we review; it can be shown to inhere in ours as well. But Abbayye's statement, II.2.B, does not go back into our case in detail; it suffices to allude to II.1.F. Then we go into another matter altogether, Simeon b. Gamaliel's ruling on the rules covering the preparation of documents; then yet another item, the receipt of a writ of divorce.

Now all that these cases have in common is the premise that we have articulated, and it is the glory of the Bavli to demonstrate that fact, time and again. Does that mean the Bavli's Mishnah exegesis falls below the standard of clarity attained in the Yerushalmi? Not at all, for at II.3 the Bavli states explicitly the exegetical proposition that the Yerushalmi has established. But here too, we present that proposition in a remarkably fresh way. Ashi sustains the proposed proposition (on which the Yerushalmi of course concurs), but then his son, Mar, takes issue with that reading; once more, a proposition is transformed into a point of contention, a thesis is offered that requires us to read the Mishnah paragraph in a contrary way, and that thesis is grounded on a close and careful reading of the formulation of the language of the Mishnah itself.

Both the Mishnah and the Bavli undertake to uncover in the laws of the Torah the philosophy that the Torah reveals. That is the upshot of the two documents—powerful and reasoned, fully instantiated polemic: many things yield one thing, and this is that one thing. Stated in the language of revelation, the Torah through many things says one thing, through many commandments, sets forth one commandment, through diversity in detail makes a single, main point. And we know what that point is. By "the integrity of truth," we then mean, the unity of all things in the One. But now, by "one" and by "whole," very specific statements are made: jurisprudence reaches upward toward philosophy, on the one side, and the teachings and rules of the Torah are wholly harmonious and cogent, on the other. The upshot is very simple: mind is one, whole, coherent; thought properly conducted yields simple truth about complex things. Comparing the Mishnah and the Bavli, as much as contrasting the Yerushalmi and the Bavli, has brought us to this conclusion. The outcome of the contrast, then, is not merely the difference that the Yerushalmi is brief and laconic while the Bavli speaks in fully spelled-out ways. Nor is it the difference that in general, the Yerushalmi's presentations are not dialectical, and the Bavli's are, for even though that difference may in general prove fixed, on occasion the Yerushalmi will expand an argument through question and answer, parry and counterthrust, and the analogy of a duel will apply to the Yerushalmi, if not consistently.

The difference is intellectual and, appropriately, comes to the surface in hermeneutics: the Bavli's composites' framers consistently treat as a question to be investigated the exegetical hypotheses that the Yerushalmi's compositions' authors happily accept as conclusive. All of the secondary devices of testing an allegation—a close reading of the formulation of the Mishnah; an appeal to the false conclusion such a close reading, absent a given formulation, might have yielded, to take the examples before us—serve that primary goal. The second recurrent difference is that the Bavli's framers find themselves constantly drawn toward questions of generalization and abstraction (once more: the law behind the laws), moving from case to principle to new case to new principle, then asking whether the substrate of principles forms a single, tight fabric. The Yerushalmi's authors rarely, if ever, pursue that chimera.

THE BAVLI'S THEOLOGY, EXPRESSED THROUGH HERMENEUTICS: In Chapter 7 we observed how the two Talmuds equally engage in a process of dismantling the Mishnah into selected paragraphs or even lone sentences, these to be read in their own, fresh context. Now we realize that the Mishnah's deconstruction forms only one phase of the larger, systematic definition of that of which the Torah's oral part consists. And that consists of sentences, at most paragraphs, but not whole chapters, and certainly not whole "books." It follows that the first rule of reading is, we read sentences on their own, but also in relationship to other sentences; documentary lines are null; large-scale, coherent propositions, such as the Mishnah read by itself composes and fully exposes, are null. Five hermeneutical rules yielding theological facts govern throughout, all of them serving to express the hermeneutics that convey the theological principles defined by the Talmud of Babylonia, which became the summa of Judaism:

[1] DEFINING THE TORAH AND THE CONTEXT FOR MEANING: The Torah consists of freestanding statements, sentences, sometimes formed into paragraphs, more often not; and we are to read these sentences both on their own—for what they say—and also in the context created by the entirety of the Torah, oral and written. Therefore the task is to set side by side and show the compatibility of discrete sentences; documents mean nothing, the Torah being one. The entirety of the Torah defines the context of meaning. All sentences of the Torah, equally, jointly and severally, form the facts out of which meaning is to be constructed.

[2] SPECIFYING THE RULES OF MAKING SENSE OF THE TORAH: Several premises

govern our reading of the sentences of the Torah, and these dictate the rules of reading. The first is that the Torah is perfect and flawless. The second is that the wording of the Torah yields meaning. The third is that the Torah contains, and can contain, nothing contradictory, incoherent, or otherwise contrary to common sense. The fourth is that the Torah can contain no statement that is redundant, banal, silly, or stupid. The fifth is that our sages of blessed memory when they state teachings of the Torah stand for these same traits of language and intellect: sound purpose, sound reasoning, sound result, in neat sentences. The task of the reader (in secular language) or the master of the Torah (in theological language, in context the two are one and the same), then, is to identify the problems of the Torah, whether written or oral, and to solve those problems. Knowing what will raise a difficulty, we also know how to resolve it.

[3] IDENTIFYING THE CORRECT MEDIUM OF DISCOURSE: Since our principal affirmation is that the Torah is perfect, and the primary challenge to that affirmation derives from the named classifications of imperfection, the proper mode of analytical speech is argument. That is because if we seek flaws, we come in a combative spirit: proof and conflict, not truth and consequence. Only by challenging the Torah sentence by sentence, at every plausible point of imperfection, are we going to show in the infinity of detailed cases the governing fact of perfection. We discover right thinking by finding the flaws in wrong thinking, the logical out of the failings of illogic. Only by sustained confrontation of opposed views and interpretations will truth result.

[4] THE HARMONY OF WHAT IS SUBJECT TO DISPUTE, THE UNITY AND INTEGRITY OF TRUTH: Finding what is rational and coherent; the final principle of hermeneutics is to uncover the rationality of dispute. Once our commitment is to sustained conflict of intellect, it must follow that our goal can only be the demonstration of three propositions, everywhere meant to govern. This is spelled out in section 9 below.

[5] KNOWING GOD THROUGH THE THEOLOGY EXPRESSED IN HERMENEUTICS: In a protracted quest for the unity of the truth, a detailed demonstration that beneath the laws is law, with a few wholly coherent principles inherent in the many, diverse rules and their cases—in that sustained quest, which defines the premise and the goal of all Talmudic discourse, Israel meets God: in mind, in intellect, where that meeting takes place. That is what is at stake in rabbinic literature, beginning to end.

9.

THE INTEGRITY OF TRUTH

The integrity of truth above all is repeatedly shown in the harmony of what is subject to dispute. How is this demonstrated? It is by finding what is rational and coherent in disagreement. Throughout the Talmud, in identifying and solving every problem of disharmony and incoherence, our goal can only be the demonstration of three propositions, everywhere meant to govern:

[1] disputes give evidence of rationality, meaning, each party has a valid, established principle in mind; without articulated rationality no one just stands by an unexplained opinion;

[2] disputes are subject to resolution, showing either that each party invokes a valid principle or that to begin with there is no dispute at all, each talking about a different thing;

[3] truth wins out, every time we show not the resolution of dispute but the rationality of the law.

The first proposition therefore proves most important. If we can demonstrate that reasonable sages can differ about equally valid propositions, for instance, which principle governs in a particular case to which two distinct and otherwise harmonious principles pertain, then schism affords evidence of not imperfection but of profound coherence. The principles are affirmed, their application subjected to conflict. So too, if disputes worked out in extended, moving arguments, covering much ground, can be brought to resolution, as is frequently the case in either a declared decision or an agreement to disagree, then the perfection of the Torah once more comes to detailed articulation in the wonder of dialectics.

If therefore I had to choose the single prevalent means for demonstrating the integrity of the truth, it would be the ubiquitous effort to show the rationality of disputes. For the Mishnah, therefore also the Tosefta, the very conduct and character of "our sages of blessed memory" in conveying their component of the Torah put forth not so much rules as conflicting opinions on rules, a vast array of disputes. How do we gain by establishing that disputes are rational? When, first of all, we can show that disputes concern the application of principles, or which of two or more principles govern in a particular case, we show that while details are subject to dispute, principles are affirmed and prevail. So the unity of truth is underscored. Second, if we find two or more sages in dispute about a given principle, one party affirming, the other party denying, the same, then our task is to show that each side has a valid reason in mind. Then the principle may be subject to dispute, but for solid reason; then the law is reasonable, but the upshot is conflicted. That too yields the consequence that the law is orderly and never capricious.

The theology that comes to expression maintains the proposition of the Torah's laws' integrity. Disputes, ubiquitous in the Mishnah and the Talmud, forming the raw materials of the writers of compositions and framers of composites, underscore the law's rationality—and therefore, in the nature of intellect, its unity. One way or the other, therefore, the stakes for the analysis of the reasoned basis for disagreement prove high. The laws yield a law, governing principles for the social order are few and coherent, and, in the here and now of Israel's life, God's rule prevails—because it should, because God has revealed in the Torah the rules of life, and those rules yield a society we can understand and trust. All of this is expressed, as usual for the Judaism of the dual Torah, whether in its scriptural or oral formulations, in concrete cases. This is how we show that the range of difference is limited and wholly rational:

MISHNAH TRACTATE BABA MESIA 10:6

A. Two [terraced] gardens, one above the other—
B. and vegetables between them—
C. R. Meir says, "[They belong to the garden] on top."
D. R. Judah says, "[They belong to the garden] below."
E. Said R. Meir, "If the one on top wants to take away his dirt, there will not be any vegetables there."
F. Said R. Judah, "If the one on the bottom wants to fill up his garden with dirt, there won't be any vegetables there."
G. Said R. Meir. "Since each party can stop the other, they consider from whence the vegetables derive sustenance [which is from the dirt (E)]."
H. Said R. Simeon, "Any [vegetables] which the ones on top can reach out and pick—lo, these are his.
I. "And the rest belong to the one down below."

One of the urgent tasks, here scarcely articulated, is to narrow the range of difference among the positions of the Mishnah authorities. For in the end, if we want to demonstrate the unity of the law, we must confront the blatant characteristic of the Mishnah as well as of other Tannaite opinion: perpetual conflict, constant debate. And the obvious flaw is: if the sages really disagree about so many things, then what are we to do and think? And if the Torah does not give us guidance on those questions of thought and action, then of what use is it, and how can it be reliable and perfect? The Mishnah's very characteristics therefore precipitated the quest for limiting the range of disagreement, on the one side, and showing agreement beneath disagreement, on the other, Before us is a classic dispute, among three authorities, about a case that scarcely requires exposition. Common sense tells us that we have to elect one or the other position or the compromise. But then how much guidance can we expect in this part of the Torah, which tells us opinions but no decisions? For such writing claims of perfection were not plausibly to be made! Here we turn to the Talmud's reading of the Mishnah's dispute, which limits the range of dispute and rationalizes the grounds for dispute:

I. 1. A. Said Raba, "As to the roots, all parties concur that they are assigned to the upper garden's owner. Where there is a dispute, it concerns the leaves. R. Meir takes the view that we assign the leaves to the roots, and R. Judah takes the view that we do not assign the leaves to the roots."

What we accomplish here is two things. First, we limit the range of the dispute; second, we demonstrate its rationality by showing the principles in conflict. The dispute concerns what is superficial, not what is at the foundations; and the dispute concerns a perfectly rational matter, to which side we assign the part not covered by either claim, the excluded middle. In fact what is subject to dispute is not law but fact: what nourishes the leaves. A good botanist can then settle the issue. If we cannot resolve the dispute, then, we both limit its range and also establish the rationality of the issue: then reasonable folk can agree to disagree, and the flaw of confusion is removed, leaving only testimony to the Torah's range of rationality: dispute about things that, after all, may reasonably be left moot.

As is ordinarily the case, in the present instance, the discussion veers off in a new direction. Our knowledge of the dialectical character of the Talmud's discourse has prepared us for that trait here, as everywhere else. But it is not unexpected for another reason besides the prevailing character of discourse; it is essential if we are to repeat the melody here too: the rationality of dispute, the coherence of truth, the consistency of sages' principles. Once we have analyzed the grounds for a disagreement and identified them as a preoccupation with the excluded middle, therefore, one absolutely required action is to ask whether we have further instances of the same disagreement, and whether the parties are consistent elsewhere with what they say here. At stake in positive answers is the proof that disputes are coherent, affecting a variety of cases—a facile way of showing the law behind the laws; that sages are consistent, invoking the same principle in diverse cases—further evidence of the cogency of the law and its authorities and in the power of a few laws to cover most situations.

The somewhat wandering quality of a given Talmudic discussion, therefore, attests not to the incapacity of editors to stick to the point. Rather, it tells us that present beneath the surface are principles of reading the Mishnah and of composing the Talmud that precipitate time and again the same exercise of analysis—that is to say, a hermeneutics of a determinate and rather uncomplicated order. Here we ask whether the authorities the point of whose disagreement has been identified in fact disagree on the same matter elsewhere; if they have, it means our reading of what is at stake gains plausibility. And if they disagree on the same principle with the same results, it means that the Torah for which Meir, Judah, and Simeon stand is coherent at its deepest layers:

> B. *The two are consistent with views expressed elsewhere, for it has been taught on Tannaite authority:*
> C. "What grows from the trunk and roots is assigned to the land-owner," the words of R. Meir.
> D. And R. Judah says, "That which grows out of the trunk belongs to the tree-owner, and what grows out of the roots belongs to the landowner."

The upshot is that the issue does occur elsewhere, and, moreover, the authorities are consistent in saying the same thing about many things. But what about redundancy?

E.   **[119A]** *But we have learned on Tannaite authority in connection with produce of a tree in the first three years after its planting:*

F.   **"A tree that grows out of the trunk or the roots of a tree that has been chopped down is liable to the laws governing the produce of a tree in the first three years after it has been planted," the words of R. Meir. R. Judah says, "A tree that grows out of the trunk is exempt, but if it grows out of the roots, it is liable" [T. Orl. 1:4A-C].**

Why do we have to be told the same thing twice? Redundancy is a flaw in an intellectually perfect writing. We are not stupid, and the Torah (here: the Mishnah and Tosefta) is not repetitious:

G.   *Both versions of the opinions of the two authorities are necessary, for had we heard only the first version, we might have thought that it is in the first version only that R. Judah takes the position that he does, because at stake is merely property, but with respect to the status of produce of a tree in the first three years after its planting, which represents a prohibition [of the Torah], I might have taken the view that he concurs with the ruling of R. Meir. And if I had in hand only the ruling of R. Meir, I might have maintained that it is here in particular that he takes the position that he does, but in the other case he concurs with R. Judah. That is why both versions of the opinions of the two authorities are necessary.*

Points of differentiation may argue that in one case the identified authorities take the position they do for considerations distinctive to that case. Or, alternatively, we may maintain that had the authorities not said the same thing two (or more) times, we should have distinguished the cases and therefore come to an inaccurate view of their true positions: how far each would go in pursuing his point, how each would respond to changes in the circumstance. Thus we have to be told more than a single case, so that we have a full view of the range and rationality of disagreement. The Torah, by the way, is perfect, because our sages of blessed memory exhibit the traits of intellectual perfection.

The goal of all argument therefore remains one: to show the unity of the law. But this is never shown in abstract terms; indeed, it is scarcely alleged in so many words. It is for us to identify the words through the repetition of the unstated point. The following abstract shows what it means, in concrete terms, to demonstrate the abstract conception of the unity of the law. First, we are going to prove that general point on the basis of a single case. Then we shall proceed to show how a variety of authorities, dealing with diverse cases, sustains the same principle. If we can show that many cases point to the same, single, principle, we are able to make considerable progress in reaching that goal of repeating the simple phrase: the law is one, so is the Torah, and so, in hierarchical succession, is the creation formed by the Mind of the Creator.

THE BAVLI'S POWER OF GENERALIZATION: Discernment consists in knowing how to generalize from the specific case, or, more to the point, knowing *that* we must do so. Generalization takes a variety of forms, some yielding a broader framework into which to locate a case, others a proposition of consequence. Accordingly, if I had to identify the single most important theological point that the Talmud sets forth, it is that the laws yield law, the truth exhibits integrity, all of the parts—the details, principles, and premises—holding together in a coherent manner. To understand how generalizations are attained, however, we cannot deal only with generalizations. How do we investigate governing categories in the context of dealing with specific cases? It is by identifying the single principle behind many, diverse cases. The hermeneutics of the Talmud guides explication toward the question, what do diverse cases have in common?

Along these same lines, that same hermeneutics wants us to show how diverse authorities concur on the same principle, dealing with diverse cases; how where there is a dispute, the dispute represents schism vs. consensus, with the weight of argument and evidence favoring consensus; where we have a choice between interpreting an opinion as schismatic and as coherent with established rule, we try to show it is not schismatic; and so on and so forth. All of these commonplace activities pursue a single goal, which is to limit the range of schism and expand the range of consensus, both in political, personal terms of authority, and, more to the point, in the framework of case and principle. That is what is meant by the integrity of truth, toward which the entire exegetical tradition extending onward from the Mishnah is aimed. Now we turn to the counterpart: the place of Scripture in rabbinic literature.

PART THREE

THE RECEPTION OF SCRIPTURE:

The Three Types of Midrash-Exegesis in Rabbinic Literature

IX

MIDRASH: WRITING WITH SCRIPTURE

1.
DEFINING MIDRASH

THE WORD "MIDRASH," TRANSLATED "EXEGESIS," PRESENTS CONFUSION, SINCE IT IS routinely used to convey three distinct, if related, meanings.[1] If someone says "the *Midrash* says," he or she may refer to

[1] a distinctive *process* of interpretation of a particular text, thus, the hermeneutic,

---

[1] For further reading and bibliography on Midrash in general (as distinct from the specific documents to be examined in the following chapters) see the following:

  Bowker, pp. 45–47: "Midrash" is a term which applies to the exegesis and interpretation of Scripture in general; Midrash becomes a vehicle of halakhah when the exegesis of Scripture produces a regulative decision or ruling. Midrash is exegesis of Scripture which attaches the exegesis to the text which it is expounding or from which it has been derived (as opposed to Mishnah, where the material is recorded independently of Scripture).

  Gary G. Porton, "Defining Midrash," in Neusner, *Study of Ancient Judaism*, I, pp. 55–92.

  Lee Haas, "Bibliography on Midrash," in Neusner, *Study of Ancient Judaism*, I, pp. 93–106.

  M. D. Herr, "Midrash," in *Encyclopaedia Judaica* 11:1507–1514: the term "Midrash"; Midrashic literature; the early Midrashim; the difference between the early Midrashim and later ones; table of the Midrash compilations according to types and periods.

[2] a particular compilation of the results of that process, thus, a book that is the composite of a set of exegeses, or

[3] a concrete unit of the working of that process of scriptural exegesis, thus the write-up of the process of interpretation as it applies to a single verse, the exegetical composition on a particular verse (or group of verses).

It follows that for clear speech the word "Midrash," standing by itself, bears no meaning. Let us consider the three distinct usages.

[1] The word "Midrash" refers to the processes of scriptural exegesis carried on by diverse groups of Jews from the time of ancient Israel to nearly the present day. Thus people say, "He produced a *Midrash* on the verse," meaning, "an exegesis." A more extreme usage produces, "Life is a *Midrash* on Scripture," meaning that what happens in the everyday world imparts meaning or significance to biblical stories and admonitions. It is difficult to specify what the word "Midrash" in Hebrew expresses that the word "exegesis" in English does not. It follows that just how "exegesis" in English differs from "Midrash" in Hebrew is not self-evident. Nor do I know why the Hebrew will serve better than the more familiar English.

Some imagine that "Midrash" for Jewish exegetes generically differs from "Exegesis" for non-Jewish ones. Each term bears its own etymological sense. "Exegesis" means "leading out," that is, drawing out the meaning intended by the author or found in the text. "Midrash" refers to what is searched out, e.g., by methodical research. The two terms refer to different aspects of the same process, that is,

---

Maccoby, p. 22–25, on the Tannaite Midrashim; p. 37, pp. 147–48 on missing Midrash compilations that have been reconstructed: Mekhilta of R. Simeon b. Yohai, Sifré Zuta on Numbers, and Mekhilta on Deuteronomy.

Stemberger-Strack, pp. 254–68: the term "Midrash"; beginnings of Midrashic exegesis; the character of rabbinic Midrash and methods; classification of the Midrashim: halakhic and aggadic, exegetical and homiletic, or expository and sermonic; country of origin; Midrash and the synagogal reading cycle (Torah, prophets, writings); synagogal sermon; petihah and hatimah.

This writer's general discussion is in *Writing with Scripture: The Authority and Uses of the Hebrew Bible in the Torah of Formative Judaism*. Philadelphia, 1989: Fortress Press. On the place of Midrash in rabbinic literature, see this writer's *The Foundations of Judaism. Method, Teleology, Doctrine*. Philadelphia, 1983–85: Fortress Press. I–III. I. *Midrash in Context. Exegesis in Formative Judaism*. Second printing: Atlanta, 1988: Scholars Press for Brown Judaic Studies. On the uses of Scripture in rabbinic literature, see *Judaism: The Classical Statement. The Evidence of the Bavli*. Chicago, 1986: University of Chicago Press; and *The Torah in the Talmud. A Taxonomy of the Uses of Scripture in the Talmuds. Tractate Qiddushin in the Talmud of Babylonia and the Talmud of the Land of Israel*. Atlanta, 1992: Scholars Press for South Florida Studies in the History of Judaism. I. *Bavli Qiddushin Chapter One*. II. *Yerushalmi Qiddushin Chapter One. And a Comparison of the Uses of Scripture by the Two Talmuds*. On the definition of Midrash and the correct modes of analysis thereof, note also the following: *Ancient Judaism and Modern Category-Formation. "Judaism," "Midrash," "Messianism," and Canon in the Past Quarter-Century*. Lanham, Maryland, 1986: University Press of America *Studies in Judaism* series; *Comparative Midrash: The Plan and Program of Genesis Rabbah and Leviticus Rabbah*. Atlanta, 1986: Scholars Press for Brown Judaic Studies; *Canon and Connection: Intertextuality in Judaism*. Lanham, Maryland, 1986: University Press of America *Studies in Judaism* series; *Midrash as Literature: The Primacy of Documentary Discourse*. Lanham, Maryland, 1987: University Press of America *Studies in Judaism* series; *Invitation to Midrash: The Working of Rabbinic Bible Interpretation. A Teaching Book*. San Francisco, 1988: Harper & Row; *The Midrash. An Introduction*. Northvale, NJ, 1990: Jason Aronson, Inc.; and *What Is Midrash?* Philadelphia, 1987: Fortress Press.

studying or re-searching the text to bring out its meaning. "Midrash" then can be said to refer to study or research, while "exegesis" speaks of the results of the search, the presentation of the meaning of the text. The two words then end up covering much of the same ground. "Midrash" stands for a perfectly respectable, rule-bound, rational, scholarly treatment of the text, as much as does "exegesis." But the words intersect over such a broad area that we are hardly required to use a foreign word when a native one serves perfectly well.[2]

In any event, what hermeneutics characterizes all exegeses produced by Jews, but no exegeses produced by non-Jews, who presumably do not produce *Midrashim* on verses but do produce exegeses of verses of the same Hebrew Scriptures, no one has said. The word "Midrash" bears no more, or less, meaning than the word "exegesis" or, some may prefer, *eisegesis*. The distinction in context makes no difference. When people mean to refer to the process that yields a given interpretation, the word "Midrash" requires qualification: Midrash exegesis.

[2] The word "Midrash" further stands for a compilation of scriptural exegeses, as in "that *Midrash* deals with the book of Joshua." In that sentence, *Midrash* refers to a compilation of exegeses, hence the statement means, "That compilation of exegeses deals with the book of Joshua." *Compilation* or *composite* in the present context clearly serves more accurately to convey meaning than *Midrash*. That is why in this introduction we speak of Midrash compilations, as in "the Midrash compilation on Exodus. . . ."

[3] The word "Midrash," finally, stands for the written-out result of a process of scriptural exegesis, that is to say, a composition (e.g., a paragraph with a beginning, middle, and end, in which a completed thought is laid forth), resulting from the process of *Midrash*. In this setting a *Midrash* refers to a paragraph or a unit of exegetical exposition, in which a verse of the Hebrew Scriptures is subjected to some form of exegesis or other. In this usage one may say, "Let me now cite the *Midrash*," meaning a particular passage of exegesis, a paragraph or other completed whole unit of exegetical thought, a composition that provides an exegesis of a particular verse. I use the word "composition" in this sense, that is, Midrash composition, the particular presentation of a given passage.

2.

THE DOCUMENTARY STRUCTURE
OF MIDRASH

For reasons spelled out in Chapter 1, this introduction to the Midrash compilations of rabbinic literature that were produced in late antiquity focuses upon the docu-

---

[2] I am glad to acknowledge with thanks Professor David Noel Freedman's clarification of this matter for me.

ments, examined one by one. Only when we know the impact of the documentary context upon the materials in a document can we take up an individual item from that document and set it into comparison and contrast with a discrete item drawn out of some other, also carefully delineated and defined, document. At the point at which we can define the traits distinctive of one documentary context we may ask about traits of an item that occur in other documentary contexts in which that item makes its appearance. Then we may inquire into the comparison and contrast of one detail, drawn from one document, with what we conceive to be a parallel or intersecting detail, drawn from another. When we describe a document, we know as fact that (1) a given method of exegesis has yielded (3) a given exegetical comment on a verse of Scripture, the result of which is now in (2) *this particular document*.

It follows that since we know the simple facts of what is found in which document, we can begin the work of describing the traits imparted by (2) that document to the (3) exegetical result of (1) the exegetical method at hand. Traits characteristic of (2) the documentary setting likewise emerge without a trace of speculation. To state matters more concretely, if a document routinely frames matters in accord with one repertoire of formal conventions rather than some other, and if it arranges its formal repertoire of types of units of discourse in one way, rather than some other, and if its compilers repeatedly propose to make one point, rather than some other, we can easily identify those traits of the passage under study that derive from the larger documentary context. Accordingly, just as we examined the reception of the Mishnah document by document, so also we work our way through the Judaic reception of the Hebrew Scriptures document by document, the document because it presents the first solid fact. Everything else then takes a position relative to that fact.

In laying emphasis on the document as the correct first point of comparison, we exclude as the appropriate point of departure approaches to the examination of Judaic Scripture exegesis that compare the results of Midrash exegesis without regard to the documentary context at all. These other approaches address either modes of exegesis, hence, comparative hermeneutics, or, much more commonly, the (mere) results of exegesis, hence, comparison of the exegesis of a verse in one document, deriving from one period and group of authorities, with the exegesis of that same verse in some other document, deriving from completely different authorities and a much earlier or much later period. If we ignore as unimportant the characteristic traits of the documentary locations of an exegesis of a verse of Scripture or of a story occurring in two or more documents, or if we treat as trivial the traits characteristic of those locative points, we do not know the rule governing both items subject to comparison. We establish no context that imparts meaning to the work of comparison. That is because we have no perspective on similarities and differences among two or more things that are compared with one another. These similarities and differences may prove merely adventitious. But we shall never know. Points of likeness may constitute mere accidents of coincidence, e.g., of internal logic of the statement of the verse of Scripture at hand. But we cannot tell. Not knowing the context of likeness or difference, we also do not know the meaning of likeness or difference. That is why the definition of the context in which discrete data make their appearance demands attention first of all.

As a matter of established fact, Scripture serves a diversity of purposes and therefore cannot establish a single definitive plane of meaning, the frame of reference against which all other things constitute variables. Scripture constitutes the neutral background, not the variable. Exegetes ("Midrashists") first of all tell us what verses of Scripture matter and, second, what we should learn from those verses. Then, as the enormous variations in reading Israelite Scripture by diverse successors and heirs prove, on its own Scripture dictates nothing but endures all things. What people tell us about the meaning of Scripture represents the outcome of the work of exegetes, not the inexorable result of the character or contents of Scripture. These are the correct questions to address:

[1] Does Scripture dictate the substance of exegesis?

[2] Or do exegetes dictate the sense they wish to impart to (or locate in) Scripture?

If the former, then the ground for comparison finds definition in a verse of Scripture. What X said, without regard to circumstance or even documentary context, compared with what Y said, viewed also with slight attention to canonical context and concrete literary circumstance, matters. If the latter, then canon and its components take pride of place, and what diverse persons said about a given verse of Scripture defines only a coincidence, unless proved on the basis of circumstance and context to constitute more than mere coincidence.

The remarkably varied history of scriptural interpretation in diverse Judaisms and Christianities tells the story of how diverse groups of believers selected diverse verses of the Hebrew Scriptures as particularly important. They then subjected those verses, and not other verses, to particular exegetical inquiry. The meanings they found in those verses answered questions they found urgent. Scripture contributed much but dictated nothing; system—circumstance and context—dictated everything and selected what Scripture might contribute in Midrash. That is why there is no "plain sense" of Scripture that bears consequence in the description, analysis, and interpretation of any Judaism or Christianity.

In this context, *Midrash* therefore means the whole extant repertoire of exegeses of verses of Scripture we possess in (2) various compilations of exegeses of Scripture, made up of (3) compositions of exegesis of verses of Scripture, guided by (1) diverse hermeneutical principles of interpretation of Scripture. Since in *Midrash* as just now defined, system, hence canon, comes first, prior to exegeses of particular verses of Scripture, all the more so prior to the hermeneutics that guides the work of exegesis, the documents that constitute the canon and contain the system form the definitive initial classification for comparative Midrash. The canon recapitulates the system, not the system, the canon; that is why "plain sense" is a chimera. In the Judaism of the dual Torah, "the plain sense" of a verse of Scripture finds its definition and validation in the systemic decision to examine that verse, and to do so in search of information defined not by the verse but by the system that has precipitated interest in it.

3.
CANONICAL RECAPITULATION OF SYSTEMS

What this fact means for the comparison of exegesis of Scripture among diverse Judaisms and Christianities is simple. System must be compared to system, not detail to detail. So too, within the canon of a given Judaism or Christianity, such as that of rabbinic Judaism, we compare a compilation of exegeses to its counterpart, thus document to document. So comparison of the repertoires of verses people chose and those they ignored yields the governing insight. Before we know the answers, we have to understand the questions people addressed to Scripture. Why so? Because a group chose a repertoire of verses distinctive to itself, rarely commenting on, therefore not confronting, verses important to other groups. When we deal with different groups talking about different things to different groups, what difference does it make to us that adventitiously and not systematically, out of all systemic context, we discover that someone reached the same conclusion as did someone else, of some other group? What else do we know if we discover such a coincidence? Parallel lines never meet, and parallel statements on the same verse may in context bear quite distinct meanings.

A single instance suffices to render these theoretical remarks concrete. Pharisees appear to have found especially interesting verses in Leviticus and Numbers that failed to attract much attention from the Evangelists. Evangelists found unusually weighty verses of Scripture in Isaiah and other prophets that the Pharisees and their heirs in the extant compilations attributed to rabbis tended to ignore. Accordingly, Scripture forms the neutral ground. Contending groups selected verses of Scripture important to the larger programs that to begin with brought them to the reading and interpretation of particular verses of Scripture. What is neutral conveys no insight, only what is subject to contention. That is why the choice of a given verse of Scripture for sustained inquiry comes prior to inquiry into the meaning or message discovered in that verse of Scripture. And that choice derives not from the neutral repertoire of Scripture but from the polemical program of the group that makes the choice. So we must describe the program and the system, and that means the canon, item by item: the documents in their canonical context, the exegeses of verses in their documentary context, then the results of exegesis. Scripture itself forms the undifferentiated background. It is the form, not the substance; the flesh, not the spirit. The fact that a single verse of Scripture generates diverse comments by itself therefore forms a statement of a merely formal character. It is a sequence of facts that may or may not bear meaning.

4.

WRITING WITH SCRIPTURE

Since the word "Midrash" cannot serve to describe in particular the reception of Israelite Scripture in rabbinic Judaism, all other Judaisms and Christianities having produced their distinctive modes of receiving the same Scripture, we require a different way of characterizing the role of the Hebrew Scriptures in rabbinic literature. Another description is simple: the sages of rabbinic Judaism wrote with Scripture. What is meant by writing with Scripture is simple. An authorship that wishes to establish an important proposition may do so by juxtaposing sequences of verses or Biblical cases (heroes, events) and, through the juxtaposition, make a point, or establish a proposition not contained within any one of the verses or cases but implicit in them all. Writing in a propositional manner we state our proposition and cite our evidence and display our argumentation. Writing with or through Scripture, we do these things:

[1] state our proposition implicitly, by citing our evidence without necessarily spelling out what we mean to prove through it, and

[2] conduct our argumentation with the reader by asking the reader to perceive the commonalities that all together point to the conclusion we wish to reach.

This may be done in a variety of ways, as most, though not all, of the rabbinic Midrash compilations will show us in due course. There are three styles of writing with Scripture. The first is verse-by-verse exegesis of a given scriptural book, with episodic compositions that set forth propositions; the second, propositional compositions formed of diverse verses and their exegesis, not organized around the sequence of verses of a single scriptural book; and the third is the repetition of the same point, again and again, in sequential exegesis of a given book of Scripture.

The earliest Midrash compilations cover the verses of a Biblical book in a sequential structure, occasionally forming a set of Midrash exegeses into a propositional composite; Sifré to Deuteronomy exemplifies that type of Midrash compilation.

The next set of Midrash compilations put forth propositions, which define the structure of large-scale compositions and composites; these do not take shape around the sequential exegesis of passages or chapters, let alone whole books, of Scripture.

The set of Midrash compilations produced at the end of late antiquity reverted to the first mode of structuring and organizing Midrash exegeses, that is, the sequential; but they adopted the second mode of argument, namely, large-scale, coherent representation of a proposition. By repeating one thing about many things, that third mode of Midrash compilation united the form of the first phase of Midrash compilation with the intellectual method of the second phase.[3]

---

[3] In Chapter 26 we shall see the context, in the documentary history of rabbinic Judaism, in which that sequence of types of Midrash compilation worked itself out. This is further explained in my *Rabbinic*

5.

THE THREE TYPES OF MIDRASH
COMPILATIONS

The relationship to Scripture and modes of use of verses of Scripture yield a taxonomy of Midrash compilations. In the Midrash compilations of rabbinic literature, (except, as we shall see in Chapter 10, Mekhilta Attributed to R. Ishmael), verses of Scripture serve not merely to prove but to instruct. Israelite Scripture constituted not merely a source of validation but a powerful instrument of profound inquiry. The framers of the various Midrash compilations set forth propositions of their own, yet in dialogue with Scripture. Scripture raised questions, set forth premises of discourse and argument, supplied facts, constituted that faithful record of the facts, rules, and meaning of humanity's, and Israel's, history that, for natural philosophy, derived from the facts of physics or astronomy. Whether or not the framers' statements accorded with the position of Scripture on a given point, merely said the simple and obvious sense of Scripture, found ample support in proof texts— none of these considerations bears material consequence. These authorships made use of Scripture, but they did so by making selections, shaping a distinctive idiom of discourse in so doing. True, verses of Scripture provided facts; they supplied proofs of propositions much as data of natural science proved propositions of natural philosophy. Writing with Scripture meant appealing to the facts that Scripture provided to prove propositions that the authorships at hand wished to prove, forming with Scripture the systems these writers proposed to construct.

Classifications of relationships to Scripture are three. The first taxonomic system, one that is visible to the naked eye, instructs us to look for evidence that a verse of the Israelite Scriptures illustrates a theme, that is to say, provides *information* on a given subject. In the context of the statement of a document, that information is systemically inert. That is markedly characteristic of Mekhilta Attributed to R. Ishmael. The first mode of relationship, therefore, is to develop an anthology on a theme. One way of forming a comprehensible statement is to draw together information on a single theme. The theme then imposes cogency on facts, which are deemed to illuminate aspects of that theme. Such a statement constitutes a topical anthology. The materials in the anthology do not, all together, add up to a statement that transcends detail. For example, they do not point toward a conclusion beyond themselves. They rather comprise a series of facts, e.g., fact 1, fact 2, fact 3. But put together, these three facts do not yield yet another one, nor do they point toward a proposition beyond themselves. They generate no generalization, prove no point, propose no proposition.

A second mode of relationship will tell us that a verse of the Israelite Scriptures

Judaism: An Historical Introduction (New York, forthcoming: Doubleday Anchor Bible Reference Library).

defines a *problem* on its own, in its own determinate limits and terms. In the setting of a document, the problem will be identified and addressed because it is systemically active. That is not at all common in Mekhilta Attributed to R. Ishmael, while Sifra for its part takes a keen interest in verses and their meanings. Yet in doing so, its authorship weaves a filigree of holy words over a polished surface of very hard wood: a wood of its own hewing and shaping and polishing. Our sense is that the recurrent allusion to verses of Scripture forms an aesthetic surface rather than a philosophical foundation for our book.

Yet a third mode points toward that utilization of Israelite Scriptures in the formation and expression of *an independent proposition*, one autonomous of the theme or even the facts contained within —proved by—those Scriptures. That is not the relationship established between Scripture and the fundamental program of some documents, e.g., Mekhilta. It does characterize the relationship between Scripture and Sifra, which is not extra-scriptural but meta-scriptural. Scripture in this function is systemically essential yet monumentally irrelevant. Sifra in that way addresses and disposes of Scripture by rewriting it in ways of Sifra's authorship's design. That is the wonder of this marvelous writing: its courage, its brilliance, its originality, above all, its stubbornness.

The routine relationship to Scripture is indicated when the focus of interest is on the exegesis of Scripture. In Mekhilta Attributed to R. Ishmael, as well as in Sifra and Sifré to Deuteronomy, we have composites of materials that find cogency solely in the words of a given verse of Scripture but in no other way. These materials string together, upon the necklace of words or phrases of a verse, diverse comments; the comments do not fit together or point to any broader conclusion; they do not address a single theme or form an anthology. Cogency derives from the (external) verse that is cited; intelligibility begins—and ends—in that verse and is accomplished by the amplification of the verse's contents. Without the verse before us, the words that follow form gibberish. But reading the words as amplifications of a sense contained within the cited verse, we can make good sense of them.

The upshot for the taxonomy of documents is simple. Where, to take up the first classification, a given theme requires illustration, the ancient Scriptures provide a useful fact. That is assuredly the case not only for Mekhilta Attributed to R. Ishmael but—by definition—for all other Midrash compilations. Indeed, those Scriptures may well form the single important treasury of facts. But the amplification of the verses of Scripture will take second place to the display of the facts important for the topic at hand; the purpose of composition is the creation of a scrapbook of materials relevant to a given theme. The verse of received Scripture will serve not to validate a proposition but only to illustrate a theme.

Where, second, the sense or meaning or implications of a given verse of Scripture defines the center of discourse, then the verse takes over and dictates the entire character of the resulting composition, and that composition we may call exegetical (substituting "eisegetical" is a mere conceit). This, we now recognize, is the principal relationship to Scripture characteristic of the Mekhilta.

And when, third, an authorship proposes to make a strong case for a given proposition, appealing to a variety of materials, there Israelite Scriptures take a subordinate position within discourse determined by a logic all its own. The theological compilations that form the third part of the Midrash compilations of rabbinic literature show us how Scripture is at once subordinated and paramount: say the same thing about many verses and Scripture itself takes on a propositional character.

6.
EXEGETICAL DISCOURSE
AND THE PENTATEUCH

One means of writing with Scripture is already familiar: compiling a sequence of Midrash interpretations that in diverse ways say the same thing. Here is an example of a sustained composition, cogent beginning to end, which makes its points through the medium of writing with Scripture. It is familiar from our discussion of the logics of coherent discourse in Chapter 3. Specifically, when we see how that medium delivers its message, we once more understand that the rabbinic canon, exemplified by the document at hand, undertakes a mode of discourse in an idiom very much its own, but within a logic of intelligible discourse entirely familiar to our own philosophical tradition, deriving as it does from the Graeco-Roman heritage.

SIFRÉ TO DEUTERONOMY I:I

1. A. "These are the words that Moses spoke to all Israel in Transjordan, in the wilderness, that is to say in the Arabah, opposite Suph, between Paran on the one side and Tophel, Laban, Hazeroth, and Dizahab, on the other" (Dt. 1:1):

   B. ["These are the words that Moses spoke" (Dt. 1:1):] Did Moses prophesy only these alone? Did he not write the entire Torah?

   C. For it is said, "And Moses wrote this Torah" (Dt. 31:9).

   D. Why then does Scripture say, "These are the words that Moses spoke" (Dt. 1:1)?

   E. It teaches that [when Scripture speaks of the words that one spoke, it refers in particular to] the words of admonition.

   F. So it is said [by Moses], "But Jeshurun waxed fat and kicked" (Dt. 32:15).

The proposition is stated at E. It is a philological one. "Speaking" in a specific sense implies a measure of rebuke or admonition. We are not offered the proposition as an introductory statement, e.g., a syllogism to be proved. The proposition occurs only in another way, at E–F. Let us proceed to follow the way in which the proposition is (1) stated, (2) illustrated and exemplified, and (3) proved—all through a barrage of cited verses of Scripture. The form is so fixed that there is no need to comment on the individual entries. Discourse requires conventional rhetoric, deemed to persuade, conventional logic, deemed to operate self-evidently and to bear its own compelling force, and the topic particular to the case at hand but part of a larger program as well. Here the rhetoric is established by repetition. The logic is worked out through the repeated appeal to "obvious" or "self-evident" truths. The topic—the proposition—recurs at every paragraph, and the whole coalesces into a single, remarkably cogent statement.

2.   A.   So too you may point to the following:

      B.   "The words of Amos, who was among the herdsmen of Tekoa, which he saw concerning Israel in the days of Uzziah, king of Judah, and in the days of Jeroboam, son of Joash, king of Israel, two years before the earthquake" (Amos 1:1):

      C.   Did Amos prophesy only concerning these [kings] alone? Did he not prophesy concerning a greater number [of kings] than any other?

      D.   Why then does Scripture say, "These are the words of Amos, [who was among the herdsmen of Tekoa, which he saw concerning Israel in the days of Uzziah, king of Judah, and in the days of Jeroboam, son of Joash, king of Israel, two years before the earthquake]" (Amos 1:1)

      E.   It teaches that [when Scripture speaks of the words that one spoke, it refers in particular to] the words of admonition.

      F.   And how do we know that they were words of admonition?

      G.   As it is said, "Hear this word, you cows of Bashan, who are in the mountain of Samaria, who oppress the poor, crush the needy, and say to their husbands, 'Bring, that we may feast'" (Amos 4:1).

      H.   ["And say to their husbands, 'Bring, that we may feast'"] speaks of their courts.

3.   A.   So too you may point to the following:

      B.   "And these are the words that the Lord spoke concerning Israel and Judah" (Jer. 30:4).

      C.   Did Jeremiah prophesy only these alone? Did he not write two [complete] scrolls?

      D.   For it is said, "Thus far are the words of Jeremiah" (Jer. 51:64).

      E.   Why then does Scripture say, "And these are the words [that the Lord spoke concerning Israel and Judah]" (Jer. 30:4)?

      F.   It teaches that [when the verse says, "And these are the words that the Lord spoke concerning Israel and Judah" (Jer. 30:4)], it speaks in particular of the words of admonition.

      G.   And how do we know that they were words of admonition?

H.   In accord with this verse: "For thus says the Lord, 'We have heard a voice of trembling, of fear and not of peace. Ask you now and see whether a man does labor with a child? Why do I see every man with his hands on his loins, as a woman in labor? and all faces turn pale? Alas, for the day is great, there is none like it, and it is a time of trouble for Jacob, but out of it he shall be saved" (Jer. 30:5–7).

4.   A.   So too you may point to the following:

B.   "And these are the last words of David" (2 Sam. 23:1).

C.   And did David prophesy only these alone? And has it furthermore not been said, "The spirit of the Lord spoke through me, and his word was on my tongue" (2 Samuel 23:2)?

D.   Why then does it say, "And these are the last words of David" (2 Sam. 23:1)?

E.   It teaches that [when the verse says, "And these are the last words of David" (2 Sam. 23:1)], it refers to words of admonition.

F.   And how do we know that they were words of admonition?

G.   In accord with this verse: "But the ungodly are as thorns thrust away, all of them, for they cannot be taken with the hand" (2 Sam. 23:6).

5.   A.   So too you may point to the following:

B.   "The words of Qohelet, son of David, king in Jerusalem" (Qoh. 1:1).

C.   Now did Solomon prophesy only these words? Did he not write three and a half scrolls of his wisdom in proverbs?

D.   Why then does it say, "The words of Qohelet, son of David, king in Jerusalem" (Qoh. 1:1)?

E.   It teaches that [when the verse says, "The words of Qohelet, son of David, king in Jerusalem" (Qoh. 1:1)], it refers to words of admonition.

F.   And how do we know that they were words of admonition?

G.   In accord with this verse: "The sun also rises, and the sun goes down . . . the wind goes toward the south and turns around to the north, it turns round continually in its circuit, and the wind returns again— that is, east and west [to its circuits. All the rivers run into the sea]" (Qoh. 1:5–7).

H.   [Solomon] calls the wicked sun, moon, and sea, for [the wicked] have no reward [coming back to them].

Let us stand back and see the matter whole. The focus is upon the exegesis of the opening words of Deuteronomy, "[These are the] words. . . ." The problem is carefully stated. And yet, without the arrangement within what is going to be a commentary on Deuteronomy, we should have no reason to regard the composition as exegetical at all. In fact, it is a syllogism, aiming at proving a particular proposition concerning word usages. Standing by itself, what we have is simply a very carefully formalized syllogism that makes a philological point, which is that the phrase "words of . . ." bears the sense of "admonition" or "rebuke." Five proofs are offered. We know that we reach the end of the exposition when at 5.H there is a minor gloss, breaking the perfect form. That is a common mode of signaling the conclusion of discourse on a given point.

7.
PHILOSOPHICAL DISCOURSE:
FROM EXEGESIS TO PROPOSITION

In Leviticus Rabbah we see how statements become intelligible not contingently, that is, on the strength of an established text, but *a priori,* that is, on the basis of a deeper logic of meaning, an independent principle of rhetorical intelligibility. The reason we say so is simple. Leviticus Rabbah is topical, not exegetical. Each of its thirty-seven chapters (in Hebrew: *parashiyyot*) pursues its given topic and develops points relevant to that topic. It is logical in that (to repeat) the discourse appeals to an underlying principle of composition and intelligibility, and that logic inheres in what is said. Logic is what joins one sentence to the next and forms the whole into paragraphs of meaning, intelligible propositions, each with its place and sense in a still larger, accessible system. Because of logic one mind connects to another, public discourse becomes possible, debate on issues of general intelligibility takes place, and an anthology of statements about a single subject becomes a composition of theorems about that subject. Accordingly, with Leviticus Rabbah rabbis take up the problem of saying what they wish to say not in an exegetical, but in a syllogistic and freely discursive, logic and rhetoric.

To appreciate what was new, let us rapidly review the prior pattern of how people wrote both with and without Scripture. To seek, through biblical exegesis, to link the Mishnah to Scripture, detail by detail, represented a well-trodden and firmly packed path. Sifra, an exegetical study of Leviticus as rabbis read the document, shows what could be done. The exegetes there cite a passage of the Mishnah verbatim and show that only through scriptural exegesis, not through the processes of reason, can we reach the correct law. Scriptural exegesis by rabbis also was a commonplace, as Genesis Rabbah indicates. Leviticus Rabbah was the first major rabbinic composition to propose to make topical and discursive statements, not episodically, as we saw in Sifré to Deuteronomy, but systematically and in a disciplined framework. Not merely a phrase-by-phrase or verse-by-verse exegesis of a document, whether the Mishnah or a book of Scripture itself, Leviticus Rabbah takes a new road. The framers of that composition undertook to offer propositions, declarative sentences (so to speak) in which, not through the exegesis of verses of Scripture in the order of Scripture but through an order dictated by their own sense of the logic of syllogistic composition, they would say what they had in mind. To begin with, they laid down their own topical program, related to, but essentially autonomous of, that of the book of Leviticus. Second, in expressing their ideas on these topics, they never undertook simply to cite a verse of Scripture and then to claim that that verse states precisely what they had in mind to begin with. Accordingly, through rather distinctive modes of expression, the framers said what they wished to say in their own way—just as had the authors of the Mishnah itself. True, in so doing, the composers of Leviticus Rabbah treated Scripture as had their predecessors. That is to say, to them as to those who had gone before, Scripture provided a rich treasury of facts.

The verse-by-verse exegetical mode of writing with Scripture is only one among three that characterize rabbinic Midrash compilations. The second is the formation of a large-scale proposition, set forth through the selection and arrangement of Midrash exegeses of unrelated verses of Scripture, all of which provide facts in behalf of a given, rather abstract proposition. This second mode of writing with Scripture moves from exegetical to propositional compositions and is exemplified by Leviticus Rabbah. How, very concretely, do the framers of Leviticus Rabbah accomplish that "writing with Scripture" of which we have spoken? When in Chapter 15 we examine a sizable sample of Leviticus Rabbah, we shall make the following observations.

The paramount and dominant exegetical construction in Leviticus Rabbah is the base verse/intersecting verse exegesis. In this construction, a verse of Leviticus is cited (hence: base verse), and another verse, from such books as Job, Proverbs, Qohelet, or Psalms, is then cited (hence: intersecting verse). The latter, not the former, is subjected to detailed and systematic exegesis. But the exegetical exercise ends up by leading the intersecting verse back to the base verse and reading the latter in terms of the former. In such an exercise, what in fact does the exegete do? The intelligent reader will read one thing in terms of something else. To begin with, it is the base verse in terms of the intersecting verse. But it also is the intersecting verse in other terms as well—a multilayered construction of analogy and parable. The intersecting verse's elements always turn out to stand for, to signify, to speak of, something other than that to which they openly refer. If water stands for Torah, a skin disease for evil speech, the reference to something for some other thing entirely, then the mode of thought at hand is simple. One thing symbolizes another, speaks not of itself but of some other thing entirely.

How shall we describe this mode of thought? We may call it an as-if way of seeing things. That is to say, it is as if a common object or symbol really represented an uncommon one. Nothing says what it means. Everything important speaks parabolically and symbolically. All statements carry deeper meaning, which inheres in other statements altogether. The profound sense, then, of the base verse emerges only through restatement within and through the intersecting verse—as if the base verse spoke of things that on the surface we do not see at all. Accordingly, if we ask the single prevalent literary construction to testify to the prevailing frame of mind, its message is that things are never what they seem. All things demand interpretation. Interpretation begins in the search for analogy, for that to which the thing is likened, hence the deep sense in which all exegesis at hand is parabolic. It is a quest for that for which the thing in its deepest structure stands.

Exegesis as we know it in Leviticus Rabbah (and not only there) consists of an exercise in analogical thinking—something is like something else, stands for, evokes, or symbolizes that which is quite outside itself. It may be the opposite of something else, in which case it conforms to the exact opposite of the rules that govern that something else. The reasoning is analogical or it is contrastive, and the fundamental logic is taxonomic. The taxonomy rests on those comparisons and contrasts we should call parabolic. In that case what lies on the surface misleads. What lies beneath or beyond the surface—there is the true reality, the world of truth and meaning. The re-presentation of that truth through the medium of Midrash exegesis joined with Midrash compilation—the synthesis of the antithetical media of the first and second stages in the unfolding of the Midrash compilations of rabbinic literature—is amply documented in Chapters 18–21.

8.
THEOLOGICAL DISCOURSE: SAYING ONE THING THROUGH MANY THINGS

To exemplify the power of a Midrash compilation to set forth a single point by repetition of that one point in response to long sequences of verses, we take up the case of Esther Rabbah Part One. The framers of that compilation addressed the issue, what is the meaning of Israel's life among the nations? How are we to live with gentile rulers? And what in the end will right the situation that we perceive as awry? The answers to these questions, specified in Chapter 21, fill the bulk of this brief Midrash compilation.

The scriptural book itself certainly defined the problem to be addressed, for these surely are issues provoked by the story of Esther, which concerns the near-catastrophe of Israel ruled by a pagan king and venal prime minister. Yet, is it not possible to read Esther Rabbah Part One and imagine that all we have in hand is a mere reprise, paraphrase, and recapitulation of the received writing? Quite to the contrary, in all its strange and determined program of exegesis and collage, arrangement and collection and restatement, the document bears no literary or rhetorical resemblance to Scripture, even while its propositional program seems so profoundly to capture the message of Scripture in not only generalities but acute detail. Scripture has provided the metaphor, but sages then identify the experience that is subject to the metaphor and illuminated by it. Israel under the Persians serves as a metaphor for Israel in the here and now; and that could have been, in the nature of things, any time and anywhere. Esther Rabbah Part One exemplifies the formation of theological discourse out of Midrash exegesis. This is accomplished by joining the form of the earliest phase of Midrash compilation with the modes of thought and argument of the second. The structure of a composition is provided by a book of Scripture, but what is said, verse after verse, turns out to repeat a single paramount point, the one specified just now.

Esther Rabbah Part One's authorship decided to compose a document concerning the book of Esther in order to make a single point. Everything else was subordinated to that definitive intention. Once the work got under way, the task was one of not exposition so much as repetition, not unpacking and exploring a complex conception, but restating the point, on the one side, and eliciting or evoking the proper attitude that was congruent with that point, on the other. The decision, viewed after the fact, was to make one statement in an enormous number of ways. This highly restricted program of thought resorted to a singularly varied vocabulary. Indeed, some might call it a symbolic vocabulary, in that messages are conveyed not through propositions but through images, whether visual or verbal. A great many ways are found to say one and the same thing. What was new to them was not the message but the medium. It was one thing to write with Scripture; that had been done before. It was quite another to write by collecting and arranging verses of Scripture in such a way that many things were made to say one thing. In Esther Rabbah Part One many things do say one thing, as will be spelled out in due course. The same is true also of the other Midrash compilations of the same classification.

9.

SYMBOLIC DISCOURSE IN VERBAL FORM
IN THE MIDDLE AND LATER
MIDRASH COMPILATIONS

In the middle and later Midrash compilations, from Genesis Rabbah through Leviticus Rabbah and routinely in all the late Midrash compilations, we find a particular form that means to conduct symbolic, as distinct from propositional and syllogistic, discourse.[4] The form, "another matter" or "another interpretation," is based upon the repeated citation, in disciplined parsing, of a verse of Scripture, and the successive imputation of various meanings, entirely cogent with one an-

---

[4] On symbolic discourse in verbal form, see this writer's *Symbol and Theology in Early Judaism.* Minneapolis, 1991: Fortress Press. On "another matter" formations, see William Scott Green, "Writing with Scripture," which is Chapter 2 of this writer's *Writing with Scripture: The Authority and Uses of the Hebrew Bible in the Torah of Formative Judaism.* Philadelphia, 1989: Fortress Press.

other, to each component of that verse. The form requires disciplined repetition of the parsed verse together with presentation of a repertoire of distinct meanings to be imputed to those components. The parsed verse then is explained in terms other than those specified by the verse when it is not parsed. When parsed, element by element, the verse is given a whole new set of meanings or reference points. And when this process is repeated, these new meanings prove multiple. If not repeated, the form is not present; not surprisingly, the form involved ordinarily bears a rhetorical signal, "another matter." The key words that are utilized in that "another matter" composite form bear meaning only in combination, having in that context no denotative sense whatsoever outside of the combination with other such verbal signs. These lists are made up of symbols in verbal form.

In sequences of three or more representations of the same parsed verse, each with its own "other matter," a restricted vocabulary of verbal representations of symbolic things recurs, with the same matter signified many times over. When we gather all of the "things"—the signs—that serve in an entire collection of these kinds of compositions, we shall see that a strikingly limited repertoire of persons, events, or actions comprises all of the lists of these "other matters." That fact standing by itself will prove only that a restricted vocabulary characterizes the "another matter" compositions and composites. But why are these words opaque signs, to be interpreted by appeal to a syntax and grammar that pertains to signs whether in verbal or iconic form, and why are they not to be classified as narrowly substantive and to be read by appeal to the conventional rules of the syntax and grammar of propositional discourse? The answer is that a symbol is a sign that transcends the details of its own representation. Can that same trait also characterize words, which surely denote, whether or not they also connote? Indeed so, in the present context at least. Let me give a theoretical instance and then state what I conceive to be the rule.

If I have a set of four components of the parsed verse, each component represented by J, K, L, and M, with words A, B, C, and D linked to each respectively, and then I have another set of the same four components of the parsed verse, with Q, R, S, and T linked to each, two sets of words require attention. The first set comprises the four components of the parsed verse: J, K, L, M. Do these have freestanding meanings? Obviously not, since the framer of the passage clearly intends to say that these four components of the parsed verse bear meaning only in combination with the repertoire of words (the A, B, C, D or Q, R, S, T of the example), and that, indeed, is the point of his composition. Then the four components of the parsed verse themselves are transformed from denotative to (at best) connotative signs.

But, in my view, they also are not connotative; they in fact are opaque and derive whatever signification they are to have only in combination, only from the linkage with the A, B, C, and D. So the four components of the parsed verse, bearing propositional, even syllogistic, meaning when standing together as a cogent statement, obeying the rules of syntax and grammar of the verse and chapter of Scripture in which they occur, in the form at hand have been taken apart ("de-constructed" being the current word). They no longer constitute denotative words or even connotative signs. They have been made opaque and gain significance only in accord with the rules of syntax and grammar of the form before us; and those rules govern symbolic discourse.

Then what about the A, B, C, and D/Q, R, S, and T-words? Can we not say that these words bear well-established and conventional meanings, denotative meanings? Well, as a matter of fact, I shall show that that is not so. For to the framer of the "another matter," composition only a restricted vocabulary is available. He may refer, e.g., to Abraham, Moses, David, Pharaoh, Sennacherib, and Nebuchad-nezzar. But, as a matter of fact, he may not refer to, e.g., Caleb, Samson, or Solomon, Cyrus or Abraham's allies. So far as Scripture defines the available repertoire, the framer of such passages, we shall see in detail, must choose from a restricted vocabulary. But do the words that the framer has in hand not bear denotative meaning, since surely David is always *that* man, the Exodus at the Sea *that* event, Sinai *that* moment?

Well, in point of fact, the mere appearance of a name by itself does not tell us where and how that name will serve, what meaning will be imputed to it, how significance will be drawn from it. "Moses" or "David" may serve in any number of sentences, and these sentences may make a vast range of points, so "Moses" or "David" functions as a mere word, just as "dog" or "king" or "table" serves as a mere word, available for combination with other words into sentences and para-graphs—always in accord with the syntax and grammar of propositional discourse.

But what about symbolic discourse? In the context of the "another matter" composition, "Moses" or "David" or "Israel at the sea" serves no propositional purpose at all—conveying no faith that, no belief that—as a (mere) sign, but is available for combination with other signs into aggregates meant to bear meaning, even to make points, in accord with the syntax and grammar solely of symbolic discourse. "David" or "Moses" in symbolic discourse bears no determinate mean-ing at all; when we see "Moses" or "the Exodus" we do not know the subject of the signification that symbolic discourse will set forth, let alone the proposition (if any) that will be laid out. Only in combination does "David" or "Moses" or "sho-far" or "menorah" gain any signification at all. And then the sense that is desired by the composer of the discourse will emerge not from the words that are used, but from the combinations that are accomplished: combinations of the (otherwise meaningless) parsed components of the verse at hand, along with the (otherwise senseless) symbolic signs that are used.

We know that a symbol is symbolic by three criteria:

[1] the thing (the sign) represented here by the word "David" or by the verbal expression of the event, "Israel at the Sea," signifies beyond its particularity;

[2] in this context the thing bears sense *only* in combination with other things;

[3] the "thing" (sign) is one of some few things, among many candidates supplied, e.g., by Scripture, that could have been used, to be repeated many times.

Whether the picture of a *menorah* on the wall of a synagogue or a reference to Abraham, Moses, and David, the Exodus from Egypt, the destruction of the Temple, or the coming of the Messiah in strings of words joined with parsed verses of Scripture, the upshot is the same. We deal with symbols, representations of objects that bear meaning beyond the details, verbal evocations of things that bear meaning beyond their particularities.

In "another matter" composites the figure of Moses, or the Exodus from Egypt, or Sennacherib, Nebuchadnezzar, and Belshazzar occur over and over again, in one combination or another. In these combinations the restricted vocabulary of symbolic discourse makes a virtually limitless number of points. In this regard, therefore, these things occur not as denotative words, where sense is limited to particular circumstance. Nor do they appear bearing determinate sense, e.g., as solely connotative words, evoking a less determinate sense, e.g., a particular emotion or an attitude that we can predict when a given word occurs. That explains why, as a matter of fact, the components of the "another matter" compositions and composites, when seen in the aggregate, require classification not as words bearing determinate meaning (however broadly constructed) but as symbols in verbal, rather than iconic, representation. The reason for that claim requires emphasis: *whatever the words mean in particular has no bearing upon their utilization in symbolic discourse.*

We know that is the fact because with the words alone in hand, we cannot predict what point the compositor will want to make, that is, the range of signification that they will be made to communicate: there is no clear limit to the possibilities of the signs "David" and "Israel at the Sea" when those "things" stand by themselves. We do not know what they may be permitted to signify and we also do not know what they may not be permitted to signify. In the combinations formed to comprise an "another matter" composition and composite, however, they conform to a syntax and grammar that impose determinate meaning upon them: each joined to the other, sign after sign after sign, bear all together a very specific sense or significance. So it is not only that viewed one by one, these words that serve in the "another matter" compositions bear meanings that transcend their own particularities. It is the simple fact that standing alone they have no determinate and conventional, predictable meanings but are opaque; they take on meaning only in combination. These "things" are signs and only signs and yield symbolic discourse and only that.

The compositor of a given "another matter" composition therefore accomplishes his goal through the combinations of things that he assembles to make his point: these things together signify this, not that. It follows that whether in iconic or verbal form, we deal with signs: words that are used as symbols as much as icons that are used as symbols. Whence significance? In symbolic discourse it must derive from combinations of one kind or another. How do these "things"—iconic and verbal alike—then serve as symbols within the definition offered at the outset? First, as I have stressed, their sense (whether propositional, intuitive, or emotional) transcends their immediate limits; or they have no intrinsic sense at all. Second, they bear their meanings only in combination, and not on their own; the rules of grammar and syntax of propositional communication do not pertain at all. The words at hand—"the Sea," "Sinai," "David," "Abraham," "the Torah"—serve as written-down symbols not in bearing meaning that is transcended but in bearing no meaning within themselves at all. In the kind of rhetoric represented by "another matter" composites, very often verbal representations of symbols are lucid only as words serving a symbolic purpose.

Symbolic discourse undertaken in verbal form proves recombinant. Only in context, in combinations with other such opaque signs, do symbols represented in verbal form begin to bear meaning, whether propositional or intuitive or emotional. The sole medium for conveying significance of any kind is to combine otherwise opaque symbols, whether conveyed in words or in iconic representation. The set of objects represented on the wall or floor of a synagogue; a list, e.g., Abraham, Isaac, Jacob, Sinai, made up of words that in context do not transcend meaning but have no fixed meaning—either constitutes symbolic discourse. Iconic symbols, of course, bear their signification only in combination. But the same is so for those words that serve only as signs, and signification takes place when, in association with the parsed components of a given verse of Scripture, the opaque symbols combine to make sense, evoke an attitude, even convey a message.

That is not to suggest that the choice of symbol is unaffected by the character of the symbol or word itself; "Moses" or "David" will stand for some few things. There are persons or events or objects that evoke certain basic responses wherever these are used. So there will be some weight in the choice of one word and not another, and the particular combinations will work themselves out within a range of determinate meanings associated with what is combined. Scripture is all-important. Still, as my example stated in abstract terms has shown, the recombinancy therefore is in two aspects:

[1] the joining in a single list of several opaque symbols, on the one side,

[2] the joining of those opaque verbal signs with the parsed components of the cited verse of Scripture, on the other. The combinations are then two and distinct; the recombinancy forms the whole into a single statement, a discourse that is wholly carried on in the syntax and grammar of symbols, not in the syntax and grammar of words at all.

That is why "Abraham" or "the destruction of the Temple" constitutes not a concept but simply a sign in the form of a word. It is a word that is opaque until made lucid by utilization in the syntactic and grammatical ways by which symbolic discourse is carried on, and the meanings imputed to those words derive from the grammar and syntax of their utilization. Just as "king" or "child" or "murder" or "love" may serve in one sentence to convey one proposition or one sentiment, and in another, a quite different proposition or sentiment, so "Abraham" or "Sennacherib" or "the pig" or "the lamb" may serve an evidently unlimited range of propositional purposes. Then how are we to interpret "Abraham" or "Sinai" or "the destruction of the Temple"? It can only be the way in which we interpret any other word: in the context defined by syntax and grammar. But in the present sort of evidence, where are we to uncover that context? It can only be in the setting of the "sentences" formed by sets of these symbols that are expressed in the form of words—opaque words, until, like all other words, they are used to make sentences.

But the sentences then are comprised of sets of opaque symbols, and to make sense of the word symbols, we have to learn how to decipher the sentences that form of those word symbols intelligible thought, whether propositional or intuitive or attitudinal. The issue, as with the visual symbols of the synagogue, then, is the same: how things combine, how we are to decipher the combinations. The medium of communication within the several compositions, which is combining and recombining symbols in verbal form, effects the formation of the entire set of compositions into a still larger, cogent statement, a statement made up of numerous statements, all of them effected through combining what are in fact words turned into symbols: recombinant symbolic speech. That is the final triumph of Midrash composition and compilation, reaching its climax in the final four Midrash compilations, those associated with the Talmud of Babylonia.

10.
THE TALMUDS AND THE MIDRASH COMPILATIONS: A COMPARISON

The sages who wrote the compositions and collected the composites of which the two Talmuds are made up, and those who wrote and compiled the Midrash compilations, in fact did exactly the same thing with the two components of the Torah, oral and written. They set their ideas into traditional form, by organizing their writings as commentaries on the received components of the Torah, oral and written, Mishnah and Scripture. But in both the Talmuds and the Midrash compilations, in providing a commentary, they obliterated the text. In "merely" paraphrasing the received Scriptures and Mishnah, they in fact reshaped both into a statement of their own making. We have already seen how the framers of the two Talmuds utilized the Mishnah for their own purposes and made it into an instrument for the re-presentation of the Torah as they wished the Torah to be received. The very act of picking and choosing tractates of the Mishnah, or books of Scripture, represented a statement of what counts. The further act of addressing to the Mishnah or Scripture questions provoked by urgent contemporary issues likewise formed an original and important statement. And, it goes without saying, even through mere paraphrase in a fresh context, the sages in both the Talmuds and the Midrash compilations reshaped the received heritage in a model of their own making.

A rapid glance at the work of the authorships of Leviticus Rabbah or Sifré to Deuteronomy (or any of their fellows) shows us the same process of re-presentation and renewal in the reception of Scripture. That examination tells us that Scripture supplies the given document of Midrash compilation with its structure, its content, its facts, its everything. But a deeper analysis also demonstrates that Scripture never provides the document with that structure, contents, and facts that it now exhibits. Everything is reshaped and reframed. Whence the paradox? Scripture as a whole does not dictate the order of discourse, let alone its character.

Just as the Talmudic authors destroyed the wholeness of the Mishnah and chose to take up its bits and pieces, so the exegetical writers did the same to Scripture. They chose in Leviticus itself a verse here, a phrase there, and, in Deuteronomy, they picked out a given set of verses for their compositions too. These then presented the pretext for propositional discourse commonly quite out of phase with the cited passage. Verses that are quoted ordinarily shift from the meanings they convey to the implications they contain, speaking about something, anything, other than what they seem to be saying. This Midrash exegesis brings renewal to Scripture, seeing everything with fresh eyes. And the result of the new vision in the Midrash compositions compiled in the documents we are now going to examine was a re-imagining of the social world envisioned by the documents at hand. For what the sages now proposed was a reconstruction of existence along the lines of the ancient design of Scripture as they read it. What that meant was that from a sequence of one-time and linear events, everything that happened was turned into a repetition of known and already experienced paradigms, hence, once more, a mythic being. The source and core of the myth, of course, derive from Scripture—Scripture reread, renewed, reconstructed along with the society that revered Scripture.

The upshot is that the mode of thought revealed by the literary construction under discussion constitutes a rather specific expression of a far more general and prevailing way of seeing things. The literary form in concrete ways says that the entirety of the biblical narrative speaks to each circumstance, that the system of Scripture as a whole not only governs, but comes prior to, any concrete circumstance of that same Scripture. Everything in Scripture is relevant everywhere else in Scripture. It must follow, the Torah (to use the mythic language of the system at hand) defines reality under all specific circumstances. Obviously we do not have to come to the specific literary traits of a given document to discover those prevailing characteristics of contemporary and later documents of the rabbinic canon. Every exercise in referring one Biblical passage to another expands the range of discourse to encompass much beyond the original referent.

These are the ways in which a single vision on how the received Torah was to be read shaped the reception of both the Mishnah and Scripture:

[1] Scripture and the Mishnah are to be read whole, because the framers pursue

issues of thought that demand that all data pertain to all times and all contexts. The authors are philosophers, looking for rules and their verification. In the Mishnah, cases are treated as exemplary, and in Scripture, stories are turned into generalizations and rules.

[2] Scripture and the Mishnah are to be read atomistically, because each of the components of the two documents—sentences, paragraphs, of the Mishnah; stories, verses of Scripture—constitutes a social fact, ever relevant to the society of which it forms a part, with that society everywhere uniform.

[3] Scripture and the Mishnah are to be read as sources of facts pertinent to historical and contemporary issues alike, because the issues at hand when worked out will indicate the prevailing laws, the rules that apply everywhere, all the time, to everyone of Israel.

Accordingly, there is no way for Scripture and the Mishnah to be read except as sources of facts about that ongoing reality that forms the focus and the center of discourse, the life of the unique social entity, Israel. The simple truth conveyed by the tale of the great man, the exemplary event of the rabbinic sage, the memorable miracle, whether in the Torah's oral or written parts—these serve equally well. The facts of Scripture stand no higher than those of the Mishnah, because, to philosophers and scientists, facts are facts, whatever their origin or point of application.

What we have in the Midrash compilations as much as in the Talmuds, therefore, is the result of the mode of thought not of prophets or historians, but of philosophers and scientists. The framers propose not to lay down, but to discover, rules governing Israel's life. As in Aristotle's natural history we find the rules of nature by identifying and classifying facts of natural life, so we find rules of society by identifying and classifying the facts of Israel's social life. In both modes of inquiry we make sense of things by bringing together like specimens and finding out whether they form a species, then bringing together like species and finding out whether they form a genus—in all, classifying data and identifying the rules that make possible the classification.

That sort of thinking lies at the deepest level of list-making, which is, as I said, a work of offering a proposition and facts (for social rules) as much as a genus and its species (for rules of nature). Once discovered, the social rules of Israel's national life of course yield explicit statements, such as that God hates the arrogant and loves the humble. The readily assembled syllogism follows: if one is arrogant, God will hate him, and if he is humble, God will love him. The logical status of these statements, in context, is as secure and unassailable as the logical status of statements about physics, ethics, or politics, as these emerge in philosophical thought. What differentiates the statements is not their logical status—as sound, scientific philosophy—but only their subject matter, on the one side, and distinctive rhetoric, on the other.

A

Exegetical Discourse
and the Pentateuch

X

MEKHILTA ATTRIBUTED TO R. ISHMAEL

(EXODUS)

1.

IDENTIFYING THE DOCUMENT

MEKHILTA ATTRIBUTED TO R. ISHMAEL[1] SEEN IN THE AGGREGATE PRESENTS A COM-posite of three kinds of materials concerning the book of Exodus.[2] The first is a set of *ad hoc* and episodic exegeses of some passages of Scripture. The second is a group of propositional and argumentative essays in exegetical form, in which theological principles are set forth and demonstrated. The third consists of topical ar-

[1] This attribution cannot be evaluated. The "Ishmael" here is presumably the colleague of Aqiba, a master in the Land of Israel at the turn of the second century. But we have no dependable historical information in the rabbinic literature on any authority, and attributions of documents to named authorities cannot be shown reliable. To the contrary, the documents accepted as authoritative or canonical are uniformly anonymous; after-the-fact attributions do not change that fact. For an account of why rabbinic literature contains no biographies, personal letters, signed books formulated in a personal style, and equivalent marks of individuality, see my *Why No Gospels in Talmudic Judaism?* Atlanta, 1988: Scholars Press for Brown Judaic Studies. The same observation applies to the other compilations that bear attributions, e.g., Pesiqta deRab Kahana; in no case can we verify that the named authority wrote or compiled the document or any of its principal parts; nor do we know why some documents bear attributions of authorship and some do not. Efforts within rabbinic literature itself to assign books to named figures, e.g., the Mishnah to Judah the Patriarch, persuade only the believers in the inerrancy

ticles, some of them sustained, many of them well crafted, about important subjects of the Judaism of the dual Torah. The document forms a sustained address to the book of Exodus, covering Ex. 12:1–23:19, Ex. 31:12–13, and Ex. 35:1–3. It comprises nine tractates, Pisha (Ex. 12:1–13:16), Beshallah (Ex. 13–17, 14–31), Shirata (Ex. 15:1–21), Vayassa (Ex. 22–17:7), Amalek (Ex. 17:8–18:27), Bahodesh (Ex. 19:1–20:26), Neziqin (Ex. 21:1–22:23), Kaspa (Ex. 22:24–23:19), and Shabbata (Ex. 31:12–17 and 35:1–3). There are eighty-two sections, subdivided into paragraphs. The division of the book of Exodus has no bearing on the lections read in the synagogue as we now know them. The document is variously dated, but ca. 250[3] is presently favored by many scholars, but rejected with reason by others.

In Mekhilta Attributed to R. Ishmael, we find a compilation of Midrash exegeses the authorship of which did not write with Scripture at all. Providing this encyclopedia of information concerning theology and normative behavior for the authorship of Mekhilta Attributed to R. Ishmael did not require a sustained demonstration of a position, whether as a whole or even in part, distinctive to that authorship and distinct from positions set forth by other authorships. These compilers encountered and utilized Scripture in a very different way. For the authorship of Mekhilta Attributed to R. Ishmael, Scripture is inert. That is to say, it is a

---

of these writings; others tend to take a position of suspended judgment. In any event there is no point in narrating the life and times of Ishmael when we open this Mekhilta, since there is no established correlation between stories about, and sayings assigned to, Ishmael, and the character and contents of this document in particular.

[2] For further reading and bibliography on the topic of this chapter, see the following:

Bowker, pp. 69–71.

M. D. Herr, "Mekhilta of R. Ishmael," *Encyclopaedia Judaica* (Jerusalem, 1971: Keter) 11:1269: the name; coverage in Exodus; division of the work; special characteristics; language; first printed editions.

Maccoby, pp. 148–72: extensive selections with commentary.

Stemberger-Strack, pp. 274–80: the name; contents and structure; character, origin, date ("an account of the origin of Mekhilta can only proceed from the individual sources. . . . The form of the individual traditions, the cited rabbis, and the historical allusions, suggest a date of final redaction in the second half of the third century"); the text, manuscripts, and printed editions.

This writer's introduction is *Mekhilta Attributed to R. Ishmael. An Introduction to Judaism's First Scriptural Encyclopaedia.* Atlanta, 1988: Scholars Press for Brown Judaic Studies.

[3] Moshe D. Herr maintains that the work was "probably compiled and redacted in Erez Israel not earlier than the end of the fourth century." The prevailing scholarly consensus assigns to the present document a place within the "halakhic Midrashim," or the "Tannaitic Midrashim," that is to say, compilations of exegeses of verses of Scripture that pertain to normative behavior, on the one side, and to the period of the authorities who produced the Mishnah, that is, the first and second centuries of the Common Era, on the other. The two current discussions are as follows: Ben Zion Wacholder, "The Date of the Mekilta de-Rabbi Ishmael," *Hebrew Union College Annual* 1968, 39:117–44, who rejects the received date and proposes one in medieval times; Günther Stemberger, "Die Datierung der Mekhilta," *Kairos* 1979, 31:81–118, who systematically proposes to refute Wacholder's position. In Wacholder's behalf, however, we have to note that if Mekilta Attributed to R. Ishmael belongs to the classification of Tannaitic Midrashim and of halakhic Midrashim, as we shall see, it is quite different from the other books in those categories, Sifra and the two Sifrés, in the indicative traits of rhetoric, logic, and topical exposition.

source of information, texts that prove propositions. It also is the foundation of the organization of discourse. But when people wish to say things, they say them *about* Scripture, not through Scripture or with Scripture.

Accordingly, what we have in Mekhilta Attributed to R. Ishmael falls into a different category altogether: the document comprises the first scriptural encyclopedia of Judaism. A scriptural encyclopedia joins together expositions of topics and disquisitions on propositions, in general precipitated by the themes of scriptural narrative or the dictates of biblical law, and collects and arranges in accord with Scripture's order and program the exegeses—paraphrases or brief explanations—of clauses of biblical verses. The nine authorships of Mekhilta Attributed to R. Ishmael treat as a given, that is to say, a corpus of facts or, more aptly, a body of tradition, what the other authorships or compilers of Midrash compositions set forth as components of a system that requires defense and demands apologetic exposition. For our authorship, the facts comprise a corpus of information, to which people require ready access. By setting forth an important component of information, that is, the data of revealed truths of the Judaism of the dual Torah, that authorship provides such access. What is needed, then, is an encyclopedia of things one should know on themes Scripture dictates, and the sequence of topics and propositions, in the order demanded by Scripture, results.

A model for long centuries to come—but for no one in the formative age—Mekhilta Attributed to R. Ishmael attracted many imitators and continuators. The conception of collecting information and holding it together upon the frame of Scripture attracted many, so that a vast literature of Midrash compilation much like this compilation came into being in succeeding periods. Not one but dozens, ultimately hundreds, of Midrash compilations, interesting, traditional, and, of course, pointless and merely informative, would fill the shelves of the library that emerged from the canon of the Judaism of the dual Torah. Accordingly, Mekhilta Attributed to R. Ishmael stood at the beginning of centuries of work carried on in the pattern set by that authorship. There would be only one Bavli, but many, many Midrash compilations—Mekhiltas, Yalquts, Midrash-this and Midrash-that—and, in due course, a secondary development would call into being commentaries to Scripture (as to the Bavli) as well. So Mekhilta Attributed to R. Ishmael formed not only a scriptural encyclopedia of Judaism, but, as it turned out, the first of many, many such compilations of revealed, received truth, set forth in the framework of the written Torah.

The sincerest compliment is imitation. We have only one Mishnah, no other writing of its kind; only one Sifra;[4] only one Leviticus Rabbah (with a document that uses some of its materials and copies its style, Pesiqta deRab Kahana, to be sure); only one Talmud of the Land of Israel; and the Talmud of Babylonia is utterly unique. But we have through time dozens of collections and arrangements of information on various scriptural books, and for the long centuries from the closure of the Talmud of Babylonia in the early seventh century to the nineteenth

---

[4] The word means "the book," and refers to the first rabbinic commentary on the book of Leviticus.

century, people reverently collected and arranged information in that essentially haphazard way, held together only by the book of Scripture at hand, that characterized this document. Whatever people wanted to say for themselves—and even the most unimaginative collector and arranger thinks to make a point, if only one of emphasis and reiteration—they said in the way the framers of Mekhilta Attributed to R. Ishmael did.

2.
TRANSLATIONS INTO ENGLISH

There are two complete translations of the Midrash compilation, and one partial translation. The first translation is Jacob Z. Lauterbach, *Mekilta de-Rabbi Ishmael. A Critical Edition on the Basis of the Manuscripts and Early Editions with an English Translation, Introduction and Notes* (Philadelphia, 1933: Jewish Publication Society of America) I–III.[5] The partial translation is Judah Goldin's, of the tractate Shirata, in his *The Song at the Sea. Being a Commentary on a Commentary in Two Parts* (New Haven, 1971: Yale University Press). The second complete translation, and first analytical one, is this writer's *Mekhilta Attributed to R. Ishmael. An Analytical Translation.* Atlanta, 1988: Scholars Press for Brown Judaic Studies. I. *Pisha, Beshallah, Shirata, and Vayassa,* and II. *Amalek, Bahodesh, Neziqin, Kaspa and Shabbata.* This translation closely adheres to that of Lauterbach in all matters of philology and text criticism.

3.
RHETORIC

A survey of the forms of Mekhilta Attributed to R. Ishmael yields the following formal repertoire:

   1. Propositional form: a proposition followed by examples, e.g., of verses or of cases.

---

[5] Lauterbach supplies no reference system apart from the quite unilluminating page-and-line-number system that was deemed serviceable in his time. Noting only lines and page numbers, he also presents an utterly undifferentiated text, so that it is difficult to conduct such studies as require differentiation between and among sizable constituents of the whole. Nor on the basis of his translation can we tell where he thinks one unit of thought ends and another begins or why one unit of completed thought has been set next to another, rather than somewhere else. The same is to be said of all other translations of rabbinic literature except for those of this writer, and it is not necessary to repeat this point throughout Part Three.

2. Proposition tested and proved: variation on the foregoing, in which a proposition is set forth and demonstrated by a sequence of factual statements.

3. Commentary form: clause of a verse + amplificatory phrase, with or without secondary expansion.

4. Dispute form, involving the statement of an issue or problem, followed by Rabbi X says . . . , Rabbi Y says . . . , very often in careful balance as to number of syllables and other formal traits.

5. Inclusionary/exclusionary form, using fixed phrases throughout to find out whether a given classification is encompassed by the statement at hand or excluded from its rule.

6. Redactional-harmonistic form: why is this passage needed? followed by another verse or treatment of the same subject, ending with a proposition that distinguishes one case from the other and shows that the Torah had to cover both.

7. The limitations of logic: protracted, dialectic argument that reason by itself will not suffice to yield a proposition so that appeal to a proof text alone suffices. This is not a narrowly syntactical form but involves a rigid organization of intellectual initiatives as much as grammatical and syntactical formations.

8. Citation form: One form not yet evidenced is Mishnah citation form, which joins to a base verse or proposition (e.g., commentary form) with the word "mikan," translated, "in this connection [sages have said]," a verbatim citation of Mishnah or Tosefta or related types of statements.

A prevailing, miscellaneous rhetorical repertoire circulates more or less promiscuously among the authorships of diverse documents. The formal plan is random and not indicative of a formal intent and program. The variation among the tractates that comprise the compilation shows that fact. Utilizing forms that serve to convey propositions, not merely ad hoc and episodic observations on this and that, our authorship sets forth propositions, either of a general character ("propositional form," "proposition tested and proved") or of a particular order, e.g., propositions of a determinate character ("limitations of reason"). Where we have a significant interest in making a general point through a plethora of specific examples ("inclusionary/exclusionary form" yielding rules out of cases, "redactional-harmonistic form" producing the proposition that Scripture does not idly repeat itself, and "limitations of logic" showing the paramount position of Scripture's taxic repertoire), the same conclusion follows. So, seen all together and overall, the rhetorical patterns, however various, characteristic of all nine tractates of Mekhilta Attributed to R. Ishmael aim to set forth first and foremost propositions of one kind or another; second, in significantly smaller proportion, commentary to passages of Exodus. In the aggregate, what we have is mainly a composite of forms, varying by tractate.

The authorships of these tractates clearly proposed to set forth a series of propositions, either of a determinate order or characteristic of a variety of cases. Pisha, Shirata, Bahodesh, Neziqin, Kaspa, and Shabbata. The authorships of Beshallah, Vayassa, and Amalek set forth something other than essentially propositional compositions. The authorships of Beshallah, Vayassa, and Amalek provide sizable proportions of phrase-by-phrase commentaries on the selected passages of the book of Exodus. The document is an encyclopedia of essentially propositional, but secondarily exegetical, rhetorical formations.

These results will take on greater meaning when we consider further Midrash compilations. We shall see that among the authorships that have chosen a limited repertoire of forms and ordered types of forms with great care so as to establish a single, encompassing proposition (not merely so as to discuss from various viewpoints a shared theme) are those of Leviticus Rabbah and Pesiqta deRab Kahana. The authorship of Sifré to Deuteronomy chose a set of forms that differ, in part if not entirely, from the choices made by the authorships of Leviticus Rabbah and Pesiqta deRab Kahana, and that authorship has also taken no interest in the order of the types of forms that they have chosen. The compositors of Sifré to Deuteronomy furthermore have had no large-scale propositional program in mind in the composition of sustained units of thought, which, in scale, are substantially smaller than those in Leviticus Rabbah and Pesiqta deRab Kahana. One may group Sifra and the two Sifrés in accord with indicative traits, differentiating all three from Genesis Rabbah, Leviticus Rabbah, and Pesiqta deRab Kahana, and, moreover, differentiate Sifra and the two Sifrés from one another.

The several canonical documents exhibit important differences in rhetoric, in the ordering of rhetorical patterns, and in the sustained cogency of a given large-scale composition. Some documents' authorships do not take an interest in the order of rhetorical patterns, other authorships exhibit keen concern for that matter. Some documents' authorships join a large number of individual units of thought to establish a single proposition, and that sustained mode of argumentation and demonstration characterizes every single principal division of those documents. Other authorships are quite content to make one point after another, with no interest in establishing out of many things one thing. These differences entirely suffice to show us that people made choices and carried them out, doing one thing, not another, in the formation of the units of thought in accord with a fixed rhetorical pattern, in the ordering of units of thought in accord with diverse rhetorical patterns, and in the composing, within a single composite, of a carefully framed proposition to be established by these ordered patterns of a limited sort. Some people did things that way, other people did things in a different way. So the differences are systematic and point to choice. It follows that the rhetorical choices of our document are not haphazard but deliberate and point toward the presence of an authorship, that is, a plan.

4.

LOGIC OF COHERENT DISCOURSE

The logic of cogent discourse of all tractates of Mekhilta Attributed to R. Ishmael serves a commentary or an encyclopedia. That is to say, approximately two-thirds of the document's individual, fully-worked-out units of thought, whether propositional or exegetical, hold together with other such units by reference not to a common argument or even theme but *only* to a prior text, shared among them all—and that seems to me the indicative and definitive trait of logic characteristic of a commentary. But the document is not only a commentary. It also bears a substantial burden of propositions, set forth in the context of a commentary but far more formidable than a mere conglomeration of a biblical clause followed by a few words of amplification would require.

Overall, the logic of the document, so far as things hold together, is that of fixed associative logic. For it is the established reference point of that text—the book of Exodus—that dictates which statement appears where and in what sequence or order in relationship to others. In a commentary, all cogent discourse should appeal solely to the logic of fixed association. But in our document, by contrast, approximately two-thirds of all molecules made up of atoms, that is, completed conglomerates of two or more units of thought, appeal for cogency to a shared proposition or theme. Accordingly, to call Mekhilta Attributed to R. Ishmael only a commentary would be excessive; but to call it solely a topical encyclopedia, which happens to be arranged in accord with the themes set forth in Scripture, would not be justified. Hence within the present set of indicative traits, we describe the document as a scriptural encyclopedia: not wholly a commentary, not entirely an encyclopedia.

5.
TOPICAL PROGRAM

Lacking all interest in cogent and sustained argumentation and demonstration of propositions set forth for argument, the authorship of Mekhilta Attributed to R. Ishmael scarcely aspires to make a full and important, well-composed and proportioned statement of its own. The nine tractates of Mekhilta Attributed to R. Ishmael, moreover, prove discrete. We have to take account of a document behind which, even at the end product, stand nine authorships, not one single authorship whose hand is evident through. For in formal and logical traits, all the more so in topical program, the nine tractates are scarcely cogent when seen whole and complete. They make no one point over and over again. They undertake no sustained, methodical analysis that joins bits and pieces of exegesis into a large-scale composition, bearing meaning. They do not pursue a single range of problems in such a way as through discrete results to demonstrate in many ways a single cogent position.

Keenly interested in setting forth what there is to know about a variety of topics, the sages who stand behind Mekhilta Attributed to R. Ishmael preserve and transmit information necessary for the reader to participate in an ongoing tradition, that is to say, a system well beyond the nascent and formative stage. For framers such as these, important questions have been settled or prove null. For it is a system that is perceived to be whole, complete, fully in place, that the information collected and set forth by our authorship attests. When people present writing in which Scripture supplies information and propositions, but not grammar and syntax of thought, Scripture plays a dominant role at the surface, but none in the substrate of the writing. That is shown here. For when facts serve not for arguing in favor of a proposition but principally for informing a readership of things it must know, then we confront not a systemic exercise expressed through sustained writing by the medium of Scripture but a traditional rite in which Scripture plays a formal role. That is to say, we find merely the repeating of the received facts so as to restate and reinforce the structure served by said facts. That accounts for our characterizing the document, assuming a provenance in late antiquity, as the first encyclopedia of Judaism, and our seeing the document as a prime example, for late antiquity, of how people did not write with Scripture but used Scripture in other ways altogether.

It follows that while the authorship of Mekhilta Attributed to R. Ishmael sets forth propositions, these overall do not serve to organize or impose cogency upon the document as a whole. That is why it is an encyclopedia, cogent in the pieces, but not overall. Only one tractate, Neziqin, clearly does exhibit fundamental cogency, since, in the main, it follows a single program of exegesis, aimed at establishing a set of uniform conceptual results. These, briefly stated, point to the conclusions that (1) cases may be generalized into rules; (2) Scripture does not repeat itself even when it covers the same legal subjects more than once; (3) the categories that make sense of reality derive from Scripture's classification of things, not from the traits of things viewed independently of Scripture. The other eight tractates into which the document is divided present a variety of conclusions.

That miscellaneous character of the whole should not obscure the fact that the parts really do form coherent statements, each on its own. Indeed, what makes the document interesting is the laconic and uncontroversial character of its discourse. Its framers clearly take for granted that what they are telling us are the established, accepted truths of the faith. That is why they can find it appropriate just to collect and present information, certain of the knowledge that everyone knows what they say is so. The main points that this Midrash compilation makes in its several parts may be conveniently divided into three classifications: (1) generalizations about the character of Scripture, (2) rules for correct conduct, and (3) theological teachings, with special reference to the relationship between Israel and God and the implications of that relationship for the fate of Israel among the nations. The first two are in volume and intellectual dimensions not imposing, the third is enormous and important, bearing the weight of the burden of our document. Miscellaneous instances are now given:

[1] Generalizations about the character of Scripture: The order in which Scripture sets forth two or more propositions does not necessarily indicate

the priority assigned to those items. Scripture itself will dictate priority. Scripture uses euphemistic language. Scripture is not bound by temporal considerations, e.g., of sequence.

[2] Rules for correct conduct: When one party pays respect to another, they speak in harmony. With the measure with which one metes out to others is one's own reward meted out. Whoever welcomes a fellow is as if one welcomed the face of the Presence of God. Do not favor either rich or poor in judging a case.

[3] Theological teachings: These add up to a great collection of the basic theses of the theology of the Judaism of the dual Torah. Let me simply state the items as they come.

Through doing religious duties Israel was redeemed, and preparation of the rite well in advance was the religious duty to which redemption for Israel would serve as reward. What God says he will do, he does. Wherever Scripture indicates that God has said something, we can find in some other passage precisely where and what he said. The upshot, of course, is that by carefully reading Scripture, we are able to identify the rules that govern history and salvation. The vindication of Moses's demands turns the demands into prophecies of precisely what would come about. This further is underlined by the careful delineation of the degradation and humiliation of Pharaoh, portrayed as running around. And then comes the striking contrast between the reverence in which Israelites hold the rule of God and the humiliation of the Egyptian ruler. People get what is coming to them. Divine punishment is inexorable, so too divine reward. When God exacts punishment of the nations, his name is made great in the world. Merit is what saved Israel at the sea. The issue to be pursued is, what sort of merit, e.g., deriving from what actions or persons? The acts of healing of the Holy One, blessed be he, are not like the acts of healing of mortals. The redemption at the sea prefigures the redemption at the end of time. Faith in God is what saves Israel.

God punishes the arrogant person by exacting a penalty precisely from that about which such a person takes pride. With that in which the nations of the world take pride before him he exacts punishment from them. Numerous cases in a long line of instances, based upon historical facts provided by Scripture, serve to demonstrate that proposition. Israel is unique among the nations. Mortals have the power to praise and glorify God. God takes many forms. The Lord is master of all media of war. The Lord needs none of those media. The Lord is a man of war, but the Lord is in no way comparable to a man of war, making war in a supernatural way, specifically by retaining, even while making war, the attributes of mercy and humanity. God is just, and God's justice insures that the worthy are rewarded and the unworthy are penalized. God responds to human actions and attitudes. Those who oppose Israel are as though they opposed God. God is unique and God's salvation at the sea will be repeated at the end of time.

Israel gained great merit because it alone was willing to accept the ten commandments. The Israelites deserve praise for accepting the Torah. The "other gods" are not really gods at all. They are called "other" for various theological reasons. Suffering is precious and will not be rejected. One must not act in regard to God the way the outsiders treat their gods. They honor their gods in good times, not in bad, but Israel, exemplified by Job, honors God in bad times as much as in good.

These fundamental principles of faith hardly exhaust the allusions to, or representations of, theological and normative statements in Mekhilta Attributed to R. Ishmael. They represent only those convictions that are spelled out in massive detail and argued with great force, the points of emphasis within a vast fabric of faith.

While familiar, these propositions form a miscellany. The characterization of the propositional message of our authorship(s) strongly suggests that we are dealing with a repertoire of standard and established, normative dogmas of the Judaism of the dual Torah. Nothing in the representation just now set forth points toward controversy or can be shown to contradict convictions contained within other documents. In Mekhilta Attributed to R. Ishmael we deal with a compilation of teachings, not a sustained argument: a systematic presentation of conventions, not a focused argument on behalf of distinct and urgent propositions.

Compared to other Midrash compilations Mekhilta Attributed to R. Ishmael therefore is abnormal in two aspects. First, it is animated by no paramount questions and does not lay out compelling and sharply etched responses to them. Second, it is not predominantly a propositional writing at all. So in its topical and propositional character, this document differs from others of its classification. If the others bear singular messages, Mekhilta Attributed to R. Ishmael speaks in eternal verities, which, in the context of controversy, enjoy the authority of accepted commonplaces, or, less cordially classified, mere banalities—theological truths, but routine and broadly acknowledged ones. If the others employ as their paramount mode of discourse propositional compositions, this compilation is first of all exegetical and miscellaneous, and only in moderate measure propositional at all. Other compilations prove points and bear a weighty message; this one does not.

6.

A SAMPLE PASSAGE

MEKHILTA. THE SECTION CALLED SHIRATA [SONGS]
CHAPTER ONE

XXVI:I.   1.   A.   "Then [Moses and the people of Israel sang this song to the Lord, saying, 'I will sing to the Lord, for he has triumphed gloriously; the horse and its rider he has thrown into the sea]'':

B. There are cases in which the word "then" refers to times past, and some in which the word "then" refers to times future:

C. "Then men began to call upon the name of the Lord" (Gen. 4:26); "Then she said, A bridegroom of blood" (Ex. 4:26); "Then sang Moses" (Ex. 15:1); "Then David said" (1 Chr. 15:2); "Then Solomon spoke" (1 Kgs. 8:12)—these are cases in which the word "then" refers to times past.

D. And there are cases in which the word "then" refers to times future:

E. "Then you shall see and be radiant" (Is. 60:5); "Then shall your light break forth as the morning" (Is. 58:8); "Then shall the lame man leap as a hart" (Is. 35:6); "Then the eyes of the blind shall be opened" (Is. 35:5); "Then shall the virgin rejoice in the dance" (Jer. 31:12); "Then our mouth will be filled with laughter . . . then they will say among the nations, The Lord has done great things with these" (Ps. 126:2)—these are cases in which the word "then" refers to times future.

2. A. Rabbi says, "What is written is not, 'Then Moses sang,' but, 'Then Moses will sing.'

B. "We turn out to derive from this passage proof on the strength of the Torah for the resurrection of the dead."

3. A. "Moses and the children of Israel":

B. Moses was equal in weight to Israel,

C. and Israel was equal in weight to Moses,

D. at the moment at which they sang the song.

4. A. Another interpretation of the clause, "Moses and the children of Israel":

B. This indicates that Moses sang the song before all Israel.

5. A. ". . . this song":

B. But is it a single song? Are there not ten in all?

C. The first was recited in Egypt: "You shall have a song, as in the night when a feast is sanctified" (Is. 30:29);

D. the second at the sea: "Then sang Moses";

E. the third at the well: "Then sang Israel" (Num. 21:17);

F. the fourth, said by Moses: "And it came to pass, when Moses had finished writing . . . Moses spoke in the ears of all the assembly of Israel the words of this song, until they were finished" (Dt. 31:24–30);

G.   the fifth, said by Joshua: "Then spoke Joshua to the Lord" (Josh. 10:12);

H.   the sixth, said by Deborah and Barak the son of Abinoam: "Then sang Deborah and Barak son of Abinoam" (Jud. 5:1);

I.   the seventh said by David: "And David spoke to the Lord the words of this song" (2 Sam. 22:1);

J.   the eighth, said by Solomon: "A Psalm, a song at the dedication of the house of David" (Ps. 30:1). [The catalog is now interrupted for an exposition of this matter. It resumes below, No. 10.]

6. A.   Now did David build it? Did not Solomon build it, as it is said, "And Solomon built the house and finished it" (1 Kgs. 6:14).

B.   So why does Scripture say, "A Psalm, a song at the dedication of the house of David" (Ps. 30:1)?

C.   Since David was prepared to give his life for the project to build it, it was named for him, and so Scripture says, "Lord, remember for David all his affliction, how he swore to the Lord and vowed to the Mighty One of Jacob, Surely I will not come into the tent of my house . . . until I find out a place for the Lord. . . . Lo, we heard of it as being in Ephrath" (Ps. 132:1–6).

D.   And elsewhere: "Now, see to your own house, David" (1 Kgs. 12:16).

E.   Accordingly, since David was prepared to give his life for the project to build it, it was named for him.

7. A.   And so you find that any matter for which a person is prepared to give his life is named for him.

B.   There are three things for which Moses was prepared to give his life, and all are named for him:

C.   He was prepared to give his life for the Torah, and it is named for him: "Remember the Torah of Moses, my servant" (Ma. 3:22).

D.   But is it not the Torah of God? "The Torah of the Lord is perfect, restoring the soul" (Ps. 19:8)?

E.   Why then is it called "Torah of Moses, my servant" (Ma. 3:22)?

F.   It is because he was prepared to give his life for it, so it was named for him.

G.   And where do we find that he was prepared to give his life for the Torah?

H.   "And he was there with the Lord" (Ex. 34:28); "Then I

stayed on the mountain forty days and forty nights" (Dt. 9:9).

I. So, since he was prepared to give his life for the Torah, it was named for him.

8. A. He was prepared to give his life for Israel, and it is named for him:

B. "Go, get down, for your people have dealt corruptly" (Ex. 32:7).

C. But were they not the people of the Lord?

D. For it is said, "Yet they are your people and your inheritance" (Dt. 9:29); "in that men said of them, 'These are the people of the Lord'" (Ez. 36:20).

E. How come Scripture says, "Go, get down, for your people have dealt corruptly" (Ex. 32:7)?

F. Since he was ready to give his life for Israel, they were named for him.

G. And where do we find that he was prepared to give his life for Israel?

H. As it is said, "And it came to pass, at that time, when Moses had grown up, that he went out to his brothers and looked at their burdens . . . and he looked this way and that way . . ." (Ex. 2:11,12).

I. So, since he was ready to give his life for Israel, they were named for him.

9. A. And he was prepared to give his life for laws, and judges therefore were named for him: "Judges and officers you shall appoint for yourself" (Dt. 16:18).

B. But is it not the fact that justice belongs to God, for it is said, "For judgment is God's" (Dt. 1:17)?

C. How come Scripture says, "Judges and officers you shall appoint for yourself" (Dt. 16:18)?

D. Since he was prepared to give his life for laws, and judges therefore were named for him.

E. And where do we find that he was prepared to give his life for laws?

F. "He went out the second day . . . and he said, 'who made you a ruler and a judge over us.' . . . Now when Pharaoh heard this thing. . . . Now the priest of Midian had seven daughters . . . and the shepherds came and drove them away" (Ex. 2:13–17).

G. It was from judges that he had fled, and to judging he returned: "He executed the righteousness of the Lord and his judgments with Israel" (Dt. 33:21).

    H.   Lo, since he was prepared to give his life for laws, and judges therefore were named for him.

10. A.   [Resuming the catalog,] the ninth, said by Jehoshaphat: "And when he had taken counsel with the people he appointed those who were to sing to the Lord and praise in the beauty of holiness, as they went out before the army, saying, 'Give thanks to the Lord for his mercy endures forever'" (2 Chr. 20:21).

    B.   Why is this mode of song of thanksgiving differentiated from all other songs of thanksgiving that are in the Torah,

    C.   in that in the case of all other songs of thanksgiving that are in the Torah it is said, "Give thanks to the Lord for he is good, for his mercy endures forever," while here we have, "Give thanks to the Lord, for his mercy endures forever"?

    D.   But it is as though there were no rejoicing before him in the heights on account of the annihilation of the wicked.

    E.   If there is no rejoicing before him in the heights on account of the annihilation of the wicked, all the more so in the case of the righteous,

    F.   one of whom weighs in the balance against the whole world,

    G.   as it is said, "But the righteous is the foundation of the world" (Prov. 10:25).

    H.   The tenth, said in the age to come: "Sing to the Lord a new song, and his praise from the end of the earth" (Is. 42:10); "Sing to the Lord a new song and his praise in the assembly of the saints" (Ps. 149:1).

11. A.   All the songs that in times past were represented in the feminine form.

    B.   Just as a woman gives birth, so the acts of salvation in times past were followed by subjugation.

    C.   But as to the salvation that is destined to come in the future, after it there will be no further subjugation.

    D.   Therefore in the case just now given, it is represented in the masculine form.

    E.   For it is said, "Ask now and see whether a man goes into labor with a child" (Jer. 30:6).

    F.   Just as a male does not give birth, so as to the salvation that is destined to come in the future, after it there will be no further subjugation:

    G.   "O Israel, saved by the Lord with an everlasting salvation" (Is. 45:17).

12. A. "[Then Moses and the people of Israel sang this song] to the Lord":

    B. "To the Lord" they said it, and they did not say it to mortals:

    C. "That the women came out of all the cities of Israel singing and dancing, to meet King Saul" (1 Sam. 18:6); "And the women sang to one another in their play" (1 Sam. 18:7).

    D. But here, "To the Lord" they said it, and they did not say it to mortals.

13. A. "[Then Moses and the people of Israel sang this song] to the Lord, saying":

    B. **R. Nehemiah says, "The Holy Spirit lighted on Israel, so they recited the song the way people recite the Shema."**

    C. **R. Aqiba says, "The Holy Spirit lighted on Israel, so they recited the song the way people recite the Hallel-Psalms."**

    D. **R. Eliezer b. Taddai says, "Moses would recite the opening words, then the Israelites would repeat them after him and complete the verse.**

    E. **"Moses would begin, saying, 'I will sing to the Lord, for he has triumphed gloriously,'**

    F. **"and the people would repeat that and conclude: 'I will sing to the Lord, for he has triumphed gloriously; the horse and its rider he has thrown into the sea.'**

    G. **"Moses would begin, saying, 'The Lord is my strength and my song,'**

    H. **"and the people would repeat that and conclude: 'The Lord is my strength and my song, and he has become my salvation.'**

    I. **"Moses would begin, saying, 'The Lord is a man of war.'**

    J. **"and the people would repeat that and conclude: 'The Lord is a man of war; the Lord is his name'"** (T. Sot. 6:2–3).

14. A. "I will sing to the Lord, for he has triumphed gloriously":

    B. "Greatness is fitting for the Lord, might is fitting for the Lord, glory and victory and majesty are fitting for the Lord."

    C. So David says, "To the Lord are greatness, might, glory and victory and majesty" (1 Chr. 29:11).

15. A. "I will sing to the Lord, for he has triumphed gloriously":

B. When a mortal king comes into a town, everybody gives praise before him, saying that he is mighty, even though he is weak; rich, even though he is poor; wise, even though he is an idiot; merciful, even though he is a sadist; that he is a judge, that he is faithful, even though none of these traits applies to him.

C. Everybody just flatters him.

D. But as to the One who spoke and brought the world into being, that is not how things are.

E. Rather, "I will sing to the Lord," who is mighty: "The Lord, mighty and awful" (Dt. 10:17); "The Lord strong and mighty, the Lord mighty in battle" (Ps. 24:8); "The Lord will go forth as a mighty man" (Is. 42:13); "There is none like you, O Lord, you are great and your name is great in might" (Jer. 10:6).

F. "I will sing to the Lord," who is rich: "Behold the Lord your God owns the heaven" (Dt. 10:14); "The earth is the Lord's and the fullness thereof" (Ps. 24:12); "The sea is his" (Ps. 95:5); "Mine is the silver and mine is the gold" (Hag. 2:8); "Behold, all souls are mine" (Ez. 18:4).

G. "I will sing to the Lord," who is wise: "The Lord by wisdom founded the earth" (Prov. 3:19); "With him are wisdom and might" (Job 12:13); "For the Lord gives wisdom" (Prov. 2:6); "He gives wisdom to the wise" (Dan. 2:21); "Who would not fear you, O King of the nations? For it befits you, since among all the wise men of the nations and in all their royalty there is none like you" (Jer. 10:7).

H. "I will sing to the Lord," who is merciful: "The Lord, the Lord, God, merciful and gracious" (Ex. 34:6); "For the Lord your God is a merciful God" (Dt. 4:31); "The Lord is good to all, and his tender mercies are over all his works" (Ps. 145:9); "To the Lord our God belong compassion and forgiveness" (Dan. 9:9).

I. "I will sing to the Lord," who is a judge: "For judgment is the Lord's" (Dt. 1:17); "God stands in the congregation of the mighty, in the midst of the judges he judges" (Ps. 82:1); "The rock, his work is perfect" (Dt. 32:4).

J. "I will sing to the Lord," who is faithful: "The faithful God" (Dt. 7:9); "A God of faithfulness" (Dt. 32:4).

K. "Greatness is fitting for the Lord, might is fitting for the Lord, glory and victory and majesty are fitting for the Lord."

16. A. "I will sing to the Lord":

B. for he is excellent, praiseworthy, and none is like him: "For who in the skies can be compared to the Lord . . . a God dread in the great council of the holy ones" (Ps. 89:7–8); "O Lord, God of hosts, who is a mighty one like you" (Ps. 89:9).

C. What is the sense of "hosts"?

D. He is [Lauterbach]: the ensign among his host.

E. So too: "And he came from the myriads holy" (Dt. 33:3), meaning [Lauterbach]: he is the ensign among his holy myriads.

F. And so David says, "There is none like you, among the gods, O Lord" (Ps. 86:8), "My beloved is white and ruddy . . . his head is as the most fine gold . . . his eyes are like doves . . . his cheeks are as a bed of spices . . . his hands are as rods of gold . . . his legs are as pillars of marble" (Song 5:10–15).

17. A. R. Yosé the Galilean says, "Lo, Scripture says, 'Out of the mouth of babies and sucklings you have founded strength' (Ps. 8:3).

B. ". . . 'babies' refers to those yet in their mothers' womb: 'or as a hidden untimely birth I had not been; as infants that never saw light' (Job 3:16).

C. ". . . 'sucklings' refers to those who feed at their mothers' breasts: 'Gather the children and those that suck the breasts' (Joel 2:16)."

D. Rabbi says, ". . . 'babies' refers to those old enough to be outside: 'To cut off the babies from the street' (Jer. 9:20); 'The babies ask for bread' (Lam. 4:4).

E. ". . . 'sucklings' refers to those who feed at their mothers' breasts: 'Gather the children and those that suck the breasts' (Joel 2:16)."

F. R. Meir says, "Even embryos in their mothers' wombs opened up their mouths and recited a song before the Omnipresent: 'Bless God in full assemblies, even the Lord, you who are from the fountain of Israel' (Ps. 68:27).

G. "And it was not Israel alone that recited the song before the Omnipresent.

H. "Even the ministering angels did so: 'O Lord, our Lord, how glorious is your name in all the earth, whose majesty is rehearsed above the heavens' (Ps. 8:2)."

No. 1 is a general proposition, to which our base verse contributes an example. Nos. 2, 3 both are singletons. The enormous composite, Nos. 5–10, bears a massive interpolation, and, once more, the whole had to have been completed prior to insertion here, since so much of the composite—Nos. 6–9—has no bearing upon the argument that is begun at 5.B. The inclusion of No. 13 seems to me more justified than Nos. 5–10, since the set of discrete sayings bears a clear relationship to our base verse. The only composition that I find genuinely well-realized is No. 15, which systematically illustrates its parable with proof texts showing how God differs from a mortal king. This proves how the authors of a single essay could realize a simple aesthetic program and do so with enormous effect. No. 16 is included because of Meir's statement, 16.F–H. Clearly, the composition, focused on Ps. 8:1–2, was assembled before the whole was inserted here, since the rest of the materials have no bearing upon our base verse.

SHIRATA CHAPTER TWO

XXVII:I. 1. A. "[I will sing to the Lord,] for he is highly exalted [Revised Standard Version: has triumphed gloriously]; [the horse and its rider he has thrown into the sea]":

B. [The use of the verb "exalt," two times, translated "highly exalted," yields this meaning:] "He has exalted me and I have exalted him."

C. "He has exalted me": in Egypt, thus: "And you shall say to Pharaoh, 'Thus says the Lord, Israel is my son, my firstborn'" (Ex. 4:22).

D. "and I have exalted him": in Egypt, thus: "You shall have a song as in the night when a feast is sanctified" (Is. 30:29).

2. A. Another teaching concerning "for he is highly exalted":

B. "He has exalted me and I have exalted him."

C. "He has exalted me": at the sea, thus: "And the angel of God . . . removed" (Ex. 14:19).

D. "and I have exalted him": at the sea when I sang a song before him, "I will sing to the Lord, for he is highly exalted."

3. A. Another teaching concerning "for he is highly exalted":

B. "He is exalted and is going to be exalted,"

C. as it is said, "For the Lord of hosts has a day upon all that is proud . . . and upon all the cedars of Lebanon . . . and upon all the high mountains . . . and upon every lofty tower . . . and upon all the ships of Tarshish . . . and the loftiness of man shall be bowed down . . . and the idols shall utterly pass away" (Is. 2:12–18).

4. A. Another teaching concerning "for he is highly exalted":

B. "He is exalted above all who take pride in themselves."

C. For with that in which the nations of the world take pride before him he exacts punishment from them.

D. For so Scripture says in connection with the men of the generation of the flood, "Their bull genders . . . they send forth their little ones . . . they sing to the timbrel and harp and rejoice" (Job 21:10–12).

E. And what is then stated? "Depart from us, we do not desire knowledge of your ways. What is the almighty that we should serve him" (Job 21:14–15).

F. They said, "Not even for a drop of rain do we need him, for 'There goes up a mist from the earth' (Gen. 2:6)."

G. Said to them the Holy One, blessed be he, "Total idiots! In the very act of goodness which I have done for you do you take pride before me? Through that same act I shall exact a penalty from you."

H. "And the rain was upon the earth forty days and forty nights" (Gen. 7:12).

5. A. R. Yosé of Damascus says, "Since they set their eyes both above and below to express their lust. So the Holy One, blessed be he, opened up against them the springs above and below so as to destroy them.

B. "For so it is said, 'All the fountains of the great deep were broken up and the windows of heaven were opened' (Gen. 7:11)."

6. A. And along these same lines, you found in connection with the men of the tower [of Babel], that with that in which they took pride before him he exacts punishment from them.

B. "Come let us build us a city" (Gen. 11:4).

C. What is said in their regard? "So the Lord scattered them abroad from thence upon the face of all the earth" (Gen. 11:8).

7. A. And along these same lines, you found in connection with the men of Sodom, that with that in which they took pride before him he exacts punishment from them.

B. "As for the earth out of it comes bread . . . the stones of it are the place of sapphires . . . that path no bird of prey knows . . . the proud beasts have not trodden it" (Job 28:5–8).

C. The men of Sodom said, "We have no need for travelers to come our way. Lo, we have food near at hand, lo, we have silver and gold, precious stones and pearls, near at hand. [Let us go and] wipe out the law of [protecting] the wayfarer [so as to remove the wayfarer] from our land."

D.   Said to them the Holy One, blessed be he, "Total idiots! On account of the act of goodness that I did for you, you take pride and you want to wipe out the law of [protecting] the wayfarer from among you. I shall wipe out the memory of you yourselves from the world."

E.   "He breaks open a shaft away from where men sojourn" (Job 28:4).

F.   "A contemptible brand . . . the tents of robbers prosper, and they that provoke God are secure" (Job. 12:5).

G.   That is what made them rebel, namely, "Whatsoever God brings into their hand" (Job 12:6).

H.   And so Scripture says, "And they were haughty and committed abominations before me" (Ez. 16:48–50).

I.   And what did it cause for them? "'As I live,' says the Lord God, 'Sodom your sister has not done . . . as you have done. . . . Behold, this was the iniquity of your sister Sodom . . . neither did she strengthen the hand of the poor and needy, and they were haughty'" (Ez. 16:48–50).

8. A.   "Before the Lord destroyed Sodom and Gomorrah they were like a garden of the Lord in the land of Egypt" (Gen. 13:10).

B.   Afterward: "And they made their father drink wine" (Gen. 19:33).

C.   Where did they get wine in the cave?

D.   The Holy One, blessed be he, made wine available for them: "And it shall come to pass on that day that the mountains shall drip sweet wine" (Joel 4:18).

E.   If that is how he provides for those who anger him, all the more so for those who carry out his will.

9. A.   So you find in the case of the Egyptians that with that in which they took pride before him he exacts punishment from them.

B.   "And he took six hundred chariots" (Ex. 14:7).

C.   Then: "Pharaoh's chariots and his host he cast into the sea, and his picked officers are sunk in the Red Sea."

10. A.   So you find in the case of Sisera that with that in which he took pride before him he exacts punishment from him.

B.   "And Sisera collected all his chariots, nine hundred chariots of iron" (Jud. 4:13).

C.   Then: "They fought from heaven, the stars in their courses fought against Sisera" (Jud. 5:20).

11. A. So you find in the case of Samson that with that in which he took pride before him he exacts punishment from him.

    B. "And Samson said to his father, 'Get her for me, for she is pleasing in my eyes'" (Jud. 14:3).

    C. Then: "And the Philistines took hold of him and put out his eyes and brought him down to Gaza" (Jud. 16:32).

    D. R. Judah says, "The beginning of his corruption was in Gaza, therefore his punishment was inflicted only in Gaza."

12. A. So you find in the case of Absalom that with that in which he took pride before him he exacts punishment from him.

    B. "Now in all Israel there was none so admired as Absalom for his beauty . . . and when he cut his hair . . ." (2 Sam. 14:25–26).

    C. R. Judah says, "He had taken the oath of a perpetual Nazirite and would cut his hair once every twelve months: 'Now it was at the end of forty years that Absalom said' (2 Sam. 15:7)."

    D. R. Yosé says, "He was a Nazirite for a specified number of days, and would cut his hair every thirty days: 'Now it was after a period of days according to the days after which he cut it' (2 Sam. 14:26)."

    E. Rabbi says, "He cut his hair every Friday, for it is the way of princes to cut their hair once a week on Friday."

    F. Now what is written thereafter? "And Absalom happened to meet the servants of David, and Absalom was riding upon his mule, and his hair got caught in the terebinth" (2 Sam. 18:9).

13. A. So you find in the case of Sennacherib that with that in which he took pride before him he exacts punishment from him.

    B. "By your messengers you have taunted the Lord . . . I have dug and drunk strange water" (2 Kgs. 19:23–24).

    C. Then: "And it happened that night that the angel of the Lord went out and killed in the camp of the Assyrians a hundred eighty-five thousand" (2 Kgs. 19:25).

    D. They say that the greatest of them was commander over a hundred eighty-five thousand, and the least was in charge of no fewer than two thousand: "How then can you turn away the face of one captain, even of the least of my master's servants" (2 Kgs. 18:24).

    E. "This is the word that the Lord has spoken concerning

him, The virgin daughter of Zion has despised you . . . whom you have taunted . . ." (2 Kgs. 19:21–22).

F.   "This day he shall halt at Nob" (Is. 10:32).

14. A.   So you find in the case of Nebuchadnezzar that with that in which he took pride before him he exacts punishment from him.

B.   "And you said in your heart, 'I will ascend to heaven . . . I will ascend above the heights of the clouds'" (Is. 14:13–14).

C.   Then: "You shall be brought down to the netherworld" (Is. 27:3).

15. A.   So you find in the case of Tyre that with that in which they took pride before him he exacts punishment from them.

B.   "You, Tyre, have said, 'I am of perfect beauty'" (Ez. 27:3).

C.   "Behold, I am against you, Tyre, and will cause many nations to come up against you" (Ez. 26:3).

16. A.   So you find in the case of the prince of Tyre that with that in which he took pride before him he exacts punishment from him.

B.   "Son of man, say to the prince of Tyre, 'Thus says the Lord God, because your heart is lifted up and you have said, I am a god'" (Ez. 28:2).

C.   Then: "You shall die the death of the uncircumcised by the hand of strangers" (Ez. 28:10).

17. A.   Lo, with that in which the nations of the world take pride before him he exacts punishment from them:

B.   "for he is highly exalted."

The use of the duplicated verb, Nos. 1–3, allows a systematic study of the reciprocal acts of exaltation, in Egypt, at the sea, then in the time to come—surely a single, protracted, and well-composed demonstration. Then we proceed to a different proposition concerning the same notion of exaltation, namely, self-aggrandizement. This yields the enormous discussion of the proposition, with that in which the nations of the world take pride before him he exacts punishment from them. Numerous cases on a long line of instances, based upon historical facts provided by Scripture, serve to demonstrate that proposition. Once more we have a sustained essay on a single proposition, which is demonstrated through a long sequence of probative cases. The proposition, God exacts punishment through the very thing in which one takes pride, could not be more effectively demonstrated.

XI

SIFRA (LEVITICUS)

1.

IDENTIFYING THE DOCUMENT

SIFRA, A COMPILATION OF MIDRASH EXEGESES ON THE BOOK OF LEVITICUS, FORMS a massive and systematic statement concerning the definition of the Mishnah in relationship to Scripture.[1] Unlike the other Midrash compilations that concern the Pentateuch, the two Sifrés and Mekhilta Attributed to R. Ishmael, the document is programmatically cogent, beginning to end, in its sustained treatment of the

---

[1] For further reading and bibliography on the topic of this chapter, see the following:

Bowker, pp. 71.

Moses D. Herr, "Sifra," *Encyclopaedia Judaica* 14:1517–1519: the name; construction (outline); language; source; editing; additions to the document; editions.

Maccoby, pp. 172–77 (selections, no introduction or analysis).

Stemberger-Strack, pp. 284–89: the name, contents, and structure; character, origin, and date; manuscripts, printed editions, translations, commentaries; a Mekhilta on Leviticus?

This writer's introductions are two, one in relationship to the Mishnah, the other in regard to the document's rhetorical, logical, and topical traits and program. The first is *Uniting the Dual Torah: Sifra and the Problem of the Mishnah*. Cambridge and New York, 1989: Cambridge University Press; the second, *Sifra in Perspective: The Documentary Comparison of the Midrashim of Ancient Judaism*. Atlanta, 1988: Scholars Press for Brown Judaic Studies. The latter conducts "comparative Midrash," treating this docu-

issues defined by the Mishnah. At the end of Chapter 5 we noted that for the heirs of the Mishnah, the relationship of the Mishnah with Scripture, in mythic language, of the oral to the written part of the Torah, required definition. The authorship of Sifra composed the one document to accomplish the union of the two Torahs, Scripture, or the written Torah, and the Mishnah, or the oral Torah.

This was achieved not merely formally by provision of proof texts from Scripture for statements of the Mishnah—as in the two Talmuds—but through a profound analysis of the interior structure of thought. It was by means of the critique of practical logic and the rehabilitation of the probative logic of hierarchical classification (accomplished through the form of *Listenwissenschaft*) in particular that the authorship of Sifra accomplished this remarkable feat of intellect. That authorship achieved the (re-)union of the two Torahs into a single cogent statement within the framework of the written Torah by penetrating into the deep composition of logic that underlay the creation of the world in its correct components, rightly classified, and in its right order, as portrayed by the Torah.

This was done in two ways. Specifically, it involved, first of all, systematically demolishing the logic that, as we saw in Chapter 5, sustains an autonomous Mishnah, which appeals to the intrinsic traits of things to accomplish classification and hierarchization. Second, it was done by demonstrating the dependency, for the identification of the correct classification of things, not upon the traits of things viewed in the abstract, but upon the classification of things by Scripture in particular. The framers of Sifra recast the two parts of the Torah into a single coherent statement through unitary and cogent discourse. So in choosing, as to structure, a book of the Pentateuch, and, as to form, the exegetical form involving paraphrase and amplification of a phrase of a base text of Scripture, the authorship of Sifra made its entire statement *in nuce*. Then by composing a document that for very long stretches simply cannot have been put together without the Mishnah and at the same time subjecting the generative logical principles of the Mishnah to devastating critique, that same authorship took up its position. The destruction of the Mishnah as an autonomous and freestanding statement, based upon its own logic, is followed by the reconstruction of (large tracts of) the Mishnah as a statement wholly within, and in accord with, the logic and program of the written Torah in Leviticus. That is what defines Sifra, the one genuinely cogent and sustained statement among the four Midrash compilations that present exegetical discourse on the Pentateuch.

The dominant approach to uniting the two Torahs, oral and written, into a single cogent statement involved reading the written Torah into the oral. In form, as we noted in the two Talmuds, this was done through inserting into the Mishnah (that is, the oral Torah) a long sequence of proof texts. The other solution required reading the oral Torah into the written one, by inserting into the written Torah

---

ment in comparison with other Midrash compilations of its class. That kind of comparative Midrash has been worked out only in the books of mine summarized in this introduction.

citations and allusions to the oral one, and, as a matter of fact, also by demonstrating, on both philosophical and theological grounds, the utter subordination and dependency of the oral Torah, the Mishnah, to the written Torah—while at the same time defending and vindicating that same oral Torah. Sifra, followed unsystematically, to be sure, by the two Sifrés, did just that. Sifra's authorship attempted to set forth the dual Torah as a single, cogent statement, doing so by reading the Mishnah into Scripture not merely for proposition but for expression of proposition. On the surface that decision represented a literary, not merely a theological, judgment. But within the deep structure of thought, it was far more than a mere matter of how to select and organize propositions.

That judgment upon the Mishnah forms part of the polemic of Sifra's authorship — but only part of it. Sifra's authorship conducts a sustained polemic against the failure of the Mishnah to cite Scripture very much or systematically to link its ideas to Scripture through the medium of formal demonstration by exegesis. Sifra's rhetorical exegesis follows a standard redactional form. Scripture will be cited. Then a statement will be made about its meaning, or a statement of law correlative to that Scripture will be given. That statement sometimes cites the Mishnah, often verbatim. Finally, the author of Sifra invariably states, "Now is that not [merely] logical?" And the point of that statement will be, Can this position not be gained through the working of mere logic, based upon facts supplied (to be sure) by Scripture?

The polemical power of Sifra lies in its repetitive demonstration that the stated position, citation of a Mishnah pericope, is not only not the product of logic, but is, and only can be, the product of exegesis of Scripture. That is only part of the matter, as I shall explain, but that component of the larger judgment of Sifra's authorship does make the point that the Mishnah is subordinated to Scripture and validated only through Scripture. In that regard, the authorship of Sifra stands at one with the position of the authorships of the other successor writings, even though Sifra's writers carried to a much more profound level of thought the critique of the Mishnah. They did so by rethinking the logical foundations of the entire Torah.

The framers of the Mishnah effect their taxonomy through the traits of things. The authorship of Sifra insists that the source of classification is Scripture. Sifra's authorship time and again demonstrates that classification without Scripture's data cannot be carried out without Scripture's data, and, it must follow, hierarchical arguments based on extra-scriptural taxa always fail. In the Mishnah we seek connection between fact and fact, sentence and sentence, by comparing and contrasting two things that are like and not alike. At the logical level the Mishnah falls into the category of familiar philosophical thought. Once we seek regularities, we propose rules. What is like another thing falls under its rule, and what is not like the other falls under the opposite rule. Accordingly, as to the species of the genus, so far as they are alike, they share the same rule. So far as they are not alike, each follows a rule contrary to that governing the other.

So the work of analysis is what produces connection, and therefore the drawing of conclusions derives from comparison and contrast: the *and,* the *equal.* The proposition, then, that forms the conclusion concerns the essential likeness of the two offices, except where they are different, but the subterranean premise is that we can explain both likeness and difference by appeal to a principle of fundamental order and unity. To make these observations concrete, we turn to the case at hand. The important contrast comes at the outset. The high priest and king fall into a single genus, but speciation, based on traits particular to the king, then distinguishes the one from the other. All of this exercise is conducted essentially independently of Scripture; the classifications derive from the system, are viewed as autonomous constructs; traits of things define classifications and dictate what is like and what is unlike.

Let us now examine one sustained example of how Sifra's authorship rejects the principles of the logic of hierarchical classification *as these are worked out by the framers of the Mishnah.* It is a critique of designating classifications of things without scriptural warrant. The critique applies to the way in which a shared logic is worked out by the other authorship. For it is not the principle that like things follow the same rule, unlike things, the opposite rule, that is at stake. Nor is the principle of hierarchical classification embodied in the argument *a fortiori* at issue. What our authorship disputes is that we can classify things on our own by appeal to their traits or indicative characteristics, that is, utterly without reference to Scripture. The argument is simple. On our own, we cannot classify species into genera. Everything is different from everything else in some way. But Scripture tells us what things are like what other things for what purposes, hence Scripture imposes on things the definitive classifications. Scripture does so—not traits we discern in the things themselves. When we see the nature of the critique, we shall have a clear picture of what is at stake when we examine, in some detail, precisely how the Mishnah's logic does its work. That is why at the outset I present a complete composition in which Sifra's authorship tests the modes of classification characteristic of the Mishnah, resting as they do on the traits of things viewed out of the context of Scripture's categories of things.

PARASHAT VAYYIQRA DIBURA DENEDABAH
PARASHAH 3[2]

V:I.   1.   A.   "[If his offering is] a burnt offering [from the herd, he shall offer a male without blemish; he shall offer it at the door of

---

[2] Sifra is divided into large sections and these are subdivided into chapters, some of which are called *parashah,* some *pereq;* I do not know why adjacent chapters will bear either the one or the other heading. Both mean, in our terms, "chapter." One of the reasons I had to invent a whole new reference system for Sifra is the confusion that results from having pereq 5 and parashah 5 side by side; another is that there was no sequential reference-system, beginning to end. What we had was the name of the large section of the book—here, *Vayyiqra Dibura Denedabah*—followed by *Pereq* or *Parashah.* Yet a third reason for redoing the entire document was that there was no division, within a given unit, between

the tent of meeting, that he may be accepted before the Lord; he shall lay his hand upon the head of the burnt offering, and it shall be accepted for him to make atonement for him]" (Lev. 1:2):

B. Why does Scripture refer to a burnt offering in particular?

C. For one might have taken the view that all of the specified grounds for the invalidation of an offering should apply only to the burnt offering that is brought as a freewill offering.

D. But how should we know that the same grounds for invalidation apply also to a burnt offering that is brought in fulfillment of an obligation [for instance, the burnt offering that is brought for a leper who is going through a rite of purification, or the bird brought by a woman who has given birth as part of her purification rite, Lev. 14, 12, respectively]?

E. It is a matter of logic.

F. Bringing a burnt offering as a freewill offering and bringing a burnt offering in fulfillment of an obligation [are parallel to one another and fall into the same classification].

G. Just as a burnt offering that is brought as a freewill offering is subject to all of the specified grounds for invalidation, so to a burnt offering brought in fulfillment of an obligation, all the same grounds for invalidation should apply.

H. No, [that reasoning is not compelling. For the two species of the genus, burnt offering, are not wholly identical and can be distinguished, on which basis we may also maintain that the grounds for invalidation that pertain to the one do not necessarily apply to the other. Specifically:] if you have taken that position with respect to the burnt offering brought as a freewill offering, for which there is no equivalent, will you take the same position with regard to the burnt offering brought in fulfillment of an obligation, for which there is an equivalent?

---

one sentence and another, or one paragraph and another, so any sort of analytical discussion was simply impossible; there was no analysis of forms, structures, and other elements of literary consequence prior to mine. The meaning here, and so throughout, then, is simple. We deal with the large section of Sifra called Vayyiqra Dibura Denedabah. In the received text, this is called Parashah 3. In my system, it is V:I.1, meaning, the fifth chapter of the entirety of Sifra; the first major propositional unit of that chapter; the first paragraph of that propositional unit; then the individual sentences are designated by letters. The same system runs throughout this presentation of the rabbinic literature. I know of no competing system for identifying sentences, paragraphs, chapters, and the like. The competing system for the two Talmuds is simply the page where a passage is found, thus, for the Talmud of Babylonia, tractate name and page number, obverse or reverse side of the page, in the standard printed editions, thus Bavli Berakhot 3a. On that basis, it is difficult to find passages and impossible to analyze their context.

[For if one is obligated to bring a burnt offering by reason of obligation and cannot afford a beast, one may bring birds, as at Lev. 14:22, but if one is bringing a freewill offering, a less expensive form of the offering may not serve.]

I. Accordingly, since there is the possibility in the case of the burnt offering brought in fulfillment of an obligation, in which case there is an acceptable equivalent [to the more expensive beast, through the less expensive birds], all of the specified grounds for invalidation [which apply to the burnt offering brought as a freewill offering, which is in any case more expensive] should not apply at all.

J. That is why in the present passage, Scripture refers simply to "burnt offering," [and without further specification, the meaning is then simple:] all the same are the burnt offering brought in fulfillment of an obligation and a burnt offering brought as a freewill offering in that all of the same grounds for invalidation of the beast that pertain to the one pertain also to the other.

2. A. And how do we know that the same rules of invalidation of a blemished beast apply also in the case of a beast that is designated in substitution of a beast sanctified for an offering [in line with Lev. 27:10, so that if one states that a given, unconsecrated beast is to take the place of a beast that has already been consecrated, the already-consecrated beast remains in its holy status, and the beast to which reference is made also becomes consecrated]?

B. The matter of bringing a burnt offering and the matter of bringing a substituted beast fall into the same classification [since both are offerings that in the present instance will be consumed upon the altar, and, consequently, they fall under the same rule as to invalidating blemishes].

C. Just as the entire protocol of blemishes applies to the one, so in the case of the beast that is designated as a substitute, the same invalidating blemishes pertain.

D. No, if you have invoked that rule in the case of the burnt offering, in which case no status of sanctification applies should the beast that is designated as a burnt offering be blemished in some permanent way, will you make the same statement in the case of a beast that is designated as a substitute? For in the case of a substituted beast, the status of sanctification applies even though the beast bears a permanent blemish! [So the two do not fall into the same classification after all, since to begin with one cannot sanctify a permanently blemished beast, which beast can never enter the status of sanctification, but through an act of substitution, a permanently blemished beast can be placed into the status of sanctification.]

E. Since the status of sanctification applies [to a substituted beast] even though the beast bears a permanent blemish, all of the specified grounds for invalidation as a matter of logic should not apply to it.

F. That is why in the present passage, Scripture refers simply to "burnt offering," [and without further specification, the meaning is then simple:] all the same are the burnt offering brought in fulfillment of an obligation and a burnt offering brought as a substitute for an animal designated as holy, in that all of the same grounds for invalidation of the beast that pertain to the one pertain also to the other.

3. A. And how do we know [that the protocol of blemishes that applies to the burnt offering brought as a freewill offering applies also to] animals that are subject to the rule of a sacrifice as a peace offering?

B. It is a matter of logic. The matter of bringing a burnt offering and the matter of bringing animals that are subject to the rule of a sacrifice as a peace offering fall into the same classification [since both are offerings and consequently under the same rule as to invalidating blemishes].

C. Just as the entire protocol of blemishes applies to the one, so in the case of animals that are subject to the rule of a sacrifice as a peace offering, the same invalidating blemishes pertain.

D. And it is furthermore a matter of an argument *a fortiori,* as follows:

E. If to a burnt offering that is valid when in the form of a bird, [which is inexpensive], the protocol of invalidating blemishes applies, to peace offerings, which are not valid when brought in the form of a bird, surely the same protocol of invalidating blemishes should also apply!

F. No, if you have applied that rule to a burnt offering, in which case females are not valid for the offering as male beasts are, will you say the same of peace offerings? For female beasts as much as male beasts may be brought for sacrifice in the status of the peace offering. [The two species may be distinguished from one another.]

G. Since it is the case that female beasts as much as male beasts may be brought for sacrifice in the status of the peace offering, the protocol of invalidating blemishes should not apply to a beast designated for use as a peace offering.

H.   That is why in the present passage, Scripture refers simply to "burnt offering," [and without further specification, the meaning is then simple:] all the same are the burnt offering brought in fulfillment of an obligation and an animal designated under the rule of peace offerings in that all of the same grounds for invalidation of the beast that pertain to the one pertain also to the other.

The systematic exercise proves for beasts that serve in three classifications of offerings, burnt offerings, substitutes, and peace offerings, that the same rules of invalidation apply throughout. The comparison of the two kinds of burnt offerings, voluntary and obligatory, shows that they are sufficiently different from one another so that as a matter of logic, what pertains to the one need not apply to the other. Then come the differences between an animal that is consecrated and one that is designated as a substitute for one that is consecrated. Finally we distinguish between the applicable rules of the sacrifice: a burnt offering yields no meat for the person in behalf of whom the offering is made, while one sacrificed under the rule of peace offerings does. We run the changes on three fundamentally different differences and show that in each case, the differences between like things are greater than the similarities

In Sifra no one denies the principle of hierarchical classification. That is an established fact, a self-evident trait of mind. The argument of Sifra's authorship is that by themselves, things do not possess traits that permit us finally to classify species into a common genus. There always are traits distinctive to a classification. Accordingly, it is the argument of Sifra's authorship that without the revelation of the Torah, we are not able to effect any classification at all, are left, that is to say, only with species, no genus, only with cases, no rules. The thrust of Sifra's authorship's attack on the Mishnah's taxonomic logic is readily discerned. Time and again, we can easily demonstrate, things have so many and such diverse and contradictory indicative traits that comparing one thing to something else, we can always distinguish one species from another. Even though we find something in common, we also can discern some other trait characteristic of one thing but not the other. Consequently, we also can show that the hierarchical logic on which we rely, the argument *a fortiori* or *qol vehomer*, will not serve. For if on the basis of one set of traits that yield a given classification, we place into hierarchical order two or more items, on the basis of a different set of traits, we have either a different classification altogether, or, much more commonly, simply a different hierarchy. So the attack on the way in which the Mishnah's authorship has done its work appeals not merely to the limitations of classification solely on the basis of traits of things. The more telling argument addresses what is, to *Listenwissenschaft*, the source of power and compelling proof: hierarchization. That is why, throughout, we must designate the Mishnah's mode of *Listenwissenschaft* a logic of hierarchical classification. Things are not merely like or unlike, therefore following one rule or its opposite. Things also are weightier or less weighty, and that particular point of likeness of difference generates the logical force of *Listenwissenschaft*.

Sifra's authorship repeatedly demonstrates that the formation of classifications is based on monothetic taxonomy. What that means is this: traits that are not only common to both items, but that are shared throughout both of the items subject to comparison and contrast, simply will not serve. These shared traits are supposed to prove that the items that are compared are alike, and therefore should be subjected to the same rule. But the allegation of comparability proves flawed. The proposition maintains that the two items are alike because they share one trait in common (thus: "monothetic taxonomy"). But I shall show you that they also exhibit traits that are different for the respective items. Then we have both likeness and difference.

Then, the argument proceeds, at every point at which someone alleges uniform, that is to say, monothetic, likeness, Sifra's authorship will demonstrate difference. Then how to proceed? Appeal is to some shared traits as a basis for classification: this is not like that, and that is not like this, but the indicative trait that both exhibit is such and so. We deal therefore with polythetic taxonomy. The self-evident problem in accepting differences among things and insisting, nonetheless, on their monomorphic character for purposes of comparison and contrast cannot be set aside: who says? That is, if I can adduce in evidence for a shared classification of things only a few traits among many characteristic of each thing, then what stops me from treating all things alike? Polythetic taxonomy opens the way to an unlimited exercise in finding what diverse things have in common and imposing, for that reason, one rule on everything. Then the very working of *Listenwissenschaft* as a tool of analysis, differentiation, comparison, contrast, and the descriptive determination of rules yields the opposite of what is desired. Chaos, not order, a mass of exceptions, no rules, a world of examples, each subject to its own regulation, instead of a world of order and proportion, composition and stability, will result.

Sifra's authorship affirms taxonomic logic when applied to the right categories. It systematically demonstrates the affirmative case, that *Listenwissenschaft* is a self-evidently valid mode of demonstrating the truth of propositions. But *the* source of the correct classification of things is Scripture and only Scripture. Without Scripture's intervention into the taxonomy of the world, we should have no knowledge at all of which things fall into which classifications and therefore are governed by which rules. How then do we appeal to Scripture to designate the operative classifications? Here is a simple example of the alternative mode of classification, one that does not appeal to the traits of things but to the utilization of names by Scripture. What we see is how by naming things in one way, rather than in another, Scripture orders all things, classifying and, in the nature of things, also hierarchizing them. Here is one example among many of how our authorship conceives the right way of logical thought to proceed:

PARASHAT VAYYIQRA DIBURA DENEDABAH
PARASHAH 4

VII:V.   1.   A.   ". . . and Aaron's sons the priests shall present the blood and throw the blood [round about against the altar that is at the door of the tent of meeting]":

B.   Why does Scripture make use of the word "blood" twice [instead of using a pronoun]?

C.   [It is for the following purpose:] How on the basis of Scripture do you know that if blood deriving from one burnt offering was confused with blood deriving from another burnt offering, blood deriving from one burnt offering with blood deriving from a beast that has been substituted therefor, blood deriving from a burnt offering with blood deriving from an unconsecrated beast, the mixture should nonetheless be presented?

D.   It is because Scripture makes use of the word "blood" twice [instead of using a pronoun].

2.   A.   It is the fact that blood deriving from beasts in the specified classifications [the blood of the sacrifice] is to be presented [on the altar, as a valid offering]. That is for the simple reason that if the several beasts while alive had been confused with one another, they might be offered up.

B.   But how do we know that even if the blood of a burnt offering were confused with that of a beast killed as a guilt offering [it is to be offered up]? [The answer is, because they fall into a single classification, namely, Most Holy Things.]

C.   I shall concede the case of the mixture of the blood of a burnt offering confused with that of a beast killed as a guilt offering; it is to be presented, for both this one and that one fall into the classification of Most Holy Things.

D.   But how do I know that if the blood of a burnt offering were confused with the blood of a beast slaughtered in the classification of peace offerings or of a thanksgiving offering [the mixture is to be presented]? [The answer, once more, is that these fall into the same classification, now for the reason that the blood of the two distinct classes of offering is sprinkled on the altar the same number of times, as is made explicit.]

E.   I shall concede the case of the mixture of the blood of a burnt offering confused with that of a beast slaughtered in the classification of peace offerings or of a thanksgiving offering; [it is to be presented], because the beasts in both classifications produce blood that has to be sprinkled four times.

F. But how do I know that if the blood of a burnt offering were confused with the blood of a beast slaughtered in the classification of a firstling or a beast that was counted as the tenth [that is, it is to serve as the tithe of that herd or flock] or of a beast designated as a passover [it is to be presented]?

G. I shall concede the case of the mixture of the blood of a burnt offering confused with that of a beast slaughtered in the classification of firstling or a beast that was counted as a tenth or of a beast designated as a passover; [it is to be presented], because Scripture uses the word "blood" two times.

H. Then while I may make that concession, might I also suppose that if the blood of a burnt offering was confused with the blood of beasts that had suffered an invalidation, it also may be offered up?

I. Scripture says, ". . . its blood" [thus excluding such a case].

J. Then I shall concede the case of a mixture of the blood of a valid burnt offering with the blood of beasts that had suffered an invalidation, which blood is not valid to be presented at all.

K. But how do I know that if such blood were mixed with the blood deriving from beasts set aside as sin offerings to be offered on the inner altar [it is not to be offered up]?

L. I can concede that the blood of a burnt offering that has been mixed with the blood deriving from beasts set aside as sin offerings to be offered on the inner altar is not to be offered up, for the one is offered on the inner altar, and the other on the outer altar [the burnt offering brought as a free-will offering, under discussion here, is slaughtered at the altar ". . . that is at the door of the tent of meeting," not at the inner altar].

M. But how do I know that even if the blood of a burnt offering was confused with the blood of sin offerings that are to be slaughtered at the outer altar, it is not to be offered up?

N. Scripture says, ". . . its blood" [thus excluding such a case].

In place of the rejecting of arguments resting on classifying species into a common genus, we now demonstrate how classification really is to be carried on. It is through the imposition upon data of the categories dictated by Scripture: Scripture's use of language. That is the force of this powerful exercise. No. 1 sets the stage, simply pointing out that the use of the word "blood" twice encompasses a case in which blood in two distinct classifications is somehow confused in the process of the conduct of the cult. In such a case it is quite proper to pour out the mixture of blood deriving from distinct sources, e.g., beasts that have served different, but comparable, purposes. We then systemically work out the limits of that rule, showing how comparability works, then pointing to cases in which comparability is set aside. Throughout the exposition, at the crucial point we invoke the formulation of Scripture, subordinating logic or in our instance the process of classification of like species to the dictation of Scripture. I cannot imagine a more successful demonstration of what the framers wish to say.

The reason for Scripture's unique power of classification is the possibility of polythetic classification that only Scripture makes possible. Because of Scripture's provision of taxa, we are able to undertake the science of *Listenwissenschaft,* including hierarchical classification, in the right way. What can we do because we appeal to Scripture, which we cannot do if we do not rely on Scripture? It is to establish the possibility of polythetic classification. We can appeal to shared traits of otherwise distinct taxa and so transform species into a common genus for a given purpose. Only Scripture makes that initiative feasible, so our authorship maintains. What is at stake? It is the possibility of doing precisely what the framers of the Mishnah wish to do. That is to join together masses of diverse data into a single, encompassing statement, to show the rule that inheres in diverse cases. In what follows, we shall see an enormous, coherent, and beautifully articulated exercise in the comparison and contrast of many things of a single genus. The whole holds together, because Scripture makes possible the statement of all things within a single rule. That is, as we have noted, precisely what the framers of the Mishnah proposed to accomplish. Our authorship maintains that only by appeal to the Torah is this feat of learning possible. If, then, we wish to understand all things all together and all at once under a single encompassing rule, we had best revert to the Torah, with its account of the rightful names, positions, and order imputed to all things.

PARASHAT VAYYIQRA DIBURA DENEDABAH
PARASHAH 11

XXII:I. 1. A. **[With reference to M. Men. 5:5:] There are those [offerings that require bringing near but do not require waving, waving but not bringing near, waving and bringing near, neither waving nor bringing near: These are offerings that require bringing near but do not require waving: the meal offering of fine flour and the meal offering prepared in the baking pan and the meal offering prepared in the frying pan, and the meal offering of cakes and the meal offering of wafers, and the meal offering of priests, and the meal offering of an anointed priest, and the**

meal offering of gentiles, and the meal offering of women, and the meal offering of a sinner. R. Simeon says, "The meal offering of priests and of the anointed priest—bringing near does not apply to them, because the taking of a handful does not apply to them. And whatever is not subject to the taking of a handful is not subject to bringing near,"] [Scripture] says, "When you present to the Lord a meal offering that is made in any of these ways, it shall be brought [to the priest who shall take it up to the altar]":

B. What requires bringing near is only the handful. How do I know that I should encompass the meal offering under the rule of bringing near?

C. Scripture says explicitly, "meal offering."

D. How do I know that I should encompass all meal offerings?

E. Scripture says, using the accusative particle, "the meal offering."

2. A. I might propose that what requires bringing near is solely the meal offering brought as a freewill offering.

B. How do I know that the rule encompasses an obligatory meal offering?

C. It is a matter of logic.

D. Bringing a meal offering as a freewill offering and bringing a meal offering as a matter of obligation form a single classification. Just as a meal offering presented as a freewill offering requires bringing near, so the same rule applies to a meal offering of a sinner [brought as a matter of obligation], which should likewise require bringing near.

E. No, if you have stated that rule governing bringing near in the case of a freewill offering, on which oil and frankincense have to be added, will you say the same of the meal offering of a sinner [Lev. 5:11], which does not require oil and frankincense?

F. The meal offering brought by a wife accused of adultery will prove to the contrary, for it does not require oil and frankincense, but it does require bringing near [as is stated explicitly at Num. 5:15].

G. No, if you have applied the requirement of bringing near to the meal offering brought by a wife accused of adultery, which also requires waving, will you say the same of the meal offering of a sinner, which does not have to be waved?

H.   Lo, you must therefore reason by appeal to a polythetic analogy [in which not all traits pertain to all components of the category, but some traits apply to them all in common]:

I.   the meal offering brought as a freewill offering, which requires oil and frankincense, does not in all respects conform to the traits of the meal offering of a wife accused of adultery, which does not require oil and frankincense, and the meal offering of the wife accused of adultery, which requires waving, does not in all respects conform to the traits of a meal offering brought as a freewill offering, which does not require waving.

J.   But what they have in common is that they are alike in requiring the taking up of a handful and they are also alike in that they require bringing near.

K.   I shall then introduce into the same classification the meal offering of a sinner, which is equivalent to them as to the matter of the taking up of a handful, and also should be equivalent to them as to the requirement of being drawn near.

L.   But might one not argue that the trait that all have in common is that all of them may be brought equally by a rich and a poor person and require drawing near, which then excludes from the common classification the meal offering of a sinner, which does not conform to the rule that it may be brought equally by a rich and a poor person [but may be brought only by a poor person,] and such an offering also should not require being brought near.

M.   [The fact that the polythetic classification yields indeterminate results means failure once more, and, accordingly,] Scripture states, "meal offering,"

N.   with this meaning: all the same are the meal offering brought as a freewill offering and the meal offering of a sinner, both this and that require being brought near.

The elegant exercise draws together the various types of meal offerings and shows that they cannot form a classification of either a monothetic or a polythetic character. Consequently, Scripture must be invoked to supply the proof for the classification of the discrete items. The important language is at H-J: these differ from those, and those from these, but what they have in common is. . . . Then we demonstrate, with our appeal to Scripture, the sole valid source of polythetic classification, M. And this is constant throughout Sifra.

While setting forth its critique of the Mishnah's utilization of the logic of comparison and contrast in hierarchical classification, the authorship of Sifra is careful not to criticize the Mishnah. Its position favors restating the Mishnah within the context of Scripture, not rejecting the conclusions of the Mishnah, let alone its authority. Consequently, when we find a critique of applied reason divorced from Scripture, we rarely uncover an explicit critique of the Mishnah, and when we find a citation of the Mishnah, we rarely uncover linkage to the ubiquitous principle that Scripture forms the source of all classification and hierarchy. When the Mishnah is cited by our authorship, it will be presented as part of the factual substrate of the Torah. When the logic operative throughout the Mishnah is subjected to criticism, the language of the Mishnah will rarely, if ever, be cited in context. The operative language in dealing with the critique of the applied logic of *Listenwissenschaft* as represented by the framers of the Mishnah ordinarily is, "is it not a matter of logic?" Then the sorts of arguments against taxonomy pursued outside of the framework of Scripture's classifications will follow. When, by contrast, the authorship of Sifra wishes to introduce into the context it has already established a verbatim passage of the Mishnah, it will ordinarily, though not always, use *mikan amru,* which, in context, means, "in this connection [sages] have said." It is a simple fact that when the intent is to demolish improper reasoning, the Mishnah's rules in the Mishnah's language rarely, if ever, occur. When the authorship of Sifra wishes to incorporate paragraphs of the Mishnah into their re-presentation of the Torah, they will do so either without fanfare, as in the passage at hand, or by the neutral joining language "in this connection [sages] have said."

The authorship of Sifra never called into question the self-evident validity of taxonomic logic. Its critique is addressed only to how the Mishnah's framers identify the origins of, and delineate, taxa. But that critique proves fundamental to the case that that authorship proposed to make. For, intending to demonstrate that "the Torah" was a proper noun, and that everything that was valid came to expression in the single, cogent statement of the Torah, the authorship at hand identified the fundamental issue. It is the debate over the way we know things. In insisting, in agreement with the framers of the Mishnah, that there are not only cases but also rules, not only species but also genera, the authorship of Sifra also made its case in behalf of the case for "the Torah" as a proper noun. This carries us to the theological foundation for Sifra's authorship's sustained critique of applied reason.

At stake is the character of the Torah. I may phrase the question in this way: exactly what do we want to learn from, or discern within, the Torah? And the answer to that question requires theological, not merely literary and philosophical, reflection on our part. For in its delineation of correct hierarchical logic, our authorship uncovered within the Torah (hence by definition, written and oral components of the Torah alike) an adumbration of the working of the mind of God. That is because the premise of all discourse is that the Torah was written by God and dictated by God to Moses at Sinai. And that will in the end explain why our authorship for its part has entered into the Torah long passages of not merely clarification but active intrusion, making itself a component of the interlocutorial process. To what end we know: it was to unite the dual Torah. The authorship of

Sifra proposed to regain access to the modes of thought that guided the formation of the Torah, oral and written alike: comparison and contrast in this way, not in that; identification of categories in one manner, not in another. Since those were the modes of thought that in our authorship's conception dictated the structure of intellect upon which the Torah, the united Torah, rested, a simple conclusion is the sole possible one.

In its analysis of the deepest structures of intellect of the Torah, the authorship of Sifra presumed to enter into the mind of God, showing how God's mind worked when God formed the Torah, written and oral alike. And there, in the intellect of God, in its judgment humanity gained access to the only means of uniting the Torah, because that is where the Torah originated. But in discerning how God's mind worked, the intellectuals who created Sifra claimed for themselves a place in that very process of thought that had given birth to the Torah. Our authorship could rewrite the Torah because, knowing how the Torah originally was written, it too could write (though not reveal) the Torah.

2.
TRANSLATIONS INTO ENGLISH

The only translation into English is this writer's *Sifra. An Analytical Translation*. Atlanta, 1988: Scholars Press for Brown Judaic Studies. I. *Introduction* and *Vayyiqra Dibura Denedabah* and *Vayiqqra Dibura Dehobah;* II. *Sav, Shemini, Tazria, Negaim, Mesora,* and *Zabim;* III. *Aharé Mot, Qedoshim, Emor, Behar,* and *Behuqotai.*

3.
RHETORIC

Three forms dictate the entire rhetorical repertoire of this document. The first, the dialectical, is the demonstration that if we wish to classify things, we must follow the taxa dictated by Scripture rather than relying solely upon the traits of the things we wish to classify. The second, the citation form, invokes the citation of passages of the Mishnah or the Tosefta in the setting of Scripture. The third is the commentary form, in which a phrase of Scripture is followed by an amplificatory clause of some sort. The forms of the document admirably expressed the polemical purpose of the authorship at hand. What they wished to prove was that a taxonomy resting on the traits of things without reference to Scripture's classifications cannot serve. They further wished to restate the oral Torah in the setting of the written Torah. And, finally, they wished to accomplish the whole by rewriting the written Torah. The dialectical form accomplishes the first purpose, the citation form the second, and the commentary form the third.

The simple commentary form is familiar in Mekhilta Attributed to R. Ishmael, in which a verse, or an element of a verse, is cited, and then a very few words explain the meaning of that verse. Second come the complex forms, in which a simple exegesis is augmented in some important way, commonly by questions and answers, so that we have more than simply a verse and a brief exposition of its elements or of its meaning as a whole. The authorship of the Sifra time and again wishes to show that prior documents, the Mishnah or Tosefta, cited verbatim, require the support of exegesis of Scripture for important propositions, presented in the Mishnah and the Tosefta not on the foundation of exegetical proof at all. In the main, moreover, the authorship of Sifra tends not to attribute its materials to specific authorities, and most of the pericopes containing attributions are shared with Mishnah and Tosefta. As we should expect, just as in Mekhilta Attributed to R. Ishmael, Sifra contains a fair sample of pericopes which do not make use of the forms common in the exegesis of specific scriptural verses and mostly do not pretend to explain the meaning of verses, but rather resort to forms typical of Mishnah and Tosefta. When Sifra uses forms other than those in which its exegeses are routinely phrased, it commonly, though not always, draws upon materials also found in Mishnah and Tosefta. It is uncommon for Sifra to make use of non-exegetical forms for materials peculiar to its compilation. To state matters simply, Sifra quotes Mishnah or Tosefta, but its own materials follow its distinctive, exegetical forms.

Every example of a complex form, that is, a passage in which we have more than a cited verse and a brief exposition of its meaning, may be called "dialectical," that is, as we saw in Chapter 4, the mode of moving or developing an idea through questions and answers, sometimes implicit, but commonly explicit. What "moves" is the argument, the flow of thought, from problem to problem. The dialectics of Sifra differs in form and purpose from that of the Talmuds. Here, the movement is generated by the raising of contrary questions and theses. There are several subdivisions of the dialectical exegesis, so distinctive as to be treated by themselves. But all exhibit a flow of logical argument, unfolding in questions and answers, characteristic, in the later literature, of the Talmud. One important subdivision of the stated form consists of those items, somewhat few in number but all rather large in size and articulation, intended to prove that logic alone is insufficient, and that only through revealed law will a reliable view of what is required be attained. The polemic in these items is pointed and obvious; logic (Hebrew: din) never wins the argument, though at a few points flaws in the text seem to suggest disjunctures in the flow of logic. To clarify these general remarks, let us now address a particular chapter of Sifra and out of its details form a theory of the repertoire of forms on which our authorship has drawn.

PARASHAT VAYYIQRA DIBURA DENEDABAH
PARASHAH 7

XIV:I. 1. A. ["If his offering to the Lord is a burnt offering of birds, he shall choose [bring near] his offering from turtledoves or pigeons. The priest shall bring it to the altar, pinch off its head, and turn it into smoke on the altar; and its blood shall be drained out against the side of the altar. He shall remove its crop with its contents and cast it into the place of the ashes, at the east side of the altar. The priest shall tear it open by its wings, without severing it, and turn it into smoke on the altar, upon the wood that is on the fire. It is a burnt offering, an offering by fire, of pleasing odor to the Lord" (Lev. 1:14–17)]:

B. "[The priest] shall bring it [to the altar]":

C. What is the sense of this statement?

D. Since it is said, "he shall choose [bring near] his offering from turtledoves or pigeons," one might have supposed that there can be no fewer than two sets of birds.

E. Accordingly, Scripture states, "[The priest] shall bring it [to the altar]" to indicate, [by reference to the "it,"] that even a single pair suffices.

Reduced to its simplest syntactic traits, the form consists of the citation of a clause of a verse, followed by secondary amplification of that clause. We may call this commentary form, meaning, the form links a clause of Scripture to a few words that amplify the sense of those words, thus, commentary on a text. The rhetorical requirement is citation plus amplification. Clearly, the form sustains a variety of expressions, e.g., the one at hand: "what is the sense of this statement . . . since it is said . . . accordingly Scripture states. . . ." But for our purposes there is no need to differentiate within the commentary form.

2. A. "The priest shall bring it to the altar, pinch off its head":

B. Why does Scripture say, "The priest . . . pinch off . . ."?

C. This teaches that the act of pinching off the head should be done only by a priest.

D. But is the contrary to that proposition not a matter of logic:

E. if in the case of a beast of the flock, to which the act of slaughter at the north side of the altar is assigned, the participation of a priest in particular is not assigned, then the act of pinching the neck, to which the act of slaughter at the north side of the altar is not assigned, surely should not involve the participation of the priest in particular!

F. That is why it is necessary for Scripture to say, "The priest . . . pinch off . . . ,"

G. so as to teach that the act of pinching off the head should be done only by a priest.

3. A. Might one compose an argument to prove that one should pinch the neck by using a knife?

B. For lo, it is a matter of logic.

C. If to the act of slaughter [of a beast as a sacrifice], for which the participation of a priest is not required, the use of a correct utensil is required, then the act of pinching the neck, for which the participation of a priest indeed is required, surely should involve the requirement of using a correct implement!

D. That is why it is necessary for Scripture to say, "The priest . . . pinch off. . . ."

4. A. Said R. Aqiba, "Now would it really enter anyone's mind that a non-priest should present an offering on the altar?

B. "Then why is it said, 'The priest . . . pinch off . . .'?

C. "This teaches that the act of pinching the neck must be done by the priest using his own finger [and not a utensil]."

5. A. Might one suppose that the act of pinching may be done either at the head [up by the altar] or at the foot [on the pavement down below the altar]?

B. It is a matter of logic:

C. If in the case of an offering of a beast, which when presented as a sin offering is slaughtered above [at the altar itself] but when slaughtered as a burnt offering is killed below [at the pavement below the altar], in the case of an offering of fowl, since when presented as a sin offering it is slaughtered down below, surely in the case of a burnt offering it should be done down below as well!

D. That is why it was necessary for Scripture to make explicit [that it is killed up by the altar itself:] "The priest shall bring it to the altar, pinch off its head, and turn it into smoke on the altar."

E. The altar is explicitly noted with respect to turning the offering into smoke and also to pinching off the head.

F. Just as the offering is turned into smoke up above, at the altar itself, so the pinching off of the head is to be done up above, at the altar itself.

The form at hand is to be characterized as a dialectical exegetical argument, in which we move from point to point in a protracted, yet very tight, exposition of a proposition. The proposition is both implicit and explicit. The implicit proposition is that "logic" does not suffice. The explicit proposition concerns the subject matter at hand. We may identify the traits of this form very simply: citation of a verse or clause + a proposition that interprets that phrase, then "it is a matter of logic" followed by the demonstration that logic is insufficient for the determination of taxa.

XIV:II. ´ 2. A. "[turn it into smoke on the altar;] and its blood shall be drained out":

B. Can one describe matters in such a way?

C. Specifically, after the carcass is turned into smoke, can one drain out the blood?

D. But one pinches the neck in accord with the way in which one turns it into smoke:

E. Just as we find that the turning of the carcass into smoke is done up to the head by itself and then the body by itself, so in the act of pinching the neck, the head is by itself and the body is by itself.

3. A. And how do we know that in the case of turning a carcass into smoke, the head is done by itself?

B. When Scripture says, "The priest [shall tear it open by its wings, without severing it,] and turn it into smoke on the altar" (Lev. 1:17),

C. lo, the turning of the body into smoke is covered by that statement.

D. Lo, when Scripture states here, "pinch off its head, and turn it into smoke on the altar," it can only mean that the head is to be turned into smoke by itself.

E. Now, just as we find that the turning of the carcass into smoke is done up to the head by itself and then the body by itself, so in the act of pinching the neck, the head is by itself and the body is by itself.

Nos. 2, 3 present in a rather developed statement the simple exegetical form. The formal requirement is not obscured, however, since all we have is the citation of a clause followed by secondary amplification. This version of the commentary form obviously cannot be seen as identical to the other; but so far as the dictates of rhetoric are concerned, there is no material difference, since the variations affect only the secondary amplification of the basic proposition, and in both cases, the basic proposition is set forth by the citation of the verse or clause followed by a sentence or two of amplification. Now we come to a simple example of how the Mishnah is introduced:

4. A. How does the priest do it?

   B. **The priest went up on the ramp and went around the circuit. He came to the southeastern corner. He would wring off its head from its neck and divide the head from the body. And he drained off its blood onto the wall of the altar [M. Zeb. 6:5B–E].**

   C. **If one did it from the place at which he was standing and downward by a cubit, it is valid. R. Simeon and R. Yohanan ben Beroqah say, "The entire deed was done only at the top of the altar" [T. Zeb. 7:9C–D].**

What we have now is the verbatim citation of a passage of the Mishnah or of the Tosefta, joined to its setting in the exegetical framework of Sifra by some sort of joining formula. Mishnah citation form requires only appropriate joining language. Among the three forms of the document, my estimate is that somewhat over half of all completed units of discourse follow commentary form; a quarter, dialectical form; and a fifth, citation form.

4.
Logic of Coherent Discourse

Just as a limited and fixed pattern of formal preferences was characteristic of the document as a whole, so a simple logical program, consisting of three logics of cogent discourse, served for every statement. Sifra's authorship made choices about how cogent and coherent statements would be made to hold together in its document. Counting each entry as a single item presents a gross and simple picture of the proportions of the types of logics we have cataloged.

Type of Logic	Number of Entries	Percentage of the Whole
Propositional	73	30.4%
Teleological	1	0.4%
Fixed-Associative	43	17.9%
Methodical-Analytical	123	51.0%
	240	99.7%

The operative logics are mainly propositional, approximately 82 percent, inclusive of propositional, teleological, and methodical-analytical compositions. An authorship intending what we now call a commentary will have found paramount use for the logic of fixed association. That logic clearly served only a modest purpose in the context of the document as a whole. Our authorship developed a tripartite program. It wished to demonstrate the limitations of the logic of hierarchical classification, such as predominates in the Mishnah; that forms a constant theme of the methodical-analytical logic. It proposed, second, to restate the Mishnah within the context of Scripture, that is, to rewrite the written Torah to make a place for the oral Torah. This is worked out in the logic of propositional discourse. And, finally, it wished in this rewriting to re-present the whole Torah as a cogent and unified document. Through the logic of fixed association it in fact did re-present the Torah. The three logics correspond, in their setting within the inner structure of cogent discourse. What the authorship of Sifra wished to prove was that a taxonomy resting on the traits of things without reference to Scripture's classifications cannot serve. They further wished to restate the oral Torah in the setting of the written Torah. And, finally, they wished to accomplish the whole by rewriting the written Torah. The dialectical form accomplished the first purpose, the citation form the second, and the commentary form the third. There is an exact correspondence between the logics of the document and its rhetorical forms.

5.
TOPICAL PROGRAM

As we realize, for its topical program the authorship of Sifra takes the book of Leviticus. For propositions Sifra's authorship presents episodic and ad hoc sentences. If we ask how these sentences form propositions other than amplifications of points made in the book of Leviticus itself, and how we may restate those propositions in a coherent way, nothing sustained and coherent emerges. Sifra does not constitute a propositional document transcending its precipitating text. But, as we have now seen in detail, that in no way bears the implication that the document's authorship merely collected and arranged this and that about the book of Leviticus. For three reasons, we must conclude that Sifra does not set forth propositions in the way in which the Rabbah compilations and Sifré to Deuteronomy do.

First, in general there is no topical program distinct from that of Scripture. Sifra remains wholly within Scripture's orbit and range of discourse, proposing only to expand and clarify what it found within Scripture. Where the authorship moves beyond Scripture, it is not toward fresh theological or philosophical thought, but rather to a quite different set of issues altogether, concerning Mishnah and Tosefta. When we describe the topical program of the document, the blatant and definitive trait of Sifra is simple: the topical program and order derive from Scripture. Just as the Mishnah defines the topical program and order for Tosefta, the Yerushalmi, and the Bavli, so Scripture does so for Sifra. It follows that Sifra takes as its structure the plan and program of the written Torah, in contrast to the decision of the framers or compilers of Tosefta and the two Talmuds.

Second, for sizable passages, the sole point of coherence for the discrete sentences or paragraphs of Sifra's authorship derives from the base verse of Scripture that is subject to commentary. That fact corresponds to the results of form analysis and the description of the logics of cogent discourse. While, as we have noted, the Mishnah holds thought together through propositions of various kinds, with special interest in demonstrating propositions through a well-crafted program of logic of a certain kind, Sifra's authorship appeals to a different logic altogether. It is one that I have set forth as fixed-associative discourse. That is not a propositional logic—by definition.

The third fundamental observation draws attention to the paramount position, within this restatement of the written Torah, of the oral Torah. We may say very simply that in a purely formal and superficial sense, a sizable proportion of Sifra consists simply of the association of completed statements of the oral Torah with the exposition of the written Torah, the whole re-presenting as one whole Torah the dual Torah received by Moses at Sinai (speaking within the Torah myth). Even at the very surface we observe a simple fact. Without the Mishnah or the Tosefta, our authorship will have had virtually nothing to say about one passage after another of the written Torah. Far more often than citing the Mishnah or the Tosefta verbatim, our authorship cites principles of law or theology fundamental to the Mishnah's treatment of a given topic, even when the particular passage of the Mishnah or the Tosefta that sets forth those principles is not cited verbatim.

It follows that the three basic and definitive topical traits of Sifra are: first, its total adherence to the topical program of the written Torah for order and plan; second, its very common reliance upon the phrases or verses of the written Torah for the joining into coherent discourse of discrete thoughts, e.g., comments on, or amplifications of, words or phrases; and third, its equally profound dependence upon the oral Torah for its program of thought: the problematic that defines the issues the authorship wishes to explore and resolve.

That brings us to the positive side of the picture. While Sifra in detail presents no paramount propositions, as a whole it demonstrates a highly distinctive and vigorously demonstrated proposition. We should drastically misunderstand the document if the miscellaneous character of the parts obscured the powerful statement made by the whole. For while in detail we cannot reconstruct a topical program other than that of Scripture, viewed in its indicative and definitive traits of rhetoric, logic, and implicit proposition, Sifra does take up a well-composed position on a fundamental issue, namely, the relationship between the written Torah, represented by the book of Leviticus, and the oral Torah, represented by the passages of the Mishnah deemed by the authorship of Sifra to be pertinent to the book of Leviticus. As we noted at the outset, Sifra joins the two Torahs into a single statement, accomplishing a re-presentation of the written Torah in topic and in program and in the logic of cogent discourse, and within that rewriting of the written Torah, a re-presentation of the oral Torah in its paramount problematic and in many of its substantive propositions. Stated simply, the written Torah provides the form; the oral Torah, the content. What emerges is not merely a united, dual Torah, but *the* Torah, stated whole and complete, in the context defined by the book of Leviticus.

6.

A SAMPLE PASSAGE

SIFRA PARASHAT BEHUQOTAI PARASHAH 1

CCLX:I.   1.   A.   ["If you walk in my statutes and observe my commandments and do them, then I will give you your rains in their season, and the land shall yield its increase, and the trees of the field shall yield their fruit. And your threshing shall last to the time of vintage, and the vintage shall last to the time for sowing; and you shall eat your bread to the full and dwell in your land securely. And I will give peace in the land, and you shall lie down and none shall make you afraid; and I will remove evil beasts from the land, and the sword shall not go through your land. And you shall chase your enemies, and they shall fall before you by the sword. Five of you shall chase a hundred, and a hundred of you shall chase ten thousand; and your enemies shall fall before you by the sword. And I will have regard for you and make you fruitful and multiply you, and will confirm my covenant with you. And you shall eat old store long kept, and you shall clear out the old to make way for the new. And I will make my abode among you, and my soul shall not abhor you. And I will walk among you and will be your God and you shall be my people. I am the Lord your God, who brought you forth out of the land of Egypt, that you should not be their slaves; and I have broken the bars of your yoke and made you walk erect" (Lev. 26:3–13).]

B.   "If you walk in my statutes":

C.   This teaches that the Omnipresent desires the Israelites to work in the Torah.

D.   And so Scripture says, "O that my people would listen to me, that Israel would walk in my ways! I would soon subdue their enemies and turn my hand against their foes" (Ps. 81:13–14).

E.   "O that you had hearkened to my commandments! Then your peace would have been like a river, and your righteousness like the waves of the sea; your offspring would have been like the sand, and your descendants like its grains; their name would never be cut off or destroyed from before me" (Isa. 48:18).

F. And so Scripture says, "Oh that they had such a mind as this always, to fear me and to keep all my commandments, that it might go well with them and with their children forever" (Dt. 5:29).

G. This teaches that the Omnipresent desires the Israelites to work in the Torah.

2. A. "If you walk in my statutes":

B. Might this refer to the religious duties?

C. When Scripture says, "and observe my commandments and do them,"

D. lo, the religious duties are covered. Then how shall I interpret, "If you walk in my statutes"?

E. It is that they should work in the Torah.

F. And so it is said, "But if you will not hearken to me."

G. Might that refer to the religious duties?

H. When Scripture says, "and will not do all these commandments,"

I. lo, the religious duties are covered.

J. If so, why is it said, "But if you will not hearken to me"?

K. It is that they should be working in the Torah.

3. A. And so Scripture says, "Remember the Sabbath day to keep it holy" (Ex. 20:8).

B. Might one suppose that what is involved is only to do so in your heart?

C. When Scripture says, "Observe [the Sabbath day]" (Dt. 5:12), lo, keeping it in the heart is covered.

D. How then am I to interpret "remember"?

E. It means that you should repeat with your mouth [the teachings concerning the Sabbath day].

F. And so Scripture says, "Remember and do not forget how you provoked the Lord your God to wrath in the wilderness, from the day you came out of the land of Egypt until you came to this place" (Dt. 9:7).

G. Might one suppose that what is involved is only to do so in your heart?

H. Scripture says, "and do not forget."

I. Lo, forgetting in the heart is covered.

J. How then am I to interpret "remember"?

K. It means that you should repeat with your mouth [the record of your behavior in the wilderness].

L. And so Scripture says, "[Take heed, in an attack of leprosy, to be very careful to do according to all that the

Levitical priests shall direct you; as I commanded them, so you shall be careful to do.] Remember what the Lord your God did to Miriam on the way as you came forth out of Egypt" (Dt. 24:9).

M.   Might one suppose that what is involved is only to do so in your heart?

N.   When Scripture says, "Take heed, in an attack of leprosy, to be very careful to do,"

O.   lo, forgetting in the heart is covered.

P.   How then am I to interpret "remember"?

Q.   It means that you should repeat with your mouth [the lessons to be learned in respect to Miriam].

R.   And so Scripture says, "Remember what Amalek did to you on the way as you came out of Egypt . . . [you shall blot out the remembrance of Amalek from under heaven; you shall not forget]" (Dt. 25:17, 19).

S.   Might one suppose that what is involved is only to do so in your heart?

T.   When Scripture says, "you shall not forget,"

U.   lo, forgetting in the heart is covered.

V.   How then am I to interpret "remember"?

W.   It means that you should repeat with your mouth [the record of Amalek].

4. A.   And so Scripture says, "And I will lay your cities waste."

B.   Might one suppose that that is of human settlement?

C.   When Scripture says, "And I will devastate the land,"

D.   lo, that covers human settlement.

E.   Then how am I to interpret, "And I will lay your cities waste"?

F.   It means there will be no wayfarers.

5. A.   And so Scripture says, "and will make your sanctuaries desolate."

B.   Might one suppose that that is desolate of offerings?

C.   When Scripture says, "and I will not smell your pleasing odors,"

D.   lo, that covers the offerings.

E.   Then how am I to interpret, "and will make your sanctuaries desolate"?

F.   They will be laid waste even of pilgrims.

6. A.   "If you walk in my statutes and observe my commandments and do them":

B.   One who studies in order to do, not one who studies not in order to do.

C. For one who studies not in order to do—it would have been better for him had he not been created.

The proposition, No. 1, that the reference is to study of Torah is demonstrated at No. 2. The rhetoric, "might this refer . . . when Scripture says . . . ," and so on, then generates a series of compositions that use the same rhetorical pattern. The pattern goes forward at Nos. 4–5, and only at No. 6 do we revert to the point that No. 1 wished to introduce: study in order to observe.

PARASHAT BEHUQOTAI PEREQ 3

CCLXIII:I. 1. A. "And you shall eat old store long kept, [and you shall clear out the old to make way for the new. And I will make my abode among you, and my soul shall not abhor you. And I will walk among you and I will be your God and you shall be my people. I am the Lord your God, who brought you forth out of the land of Egypt, that you should not be their slaves; and I have broken the bars of your yoke and made you walk erect]:"

B. This teaches that whatever is better aged tastes better than its fellow.

C. ". . . old":

D. I know only that the rule applies to wine, which customarily is kept for aging. How do I know that the same rule applies to everything that is allowed to age?

E. Scripture says, "Old store long kept."

2. A. ". . . and you shall clear out the old to make way for the new":

B. The granaries will be full of new grain, and the storage bins will be full of the old,

C. so you will wonder how we shall take out the old on account of the new harvest.

3. A. "And I will make my abode among you":

B. this refers to the house of the sanctuary.

4. A. ". . . and my soul shall not abhor you":

B. Once I shall redeem you, I shall never again reject you.

5. A. "And I will walk among you":

B. The matter may be compared to the case of a king who went out to stroll with his sharecropper in an orchard.

C. But the sharecropper hid from him.

D. Said the king to that sharecropper, "How come you're hiding from me? Lo, I am just like you."

E.   So the Holy One, blessed be He, said to the righteous, "Why are you trembling before me?"

F.   So the Holy One, blessed be He, is destined to walk with the righteous in the Garden of Eden in the coming future, and the righteous will see him and tremble before him,

G.   [and he will say to them,] "[How come you're trembling before me?] Lo, I am just like you."

6. A.   Might one suppose that my fear will not be upon you?

B.   Scripture says, "and I will be your God and you shall be my people."

C.   "If you do not believe in me through all these things, nonetheless 'I am the Lord your God, who brought you forth out of the land of Egypt.'

D.   "I am the one who did wonders for you in Egypt. I am the one who is going to do for you all these wonders."

7. A.   ". . . that you should not be their slaves":

B.   What is the point of Scripture here?

C.   Since it is said, "And he redeemed you from the house of slavery" (Dt. 7:8), might one suppose that they were slaves to slaves?

D.   ". . . their slaves":

E.   they were slaves to kings, not slaves to slaves.

8. A.   ". . . and I have broken the bars of your yoke":

B.   The matter may be compared to the case of a householder who had a cow for plowing, and he lent it to someone else to plow with it.

C.   That man had ten sons. This one came and plowed with it and went his way, and that one came and plowed with it and went his way, so that the cow got tired and crouched down.

D.   All the other cows came back, but that cow did not enter the fold.

E.   The owner hardly agreed to accept consolation from that man, but he went and broke the yoke and cut off the carved ends of the yoke.

F.   So is Israel in this world.

G.   One ruler comes along and subjugates them and then goes his way, then another ruler comes along and subjugates them and goes his way, so that the furrow is very long.

H.   So it is said, "Plowmen plowed across my back; they made long furrows. [The Lord, the righteous one, has snapped the cords of the wicked]" (Ps. 129:3–4).

> I. Tomorrow, when the end comes, the Holy One, blessed be He, will not say to the nations, "Thus and so have you done to my children!"
>
> J. Rather, he will immediately come and break the yoke and cut off the ends of the yoke.
>
> K. For it is said, "and I have broken the bars of your yoke."
>
> L. And further, "The Lord has snapped the cords of the wicked."
>
> 9. A. ". . . and made you walk erect":
>
>   B. R. Simeon says, "Two hundred cubits in height."
>
>   C. R. Judah says, "A hundred, like the first Adam."
>
>   D. I know that that statement applies only to men. How do I know that it applies to women too?
>
>   E. Scripture says, "[For our sons are like saplings, well tended in their youth;] our daughters are like cornerstones, trimmed to give shape to a palace" (Ps. 144:12).
>
>   F. And how high was the cornerstone of the temple? A hundred cubits.
>
> 10. A. Another teaching concerning the clause, "and made you walk erect":
>
>   B. Upright, not fearful of anyone.

The eschatological focus is made sharp at No. 4. The polemic throughout is now uniform: Israel is destined to be redeemed in the future, and when that happens, it will be for all time. Then the return to Zion and rebuilding of the Temple did not fulfill the prophecies of redemption; Israel will have a future redemption, of which the prophets, including Moses, spoke. The text of No. 5 is somewhat flawed, but the sense is readily recovered. No. 6 reworks the materials at hand for the same purpose. No. 8 once more is explicit, with its parable of how God's redemption of Israel will take place: with impatience, when it comes.

PARASHAT BEHUQOTAI PEREQ 8

> CCLXIX:I. 1. A. "And you shall perish among the nations, [and the land of your enemies shall eat you up. And those of you that are left shall pine away in your enemies' lands because of their iniquity; and also because of the iniquities of their fathers they shall pine away like them]":
>
>   B. R. Aqiba says, "This refers to the ten tribes who went into exile in Media."
>
>   C. Others say, "'And you shall perish among the nations': The reference to 'perishing' speaks only of going into exile.

D.   "Might one suppose that the sense is literal [that Israel really will perish among the nations]?

E.   "When Scripture says, 'and the land of your enemies shall eat you up,' lo, we find a reference to literally perishing.

F.   "Then how am I to interpret 'And you shall perish among the nations'?

G.   "The reference to 'perishing' speaks only of going into exile."

2.   A.   "And those of you that are left shall pine away in your enemies' lands because of their iniquity":

B.   The sense of "pining away" is on account of their iniquity.

3.   A.   ". . . and also because of the iniquities of their fathers they shall pine away like them":

B.   Now has not the Omnipresent already assured Israel that he will not judge the fathers on account of the sons or the sons on account of the fathers?

C.   For it is said, "The fathers shall not be put to death for the children, nor shall the children be put to death for the fathers; every man shall be put to death for his own sin" (Dt. 24:16).

D.   If so, why is it said, "and also because of the iniquities of their fathers they shall pine away like them"?

E.   When for generation after generation they are enthralled in the deeds of their fathers, then they are judged on their account.

"Exile" is taken to fulfill the curse of "perishing," and then comes the religious duty of "pining away." The important clarification comes at Nos. 2–3, which draw into alignment a variety of pertinent verses.

CCLXIX:II.   1.   A.   "But if they confess their iniquity and the iniquity of their fathers [in their treachery which they committed against me, and also in walking contrary to me, so that I walked contrary to them and brought them into the land of their enemies; if then their uncircumcised heart is humbled and they make amends for their iniquity; then I will remember my covenant with Jacob, and I will remember my covenant also with Isaac and my covenant also with Abraham, and I will remember the land. But the land shall be left by them and enjoy its sabbaths while it lies desolate

without them; and they shall make amends for their
iniquity, because they spurned my ordinances, and
their soul abhorred my statutes. Yet for all that, when
they are in the land of their enemies, I will not spurn
them, neither will I abhor them so as to destroy them
utterly and break my covenant with them; for I am
the Lord their God; but I will for their sake remember
the covenant with their forefathers whom I brought
forth out of the land of Egypt in the sight of the nations, that I might be their God: I am the Lord. These
are the statutes and ordinances and laws which the
Lord made between him and the people of Israel on
Mount Sinai by Moses]" (Lev. 26:40–46):

B.　This is how things are as to repentance,

C.　for as soon as they confess their sins, I forthwith revert
and have mercy on them,

D.　as it is said, "But if they confess their iniquity and the
iniquity of their fathers in their treachery which they
committed against me."

2.　A.　". . . and also in walking contrary to me, so that I
walked contrary to them":

B.　In this world they treated my laws in a casual way, so
I shall treat them in a casual way in this world."

3.　A.　". . . and brought them into the land of their enemies":

B.　This is a good deal for Israel.

C.　For the Israelites are not to say, "Since we have gone
into exile among the gentiles, let us act like them."

D.　[God speaks:] "I shall not let them, but I shall call
forth prophets against them, who will bring them
back to the right way under my wings."

E.　And how do we know?

F.　"What is in your mind shall never happen, the
thought, 'Let us be like the nations, like the tribes of
the countries, and worship wood and stone.' 'As I
live,' says the Lord God, 'surely with a mighty hand
and an outstretched arm and with wrath poured out,
I will be king over you. [I will bring you out from
the peoples and gather you out of the countries
where you are scattered, with a mighty hand and an
outstretched arm and with wrath poured out]'" (Ez.
20:33–4).

G.　"Whether you like it or not, with or without your
consent, I shall establish my dominion over you."

4. A. "... if then their uncircumcised heart is humbled and they make amends for their iniquity":

    B. This is how things are as to repentance,

    C. for as soon as they humble their heart in repentance, I forthwith revert and have mercy on them,

    D. as it is said, "if then their uncircumcised heart is humbled and they make amends for their iniquity."

5. A. "... then I will remember my covenant with Jacob, [and I will remember my covenant also with Isaac and my covenant also with Abraham]":

    B. Why are the patriarchs listed in reverse order?

    C. It is to indicate, if the deeds of Abraham are not sufficient, then the deeds of Isaac, and if the deeds of Isaac are not worthy, then the deeds of Jacob.

    D. Each one of them is worthy that the world should depend upon his intervention.

6. A. And why with reference to Abraham and Jacob are remembrance mentioned, but not with respect to Isaac?

    B. His ashes are regarded as though he were scooped up on the altar.

    C. And why with respect to Abraham and Isaac, but not with respect to Jacob, is there mention of "also"?

    D. This teaches that the bier of Jacob our father was without flaw [since he did not produce an evil son, unlike Abraham with Ishmael and Isaac with Esau].

7. A. I know only that the patriarchs are covered. How about the matriarchs?

    B. Scripture uses the accusative particle, and the accusative particle encompasses only the matriarchs,

    C. as it is said, "There they buried Abraham and [the accusative particle] Sarah his wife" (Gen. 49:31).

8. A. And how do we know that the covenant is made with the land?

    B. Scripture says, "and I will remember the land."

9. A. "But the land shall be left by them and enjoy its sabbaths [while it lies desolate without them]":

    B. "I said to them to sow for me for six years and release the year for me for one year, so that they might know that the land is mine.

    C. "But that is not what they did, get up and go into exile from it, so that it may enjoy release on its own for all the years of release that it owes to me."

D. For it is said, "But the land shall be left by them and enjoy its sabbaths while it lies desolate without them, and they shall make amends for their iniquity."

10. A. ". . . because and because, [that is, for this item and for that item, exactly] [they spurned my ordinances, and their soul abhorred my statutes]":

B. Now did I collect item by item from Israel? And did I not exact punishment for them only for one out of a hundred sins that they committed before me?

C. Why then is it said, "because" [as though the penalty were exact]?

D. It is because "they spurned my ordinances"—this refers to the laws;

E. and because "their soul abhorred my statutes"—this refers to the exegeses of Scripture.

11. A. "[Yet for all] that"—this refers to the sin committed in the Wilderness.

B. ". . . yet for"—this refers to the sin of Baal Peor.

C. ". . . yet for all that"—this refers to the sin involving the kings of the Amorites.

12. A. "[Yet for all that, when they are in the land of their enemies,] I will not spurn them, neither will I abhor them so as to destroy them utterly":

B. Now what is left for them, but that they not be spurned nor abhorred? For is it not the fact that all the good gifts that had been given to them were now taken away from them?

C. And were it not for the Scroll of the Torah that was left for them, they would in no way be different from the nations of the world!

D. But "I will not spurn them"—in the time of Vespasian.

E. ". . . neither will I abhor them"—in the time of Greece.

F. ". . . so as to destroy them utterly and break my covenant with them"—in the time of Haman.

G. ". . . for I am the Lord their God"—in the time of Gog.

13. A. And how do we know that the covenant is made with the tribal fathers?

B. As it is said, "but I will for their sake remember the covenant with their forefathers whom I brought forth out of the land of Egypt":

C.   This teaches that the covenant is made with the tribal fathers.

14. A.   "These are the statutes and ordinances and Torahs":

B.   ". . . the statutes": this refers to the exegeses of Scripture.

C.   ". . . and ordinances": this refers to the laws.

D.   ". . . and Torahs": this teaches that two Torahs were given to Israel, one in writing, the other oral.

E.   Said R. Aqiba, "Now did Israel have only two Torahs? And did they not have many Torahs given to them? 'This is the Torah of burnt-offering' (Lev. 6:2), 'This is the Torah of the meal offering' (Lev. 6:27), 'This is the Torah of the guilt offering' (Lev. 7:1), 'This is the Torah of the sacrifice of peace offerings' (Lev. 7:11), 'This is the Torah: when a man dies in a tent' (Num. 19:1)."

15. A.   ". . . which the Lord made between him and the people of Israel [on Mount Sinai by Moses]":

B.   Moses had the merit of being made the intermediary between Israel and their father in heaven.

C.   ". . . on Mount Sinai by Moses":

D.   This teaches that the Torah was given, encompassing all its laws, all its details, and all their amplifications, through Moses at Sinai.

Some of the items begin to reveal a protocol or pattern, e.g., Nos. 2, 3, 4, 9, 14. But overall, the impression I gain is one of a miscellany, since I see no polemical and well-focused proposition. The exegesis of the verse involving the patriarchs is full and rich, Nos. 5, 6, 7. The *heilsgeschichtliche* exercises, e.g., No. 11, 12, are not sustained and lack conviction; the order is wrong, and no point is drawn from them. The upshot is that the methodical and rigorous discourse established with reference to the legal passages finds no counterpart here.

XII

SIFRÉ TO NUMBERS

1.

IDENTIFYING THE DOCUMENT

SIFRÉ TO NUMBERS[1] PROVIDES A MISCELLANEOUS READING OF MOST OF THE BOOK of Numbers, but examining the implicit propositions of the recurrent forms of the document yields a clear-cut purpose.[2] The document follows no topical program; but it also is unlike Mekhilta Attributed to R. Ishmael because of its recurrent effort to prove a few fundamental points. True, these are general and not limited

---

[1] The word *sifré* corresponds to the Hebrew *sefarim,* "books." It is explained by Moses D. Herr, in the article cited in the next note, as follows: "As early as Amoraic times the word sifré was employed as the designation for a collection of *halakhic beraitot* [legal rulings not found in the Mishnah but enjoying authoritative status], and also used for a collection of *beraitot* containing *halakhot* [legal rulings] derived from exegesis of biblical verses."

[2] For further reading and bibliography on the topic of this chapter, see the following:

Bowker, pp. 71–72.

Moses D. Herr, "Sifrei," *Encyclopaedia Judaica* 14:1519–21: coverage of Numbers, distinction from Sifré to Deuteronomy; characteristics; origin in the school of Aqiba; commentaries; critical editions.

Maccoby does not introduce this document.

to a given set of cases or issues, so that the successive compositions that comprise
Sifré to Numbers yield no propositional program. But the recurrent proofs of discrete propositions that time and again bear one and the same implication do accumulate and when we see what is implicit in the various explicit exercises, we find
a clear-cut and rather rich message indeed.

The document as a whole through its fixed and recurrent formal preferences
or literary structures makes two complementary points: (1) Reason unaided by
Scripture produces uncertain propositions. (2) Reason operating within the limits
of Scripture produces truth. These two principles are never articulated but left
implicit in the systematic reading of most of the book of Numbers, verse by verse.
The exegetical forms stand for a single proposition: the human mind joins God's
mind when humanity receives and sets forth the Torah. The Torah opens the road
into the mind of God, and our minds can lead us on that road, because our mind
and God's mind are comparable. We share a common rationality. Only when we
examine the rhetorical plan and then in search of the topical program reconsider
the forms of the document does this propositional program emerge.

As with Sifra, therefore, Sifré to Numbers follows no topical program distinct
from that of Scripture, which is systematically clarified, as we shall see in our
sample of the document below. An interest in the relations to Scripture of the
Mishnah and Tosefta, a concern with the dialectics characteristic of Sifra—these
occur episodically, but scarcely define the character of the document. Its topical
program and order derive from Scripture. As with Sifra, here too, as we have
already noticed, the sole point of coherence for the discrete sentences or paragraphs derives from the base verse of Scripture that is subject to commentary.
At the same time, if we examine the incremental message, the cumulative effect
of the formal traits of speech and thought revealed in the uniform rhetoric and
syntax of the document, we may discern a propositional program that is implicit
in the rhetoric and logic of the compilation. What is required here is the
articulation of the general consequences of numerous specific exegetical exercises.

If our authorship met the sets of writers whose consensus stands behind Sifra
and Sifré to Deuteronomy, the several groups would find it difficult to distinguish
themselves, one from the next. For one principal point of emphasis we discern in
our document takes an equally central role in the propositional, topical program
of the other two compilations, Sifra and Sifré to Deuteronomy. It is the insistence
on the principle that logic alone cannot suffice, and that all law must in the end
derive from the written part of the Torah. The single sustained proposition of the
several writings is that truth derives from Scripture, not from reason unaided by

Stemberger-Strack, pp. 290–93: translation; the name; contents and structure; character, origin,
        date (after the middle of the third century); manuscripts, printed editions, commentaries.
This writer's introduction is in *Sifré to Numbers. An American Translation*. II. *59–115*. Atlanta, 1986:
Scholars Press for Brown Judaic Studies.

revelation. But a further proposition will attract our attention. By the very labor of explaining the meaning of verses of Scripture, the rabbinic exegetes laid claim to participate in the work of revelation. And by distinguishing their contribution from the received text of the Torah, they announced their presence within the process of revelation. In these two ways the exegetes who made up Sifra and the two Sifrés announced not one but two fundamental propositions. The first is that God's revelation in the written Torah takes priority. The second is that man's reason in the exegesis of the written Torah enjoys a full and legitimate place in the unfolding of the lessons of Sinai. No one can doubt that our authorship concurs on both principles.

The rhetorical form of both documents underlines the topical program contained in the first of the two propositions. For if I want to underline over and over again the priority of not proposition, hence reason, but process, hence the exegesis of Scripture, my best choice is an obvious one. Begin at all points with a verse of Scripture and demonstrate that only by starting with the word choices and propositions of that verse of Scripture, all further progress of interpretation commences. But the second proposition, that man (then, now: men and women) has a place in the process of revealing the Torah of Sinai, comes to expression in the careful separation of the cited verse of the written Torah from the contribution of the contemporary exegete. In that formal preference too, the authorship made a major point and established—if implicitly—a central syllogism: God's will follows the rules of reason. Man can investigate the consequences of reason as expressed in God's will. Therefore man can join in the labor of exploring God's will in the Torah.

Consequently, the authorships of all three Midrash compilations make their powerful case by their rhetorical program, which relies first and foremost on the citation and gloss of a verse of Scripture, as much as by their proposition and syllogism: only by Scripture does truth gain certainty. The appeal to Scripture, however, comes once the proposition is established, and that appeal then dictates the rhetoric and topic alike. Only when we know what question we bring to Scripture may we devise appropriate formal and programmatic policies for our Midrash exegesis and Midrash compilation alike. A second formal preference in all three documents, in addition to the exegetical form, makes the same point. The other form involves citation of a passage of the Mishnah followed by an extensive discourse on how the verse of Scripture that pertains to the topic of that Mishnah passage must contribute its facts, revealed at Sinai, if we wish to know the truth. Reason alone, which is systematically tested through a sequence of propositions shown to fail, will not serve.

The rhetorical plan of Sifra and Sifré to Numbers and Sifré to Deuteronomy shows that the exegetes, while working verse by verse, in fact have brought a considerable program to the reading of the books of Leviticus, Numbers, and Deuteronomy, respectively. The authorships of Sifra and the two Sifrés share that program, when they cite a verse of Scripture and then a passage of the Mishnah. The proposition, then, in all three writings concerns the interplay of the oral Torah, represented by the Mishnah, with the written Torah, represented by the book of Leviticus or Numbers or Deuteronomy. That question demanded, in the authorships' view, not an answer comprising mere generalities. They wished to show their results through details, masses of details, and, like the rigorous philosophers that they were, they furthermore argued essentially through an inductive procedure, amassing evidence that in its accumulation made the point at hand.

The syllogism about the priority of the revelation of the written Torah in the search for truth is nowhere expressed in so many words, because the philosopher-exegetes of the rabbinic world preferred to address an implicit syllogism and to pursue or to test that syllogism solely in a sequence of experiments on a small scale. The three authorships therefore find in the Mishnah and Tosefta a sizable laboratory for the testing of propositions. We have therefore to ask, "At what points do Sifra's and the two Sifrés' authorships and those of the Mishnah and Tosefta share a common agenda of interests, and at what points does one compilation introduce problems, themes, or questions unknown to the other?"

The answers to these questions for the three Midrash compilations are various. The one for Sifra will show that Sifra and Mishnah and Tosefta form two large concentric circles, sharing a considerable area in common. Sifra, however, exhibits interests peculiar to itself. On the criterion of common themes and interests, Mishnah and Tosefta and Sifra exhibit a remarkable unity. The authorships of the two Sifrés in diverse measure join in that united front on a basic issue. The authorship of Sifré to Numbers, for its part, took up a pentateuchal book that in no way focuses upon the topics paramount also in the Mishnah and the Tosefta, in the way in which the book of Leviticus covers subjects that take a prominent position in the later law codes. Consequently, we cannot find in Sifré to Numbers a counterpart to the stress on the matters we have located in Sifra. Still, the established polemic about the priority of Scripture over unaided reason does take its place. Accordingly, we can show that Sifra and the two Sifrés join together in a single species of the genus Midrash compilation.

2.

TRANSLATIONS INTO ENGLISH

The first complete English translation is this writer's *Sifré to Numbers. An American Translation.* (Atlanta, 1986: Scholars Press for Brown Judaic Studies) I. *1–58*, and II. *59–115*. The completion, III. *116–61*, by William Scott Green, is due in 1995. Some of the as-yet-untranslated passages are in the incomplete work by Paul P. Levertoff, *Midrash Sifre on Numbers. Selections from Early Rabbinic Scriptural Interpretations.* With an Introduction by G. H. Box (London, 1916).

3.

RHETORIC

Two forms encompass all of the literary structures of Sifré to Numbers. These are exemplified in the catalog that follows.

EXTRINSIC EXEGETICAL FORM: The form consists of the citation of an opening verse, followed by an issue stated in terms extrinsic to the cited verse. That is to say, no word or phrase of the base verse (that is, the cited verse at the beginning) attracts comment. Rather a general rule of exegesis is invoked. The formal traits are: (1) citation of a base verse from Numbers, (2) a generalization ignoring clauses or words in the base verse, (3) a further observation without clear interest in the verse at hand. But the whole is linked to the theme of the base verse—and to that alone. So an extrinsic exegetical program comes to bear. One example of the form involves syllogistic argument on the meaning of words or phrases, in which the base verse of Numbers occurs as one among a set of diverse items, as in the following instance:

I.III. 1. A. R. Judah b. Beterah says, "The effect of a commandment stated in any context serves only [1] to lend encouragement.

   B. "For it is said, 'But command Joshua and encourage and strengthen him' (Deut. 3:28).

   C. "Accordingly, we derive the lesson that strength is granted only to the strong, and encouragement only to the stout of heart."

   D. R. Simeon b. Yohai says, "The purpose of a commandment in any context is only [2] to deal with the expenditure of money, as it is said, 'Command the children of Israel to bring you pure oil from beaten olives for the lamp, that a light may be kept burning continually outside the veil of the testimony in the tent of meeting. Aaron shall keep it in order from evening to morning before the Lord continually; it shall be a statute forever throughout your generations' (Lev. 24:2). 'Command the people of Israel that they put out of the camp every leper and every one having a discharge, and every one that is unclean through contact with the dead' (Num. 5:1–2). 'Command the children of Israel that they give to the Levites from the inheritance of their possession cities to dwell in, and you shall give to the Levites pasture lands round about the cities' (Num. 35:2). 'Command the people of Israel and say to them, "My offering, my food for my offerings by fire, my pleasing odor you shall take heed to offer to me in its due season"' (Num. 28:2). Lo, we see in all these cases that the purpose of a commandment is solely to bring about the expenditure of money.

E.   "There is one exception, and what is that? It is this verse:
      'Command the people of Israel and say to them, "When you
      enter the land of Canaan, this is the land that shall fall to you
      for an inheritance, the land of Canaan in its full extent"'
      (Num. 34:2).

F.   "You must give encouragement to them in the matter of the
      correct division of the land."

G.   And Rabbi [Judah the Patriarch] says, "The use of the word
      'commandment' in all passages serves only for the purpose of
      [3] imparting an admonition [not to do a given action], along
      the lines of the following: 'And the Lord God commanded
      the man, saying, "You may freely eat of every tree of the gar-
      den, but of the tree of the knowledge of good and evil you
      shall not eat"' (Gen. 2:16)."

In the INTRINSIC EXEGETICAL FORM the verse itself is clarified. In the first instance, the exegesis derives from the contrast with another verse that makes the
same point. But the formal trait should not be missed. It is that the the focus is on
the base verse and not on a broader issue. We may call this an intrinsic exegetical
form, in that the focus of exegesis is on the verse, which is cited and carefully
spelled out. We shall know that we have it when the base verse is cited, clause by
clause or in other ways, and then given an ample dose of attention. Since the
present category presents numerous variations, we shall subdivide as we go along.
The key words of the species of the genus at hand will supply the basis for differentiation, as will be clear throughout. In the first example, the exegesis asks the
purpose of a given passage, and the form requires the citation of the base verse plus
"For what purpose is this passage presented?"

I:I. 1.   A.   "The Lord said to Moses, 'Command the people of Israel that
                 they put out of the camp [every leper and every one having a
                 discharge, and every one that is unclean through contact with
                 the dead]'" (Num. 5:1–2).

           B.   For what purpose is this passage presented?

           C.   Because it is said, "But the man who is unclean and does not
                 cleanse himself [that person shall be cut off from the midst of
                 the assembly, since he has defiled the sanctuary of the Lord,
                 because the water for impurity has not been thrown upon
                 him, he is unclean]" (Num. 19:20).

           D.   Consequently, we are informed of the penalty [for contami-
                 nating the sanctuary]. But where are we informed of the ad-
                 monition not to do so?

           E.   Scripture accordingly states, "Command the people of Israel
                 that they put out of the camp every leper and every one hav-

ing a discharge, and every one that is unclean through contact with the dead" (Num. 5:1–2).

F. Lo, here is an admonition that unclean persons not come into the sanctuary ["out of the camp"] in a state of uncleanness. [Consequently, the entire transaction—admonition, then penalty—is laid forth.]

In another version, we find the rudiments of a dialectical argument, that is, a proposition is announced, then challenged, and the argument moves in its own direction. Here we have the citation of a word or clause in the base verse, followed by a declarative sentence explaining the purpose and meaning of the cited passage. Then we ask, "You say this, but perhaps it means that." Then we proceed to justify the original statement. This is a fine example of the dialectical exegesis of an intrinsic character.

I:II.   1.   A.   "Command" (Num. 5:2):

B. The commandment at hand is meant both to be put into effect immediately and also to apply for generations to come.

C. You maintain that the commandment at hand is meant both to be put into effect immediately and also to apply for generations to come.

D. But perhaps the commandment is meant to apply only after a time [but not right away, at the moment at which it was given].

E. [We shall now prove that the formulation encompasses both generations to come and also the generation to whom the commandment is entrusted.] Scripture states, "The Lord said to Moses, 'Command the people of Israel that they put out [of the camp every leper and every one having a discharge, and every one that is unclean through contact with the dead. You shall put out both male and female, putting them outside the camp, that they may not defile their camp, in the midst of which I dwell.'] And the people of Israel did so and drove them outside the camp, as the Lord said to Moses, *so the people of Israel did*" (Num. 5:1–4). [The verse itself makes explicit the fact that the requirement applied forthwith, not only later on.]

F. Lo, we have learned that the commandment at hand is meant to be put into effect immediately.

G. How then do we derive from Scripture the fact that it applies also for generations to come? [We shall now show that the same word used here, "command," pertains to generations to come and not only to the generation at hand.]

H. Scripture states, "Command the children of Israel to bring you pure oil from beaten olives [for the lamp, that a light may be kept burning continually outside the veil of the testimony in the tent of meeting. Aaron shall keep it in order from evening to morning before the Lord continually; it shall be a statute forever throughout your generations]" (Lev. 24:2).

I. Lo, we here derive evidence that the commandment at hand is meant both to be put into effect immediately and also to apply for generations to come, [based on the framing of the present commandment].

J. How, then, do we derive evidence that all of the commandments that are contained in the Torah [apply in the same way]? [We wish now to prove that the language, "command," always bears the meaning imputed to it here.]

K. R. Ishmael maintained, "Since the bulk of the commandments stated in the Torah is presented without further amplification, while in the case of one of them [namely, the one at hand], Scripture has given explicit details, that commandment [that has been singled out] is meant both to be put into effect immediately and also to apply for generations to come. Accordingly, I apply to all of the other commandments in the Torah the same detail, so that in all cases the commandment is meant both to be put into effect immediately and also to apply for generations to come."

Dialectics consists of a sequence of arguments about the meaning of a passage, in which the focus is upon the base verse, and a sequence of possibilities is introduced to spell out the meaning of that verse. At issue is not the power of logic but the meaning of the base verse; nonetheless, that issue is pursued through an argument of many stages.

I:IV. 1. A. "[The Lord said to Moses, 'Command the people of Israel that] they put out of the camp [every leper and every one having a discharge, and every one that is unclean through contact with the dead']" (Num. 5:1–2).

B. Is it from the [innermost] camp, of the Presence of God, or should I infer that it is only from the camp of the Levites?

C. Scripture states, ". . . they put out them of the camp." [The sense is that they are to be put outside of the camp of the Presence.]

D. Now even if Scripture had not made the matter explicit, I could have suggested the same proposition on the basis of reasoning [that they should be put outside of the camp of the Presence]:

E.   If unclean people are driven out of the camp that contains the ark, which is of lesser sanctity, all the more so should they be driven out of the camp of the Presence of God, which is of greater sanctity.

F.   But if you had proposed reasoning on that basis, you would have found yourself in the position of imposing a penalty merely on the basis of reason [and not on the basis of an explicit statement of Scripture, and one does not impose a penalty merely on the basis of reason].

G.   Then why is it stated: ". . . they put out of the camp"?

H.   Making that matter explicit in Scripture serves to teach you that penalties are not to be imposed merely on the basis of logic [but require explicit specification in Scripture]. [That is, Scripture made a point that reason could have reached, but Scripture made the matter explicit so as to articulate a penalty applicable for violating the rule.]

I.   [Rejecting that principle,] Rabbi says, "It is not necessary for Scripture to make the matter explicit, since it is a matter of an argument *a fortiori*:

J.   "If the unclean people are driven out of the camp that contains the ark, which is of lesser sanctity, all the more so should they be driven out of the camp of the Presence of God, which is of greater sanctity.

K.   "Then why is it stated: '. . . they put out of the camp every leper and every one having a discharge, and every one that was unclean through contact with the dead'?

L.   "[By specifying that all three are put out of the camp,] Scripture thereby served to assign to them levels or gradations [of uncleanness, with diverse rules affecting those levels, as will now be spelled out. Since we know that that rule applies to the ostracism of the leper, the specification that the others also are to be put out of the camp indicates that a singular rule applies to each of the categories. If one rule applied in common, then the specification with respect to the leper alone would have sufficed to indicate the rule for all others.]"

M.   [We review the distinctions among several gradations of uncleanness affecting human beings, inclusive of the three at hand: the leper, the one having a discharge, and the one unclean through contact with the dead.] "The Lord said to Moses, 'Command the people of Israel that they put out of the camp every leper and every one having a discharge, and every one that is unclean through contact with the dead'" (Num. 5:1–2).

N.   Shall I then draw the conclusion that all three of those listed [the leper, the one affected by a discharge, the one unclean with corpse-uncleanness] are to remain in the same locale [in relationship to the Temple]?

O.   With respect to the leper, Scripture states explicitly, "He shall dwell by himself; outside of the camp shall be his dwelling" (Lev. 13:46).

P.   Now the leper fell into the same category as the others, and he has been singled out from the general category, thereby serving to impose a single rule on the category from which he has been singled out.

Q.   [And this is the rule applicable to the leper and hence to the others from among whom he has been singled out:] Just as in the case of the leper, who is subject to a most severe form of uncleanness, and who also is subjected to a more severe rule governing ostracism than that applying to his fellow, so all who are subject to a more severe form of uncleanness likewise are subject to a more severe rule of ostracism than that applying to his fellow.

R.   On this basis sages listed distinctions that apply to those that are unclean [since a different rule applies to each of them, in descending order of severity, as is now spelled out]:

S.   To any object that one affected by a flux imparts uncleanness, a leper imparts uncleanness. A leper is subject to a more severe rule, however, in that a leper imparts uncleanness through an act of sexual relations.

T.   To any object that one unclean with corpse-uncleanness imparts uncleanness, one affected by a flux imparts uncleanness. But a more severe rule affects one affected by a flux, in that he imparts uncleanness to an object located far beneath a rock in the deep [imparting uncleanness to that deeply buried object merely by the application of the pressure of his weight, while one unclean with corpse-uncleanness does not impart uncleanness merely by pressure of his weight].

U.   To any object that one unclean by reason of waiting for sunset after immersion imparts uncleanness one unclean by corpse-uncleanness imparts uncleanness. A more severe rule applies to one unclean by corpse-uncleanness, for he imparts uncleanness to a human being [which is not the case of one who is unclean because he has immersed and remains unclean until sunset].

V.   What is made unfit by one who has not yet completed his
rites of atonement [for having become unclean, by presenting
a purification offering] following uncleanness and purification
is made unfit by one who awaits for sunset to complete his
process of purification. A more strict rule applies to one
awaiting sunset for the completion of his rite of purification,
for he imparts unfitness to food designated for priestly rations
[while the one who has completed his rites of purification
but not yet offered the atonement sacrifice on account of his
uncleanness does not impart unfitness to priestly rations that
he may touch].

The dominant form of Sifra, the demonstration of the fallacy of logic uncor-
rected by exegesis of Scripture, produces in Sifré to Numbers yet another moving,
or dialectical, exegetical form, but while the basic trait is familiar—a sequence of
shifts and turns in the possibility of interpretation, all of them subjected to close
logical scrutiny—the purpose is different. And the purpose comes to expression
not in content, particular to diverse passages, but in form.

The formal indicator is the presence of the question, in one of several versions:
is it not a matter of logic? That is the never-failing formal indicator. From that
clause we invariably move on to a set of arguments of a highly formalized character
on taxonomic classification: what is like, or unlike? What is like follows a given
rule, what is unlike follows the opposite rule, and it is for us to see whether the
likenesses or unlikenesses prevail. The argument is formalized to an extreme, and
there are very few variations among our document's exempla of this form, though
one—the matter of length—should not be missed. The exegesis of the verse at
hand plays no substantial role, beyond its initial introduction. What is critical is the
issue of the reliability of logic. The base verse before us contributes virtually nothing and in no way serves as the foundation for the composition at hand.

An inquiry into the scriptural basis for a passage of the Mishnah, occurs. The
sole important difference from Sifra, of course, is that in Sifré to Numbers, this
form is merely occasional, not indicative of the program of the document as a
whole. What we have is simply a citation of the verse plus a law in a prior writing
(Mishnah, Tosefta) which the verse is supposed to sustain. The formal traits require
(1) citation of a verse, with or without comment, followed by (2) verbatim citation
of a passage of the Mishnah or the Tosefta.

I:IX. 1. A.   "[You shall put out both male and female, putting them outside the camp], that they may not defile their camp, [in the
midst of which I dwell]":

B.   On the basis of this verse, the rule has been formulated:

C.   **There are three camps, the camp of Israel, the camp
of the Levitical priests, and the camp of the Presence**

> **of God. From the gate of Jerusalem to the Temple mount is the camp of Israel, from the gate of the Temple mount to the Temple courtyard is the camp of the Levitical priesthood, and from the gate of the courtyard and inward is the camp of the Presence of God [T. Kelim 1:12].**

A variation on the foregoing presents a statement of a rule, in which the Mishnah or Tosefta is not cited verbatim. That is the undefined side. But the rule that is presented is not intrinsic to the verse at hand, in that the verse does not refer in any way to the case or possibility framed as the issue. In that case we do not have a clear-cut exegesis of the verse in its own terms. But we also do not have an example of the linking of Scripture to the Mishnah. An example of this type follows:

III:I.   1.   A.   "[And the Lord said to Moses, 'Say to the people of Israel, When a man or woman commits any of the sins that men commit by breaking faith with the Lord, and that person is guilty,] he shall confess his sin which he has committed [and he shall make full restitution for his wrong, adding a fifth to it, and giving it to him to whom he did the wrong']" (Num. 5:5–10).

                B.   But [in stressing "his sin," Scripture makes it clear that he does not have to make confession] for what his father did.

                C.   For if one said to him, "Give me the bailment that I left with your father," and he says, "You left no bailment" [and the other says] "I impose an oath on you," and the first says, "Amen,"

                D.   [and if] after a while the [son] remembers [that a bailment indeed had been left and must be handed over]—

                E.   should I conclude that the son is liable [to make confession, not merely to hand over the bailment]?

                F.   Scripture says, "He shall confess his sin which *he* has committed," but he does not make confession for what his father did.

The proof text serves for a proposition given in apodictic form. The point is that the son does not confess the father's sin, though he has to make up for it. Scripture then sets forth the stated law by its stress. We shall now derive laws from the verses at hand to cover further such situations.

4.

LOGIC OF COHERENT DISCOURSE

The paramount logic that joins composition to composition is, of course, fixed-associative. The same serves for a fair number of composites; a very small number are shaped into propositional statements. In all, the document relies principally on the sequence of verses of the book of Numbers for the joining of its compositions.

5.

TOPICAL PROGRAM

Let us now characterize the formal traits of Sifré to Numbers as a commentary, since, as noted at the outset, it is here that we identify the implicit propositional program of the document's compilers and the writers of the bulk of its compositions. These we have reduced to two classifications, based on the point of origin of the verses that are cataloged or subjected to exegesis: exegesis of a verse in the book of Numbers in terms of the theme or problems of that verse, hence, intrinsic exegesis; exegesis of a verse in Numbers in terms of a theme or polemic not particular to that verse, hence, extrinsic exegesis.

THE FORMS OF EXTRINSIC EXEGESIS: The implicit message of the external category proves simple to define, since the several extrinsic classifications turn out to form a cogent polemic. Let me state the recurrent polemic of external exegesis.

The Syllogistic Composition: Scripture supplies hard facts, which, properly classified, generate syllogisms. By collecting and classifying facts of Scripture, therefore, we may produce firm laws of history, society, and Israel's everyday life. The diverse compositions in which verses from various books of the Scriptures are compiled in a list of evidence for a given proposition—whatever the character or purpose of that proposition—make that one point. And given their power and cogency, they make the point stick.

The Fallibility of Reason Unguised by Scriptural Exegesis: Scripture alone supplies reliable basis for speculation. Laws cannot be generated by reason or logic unguided by Scripture. Efforts at classification and contrastive-analogical exegesis, in which Scripture does not supply the solution to all problems, prove few and far between. This polemic forms the obverse of the point above. So when extrinsic issues intervene in the exegetical process, they coalesce to make a single point. Let me state that point with appropriate emphasis on the recurrent and implicit message of the forms of external exegesis: Scripture stands paramount; logic, reason, analytical processes of classification and differentiation, secondary. Reason not built on scriptural foundations yields uncertain results. The Mishnah itself demands scriptural bases.

What about the polemic present in the intrinsic exegetical exercises? This clearly does not allow for ready characterization. As we saw, at least three intrinsic exegetical exercises focus on the use of logic, specifically, the logic of classification, comparison, and contrast of species of a genus, in the explanation of the meaning of verses of the book of Numbers. The internal dialectical mode, moving from point to point as logic dictates, underlines the main point already stated: logic produces possibilities, Scripture chooses among them. Again, the question, why is this passage stated? commonly produces an answer generated by further verses of Scripture, e.g., this matter is stated here to clarify what otherwise would be confusion left in the wake of other verses. So Scripture produces problems of confusion and duplication, and Scripture—and not logic, not differentiation, not classification—solves those problems.

To state matters simply: Scripture is complete, harmonious, perfect. Logic not only does not generate truth beyond the limits of Scripture but also plays no important role in the harmonization of difficulties yielded by what appear to be duplications or disharmonies. These forms of internal exegesis then make the same point that the extrinsic ones do.

In so stating, of course, we cover all but the single most profuse category of exegesis, which we have treated as simple and undifferentiated: (1) verse of Scripture or a clause, followed by (2) a brief statement of the meaning at hand. Here I see no unifying polemic in favor of, or against, a given proposition. The most common form also proves the least pointed: X bears this meaning, Y bears that meaning, or, as we have seen, citation of verse X, followed by [what this means is]. . . . Whether simple or elaborate, the upshot is the same. What can be at issue when no polemic expressed in the formal traits of syntax and logic finds its way to the surface? What do I do when I merely clarify a phrase? Or, to frame the question more logically: what premises must validate my *intervention*, that is, my willingness to undertake to explain the meaning of a verse of Scripture? These justify the labor of intrinsic exegesis as we have seen its results here:

[1] My independent judgment bears weight and produces meaning. I—that is, my mind—therefore may join in the process.

[2] God's revelation to Moses at Sinai requires my intervention. I have the role, and the right, to say what that revelation means.

[3] What validates my entry into the process of revelation is the correspondence between the logic of my mind and the logic of the document.

Only if I think in accord with the logic of the revealed Torah can my thought processes join issue in clarifying what is at hand: the unfolding of God's will in the Torah. To state matters more accessibly: if the Torah does not make statements in accord with a syntax and a grammar that I know, I cannot so understand the Torah as to explain its meaning. But if I can join in the discourse of the Torah, it is because I speak the same language of thought: syntax and grammar at the deepest levels of my intellect.

[4] Then to state matters affirmatively and finally: since a shared logic of syntax and grammar joins my mind to the mind of God as revealed in the Torah, I can say what a sentence of the Torah means. So I too can amplify, clarify, expand, revise, rework: that is to say, create a commentary. So the work of commenting upon the written Torah bears profound consequence for the revelation of the Torah, the sage becoming partner with God in the giving of the Torah. In that conclusion, we find ourselves repeating the main point that Sifra yields in the description of rabbinic literature as a whole.

6.

A Sample Passage

We consider as our sample passage the way in which Sifré to Numbers reads Num. 7:1–6, because, when we come to Pesiqta deRab Kahana, we shall have the occasion to see how a different document chooses to interpret the same passage. This will underline the documentary character of the Midrash compilations, that is to say, the paramount and definitive role that the framers of documents play in the contents of those documents' Midrash exegeses. The way in which Scripture is read in a given document's Midrash exegeses turns out to differ from the way in which another document's Midrash exegeses treat the same passage. Only when we compare the sample of Sifré to Numbers with the sample of Pesiqta deRab Kahana will that fact become strikingly clear as a dominant characteristic of rabbinic literature throughout, a literature made up of distinct and ordinarily free-standing and autonomous compilations of compositions that, in the main, serve the document in which they occur and no other. What we see in this Sifré's reading of Num. 7:1ff. is what we should by now expect: a systematic and close reading, verse by verse, with slight attention to issues of coherence and large-scale meaning— exegesis pure and simple.

SIFRÉ TO NUMBERS 44

XLIV:I.   1.   A.   "On the day when Moses had finished setting up the tabernacle [and had anointed and consecrated it with all its furnishings and had anointed and consecrated the altar with all its utensils, the leaders of Israel, heads of their fathers' houses, the leaders of the tribes, who were over those who were numbered, offered and brought their offerings before the Lord, six covered wagons and twelve oxen, a wagon for every two of the leaders, and for each one an ox, they offered them before the tabernacle. Then the Lord said to Moses, 'Accept these from them, that they may be used in doing the service of the tent of meeting, and give them to the Levites, to each man according to his service.' So Moses took the wagons and the oxen and gave them to the Levites]" (Num. 7:1–6):

B.   Scripture indicates that for each of the seven days of consecrating the tabernacle, Moses would set up the tabernacle, and every morning he would anoint it and dismantle it. But on that day he set it up and anointed it, but he did not dismantle it. [On the prior days he set up the tabernacle and dismantled it. On the eighth day, he set it up but did not dismantle it.]

C.   R. Yosé b. R. Judah: "Also on the eighth day he set it up and dismantled it, for it is said, 'And in the first month in the second year on the first day of the month the tabernacle was erected' (Ex. 30:17). On the basis of that verse we learn that on the twenty-third day of Adar, Aaron and his sons, the tabernacle and the utensils were anointed."

XLIV:I. 2. A.   On the first day of the month the tabernacle was set up, on the second the red cow was burned [for the purification rite required at Num. 19], on the third day water was sprinkled from it in lieu of the second act of sprinkling, the Levites were shaved.

B.   On that same day the Presence of God rested in the tabernacle, as it is said, "Then the cloud covered the tent of meeting, and the glory of the Lord filled the tabernacle, and Moses was not able to enter the tent of meeting, because the cloud abode upon it" (Ex. 40:34).

C.   On that same day the heads offered their offerings, as it is said, "He who offered his offering the first day . . ." (Num. 7:12). Scripture uses the word "first" only in a setting when "first" introduces all of the days of the year.

D.   On that day fire came down from heaven and consumed the offerings, as it is said, "And fire came forth from before the Lord and consumed the burnt offering and the fat upon the altar" (Lev. 9:24).

E.   On that day the sons of Aaron offered strange fire, as it is said, "Now Nadab and Abihu, the sons of Aaron, each took his censer and put fire in it . . . and offered unholy fire before the Lord, such as he had not commanded them" (Lev. 10:1).

F.   "And they died before the Lord . . ." (Lev. 10:2): they died before the Lord, but they fell outside [of the tabernacle, not imparting corpse uncleanness to it].

G. How so? They were on their way out.

H. R. Yosé says, "An angel sustained them, as they died, until they got out, and they fell in the courtyard, as it is said, 'And Moses called Mishael and Elzaphan, the sons of Uzziel the uncle of Aaron, and said to them, "Draw near, carry your brethren from before the sanctuary out of the camp"' (Lev. 10:4). What is stated is not, 'From before the Lord,' but, 'from before the sanctuary.'"

I. R. Ishmael says, "The context indicates the true state of affairs, as it is said, 'And they died before the Lord,' meaning, they died inside and fell inside. How did they get out? People dragged them with iron ropes."

The expansion and amplification of the base verse runs through No. 1. From that point, No. 2, we deal with the other events of that same day, surveying the several distinct narratives which deal with the same thing, Ex. 40, Lev. 9–10, and so on. This produces the effect of unifying the diverse scriptural accounts into one tale, an important and powerful exegetical result. One of the persistent contributions of our exegetes is to collect and harmonize a diversity of verses taken to refer to the same day, event, or rule.

XLIV:II. 1. A. ". . . and had anointed and consecrated it with all its furnishings and had anointed and consecrated the altar with all its utensils":

B. Might I infer that as each utensil was anointed, it was sanctified?

C. Scripture says, ". . . and had anointed and consecrated it with all its furnishings and had anointed and consecrated the altar with all its utensils," meaning that not one of them was sanctified until all of them had been anointed. [The process proceeded by stages.]

XLIV:II. 2. A. ". . . and had anointed and consecrated it with all its furnishings and had anointed and consecrated the altar with all its utensils":

B. The anointing was done both inside and outside [of the utensil].

C. R. Josiah says, "Utensils meant to hold liquids were anointed inside and outside, but utensils meant to hold dry stuffs were anointed on the inside but not anointed on the outside."

D. R. Jonathan says, "Utensils meant to hold liquids were anointed inside and not outside, but utensils meant to hold dry stuffs not anointed.

E. "You may know that they were not consecrated, for it is said, 'You shall bring from your dwellings two loaves of bread to be waved, made of two-tenths of an ephah' (Lev. 23:17). Then when do they belong to the Lord? Only after they are baked." [The bread was baked in utensils at home, so the utensils were not consecrated.]

XLIV:II. 3. A. Rabbi says, "Why is it said, '. . . and had anointed and consecrated it'? And is it not already stated, '. . . and had anointed and consecrated it'?

B. "This indicates that with the anointing of these utensils all future utensils were sanctified [so that the sanctification of the tabernacle enjoyed permanence and a future tabernacle or Temple did not require a rite of sanctification once again]."

No. 1 clarifies the rite of sanctification, aiming at the notion that the act of consecration covered everything at once, leading to the future conclusion, at the end, that that act also covered utensils later on to be used in the cult. No. 3 goes over that same ground. No. 2 deals with its own issue, pursuing the exegesis of the verse at hand. Its interest in the consecration of the utensils is entirely congruent with No. 3, because it wants to know the status of utensils outside of the cult, and, while they serve the purpose of the cult as specified, still, they are not deemed to have been consecrated.

SIFRÉ TO NUMBERS 45

XLV:I. 1. A. "[On the day when Moses had finished setting up the tabernacle and had anointed and consecrated it with all its furnishings and had anointed and consecrated the altar with all its utensils] the leaders of Israel, [heads of their fathers' houses, the leaders of the tribes, who were over those who were numbered], offered [and brought their offerings before the Lord, six covered wagons and twelve oxen, a wagon for every two of the leaders, and for each one an ox, they offered them before the tabernacle. Then the Lord said to Moses, 'Accept these from them, that they may be used in doing the service of the tent of meeting, and give them to the Levites, to each man according to his service.' So Moses took the wagons and the oxen and gave them to the Levites]" (Num. 7:1–6):

B. May I infer that they had been ordinary people who were elevated?

C. Scripture says, "heads of their fathers' houses."

D. And they were not merely "heads of their fathers' houses," but also "the leaders of the tribes, who were over those who were numbered."

E. They were leaders, sons of leaders.

XLV:I. 2. A. ". . . the leaders of the tribes, who were over those who were numbered":

B. They were the same ones who had been appointed over them in Egypt, as it is said, "And the leaders of the children of Israel smote . . ." (Ex. 5:14).

The interest is in showing the distinguished origins of the Israelite leadership.

XLV:II. 1. A. ". . . six covered wagons [and twelve oxen, a wagon for every two of the leaders, and for each one an ox, they offered them before the tabernacle]":

B. The word "covered" means only "decorated," for they lacked for nothing.

C. Rabbi says, "The word 'covered' means only 'canopied,' and even though there is no firm proof for that proposition, there is at least some indication of it: 'And they shall bring all your brethren from all the nations as an offering to the Lord, upon horses and in chariots and in litters and upon mules and upon dromedaries to my holy mountain, Jerusalem, says the Lord' (Is. 66:20)."

XLV:II. 2. A. ". . . six covered wagons and twelve oxen, a wagon for every two of the leaders, and for each one an ox, they offered them before the tabernacle.

B. May I infer that there was a wagon for each one?

C. Scripture says, ". . . a wagon for every two of the leaders."

D. May I infer there was an ox for every two of the leaders?

E. Scripture says, ". . . and for each one an ox."

XLV:II. 3. A. They came and took up positions before the tabernacle, but Moses did not accept anything from them, until it was stated to him by the mouth of the Holy One, "Accept these from them, that they may be used in doing the service of the tent of meeting."

B. Lo, mortals thus brought their judgment into accord with the judgment on high.

XLV:II. 4. A. R. Nathan says, "And why in the present matter did the princes bring voluntary gifts first [rather than waiting for the community to do so], while in the work of the making of the tabernacle they in fact did not volunteer to begin with [but let the community give and only afterward they made their contribution]?

B.   "Well, this is how the leaders had earlier reasoned matters out: 'Let the community contribute what they will, and what is still needed after they have given we shall make up.'

C.   "When the princes realized that the community had provided all that was needed, as it is said, 'And the work was sufficient,' (Ex. 34:4), the princes said, 'What is left for us to do?'

D.   "So the princes brought the precious stones for the ephod.

E.   "That is why, in the present case, the princes brought their voluntary offering first [so as not to be left out]."

No. 1 provides the explanation of a word, and No. 2 proceeds to a phrase. No. 3 restates what the text says and explains the implications of the matter, and No. 4 draws into relationship two distinct accounts of gifts to the sanctuary, explaining in a striking way the difference in the detail of the two pictures.

SIFRÉ TO NUMBERS 46

XLVI:I.   1.   A.   "So Moses took the wagons and the oxen and gave them to the Levites" (Num. 7:1–6):

B.   Lo, Moses took them and divided them up on his own initiative.

XLVI:I.   2.   A.   "The two wagons and the four oxen he gave to the sons of Gershom, and the four wagons and the eight oxen he gave to the sons of Merari,"

B.   Because Eleazar had sixteen sons, and Ithamar, eight.

C.   As it is said, "The male heads of families proved to be more numerous in the line of Eleazar than in that of Ithamar, so that sixteen heads of families were grouped under the line of Eleazar and eight under that of Ithamar. He organized them by drawing lots among them, for there were sacred officers and offices of God in the line of Eleazar and in that of Ithamar" (1 Chr. 24:4–6).

No. 1 draws its own conclusions from the cited verse, and No. 2 proceeds to relate the present division to the materials available elsewhere, a common exegetical interest.

XLVI:II.   1.   A.   "He gave none to the Kohathites, because the service laid upon them was that of the holy things: these they had to carry themselves on their shoulders" (Num. 7:9):

B.   R. Nathan, "On the basis of what is said here we see what David missed, for the Levites did not bear the ark, but they bore the wagon, as it is said, 'They mounted the ark of God on a new cart and conveyed it from the house of Abinadab on the hill' (1 Sam. 6:3).

C. "'The Lord was angry with Uzzah and struck him down there for his rash act, so he died there beside the ark of God' (2 Sam. 6:7).

D. "'David was vexed because the Lord's anger had broken out upon Uzzah, and he called the place Perez-uzzah, the name it still bears' (2 Sam 6:8).

E. "Ahitophel said to David, 'Should you not have learned the lesson of Moses, your master, for the Levites bore the ark only on their shoulders, as it says, "He gave none to the Kohathites, because the service laid upon them was that of the holy things: these they had to carry themselves on their shoulders."'

F. "Lo, David then sent and had it carried by shoulder, as it is said, 'And David summoned Zadok and Abiathar the priests, together with the Levites, Uriel, Asaiah, Joel, Shemaiah, Eliel, and Amminadab, and said to them, You who are heads of families of the Levites, hallow yourselves, you and your kinsmen, and bring up the ark of the Lord, the God of Israel, to the place which I have prepared for it. . . . So the priests and the Levites hallowed themselves to bring up the ark of the Lord, the God of Israel, and the Levites carried the ark of God, bearing it on their shoulders with poles, as Moses had prescribed at the command of the Lord' (1 Chr. 15:11–15)."

XLVI:II.   2.   A.   "This was their order of duty for the discharge of their service when they entered the house of the Lord, according to the rule prescribed for them by their ancestor Aaron, who had received his instructions from the Lord, the God of Israel" (1 Chr. 24:19):

B. Where did he give a commandment? He gave nothing at all to the sons of Kohath. So lo, the sons of the Levites in no way innovated, but everything was done on the instructions of Moses, and Moses did everything at the instructions of the Almighty.

No. 1 is important in underlining David's error in not following the precedent established here by Moses and the Levites, carrying the ark not on the wagon but on their shoulders. David then corrected himself, following the proper precedent. No. 2 then underlines the matter that the precedent of the base verse guided the Levites later on. What we see, then, is a harmonization of diverse materials on the same important theme.

SIFRÉ TO NUMBERS 47

XLVII:I. 1. A. "And the leaders presented offerings for the dedication of the altar [on the day it was anointed; and the leaders offered their offering before the altar. And the Lord said to Moses, 'They shall offer their offerings, one leader each day, for the dedication of the altar.' He who offered his offering the first day was Nahshon the son of Amminadab of the tribe of Judah; and his offering was one silver plate whose weight was a hundred and thirty shekels, one silver basin of seventy shekels according to the shekel of the sanctuary, both of them full of fine flour mixed with oil for a cereal offering; one golden dish of ten shekels, full of incense; one young bull, one ram, one male lamb a year old, for a burnt offering; one male goat for a sin offering; and for the sacrifice of peace offerings, two oxen, five rams, five male goats, and five male lambs a year old. This was the offering of Nahshon the son of Amminadab]" (Num. 7:10–17):

B. The Scripture thus indicates that just as the princes made voluntary gifts for the work of building the tabernacle, so they did for the dedication of the tabernacle.

XLVII:I. 2. A. "And the leaders offered offerings for the dedication of the altar . . . and the leaders offered their offering before the altar":

B. They came and stood before the altar, but Moses did not accept the offerings from them, until he was so instructed by the word of the Holy One: "Let them make their offerings for the dedication of the altar."

C. Moses still did not know the proper manner in which they were to make their offerings, whether by the order dictated for the journeys, whether by the order dictated by the generations in which the tribal founders had been born, until he was instructed by the explicit statement of the Holy One, blessed be he, "Let them offer in accord with the order governing their journeys," as it is said, "And it came to pass." For the words "and it came to pass" indicate solely what was said to Moses on the authority of the Holy One, so they offered in accord with the order governing their journeys.

D. But Moses still did not know how the princes were to make their offerings, specifically, whether it was to be done all at once, or each one on his own day, until he was so instructed that each was to offer on his own day, as it is said, "They shall offer their offerings, one leader each day, for the dedication of the altar."

E.   The princes make voluntary offerings, but ordinary people do not do so. Why then does Scripture say, "'They shall offer their offerings, one leader each day, for the dedication of the altar" [specifying that the princes did it, when we know that only they could do it]?

F.   It was because Nahshon was a king, and he made the offering first. So people should not say, "Lo, because I made the offering first, I shall make an offering with everyone else, day by day." Therefore it is said, "They shall offer their offerings, *one leader* each day, for the dedication of the altar."

We begin with the simple clarification of the donation of the princes: not only for building the tabernacle, but also for dedicating the altar. Then, No. 2, we underline that each detail of the process of dedication was dictated by divine instructions. This would underline the polemic that the original work of sanctification imparted to the cult an indelible character of holiness. It is difficult to find a single point that does not begin in the amplification of the statements of Scripture.

XIII

SIFRÉ TO DEUTERONOMY

1.

IDENTIFYING THE DOCUMENT

OUT OF CASES AND EXAMPLES, SAGES SEEK GENERALIZATIONS AND GOVERNING PRIN-
ciples. Since in the book of Deuteronomy, Moses explicitly sets forth a vision of
Israel's future history, sages in Sifré to Deuteronomy examined that vision to uncover the rules that explain what happens to Israel.[1] That issue drew attention from
cases to rules, with the result that in the book of Deuteronomy, they set forth a

---

[1] For further reading and bibliography on the topic of this chapter, see the following:

Bowker, pp. 71–72.

Steven D. Fraade, *From Tradition to Commentary. Torah and its Interpretation in the Midrash Sifré to
Deuteronomy*. Albany, 1991: State University of New York Press.

Moses D. Herr, "Sifrei," *Encyclopaedia Judaica* 14:1519–21: coverage of Numbers, distinction from
Sifré to Deuteronomy; Sifré to Deuteronomy; characteristics; origin in the school of Aqiba;
commentaries; critical editions.

Maccoby, pp. 177–81 (selections, no introduction or analysis).

Stemberger-Strack, pp. 294–99: contents and structure; critical editions, translations; character,
origin, date (late third century); commentaries.

This writer's introduction is *Sifré to Deuteronomy. An Introduction to the Rhetorical, Logical, and Topical
Program*. Atlanta, 1987: Scholars Press for Brown Judaic Studies.

systematic account of Israel's future history, the key to Israel's recovery of command of its destiny. Like Sifra, Sifré to Deuteronomy pursues a diverse topical program in order to demonstrate a few fundamental propositions. The survey of the topical and propositional program of Sifré to Deuteronomy dictates what is truly particular to that authorship. It is its systematic mode of methodical analysis, in which it does two things. First, the document's compilers take the details of cases and carefully re-frame them into rules pertaining to all cases. The authorship therefore asks those questions of susceptibility to generalization ("generalizability") that first-class philosophical minds raise. And it answers those questions by showing what details restrict the prevailing law to the conditions of the case, and what details exemplify the encompassing traits of the law overall. These are, after all, the two possibilities. The law is either limited to the case and to all cases that replicate this one, or the law derives from the principles exemplified, in detail, in the case at hand. Essentially, as a matter of both logic and topical program, our authorship has reread the legal portions of the book of Deuteronomy and turned Scripture into what we now know is the orderly and encompassing code supplied by the Mishnah. To state matters simply, this authorship "Mishna-izes" Scripture. We find in Sifré to Numbers no parallel to this dominant and systematic program of Sifré to Deuteronomy.

But in other aspects, the document presents no surprises. In the two Sifrés and Sifra we find a recurrent motif, intense here, episodic there, of how the written component of the Torah, that is, revelation in written form, serves as the sole source of final truth. Logic or reason untested against Scripture produces flawed or unreliable results. The Torah, read as rabbis read it, and that alone proves paramount. Reason on its own is subordinate. For their search for the social rules of Israel's society, the priority of the covenant as a reliable account of the workings of reality, and the prevailing laws of Israel's history decreed by the terms of the covenant, their fundamental claim is the same. There are rules and regularities, but reason alone will not show us what they are. A systematic and reasoned reading of the Torah—the written Torah—joined to a sifting of the cases of the Torah in search of the regularities and points of law and order—these are what will tell the prevailing rule. A rule of the Mishnah and its account of the here and now of everyday life rests upon the Torah, not upon (mere) logic. A rule of Israel's history, past, present, and future, likewise derives from a search for regularities and points of order identified not by logic alone, but by logic addressed to the Torah. So there are these modes of gaining truth that apply equally to Mishnah and Scripture. There is logic, applied reason, and practical wisdom, such as sages exhibit; there is the corpus of facts supplied by Scripture, read as sages read it. These two together form God's statement upon the world today.

The topical program of the document intersects at its fundamental propositions with programs of other authorships—beginning, after all, with those of Scripture itself. The writers and compilers and compositors of Deuteronomy itself will have found entirely familiar such notions as the conditional character of Israel's possession of the land of Israel, the centrality of the covenant in Israel's relationship with

God and with the other nations of the world, the decisive role of the covenant in determining Israel's own destiny, and the covenantal responsibilities and standing of Israel's leadership—surely a considerable motif in the very structure of the book of Deuteronomy itself, beginning and end in particular. The reader may well wonder how we may treat as a distinctive authorship a group of writers who simply go over ground familiar in the received literature. In some important ways the authorship of Sifré to Deuteronomy makes a statement that is very much its own. That fact becomes clear when we consider the document's rhetorical, logical, and topical characteristics.

2.
TRANSLATIONS INTO ENGLISH

There are two complete translations into English, Reuven Hammer, *Sifre. A Tannaitic Commentary on the Book of Deuteronomy. Translated from the Hebrew with Introduction and Notes.* New Haven and London, 1986: Yale University Press. Yale Judaica Series XXIII, and this writer's *Sifré to Deuteronomy. An Analytical Translation.* Atlanta, 1987: Scholars Press for Brown Judaic Studies. I. *Pisqaot One through One Hundred Forty-Three. Debarim, Waethanan, Eqeb, Re'eh,* and II. *Pisqaot One Hundred Forty-Four through Three Hundred Fifty-Seven. Shofetim, Ki Tese, Ki Tabo, Nesabim, Ha'azinu, Zot Habberakhah.* The only difference between them is that Hammer's has no analytical reference system of any kind and lacks a systematic introduction to the document.

3.
RHETORIC

Nine recurrent patterns prove dominant in Sifré to Deuteronomy. Because of the close relationship between rhetorical conventions and logical necessities for coherent discourse, we distinguish among them by the presence of propositions, explicit and then implicit, and how these are argued or proved.

I.   *Propositions Stated Explicitly and Argued Philosophically*   1. *The Proposition and Its Syllogistic Argument:* This form is made up of simple sentences, in one way or another, which set forth propositions and demonstrate them by amassing probative facts, e.g., examples. The patterning of the individual sentences varies.

But the large-scale rhetoric, involving the presentation of a proposition, in general terms, and then the amassing of probative facts (however the sentences are worded), is essentially uniform. What we have are two or more sentences formed into a proposition and an argument, by contrast to those that are essentially single-ton sentences, rather than components of a more sustained discourse. These items ordinarily deal with matters of proper conduct or right action, hence *halakhic* is-sues. There is a two-layer discourse in them, since, at the superficial level, they yield only a detail of a law, that is, thus and so is the rule here; but at the deep layer of thought, they demonstrate a prevailing and global proposition, that applies—it is implied—throughout, not only to a single case. Overall, rhetorical analysis draws our attention to modes of stating a middle-level proposition, affecting a variety of verses and their cases. Then we move onward, to the low-level proposition, that pertains only to a single case, and, finally, we turn to a global proposition, which affects a broad variety of cases and homogenizes them. These distinctions are meant to explain the classification system represented here. The absence of a coun-terpart in Sifra does not require proof.

2. *The Proposition Based on the Classification of Probative Facts:* The prevailing pat-tern here is not vastly changed. This is different from the foregoing only in a minor matter. In this case we shall propose to prove a proposition, e.g., the meaning of a word, by classifying facts that point toward that proposition. In the forego-ing, the work of proof is accomplished through listing proofs made up of diverse facts. The difference between the one and the other is hardly very considerable, but I think we can successfully differentiate among the formal patterns through the stated criterion. However, one may reasonably argue that this catalog and the foregoing list essentially the same formal patterns of language or argument. In many of these instances, we have a complex development of a simple exegesis, and it is at the complexity—the repeated use of a simple pat-tern—that the propositional form(s) reach full exposure. Sifra's authorship has no use for such a pattern.

3. *The Proposition Based on the Recurrent Opinions of Sages:* This is another varia-tion, in that the nature of the evidence shifts, and, it follows, also the patterning of language. Here we shall have the attribution constantly present, e.g., X says, and that does form an important rhetorical indicator. We may say flatly that this form is not characteristic of our authorship and accomplishes none of its goals. It is a commonplace in the Mishnah, inclusive of tractate Abot, and in the Tosefta; large-scale compositions in the Yerushalmi and the Bavli follow the same pattern; and other large-scale compositions will be drawn together because a sequence of simple declarative sentences on diverse topics, whether or not related in theme, bears the same attribution. The omission of this pattern here therefore is notewor-thy and constitutes a decision for one pattern and against another. I know of no material equivalent in Sifra.

4-5. *The Narrative and Its Illustrated Proposition: Scriptural Story. Also: The Parable as Illustration of an Established Proposition:* The construction in which a proposition is established and then illustrated in a narrative, whether parable, scriptural story, or other kind of narrative, is treated in a single rubric. The formal-structural uniformity justifies doing so. We may find varieties of patterns of sentences, e.g., parables as against stories. But the narrative is always marked by either, "he said to him . . . he said to him . . . ," for the story, or counterpart indications of a select pattern of forming and arranging sentences, for the parable. The authorship of Sifré Deuteronomy has resorted to a very limited repertoire of patterns of language, and "narrative," a gross and hardly refined classification, suffices. For narratives, viewed as an encompassing formal category, do not play a large role in defining (therefore differentiating) the rhetorical-logical program of our authorship. Sifra's authorship scarcely presents stories of this kind.

II. ***Propositions Stated Implicitly but Argued Philosophically*** *6. Implicit Propositions:* These items involve lists of facts, but lack that clear statement of the proposition that the facts establish. What we have here are complexes of tightly joined declarative sentences, many of them (in the nature of things) in that atom-pattern, "commentary form," but all of them joined into a much larger set of (often) highly formalized statements. Hence I characterize this form as an implicit proposition based on facts derived from exegesis. For obvious reasons, there is no counterpart in Sifra.

III. ***Facts That Do Not Yield Propositions Beyond Themselves*** *7. Exegetical Form with No Implicit Proposition:* This simple exegetical form presents a single fact, a discrete sentence, left without further development and without association or affinity with surrounding statements—once more, "commentary form." The form is as defined: clause + phrase. In Sifra this is the single most common pattern, as we saw. But in Sifré to Deuteronomy that same form in the propositional compositions rarely occurs without development, and if I had to specify the one fundamental difference between the nonpropositional exegetical form (such as we find in Sifra and Sifré to Numbers and in some measure in Sifré to Deuteronomy) and all other forms, it is in the simplicity of the one as against the complexity of the other. Or, to state matters more bluntly, excluding narrative, the sole rhetorical building block of any consequence in Sifra, Sifré to Numbers, and Sifré to Deuteronomy is the simple exegetical one, consisting of *clause + phrase = sentence.*

What differentiates Sifra from Sifré to Deuteronomy is that here all other forms develop the simple atom of exegetical form into a complex molecule, but the "exegetical form with no implicit proposition" remains at the atomic level (if not an even smaller particle than the atom) and never gains the dimensions of a molecular composite. These therefore constitute entirely comprehensible sense units, that is, simple sentences on their own, never formed into paragraphs, and define the lowest rhetorical form of our document. The other rhetorical forms build these simple sense units or sentences into something more complex. That fact of rhetoric accounts also for our having—willy-nilly—to appeal to considerations of logical cogency in our analysis of rhetoric and form.

IV. Facts That Do Not Yield Propositions Particular to the Case at Hand

8. *Dialectical Exegesis with No Implicit Proposition Pertinent to the Case at Hand but with Bearing on Large-Scale Structural Issues:* Here we deal with the same pattern that in Sifra we have called dialectical-exegetical form. The purpose of the form in Sifra is limited to the two purposes of, first, exclusionary-inclusionary inquiry, and, second, the critique of non-scripturally-based taxonomy, while in Sifré to Deuteronomy a variety of propositions will be served. This form is made up of a series of closely joined thought units or sentences. Hence they present us with two or more sentences that constitute joined, propositional paragraphs. But the rhetorical traits are so much more particular, and their net effect so much more distinctive, that I treat them as a quite distinct rhetorical phenomenon. Moreover, these are the most patterned, the most formed, of all formal compositions at hand. They require sustained exposition of a proposition, not a simple proposition plus probative facts. They all make two points, as I have already pointed out, one at the surface, the other through the deep structure. Strictly speaking, as sustained and complex forms, all of these items conform most exactly to the fundamental definition of a rhetorical form language that coheres to a single pattern. And the pattern is one of both rhetoric and logic.

Two such patterns are, first, the systematic analytical exercise of restricting or extending the application of a discrete rule, ordinarily signified through sereotyped language; second, the demonstration that logic without revelation in the form of a scriptural formulation and exegesis produces unreliable results. There are other recurrent patterns of complex linguistic formation matched by sustained thought that conform to the indicative traits yielded by these two distinct ones. The form invariably involves either the exercise of generalization through extension or restriction of the rule to the case given in Scripture or the demonstration that reason unaided by Scripture is not reliable. The formal traits are fairly uniform, even though the intent—the upshot of the dialectical exegesis—varies from instance to instance. Very often these amplifications leave the base verse far behind, since they follow a program of their own, to which the base verse and its information are at best contributory. One of the ways in which this formalization of language differs from the foregoing is that the exegesis that is simple in form always is closely tied to the base verse, while the one that pursues larger-scale structural issues very frequently connects only very loosely to the base verse. Another persistent inquiry, external to any given verse and yielding, in concrete terms, no general rule at all, asks how to harmonize two verses, the information of which seems to conflict. The result is a general proposition that verses are to be drawn into alignment with one another. Here, we see, we are entirely at home. Sifra and Sifré to Deuteronomy have in common the usage of the dialectical-exegetical form for pretty much the same purposes. A highly restricted repertoire of formal possibilities therefore confronted the writers of materials now collected in Sifré to Deuteronomy.

4.
LOGIC OF COHERENT DISCOURSE

The paramount logic of Sifré to Deuteronomy is not exegetical but propositional. Most units of cogent discourse in Sifré to Deuteronomy appeal for cogency to propositions, not to fixed associations, such as characterize commentaries and other compilations of exegeses of verses of Scripture:

Propositional Units of Cogent Discourse	*Non-propositional Units of Cogent Discourse*	
Fixed-Associative	159	13.9%
Propositional	690	60.4%
Narrative	61	5.3%
Methodical-Analytical	232	20.3%

More than 85 percent of all itemized units of discourse—the second, third, and fourth entries on the list—find cogency through one or another mode of propositional logic. That figure is confirmed by yet another. Of the propositional units of cogent discourse, 70.1 percent in fact constitute propositional discourse, 6.2 percent find cogency in narrative, and 23.6 percent in the methodical-analytical mode. Since that mode presents not one but two propositions, we find ourselves on firm ground in maintaining that the logic of Sifré to Deuteronomy is a logic not of exegesis but of sustained proposition of one kind or another. Our document's authorship links one sentence to another by appeal to connections of proposition, not mere theme, and only occasionally asks the structure of a verse or sequence of verses to sustain the intelligible joining of two or more sentences into a coherent and meaningful statement.

Do the rhetoric and logic of our document derive from the (supposed) purpose of the authorship of forming a commentary? Not at all. On the contrary, in general, the logic of our document is sustained, propositional, mostly philosophical, and not that of commentary. What holds things together for our authorship does not rely upon the verse at hand to impose order and cogency upon discourse. The authorship of this document ordinarily appeals to propositions to hold two or more sentences together. If, by definition, a commentary appeals for cogency to the text that the commentators propose to illuminate, then ours is a document that is in no essential way a commentary. The logic is not that of a commentary, and the formal repertoire shows strong preference for other than commentary form. So far as commentary dictates both its own rhetoric and its own logic, this is no commentary. It is, in fact, a highly argumentative, profoundly well-crafted, and cogent set of propositions. We may indeed speak of a message, a topical program, such as, in general, a commentary that in form appeals to a clause of a verse and a phrase of a sentence, and in logic holds things together through fixed associations, is not apt to set forth. A commentary makes statements about meanings of verses, but it does not make a set of cogent statements of its own. I have now shown that in rhetoric and in logic Sifré to Deuteronomy takes shape in such a way as to yield a statement, or a set of cogent statements. Such a document as ours indicates that an authorship has found a need for propositions to attain cogency or impart connections to two or more sentences, calls upon narrative, demands recurrent methodical analyses. The text that is subjected to commentary only occasionally is asked to join sentence to sentence.

Let us now compare Sifra and Sifré to Deuteronomy, to show that these observations indeed do effect the differentiation of otherwise closely aligned documents.

SIFRA

Type of Logic	Number of Entries	Percentage of the Whole
Propositional	73	30.4%
Narrative/		
Teleological	1	0.4%
Fixed-Associative	43	17.9%
Methodical-Analytical	123	51.0%
	240	99.7%

SIFRÉ TO DEUTERONOMY

Type of Logic	Number of Entries	Percentage of the Whole
Propositional	690	60.4%
Narrative/		
Teleological	61	5.3%
Fixed-Associative	59	13.9%
Methodical-		
Analytical	232	20.3%
	1142	99.9%

In Sifré to Deuteronomy, of the propositional units of cogent discourse, 60.4 percent in fact constitute propositional discourse, 5.3 percent find cogency in narrative, and 20.3 percent in the methodical-analytical mode. Since that mode presents not one but two propositions, we find ourselves on firm ground in maintaining that the logic of Sifré to Deuteronomy is a logic not of exegesis but of sustained proposition of one kind or another. The differences between Sifra and Sifré to Deuteronomy are these:

1. *Propositional logic:* Sifré to Deuteronomy contains two times the proportion of propositional compositions. Sifré to Deuteronomy is a highly propositional compilation, while Sifra is not.

2. *Teleological logic:* Sifré to Deuteronomy contains thirteen times the proportion of narrative compositions. Since teleological logic is propositional in its foundation, that disproportion is readily understood.

3. *Fixed-associative logic:* The two documents make use of approximately the same proportions of this mode of stringing sentences or facts together, 17.9 percent against 13.9 percent, a differential of 1.2 times the proportion in Sifra over Sifré to Numbers. That does not seem to me a significant difference, given the rough and ready mode of classification employed at this stage in the work.

4. *Methodical-analytical logic:* Sifra's authorship presents *two and a half* times the proportion of completed units of thought held together by the logic of systematic methodical analysis than does that of Sifré to Deuteronomy. The message of Sifra—as we saw in Chapter 11—depends upon repetition of a single, highly abstract proposition expressed in concrete terms. Hence the repetition of the same inquiry over a sizable number of diverse entries makes the point Sifra's authorship wishes to make. Sifré to Deuteronomy makes its points as propositions, not as repeated demonstrations of fundamental attributes of thought, which is the paramount medium of thought and expression of Sifra.

The authorship of Sifra has a very clear notion of precisely the questions it wishes persistently to address and it follows that program through the majority of the pericopes of its document. These questions then form the distinctive trait of mind of Sifra in comparison to Sifré to Deuteronomy. The resort to teleological logic in both documents is negligible in proportion to the whole. The utilization of fixed-associative logic is pretty much in equal proportions; and Sifré to Deuteronomy is characterized by an interest in propositional discourse, while in Sifra that mode of discourse is subsumed under the logic of fixed analysis.

5.

TOPICAL PROGRAM

Four principal topics encompass the document's propositions, of which the first three correspond to the three relationships into which Israel entered: with heaven, on earth, and within. These yield systematic statements that concern the relationships between Israel and God, with special reference to the covenant, the Torah, and the land; Israel and the nations, with interest in Israel's history, past, present, and future, and how that cyclic is to be known; Israel on its own terms, with focus upon Israel's distinctive leadership. The fourth rubric encompasses not specific *ad hoc* propositions that form aggregates of proofs of large truths, but rather, prevailing modes of thought, demonstrating the inner structure of intellect in our document, yielding the formation, out of the cases of Scripture, of encompassing rules.

ISRAEL AND GOD: THE IMPLICATIONS OF THE COVENANT: The basic proposition, spelled out in detail, is that Israel stands in a special relationship with God, and that relationship is defined by the contract, or covenant, that God made with Israel. The covenant comes to particular expression in our document in two matters, first, the land, second, the Torah. Each marks Israel as different from all other nations, on the one side, and as selected by God, on the other. In these propositions, sages situate Israel in the realm of heaven, finding on earth the stigmata of covenanted election and concomitant requirement of loyalty and obedience to the covenant.

First comes the definition of those traits of God that our authorship finds pertinent. God sits in judgment upon the world, and his judgment is true and righteous. God punishes faithlessness. But God's fundamental and definitive trait is mercy. The way of God is to be merciful and gracious. The basic relationship of Israel to God is one of God's grace for Israel. God's loyalty to Israel endures, even when Israel sins. When Israel forgets God, God is pained. Israel's leaders, whatever their excellence, plead with God only for grace, not for their own merit. Correct attitudes in prayer derive from the need for grace, Israel having slight merit on its own account. Israel should follow only God, carrying out religious deeds as the covenant requires, in accord with the instructions of prophets. Israel should show mercy to others, in the model of God's merciful character.

Second, the contract, or covenant, produces the result that God has acquired Israel, which God created. The reason is that only Israel accepted the Torah, among all the nations, and that is why God made the covenant with Israel in particular. Why is the covenant made only with Israel? The gentiles did not accept the Torah, Israel did, and that has made all the difference. Israel recognized God forthwith; the very peace of the world and of nature depends upon God's giving the Torah to Israel. That is why Israel is the sole nation worthy of dwelling in the palace of God and that is the basis for the covenant too. The covenant secures for Israel an enduring relationship of grace with God. The covenant cannot be revoked and endures forever. The covenant, terms of which are specified in the Torah, has duplicate terms: if you do well, you will bear a blessing, and if not, you will bear a curse.

That is the singular mark of the covenant between God and Israel. A mark of the covenant is the liberation from Egypt, and that sufficed to impose upon Israel God's claim for their obedience. An important sign of the covenant is the possession of the land. Part of the covenant is the recognition of merit of the ancestors. In judging the descendants of the patriarchs and matriarchs, God promised, in making the covenant, recognition of the meritorious deeds of the ancestors. The conquest of the land and inheriting it are marks of the covenant, which Israel will find easy because of God's favor. The inheritance of the land is a mark of merit, inherited from the ancestors. The land is higher than all others and more choice. All religious duties are important, those that seem trivial as much as those held to be weightier.

God always loves Israel. That is why Israel should carry out the religious duties of the Torah with full assent. All religious duties are equally precious. Israel must be wholehearted in its relationship with God. If it is, then its share is with God, and if not, then not. But Israel may hate God. The right attitude toward God is love, and Israel should love God with a whole heart. The reason that Israel rebels against God is prosperity. Then people become arrogant and believe that their prosperity derives from their own efforts. But that is not so, and God punishes people who rebel to show them that they depend upon God. When Israel practices idolatry, God punishes it, e.g., through exile, through famine, through drought, and the like. Whether or not Israel knows or likes the fact, it is the fact that Israel therefore has no choice but to accept God's will and fulfill the covenant.

The heaven and the earth respond to the condition of Israel and therefore carry out the stipulations of the covenant. If Israel does not carry out religious duties concerning heaven, then heaven bears witness against it. That centers on the Land of Israel in particular. Possession of the land is conditional, not absolute. It begins with grace, not merit. It is defined by the stipulation that Israel observe the covenant, in which case Israel will retain the land. If Israel violates the covenant, Israel will lose the land. When Israel inherits the land, in obedience to the covenant and as an act of grace bestowed by God, it will build the Temple, where Israel's sins will find atonement. The conquest of the land itself is subject to stipulations, just as possession of the land, as an act of God's grace, is marked by religious obligations. If Israel rebels or rejects the Torah, it will lose the land, just as the Canaanites did for their idolatry.

The land is not the only, or the most important, mark of the covenant. It is the fact that Israel has the Torah which shows that Israel stands in a special relationship to God. The Torah is the source of life for Israel. It belongs to everyone, not only the aristocracy. Children should start studying the Torah at the earliest age possible. The study of the Torah is part of the fulfillment of the covenant. Even the most arid details of the Torah contain lessons, and if one studies the Torah, the reward comes both in this world and in the world to come.

The possession of the Torah imposes a particular requirement, involving an action. The most important task of every male Israelite is to study the Torah, which involves memorizing, and not forgetting, each lesson. This must go on every day and all the time. Study of the Torah should be one's main obligation, prior to all others. The correct motive is not for the sake of gain, but for the love of God and the desire for knowledge of God's will. People must direct heart, eyes, ears to teachings of the Torah. Study of the Torah transforms human relationships, so that strangers become the children of the master of the Torah whom they serve as disciples. However unimportant the teaching or the teacher, all is as if on the authority of Moses at Sinai. When a person departs from the Torah, that person becomes an idolator. Study of the Torah prevents idolatry.

ISRAEL AND THE NATIONS: THE MEANING OF HISTORY: The covenant, through the Torah of Sinai, governs not only the ongoing life of Israel but also the state of human affairs universally. The history of Israel forms a single, continuous cycle, in that what happened in the beginning prefigures what will happen at the end of time. Events of Genesis are re-enacted both in middle history, between the beginning and the end, and also at the end of times. So the traits of the tribal founders dictated the history of their families to both the here and now and also the eschatological age. Moses was shown the whole of Israel's history, past, present, future. The times of the patriarchs are re-enacted in the messianic day. That shows how Israel's history runs in cycles, so that events of ancient times prefigure events now. The prophets, beginning with Moses, describe those cycles. What happens bears close ties to what is going to happen. The prophetic promises too were realized in Temple times, and will be realized at the end of time.

The periods in the history of Israel, marked by the exodus and wandering, the inheritance of the land and the building of the Temple, the destruction, are all part of a divine plan. In this age Rome rules, but in the age to come, marked by the study of the Torah and the offering of sacrifices in the Temple cult, Israel will be in charge. That is the fundamental pattern and meaning of history. The Holy Spirit makes possible actions that bear consequences only much later in time. The prefiguring of history forms the dominant motif in Israel's contemporary life, and the re-enacting of what has already been forms a constant. Israel therefore should believe, if not in what is coming, then in what has already been. The very names of places in the land attest to the continuity of Israel's history, which follows rules that do not change. The main point is that while Israel will be punished in the worst possible way, Israel will not be wiped out.

But the cyclical character of Israel's history should not mislead. Events follow a pattern, but knowledge of that pattern, which is provided by the Torah, permits Israel both to understand and to affect its own destiny. Specifically, Israel controls its own destiny through its conduct with God. Israel's history is the working out of the effects of Israel's conduct, moderated by the merit of the ancestors. Abraham effected a change in God's relationship to the world. But merit, which makes history, is attained by one's own deeds as well. The effect of merit, in the nation's standing among the other nations, is simple. When Israel enjoys merit, it gives testimony against itself, but when not, then the most despised nation testifies against it.

But God is with Israel in time of trouble. When Israel sins, it suffers. When it repents and is forgiven, it is redeemed. For example, Israel's wandering in the wilderness took place because of the failure of Israel to attain merit. Sin is what causes the wandering in the wilderness. People rebel because they are prosperous. The merit of the ancestors works in history to Israel's benefit. What Israel does not merit on its own, at a given time, the merit of the ancestors may secure in any event. The best way to deal with Israel's powerlessness is through Torah study; the vigor of engagement with Torah study compensates for weakness.

It goes without saying that Israel's history follows a set time, e.g., at the fulfillment of a set period of time, an awaited event will take place. The prophets prophesy concerning the coming of the day of the Lord. Accordingly, nothing is haphazard, and all things happen in accord with a plan. That plan encompasses this world, the time of the Messiah, and the world to come, in that order. God will personally exact vengeance at the end of time. God also will raise the dead. Israel has overcome difficult times and can continue to do so. The task ahead is easier than the tasks already accomplished. Israel's punishment is only once, while the punishment coming upon the nations is unremitting. Peace is worthwhile and everyone needs it. Israel's history ends in the world to come or in the days of the Messiah. The righteous inherit the Garden of Eden. The righteous in the age to come will be joyful.

God acts in history and does so publicly, in full light of day. That is to show the nations who is in charge. The Torah is what distinguishes Israel from the nations. All the nations had every opportunity to understand and accept the Torah, and all declined it; that is why Israel was selected. And that demonstrates the importance of both covenant and the Torah, the medium of the covenant. The nations even had a prophet, comparable to Moses, who was Balaam. The nations have no important role in history, except as God assigns them a role in relationship to Israel's conduct. The nations are estranged from God by idolatry. That is what prevents goodness from coming into the world. The name of God rests upon Israel in greatest measure. Idolators do not control heaven. The greatest sin an Israelite can commit is idolatry, and those who entice Israel to idolatry are deprived of the ordinary protections of the law. God is violently angry at the nations because of idolatry. As to the nations' relationships with Israel, they are guided by Israel's condition. When Israel is weak, the nations take advantage, when strong, they are sycophantic. God did not apportion love to the nations of the world as he did to Israel.

ISRAEL AT HOME: THE COMMUNITY AND ITS GOVERNANCE: A mark of God's favor is that Israel has (or, has had and will have) a government of its own. Part of the covenantal relationship requires Israel to follow leaders whom God has chosen and instructed, such as Moses and the prophets. Accordingly, Israel is to establish a government and follow sound public policy. Its leaders are chosen by God. Israel's leaders, e.g., prophets, are God's servants, and that is a mark of the praise that is owing to them. They are to be in the model of Moses, humble, choice, select, well-known. Moses was the right one to bestow a blessing, Israel's people were the right ones to receive the blessing.

Yet all leaders are mortal; even Moses died. The saints are leaders ready to give their lives for Israel. The greatest of them enjoy exceptionally long life. But the sins of the people are blamed on their leaders. The leaders depend on the people to keep the Torah, and Moses thanked them in advance for keeping the Torah after he died. The leaders were to be patient and honest, to give a full hearing to all sides, to make just decisions, in a broad range of matters. To stand before the judge is to stand before God. God makes sure that Israel does not lack for leadership. The basic task of the leader is both to rebuke and also to console the people.

The rulers of Israel are servants of God. The prophets exemplify these leaders, in the model of Moses, and Israel's rulers act only on the instruction of prophets. Their authority rests solely on God's favor and grace. At the instance of God, the leaders of Israel speak, in particular, words of admonition. These are delivered before death, when the whole picture is clear, so that people can draw the necessary conclusions. These words, when Moses spoke them, covered the entire history of the community of Israel. The leaders of Israel address admonition to the entire community at once. No one is excepted. But the Israelites can deal with the admonition. They draw the correct conclusions. Repentance overcomes sin, as at the sin of the golden calf. The Israelites were contentious, nitpickers, and litigious, and, in general, they gave Moses a difficult time. Their descendants should learn not to do so. Israel should remain united and obedient to its leaders. The task of the community is to remain united. When the Israelites are of one opinion below, God's name is glorified above.

THE LAWS AND LAW: THE STRUCTURE OF INTELLECT: The explicit propositional program of our document is joined by a set of implicit ones. These comprise repeated demonstration of a point never fully stated. The implicit propositions have to do with the modes of correct analysis and inquiry that pertain to the Torah. There are two implicit propositions that predominate. The first, familiar (as I shall show presently) from other compilations, is that pure reason does not suffice to produce reliable results. Only through linking our conclusions to verses of Scripture may we come to final and fixed conclusions. The implicit proposition, demonstrated many times, may therefore be stated very simply. The Torah (written) is the sole source of reliable information. Reason undisciplined by the Torah yields unreliable results.

The second of the two recurrent modes of thought is the more important. Indeed, we shall presently note that it constitutes the one substantial, distinctive statement made by our authorship. It is the demonstration that many things conform to a single structure and pattern. We can show this uniformity of the law by addressing the same questions to disparate cases and, in so doing, composing general laws that transcend cases and form a cogent system. What is striking, then, is the power of a single set of questions to reshape and reorganize diverse data into a single cogent set of questions and answers, all things fitting together into a single, remarkably well-composed structure. Not only so, but when we review the numerous passages at which we find what in the logical repertoire I called methodical-analytical logic, we find a single program. It is an effort to ask whether a case of Scripture imposes a rule that limits or imparts a rule that augments the application of the law at hand.

A systematic reading of Scripture permits us to restrict or to extend the applicability of the detail of a case into a rule that governs many cases. A standard repertoire of questions may be addressed to a variety of topics, to yield the picture of how a great many things make essentially a single statement. This seems to me the single most common topical inquiry in our document. It covers most of the laws of Deut. 12–26. I have not cataloged the laws of history, which generalize from a case and tell us how things always must be; the list of explicit statements of the proposition that the case at hand is subject to either restriction or augmentation, that the law prevailing throughout is limited to the facts at hand or exemplified by those facts, would considerably add to this list. The size, the repetitious quality, the obsessive interest in augmentation and restriction, generalization and limitation—these traits of logic and their concomitant propositional results form the centerpiece of the whole.

In a few units of thought I discern no distinctive message, one that correlates with others to form a proposition of broad implications. Perhaps others can see points that transcend the cases at hand. These items would correspond to ones we should expect from an authorship that remained wholly within Scripture's range of discourse, proposing only to expand and clarify what it found within Scripture. Were our document to comprise only a commentary, then the messages of Scripture, delivered within the documentary limits of Scripture—that is, verse by verse, in a sustained statement solely of what Scripture says restated in paraphrase— would constitute the whole of the catalog of this chapter. We now see that that is far from the fact. Relative to the size of the document as a whole, these items do not seem to me to comprise an important component of the whole. They show that had our authorship wished only to amplify and restate the given, without presenting their own thought through the medium of Scripture (as through other media), they had every occasion and means of doing so. But they did so only in a limited measure.

6.

A SAMPLE PASSAGE

SIFRÉ TO DEUTERONOMY PISQA I:I

1. A. "These are the words that Moses spoke to all Israel in Transjordan, in the wilderness, that is to say in the Arabah, opposite Suph, be-

tween Paran on the one side and Tophel, Laban, Hazeroth, and Dizahab, on the other" (Dt. 1:1):

B. ["These are the words that Moses spoke" (Dt. 1:1):] Did Moses
prophesy only these alone? Did he not write the entire Torah?

C. For it is said, "And Moses wrote this Torah" (Dt. 31:9).

D. Why then does Scripture say, "These are the words that Moses
spoke" (Dt. 1:1)?

E. It teaches that [when Scripture speaks of the words that one spoke,
it refers in particular to] the words of admonition.

F. So it is said [by Moses], "But Jeshurun waxed fat and kicked" (Dt.
32:15).

2. A. So too you may point to the following:

B. "The words of Amos, who was among the herdmen of Tekoa, which
he saw concerning Israel in the days of Uzziah, king of Judah, and in
the days of Jeroboam, son of Joash, king of Israel, two years before
the earthquake" (Amos 1:1):

C. Did Amos prophesy only concerning these [kings] alone? Did he not
prophesy concerning a greater number [of kings] than any other?

D. Why then does Scripture say, "These are the words of Amos, [who
was among the herdmen of Tekoa, which he saw concerning Israel
in the days of Uzziah, king of Judah, and in the days of Jeroboam, son
of Joash, king of Israel, two years before the earthquake]" (Amos 1:1)

E. It teaches that [when Scripture speaks of the words that one spoke,
it refers in particular to] the words of admonition.

F. And how do we know that they were words of admonition?

G. As it is said, "Hear this word, you cows of Bashan, who are in the
mountain of Samaria, who oppress the poor, crush the needy, and
say to their husbands, 'Bring, that we may feast'" (Amos 4:1).

H. ["And say to their husbands, 'Bring, that we may feast'"] speaks of
their courts [of justice].

3. A. So too you may point to the following:

B. "And these are the words that the Lord spoke concerning Israel and
Judah" (Jer. 30:4).

C. Did Jeremiah prophesy only these words of prophecy alone? Did he
not write two [complete] scrolls?

D. For it is said, "Thus far are the words of Jeremiah" (Jer. 51:64)

E. Why then does Scripture say, "And these are the words [that the Lord
spoke concerning Israel and Judah]" (Jer. 30:4)?

F. It teaches that [when the verse says, "And these are the words that
the Lord spoke concerning Israel and Judah" (Jer. 30:4)], it speaks in
particular of the words of admonition.

G. And how do we know that they were words of admonition?

H. In accord with this verse: "For thus says the Lord, 'We have heard a voice of trembling, of fear and not of peace. Ask you now and see whether a man does labor with a child? Why do I see every man with his hands on his loins, as a woman in labor? and all faces turn pale? Alas, for the day is great, there is none like it, and it is a time of trouble for Jacob, but out of it he shall be saved" (Jer. 30:5–7).

4.   A.   So too you may point to the following:

    B.   "And these are the last words of David" (2 Sam. 23:1).

    C.   And did David prophesy only these alone? And has it furthermore not been said, "The spirit of the Lord spoke through me, and his word was on my tongue" (2 Sam. 23:2)?

    D.   Why then does it say, "And these are the last words of David" (2 Sam. 23:1)?

    E.   It teaches that [when the verse says, "And these are the last words of David" (2 Sam. 23:1)], it refers to words of admonition.

    F.   And how do we know that they were words of admonition?

    G.   In accord with this verse: "But the ungodly are as thorns thrust away, all of them, for they cannot be taken with the hand" (2 Sam. 23:6).

5.   A.   So too you may point to the following:

    B.   "The words of Qohelet, son of David, king in Jerusalem" (Qoh. 1:1).

    C.   Now did Solomon prophesy only these words? Did he not write three and a half scrolls of his wisdom in proverbs?

    D.   Why then does it say, "The words of Qohelet, son of David, king in Jerusalem" (Qoh. 1:1)?

    E.   It teaches that [when the verse says, "The words of Qohelet, son of David, king in Jerusalem" (Qoh. 1:1)], it refers to words of admonition.

    F.   And how do we know that they were words of admonition?

    G.   In accord with this verse: "The sun also rises, and the sun goes down . . . the wind goes toward the south and turns around to the north, it turns round continually in its circuit, and the wind returns again— that is, east and west [to its circuits. All the rivers run into the sea]" (Qoh. 1:5–7).

    H.   [Solomon] calls sun, moon, and sea "the wicked" for [the wicked] have no reward [coming back to them].

The focus is upon the exegesis of the opening word of Deuteronomy, "words. . . ." The problem is carefully stated. And yet without the arrangement within what is going to be a commentary on Deuteronomy, we should have no reason to regard the composition as exegetical at all. In fact, it is a syllogism, aiming at proving a particular proposition concerning word usages. Standing by itself, what we have is simply a very carefully formalized syllogism that makes a philological point, which is that the word "words of . . ." bears the sense of "admonition" or "rebuke." Five proofs are offered. We know that we reach the end of the exposition when, at

5.H, there is a minor gloss, breaking the perfect form. That is a common mode of signaling the conclusion of discourse on a given point.

SIFRÉ TO DEUTERONOMY PISQA I:II

1. A. ". . . to all Israel":
   B. [Moses spoke to the entire community all at once, for] had he admonished only part of them, those who were out at the market would have said, "Is this what you heard from the son of Amram? And did you not give him such-and-such an answer? If we had been there, we should have answered him four or five times for every word he said!"
2. A. Another matter concerning ". . . to all Israel]":
   B. This teaches that Moses collected all of them together, from the greatest to the least of them, and he said to them, "Lo, I shall admonish you. Whoever has an answer—let him come and say it."

We proceed to the next word in the base verse, but now our comment is particular to the verse. The explanation of why Moses spoke to everyone is then clear. On the one hand, it was to make certain that there was no one left out, so No. 1. On the other, it was to make certain that everyone had a say, so No. 2. These two points then complement one another.

SIFRÉ TO DEUTERONOMY PISQA I:III

1. A. Another matter concerning ". . . to all Israel":
   B. This teaches that all of them were subject to admonition but quite able to deal with the admonition.
2. A. Said R. Tarfon, "By the Temple service! [I do not believe] that there is anyone in this generation who can administer an admonition."
   B. Said R. Eleazar ben Azariah, "By the Temple service! [I do not believe] that there is anyone in this generation who can accept admonition."
   C. Said R. Aqiba, "By the Temple service! [I do not believe] that there is anyone in this generation who knows how to give an admonition."
   D. Said R. Yohanan ben Nuri, "I call to give testimony against me heaven and earth [if it is not the case that] more than five times was R. Aqiba criticized before Rabban Gamaliel in Yavneh, for I would lay complaints against him, and [Gamaliel therefore] criticized him. Nonetheless, I know that [each such criticism] added to [Aqiba's] love for me.
   E. "This carries out the verse, 'Do not criticize a scorner, lest he hate you, but reprove a wise person, and he will love you' (Prov. 9:8)."

Nos. I:III.1 and I:III.2 are quite separate units of thought, each making its own point. Shall we say that all we have, at I:I–III, is a sequence of three quite disparate propositions? In that case, the authorship before us has presented nothing more than a scrapbook of relevant comments on discrete clauses. I think otherwise. It seems to me that in I:I–III as the distinct and complete units of thought unfold we have a proposition, fully exposed, composed by the setting forth of two distinct facts, which serve as established propositions to yield the syllogism of I:III. But the syllogism is not made explicitly, rather it is placed on display by the (mere) juxtaposition of **I:I** and **I:II** and then the final proposition, I:III.1, followed by a story making the same point as the proposition. The exegesis now joins the (established) facts (1) that Moses rebuked Israel and (2) that all Israel was involved. The point is (3) that Israel was able to deal with the admonition and did not reject it. No. 2 then contains a story that makes explicit and underlines the virtue spun out of the verse. Aqiba embodies that virtue, the capacity—the wisdom—to accept rebuke. The upshot, then, is that the authorship wished to make a single point in assembling into a single carefully ordered sequence I:I–III, and it did so by presenting two distinct propositions, at I:I, I:II, and then, at I:III, recast the whole by making a point drawing upon the two original, autonomous proofs. Joining I:I and I:II then led directly to the proposition at which the authorship was aiming. We have much more than an assembly of information on diverse traits or points of verses, read word by word. It is, rather, a purposeful composition, made up of what clearly are already available materials.

SIFRÉ TO DEUTERONOMY PISQA I:IV

1. A. "On the other side of the Jordan" (Dt. 1:1):
   B. This teaches that he admonished them concerning things that they had done on the other side of the Jordan.

I:V

1. A. "In the wilderness" (Dt. 1:1):
   B. This teaches that he admonished them concerning things that they had done in the wilderness.
2. A. Another matter concerning "In the wilderness" (Dt. 1:1):
   B. This teaches that they would take their little sons and daughters and toss them into Moses' bosom and say to him, "Son of Amram, what ration have you prepared for these? What living have you prepared for these?"
   C. R. Judah says, "Lo, Scripture says [to make this same point], 'And the children of Israel said to them, "Would that we had died by the hand of the Lord in the land of Egypt [when we sat by the fleshpots, when we ate bread . . . for you have brought us forth to this wilderness to kill the whole assembly with hunger]" (Ex. 16:3).'"

3. A. Another matter concerning "In the wilderness" (Dt. 1:1):

   B. This encompasses everything that they had done in the wilderness.

SIFRÉ TO DEUTERONOMY PISQA I:VI

1. A. "In the Plain" (Dt. 1:1):

   B. This teaches that he admonished them concerning things that they had done in the Plains of Moab.

   C. So Scripture says, "And Israel dwelt in Shittim [and the people began to commit harlotry with the daughters of Moab" (Num. 25:1).

SIFRÉ TO DEUTERONOMY PISQA I:VII

1. A. "Over against Suph [the sea]" (Dt. 1:1):

   B. This teaches that he admonished them concerning things that they had done at the sea.

   C. For they rebelled at the sea and turned their back on Moses' days.

2. A. R. Judah says, "They rebelled at the sea, and they rebelled within the sea.

   B. "And so Scripture says, 'They rebelled at the sea, even in the sea itself' (Psa. 106:7)."

3. A. Is it possible to suppose that he admonished them only at the outset of a journey? How do we know that he did so between one journey and the next?

   B. Scripture says, "Between Paran and Tophel" (Dt. 1:1).

4. A. "Between Paran and Tophel" (Dt. 1:1):

   B. [The word "Tophel" bears the sense of] disparaging words with which they disparaged the manna.

   C. And so does Scripture say, "And our soul loathed this light bread" (Num. 21:5).

   D. [God] said to them, "Fools! Even royalty choose for themselves only light bread, so that none of them should suffer from vomiting or diarrhea. For your part, against that very act of kindness that I have done for you, you bring complaints before me.

   E. "It is only that you continue to walk in the foolishness of your father, for I said, 'I will make a helpmeet for him' (Gen. 2:18), while he said, 'The woman whom you gave to be with me gave me of the tree and I ate' (Gen. 3:12)."

The words of admonition, now fully exposed, apply to a variety of actions of the people. That is the main point of I:IV–VII. The matter is stated in a simple way at I:IV, I.V.1 (with an illustration at I:V.2), I:V.3, I:VI, I:VII. After the five illustrations of the proposition that the admonition covered the entire past, we proceed to a secondary expansion, I:VII.2, 3, which itself is amplified at I:VII.4.

The main structure is clear, and the proposition is continuous with the one with which we began: Moses admonished Israel, all Israel, which could take the criticism, and covered the entire list of areas where it had sinned, which then accounts for the specification of the various locations mentioned by Dt. 1:1. When we realize what is to come, we understand the full power of the proposition, which is syllogistic though in exegetical form. It is to indicate the character and encompassing program of the book of Deuteronomy—nothing less.

SIFRÉ TO DEUTERONOMY PISQA I:VIII

1. A. "And Hazeroth" (Dt. 1:1):
   B. [God] said to them, "Ought you not to have learned from what I did to Miriam in Hazeroth?
   C. "If to that righteous woman, Miriam, I did not show favor in judgment, all the more so to other people!"
2. A. Another matter: now if Miriam, who gossiped only against her brother, who was younger than herself, was punished in this way, one who gossips against someone greater than himself all the more so!
3. A. Another matter: Now if Miriam, whom when she spoke, no person heard, but only the Omnipresent alone, in line with this verse, "And the Lord heard . . . ," (Num. 12:2), was punished, one who speaks ill of his fellow in public all the more so!

The basic point is made at the outset and the case is then amplified. The sin concerning which Moses now admonished the people was that of gossiping, and the connection to Miriam is explicit. The argument that each place-name concerns a particular sin thus is carried forward. The entire discourse exhibits remarkable cogency.

SIFRÉ TO DEUTERONOMY PISQA I:IX

1. A. "And Dizahab" (Dt. 1:1):
   B. [Since the place-name means, "of gold," what he was] saying to them [was this:] "Lo, [following Finkelstein's text and comment] everything you did is forgiven. But the deed concerning the [golden] calf is worst of them all." [Hammer: "I would have overlooked everything that you have done, but the incident of the golden calf is to me worse than all the rest put together."]
2. A. R. Judah would say, "There is a parable. To what may the case be compared? To one who made a lot of trouble for his fellow. In the end he added yet another. He said to him, 'Lo, everything you did is forgiven. But this is the worst of them all.'
   B. "So said the Omnipresent to Israel, 'Lo, everything you did is for-

given. But the deed concerning the [golden] calf is worst of them all.'"

The place-name calls to mind the sin of the golden calf. This is made explicit as a generalization at No. 1, and then, No. 2, Judah restates the matter as a story.

SIFRÉ TO DEUTERONOMY PISQA I:X

1. A. R. Simeon says, "There is a parable. To what may the case [of Israel's making the calf of gold] be compared? To one who extended hospitality to sages and their disciples, and everyone praised him.
   B. "Gentiles came, and he extended hospitality to them. Thieves came and he extended hospitality to them.
   C. "People said, 'That is so-and-so's nature—to extend hospitality [indiscriminately] to anyone at all.'
   D. "So did Moses say to Israel, '[*Di zahab,* meaning "enough gold," yields the sense] there is enough gold for the tabernacle, enough gold also for the calf!'"
2. A. R. Benaiah says, "The Israelites have worshiped idolatry. Lo, they are liable to extermination. Let the gold of the tabernacle come and effect atonement for the gold of the calf."
3. A. R. Yosé b. Haninah says, "'And you shall make an ark cover of pure gold' (Ex. 25:17).
   B. "Let the gold of the ark cover come and effect atonement for the gold of the calf."
4. A. R. Judah says, "Lo, Scripture states, 'In the wilderness, in the plain.'
   B. "These are the ten trials that our fathers inflicted upon the Omnipresent in the wilderness.
   C. "And these are they: two at the sea, two involving water, two involving manna, two involving quails, one involving the calf, and one involving the spies in the wilderness."
   D. Said to him R. Yosé b. Dormasqit, "Judah, my honored friend, why do you distort verses of Scripture for us? I call to testify against me heaven and earth that we have made the circuit of all of these places, and each of the places is called only on account of an event that took place there [and not, as you say, to call to mind Israel's sin].
   E. "And so Scripture says, 'And the herdsmen of Gerar strove with the herdsmen of Isaac, saying, "The water is ours." And he called the name of the well Esek, because they contended with him' (Gen. 26:29). 'And he called it Shibah' (Gen. 26:33)."

I:X.1–3 carries forward the matter of Dizahab and amplifies upon the theme, not the proposition at hand. No. 4 then presents a striking restatement of the basic proposition, which has been spelled out and restated in so many ways. It turns out that Judah takes the position implicit throughout and made explicit at I:X.4. There is then a contrary position, at D. We see, therefore, how the framers have drawn upon diverse materials to present a single, cogent syllogism, the one then stated in most succinct form by Judah. The contrary syllogism, that of Yosé, is not spelled out, since amplification is hardly possible. Once we maintain that each place has meaning only for what happened in that particular spot, the verse no longer bears the deeper meaning announced at the outset—admonition or rebuke, specifically for actions that took place in various settings and that are called to mind by the list of words (no longer place-names) of Dt. 1:1.

SIFRÉ TO DEUTERONOMY PISQA I:XI

1. A. Along these same lines [of dispute between Judah and Yosé:]
   B. R. Judah expounded, "'The burden of the word of the Lord. In the land of Hadrach, and in Damascus, shall be his resting place, for the Lord's is the eye of man and all the tribes of Israel' (Zech. 9:1):
   C. "[Hadrach] refers to the Messiah, who is sharp [*hard*] toward the nations, but soft [*rakh*] toward Israel."
   D. Said to him R. Yosé b. Dormasqit, "Judah, my honored friend, why do you distort verses of Scripture for us? I call to testify against me heaven and earth that I come from Damascus, and there is a place there that is called Hadrach."
   E. He said to him, "How do you interpret the clause, 'and in Damascus, shall be his resting place'?"
   F. [Yosé] said to him, "How do we know that Jerusalem is destined to touch the city-limits of Damascus? As it is said, 'and in Damascus, shall be his resting place. And 'resting place' refers only to Jerusalem, as it is said, 'This is my resting place forever' (Ps. 132:14)."
   G. [Judah] said to him, "How then do you interpret the verse, 'And the city shall be built upon its own mound' (Jer. 30:18)?"
   H. [Yosé] said to him, "That it is not destined to be moved from its place."
   I. [Yosé continued,] saying to him, "How do I interpret the verse, 'And the side chambers were broader as they wound about higher and higher; for the winding about of the house went higher and higher round about the house, therefore the breadth of the house continued upward' (Ez. 41:7)? It is that the Land of Israel is destined to expand outward on all sides like a fig tree that is narrow below and broad above. So the gates of Jerusalem are destined to reach Damascus.
   J. "And so too Scripture says, 'Your nose is like the tower of Lebanon, which looks toward Damascus' (Song 7:5).
   K. "And the exiles will come and encamp in it, as it is said, 'And in Damascus shall be his resting place' (Zech. 9:1).

L.   "'And it shall come to pass in the end of days that the mountain of
the Lord's house shall be established at the top of the mountains and
shall be exalted above the hills, and all nations shall flow into it, and
many peoples shall go and say . . .' (Is. 2:2–3)."

SIFRÉ TO DEUTERONOMY PISQA I:XII

1. A.   Along these same lines [of dispute between Judah and Yosé:]
    B.   R. Judah expounded, "'And he made him to ride in the second char-
iot which he had, and they cried before him, "Abrech"' (Gen.
41:43):
    C.   "[Abrech] refers to Joseph, who is a father [*ab*] in wisdom, but soft
[*rakh*] in years."
    D.   Said to him R. Yosé b. Dormasqit, "Judah, my honored friend, why
do you distort verses of Scripture for us? I call to testify against me
heaven and earth that the meaning of Abrech pertains to knees and
is simply, 'I shall cause them to bend their knees' [appealing to the
causative applied to the root for "knee"].
    E.   "For everyone came and went under his authority, as Scripture says,
'And they set him over all of Egypt' (Gen. 41:43)."

I:XI–XII simply lay out further instances of the same hermeneutical dispute
between Judah and Yosé. All three items—I:X–XII—form a single cogent dispute
on its own terms. Then the composite establishes a distinct statement, which concerns figurative, as against literal, interpretation. The whole found an appropriate
place here, at I:X.4.

B

Philosophical Discourse:
From Exegesis to Proposition

XIV

Genesis Rabbah

1.

Identifying the Document

WHILE MEKHILTA ATTRIBUTED TO R. ISHMAEL, SIFRA, AND SIFRÉ TO NUMBERS, LIKE the Mishnah, cover many topics and yield no prominent propositional program but only implicit principles of thought, the second set of Midrash compilations, produced in the fifth and early sixth centuries, which accompany the Talmud of the Land of Israel, form highly propositional statements. The first of the group, Genesis Rabbah,[1] makes the same point many times and sets forth a coherent and original account of the book of Genesis.[2] The next set, Leviticus Rabbah, Pesiqta

---

[1] The word *rabbah* means "great," so one may interpret the title of the compilation to mean "amplification of the book of Genesis." But that is only a suggestion.

[2] For further reading and bibliography on the topic of this chapter, see the following:

> Bowker, pp. 72–77: the homiletic Midrashim: a number of works which have made a collection of synagogue sermons; Midrash Rabbah (= Pentateuch, Song of Songs, Ruth, Lamentations, Ecclesiastes, and Esther), pp. 77–78. Genesis Rabbah, pp. 78–79.

> Moses D. Herr, "Genesis Rabbah," *Encyclopaedia Judaica* 7:399–401: the title, structure, language, redaction, later additions, editions; apparently edited at about the same time as the Talmud of the Land of Israel, not later than 425.

> Maccoby, pp. 226–29 (sample passage).

> Stemberger-Strack, pp. 300–08: the name, contents, and structure; sources of Genesis Rabbah;

deRab Kahana, and Pesiqta Rabbati,[3] provide well-argued syllogistic arguments, entirely leaving behind the structure of verse-by-verse exposition. Generally thought to have been closed ("redacted") at ca. 400–450 C.E., sometime after the Talmud of the Land of Israel had been redacted, Genesis Rabbah transforms the book of Genesis from a genealogy and family history of Abraham, Isaac, Jacob, then Joseph into a book of the laws of history and rules of the salvation of Israel: the deeds of the founders become omens and signs for the final generations.

The single most important proposition of the authorship[4] of Genesis Rabbah is that in the story of the beginnings of creation, humanity, and Israel, we find the message of the meaning and end of the life of the Jewish people in the here and now of the fifth century. The deeds of the founders supply signals for the children about what is going to come in the future. So the biography of Abraham, Isaac, and Jacob also constitutes a protracted account of the history of Israel later on.

Genesis Rabbah is a composite document. As with the Talmud that it accompanies, so in Genesis Rabbah, some of the material in the compilation can be shown to have been put together before that material was used for the purposes of the compilers. Many times a comment entirely apposite to a verse of Genesis has been joined to a set of comments in no way pertinent to the verse at hand. Proof for a given syllogism, furthermore, will derive from a verse of Genesis as well as from numerous verses of other books of the Bible. Such a syllogistic argument therefore has not been written for exegetical purposes particular to the verse at hand. On the contrary, the particular verse subject to attention serves that other, propositional plan; it is not the focus of discourse; it has not generated the comment but merely provided a proof for a syllogism. That is what it means to say that a proposition yields an exegesis. That fundamental proposition, displayed throughout Genesis Rabbah, which yields the specific exegeses of many of the verses of

---

redaction and date (after 400); the text: manuscripts, Genizah fragments, printed editions, translations, commentaries.

This writer's introductions to the document are in *Comparative Midrash: The Plan and Program of Genesis Rabbah and Leviticus Rabbah*. Atlanta, 1986: Scholars Press for Brown Judaic Studies; *Genesis and Judaism: The Perspective of Genesis Rabbah. An Analytical Anthology*. Atlanta, 1986: Scholars Press for Brown Judaic Studies; and *Confronting Creation: How Judaism Reads Genesis. An Anthology of Genesis Rabbah*. Columbia, 1991: University of South Carolina Press.

[3] *Pisqa* means "chapter," *pesiqta* being the plural; hence "chapters attributed to R. Kahana," and "amplified chapters" might serve to render these titles more accessible.

[4] Those responsible for compiling the compositions that are made into the composite document as a whole. Since some materials were formulated on their own, prior to inclusion in the document in which they are now located, we have to distinguish between the author of a composition, whole and complete in its own terms, and the authorship of a composite of such compositions. On the formation of compositions prior to their inclusion in composite documents, see my *Making the Classics in Judaism: The Three Stages of Literary Formation*. Atlanta, 1990: Scholars Press for Brown Judaic Studies; and on the distinction between composition and composite, note *The Rules of Composition of the Talmud of Babylonia. The Cogency of the Bavli's Composite*. Atlanta, 1991: Scholars Press for South Florida Studies in the History of Judaism.

the book of Genesis and even whole stories, is that the beginnings point toward the endings, and the meaning of Israel's past points toward the message that lies in Israel's future. The things that happened to the fathers and mothers of the family, Israel, provide a sign for the things that will happen to the children later on.

What is at stake is the discovery, among the facts provided by the written Torah, of the social rules that govern Israel's history. At stake is the search for the order yielded by the chaos of uninterpreted data. It follows that as with the Mishnah, the governing mode of thought is that of natural philosophy. It involves the classification of data by shared traits, yielding descriptive rules, the testing of propositions against the facts of data, the whole aimed at the discovery of underlying rules out of a multiplicity of details, in all, the proposing and testing, against the facts provided by Scripture, of the theses of Israel's salvation that demanded attention just then. But the issues were not so much philosophical as religious, in the sense that while philosophy addressed questions of nature and rules of enduring existence, religion asked about issues of history and God's intervention in time. Within that rough and ready distinction between nature, supernature, and sanctification, typified by the Mishnah and the Tosefta and the legal enterprise in general, on the one side, and society, history, and salvation, typified by Genesis Rabbah, Leviticus Rabbah, Pesiqta deRab Kahana, and the theological inquiry into teleology, on the other, we may distinguish our documents.

Specifically, we may classify the document before us and its successors and companions as works of profound theological inquiry into God's rules for history and society in the here and now and for salvation at the end of historical time. That fundamental proposition concerning the search, in the account of the beginnings, of the ending and meaning of Israel's society and history—hence the rules that govern and permit knowledge of what is to come—constitutes the generative proposition that yielded the specific exegesis of the book of Genesis in Genesis Rabbah.

Genesis Rabbah in its final form emerges from that momentous century in which the Roman Empire passed from pagan to Christian rule and in which, in the aftermath of Julian's abortive reversion to paganism, in ca. 360, which endangered the Christian character of the Roman Empire, Christianity adopted that politics of repression of paganism that rapidly engulfed Judaism as well. The issue confronting Israel in the Land of Israel therefore proved immediate: the meaning of the new and ominous turn of history, the implications of Christ's worldly triumph for the other-worldly and supernatural people, Israel, whom God chooses and loves. The message of the exegete-compositors addressed the circumstance of historical crisis and generated remarkable renewal, a rebirth of intellect in the encounter with Scripture, now in quest of the rules not of sanctification—these had already been found—but of salvation. So the book of Genesis, which portrays how all things had begun, would testify to the message and the method of the end: the coming salvation of patient, hopeful, enduring Israel.

That is why in the categories of philosophy, including science and society, and religion, including a prophetic interpretation of history and teleology, Genesis Rabbah presents a deeply *religious* view of Israel's historical and salvific life, in much the same way that the Mishnah provides a profoundly *philosophical* view of Israel's everyday and sanctified existence. Just as the main themes of the Mishnah evoke the consideration of issues of being and becoming, the potential and the actual, mixtures and blends, and other problems of physics, all in the interest of philosophical analysis, so Genesis Rabbah presents its cogent and coherent agendum as well. That program of inquiry concerns the way in which, in the book of Genesis, God set forth to Moses the entire scope and meaning of Israel's history among the nations and salvation at the end of days. The mode of thought by which the framers of Genesis Rabbah work out their propositions dictates the character of their exegesis, as to rhetoric, logical principle of cogent and intelligible discourse, and, as is clear, even as to topic.

In the view of the framers of the compilation, the entire narrative of Genesis is so formed as to point toward the sacred history of Israel, the Jewish people: its slavery and redemption; its coming Temple in Jerusalem; its exile and salvation at the end of time. In the reading of the authors at hand, therefore, the powerful message of Genesis proclaims that the world's creation commenced a single, straight line of events, leading in the end to the salvation of Israel and through Israel of all humanity. That message—that history heads toward Israel's salvation—the sages derived from the book of Genesis and contributed to their own day. Therefore in their reading of Scripture a given story will bear a deeper truth about what it means to be Israel, on the one side, and what in the end of days will happen to Israel, on the other. True, their reading makes no explicit reference to what, if anything, had changed in the age of Constantine. But we do find repeated references to the four kingdoms, Babylonia, Media, Greece, Rome—and beyond the fourth will come Israel, fifth and last. So sages' message, in their theology of history, was that the present anguish prefigured the coming vindication of God's people.

It follows that sages read Genesis as the history of the world with emphasis on Israel. So the lives portrayed, the domestic quarrels and petty conflicts with the neighbors, all serve to yield insight into what was to be. Why so? Because the deeds of the patriarchs taught lessons on how the children were to act, and, it further followed, the lives of the patriarchs signaled the history of Israel. Israel constituted one extended family, and the metaphor of the family, serving the nation as it did, imparted to the stories of Genesis the character of a family record. History become genealogy conveyed the message of salvation. These propositions really laid down the same judgment, one for the individual and the family, the other for the community and the nation, since there was no differentiating one from the other. Every detail of the narrative therefore served to prefigure what was to be, and Israel found itself, time and again, in the revealed facts of the history of the creation of the world, the decline of humanity down to the time of Noah, and, finally, its ascent to Abraham, Isaac, and Israel.

2.

TRANSLATIONS INTO ENGLISH

The first complete translation into English is H. Freedman and Maurice Simon, ed., *Midrash Rabbah. Translated into English. With Notes, Glossary, and Indices* (London, 1939: Soncino Press). I. *Genesis. In Two Volumes*. Translated by H. Freedman. The second, and the first form-analytical translation, is this writer's *Genesis Rabbah. The Judaic Commentary on Genesis. A New American Translation*. Atlanta, 1985: Scholars Press for Brown Judaic Studies. I. *Genesis Rabbah. The Judaic Commentary on Genesis. A New American Translation. Parashiyyot One through Thirty-Three. Genesis 1:1–8:14;* II. *Parashiyyot Thirty-Four through Sixty-Seven. Genesis 8:15–28:9;* and III. *Parashiyyot Sixty-Eight through One Hundred. Genesis 28:10–50;26.*

3.

RHETORIC

The document undertakes two tasks. First comes the exegesis of clauses of verses, read in sequence, just as we noted in Sifra and Sifré to Numbers. Second, a not-quite-fresh, but vigorous and now-fully-exploited, exegetical technique involves the introduction, at the beginning of a sustained composition, of a verse other than the one under analysis. That other verse intersects with the verse under discussion, and—as before, with Sifré to Numbers—the one is called the intersecting verse and the other the base verse. This formal arrangement of verses predominates from Genesis Rabbah forward. The power of this form—the juxtaposition of two verses, one derived from the document at hand, the other from some other document altogether—which will dominate from the present document (ca. 400–450 C.E.) onward, is simple. On the surface, the intersecting verse expands the frame of reference of the base verse, introducing data otherwise not present. But just beneath the surface lies the implicit premise: both the intersecting verse and the base verse make the same point, and, in their meeting, each rises out of its narrow framework as a detail or an instance of a rule and testifies to the larger picture, the encompassing rule itself. The intersecting-verse/base-verse construction therefore yields a proposition that transcends both verses and finds proof in the cases of each, and that powerful way of composing something new forms the centerpiece of the present document and the two that follow.

The reason that this rhetorical program—intersecting verse/base verse—serves so well derives from the program of the document. It is to demonstrate that there are reliable rules that govern Israel's history, specifically to discover and validate those fixed and governing rules within the details of stories of the origins of the family of Abraham, Isaac, and Jacob, which Israel now constitutes. A process of search for the governing laws of history and society requires not specific cases but general rules, and an inductive process will demand that sages generate rules out of cases. The meeting of rhetoric, logic, and topic takes place here. Putting together the cases represented by two verses, one deep within the narrative of Genesis, the other far distant from that narrative, the exegetes found it possible to state a case and along with the case to point toward an implicit generalization yielded by the two or more cases at hand. The rhetoric involves the recurrent arrangement of verses; the logic, the inquiry into the general rule that holds together two cases and makes of them a single statement of an overriding law; and the topic, the direction of the history of Israel, specifically, its ultimate salvation at the end of time.

The first of the three forms of the document is the recurrent mode of organization, namely, the base-verse/intersecting-verse construction. In the sort of passage under discussion, (1) a verse of the book of Genesis will be followed by (2) a verse from some other book of the Hebrew Scriptures. The latter (2) will then be subjected to extensive discussion. But in the end the exposition of the intersecting verse will shed some light, in some way, upon (1) the base verse, cited at the outset. The second paramount form, which always follows in sequence as well, is the exegesis of a verse, which is familiar: a verse of the book of Genesis will be subjected to sustained analysis and amplification. But this analysis does not refer to some other intersecting verse. What we find instead are numerous proof texts, or there may be no proof texts at all. Finally, the syllogism form will cite a variety of verses, drawn from a broad range of books of the Hebrew Scriptures, ordinarily composed in a list of like grammatical and syntactical entries.

In the aggregate Genesis Rabbah conforms to two important literary patterns. First we are able to classify the bulk of its completed units of thought among three forms or patterns, as specified. Second, the formal types of units of discourse are arranged in accord with a single set of preferences, with the intersecting verse/base verse always standing at the head of a composite, followed by the exegetical form. Within the formal structures may be discerned miscellaneous material as well. Form I, for example, with its reference to an intersecting verse followed by its treatment of the base verse, not uncommonly carried in its wake materials of a formally quite miscellaneous character. Form II still more commonly permits characterization only in the simplest way: first comes the citation of a verse of the book of Genesis, then comes some sort of comment on that verse. Within the requirements of so simple a pattern, a variety of arrangements and formulations found ample place. Form III, to be sure, presents more striking formal traits, with its emphasis upon the construction of a list of facts to prove a given proposition. In the cases of Form II and Form III, the patterns find a place not in the center but at the edges of the compositions in which they occur.

These forms make only a superficial, external impact on the compositions in which they occur.

4.
LOGIC OF COHERENT DISCOURSE

Genesis Rabbah is made up of one hundred *parashiyyot* or chapters, and each *parashah* or chapter is comprised of from as few as five to as many as fifteen subdivisions. Genesis Rabbah is a huge document, probably five times larger than the book of Genesis itself. The hundred chapters' subdivisions in the main formed cogent statements. That is to say, words joined together to form autonomous statements, sentences. Sentences then coalesced into cogent propositions, paragraphs. Paragraphs then served a larger purpose, forming a cogent proposition of some sort. All together, therefore, discrete words turned into sentences, and sentences into whole thoughts, that we can discern and understand. The smallest whole units of thought of Genesis Rabbah contain cogent thought. We can discern the ideas presented in the composition at hand. The use of the word "composition" is justified: there is thought, in logical sequence, in proportion, in order, with a beginning, a middle, and an end. Genesis Rabbah, then, is composed of a long sequence of these smallest whole units of thought, strung together for some purpose or other.

What differentiates this document from its predecessors, as noted at the outset, is that these smallest whole units of discourse or thought join together for a larger purpose. The document intellectually is more than an anthology of discrete passages. How so? Among all the diverse smaller units of discourse, sayings, stories, exegeses of verses of Scripture, protracted proofs of a single proposition, and the like, ordinarily served a purpose cogent to the whole subdivision of a *parashah*. That is to say, whatever finished materials are present have been made by the compositors—the authorities who selected the smallest completed units of thought and arranged them as we now have them—to serve their goals, that is, the purposes of the compositors of the larger unit of thought of which the several smallest units of thought now form a part. That is why form analysis worked its way from the largest components of the document, the *parashiyyot,* to the next largest, and so on down.

The analysis of the logic of coherent discourse shows a kind of writing not apparent in rabbinic literature in prior documents. The coherence of the document derives from the program of the document as a whole, rather than from the joining of the smaller into the larger units of discourse and thought. True, we find compositions that present syllogistic arguments; we find passages joined by the teleological logic of narrative; and the compilation has its share of passages that hold together only through the logic of fixed association. But, overall, the document holds together through what we may call the governing purpose of the entire compilation, not only the sewing together of its components. What accomplishes the ultimate unification of the writing is that the framers of Genesis Rabbah wished to do two things:

First, they proposed to read the book of Genesis in light of other books of the Hebrew Scriptures, so underlining the unity of the Scriptures.

Second, they planned to read the book of Genesis phrase by phrase, so emphasizing the historical progression of the tale at hand, from verse to verse, from event to event.

So the book of Genesis now presents more than a single dimension. It tells the story of things that happened. The exegetes explain the meaning of these events, adding details and making explicit the implicit, unfolding message. Read from beginning to end, time in the beginning moved in an orderly progression. The book of Genesis also tells the laws that govern Israel's history. These laws apply at all times and under all circumstances. Facts of history, emerging at diverse times and under various circumstances, attest to uniform and simple laws of society and of history. That is why verses of Scripture originating here, there, everywhere, all serve equally well to demonstrate the underlying rules that govern. Read out of all historical sequence but rather as a set of exemplifications of recurrent laws, the stories of Genesis do not follow a given order, a single sequence of timely events. Time now moves in deep, not shallow, courses; time is cyclical, or, more really, time matters not at all. The long stretches of timeless rules take over. Sequential exegeses, citing and commenting on verses, classified as Form II, express the former of the two dimensions; and exercises in the clarification of a verse of Genesis through the message of a verse in another book of the Scriptures altogether, on the one side, and propositional or syllogistic compositions, on the other, Forms I and III, express the latter. The book of Genesis is made greater than its first reading would suggest. Hence, Genesis Rabbah, meaning (from a later angle of vision only) a greater conception of the book of Genesis, vastly expands the dimensions of the story of the creation of the world, humanity, and Israel. The document finds its coherence in the vast conception that it wishes to put forth.

5.

TOPICAL PROGRAM

In Genesis Rabbah the entire narrative of Genesis is so formed as to point toward the sacred history of Israel, the Jewish people: its slavery and redemption; its coming Temple in Jerusalem; its exile and salvation at the end of time. The powerful message of Genesis in Genesis Rabbah proclaims that the world's creation commenced a single, straight line of events, leading in the end to the salvation of Israel and, through Israel, all humanity. Israel's history constitutes the counterpart of creation, and the laws of Israel's salvation form the foundation of creation. Therefore a given story out of Genesis, about creation, events from Adam to Noah and Noah to Abraham, the domestic affairs of the patriarchs, or Joseph, will bear a deeper message about what it means to be Israel, on the one side, and what in the end of days will happen to Israel, on the other. So the persistent theological program requires sages to search in Scripture for meaning for their own circumstance and for the condition of their people. The single most important proposition of Genesis Rabbah is that in the story of the beginnings of creation, humanity, and Israel, we find the message of the meaning and end of the life of the Jewish people. The deeds of the founders supply signals for the children about what is going to come in the future. So the biography of Abraham, Isaac, and Jacob also constitutes a protracted account of the history of Israel later on. If the sages could announce a single syllogism and argue it systematically, that is the proposition upon which they would insist.

As a corollary to the view that the biography of the fathers prefigures the history of the descendants, sages maintained that the deeds of the children—the holy way of life of Israel—must follow the model established by the founders long ago. So they looked in Genesis for the basis for the things they held to be God's will for Israel. And they found ample proof. Sages invariably searched the stories of Genesis for evidence of the origins not only of creation and of Israel, but also of Israel's cosmic way of life, its understanding of how, in the passage of nature and the seasons, humanity worked out its relationship with God. The holy way of life that Israel lived through the seasons of nature therefore would make its mark upon the stories of the creation of the world and the beginning of Israel.

Part of the reason sages pursued the interest at hand derived from polemic. From the first Christian century theologians of Christianity maintained that salvation did not depend upon keeping the laws of the Torah. Abraham, after all, had been justified and he did not keep the Torah, which, in his day, had not yet been given. So sages time and again would maintain that Abraham indeed kept the entire Torah even before it had been revealed. They further attributed to Abraham, Isaac, and Jacob rules of the Torah enunciated only later on, for example, the institution of prayer three times a day. But the passage before us bears a different charge. It is to Israel to see how deeply embedded in the rules of reality were the patterns governing God's relationship to Israel. That relationship, one of human sin and atonement, divine punishment and forgiveness, expresses the most fundamental laws of human existence.

The world was created for Israel, and not for the nations of the world. At the end of days everyone will see what only Israel now knows. Since sages read Genesis as the history of the world with emphasis on Israel, the lives portrayed, the domestic quarrels and petty conflicts with the neighbors, as much as the story of creation itself, all serve to yield insight into what was to be. We now turn to a detailed examination of how sages spelled out the historical law at hand. The lives of the patriarchs signaled the history of Israel. Every detail of the narrative therefore served to prefigure what was to be, and Israel found itself, time and again, in the revealed facts of the history of the creation of the world, the decline of humanity down to the time of Noah, and, finally, its ascent to Abraham, Isaac, and Israel. In order to illustrate the single approach to diverse stories, whether concerning Creation, Adam, and Noah, or concerning Abraham, Isaac, and Jacob, we focus on two matters: Abraham, on the one side, and Rome, on the other. In the former we see that Abraham serves as well as Adam to prove the point of it all. In the latter we observe how, in reading Genesis, the sages who compiled Genesis Rabbah discovered the meaning of the events of their own day.

One rule of Israel's history is yielded by the facts at hand. Israel is never left without an appropriate hero or heroine. The relevance of the long discourse becomes clear at the end. Each story in Genesis may forecast the stages in Israel's history later on, beginning to end. A matter of deep concern focused sages' attention on the sequence of world empires to which, among other nations, Israel was subjugated: Babylonia, Media, Greece, and Rome—Rome above all. What will follow? Sages maintained that beyond the rule of Rome lay the salvation of Israel:

XLII:IV. 1. A. "And it came to pass in the days of Amraphel" (Gen. 14:1):

4. A. Another matter: "And it came to pass in the days of Amraphael, king of Shinar" (Gen. 14:1) refers to Babylonia.

B. "Arioch, king of Ellasar" (Gen. 14:1) refers to Greece.

C. "Chedorlaomer, king of Elam" (Gen. 14:1) refers to Media.

D. "And Tidal, king of Goiim [nations]" (Gen. 14:1) refers to the wicked government [Rome], which conscripts troops from all the nations of the world.

E. Said R. Eleazar bar Abina, "If you see that the nations contend with one another, look for the footsteps of the king-messiah. You may know that that is the case, for lo, in the time of Abraham, because the kings struggled with one another, a position of greatness came to Abraham."

Obviously, No. 4 presents the most important reading of Gen. 14:1, since it links the events of the life of Abraham to the history of Israel and even ties the whole to the messianic expectation. I suppose that any list of four kings will provoke inquiry into the relationship of the entries of that list to the four kingdoms among which history, in Israel's experience, is divided. The process of history flows in both directions. Just as what Abraham did prefigured the future history of Israel, so what the Israelites later on were to do imposed limitations on Abraham. Time and again events in the lives of the patriarchs prefigure the four monarchies, among which the fourth, last, and most intolerable was Rome.

Genesis is read as if it portrayed the history of Israel and Rome. For that is the single obsession binding sages of the document at hand to common discourse with the text before them. Why Rome in the form it takes in Genesis Rabbah? And how come the obsessive character of the sages' disposition of the theme of Rome? Were their picture merely of Rome as tyrant and destroyer of the Temple, we should have no reason to link the text to the problems of the age of redaction and closure. But now it is Rome as Israel's brother, counterpart, and nemesis, Rome as the one thing standing in the way of Israel's, and the world's, ultimate salvation. So the stakes are different, and much higher. It is not a political Rome but a Christian and messianic Rome that is at issue: Rome as surrogate for Israel, Rome as obstacle to Israel. Why? It is because Rome now confronts Israel with a crisis, and, I argue, the program of Genesis Rabbah constitutes a response to that crisis. Rome in the fourth century became Christian. Sages respond by facing that fact quite squarely and saying, "Indeed, it is as you say, a kind of Israel, an heir of Abraham as your texts explicitly claim. But we remain the sole legitimate Israel, the bearer of the birthright—we and not you. So you are our brother: Esau, Ishmael, Edom." And the rest follows.

By rereading the story of the beginnings, sages discovered the answer and the secret of the end. Rome claimed to be Israel, and, indeed, sages conceded, Rome shared the patrimony of Israel. That claim took the form of the Christians' appropriation of the Torah as "the Old Testament," so sages acknowledged a simple fact in acceding to the notion that in some way, Rome too formed part of Israel. But it was the rejected part, the Ishmael, the Esau, not the Isaac, not the Jacob. The advent of Christian Rome precipitated the sustained, polemical, and, I think, rigorous and well-argued rereading of beginnings in light of the end. Rome then marked the conclusion of human history as Israel had known it. Beyond? The coming of the true Messiah, the redemption of Israel, the salvation of the world, the end of time. So the issues were not inconsiderable, and when the sages spoke of Esau/Rome, as they did often, they confronted the life-or-death decision of the day.

We consider a single example of how ubiquitous is the shadow of Ishmael/Esau/Edom/Rome. Whenever sages reflect on future history, their minds turn to their own day. They found the hour difficult, because Rome, now Christian, claimed that very birthright and blessing that they understood to be theirs alone. Christian Rome posed a threat without precedent. Now another dominion, besides Israel's, claimed the rights and blessings that sustained Israel. Wherever in Scripture they turned, sages found comfort in the iteration that the birthright, the blessing, the Torah, and the hope—all belonged to them and to none other. As the several antagonists of Israel stand for Rome in particular, so the traits of Rome, as sages perceived them, characterized the Biblical heroes.

6.

A SAMPLE PASSAGE

GENESIS RABBAH *PARASHAH* SEVENTY
TO GENESIS 28:20–29:30

LXX:I. 1. A. "Then Jacob made a vow, saying, 'If God will be with me and will keep me in this way that I go and will give me bread to eat and clothing to wear, so that I come again to my father's house in peace, then the Lord shall be my God. And this stone, which I have set up for a pillar, shall be God's house; and of all that you give me, I will give the tenth to you'" (Gen. 28:20–22):

B. "I will perform for you my vows, which my lips have uttered and my mouth has spoken when I was in distress" (Ps. 66:13–14).

C. Said R. Isaac the Babylonian, "One who takes a vow carries out a religious duty [if he does so in time of stress]."

D. What is the meaning of the statement, "Then Jacob made a vow, saying"? "Saying" to the future generations, so that they too will take vows in a time of stress.

Here we see the working of the base-verse/intersecting-verse construction, and we can immediately explain the choice of the intersecting verse. What attracts the exegete's attention in Gen. 28:20 is the simple fact that Jacob has taken a vow, and the intersecting verse, Ps. 66:13–14, then underlines that fact. R. Isaac evaluates vow-taking, subjected to criticism, by saying that it can represent a meritorious action. Paragraph D repeats the basic syllogism of Genesis Rabbah: what the founders do, the children carry on, and what happens to the founders tells what will happen to the children, and, finally, the merit accumulated by the founders serves the children later on as their inheritance and source of protection. The amplification of the opening encounter of base verse and intersecting verse follows. This order—base verse, then intersecting verse—will be reversed in the later compilations, which will begin in the distant reaches of Scripture and only slowly and unpredictably recover the point articulated in what becomes the base verse.

2. A. Jacob was the first to take a vow, therefore whoever takes a vow should make it depend only upon him.

B. Said R. Abbahu, "It is written, *'How he swore to the Lord and vowed to the mighty one of Jacob'* (Ps. 132:2).

> C.   "What is written is not, 'how he [David] swore to the Lord and vowed to the mighty one of Abraham' or 'of Isaac,' but 'of Jacob.'"
>
> D.   "He made the vow depend upon the first person ever to take a vow."

The theme of the passage, taking vows, produces two important points. First is that of No. 1, that while vowing in general does not meet sages' approval, in times of stress it does, and Jacob is the example of that fact. Then, No. 2, Jacob is the one who started the practice of vowing, so Jacob is the one to whom vows are referred as in the cited passage. These two intersecting verses do not receive detailed exegesis on their own; they contribute themes and propositions. So the passage is not like those in which a long sequence of comments either brings the intersecting verse back to the base verse or reads the intersecting verse as an expression of the views of the principle of the base verse. Later on Jacob's failure to keep his vow in a prompt way elicits comment.

> LXX:II.   1.   A.   R. Yudan in the name of R. Idi: "It is written. *Then the people rejoiced, for they offered willingly. Wherefore David blessed the Lord before all the congregation, and David said, "Blessed be you, O Lord, the God of Israel our father"'* (1 Chr. 29:9–10).
>
> B.   "It was because they were engaged in carrying out religious duties that were acts of free will and that matters were successful that they rejoiced.
>
> C.   "What is the meaning of the statement, *'Wherefore David blessed the Lord before all the congregation, and David said, "Blessed be you, O Lord, the God of Israel our father"'*? Specifically, we note that what is written is not, 'the God *of Abraham, Isaac,* and Israel,' but only 'God of Israel'?
>
> D.   "He made the vow depend upon the first person ever to take a vow."
>
> E.   Said R. Yudan, "From the document at hand [the Torah, not merely the Writings] we do not lack further proof of that same fact. For example, *'And Israel vowed'* (Num. 21:2), meaning, our father, Israel.
>
> F.   *" 'Then Jacob made a vow.' "*

The same point now recurs, with a different set of proof texts. The rhetorically noteworthy point is at F: we revert to the base verse, and this will form a bridge to the systematic exposition of that base verse, which now begins.

LXX:III.   1.   A.   *"Then Jacob made a vow":*

B.   Four made a vow, two vowed and lost out, and two vowed and benefited.

C.   Israel took a vow and Hannah took a vow, and they benefited.

D.   Jephthah took a vow and lost out, Jacob took a vow and lost out. [Freedman, *Genesis Rabbah*, p. 637, n. 2: His (Jacob's) vow was superfluous, since he had already received God's promise and therefore he lost thereby.]

The fragmentary comment serves the purpose of removing the impression that the text of Scripture goes over the same ground twice and contradicts itself. This same problem will be solved in a different way in what follows. Since, as we know, the pentateuchal books, including Genesis, are composed of a number of prior strands, some of which go over the same ground two or more times, the text itself, read by sages as single, linear, and unitary, presents its own problems for sages' attention.

LXX:IV.   1.   A.   R. Aibu and R. Jonathan:

B.   One of them said, "The passage states matters out of the proper order."

C.   The other said, "The passage is entirely in the proper order."

D.   The one who has said, "The passage states matters out of the proper order" points to the following: *"And lo, I am with you"* (Gen. 28:15) contrasts to the statement, "Then Jacob made a vow, saying, *'If God will be with me.'"*

E.   The other who has said, "The passage is entirely in the proper order" has then to explain the statement, "If God will be with me" in light of the statement already at hand.

F.   His point is this: "If he will be with me" means "if all of the conditions that he has stipulated with me will be carried out," [then I will keep my vow].

2.   A.   R. Abbahu and rabbis:

B.   R. Abbahu said, "If God will be with me and will keep me in *'this way'* refers to protection from gossip, in line with this usage: *'And they turn their tongue in the way of slander* [Freedman, p. 637, n. 4], *their bow of falsehood'* (Jer. 9:2).

C.   "'. . . *will give me bread to eat'* refers to protection from fornication, in line with this usage: *'Neither has he kept* back anything from me, except the bread which he ate' (Gen. 39:9), a euphemism for sexual relations with his wife.

D. "'. . . so that I come again to my father's house in peace' refers to bloodshed.

E. "'. . . then the Lord shall be my God' so that I shall be protected from idolatry.'"

F. Rabbis interpreted the statement "*this way*" to speak of all of these.

G. [The rabbis' statement now follows:] "Specifically: '*If God will be with me and will keep me in this way that I go*' [by referring only to "way"] contains an allusion to idolatry, fornication, murder, and slander.

H. "'*Way*' refers to idolatry: '*They who swear by the sin of Samaria and say, As your god, O Dan, lives, and as the way of Beer sheba lives*' (Amos 8:14).

I. "'*Way*' refers to adultery: '*So is the way of an adulterous woman*' (Prov. 30:20).

J. "'*Way*' refers to murder: '*My son, do not walk in the way of them, restrain your foot from their path, for their feet run to evil and they make haste to shed blood*' (Prov. 1:15–16).

K. "'*Way*' refers to slander: '*And he heard the words of Laban's sons, saying, "Jacob has taken away [everything that belonged to our father]"*' (Gen. 31:1)."

No. 1 goes over the problem of the preceding and makes it explicit. No. 2 then subjects the verse to a close exegesis, with the standard repertoire of mortal sins—murder, fornication, slander—now read into the verse. Jacob asks God's protection to keep himself from sinning. That interpretation rehabilitates Jacob, since the picture in Scripture portrays a rather self-centered person, and now Jacob exhibits virtue.

LXX:V. 1. A. "*. . . will give me bread to eat and clothing to wear*":

B. Aqilas the proselyte came to R. Eliezer and said to him, "Is all the gain that is coming to the proselyte going to be contained in this verse: '*. . . and loves the proselyte, giving him food and clothing*' (Deut. 10:18)?"

C. He said to him, "And is something for which the old man [Jacob] beseeched going to be such a small thing in your view, namely, '*. . . will give me bread to eat and clothing to wear*'? [God] comes and hands it over to [a proselyte] on a reed [and the proselyte does not have to beg for it.]"

D. He came to R. Joshua, who commenced by saying

words to appease him: "'*Bread*' refers to Torah, as it is said, '*Come, eat of my bread*' (Prov. 9:5). '*Clothing*' refers to the cloak of a disciple of sages.

E.   "When a person has the merit of studying the Torah, he has the merit of carrying out a religious duty. [So the proselyte receives a great deal when he gets bread and clothing, namely, entry into the estate of disciples].

F.   "And not only so, but his daughters may be chosen for marriage into the priesthood, so that their sons' sons will offer burnt-offerings on the altar. [So the proselyte may also look forward to entry into the priests' caste. That statement will now be spelled out.]

G.   "'*Bread*' refers to the show-bread.

H.   "'*Clothing*' refers to the garments of the priesthood.

I.   "So lo, we deal with the sanctuary.

J.   "How do we know that the same sort of blessing applies in the provinces? '*Bread*' speaks of the dough-offering [that is separated in the provinces], while '*clothing*' refers to the first fleece [handed over to the priest]."

The interpretation of "bread" and "clothing" yields its own message, intersecting only at one point with the passage at hand. So at issue in this composition is not the exegesis of our base verse but the meaning of "bread" and "clothing" as applied to the proselyte. We now see how the components of the base verse are reread in terms of the base values of sages themselves: Torah and cult. Sages regard study of Torah as equivalent to a sacrifice, and the sage as equivalent to the priest. This typological reading of Israel's existence then will guide sages' interpretation of such specific passages as the one before us.

LXX:VI.   1.   A.   "*. . . so that I come again to my father's house in peace, then the Lord shall be my God*" (Gen. 28:20–22):

B.   R. Joshua of Sikhnin in the name of R. Levi: "The Holy One, blessed be he, took the language used by the patriarchs and turned it into a key to the redemption of their descendants."

Now comes the main event in our passage: the reading, in the light of Israel's future history, that is, the story of Israel's salvation, of the deeds of the matriarchs and patriarchs and of God's love for them.

C.   "Said the Holy One, blessed be he, to Jacob, 'You have said, "*Then the Lord shall be my God.*" By your life, all of the acts of goodness, blessing, and consolation which I am going to carry out for your descendants I shall bestow only by using the same language:

D.   "'"Then in that day, living waters shall go out from Jerusalem" (Zech. 14:8). "Then in that day a man shall rear a young cow and two sheep" (Is. 7:21). "Then, in that day, the Lord will set his hand again the second time to recover the remnant of his people" (Is. 11:11). "Then, in that day, the mountains shall drop down sweet wine" (Joel 4:18). "Then, in that day, a great horn shall be blown and they shall come who were lost in the land of Assyria" (Is. 27:13).'"*

The union of Jacob's biography and Israel's history yields the passage at hand. The explicit details, rather conventional in character, are less interesting than the basic syllogism, which is implicit and ubiquitous.

Another approach to the interpretation of Scripture in which this document's framers pioneered is the imputation to a single verse of a wide variety of coherent, alternative readings. Later on this exegetical mode would be given its own form, introduced by Hebrew words meaning "another matter," and a long sequence of "other matters" would be strung together. In fact, all of the "other matters" turn out to say the same thing, only in different ways, or to convey a single, coherent attitude, emotion, sentiment, or conception. But in the following, we find the substance of the hermeneutics, but not the form it would ultimately be given.

LXX:VIII.   1.   A.   *"Then Jacob lifted up his feet"* (Gen. 29:1):

            B.   Said R. Aha, "'A tranquil heart is the life of the flesh' (Prov. 14:30).

            C.   "Since he had been given this good news, his heart carried his feet.

            D.   "So people say: 'The stomach carries the feet.'"

What captures attention is the happiness that is expressed in the description of Jacob's onward journey. The good news carried him forward. But I do not see at this point what this good news ("gospel") represents. However, what follows more than fills the gap. It is the gospel of Israel: its salvation, worked out in the principal components of its holy way of life of sanctification. So the base and intersecting verses prepare the way for a powerful and sustained statement. In the following protracted, six-part interpretation of the simple verse about seeing a well in the field, we see the full power of Midrash as proposition yielding exegesis. Elements of both sanctification and salvation are joined in a remarkable message.

        2.   A.   *"As he looked, he saw a well in the field"*:

            B.   R. Hama bar Hanina interpreted the verse in six ways

[that is, he divides the verse into six clauses and systematically reads each of the clauses in light of the others
and in line with an overriding theme]:

C.   "*'As he looked, he saw a well in the field':* this refers to the
well [of water in the wilderness, Num. 21:17].

D.   "*'. . . and lo, three flocks of sheep lying beside it':* specifically, Moses, Aaron, and Miriam.

E.   "*'. . . for out of that well the flocks were watered':* from there
each one drew water for his standard, tribe, and family."

F.   "*And the stone upon the well's mouth was great":*

G.   Said R. Hanina, "It was only the size of a little sieve."

H.   [Reverting to Hama's statement:] "*'. . . and put the stone
back in its place upon the mouth of the well':* for the coming journeys."

Thus the first interpretation applies the passage at hand to the life of Israel in the
wilderness. The premise is the prevailing syllogism: Israel's future history is lived
out, the first time around, in the lives of the patriarchs and matriarchs.

3.   A.   "*'As he looked, he saw a well in the field':* refers to Zion.

B.   "*'. . . and lo, three flocks of sheep lying beside it':* refers to
the three festivals.

C.   "*'. . . . for out of that well the flocks were watered':* from
there they drank of the Holy Spirit.

D.   "*'. . . The stone on the well's mouth was large':* this refers
to the rejoicing of the house of the water-drawing."

E.   Said R. Hoshaiah, "Why is it called 'the house of the
water drawing'? Because from there they drink of the
Holy Spirit."

F.   [Resuming Hama b. Hanina's discourse:] "*'. . . and
when all the flocks were gathered there':* coming from *'the
entrance of Hamath to the brook of Egypt'* (1 Kgs. 8:66).

G.   "*'. . . the shepherds would roll the stone from the mouth of
the well and water the sheep':* for from there they would
drink of the Holy Spirit.

H.   "*'. . . and put the stone back in its place upon the mouth of
the well':* leaving it in place until the coming festival."

Thus the second interpretation reads the verse in light of the Temple celebration
of the Festival of Tabernacles.

4.   A.   "*'. . . As he looked, he saw a well in the field':* this refers
to Zion.

B.   *" '. . . and lo, three flocks of sheep lying beside it':* this refers to the three courts, concerning which we have learned in the Mishnah: **There were three courts there, one at the gateway of the Temple mount, one at the gateway of the courtyard, and one in the chamber of the hewn stones [M. San. 11:2].**

C.   *" '. . . for out of that well the flocks were watered':* for from there they would hear the ruling.

D.   *" 'The stone on the well's mouth was large':* this refers to the high court that was in the chamber of the hewn stones.

E.   *" '. . . and when all the flocks were gathered there':* this refers to the courts in session in the Land of Israel.

F.   *" '. . . the shepherds would roll the stone from the mouth of the well and water the sheep':* for from there they would hear the ruling.

G.   *" '. . . and put the stone back in its place upon the mouth of the well':* for they would give and take until they had produced the ruling in all the required clarity."

The third interpretation reads the verse in light of the Israelite institution of justice and administration. The intrusion of the cited passage of the Mishnah alerts us to the striking difference between our document and Sifra and Sifré to Numbers. The Mishnah passage serves as mere illustration. It does not generate the question to be answered, nor does it come under detailed amplification itself. It is in no way a focus of interest.

5. A.   *" 'As he looked, he saw a well in the field':* this refers to Zion.

B.   *" '. . . and lo, three flocks of sheep lying beside it':* this refers to the first three kingdoms [Babylonia, Media, Greece].

C.   *" '. . . for out of that well the flocks were watered':* for they enriched the treasures that were laid up in the chambers of the Temple.

D.   *" '. . . The stone on the well's mouth was large':* this refers to the merit attained by the patriarchs.

E.   *" '. . . and when all the flocks were gathered there':* this refers to the wicked kingdom, which collects troops through levies from all the nations of the world.

F.   *" '. . . the shepherds would roll the stone from the mouth of the well and water the sheep':* for they enriched the treasures that were laid up in the chambers of the Temple.

G.   *" '. . . and put the stone back in its place upon the mouth of the well'*: in the age to come the merit attained by the patriarchs will stand [in defense of Israel]."

So the fourth interpretation interweaves the themes of the Temple cult and the domination of the four monarchies.

6. A. "'*As he looked, he saw a well in the field*': this refers to the sanhedrin.

    B. "'. . . *and lo, three flocks of sheep lying beside it*': this alludes to the three rows of disciples of sages that would go into session in their presence.

    C. "'*for out of that well the flocks were watered*': for from there they would listen to the ruling of the law.

    D. "'. . . *The stone on the well's mouth was large*': this refers to the most distinguished member of the court, who determines the law decision.

    E. "'. . . *and when all the flocks were gathered there*': this refers to disciples of the sages in the Land of Israel.

    F. "'. . . *the shepherds would roll the stone from the mouth of the well and water the sheep*': for from there they would listen to the ruling of the law.

    G. "'. . . *and put the stone back in its place upon the mouth of the well*': for they would give and take until they had produced the ruling in all the required clarity."

The fifth interpretation again reads the verse in light of the Israelite institution of legal education and justice.

7. A. "'*As he looked, he saw a well in the field*': this refers to the synagogue.

    B. "'. . . *and lo, three flocks of sheep lying beside it*': this refers to the three who are called to the reading of the Torah on weekdays.

    C. "'. . . *for out of that well the flocks were watered*': for from there they hear the reading of the Torah.

    D. "'. . . *The stone on the well's mouth was large*': this refers to the impulse to do evil.

    E. "'. . . *and when all the flocks were gathered there*': this refers to the congregation.

    F. "'. . . *the shepherds would roll the stone from the mouth of the well and water the sheep*': for from there they hear the reading of the Torah.

    G. "'. . . *and put the stone back in its place upon the mouth of*

*the well': for once they go forth [from the hearing of
the reading of the Torah] the impulse to do evil reverts
to its place."*

The sixth and last interpretation turns to the twin themes of the reading of the
Torah in the synagogue and the evil impulse, temporarily driven off through the
hearing of the Torah. The six themes read in response to the verse cover (1) Israel
in the wilderness, (2) the Temple cult on festivals with special reference to Tabernacles, (3) the judiciary and government, (4) the history of Israel under the four
kingdoms, (5) the life of sages, and (6) the ordinary folk and the synagogue. The
whole is an astonishing repertoire of fundamental themes of the life of the nation,
Israel: at its origins in the wilderness, in its cult, in its institutions based on the
cult, in the history of the nations, and, finally, in the twin social estates of sages
and ordinary folk, matched by the institutions of the master-disciple circle and
the synagogue. The vision of Jacob at the well thus encompassed the whole
of the social reality of Jacob's people, Israel. The labor of interpreting this same
passage in the profound, typological context already established now goes
forward.

LXX:IX. 1. A.   R. Yohanan interpreted the statement in terms of Sinai:
             B.   "'*As he looked, he saw a well in the field*': this refers to
                  Sinai.
             C.   "'. . . *and lo, three flocks of sheep lying beside it*': these
                  stand for the priests, Levites, and Israelites.
             D.   "'. . . *for out of that well the flocks were watered*': for from
                  there they heard the ten commandments.
             E.   "'. . . *The stone on the well's mouth was large*': this refers
                  to the Presence of God."
             F.   ". . . *and when all the flocks were gathered there*":
             G.   R. Simeon b. Judah of Kefar Akum in the name of
                  R. Simeon: "All of the flocks of Israel had to be pres-
                  ent, for if any one of them had been lacking, they
                  would not have been worthy of receiving the Torah."
             H.   [Returning to Yohanan's exposition:] "'. . . *the shep-
                  herds would roll the stone from the mouth of the well and water
                  the sheep*': for from there they heard the Ten Com-
                  mandments.
             I.   "'. . . *and put the stone back in its place upon the mouth of
                  the well*': '*You yourselves have seen that I have talked with
                  you from heaven*' (Ex. 20:19)."

Yohanan's exposition adds what was left out, namely, reference to the revelation
of the Torah at Sinai. As though the demonstration of the ubiquitous syllogism

that Israel's history is the story of the lives of the founders, we now go over the same proposition again, with utterly fresh materials. That shows that the proposed syllogism states the deep structure of reality, the syntax that permits words to make diverse, yet intelligible, statements. Once we have taken up the challenge of the foregoing, a still greater task requires us to make the same basic point in utterly different cases, and that allows us definitively to demonstrate that syllogism as it is tested against diverse cases presented by Scripture's facts.

LXX:X.   1.   A.   "Jacob said to them, 'My brothers, where do you come from?' They said, 'We are from Haran'" (Gen. 29:40):

B.   R. Yosé bar Haninah interpreted the verse at hand with reference to the Exile.

C.   "'Jacob said to them, "My brothers, where do you come from?"' They said, "We are from Haran": that is, 'We are flying from the wrath of the Holy One, blessed be he.' [Here there is a play on the words for "Haran" and "wrath," which share the same consonants.]

D.   "'He said to them, "Do you know Laban the son of Nahor?"' The sense is this, 'Do you know him who is destined to bleach your sins as white as snow?' [Here there is a play on the words for "Laban" and "bleach," which share the same consonants.]

E.   "'They said, "We know him." He said to them, "Is it well with him?" They said, "It is well."' On account of what sort of merit?

F.   [Yosé continues his interpretation:] "'[The brothers go on,] ". . . and see, Rachel his daughter is coming with the sheep"' (Gen. 29:6–7).

G.   "That is in line with this verse: 'Thus says the Lord, "A voice is heard in Ramah, lamentation and bitter weeping, Rachel weeping for her children. She refuses to be comforted." Thus says the Lord, "Refrain your voice from weeping . . . and there is hope for your future," says the Lord, and your children shall return to their own border"' (Jer. 31:15–16)."

Now the history of the redemption of Israel is located in the colloquy between Jacob and Laban's sons. The themes pour forth in profusion, forming propositions of a subordinate character.

LXX:XI.   1.   A.   ["He said to them, 'Is it well with him?' They said, 'It is well; and see, Rachel his daughter is coming with the sheep'" (Lev. 29:6–7)]: "He said to them, 'Is it well with him?'" "Is there peace between him and you?"

B.   *"They said, 'It is well.'* And if it is gossip that you want, *'see, Rachel his daughter is coming with the sheep.'"*

C.   That is in line with this saying: *"Women like gossip."*

2.   A.   *"He said, 'Behold, it is still [high day, it is not time for the animals to be gathered together; water the sheep and go, pasture them.' But they said, 'We cannot until all the flocks are gathered together, and the stone is rolled from the mouth of the well; then we water the sheep']"* (Gen. 29:7–8):

B.   He said to them, "If you are hired hands, *'it is still high day.'* [You have no right to water the flock so early in the day.]

C.   *"If you are shepherding your own flock: 'It is not time for the animals to be gathered together.'* [It is not in your interest to do so.]"

3.   A.   *"They said, 'We cannot. . . .' While he was still speaking with them, Rachel came"* (Gen. 29:9):

B.   Said Rabban Simeon b. Gamaliel, "Come and note the difference between one neighborhood and the next.

C.   "Elsewhere [in Midian, when the daughters of Jethro came to water their flocks,] there were seven women, and the shepherds wanted to give them a hard time, as it is said, *'And the shepherds came and drove them away'* (Ex. 2:17).

D.   "Here, by contrast, there was only one woman, and yet not one of them laid a hand on her, because *'The angel of the Lord encamps around about those who fear him and delivers them'* (Ps. 34:8).

E.   "This refers to those who live in a neighborhood of those who fear him."

Nos. 1, 2 articulate the conversation between Jacob and the shepherds. No. 3 draws a more general conclusion, using the verse at hand to demonstrate the contrast necessary for the syllogism. It is safer to live in a Jewish neighborhood.

LXX:XII.   1.   A.   *"Now when Jacob saw Rachel, the daughter of Laban his mother's brother, and the sheep of Laban, his mother's brother, Jacob went up and rolled the stone [from the well's mouth and watered the flock of Laban his mother's brother. Then Jacob kissed Rachel and wept aloud. And Jacob told Rachel that he was Rebecca's son, and she ran and told her father]"* (Gen. 29:10–12):

B.   Said R. Yohanan, "He did it without effort, like someone who takes a stopper out of a flask."

2.   A.   *"Then Jacob kissed Rachel"*:

What follows is yet another mode of inquiry, namely, the laying out of a proposition by means of a list. The list collects the relevant data, and the proposition sorts out among the data the classifications that render the facts intelligible. In this pursuit of natural philosophy or science accomplished through list-making and classification of data on lists, sages turn to Scripture, rather than to nature, but the mode of inquiry is the same. In this composition the cited verse plays no important role. It is tacked on, simply a fact which joins the prepared list to the larger context of the document at hand.

    B.   Every form of kissing is obscene except for three purposes, the kiss upon accepting high office, the kiss upon seeing someone at an interval after an absence, and the kiss of departure.

    C.   The kiss upon accepting high office: *"Then Samuel took the vial of oil and poured it upon his head and kissed him"* (1 Sam. 10:1).

    D.   The kiss upon seeing someone at an interval [after an absence]: *"And he went and met him in the mountain of God and kissed him"* (Ex. 4:27).

    E.   The kiss of departure: *"And Orpah kissed her mother-in-law"* (Ruth 1:4).

    F.   Said R. Tanhuma, "Also the kiss exchanged among kin: *'Then Jacob kissed Rachel.'"*

3.   A.   *"And he wept aloud"*:

    B.   Why did Jacob weep?

    C.   [Jacob thus] said, "Concerning Eliezer [Abraham's majordomo, who went to find a wife for Abraham's son, Isaac] when he went to bring Rebecca [to Isaac as Isaac's wife], it is written in his regard: *'and the servant took ten camels'* (Gen. 24:10). But I do not have even a ring or a bracelet." [That is why he wept.]

4.   A.   Another matter:

    B.   Why did Jacob weep?

    C.   Because he foresaw that she would not be buried with him.

    D.   That is in line with this statement that Rachel made to Leah: *"Therefore he shall lie with you tonight"* (Gen. 30:15).

    E.   "With you he will sleep, and not with me."

5.   A.   Another matter:

    B.   Why did Jacob weep?

C. Because he saw that men were whispering with one another, saying, "Has this one now come to create an innovation in sexual licentiousness among us? [That is something we cannot permit.]"

D. For from the moment that the world had been smitten on account of the generation of the flood, the nations of the world had gone and fenced themselves away from fornication.

E. That is in line with what people say: "People of the east are meticulous about sexual purity."

No. 1 supplies a minor gloss. No. 2 uses the base verse as part of a syllogistic statement. No. 3 answers an obvious question. Nos. 4, 5 answer the same question.

LXX:XIX. 1. A. *"So Laban gathered together all the men of the place and made a feast"* (Gen. 29:22):

B. He brought together all of the men of the place. He said to them, "You know that we were in need of water. But once this righteous man came, the water has been blessed. [So let's keep him around here.]"

C. They said to him, "What is good for you is what you should do."

D. He said to them, "Do you want me to deceive him and give him Leah, and, since he loves Rachel more, he will stay and work here with you for another seven years?"

E. They said to him, "What is good for you is what you should do."

F. He said to them, "Give me your pledge that none of you will inform him."

G. They gave him their pledge. Then he went and with the pledges the neighbors had given got them wine, oil and meat.

H. What follows is that he was called Laban the deceiver, since he deceived even the people who lived in his own town.

I. All that day the people were praising him. When the evening came, he said to them, "Why are you doing this?"

J. They said to him, "On your account benefits have been coming to us," and they sang praises before him, saying, *"Hey, Leah, Hey, Leah."*

K.   In the evening they came to bring her in and they put
     out the lamps. He said to them, "Why so?"

L.   They said to him, "Do you want us to be indecent the
     way you are? [Here we do not have sexual relations in
     the light.]"

M.   All that night he would use the name of Rachel and
     she answered him. In the morning: *"And in the morning,
     behold, it was Leah"* (Gen. 29:24–25)!

N.   He said, "How could you have deceived me, you
     daughter of a deceiver?"

O.   She said to him, "And is there a book without faithful
     readers? [I know your story and so I followed your ex-
     ample.] Did not your father call you 'Esau,' and you
     answered him accordingly? So you called me by a name
     other than my own, and I answered you accordingly."

2.   A.   *"And Jacob said to Laban, 'What is this that you have done
          to me? Did I not serve with you for Rachel? Why then
          have you deceived me?' And Laban said, 'It is not so done
          in our country, to give the younger before the firstborn. . . .
          Complete the week of this one and we will give you the other
          also in return for serving me another seven years'"* (Gen.
          29:25–27):

     B.   Said R. Jacob bar Aha, "On the basis of this statement
          we learn the rule that people may not confuse one oc-
          casion for rejoicing with some other."

No. 1 presents a sustained amplification of details of the story, ending with a
stunning and apt observation about the appropriate conduct of Leah with Jacob.
No. 2, by contrast, just draws a moral. The reference to the deeds of the patriarchs
and matriarchs does not always yield complimentary judgments. Quite to the contrary, Jacob's conduct with Isaac accounts for Leah's conduct with Jacob. We look
in vain for traces of sentimentality in the intellect of the exegetes at hand, who
were engaged in a solemn search for the rules of life, not in a systematic apologetic
for a merely sacred text.

In Genesis Rabbah the sages show in detail the profound depths of the story
of the creation of the world and Israel's founding family. Bringing their generative
proposition about the character of the Scripture to the stories at hand, they systematically found in the details of the tales the history of the people Israel portrayed
in the lives and deeds of the founders, the fathers and the mothers of this book
of the Torah. It is no accident that the exegetes of the book of Genesis invoke
large-scale constructions of history to make fundamental judgments about society—Israel's society. Nor is it merely happenstance that the exegetes bring into
juxtaposition distinct facts—passages—of scriptural history or appeal to a typologi-

cal reading of the humble details of the scriptural tale, the simple statement that the shepherds had brought their flocks to the well, for example. A large proposition has governed the details of exegesis, and the individual verses commonly, though not always, address their facts in the proof of an encompassing hypothesis, a theorem concerning Israel's fate and faith.

XV

LEVITICUS RABBAH

1.

IDENTIFYING THE DOCUMENT

WHEN WE COME TO LEVITICUS RABBAH,[1] WE FIND THE INTEREST IN VERSE SUC-
ceeding verse has waned, while the proposition comes to the fore as the definitive
and dominant organizing motif throughout. With Genesis Rabbah, the Sifra's and
Sifré's mode of exegesis of verses and their components, one by one in sequence,
comes to its conclusion and a new approach commences. The mixed character of
Genesis Rabbah, joining propositional to exegetical rhetoric in order to make
points of both general intelligibility and also very specific and concrete amplification of detail, marks a transitional moment in the workings of Midrash. Exactly
what did the framers of Leviticus Rabbah learn when they opened the book of
Leviticus? To state the answer in advance, when they read the rules of sanctification
of the priesthood, they heard the message of the salvation of all Israel. Leviticus
became the story of how Israel, purified from social sin and sanctified, would be
saved.

---

[1] As before, *rabbah* means "great," and hence an interpretation of the title would be "an amplification"
or "an expansion" of the book of Leviticus.

The framers of Leviticus Rabbah, closed in the mid–fifth century, set forth, in the thirty-seven *parashiyyot* or chapters into which their document is divided, thirty-seven well-crafted propositions.[2] They made no pretense at a systematic exegesis of sequences of verses of Scripture, abandoning the verse-by-verse mode of organizing discourse. They struck out on their own to compose a means of expressing their propositions in a more systematic and cogent way. Each of the thirty-seven chapters proves cogent, and all of them spell out their respective statements in an intellectually economical, if rich, manner. Each *parashah* makes its own point, but all of them furthermore form a single statement.

The message of Leviticus Rabbah—congruent with that of Genesis Rabbah— is that the laws of history may be known, and that these laws, so far as Israel is concerned, focus upon the holy life of the community. If Israel then obeys the laws of society aimed at Israel's sanctification, then the foreordained history, resting on the merit of the ancestors, will unfold as Israel hopes. So there is no secret to the meaning of the events of the day, and Israel, for its part, can affect its destiny and effect salvation. The authorship of Leviticus Rabbah has thus joined the two great motifs, sanctification and salvation, by reading a biblical book, Leviticus, that is devoted to the former in the light of the requirements of the latter. In this way they made their fundamental point, which is that salvation at the end of history depends upon sanctification in the here and now.

To prove these points, the authors of the compositions make lists of facts that bear the same traits and show the working of rules of history. It follows that the mode of thought brought to bear upon the theme of history remains exactly the same as in the Mishnah: list-making, with data exhibiting similar taxonomic traits drawn together into lists based on common monothetic traits or definitions. These lists then through the power of repetition make a single enormous point or prove a social law of history. The catalogs of exemplary heroes and historical events serve a further purpose. They provide a model of how contemporary events are to be absorbed into the biblical paradigm. Since biblical events exemplify recurrent happenings, sin and redemption, forgiveness and atonement, they lose their one-time

---

[2] For further reading and bibliography on the topic of this chapter, see the following:

Bowker, pp. 80–81.

J. Heinemann, "Leviticus Rabbah," *Encyclopaedia Judaica* 11:147–50: fifth-century redaction in the Land of Israel; description of the document and its contents; survey of a *parashah*, construction of the *parashiyyot;* relationship to Pesiqta deRab Kahana.

Maccoby does not explain why, while he includes Genesis Rabbah in "early rabbinic writings," he excludes Leviticus Rabbah, which I do not find mentioned in his introduction.

Stemberger-Strack, pp. 313–17: text; the name, contents and structure; redaction and time of origin (400–500).

This writer's introductions to the document are as follows: *The Integrity of Leviticus Rabbah. The Problem of the Autonomy of a Rabbinic Document.* Chico, CA 1985: Scholars Press for Brown Judaic Studies; *Comparative Midrash: The Plan and Program of Genesis Rabbah and Leviticus Rabbah.* Atlanta, 1986: Scholars Press for Brown Judaic Studies; and *Judaism and Scripture: The Evidence of Leviticus Rabbah.* Chicago, 1986: University of Chicago Press.

character. At the same time and in the same way, current events find a place within the ancient, but eternally present, paradigmatic scheme. So no new historical events, other than exemplary episodes in lives of heroes, demand narration because, through what is said about the past, what was happening in the times of the framers of Leviticus Rabbah would also come under consideration.

This mode of dealing with Biblical history and contemporary events produces two reciprocal effects. The first is the mythicization of biblical stories, their removal from the framework of ongoing, unique patterns of history and sequences of events and their transformation into accounts of things that happen all the time. The second is that contemporary events too lose all of their specificity and enter the paradigmatic framework of established mythic existence. So (1) Scripture's myth happens every day, and (2) every day produces re-enactment of Scripture's myth.

The focus of Leviticus Rabbah's laws of history is upon the society of Israel, its national fate and moral condition. Indeed, nearly all of the *parashiyyot* of Leviticus Rabbah turn out to deal with the national, social condition of Israel, and this in three contexts: (1) Israel's setting in the history of the nations, (2) the sanctified character of the inner life of Israel itself, (3) the future, salvific history of Israel. So the Biblical book that deals with the tabernacle in the wilderness, which sages understood to form the model for the holy Temple later on built in Jerusalem, now is shown to address the holy people. That is no paradox, rather a logical next step in the exploration of sanctification. Leviticus really discusses not the consecration of the cult but the sanctification of the nation—its conformity to God's will laid forth in the Torah, and God's rules. Leviticus Rabbah executes the paradox of shifting categories, applying to the nation—not a locative category—and its history the category that in the book subject to commentary pertained to the holy place—a locative category—and its eternal condition. The nation now is like the cult then, the ordinary Israelite now like the priest then. The holy way of life lived now, through acts to which merit accrues, corresponds to the holy rites then. The process of metamorphosis is full, rich, complete. When everything stands for something else, the something else repeatedly turns out to be the nation. This is what our document spells out in exquisite detail, yet never missing the main point.

The message of Leviticus Rabbah paradoxically attaches itself to the book of Leviticus, as if that book had come from prophecy and addressed the issue of salvation. But it came from the priesthood and spoke of sanctification. The paradoxical syllogism—the as-if reading, the opposite of how things seem—of the composers of Leviticus Rabbah therefore reaches simple formulation. In the very setting of sanctification the authors find the promise of salvation. In the topics of the cult and the priesthood they uncover the national and social issues of the moral life and redemptive hope of Israel. The repeated comparison and contrast of priesthood and prophecy, sanctification and salvation, turn out to produce a complement, which comes to most perfect union in the text at hand.

What we have in Leviticus Rabbah is the result of the mode of thought not of prophets or historians, but of philosophers and scientists. The framers propose not to lay down, but to discover, rules governing Israel's life. As we find the rules of nature by identifying and classifying facts of natural life, so we find rules of society by identifying and classifying the facts of Israel's social life. In both modes of inquiry we make sense of things by bringing together like specimens and finding out whether they form a species, then bringing together like species and finding out whether they form a genus—in all, classifying data and identifying the rules that make possible the classification. That sort of thinking lies at the deepest level of list-making, which is work of offering a proposition and facts (for social rules) as much as a genus and its species (for rules of nature). Once discovered, the social rules of Israel's national life yield explicit statements, such as that God hates the arrogant and loves the humble. The logical status of these statements, in context, is as secure and unassailable as the logical status of statements about physics, ethics, or politics, as these emerge in philosophical thought. What differentiates the statements is not their logical status—as sound, scientific philosophy—but only their subject matter, on the one side, and distinctive rhetoric, on the other.

FROM COMMENTARY TO PROPOSITIONAL STATEMENTS: The framers of Leviticus Rabbah treat topics, not particular verses. They make generalizations that are freestanding. They express cogent propositions through extended compositions, not episodic ideas. Earlier, in Genesis Rabbah, as we have seen, things people wished to say were attached to predefined statements based on an existing text, constructed in accord with an organizing logic independent of the systematic expression of a single, well-framed idea. That is to say, the sequence of verses of Genesis and their contents played a massive role in the larger-scale organization of Genesis Rabbah and expression of its propositions. Now the authors of Leviticus Rabbah so collected and arranged their materials that an abstract proposition emerges. That proposition is not expressed only or mainly through episodic restatements, assigned, as I said, to an order established by a base text (whether Genesis or Leviticus, or a Mishnah tractate, for that matter). Rather it emerges through a logic of its own.

What is new is the move from an essentially exegetical mode of logical discourse to a fundamentally philosophical one. It is the shift from discourse framed around an established (hence old) text to syllogistic argument organized around a proposed (hence new) theorem or proposition. What changes, therefore, is the way in which cogent thought takes place, as people moved from discourse contingent on some prior principle of organization to discourse autonomous of a ready-made program inherited from an earlier paradigm. When they read the rules of sanctification of the priesthood, the sages responsible for Leviticus Rabbah heard the message of the salvation of all Israel. Leviticus became the story of how Israel, purified from social sin and sanctified, would be saved.

The authors of Leviticus Rabbah express their ideas first by selecting materials already written for other purposes and using them for their own, second by composing materials, and third by arranging both in *parashiyyot* into an order through which propositions may reach expression. This involves both the modes of thought, and the topical program, and also the unifying proposition of the document as a whole. To summarize:

[1] The principal mode of thought required one thing to be read in terms of another, one verse in light of a different verse (or topic, theme, symbol, idea), one situation in light of another.

[2] The principal subject of thought is the moral condition of Israel, on the one side, and the salvation of Israel, on the other.

[3] The single unifying proposition—the syllogism at the document's deepest structure—is that Israel's salvation depends upon its moral condition.

It follows that Leviticus Rabbah constitutes not merely diverse thoughts but a single, sustained composition. The authors do so through a rich tapestry of unstated propositions that are only illustrated, delineated at the outset, by the statement of some propositions. And these also are illustrated. It is, in a word, a syllogism by example—that is, by repeated appeal to facts—rather than by argument alone. For in context, an example constitutes a fact. The source of many examples or facts is Scripture, the foundation of all reality. Accordingly, in the context of Israelite life and culture, in which Scripture recorded facts, we have a severely logical, because entirely factual, statement of how rightly organized and classified facts sustain a proposition. In context that proposition is presented as rigorously and critically as the social rules of discourse allowed.

The authors of the document's compositions and composites transformed scriptural history from a sequence of one-time events, leading from one place to some other, into an ever-present mythic world. No longer does Scripture speak of only one Moses, one David, one set of happenings of a distinctive and never-to-be-repeated character. Now whatever happens of which the thinkers propose to take account must enter and be absorbed into that established and ubiquitous pattern and structure founded in Scripture. It is not that biblical history repeats itself. Rather, biblical history no longer constitutes history at all, that is, history as a linear, purposeful, continuous story of things that happened once, long ago, and pointed to some one moment in the future. Rather it becomes an account of things that happen every day—hence, an ever-present mythic world. In this way the basic trait of history in the salvific framework, its one-timeness and linearity, is reworked into the generative quality of sanctification, its routine and everyday, ongoing reality. When history enters a paradigm, it forms an exercise within philosophy, the search for the rules and regularities of the world. That is the profound achievement of the document before us.

And that is why, in Leviticus Rabbah, Scripture—the book of Leviticus—as a whole does not dictate the order of discourse, let alone its character. In this document the authorship at hand chose in Leviticus itself an isolated verse here, an odd phrase there. These then presented the pretext for propositional discourse commonly quite out of phase with the cited passage. The verses that are quoted ordinarily shift from the meanings they convey to the implications they contain, speaking about something, anything, other than what they seem to be saying. So the *as-if* frame of mind brought to Scripture precipitates renewal of Scripture, requiring the seeing of everything with fresh eyes. And the result of the new vision was a re-imagining of the social world envisioned by the document at hand, I mean, the everyday world of Israel in its Land in that same difficult time at which Genesis Rabbah was taking shape, sometime in the fifth century and the first century after the conversion of Constantine and the beginning of the Christian chapter of Western civilization. For what the sages now proposed was a reconstruction of existence along the lines of the ancient design of Scripture as they read it. What that meant was that from a sequence of one-time and linear events, everything that happened was turned into a repetition of known and already experienced paradigms, hence, once more, a mythic being. The source and core of the myth derive from Scripture—Scripture reread, renewed, reconstructed along with the society that revered Scripture.

2.
TRANSLATIONS INTO ENGLISH

The first complete translation into English is H. Freedman and Maurice Simon, eds., *Midrash Rabbah. Translated into English. With Notes, Glossary, and Indices* (London, 1939: Soncino Press). IV. *Leviticus. Chapters I–XIX* translated by J. Israelstam. *Chapters XX–XXXVII* translated by Judah J. Slotki. The second, and first form-analytical translation, is in this writer's *Judaism and Scripture: The Evidence of Leviticus Rabbah*. Chicago, 1986: University of Chicago Press. This translation also is the first to present in English the critical text and commentary of Mordecai Margulies, *Midrash Wayyikra Rabbah. A Critical Edition Based on Manuscripts and Genizah Fragments with Variants and Notes* (Jerusalem, 1953 et seq., The Minister of Education and Culture of Israel and the Louis M. and Minnie Epstein Fund of the American Academy for Jewish Research) I–IV.

3.
RHETORIC

While Leviticus Rabbah focuses the discourse of each of its thirty-seven *parashiyyot* on a verse of the book of Leviticus, these verses in no way are sequential, e.g., Lev. 1:1, then Lev. 1:2, in the way in which the structure of Genesis Rabbah dictates exegesis of the verses of the book of Genesis, read in sequence. This document's chapters work out theses on a sequence of themes, for example, the evils of gossip or of drink, the unique character of Moses, and the like. But the respective themes cover a variety of propositions, and a *parashah* ordinarily displays and demonstrates more than a single cogent syllogism.

The single most striking recurrent literary structure of Leviticus Rabbah is the base-verse/intersecting-verse construction, already familiar from Genesis Rabbah, and to be repeated in Pesiqta deRab Kahana. In such a construction, a base verse, drawn from the book of Leviticus, is juxtaposed to an intersecting verse, drawn from any book other than a pentateuchal one. Then this intersecting verse is subjected to systematic exegesis. On the surface the exegesis is out of all relationship with the base verse. But in a stunning climax, all of the exegeses of the intersecting verse are shown to relate to the main point the exegete wishes to make about the base verse. What that means is that the composition as a whole is so conceived as to impose meaning and order on all of the parts, original or ready-made, of which the author of the whole has made use.

Another classification of rhetorical pattern, familiar from Sifra and Sifré to Numbers as well as from Genesis Rabbah, derives from the clause-by-clause type of exegesis of the base verse, with slight interest in intersecting verses or in illustrative materials deriving from other books of Scripture. The base verse in this classification defines the entire frame of discourse, either because of its word choices or because of its main point. Where verses of other passages are quoted, they serve not as the focus of discourse but only as proof texts or illustrative texts. They therefore function in a different way from the verses adduced in discourse in the first two classifications, for, in those former cases, the intersecting verses form the center of interest. The categories of units of discourse also explain the order of arrangement of types of units of discourse. First will come the base-verse/intersecting-verse construction; then will come intersecting-verse/base-verse construction; finally we shall have clause-by-clause exegetical constructions.

In the base-verse/intersecting-verse exegesis characteristic of Leviticus Rabbah, exegetes read one thing in terms of something else. To begin with, it is the base verse in terms of the intersecting verse. It also is the intersecting verse in other terms as well—a multiple-layered construction of analogy and parable. The intersecting verse's elements always turn out to stand for, to signify, to speak of, something other than that to which they openly refer. If water stands for Torah, skin disease for evil speech, the reference to something for some other thing entirely, then the mode of thought at hand is simple. One thing symbolizes another, speaks not of itself but of some other thing entirely. It is as if a common object or symbol really represented an uncommon one. Nothing says what it means. All statements carry deeper meaning, which inheres in other statements altogether. The profound sense, then, of the base verse emerges only through restatement within and through the intersecting verse—as if the base verse spoke of things that on the surface we do not see at all. Accordingly, if we ask the single prevalent literary construction to testify to the prevailing frame of mind, its message is that things are never what they seem.

4.
LOGIC OF COHERENT DISCOURSE

The paramount logic that imposes coherence on the *parashiyyot* and their subdivisions is not only propositional but syllogistic. The syllogistic argument of Leviticus Rabbah rests on the simple equation: if X, then Y; if not X, then not Y. If Israel carries out its moral obligations, then God will redeem Israel. If Israel does not, then God will punish Israel. This simple statement is given innumerable illustrations. These include, for example, that Israel in times past repented, therefore God saved it. Israel in times past sinned, therefore God punished it. Other sorts of statements follow suit. God loves the humble and despises the haughty. Therefore God saves the humble and punishes the haughty. In the same terms, if anyone is humble, then God will save him or her, and if one is haughty, then God will punish the arrogant person. Accordingly, if one condition is met, then another will come about. And the opposite also is the fact.

True, the document does not express these syllogisms in the form of arguments at all. Rather they come before us as lists of statements of fact, and the facts upon which numerous statements rest derive from Scripture. So, on the surface, there is not a single statement in the document that a Graeco-Roman logician would have understood, since the formal patterns of Graeco-Roman logic do not make an appearance. Yet once we translate the statements the authors do make into the language of abstract discourse, we find exact correspondences between the large-scale propositions of the document and the large-scale syllogisms of familiar logic. Along these same lines, we may find numerous individual examples in which, in exquisite detail, the syllogistic mode at hand—if X, then Y; if not X, then not Y—defines the pattern of discourse. We find both brief and simple propositions that make sense of large-scale compositions, e.g., on humility and arrogance, and also an overall scheme of proposition and argument.

As we saw in Chapter 5, the Mishnah makes its principal points by collecting three or five examples of a given rule. The basic rule is not stated, but it is exemplified through the several statements of its application. The reader then may infer the generalization from its specific exemplifications. Sometimes, but not often, the generalization will be made explicit. The whole then constitutes an exercise in rhetoric and logic carried out through list-making. And the same is true in Leviticus Rabbah. But it makes lists of things different from those of the Mishnah: events, not everyday situations. The framers of Leviticus Rabbah revert to sequences of events, all of them exhibiting the same definitive traits and the same ultimate results, e.g., arrogance, downfall, not one time but many; humility, salvation, over and over again, and so throughout. Indeed, if we had to select a single paramount trait of argument in Leviticus Rabbah, it would be the theorem stated by the making of a list of similar examples. The search for the rules lies through numerous instances that, all together, yield the besought rule.

In context, therefore, we have in Leviticus Rabbah the counterpart to the list-making that defined the labor of the philosophers of the Mishnah. Through composing lists of items joined by a monothetic definitive trait, the framers produce underlying or overriding rules always applicable. Here too, through lists of facts of history, the foundations of social life rise to the surface. All of this, we see, constitutes a species of a molecular argument, framed in very definite terms, e.g., Nebuchadnezzar, Sennacherib, David, Josiah did so-and-so with such-and-such result. So, as we said, the mode of argument at hand is the assembly of instances of a common law. The argument derives from the proper construction of a statement of that law in something close to a syllogism. The syllogistic statement often, though not invariably, occurs at the outset—all instances of so-and-so produce such-and-such a result—followed by the required catalog.

The conditional syllogisms of our composition over and over again run through the course of history. The effort is to demonstrate that the rule at hand applies at all times, under all circumstances. Why so? It is because the conditional syllogism must serve under all temporal circumstances. The recurrent listing of events subject to a single rule runs as often as possible through the course of all of human history, from creation to the fourth monarchy (Rome), which, everyone knows, is the end of time prior to the age that is coming. Accordingly, the veracity of rabbinic conditional arguments depends over and over again on showing that the condition holds at all times.

Accordingly, when we listen to the framers of Leviticus Rabbah, we see how statements in the document at hand thus become intelligible not contingently, that is, on the strength of an established text, but *a priori,* that is, on the basis of a deeper logic of meaning and an independent principle of rhetorical intelligibility. Leviticus Rabbah is topical, not exegetical in any received sense. Each of its thirty-seven *parashiyyot* pursues its given topic and develops points relevant to that topic. It is logical in that (to repeat) discourse appeals to an underlying principle of composition and intelligibility, and that logic inheres in what is said. Logic is what joins one sentence to the next and forms the whole into paragraphs of meaning, intelligible propositions, each with its place and sense in a still larger, accessible system. Because of logic one mind connects to another, public discourse becomes possible, debate on issues of general intelligibility takes place, and an anthology of statements about a single subject becomes a composition of theorems about that subject.

In this sense, after the Mishnah, Leviticus Rabbah constitutes the next major logical composition in the rabbinic canon. Accordingly, with Leviticus Rabbah rabbis take up the problem of saying what they wish to say not in an exegetical, but in a syllogistic and freely discursive, logic and rhetoric. It was a pioneering document, but the next set of successors, those associated with the Talmud of Babylonia, reverted to the received form of verse-by-verse commentary, even while accomplishing the same goal of a broad-ranging syllogistic discourse—a synthesis of the form of verse-by-verse exegesis and sustainedly propositional presentation.

5.

Topical Program

The recurrent message of the document may be stated in a brief way. God loves Israel, so gave it the Torah, which defines its life and governs its welfare. Israel is alone in its category (*sui generis*), so what is a virtue to Israel is a vice to the nations, life-giving to Israel, poison to the gentiles. True, Israel sins, but God forgives that sin, having punished the nation on account of it. Such a process has yet to come to an end, but it will culminate in Israel's complete regeneration. Meanwhile, Israel's assurance of God's love lies in the many expressions of special concern, for even the humblest and most ordinary aspects of the national life: the food the nation eats, the sexual practices by which it procreates. These life-sustaining, life-transmitting activities draw God's special interest, as a mark of his general love for Israel. Israel then is supposed to achieve its life in conformity with the marks of God's love.

These indications moreover signify also the character of Israel's difficulty, namely, subordination to the nations in general, but to the fourth kingdom, Rome, in particular. Both food laws and skin diseases stand for the nations. There is yet another category of sin, also collective and generative of collective punishment, and that is social. The moral character of Israel's life, the treatment of people by one another, the practice of gossip and small-scale thuggery—these too draw down divine penalty. The nation's fate therefore corresponds to its moral condition. The moral condition, however, emerges not only from the current generation. Israel's richest hope lies in the merit of the ancestors, thus in the scriptural record of the merits attained by the founders of the nation, those who originally brought it into being and gave it life.

The world to come will right all presently unbalanced relationships. What is good will go forward, what is bad will come to an end. The simple message is that the things people revere, the cult and its majestic course through the year, will go on; Jerusalem will come back, so too the Temple, in all their glory. Israel will be saved through the merit of the ancestors, atonement, study of Torah, practice of religious duties. The prevalence of the eschatological dimension in the formal structures, with its messianic and other expressions, here finds its counterpart in the repetition of the same few symbols in the expression of doctrine.

The theme of the moral life of Israel produces propositions concerning not only the individual but, more important, the social virtues that the community as a whole must exhibit. First of all, the message to the individual constitutes a revision, for this context, of the address to the nation: humility as against arrogance, obedience as against sin, constant concern not to follow one's natural inclination to do evil or to overcome the natural limitations of the human condition. Israel must accept its fate, obey and rely on the merits accrued through the ages and God's special love. The individual must conform, in ordinary affairs, to this same paradigm of patience and submission. Great men and women, that is, individual heroes within the established paradigm, conform to that same pattern, exemplifying the national virtues. Among these, Moses stands out; he has no equal. The special position of the humble Moses is complemented by the patriarchs and by David, all of whom knew how to please God and left as an inheritance to Israel the merit they had thereby attained.

If we now ask about further recurring themes or topics, there is one so commonplace that we should have to list the majority of paragraphs of discourse in order to provide a complete list. It is the list of events in Israel's history, meaning, in this context, Israel's history solely in scriptural times, down through the return to Zion. The one-time events of the generation of the flood, Sodom and Gomorrah, the patriarchs and the sojourn in Egypt, the exodus, the revelation of the Torah at Sinai, the golden calf, the Davidic monarchy and the building of the Temple, Sennacherib, Hezekiah, and the destruction of northern Israel, Nebuchadnezzar and the destruction of the Temple in 586, the life of Israel in Babylonian captivity, Daniel and his associates, Mordecai and Haman—these events occur over and over again. They turn out to serve as paradigms of sin and atonement, steadfastness and divine intervention, and equivalent lessons.

We find, in fact, a fairly standard repertoire of scriptural heroes or villains, on the one side, and conventional lists of Israel's enemies and their actions and downfall, on the other. The boastful, for instance, include the generation of the flood, Sodom and Gomorrah, Pharaoh, Sisera, Sennacherib, Nebuchadnezzar, the wicked empire (Rome)—contrasted to Israel, "despised and humble in this world." The four kingdoms recur again and again, always ending with Rome, with the repeated message that after Rome will come Israel. But Israel has to make this happen through its faith and submission to God's will. Lists of enemies ring the changes on Cain, the Sodomites, Pharaoh, Sennacherib, Nebuchadnezzar, Haman.

At the center of the pretense, that is, the as-if mentality of Leviticus Rabbah and its framers, we find a simple proposition. Israel is God's special love. That love is shown in a simple way. Israel's present condition of subordination derives from its own deeds. It follows that God cares, so Israel may look forward to redemption on God's part in response to Israel's own regeneration through repentance. When the exegetes proceeded to open the scroll of Leviticus, they found numerous occasions to state that proposition in concrete terms and specific contexts. The sinner brings on his own sickness. But God heals through that very ailment. The nations of the world govern in heavy succession, but Israel's lack of faith guaranteed their rule and Israel's moment of renewal will end gentile rule. Israel's leaders—priests, prophets, kings—fall into an entirely different category from those of the nations, as much as does Israel. In these and other concrete allegations, the same classical message comes forth. Israel's sorry condition in no way testifies to Israel's true worth—the grandest pretense of all. All of the little evasions of the primary sense in favor of some other testify to this, the great denial that what is, is what counts.

Leviticus Rabbah makes that statement with art and imagination. But it is never subtle about saying so.

Salvation and sanctification join together in Leviticus Rabbah. The laws of the book of Leviticus, focused as they are on the sanctification of the nation through its cult, in Leviticus Rabbah indicate the rules of salvation as well. The message of Leviticus Rabbah attaches itself to the book of Leviticus, as if that book had come from prophecy and addressed the issue of the meaning of history and Israel's salvation. But the book of Leviticus came from the priesthood and spoke of sanctification. The paradoxical syllogism—the as-if reading, the opposite of how things seem—of the composers of Leviticus Rabbah therefore reaches simple formulation. In the very setting of sanctification we find the promise of salvation. In the topics of the cult and the priesthood we uncover the national and social issues of the moral life and redemptive hope of Israel. The repeated comparison and contrast of priesthood and prophecy, sanctification and salvation, turn out to produce a complement, which comes to most perfect union in the text at hand.

The focus of Leviticus Rabbah and its laws of history is upon the society of Israel, its national fate and moral condition. Indeed, nearly all of the *parashiyyot* of Leviticus Rabbah turn out to deal with the national, social condition of Israel, and this in three contexts: (1) Israel's setting in the history of the nations, (2) the sanctified character of the inner life of Israel itself, (3) the future, salvific history of Israel. So the biblical book that deals with the Tabernacle, identified by the sages as the holy Temple, now is shown to address the holy people. Leviticus really discusses not the consecration of the cult but the sanctification of the nation—its conformity to God's will laid forth in the Torah, and God's rules. So when we review the document as a whole and ask what is that something else that the base text is supposed to address, it turns out that the sanctification of the cult stands for the salvation of the nation. So the nation now is like the cult then, the ordinary Israelite now like the priest then. The holy way of life lived now, through acts to which merit accrues, corresponds to the holy rites then. The process of metamorphosis is full, rich, complete. When everything stands for something else, the something else repeatedly turns out to be the nation. This is what our document spells out in exquisite detail, yet never missing the main point.

6.

A SAMPLE PASSAGE

The treatment of the festival of Tabernacles, part of which follows, allows us to see the transformation of facts into laws of history and the social order. The operative proposition remains comprehensive and simple: Israel's history is explained by Israel's moral condition, therefore Israel itself commands its own destiny, by the will of God.

LEVITICUS RABBAH PARASHAH THIRTY

XXX:I. 1. A. "[On the fifteenth day of the seventh month, when you have gathered in the produce of the land, you shall keep the feast of the Lord seven days. . . .] And you shall take on the first day [the fruit of goodly trees, branches of palm trees and boughs of leafy trees and willows of the brook, and you shall rejoice before the Lord your God for seven days]" (Lev. 23:39–40).

B. R. Abba bar Kahana commenced [discourse by citing the following verse]: "Take my instruction instead of silver, [and knowledge rather than choice gold]" (Prov. 8:10).

C. Said R. Abba bar Kahana, "Take the instruction of the Torah instead of silver.

D. "'Why do you weigh out money? Because there is no bread' (Is. 55:2).

E. "'Why do you weigh out money to the sons of Esau [Rome]? [It is because] "there is no bread," because you did not sate yourselves with the bread of the Torah.

F. "'And [why] do you labor? Because there is no satisfaction' (Is. 55:2)."

G. "'Why do you labor while the nations of the world enjoy plenty? 'Because there is no satisfaction,' that is, because you have not sated yourselves with the wine of the Torah.

H. "For it is written, 'Come, eat of my bread, and drink of the wine I have mixed' (Prov. 9:5)."

2. A. R. Berekhiah and R. Hiyya, his father, in the name of R. Yosé b. Nehori, said, "It is written, 'I shall punish all who oppress him' (Jer. 30:20) even those who collect funds for charity [and in doing so, treat people badly], except [for those who collect] the wages to be paid to teachers and repeaters of Mishnah traditions.

B. "For they receive [as a salary] only compensation for the loss of their time, [which they devote to teaching and learning rather than to earning a living].

C. "But as to the wages [for carrying out] a single matter

in the Torah, no creature can pay the [appropriate] fee in reward."

3.   A.   It has been taught: On the New Year, a person's sustenance is decreed [for the coming year],

      B.   except for what a person pays out [for food in celebration] of the Sabbath, festivals, the celebration of the New Month,

      C.   and for what children bring to the house of their master [as his tuition].

      D.   If he adds [to what is originally decreed], [in Heaven] they add to his [resources], but if he deducts [from what he should give], [in Heaven] they deduct [from his wealth]. [Margulies, p. 688, n. to 1.5, links this statement to Prov. 8:10.]

4.   A.   R. Yohanan was going up from Tiberias to Sepphoris. R. Hiyya bar Abba was supporting him. They came to a field. He said, "This field once belonged to me, but I sold it in order to acquire merit in the Torah."

      B.   They came to a vineyard, and he said, "This vineyard once belonged to me, but I sold it in order to acquire merit in the Torah."

      C.   They came to an olive grove, and he said, "This olive grove once belonged to me, but I sold it in order to acquire merit in the Torah."

      D.   R. Hiyya began to cry.

      E.   Said R. Yohanan, "Why are you crying?"

      F.   He said to him, "It is because you left nothing over to support you in your old age."

      G.   He said to him, "Hiyya, my disciple, is what I did such a light thing in your view? I sold something which was given in a spell of six days [of creation] and in exchange I acquired something which was given in a spell of forty days [of revelation].

      H.   "The entire world and everything in it was created in only six days, as it is written, 'For in six days the Lord made heaven and earth' (Ex. 20:11).

      I.   "But the Torah was given over a period of forty days, as it was said, 'And he was there with the Lord for forty days and forty nights' (Ex. 34:28).

      J.   "And it is written, 'And I remained on the mountain for forty days and forty nights'" (Deut. 9:9).

5.   A.   When R. Yohanan died, his generation recited concerning him [the following verse of Scripture]: "If a

man should give all the wealth of his house for the love" (Song 8:7), with which R. Yohanan loved the Torah, "he would be utterly destitute" (Song 8:7).

B. When R. Hoshaiah of Tiria died, they saw his bier flying in the air. His generation recited concerning him [the following verse of Scripture]: "If a man should give all the wealth of his house for the love," with which the Holy One, blessed be he, loved Abba Hoshaiah of Tiria, "he would be utterly destitute" (Song 8:7).

C. When R. Eleazar b. R. Simeon died, his generation recited concerning him [the following verse of Scripture]: "Who is this who comes up out of the wilderness like pillars of smoke, perfumed with myrrh and frankincense, with all the powders of the merchant?" (Song 3:6).

D. What is the meaning of the clause, "With all the powders of the merchant"?

E. [Like a merchant who carries all sorts of desired powders,] he was a master of Scripture, a repeater of Mishnah traditions, a writer of liturgical supplications, and a poet.

6. A. Said R. Abba bar Kahana, "On the basis of the reward paid for one act of 'taking,' you may assess the reward for [taking] the palm branch [on the festival of Tabernacles].

B. "There was an act of taking in Egypt: 'You will take a bunch of hyssop' (Ex. 12:22).

C. "And how much was it worth? Four *manehs*.

D. "Yet that act of taking is what made Israel inherit the spoil at the sea, the spoil of Sihon and Og, and the spoil of the thirty-one kings.

E. "Now the palm-branch, which costs a person such a high price, and which involves so many religious duties—how much the more so [will a great reward be forthcoming on its account]!"

F. Therefore Moses admonished Israel, saying to them, "And you shall take on the first day . . ." (Lev. 23:40).

1.B seems to me to employ Is. 55:2 as an intersecting verse for the base verse of Prov. 8:10. That, at any rate, is the force of the exegesis of 1.C–G. Then the citation of Prov. 9:5 presents a secondary expansion of what has been said about Is. 55:2, that is, 1.F–G lead us directly to H. What has happened to Lev. 23:39? In fact, 1.B–H are inserted whole because of the use of the key word "take," at Lev. 23:39 and Prov. 8:10. From that point, Lev. 23:39 plays no role whatsoever. It is only at No. 6 that Lev. 23:39—with stress on the word "take"—recurs. The theme of the intervening passages is established at 1.B, namely, Torah and the value and importance of study of Torah. Nos. 2, 3, 4, and 5 all present variations on amplifications of that theme. I cannot follow Margulies in linking No. 3 to the intersecting verse. No. 5 is attached because of No. 4, and No. 4 because of its homily on the Torah. Since No. 6 ignores all that has gone before, and since No. 6 alone alludes to 1.A, we have to regard as remarkable the insertion of the rather sizable construction, 1.B through 5.E. In some other passages we see subtle connections between the base verse, or, at least, the theme of the base verse, and the exegesis of the intersecting verse, and the secondary exegetical expansions of verses introduced in connection with the intersecting one. But here I see none. Even the key word, "take," does not recur beyond the intersecting verse. So the editorial principle accounting for the inclusion of 1.B–5.E is the occurrence of a single shared word, that alone. That seems to me uncommon in our document. As to No. 6, the homily rests on the key word, "take," and that is made explicit. But No. 6 does not rest upon the exegesis of any intersecting verse; it is a simple exegetical homily. 6.F is secondary, a redactional filling we shall see again.

XXX:II. 1. A. "You show me the path of life, [in your presence] there is fullness of joy" (Ps. 16:11).

B. Said David before the Holy One, blessed be he, "Show me the open gateway to the life of the world to come."

2. A. R. Yudan said, "David said before the Holy One, blessed be he, 'Lord of the ages, Show me the path of life.'"

B. "Said the Holy One, blessed be he, to David, 'If you seek life, look for fear, as it is said, "The fear of the Lord prolongs life"'" (Prov. 10:27).

C. R. Azariah said, "The Holy One, blessed be he, said to David, 'David, if you seek life, look for suffering (YYSWRYN), as it is said, "The reproofs of discipline (MWSR) are the way of life"'" (Prov. 6:23).

D. Rabbis say, "The Holy One, blessed be he, said to David, 'David, if you seek life, look for Torah,' as it is said, 'It is a tree of life to those that hold fast to it'" (Prov. 3:18).

E. R. Abba said, "David said before the Holy One, blessed be he, 'Lord of the ages, "Show me the path of life."'"

F. "Said to him the Holy One, blessed be he, 'Start fighting and exert yourself! Why are you puzzled? Work and eat: "Keep my commandments and live"'" (Prov. 4:4).

3. A. "The fullness (SWB') of joy" (Ps. 16:11):

B.   Satisfy (SB'NW) us with five joys: Scripture, Mishnah, Talmud, Supplements, and Lore.

4.   A.   Another matter: "In your presence is the fullness of joy" (Ps. 16:11):

B.   Read not "fullness (SWB')" but "seven (SB')." These are the seven groups of righteous men who are going to welcome the Presence of God. [The Hebrew, "receive the face," ordinarily yields "welcome."]

C.   And their face is like the sun, moon, firmament, stars, lightning, lilies, and the pure candelabrum that was in the house of the sanctuary.

D.   How do we know that it is like the sun? As it is said, "Clear as the sun" (Song 6:10).

E.   How do we know that it is like the moon? As it is said, "As lovely as the moon" (Song 6:10).

F.   How do we know that it is like the firmament? As it is said, "And they that are wise shall shine as the brightness of the firmament" (Dan. 12:3).

G.   How do we know that it is like the stars? As it is said, "And they that turn the many to righteousness as the stars forever and ever" (Dan. 12:3).

H.   And how do we know that it is like the lightning? As it is said, "Their appearance is like torches, they run to and fro like lightning" (Nah. 2:5).

I.   How do we know that it is like lilies? As it is said, "For the leader: upon the lilies" (Ps. 80:1).

J.   How do we know that it will be like the pure candelabrum? As it is said, "And he said to me, 'What do you see?' And I said, 'I looked and behold [there was] a candelabrum all of gold'" (Zech. 4:2).

5.   A.   "At your right hand is bliss for evermore" (Ps. 16:11).

B.   Said David before the Holy One, blessed be he, "Lord of the ages, now who will tell me which group is the most beloved and blissful of them all?"

C.   There were two Amoras [who differed on this matter]. One of them said, "It is the group that comes as representative of the Torah and commandments, as it is said, 'With a flaming fire at his right hand'" (Deut. 33:2).

D.   And the other said, "This refers to the scribes, the Mishnah repeaters, and those who teach children in their fear, who are going to stand at the right hand of the Holy One, blessed be he.

E.   "That is in line with the following verse of Scripture:

'I keep the Lord always before me, because he is at my right hand, I shall not be moved'" (Ps. 16:8).

    F.   "[You show me the path of life, in your presence there is fullness of joy,] in your right hand are pleasures for evermore" (Ps. 16:11).

6.   A.   Another matter: "You show me the path of life" (Ps. 16:11) speaks of Israel.

    B.   Israel stated before the Holy One, blessed be he, "Lord of the ages, 'Show me the path of life.'"

    C.   Said to them the Holy One, blessed be he, "Lo, you have the ten days of repentance between the New Year and the Day of Atonement."

7.   A.   "In your presence there is fullness (SWB') of joy" (Ps. 16:11):

    B.   Read only "seven (SB') joys." These are the seven religious duties associated with the Festival [Tabernacles].

    C.   These are they: the four species that are joined in the palm branch, [the building of] the tabernacle, [the offering of] the festal sacrifice, [the offering of] the sacrifice of rejoicing.

8.   A.   What is the meaning of the phrase, "In your right hand are pleasures for evermore (NSH)" (Ps. 16:11)?

    B.   Said R. Abin, "This refers to the palm branch. It is comparable to one who is victor (NWSH) and so takes the branch as [a sign of his victory].

    C.   "The matter may be compared to two who came before a judge. Now we do not know which one of them is the victor. But it is the one who takes the palm branch in his hand who we know to be the victor.

    D.   "So is the case of Israel and the nations of the world. The [latter] come and draw an indictment before the Holy One, blessed be he, on the New Year, and we do not know which party is victor.

    E.   "But when Israel goes forth from before the Holy One, blessed be he, with their palm branches and their citrons in their hands, we know that it is Israel that is the victor."

    F.   Therefore Moses admonishes Israel, saying to them, "And you shall take on the first day . . . [branches of palm trees]" (Lev. 23:40).

The base verse is not explicitly cited, but the intersecting verse—Ps. 16:11—leads us to it, after a long and majestic sequence of exegeses of the three elements of the intersecting verse. When we reach the base verse, the connection turns out to be tight and persuasive. Nos. 6–8 show us the ideal form, that is, a clause-by-clause reading of the intersecting verse within a coherent hermeneutic. If then we look back to the earlier materials, Nos. 2–5, we find a somewhat less cogent exegesis of the three clauses. No. 2 reads the verse as a statement by David. No. 4 would look to be interpolated, were it not for No. 5, which brings us back to David, and which refers to the materials expounded at No. 4. Then the original repertoire of key words—"Torah," "commandments," and the like—is reviewed. Nos. 6–8 go over the same verse with respect to Israel, introducing the matters of the New Year, the Day of Atonement, and the Festival. Then each clause suitably links to the several themes at hand. 8.F is tacked on.

XXX:III. 1. A. "He will regard the prayer of the destitute [and will not despise their supplication]" (Ps. 102:17).

B. Said R. Abin, "We are unable to make sense of David's character. Sometimes he calls himself king, and sometimes he calls himself destitute.

C. "How so? When he foresaw that righteous men were going to come from him, such as Asa, Jehoshaphat, Hezekiah, and Josiah, he would call himself king as it is said, 'Give the king your judgments, O God' (Ps. 72:1).

D. "When he foresaw that wicked men would come forth from him, for example, Ahaz, Manasseh, and Amon, he would call himself destitute, as it is said, 'A prayer of one afflicted, when he is faint [and pours out his complaint before the Lord]' (Ps. 102:1)."

2. A. R. Alexandri interpreted the cited verse (Ps. 102:1) to speak of a worker. [The one afflicted is the worker. The word for "faint," 'TP, bears the meaning "cloak oneself," hence "in prayer." The worker then has delayed his prayer, waiting for the overseer to leave, at which point he can stop and say his prayer. So he postpones his prayer (Margulies).] [So Alexandri says], "Just as a worker sits and watches all day long for when the overseer will leave for a bit, so he is late when he says [his prayer], [so David speaks at Ps. 102:1: 'Hear my prayer, O Lord; let my cry come to you']."

B. "That [interpretation of the word 'TP] is in line with the use in the following verse: 'And those cattle and sheep that were born late belonged to Laban'" (Gen. 30:42).

C. What is the meaning of "those that were born late"?

D. R. Isaac bar Haqqolah said, "The ones that tarried."

3. A. Another interpretation: "He will regard the prayer of the destitute individual [and will not despise their supplication]" (Ps. 102:17):

B. Said R. Simeon b. Laqish, "As to this verse, the first half of it is not consistent with the second half, and vice versa.

C. "If it is to be, 'He will regard the prayer of the destitute [individual],' he should then have said, 'And will not despise *his* supplication.'

D. "But if it is to be, 'He will not despise *their* supplication,' then he should have said, 'He will regard the prayer of those who are destitute.'

E. "But [when David wrote,] 'He will regard the prayer of the individual destitute,' this [referred to] the prayer of Manasseh, king of Judah.

F. "And [when David wrote,] 'He will not despise their supplication,' this [referred to] his prayer and the prayer of his fathers.

G. "That is in line with the following verse of Scripture: 'And he prayed to him, and he was entreated (Y'TR) of him'" (2 Chron. 33:13).

H. What is the meaning of the phrase, "He was entreated of him"?

I. Said R. Eleazar b. R. Simeon, "In Arabia they call a breach an *athirta* [so an opening was made for his prayer to penetrate to the Throne of God]" (Slotki, p. 385, n. 3).

J. "And he brought him back to Jerusalem, his kingdom" (2 Chron. 33:13).

K. How did he bring him back?

L. R. Samuel b. R. Jonah said in the name of R. Aha, "He brought him back with a wind.

M. "That is in line with the phrase, 'He causes the wind to blow.'"

N. At that moment: "And Manasseh knew that the Lord is God" (2 Chron. 33:13). Then Manasseh said, "There is justice and there is a judge."

4. A. Another interpretation: "He will regard the prayer of the destitute" (Ps. 102:17) refers to the generation of Mordecai.

B. "And will not despise their supplication"—for he did not despise either his prayer or the prayer of his fathers.

5. A. R. Isaac interpreted the verse to speak of these genera-

tions that have neither king nor prophet, neither priest nor Urim and Thummim, but who have only this prayer alone.

B. "Said David before the Holy One, blessed be he, 'Lord of the ages, "Do not despise their prayer. 'Let this be recorded for a generation to come'"'" (Ps. 102:18).

C. "On the basis of that statement, [we know that] the Holy One, blessed be he, accepts penitents.

D. "'So that a people yet unborn may praise the Lord' [Ps. 102:18].

E. "For the Holy One, blessed be he, will create them as a new act of creation."

6. A. Another interpretation: "Let this be recorded for a generation to come" (Ps. 102:18):

B. This refers to the generation of Hezekiah, which was tottering toward death.

C. "So that a people yet unborn may praise the Lord" (Ps. 102:18): for the Holy One, blessed be he, created them in a new act of creation.

7. A. Another interpretation: "Let this be recorded for a generation to come" (Ps. 102:18):

B. This refers to the generation of Mordecai, which was tottering toward death.

C. "So that a people yet unborn may praise the Lord" (Ps. 102:18): for the Holy One, blessed be he, created them in a new act of creation.

8. A. Another interpretation: "Let this be recorded for a generation to come" (Ps. 102:18):

B. This refers to these very generations, which are tottering to death.

C. "So that a people yet unborn may praise the Lord" (Ps. 102:18):

D. For the Holy One, blessed be he, is going to create them anew, in a new act of creation.

9. A. What do we have to do [in order to reach that end]? Take up the palm branch and citron and praise the Holy One, blessed be he.

B. Therefore Moses admonishes Israel, saying, "You shall take on the first day . . ." (Lev. 23:30).

Until the very final lines, No. 9, we have no reason at all to associate the exegesis of Ps. 102:17–18 with the theme of the Festival. On the contrary, all of the materials are independent of the present "base verse," and none of them hints at what is to come at the end. On that basis I regard the construction as complete prior to its insertion here, with a redactional hand contributing only No. 9 to validate the inclusion of an otherwise irrelevant exegetical exercise. The established pattern—the tripartite exegesis of Ps. 102:17, 18—is worked out at No. 1 (supplemented by Nos. 2 and 3), then Nos. 4–8.

XXX:IV. 1. A. "'Let the field exult and everything in it.' [Then shall all the trees of the wood sing for joy before the Lord, for he comes, for he comes to judge the earth]" (Ps. 96:12–13).

B. "Let the field exult" refers to the world, as it is said, "And it came to pass, when they were in the field" (Gen. 4:8) [and determined to divide up the world between them].

C. "And everything in it" refers to creatures.

D. That is in line with the following verse of Scripture: "The earth is the Lord's, and all that is in it" (Ps. 24:1).

E. "Then shall all the trees of the wood sing for joy" (Ps. 96:12).

F. Said R. Aha, "The forest and all the trees of the forest.

G. "The forest refers to fruit-bearing trees.

H. "'And all the trees of the forest' encompasses those trees that do not bear fruit."

I. Before whom? "Before the Lord" (Ps. 96:14).

J. Why? "For he comes" on New Year and on the Day of Atonement.

K. To do what? "To judge the earth: He will judge the world with righteousness, and the peoples with his truth" (Ps. 96:13).

L. On that basis what do we have to do? We take a citron, boughs of leafy trees, a palm branch, and a willow [branch], and give praise before the Holy One, blessed be he: "And you shall take on the first day . . ." (Lev. 23:40).

Ps. 96:12–14 supplies direct connections to the theme of Tabernacles, with its reference to trees of the wood, exultation and rejoicing, judgment, and the like. These topics are explicitly read into the intersecting verse at the end, but I am inclined to see the whole as a single and unified construction, with 1.F–H as an interpolated comment.

XXX:V. 1. A. "I wash my hands in innocence [and go about your altar, O Lord, singing aloud a song of thanksgiving, and telling all your wondrous deeds]" (Ps. 26:6–7).

    B.   [What I require I acquire] through purchase, not theft.

    C.   For we have learned there: "A stolen or dried-up palm branch is invalid. And one deriving from an *asherah* or an apostate town is invalid" (M. Suk. 3:1A–B).

    D.   "And go about your altar, O Lord" (Ps. 26:7).

    E.   That is in line with what we have learned there (M. Suk. 4:5): Every day they circumambulate the altar one time and say, "We beseech you, O Lord, save now. We beseech you, O Lord, make us prosper now (Ps. 118:25). R. Judah says, "I and he—save now." On that day they circumambulate the altar seven times.

2.   A.   "Singing aloud a song of thanksgiving" (Ps. 26:7)—this refers to the offerings.

    B.   "And telling all your wondrous deeds" (Ps. 26:7):

    C.   Said R. Abin, "This refers to the *Hallel* Psalms [Ps. 113–18], which contain [praise for what God has done] in the past, also [what he has done] during these generations, as well as what will apply to the days of the Messiah, to the time of Gog and Magog, and to the age to come.

    D.   "'When Israel went forth from Egypt' [Ps. 114:1] refers to the past.

    E.   "'Not for us, O Lord, not for us' [Ps. 115:1] refers to the present generations.

    F.   "'I love for the Lord to hear' [Ps. 116:1] refers to the days of the Messiah.

    G.   "'All the nations have encompassed me' [Ps. 118:10] speaks of the time of Gog and Magog.

    H.   "'You are my God and I shall exalt you' [Ps. 118:28] speaks of the age to come."

No. 1 makes a point quite distinct from No. 2. "The innocence" of Ps. 26:6 refers to the fact that one must not steal the objects used to carry out the religious duty of the waving of the palm branch on Tabernacles. I assume that the allusion to Tabernacles in Ps. 26:6–7 is found in the referring to circumambulating the altar, such as is done in the rite on that day, as 1.C makes explicit. No. 2 then expands on the cited verse in a different way. To be sure, the *Hallel* Psalms are recited on Tabernacles, but they serve all other festivals as well. Only No. 1 therefore relates to the established context of Lev. 23:40. It follows that the exegeses of Ps. 26:6–7 were assembled and only then utilized—both the relevant and also the irrelevant parts—for the present purpose.

Now we turn from the base-verse/intersecting-verse compositions to the systematic reading of the verse under study, Lev. 23:40. This order—base verse/intersecting verse, then verse-by-verse exegesis—is absolutely fixed for this document and all others that combine the two forms. It serves our purpose to give only part of the remainder of the *parashah*.

XXX:VI. 1. A. "And you will take for yourselves" (Lev. 23:40).

B. R. Hiyya taught, "[You take the required species] through purchase and not through thievery."

C. "For yourselves"—for every one of you. They must be yours and not stolen.

2. A. Said R. Levi, "One who takes a stolen palm branch— to what is he comparable? To a thief who sat at the crossroads and mugged passersby.

B. "One time a legate came by, to collect the taxes for that town. [The thug] rose before him and mugged him and took everything he had. After some time the thug was caught and put in prison. The legate heard and came to him. He said to him, 'Give back what you grabbed from me, and I'll argue in your behalf before the king.'

C. "He said to him, 'Of everything that I robbed and of everything that I took, I have nothing except for this rug that is under me, and it belongs to you.'

D. "He said to him, 'Give it to me, and I'll argue in your behalf before the king.'

E. "He said to him, 'Take it.'

F. "He said to him, 'You should know that tomorrow you are going before the king for judgment, and he will ask you and say to you, "Is there anyone who can argue in your behalf," and you may say to him, "I have the legate, Mr. So-and-so, to speak in my behalf," and he will send and call me, and I shall come and argue in your behalf before him.'

G. "The next day they set him up for judgment before the king. The king asked him, saying to him, 'Do you have anyone to argue in your behalf?'

H. "He said to him, 'I have a legate, Mr. So-and-so, to speak in my behalf.'

I. "The king sent for him. He said to him, 'Do you know anything to say in behalf of this man?'

J. "He said to him, 'I do indeed have knowledge. When you sent me to collect the taxes of that town, he rose up before me and mugged me and took everything that I had. That rug that belongs to me gives testimony against him.'

K. "Everyone began to cry out, saying, 'Woe for this one, whose defense attorney has turned into his prosecutor.'

L.   "So a person acquires a palm branch to attain merit
     through it. But if it was a stolen one, [the branch] cries
     out before the Holy One, blessed be he, 'I am stolen!
     I am taken by violence.'

M.   "And the ministering angels say, 'Woe for this one,
     whose defense attorney has turned into his prosecutor!'"

The theme of the preceding, the prohibition against using a stolen palm
branch, is given two further treatments. Except in a formal way none of this pretends to relate to the specific verses of Lev. 23:40ff., nor do we find an intersecting verse.

XXX:VII.   1.   A.   "[On the fifteenth day of the seventh month, when
                     you have gathered the produce of the land, you shall
                     keep the feast of the Lord seven days;] on the first day
                     [shall be a solemn rest]" (Lev. 23:40).

                B.   This in fact is the fifteenth day, yet you speak of the
                     first day!

                C.   R. Mana of Sheab and R. Joshua of Sikhnin in the
                     name of R. Levi said, "The matter may be compared
                     to the case of a town that owed arrears to the king, so
                     the king went to collect [what was owing]. [When he
                     had reached] ten *mils* [that is, about a half a mile from
                     the town], the great men of the town came forth and
                     praised him. He remitted a third of their [unpaid] tax.
                     When he came within five *mils* of the town, the
                     middle-rank people came out and acclaimed him, so he
                     remitted yet another third [of what was owing to him].
                     When he entered the town, men, women, and children
                     came forth and praised him. He remitted the whole [of
                     the tax].

                D.   "Said the king, 'What happened happened. From now
                     on we shall begin keeping books [afresh].'

                E.   "So on the eve of the New Year, the great men of the
                     generation fast, and the Holy One, blessed be he, re-
                     mits a third of their [that is, Israel's] sins. From the New
                     Year to the Day of Atonement outstanding individuals
                     fast, and the Holy One, blessed be he, remits a third of
                     their [that is, Israel's] sins. On the Day of Atonement
                     all of them fast, men, women, and children, so the
                     Holy One, blessed be he, says to Israel, 'What hap-
                     pened happened. From now on we shall begin keeping
                     books [afresh].'"

2. A. Said R. Aha, "'For with you there is forgiveness' [Ps. 80:4]. From the New Year forgiveness awaits you.

    B. "Why so long? 'So that you may be feared' [Ps. 80:4]. To put your fear into creatures.

    C. "From the Day of Atonement to the Festival, all the Israelites are kept busy with doing religious duties. This one takes up the task of building his booth, that one preparing his palm branches. On the first day of the Festival, all Israel stands before the Holy One, blessed be he, with their palm branches and citrons in their hands, praising the name of the Holy One, blessed be he. The Holy One, blessed be he, says to them, 'What happened happened. From now on we shall begin keeping books [afresh].'"

    D. Therefore Moses admonished Israel: "And you shall take on the first day . . ." (Lev. 23:40).

Nos. 1 and 2 go over the same matter. It seems to me that Aha's version puts into concrete terms the basic point of Levi's. 2.D is out of place, since it ignores the antecedent materials and takes as its proof text a formula in no way important in the preceding. Once more the ultimate redactor's hand is in evidence.

Now we come to one of the most interesting types of later Midrash composition, the "another interpretation" or "another matter" formulations. We have already examined one of these, in Genesis Rabbah. Here is a much richer example of the same.

XXX.VIII. 1. A. "On the first day" (Lev. 23:40):

        B. By day and not by night.

        C. "On the . . . day"—even on the Sabbath.

        D. "On the *first* day"—only the first day [of the Festival] overrides the restrictions [of Sabbath rest. When the Sabbath coincides with other than the first day of the Festival, one does not carry the palm branch.]

    2. A. "[And you shall take . . .] the fruit of a goodly tree [branches of palm trees and boughs of leafy trees and willows of the brook]" (Lev. 23:40).

        B. R. Hiyya taught, "'A tree': the taste of the wood and fruit of which is the same. This is the citron."

        C. "Goodly (HDR)": Ben Azzai said, "[Fruit] that remains [HDR] on its tree from year to year."

        D. Aqilas the proselyte translated [HDR] as, "That which dwells by water (Greek: *hudor*)."

        E. "Branches of a palm tree" (Lev. 23:40): R. Tarfon says,

"[As to the branch of a palm tree (KPWT)], it must be bound. If it was separated, one has to bind it up."

F.   "Boughs of leafy trees": The branches of which cover the wood. One has to say, "This is the myrtle."

G.   "Willows of the brook": I know only that they must come from a brook. How do I know that those that come from a valley or a hill [also are valid]? Scripture says, "*And* willows of a brook."

H.   Abba Saul says, "'*And* willows of the brook' refers to the requirement that there be two, one willow for the palm branch, and a willow for the sanctuary."

I.   R. Ishmael says, "'The fruit of goodly trees' indicates one; 'branches of palm tree' also one; 'boughs of leafy trees,' three; 'willows of the brook,' two. Two [of the myrtles] may have the twigs trimmed at the top, and one may not."

J.   R. Tarfon says, "Even all three of them may be trimmed."

XXX:IX. 1. A.   Another interpretation: "The fruit of goodly (HDR) trees": this refers to the Holy One, blessed be he, concerning whom it is written, "You are clothed with glory and majesty (HDR)" (Ps. 104:1).

B.   "Branches of palm trees": this refers to the Holy One, blessed be he, concerning whom it is written, "The Righteous One shall flourish like a palm tree" (Ps. 92:13).

C.   "Boughs of leafy trees": this refers to the Holy One, blessed be he, concerning whom it is written, "And he stands among the leafy trees" (Zech. 1:8).

D.   "And willows of the brook": this refers to the Holy One, blessed be he, concerning whom it is written, "Extol him who rides upon the willows, whose name is the Lord" (Ps. 68:5).

The base text is systematically read in line with intersecting verses referring to God. The species are read as symbolizing, in sequence, God, the patriarchs and matriarchs, Torah institutions, and Israel.

XXX:X. 1. A.   Another interpretation: "The fruit of goodly (HDR) trees" (Lev. 23:40):

B.   This refers to Abraham, whom the Holy One, blessed be he, honored (HDR) with a goodly old age,

C. as it is said, "And Abraham was an old man, growing old in years" (Gen. 24:1).

D. And it is written, "And you will honor (HDR) the face of an old man" (Lev. 19:32).

E. "Branches (KPWT) of palm trees" (Lev. 23:40):

F. This refers to Isaac, who was tied (KPWT) and bound upon the altar.

G. "And boughs of leafy trees" (Lev. 23:40):

H. This refers to Jacob. Just as a myrtle is rich in leaves, so Jacob was rich in children.

I. "Willows of the brook" (Lev. 23:40):

J. This refers to Joseph. Just as the willow wilts before the other three species do, so Joseph died before his brothers did.

2. A. Another interpretation: "The fruit of goodly trees" (Lev. 23:40):

B. This refers to Sarah, whom the Holy One, blessed be he, honored with a goodly old age, as it is said, "And Abraham and Sarah were old" (Gen. 18:11).

C. "Branches of palm trees" (Lev. 23:40): this refers to Rebecca. Just as a palm tree contains both edible fruit and thorns, so Rebecca produced a righteous and a wicked son [Jacob and Esau].

D. "Boughs of leafy trees" (Lev. 23:40): this refers to Leah. Just as a myrtle is rich in leaves, so Leah was rich in children.

E. "And willows of the brook" (Lev. 23:40): this refers to Rachel. Just as the willow wilts before the other three species do, so Rachel died before her sister.

The powerful result of the exegesis is to link the species of the Festival to the patriarchs and matriarchs of Israel. It is continuous with the foregoing, linking the species to God, and with what is to follow, as the species will be compared to Israel's leadership, on the one side, as well, finally, to ordinary people, on the other.

XXX:XI. 1. A. Another interpretation: "The fruit of goodly trees" (Lev. 23:40): this refers to the great Sanhedrin of Israel, which the Holy One, blessed be he, honored (HDR) with old age, as it is said, "You will rise up before old age" (Lev. 19:32).

B. "Branches (KPWT) of palm trees" (Lev. 23:40): this refers to disciples of sages, who compel (KWPYN) themselves to study Torah from one another.

C. "Boughs of leafy trees": this refers to the three rows of disciples who sit before them.

D. "And willows of the brook" (Lev. 23:40): this refers to the court scribes, who stand before them, one on the right side, the other on the left, and write down the opinions of those who vote to acquit and those who vote to convict.

XXX:XII. 1. A. Another interpretation: "The fruit of goodly trees" refers to Israel.

B. Just as a citron has both taste and fragrance, so in Israel are people who have [the merit of both] Torah and good deeds.

C. "Branches of palm trees" (Lev. 23:30) refers to Israel. Just as a palm has a taste but no fragrance, so in Israel are people who have [the merit of] Torah but not of good deeds.

D. "Boughs of leafy trees" refers to Israel. Just as a myrtle has a fragrance but no taste, so in Israel are people who have the merit of good deeds but not of Torah.

E. "Willows of the brook" refers to Israel. Just as a willow has neither taste nor fragrance, so in Israel are those who have the [merit] neither of Torah nor of good deeds.

F. What does the Holy One, blessed be he, do for them? Utterly to destroy them is not possible.

G. Rather, said the Holy One, blessed be he, "Let them all be joined together in a single bond, and they will effect atonement for one another.

H. "And if you have done so, at that moment I shall be exalted."

I. That is in line with the following verse of Scripture: "He who builds his upper chambers in heaven" (Amos 9:6).

J. And when is he exalted? When they are joined together in a single bond, as it is said, "When he has founded his bond upon the earth" (Amos 9:6).

K. Therefore Moses admonishes Israel: "And you shall take . . . " (Lev. 23:40).

The final exegesis reaches its climax here, concluding, then, with the redactional subscript. The composition follows a single program, from beginning to end, as it rehearses the several intersecting realms of Judaic symbol systems. Always at the climax come Torah and good deeds. 1.K is tacked on.

XVI

PESIQTA deRab KAHANA

1.

IDENTIFYING THE DOCUMENT

A COMPILATION OF TWENTY-EIGHT PROPOSITIONAL DISCOURSES, PESIQTA DERAB
Kahana (*pisqa* yields "chapter," so the plural can be rendered, "chapters attributed
to R. Kahana"), innovates because it appeals for its themes and lections to the
liturgical calendar, rather than to a pentateuchal book.[1] Pesiqta deRab Kahana
marks a stunning innovation in Midrash compilation because it abandons the pre-

---

[1] For further reading and bibliography on the topic of this chapter, see the following:

Bowker, pp. 74–75.

Maccoby omits this document from his introduction.

Bernard Mandelbaum, "Pesikta deRav Kahana," *Encyclopaedia Judaica* 13:333–34: the identification
of the document; the original structure of the document and manuscript evidence; the manuscripts of the document; the original order followed the cycle of the Jewish calendar from the
New Year through the Sabbath before the next New Year.

Stemberger-Strack, pp. 317–22: translation; the name, contents and structure, redaction and date
(various).

This writer's introduction is *Pesiqta deRab Kahana. An Analytical Translation and Explanation*. II.
15–28. With an Introduction to Pesiqta deRab Kahana. Atlanta, 1987: Scholars Press for Brown Judaic

tense that fixed associative connections derive solely from Scripture. Rather, the document follows the synagogal lections. The text that governs the organization of Pesiqta deRab Kahana comprises a liturgical occasion of the synagogue, which is identical to a holy day. The text has told our authorship what topic it wishes to take up—and therefore also what verses of Scripture (if any) prove suitable to that topic and its exposition. The liturgy and *pisqaot* correspond as follows:

Months	Holy Days	Pisqaot
Adar-Nisan-Sivan	Passover-Pentecost:	*Pisqaot 2–12*
	(possible exception:	*Pisqa 6)*
Tammuz-Ab-Elul	The Ninth of Ab:	*Pisqaot 13–22*
Tishré	Tishré 1–22:	*Pisqaot 23–28*

Only Pisqa 1 (possibly also Pisqa 6) falls out of synchronic relationship with a long sequence of special occasions in the synagogal lections. The twenty-eight *parishiy-yot* of Pesiqta deRab Kahana in order follow the synagogal lections from early spring through fall, in the Western calendar, from late February or early March through late September or early October, approximately half of the solar year, twenty-seven weeks, and somewhat more than half of the lunar year. On the very surface, the basic building block is the theme of a given lectionary Sabbath—that is, a Sabbath distinguished by a particular lection—and not the theme dictated by a given passage of Scripture, let alone the exposition of the language or proposition of such a scriptural verse. The topical program of the document may be defined very simply: expositions of themes dictated by special Sabbaths or festivals and their lections.

Pisqa	Base Verse	Topic or Occasion
1.	*On the day Moses completed* (Num. 7:1)	Torah lection for the Sabbath of Hanukkah
2.	*When you take the census* (Ex. 30:12)	Torah lection for the Sabbath of Sheqalim, first of the four Sabbaths prior to the advent of Nisan, in which Passover falls
3.	*Remember Amalek* (Deut. 25:17–19)	Torah lection for the Sabbath of Zakhor, second of the four Sabbaths prior to the advent of Nisan, in which Passover falls
4.	*Red heifer* (Num. 19:1ff.)	Torah lection for the Sabbath of Parah, third of the four Sabbaths prior to the advent of Nisan, in which Passover falls

Studies. *From Tradition to Imitation. The Plan and Program of Pesiqta deRab Kahana and Pesiqta Rabbati.* Atlanta, 1987: Scholars Press for Brown Judaic Studies.

Pisqa	Base Verse	Topic or Occasion
5.	*This month* (Ex. 12:1–2)	Torah lection for the Sabbath of Hahodesh, fourth of the four Sabbaths prior to the advent of Nisan, in which Passover falls
6.	*My offerings* (Num. 28:1–4)	Torah lection for the New Moon, which falls on a weekday
7.	*It came to pass at midnight* (Ex. 12:29–32)	Torah lection for the first day of Passover
8.	*The first sheaf* (Lev. 23:11)	Torah lection for the second day of Passover, on which the first sheaves of barley were harvested and waved as an offering
9.	*When a bull or sheep or goat is born* (Lev. 22:26)	Lection for Passover
10.	*You shall set aside a tithe* (Deut. 14:22)	Torah lection for Sabbath during Passover in the Land of Israel or for the eighth day of Passover outside of the Land of Israel
11.	*When Pharaoh let the people go* (Ex. 13:17–18)	Torah lection for the Seventh Day of Passover
12.	*In the third month* (Ex. 19:1ff.)	Torah lection for Pentecost
13.	*The words of Jeremiah* (Jer. 1:1–3)	Prophetic lection for the first of three Sabbaths prior to the Ninth of Ab
14.	*Hear* (Jer. 2:4–6)	Prophetic lection for the second of three Sabbaths prior to the Ninth of Ab
15.	*How lonely sits the city* (Lam. 1:1–2)	Prophetic lection for the third of three Sabbaths prior to the Ninth of Ab
16.	*Comfort* (Is. 40:1–2)	Prophetic lection for the first of three Sabbaths following the Ninth of Ab
17.	*But Zion said* (Is. 49:14–16)	Prophetic lection for the second of three Sabbaths following the Ninth of Ab
18.	*O afflicted one, storm tossed* (Is. 54:11–14)	Prophetic lection for the third of three Sabbaths following the Ninth of Ab
19.	*I even I am he who comforts you* (Is. 51:12–15)	Prophetic lection for the fourth of three Sabbaths following the Ninth of Ab
20.	*Sing aloud, O barren woman* (Is. 54:1ff.)	Prophetic lection for the fifth of three Sabbaths following the Ninth of Ab
21.	*Arise, Shine* (Is. 60:1–3)	Prophetic lection for the sixth of three Sabbaths following the Ninth of Ab
22.	*I will greatly rejoice in the Lord* (Is. 61:10–11)	Prophetic lection for the seventh of three Sabbaths following the Ninth of Ab
23.	*The New Year*	No base verse indicated. The theme is God's justice and judgment.

Pisqa	Base Verse	Topic or Occasion
24.	*Return O Israel to the Lord your God* (Hos. 14:1–3)	Prophetic lection for the Sabbath of Repentance between New Year and Day of Atonement
25.	*Selihot*	No base verse indicated. The theme is God's forgiveness.
26.	*After the death of the two sons of Aaron* (Lev. 16:1ff.)	Torah lection for the Day of Atonement
27.	*And you shall take on the first day* (Lev. 23:39–43)	Torah-lection for the first day of the Festival of Tabernacles
28.	*On the eighth day* (Num. 29:35–39)	Torah lection for the Eighth Day of Solemn Assembly

This catalog draws our attention to three eccentric *pisqaot,* distinguished by their failure to build discourse upon the base verse. These are No. 4, which may fairly claim that its topic, the red cow, occurs in exact verbal formulation in the verses at hand; No. 23, the New Year, and No. 25, *Selihot.* The last-named may or may not take an integral place in the structure of the whole. But the middle item, the New Year, on the very surface is essential to a structure that clearly wishes to follow the line of holy days onward through the Sabbath of Repentance, the Day of Atonement, the Festival of Tabernacles, and the Eighth Day of Solemn Assembly.

It follows that unlike Genesis Rabbah and Leviticus Rabbah, the document focuses upon the life of the synagogue. Its framers set forth propositions in the manner of the authorship of Leviticus Rabbah. But these are framed by appeal not only to the rules governing the holy society, as in Leviticus Rabbah, but also to the principal events of Israel's history, celebrated in the worship of the synagogue. What we do not find in this Midrash compilation is exposition of pentateuchal or prophetic passages, verse by verse; the basis chosen by our authorship for organizing and setting forth its propositions is the character and theme of holy days and their special synagogue Torah lections. That is, all of the selected base verses upon which the *parashiyyot* or chapters are built, pentateuchal or prophetic, are identified with synagogal lections for specified holy days, special Sabbaths, or festivals.

The contrast to the earlier compilations—this one is generally assigned to ca. 500—is striking. The framers of Sifra and Sifré to Numbers and Sifré to Deuteronomy follow the verses of Scripture and attach to them whatever messages they wish to deliver. The authorship of Genesis Rabbah follows suit, though less narrowly guided by verses and more clearly interested in their broader themes. The framers of Leviticus Rabbah attached rather broad, discursive, and syllogistic statements to verses of the book of Leviticus, but these verses do not follow in close sequence, one, then the next, as in Sifra and documents like it. That program of exposition of verses of Scripture read in or out of sequence, of organization of discourse in line with Biblical books, parallel to the Tosefta's and Talmuds' authorships' exposition of passages of the Mishnah, read in close sequence or otherwise, we see, defines what our authorship has not done. Pesiqta deRab Kahana has been assembled so as to exhibit a viewpoint, a purpose of its particular authorship, one quite distinctive, in its own context (if not in a single one of its propositions!), to its framers or collectors and arrangers.

2.
TRANSLATIONS INTO ENGLISH

The first translation of the document is William G. (Gershon Zev) Braude and Israel J. Kapstein, *Pesikta de-Rab Kahana. R. Kahana's Compilation of Discourses for Sabbaths and Festal Days* (Philadelphia, 1975: Jewish Publication Society of America). The second, and the first analytical translation, is this writer's *Pesiqta deRab Kahana. An Analytical Translation and Explanation. I. 1–14. II. 15–28. With an Introduction to Pesiqta deRab Kahana* (Atlanta, 1987: Scholars Press for Brown Judaic Studies). It also is the only translation of the critical text by Bernard Mandelbaum, *Pesiqta deRab Kahana. According to an Oxford Manuscript. With Variants from All Known Manuscripts and Genizoth Fragments and Parallel Passages. With Commentary and Introduction* (New York, 1962: Jewish Theological Seminary of America).

3.
RHETORIC

Following the model of Leviticus Rabbah, Pesiqta deRab Kahana consists of twenty-eight syllogisms, each presented in a cogent and systematic way by the twenty-eight pisqaot, (the Hebrew plural) respectively. Each *pisqa* or chapter (simply a different word for *parashah,* with the Aramaic plural, *pesiqta*) contains an implicit proposition, and that proposition may be stated in a simple way. It emerges from the intersection of an external verse with the base verse that recurs through the *pisqa,* and then is restated by the systematic dissection of the components of the base verse, each of which is shown to say the same thing as all the others.

A *pisqa* in Pesiqta deRab Kahana systematically presents a single syllogism, which is expressed through the contrast of an external verse with the base verse— hence, the base-verse/intersecting-verse form. In this form the implicit syllogism is stated through the intervention of an contrastive verse into the basic proposition established by the base verse. The second type of material proceeds to the systematic exegesis of the components of the base verse on their own, hence through the exegetical form. There is a third form, a syllogistic list, familiar from the Mishnah and prior Midrash compilations as well. The first two forms occur in the same sequence, because the former of the two serves to declare the implicit syllogism, and the latter, to locate that implicit syllogism in the base verse itself. The third will then be tacked on at the end. Otherwise it would disrupt the exposition of the implicit syllogism. All of these forms are familiar and require no further explanation.

4.

Logic of Coherent Discourse

The document as a whole appeals to the fixed associations defined by synagogal lections, in sequence. The individual compositions are syllogistic.

5.

Topical Program

These synagogal discourses, read in their entirety, form a coherent statement of three propositions:

[1] God loves Israel, that love is unconditional, and Israel's response to God must be obedience to the religious duties that God has assigned, which will produce merit. Israel's obedience to God is what will save Israel. That means doing the religious duties as required by the Torah, which is the mark of God's love for—and regeneration of—Israel. The tabernacle symbolizes the union of Israel and God. When Israel does what God asks above, Israel will prosper down below. If Israel remembers Amalek down below, God will remember Amalek up above and will wipe him out. A mark of Israel's loyalty to God is remembering Amalek. God does not require the animals that are sacrificed, since man could never match God's appetite, if that were the issue, but the savor pleases God (as a mark of Israel's loyalty and obedience). The first sheaf returns to God God's fair share of the gifts that God bestows on Israel, and those who give it benefit, while those who hold it back suffer. Observing religious duties, typified by the rites of the Festival, brings a great reward of that merit that ultimately leads to redemption. God's ways are just, righteous, and merciful, as shown by God's concern that the offspring remain with the mother for seven days. God's love for Israel is so intense that he wants to hold the people back for an extra day after the Festival in order to spend more

time with them, because, unlike the nations of the world, Israel knows how to please God. This is a mark of God's love for Israel.

[2] God is reasonable and when Israel has been punished, it is in accord with God's rules. God forgives penitent Israel and is abundant in mercy. Laughter is vain because it is mixed with grief. A wise person will not expect too much joy. But when people suffer, there ordinarily is a good reason for it. That is only one sign that God is reasonable and that God never did anything lawless and wrong to Israel or made unreasonable demands, and there was, therefore, no reason for Israel to lose confidence in God or to abandon him. God punished Israel, to be sure. But this was done with reason. Nothing happened to Israel of which God did not give fair warning in advance, and Israel's failure to heed the prophets brought about her fall. And God will forgive a faithful Israel. Even though the Israelites sinned by making the golden calf, God forgave them and raised them up. On the New Year, God executes justice, but the justice is tempered with mercy. The rites of the New Year bring about divine judgment and also forgiveness because of the merit of the fathers. Israel must repent and return to the Lord, who is merciful and will forgive it for its sins. The penitential season of the New Year and Day of Atonement is the right time for confession and penitence, and God is sure to accept penitence. By exercising his power of mercy, the already-merciful God grows still stronger in mercy.

[3] God will save Israel personally at a time and circumstance of his own choosing. Israel may know what the future redemption will be like, because of the redemption from Egypt. The paradox of the red cow, that what imparts uncleanness, namely, touching the ashes of the red cow, produces cleanness, is part of God's ineffable wisdom, which man cannot fathom. Only God can know the precise moment of Israel's redemption. That is something man cannot find out on his own. But God will certainly fulfill the predictions of the prophets about Israel's coming redemption. The Exodus from Egypt is the paradigm of the coming redemption. Israel has lost Eden—but can come home, and, with God's help, will. God's unique power is shown through Israel's unique suffering. In God's own time, he will redeem Israel.

To develop this point, the authorship proceeds to further facts, worked out in its propositional discourses. The lunar calendar, particular to Israel, marks Israel as favored by God, for the new moon signals the coming of Israel's redemption, and the particular new moon that will mark the actual event is that of Nisan. When God chooses to redeem Israel, Israel's enemies will have no power to stop him, because God will force Israel's enemies to serve Israel, because of Israel's purity and loyalty to God. Israel's enemies are punished, and what they propose to do to Israel, God does to them. Both directly and through the prophets, God is the source of true comfort, which he will bring to Israel.

Israel thinks that God has forsaken it. But it is Israel who forsook God. God's love has never failed, and will never fail. Even though he has been angry, his mercy still is near and God has the power and will to save Israel. God has designated the godly for himself and has already promised to redeem them. He will assuredly do so. God personally is the one who will comfort Israel. While Israel says there is no comfort, in fact, God will comfort Israel. Zion/Israel is like a barren woman, but Zion will bring forth children, and Israel will be comforted. Both God and Israel will bring light to Zion, which will give light to the world. The rebuilding of Zion will be a source of joy for the entire world, not for Israel alone. God will rejoice in Israel, Israel in God, like bride and groom.

6.

A SAMPLE PASSAGE

We consider the way in which this compilation treats Num. 7:1, which we have already read through the eyes of the authors of Sifré to Numbers, and which, in Chapter 17, we shall examine from the perspective of the writers of Pesiqta Rabbati.

PISQA ONE

On the day that Moses completed the setting up of the Tabernacle, he anointed and consecrated it (Num. 7:1)

I:I.   1.   A.   *I have come back to my garden, my sister, my bride* (Song 5:1):
            B.   R. Azariah in the name of R. Simon said, "[The matter may be compared to the case of] a king who became angry at a noblewoman and drove her out and expelled her from his palace. After some time he wanted to bring her back. She said, 'Let him renew in my behalf the earlier state of affairs, and then he may bring me back.'
            C.   "So in former times the Holy One, blessed be he, would receive offerings from on high, as it is said, *And the Lord smelled the sweet odor* (Gen. 8:21). But now he will accept them down below."
       2.   A.   *I have come back to my garden, my sister, my bride* (Song 5:1):
            B.   Said R. Hanina, "The Torah teaches you proper conduct,
            C.   "specifically, a groom should not go into the marriage canopy until the bride gives him permission to do so: *Let my beloved come into his garden* (Song 4:16), after which, *I have come back to my garden, my sister, my bride* (Song 5:1)."
       3.   A.   R. Tanhum, son-in-law of R. Eleazar b. Abina, in the name of R. Simeon b. Yosni: "What is written is not, 'I have come into the garden,' but rather, *I have come back to my garden.* That is, 'to my [Mandelbaum:] canopy.'

B. "That is to say, to the place in which the the principal [presence of God] had been located to begin with.

C. "The principal locale of God's presence had been among the lower creatures, in line with this verse: *And they heard the sound of the Lord God walking about* (Gen. 3:8)."

4. A. [*And they heard the sound of the Lord God walking about* (Gen. 3:8):] Said R. Abba bar Kahana, "What is written is not merely 'going,' but 'walking about,' that is, 'walking away from.'"

B. *And man and his wife hid* (Gen. 3:8):

C. Said R. Aibu, "At that moment the first man's stature was cut down and diminished to one hundred cubits."

5. A. Said R. Isaac, "It is written, *The righteous will inherit the earth* (Ps. 47:29). Where will the wicked be? Will they fly in the air?

B. "Rather, the sense of the clause, *they shall dwell thereon in eternity* is, 'they shall bring the presence of God to dwell on the earth.'"

6. A. [Reverting to 3.C,] the principal locale of God's presence had been among the lower creatures, but when the first man sinned, it went up to the first firmament.

B. The generation of Enosh came along and sinned, and it went up from the first to the second.

C. The generation of the flood [came along and sinned], and it went up from the second to the third.

D. The generation of the dispersion [came along] and sinned, and it went up from the third to the fourth.

E. The Egyptians in the time of Abraham our father [came along] and sinned, and it went up from the fourth to the fifth.

F. The Sodomites [came along], and sinned . . . from the fifth to the sixth.

G. The Egyptians in the time of Moses . . . from the sixth to the seventh.

H. And, corresponding to them, seven righteous men came along and brought it back down to earth:

I. Abraham our father came along and acquired merit, and brought it down from the seventh to the sixth.

J. Isaac came along and acquired merit and brought it down from the sixth to the fifth.

K. Jacob came along and acquired merit and brought it down from the fifth to the fourth.

L. Levi came along and acquired merit and brought it down from the fourth to the third.

M. Kohath came along and acquired merit and brought it down from the third to the second.

N. Amram came along and acquired merit and brought it down from the second to the first.

O. Moses came along and acquired merit and brought it down to earth.

P. Therefore it is said, *On the day that Moses completed the setting up of the tabernacle, he anointed and consecrated it* (Num. 7:1).

The selection of the intersecting verse, Song 5:1, rests on the appearance of the letters KLT, meaning "completed," but yielding also the word KLH, meaning "bride." The exegete wishes to make the point that in building the tabernacle, Moses has brought God down to earth, 6.P. This he accomplishes by bringing the theme of "garden, bride" together with the theme of the union of God and Israel. The parable at 1.B then is entirely apt, since it wishes to introduce the notion of God's having become angry with humanity but then reconciled through Israel in the sacrificial cult. 1.B then refers to the fall from grace, with Israel as the noble spouse who insists that the earlier state of affairs be restored. C then makes explicit precisely what is in mind, a very effective introduction to the whole. No. 2 pursues the exegesis of the intersecting verse, as does No. 3, the latter entirely apropos. Because of 3.C, No. 4 is tacked on; it continues the exegesis of the proof text but has no bearing on the intersecting verse. But No. 5 does—at least in its proposition, if not in its selection of proof texts. No. 6 then brings us back to 3.C, citing the language of the prior component and then making the point of the whole quite explicit. Even with the obvious accretions at Nos. 4 and 5, the whole hangs together and makes its point—the intersecting verse, Song 5:1; the base verse, Num. 7:1—in a cogent way.

I:II. 1. A. *King Solomon made a pavilion for himself* (Song 3:9). [The New English Bible: *The palanquin which King Solomon had made for himself was of wood from Lebanon. Its poles he made of silver, its headrest of gold; its seat was of purple stuff, and its lining was of leather*]:

B. *Pavilion* refers to the tent of meeting.

C. *King Solomon made a . . . for himself:* he is the king to whom peace [*shalom/shelomoh*] belongs.

2. A. Said R. Judah bar Ilai, "[The matter may be compared to the case of] a king who had a little girl. Before she grew up and reached puberty, he would see her in the marketplace and chat with her, or in alleyways and chat with her. But when she grew up and reached puberty, he said, 'It is not fitting for the dignity of my daughter that I should talk with her in public. Make a pavilion for her, so that I may chat with her in the pavilion.'

B. "So, to begin with: *When Israel was a child in Egypt, then in my love of him, I used to cry out* (Hos. 11:1). In Egypt they saw me: *And I passed through the Land of Israel* (Ex. 12:12). At the sea they saw me: *And Israel saw the great hand* (Ex. 14:31). At Sinai they saw me: *Face to face the Lord spoke with you* (Deut. 5:4).

C. "But when they received the Torah, they became a fully-grown nation for him. So he said, 'It is not appropriate to the dignity of my children that I should speak with them in public. But make me a tabernacle, and I shall speak from the midst of the tabernacle.'

D. "That is in line with this verse: *And when Moses entered the tent of the presence to speak with God, he heard the voice speaking from above the cover over the ark of the pact from between the two cherubim: the voice spoke to him* (Num. 7:89)."

3. A. [*The palanquin that King Solomon had made for himself was of wood from Lebanon. Its poles he made of silver, its headrest of gold; its seat was of purple stuff, and its lining was of leather*] . . . *was of wood from Lebanon. Make for the tabernacle planks of acacia-wood as uprights* (Ex. 26:15).

B. *Its poles he made of silver: The hooks and bands on the posts shall be of silver (Ex. 27:10).*

C. . . . *its headrest of gold: Overlay the planks with gold, make rings of gold on them to hold the bars* (Ex. 26:29).

D. . . . *its seat was of purple stuff: Make a veil of finely woven linen and violet, purple, and scarlet yarn* (Ex. 26:31).

E. . . . *and its lining was of leather:*

F. R. Yudan says, "This refers to the merit accruing on account of the Torah and the righteous."

G. R. Azariah in the name of R. Judah bar Simon says, "This refers to the Presence of God."

4. A. Said R. Aha bar Kahana, "It is written, *And there I shall meet with you* (Ex. 25:22),

B. "to teach that even what is on the outside of the ark cover is not empty of God's presence."

5. A. A gentile asked Rabban Gamaliel, saying to him, "On what account did the Holy One, blessed be he, reveal himself to Moses in a bush?"

B. He said to him, "If he had revealed himself to him in a carob tree or a fig tree, what might you have said?

C. "It is so as to indicate that there is no place in the earth that is empty of God's presence."

6. A. R. Joshua of Sikhnin in the name of R. Levi: "To what may the tent of meeting be compared?

B.   "To an oceanside cave. The sea tide flows and engulfs the cave, which is filled by the sea, but the sea is not diminished.

C.   "So the tent of meeting is filled with the splendor of the presence of God."

D.   Therefore it is said, *On the day that Moses completed the setting up of the tabernacle, he anointed and consecrated it* (Num. 7:1).

Seen by itself, No. 1 has no bearing upon the larger context, but it does provide a good exegesis of Song 3:9 in terms of the theme at hand, the tabernacle. The point of No. 2 is that the purpose of the tabernacle was to make possible appropriate communication between a mature Israel and God. Then the two items are simply distinct workings of the theme of the tabernacle, one appealing to Song 3:9; the other, Num. 7:89.

I:III.   1.   A.   [Continuing the exegesis of the successive verses of Song 3:9ff.] *Come out, daughters of Jerusalem, you daughters of Zion, come out and welcome King Solomon, wearing the crown with which his mother has crowned him, on his wedding day, on his day of joy* (Song 3:11) [Braude and Kapstein: *Go forth, O younglings whose name Zion indicates that you bear a sign*]:

B.   Sons who are marked [a play on the letters that stand for the word *"come out"*] for me by the mark of circumcision, by not cutting the corners of the head [in line with Lev. 19:27], and by wearing show-fringes.

2.   A.   *[. . . and welcome] King Solomon:*

B.   The king to whom peace belongs.

3.   A.   Another interpretation: *and welcome King Solomon:*

B.   The King [meaning God] who brings peace through his deeds among his creatures.

C.   He caused the fire to make peace with our father Abraham, the sword with our father Isaac, the angel with our father Jacob.

D.   It is the king who brings peace among his creatures.

E.   Said R. Yohanan, "*Merciful dominion and fear are with him* (Job 25:2) [that is, are at peace with him]."

F.   Said R. Jacob of Kefar Hanan, "*Merciful dominion* refers to the angel Michael, and *fear* to the angel Gabriel.

G.   "*With him* means that they make peace with him and do not do injury to one another."

H.   Said R. Yohanan, "The sun has never laid eyes on the blemished part of the moon [the black side], nor does one star take precedence over another one, nor does a planet lay eyes on the one above it."

I.   Said Rabbi, "All of them traverse as it were a spiral staircase."

4. A.   It is written, *Who lays the beams of your upper chambers in the waters, who makes the flaming fires your ministers* (Ps. 104:2–3):

B.   R. Simeon b. Yohai taught, "The firmament is of water, the stars of fire, and yet they dwell with one another and do not do injury to one another.

C.   "The firmament is of water and the angel is of fire, and yet they dwell with one another and do not do injury to one another."

D.   Said R. Abin, "It is not the end of the matter [that there is peace between] one angel and another. But even the angel himself is half fire and half water, and yet they make peace."

E.   The angel has five faces—*The angel's body was like beryl, his face as the appearance of lightning, his eyes as torches of fire, his arms and feet like in color to burnished brass, and the sound of his words like the sound of a roaring multitude* (Dan. 10:6)—[yet none does injury to the other].

5. A.   *So there was hail and fire flashing continually amid the hail* (Ex. 9:24):

B.   R. Judah says, "There was a flask of hail filled with fire."

C.   R. Nehemiah said, "Fire and hail, mixed together."

D.   R. Hanin said, "In support of the position of R. Judah is the case of the pomegranate in the pulp of which seeds can be discerned."

E.   R. Hanin said, "As to R. Nehemiah's position, it is the case of a crystal lamp in which are equivalent volumes of water and oil, which together keep the flame of the wick burning above the water and the oil."

6. A.   [*So there was hail and fire flashing continually amid the hail* (Ex. 9:24)]: What is the meaning of *flashing continually*?

B.   Said R. Judah bar Simon, "Each one is eager in its [Braude and Kapstein reader, p. 10] determination to carry out their mission."

C.   Said R. Aha, "[The matter may be compared to the case of] a king, who had two tough legions, who competed with one another, but when the time to make war in behalf of the king came around, they made peace with one another.

D.   "So is the case with the fire and hail, they compete with one another, but when the time came to carry out the war of the Holy One, blessed be he, against the Egyptians, then: *So there was hail and fire flashing continually amid the hail* (Ex. 9:24)—one miracle within the other [more familiar one, namely, that the hail and fire worked together]."

7. A. *[Come out, daughters of Jerusalem, you daughters of Zion, come out and welcome King Solomon,] wearing the crown with which his mother has crowned him, on his wedding day, [on his day of joy]* (Song 3:11):

B. Said R. Isaac, "We have reviewed the entire Scripture and have not found evidence that Bathsheba made a crown for her son, Solomon. This refers, rather, to the tent of meeting, which is crowned with blue and purple and scarlet."

8. A. Said R. Hunia, "R. Simeon b. Yohai asked R. Eleazar b. R. Yosé, 'Is it possible that you have heard from your father what was the crown with which his mother crowned him?'

B. "He said to him, 'The matter may be compared to the case of a king who had a daughter, whom he loved even too much. He even went so far, in expressing his affection for her, as to call her 'my sister.' He even went so far, in expressing his affection for her, as to call her 'my mother.'

C. "So at the outset, the Holy One, blessed be he, expressed his affection for Israel by calling them, 'my daughter': *Hear, O daughter, and consider* (Ps. 45:11). Then he went so far, in expressing his affection for them, as to call them, 'my sister': *My sister, my bride* (Song 5:1). Then he went so far, in expressing his affection for them, as to call them, 'my mother': *Attend to me, O my people, and give ear to me, O my nation* (Is. 51:4). The letters that are read as "my nation" may also be read as 'my mother.'" [The distinction between the *ayin* sound, a rough breathing, and the *aleph* sound, no rough breathing, is thus obscured for exegetical purposes, so that it is as if the one letter, yielding "my nation," were interchangeable with the other, producing "my mother."]

D. R. Simeon b. Yohai stood and kissed him on his brow.

E. He said to him, "Had I come only to hear this teaching, it would have been enough for me."

9. A. R. Joshua of Sikhnin taught in the name of R. Levi: "When the Holy One, blessed be he, said to Moses, 'Make me a tabernacle,' Moses might have brought four poles and spread over them [skins to make] the tabernacle. This teaches, therefore, that the Holy One, blessed be he, showed Moses on high red fire, green fire, black fire, and white fire.

B. "He said to him, 'Make me a tabernacle.'

C. "Moses said to the Holy One, blessed be he, 'Lord of the ages, where am I going to get red fire, green fire, black fire, or white fire?'

D. "He said to him, '*After the pattern which is shown to you on the mountain*' (Ex. 25:40).'"

10. A. R. Berekhiah in the name of R. Levi: "[The matter may be compared to the case of] a king who appeared to his household clothed in a garment [Braude and Kapstein reader, p. 11] covered entirely with precious stones.

B. "He said to him, 'Make me one like this.'

C. "He said to him, 'My lord, O king, where am I going to get myself a garment made entirely of precious stones?'

D. "He said to him, 'You in accord with your raw materials and I in accord with my glory.'

E. "So said the Holy One, blessed be he, to Moses, 'Moses, if you make what belongs above down below, I shall leave my council up here and go down and reduce my Presence so as to be among you down there.'

F. "Just as up there: *seraphim are standing* (Is. 6:2), so down below: *boards of shittim-cedars are standing* (Ex. 26:15).

G. "Just as up there are stars, so down below are the clasps."

H. Said R. Hiyya bar Abba, "This teaches that the golden clasps in the tabernacle looked like the fixed stars of the firmament."

11. A. [*Come out, daughters of Jerusalem, you daughters of Zion, come out and welcome King Solomon, wearing the crown with which his mother has crowned him,*] *on his wedding day,* [*on his day of joy*] (Song 3:11):

B. . . . *on his wedding day* [B&K, p. 12:] the day he entered the tent of meeting.

C. . . . *on his day of joy:*

D. this refers to the tent of meeting.

E. Another interpretation of the phrase, *on his wedding day, on his day of joy* (Song 3:11):

F. . . . *on his wedding day* refers to the tent of meeting.

G. . . . *on his day of joy* refers to the building of the eternal house.

H. Therefore it is said, *On the day that Moses completed the setting up of the tabernacle, he anointed and consecrated it* (Num. 7:1).

The exegesis of Song 3:11 now receives attention in its own terms, our point of departure having been forgotten. No. 1 simply provides a play on one of the words of the verse under study. Nos. 2–6 proceed to work on the problem of the name of the king, Solomon. We have a striking and fresh approach at Nos. 2–3: the reference is now to God as King, and the name, Solomon, then is interpreted as God's function of bringing peace both among his holy creatures, the patriarchs and the angels, and among the elements of natural creation. Both topics are introduced and then, at Nos. 4–6, the latter is worked out. God keeps water and fire working together and to do his bidding, they do not injure one another. The proof text, Ex. 9:24, then leads us in its own direction, but at No. 6 discourse returns to the main point. No. 7 moves us on to a fresh issue, namely, Solomon himself. And now we see the connection between the passage and our broader theme, the tabernacle. The Temple is now compared to a crown. No. 8 pursues the interpretation of the same clause. But the point of interest is the clause, not the theme under broader discussion, so what we have is simply a repertoire of exegeses of the cited verse. No. 9 carries forward the theme of making the tabernacle. It makes the point that Moses was to replicate the colors he had seen on high. I see no connection to the preceding. It is an essentially fresh initiative. No. 10 continues along that same line, now making yet another point, which is that the tabernacle on earth was comparable to the abode of God in heaven. No. 11 brings us back to our original verse. We take up a clause-by-clause interpretation of the matter. No. 11.H is an editorial subscript, with no connection to the foregoing except the rather general thematic one. But the original interest in working on the theme of the building of the tabernacle as Israel's wedding day to God is well expressed, beginning to end.

I:IV.   1.   A.   *Who has ever gone up to heaven and come down again? Who has cupped the wind in the hollow of his hands? Who has bound up the waters in the fold of his garment? Who has fixed the boundaries of the earth? What is his name or his son's name, if you know it?* (Prov. 30:4):

B.   . . . *Who has ever gone up to heaven:* this refers to the Holy One, blessed be he, as it is written, *God has gone up to the sound of the trumpet* (Ps. 37:6).

C.   . . . *and come down again: The Lord came down onto Mount Sinai* (Ex. 19:20).

D.   . . . *Who has cupped the wind in the hollow of his hands: In whose hand is the soul of all the living* (Job 12:10).

E.   . . . *Who has bound up the waters in the fold of his garment: He keeps the waters penned in dense cloud-masses* (Job 26:8).

F.   . . . *Who has fixed the boundaries of the earth:* . . . *who kills and brings to life* (1 Sam. 2:6).

G.   . . . *What is his name:* his name is the Rock, his name is the Almighty, his name is the Lord of Hosts.

H.   *or his son's name, if you know it: My son, my firstborn is Israel* (Ex. 4:22).

2.   A.   Another interpretation of the verse, *Who has ever gone up to heaven:* Who is the one whose prayer goes up to heaven and brings down rain?

B.   This is one who with his hands sets aside the tithes that he owes, who brings dew and rain into the world.

C. *Who has cupped the wind in the hollow of his hands? Who has bound up the waters in the fold of his garment? Who has fixed the boundaries of the earth?* Who is the one whose prayer does not go up to heaven and bring down rain?

D. This is one who with his hands does not set aside the tithes that he owes, who does not bring dew and rain into the world.

3. A. Another interpretation of the verse, *Who has ever gone up to heaven*:

B. This refers to Elijah, concerning whom it is written, *And Elijah went up in a whirlwind to heaven* (2 Kgs. 2:11).

C. *... and come down again: Go down with him, do not be afraid* (2 Kgs. 1:16).

D. *Who has cupped the wind in the hollow of his hands: Lord, God of Israel, before whom I stand* (1 Kgs. 17:1).

E. *Who has bound up the waters in the fold of his garment: And Elijah took his mantle and wrapped it together and smote the waters and they were divided* (1 Kgs. 2:8).

F. *Who has fixed the boundaries of the earth: And Elijah said, See your son lives* (1 Kgs. 17:23).

4. A. Another interpretation of the verse, *Who has ever gone up to heaven and come down again*:

B. This refers to Moses, concerning whom it is written, *And Moses went up to God* (Ex. 19:3).

C. *... and come down again: And Moses came down from the mountain* (Ex. 19:14).

D. *Who has cupped the wind in the hollow of his hands: As soon as I have gone out of the city, I shall spread my hands out to the Lord* (Ex. 9:29).

E. *Who has bound up the waters in the fold of his garment: The floods stood upright as a heap* (Ex. 15:8).

F. *Who has fixed the boundaries of the earth*: this refers to the tent of meeting, as it is said, *On the day on which Moses completed setting up the tabernacle* (Num. 7:1)—for the entire world was set up with it.

5. A. R. Joshua b. Levi in the name of R. Simeon b. Yohai: "What is stated is not 'setting up the tabernacle [without the accusative particle, *et*],' but 'setting up + *the accusative particle* + the tabernacle,' [and since the inclusion of the accusative particle is taken to mean that the object is duplicated, we understand the sense to be that he set up a second tabernacle along with the first].

B. "What was set up with it? It was the world that was set up with [the tabernacle, that is, the tabernacle represented the cosmos].

C. "For until the tabernacle was set up, the world trembled, but after the tabernacle was set up, the world rested on firm foundations."

D. Therefore it is said, *On the day that Moses completed the setting up of the tabernacle, he anointed and consecrated it* (Num. 7:1).

The intersecting verse, Prov. 30:4, is systematically applied to God, to tithing, then Elijah, finally Moses, at which point the exposition comes to a fine editorial conclusion. I cannot imagine a more representative example of the intersecting-verse/base-verse exposition. No. 5 is tacked on because it provides a valuable complement to the point of No. 4.

I:V. 1. A. Another interpretation of the verse: *On the day that Moses completed the setting up of the tabernacle, he anointed and consecrated it* (Num. 7:1):

B. The letters translated as "completed" are so written that they can be read "bridal," that is, on the day on which [Israel, the bride] entered the bridal canopy.

2. A. R. Eleazar and R. Samuel bar Nahmani:

B. R. Eleazar says, "*On the day that Moses completed* means on the day on which he left off setting up the tabernacle day by day."

C. It has been taught on Tannaite authority: Every day Moses would set up the tabernacle, and every morning he would make his offerings on it and then take it down. On the eighth day [to which reference is made in the verse, *On the day that Moses completed the setting up of the tabernacle, he anointed and consecrated it*] he set it up but did not take it down again.

D. Said R. Zeira, "On the basis of this verse we learn the fact that an altar set up on the preceding night is invalid for the offering of sacrifices on the next day."

E. R. Samuel bar Nahmani says, "Even on the eighth day he set it up and took it apart again."

F. And how do we know about these dismantlings?

G. It is in line with what R. Zeira said, "*On the day that Moses completed* means on the day on which he left off setting up the tabernacle day by day."

3. A. R. Eleazar and R. Yohanan:

B. R. Eleazar said, "*On the day that Moses completed* means on the day on which demons ended their spell in the world.

C.   "What is the scriptural basis for that view?

D.   "*No evil thing will befall you, nor will any demon come near you*
[B&K p. 15] *by reason of your tent* (Ps. 91:10)—on the day on
which demons ended their spell in the world."

E.   Said R. Yohanan, "What need do I have to derive the lesson
from another passage? Let us learn it from the very passage
in which the matter occurs: *May the Lord bless you and keep
you* (Num. 6:24)—keep you from demons."

4.   A.   R. Yohanan and R. Simeon b. Laqish:

B.   R. Yohanan said, "*On the day that Moses completed* means on
the day on which hatred came to an end in the world. For
before the tabernacle was set up, there was hatred and envy,
competition, contention, and strife in the world. But once
the tabernacle was set up, love, affection, comradeship,
righteousness, and peace came into the world.

C.   "What is the verse of Scripture that so indicates?

D.   "*Let me hear the words of the Lord, are they not words of peace,
peace to his people and his loyal servants and to all who turn and
trust in him? Deliverance is near to those who worship him, so that
glory may dwell in our land. Love and fidelity have come together,
justice and peace join hands* (Ps. 85:8–10)."

E.   Said R. Simeon b. Laqish, "What need do I have to derive
the lesson from another passage? Let us learn it from the
very passage in which the matter occurs: *and give you peace.*"

5.   A.   [*On the day that Moses completed*] *the setting up of the tabernacle,
[he anointed and consecrated it]*:

B.   R. Joshua b. Levi in the name of R. Simeon b. Yohai:
"What is stated is not 'setting up the tabernacle [without the
accusative particle, *et*],' but 'setting up + *the accusative particle*
+ the tabernacle,' [and since the inclusion of the accusative
particle is taken to mean that the object is duplicated, we
understand the sense to be that he set up a second tabernacle
along with the first].

C.   "What was set up with it? It was the world that was set
up with [the tabernacle, that is, the tabernacle represented
the cosmos].

D.   "For until the tabernacle was set up, the world trembled,
but after the tabernacle was set up, the world rested on
firm foundations."

We work our way through the clause, *on the day that Moses completed.* No. 1
goes over familiar ground. It is a valuable review of the point of stress, the meaning
of the word "completed." No. 2 refers to the claim that from day to day Moses

would set up and take down the tent, until on the day at hand, he left it standing; so the "completed" bears the sense of ceasing to go through a former procedure. The word under study bears the further sense of "coming to an end," and therefore at Nos. 3, 4, we ask what came to an end when the tabernacle was set up. The matched units point to demons, on the one side, and hatred, on the other. No. 5 moves us along from the word KLT to the following set, *accusative + tabernacle.*

I:VI.   1.   A.   *[On the day that Moses completed the setting up of the tabernacle], he anointed and consecrated it:*

B.   Since it is written, *he anointed and consecrated it,* why does it also say, *he anointed them and consecrated them* (Num. 7:1)?

C.   R. Aibu said, "R. Tahalipa of Caesarea, and R. Simeon:

D.   "One of them said, 'After he had anointed each one, he then anointed all of them simultaneously.'

E.   "The other said, '*And he anointed them* refers to an anointing in this world and another anointing in the world to come.'"

2.   A.   Along these same lines: *You shall couple the tent together* (Ex. 26:11), *You shall couple the curtains* (Ex. 26:6):

B.   R. Judah and R. Levi, R. Tahalipa of Caesarea and R. Simeon b. Laqish:

C.   One of them said, "Once he had coupled them all together, he went back and coupled them one by one."

D.   The other said, "*You shall couple the curtains and it shall be one* meaning, one for measuring, one for anointing."

I:VII.   1.   A.   *The chief men of Israel, heads of families—that is, the chiefs of the tribes, [who had assisted in preparing the detailed lists] came forward and brought their offering before the Lord* (Num. 7:2):

B.   [(Following B&K, p. 16:) The word for *tribes* can mean *rods,* so we understand the meaning to be, they had exercised authority through rods] in Egypt.

C.   . . . *who had assisted in preparing the detailed lists:* the standards.

2.   A.   . . . *came forward and brought their offering before the Lord , six covered wagons [and twelve oxen, one wagon from every two chiefs and from each one an ox]* (Num. 7:2):

B.   The six corresponded to the six days of creation.

C.   The six corresponded to the six divisions of the Mishnah.

D.   The six corresponded to the six matriarchs: Sarah, Rebecca, Rachel, Leah, Bilhah, and Zilpah.

E.   Said R. Yohanan, "The six corresponded to the six religious duties that pertain to a king: *[1] He shall not have too many wives* (Deut. 17:17), *[2] He shall not have too many horses* (Deut. 17:16), *[3] He shall not have too much silver and gold* (Deut. 17:17), *[4] He shall not pervert justice, [5] show favor, or [6] take bribes* (Deut. 16:9)."

3. A. The six corresponded to the six steps of the throne. How so?

    B. When he goes up to take his seat on the first step, the herald goes forth and proclaims, *He shall not have too many wives* (Deut. 17:17).

    C. When he goes up to take his seat on the second step, the herald goes forth and proclaims, *He shall not have too many horses* (Deut. 17:16).

    D. When he goes up to take his seat on the third step, the herald goes forth and proclaims, *He shall not have too much silver and gold* (Deut. 17:17).

    E. When he goes up to take his seat on the fourth step, the herald goes forth and proclaims, *He shall not pervert justice.*

    F. When he goes up to take his seat on the fifth step, the herald goes forth and proclaims, . . . *or show favor.*

    G. When he goes up to take his seat on the sixth step, the herald goes forth and proclaims, . . . *or take bribes* (Deut. 16:9).

    H. When he comes to take his seat on the seventh step, he says, "Know before whom you take your seat."

4. A. *And the top of the throne was round behind* (1 Kgs. 10:19):

    B. Said R. Aha, "It was like the throne of Moses."

    C. *And there were arms on either side of the throne by the place of the seat* (1 Kgs. 10:19):

    D. How so? There was a scepter of gold suspended from behind, with a dove on the top, and a crown of gold in the dove's mouth, and he [Moses] would sit under it on the Sabbath, and it would touch but not quite touch [I am not sure whether the "it" is the dove, scepter, crown, or what.]

5. A. The six corresponded to the six firmaments.

    B. But are they not seven?

    C. Said R. Abia, "The one where the King dwells is royal property [not counted with what belongs to the world at large]."

We proceed with the detailed exposition of the verse at hand. The focus of interest, after No. 1, is on the reason for bringing six wagons. The explanations, Nos. 2 (+ 3–4), 5, relate to the creation of the world, the Torah, the life of Israel, the religious duties of the king, and the universe above. The underlying motif, the tabernacle as the point at which the supernatural world of Israel meets the supernatural world of creation, is carried forward.

I:VIII. 1. A. *[. . . came forward and brought their offering before the Lord, six] covered [wagons and twelve oxen, one wagon from every two chiefs and from each one an ox]* (Num. 7:2):

    B. The word for "covered wagons" may be read to yield these meanings:

C. like a lizard-skin [B&K, p. 17: "it signifies that the outer surface of the wagons' frames was as delicately reticulated as the skin of a lizard"];

D. [and the same word may be read to indicate that the wagons were] decorated, or fully equipped.

E. It has been taught in the name of R. Nehemiah, "They were like a bent bow."

2. A. . . . *twelve oxen, one wagon from every two chiefs . . . :*

B. This indicates that two chiefs would together bring one wagon, while each tribe gave an ox.

3. A. *These they brought forward before the tabernacle* (Num. 7:3):

B. This teaches that they turned them into their monetary value and sold them to the congregation at large [so that everyone had a share in the donation].

4. A. *And the Lord spoke to Moses and said, ["Accept these from them: they shall be used for the service of the tent of the presence"]* (Num. 7:45):

B. What is the meaning of the word, *and said?*

C. R. Hoshaia taught, "The Holy One, blessed be he, said to Moses, 'Go and say to Israel words of praise and consolation.'

D. "Moses was afraid, saying, 'But is it not possible that the holy spirit has abandoned me and come to rest on the chiefs?'

E. "The Holy One said to him, 'Moses, had I wanted them to bring their offering, I should have said to you to 'say to them,' [so instructing them to do so], but *Take—it is from them [at their own volition, not by my inspiration]* (Num. 7:5) is the language that means, they did it on their own volition [and have not received the holy spirit].'"

5. A. And who gave them the good ideas [of making the gift]?

B. It was the tribe of Issachar who gave them the good idea, in line with this verse: *And of the children of Issachar came men who had understanding of the times* (1 Chr. 12:33).

C. What is the sense of *the times?*

D. R. Tanhuma said, "The ripe hour [*kairos*]."

E. R. Yosé bar Qisri said, "Intercalating the calendar."

F. *They had two hundred heads* (1 Chr. 12:33):

G. This refers to the two hundred heads of sanhedrins that were produced by the tribe of Issachar.

H. *And all of their brethren were subject to their orders* (1 Chr. 12:33):

I. This teaches that the law would accord with their rulings.

J. They said to the community, "Is this tent of meeting which you are making going to fly in the air? Make wagons for it, which will bear it."

6. A. Moses was concerned, saying, "Is it possible that one of the wagons might break, or one of the oxen die, so that the offering of the chiefs might be invalid?"

   B. Said to Moses the Holy One, blessed be he, "*They shall be used for the service of the tent of the presence* (Num. 7:5).

   C. "To them has been given a long-term existence."

7. A. How long did they live?

   B. R. Yudan in the name of R. Samuel bar Nahman, R. Hunia in the name of Bar Qappara, "*In Gilgal they sacrificed the oxen* (Hos. 12:12)."

   C. And where did they offer them up?

   D. R. Abba bar Kahana said, "In Nob they offered them up."

   E. R. Abbahu said, "In Gibeon they offered them up."

   F. R. Hama bar Hanina said, "In the eternal house [of Jerusalem] they offered them up."

   G. Said R. Levi, "A verse of Scripture supporting the view of R. Hama bar Hanina: *Solomon offered a sacrifice of peace offerings, which he slaughtered for the Lord, twenty-two thousand oxen* (1 Kgs. 8:63)."

   H. It was taught in the name of R. Meir, "They endure even to now, and they never produced a stink, got old, or produced an invalidating blemish."

   I. Now that produces an argument *a fortiori*:

   J. If the oxen who cling to the work of the making of the tent of meeting were given an eternal existence, Israel, who cling to the Holy One, blessed be he, how much the more so!

   K. *And you who cling to the Lord your God are alive, all of you, this day* (Deut. 4:4).

The exegesis of the verse in its own terms leads us through the several phrases, Nos. 1, 2, 3. No. 4, continuing at No. 6, with an important complement at No. 5, goes on to its own interesting question. No. 7 serves No. 6 as No. 6 serves No. 5.

XVII

PESIQTA RABBATI

1.

IDENTIFYING THE DOCUMENT

IN PRESENTING PROPOSITIONAL COMPOSITIONS, ORGANIZED TOPICALLY RATHER than exegetically, Pesiqta Rabbati[1] stands third in line, from Leviticus Rabbah through Pesiqta deRab Kahana, and can best be understood only in the context of its antecedents.[2] The authorship of Leviticus Rabbah received from the authorship of Genesis Rabbah, where, in the unfolding of the literature, they first occur,

---

[1] *Pisqa* means "chapter," with the plural *pesiqta; rabbati* means "great," hence, "augmented chapters" would be a rough translation for the title of this document.

[2] For further reading and bibliography on the topic of this chapter, see the following:

Bowker, pp. 76–77.

Maccoby omits this document from his introduction.

Daniel Sperber, "Pesikta Rabbati," *Encyclopaedia Judaica* 13:335–36: fragments; manuscripts; meaning of the title; description of the document: probably covered the full year, but the end has been lost; a work of the Land of Israel of the sixth or seventh century.

Stemberger-Strack, pp. 322–29: text; translations; the name; contents and text; redaction and compilation (composite work, "a lengthy process of development must be assumed, sixth or seventh century is an appropriate time frame").

This writer's discussion of the traits of the document is in *From Tradition to Imitation. The Plan and*

two interesting forms. The authorship of Leviticus Rabbah revised these forms and imposed upon them a stunning discipline, making of them modes of subtle and compelling persuasion in the service of an implicit syllogism. The framers of Pesiqta deRab Kahana took the bold step of leaving behind the exegetical structure entirely and adopting that of the calendar, which is the natural development of the decision to write propositionally and not exegetically.

What happened then was that the authorship represented in Pesiqta Rabbati took over these same forms and, not understanding their integrity and vitality, merely copied them without utilizing the potential force for compelling statement of an implicit syllogism that the forms, in the hands of the authorship of the earlier authorships, had made available. They went through motions without real understanding, and even their own innovations proved in my view lifeless and merely interesting. So the Midrash compilation as a pointed and purposeful act of literature, which had begun its life in Genesis Rabbah and Leviticus Rabbah, and in Pesiqta deRab Kahana had become a mode of argument of remarkable subtlety and force, turned into a collection of information—in places a collage, in places a mere scrapbook of this and that upon a common theme, but nowhere a text of integrity such as the Midrash compilation had been. Propositional argument gave way to thematic exposition, and the intellectual vigor of Leviticus Rabbah and Pesiqta deRab Kahana went to waste.

The *pisqa* of the earlier Pesiqta ordinarily presents a proposition worked out in a well-composed syllogism; it commonly makes a single point, fully spelled out and carefully instantiated, which will be generated to begin with by that intersection. The *pisqa* in the later Pesiqta, Pesiqta Rabbati, by contrast works through a fixed theme, but more often than not delivers miscellaneous messages concerning that theme, and, in any event, through its several components does not ordinarily argue in favor of (or against) a single important proposition. It follows that while the *pisqa* of Pesiqta deRab Kahana proves remarkably cogent in its mode of discourse, repeatedly saying one thing through diverse media, the *pisqa* in the later Pesiqta tends to be propositionally diffuse. It begins with a legal colloquy on practical law, which in context represents a promising innovation. But then, more often than not, it moves forward simply saying different things about one topic. That is why the *pisqa* of Pesiqta Rabbati may fall into the category of a collage, with its cogent message made up of discrete yet mutually illuminating parts, or it may appear to be little more than a scrapbook on a single topic. But it rarely, if ever, exhibits that syllogistic integrity that won admiration for the authorship of Pesiqta deRab Kahana.

Imitating Pesiqta deRab Kahana's framers, those who wrote the fifty-three compositions of Pesiqta Rabbati and compiled them put forth fifty-three distinct *pisqaot* or chapters, which focus on liturgical occasions. Though derivative and

---

Program of Pesiqta deRab Kahana and Pesiqta Rabbati. Atlanta, 1987: Scholars Press for Brown Judaic Studies.

imitative, the document does a creditable job of carrying forward the program of the prior Pesiqta's authors and compositors. A brief survey of the contents suffices. The order accords with the lunar events of Judaism, from Hanukkah in December through the Days of Awe and Tabernacles in the following September and October.

Pisqa 1 treats the lesson for a New Moon which coincides with the Sabbath. Nos. 2–9 deal with the lessons read during the eight days of the Hanukkah festival. Nos. 10–16 deal with the five special Sabbaths, the first four coming prior to Passover (Sheqalim, Zakhor, Parah, Hahodesh), and finally, for the first Sabbath in Nisan. Nos. 17–19 (48, 49) take up the lessons for Passover. Nos. 20–25 cover lessons for Pentecost. Nos. 26–29/30 deal with three Sabbaths of mourning prior to the Ninth of Ab. Nos. 29/30A–37 deal with the lessons for the seven Sabbaths of Consolation after the Ninth of Ab. Nos. 38–47 take up the New Year, the Sabbath of Repentance, and the Day of Atonement. Nos. 51, 52 deal with Tabernacles and the Eighth Day of Solemn Assembly. Only No. 53 is not associated with a particular holy day or special occasion of the synagogue lections. In no way, therefore, do the order or selections of passages of Pesiqta Rabbati differ from those of Pesiqta deRab Kahana. Some of the compositions are lifted from the prior Pesiqta, most being original to the later one.

The authorship of Pesiqta Rabbati made use of a fixed and limited repertoire of large-scale literary structures. These it has ordered in diverse ways, so the authorship found no important message to be delivered through the sequence in which the types of forms would be utilized. The same authorship pursued a variety of modes of cogent discourse, sometimes appealing to the theme to hold together whatever materials they chose to display, sometimes delivering a rather general message in connection with that theme, and, on occasion, sometimes choosing to lay down a very specific syllogism in connection with a theme. These traits take on significance when we compare Midrash to Midrash, that is to say, Pesiqta Rabbati to Pesiqta deRab Kahana. For that purpose in section 7 of this chapter we address the way in which three compilations, Pesiqta Rabbati, Pesiqta deRab Kahana, and Sifré to Numbers, treat Num. 7:1.

It remains to observe that an introduction to rabbinic literature in medieval times will find in the area of exegesis of the written Torah many more Midrash compilations and other documents akin to Pesiqta Rabbati—collections and arrangements of information by topic—than those similar to Leviticus Rabbah and Pesiqta deRab Kahana, sustained, argumentative, compelling presentations of well-crafted propositions. For medieval times, collecting and arranging by theme predominated, so Midrash compilation lost its intellectual energy, and the main events of disciplined thought took place in philosophy, whether rational or mystical, on the one side, and the theoretical expansion of law, on the other.

2.
TRANSLATIONS INTO ENGLISH

The first translation is that of William G. Braude, *Pesikta Rabbati. Discourses for Feasts, Fasts, and Special Sabbaths* (New Haven and London, 1968: Yale University Press) I–II. In connection with the comparative study *From Tradition to Imitation (The Plan and Program of Pesiqta deRab Kahana and Pesiqta Rabbati.* Atlanta, 1987: Scholars Press for Brown Judaic Studies); this writer made a fresh, form-analytical translation of Pisqaot 1–5 and 15.

3.
RHETORIC

As usual, we may classify all the large-scale compositions of Pesiqta Rabbati within a limited set of literary structures. These are (1) the legal colloquy, which itself follows a fairly restrictive pattern in that the form opens with a narrowly legal question, which moves toward a broader, propositional conclusion; (2) the intersecting-verse/base-verse construction, the exegetical form, and (3) the propositional list. The legal colloquy commences, "May our master instruct us . . . our masters have taught us . . . ," and this then is followed by a secondary lesson. The intersecting-verse/base-verse construction itself is composed of a variety of clearly formalized units, e.g., exegesis of verses of Scripture and the like. The exegetical form invariably consists of the citation of a verse of Scripture followed by a few words that impute to that verse a given meaning; this constant beginning may then be followed by a variety of secondary accretions which themselves exhibit no persistent formal traits. The propositional list is remarkably cogent in both its formal traits and its principle of cogency. In Pesiqta Rabbati we find one fixed order: the legal colloquy always comes first. But event that form serves diverse purposes, since in some *pisqaot* it announces a proposition which will be spelled out and restated in exegetical form as well, while in others the legal colloquy introduces a theme but no proposition in connection with that theme. From that point we may find no fixed order at all.

4.
LOGIC OF COHERENT DISCOURSE

As in the antecedent compilation, the document as a whole appeals to the fixed associations defined by synagogal lections, in sequence. The individual compositions are syllogistic. It is difficult to discover as a general or indicative trait of Pesiqta Rabbati a sustained effort at making a cogent and single statement. That means that the authorship of the document as a whole found itself contented with a variety of types of logical discourse. As noted, some of the *pisqaot* treat a single topic, but only in a miscellaneous way, not setting forth a proposition and its proof. The propositions associated with that topic would scarcely cohere to form a single cogent statement. In that case the document constitutes a scrapbook. Other *pisqaot* draw a variety of statements into juxtaposition so that while not coherent, when viewed all together, those statements would form a single significant judgment upon a theme, hence, a collage.

5.
TOPICAL PROGRAM

Briefly cataloged above, the topics covered by Pesiqta Rabbati go over precisely the same liturgical calendar as Pesiqta deRab Kahana, and do so in pretty much the same way. The imitative character of the later Pesiqta—form and substance alike—is proven by a simple fact. The authorship of Pesiqta Rabbati has simply recapitulated the liturgical program of the authorship of the earlier Pesiqta. But when, in section 7 below, we compare the two Pesiqtas' treatment of the same verse of Scripture, we shall see in Pesiqta Rabbati's exposition not only recapitulation but also fresh initiatives. So the main difference between the documents is in the greater cogency attained by the earlier of the two.

6.
A SAMPLE PASSAGE

PESIQTA RABBATI PISQA FIVE
CONCERNING THE SABBATH OF HANUKKAH

And it came to pass on the day that Moses completed setting up the tabernacle, [he anointed and consecrated it; he also anointed and consecrated its equipment, and the altar and its vessels. The chief men of Israel, heads of families, that is, the chiefs of the tribes who had assisted in preparing the detailed lists, came forward and brought their offering before the Lord] (Num. 7:1–2).

V:I.   1.   A.   May our master instruct us [concerning the correct procedure when one person reads aloud from the Hebrew of

Scripture and another translates the passage into Aramaic
for the community? Specifically may the same person both
read the text and also translate it? May the one who translates the text do so by reading from a written document,
thus giving the impression of reading aloud from an Aramaic, rather than Hebrew, original?]:

B.   What is the law as to having the one who translates the
Torah lection actually read aloud the Torah lection itself?

C.   What is the law as to permitting the one who translates the
Torah lection to read aloud from a written text?

D.   Our rabbis have taught:

E.   It is forbidden [for the one who pronounces the translation]
to glance at a written text, and it also is forbidden for the
one who reads the Hebrew text of the Torah aloud to raise
his eyes from the Torah.

F.   For the Torah has been given only in writing, as it is said, *I
shall write on the tablets . . .* (Ex. 34:1).

G.   And it also is forbidden for the one who pronounces the
translation to set his eyes upon the Torah text [so that he
does not give the wrong impression that he is reading an
Aramaic original].

H.   Said R. Judah b. Pazzi, "There is a verse of Scripture that
makes this point explicitly: *The Lord said to Moses, Write these
words* (Ex. 34:27), lo, this refers to Scripture, which was
given in writing.

I.   *"For these words are given orally* [and not in writing] (Ex.
34:27), lo, [this refers] to the translation into Aramaic,
which is to be stated orally."

2.   A.   Said R. Judah b. R. Shalom, "Moses wanted the Mishnah
to be handed on in writing. The Holy One, blessed be he,
foresaw that the nations were going to translate the Torah,
proclaiming it in Greek, saying that they are Israel.

B.   "Said the Holy One, blessed be he, to Moses, 'Now Moses,
the nations of the world are destined to claim, "We are Israel, we are the true children of the Omnipresent," while
Israel will say, "We are the children of the Omnipresent."
And then the scales will be evenly balanced.'

C.   "Said the Holy One, blessed be he, to the nations, 'Now if
you say that you are my children, I shall know the truth
only by reference to who has my mysteries in his possession. They are the ones who are my children.'

D.   "Then the nations will say to him, 'And what are these
mysteries of yours?'

E.   "He will say to them, 'These mysteries are the Mishnah.'"

F.   Now how is all of this to be derived from exegesis?

G.   Said R. Judah the Levite, son of R. Shalom, "Said the Holy One, blessed be he, to Moses, 'How can you want the Mishnah to be written down? How are we to tell the difference between Israel and the nations of the world?'

H.   "It is written, '*If I should write for him the larger part of my Torah, then he would have been seen as a stranger* (Hos. 8:12)— if so, they would have been held to be strangers [being unable to point to their knowledge of the Mishnah as evidence of their unique calling].'"

No. 1 and No. 2 do not relate, since what is oral for No. 1 is the translation of Scripture from Hebrew to Aramaic, while what is at issue at No. 2 is the Mishnah as a document to be memorized and not written down. The point of No. 1 is that the law requires preserving a clear distinction between what is written, which is Scripture in Hebrew, and what is presented orally and not as though read, which is the translation of Scripture into the vernacular. No. 2 makes the quite separate point that while the nations of the world have possession, in Greek, of Scripture, only Israel has possession of God's *gnosis*, the Mishnah, which is learned by memory.

V:II.   1.   A.   Another interpretation of the verse, *If I should write for him the larger part of my Torah, then he would have been seen as a stranger* (Hos. 8:12):

B.   This is one of the three matters for which Moses was prepared to give his life, on account of which the Holy One, blessed be he, gave them in his name [in line with the sense of the verse, I should write *for him*, meaning, *in his name*].

C.   The three are the rule of justice, the Torah, and the building of the tabernacle in the wilderness.

D.   How do we know that that is so of the Torah? *Remember the Torah of Moses, my servant* (Mal. 3:22).

E.   The rule of justice: *Moses the lawgiver . . . maintained the righteous judgments of the Lord and his ordinances among Israel* (Deut. 33:21).

F.   How do we know that Moses was prepared to give his life for the sake of the tabernacle:

G.   R. Hiyya b. Joseph said, "On each of the seven days of the consecration of the tabernacle, Moses would dismantle the tabernacle twice a day and then set it up again [thus, morning and evening, for the obligatory daily whole offering done twice a day]."

H.   R. Hanina the Elder said, "Three times a day he would dismantle it and then erect it."

I.   And should you suppose that someone of the tribe of Levi would give him a hand, our masters have said, "He by himself would dismantle it, and no person of Israel helped him in any way.

J.   "How [do we know that Moses did it by himself]? As it is said, *And it came to pass on the day that Moses completed setting up the tabernacle, [he anointed and consecrated it; he also anointed and consecrated its equipment, and the altar and its vessels. The chief men of Israel, heads of families, that is, the chiefs of the tribes who had assisted in preparing the detailed lists, came forward and brought their offering before the Lord]* (Num. 7:1–2). [All that the others did was make the lists and then give their own offering. Moses did the rest.]"

The insertion of this entire composition, covering V:I.2 and V:II, is now clearly to lead us to the conclusion of J. The relevant point then is that Moses did the work by himself, sacrificially, and therefore Scripture credits to him the making of the tabernacle. Braude reads the proof text, *And it came to pass on the day that Moses' strength had all but given out because of the settings up of the tabernacle,* which has the merit of translating the proof text, with its use of the letters KLH, which can mean "be completed," and, by extension, "exhaust," within the context of the sense intended here: self-sacrifice.

V:III.   1.   A.   Thus did R. Tanhuma b. R. Abba commence discourse: *Who has ascended heaven and come down? [Who has gathered up the wind in the hollow of his hand? Who has wrapped the waters in his garment? Who has established all the extremities of the earth? What is his name or his son's name, if you know it? Every word of God is pure, a shield to those who take refuge in him. Do not add to his words, lest he indict you and you be proved a liar]* (Prov. 30:4):

B.   "This verse of Scripture is to be expounded with reference to God and Moses.

C.   "How so?

D.   "*Who has ascended heaven and come down?*

E.   "This refers to the Holy One, blessed be he: *God has gone up amid acclamation* (Ps. 47:6).

F.   "The matter may be compared to the case of a mortal king who was going from one place to another. They bring trumpets and sound them before him. So did they do before the Holy One, blessed be he, as in the following verse:

With trumpets at the blast of the horn raise a shout before the Lord King (Ps. 98:6).

G. "... *and come down:* this refers to the Holy One, blessed be he: *And the Lord came down on Mount Sinai* (Ex. 19:20).

H. "*Who has gathered up the wind in the hollow of his hand?*

I. "This refers to the Holy One, blessed be he: *In whose hand is the soul of every living thing, and the breath of all mankind* (Job 12:10).

J. "*Who has wrapped the waters in his garment?*

K. "This refers to the Holy One, blessed be he: *He binds up the waters in his thick clouds* (Job 26:8).

L. "*Who has established all the extremities of the earth?* [Braude: Who has raised up all those who have come to their end upon the earth?]

M. "This refers to the Holy One, blessed be he, who revives the dead: *Your dead shall live, my dead bodies shall arise* (Is. 26:19), also: *The Lord kills and brings alive* (1 Sam. 2:6).

N. "*What is his name?*

O. "It is God, the Almighty, of Hosts, the Lord. What is his name? It is the Lord: *I am the Lord, that is my name* (Is. 42:8).

P. "... *or his son's name, if you know it:*

Q. "This refers to Israel: *Thus says the Lord, Israel is my son, my firstborn* (Ex. 4:22)."

2. A. *Who has ascended heaven and come down?*

B. Who is this one, whose prayer goes up to heaven and brings down rain?

C. This is one who shares out the tithes that he owes [not by exact calculation] but merely by fistfuls.

D. *Who has gathered up the wind in the hollow of his hand?*

E. This is one who does not divide up the tithes that he owes in the proper manner. He holds back rain.

3. A. Another interpretation: *Who has ascended heaven and come down?*

B. This refers to Elijah: *Elijah went up by a whirlwind into heaven* (2 Kgs. 2:11).

C. ... *and come down?*

D. *Go down with him, do not be afraid* (2 Kgs. 1:15).

E. *Who has gathered up the wind in the hollow of his hand?*

F. *As the Lord, God of Israel, lives, before whom I stand, there shall not be dew nor rain these years* (1 Kgs. 17:1).

G. *Who has wrapped the waters in his garment?*

H. *Elijah took his cloak and wrapped it together and smote the waters and they were divided* (1 Kgs. 2:8).

I. *Who has established all the extremities of the earth?*

J. *And Elijah said, See, your son lives* (1 Kgs. 17:23).

4. A. Another interpretation: *Who has ascended heaven and come down?*

B. This refers to Moses: *And Moses went up to God* (Ex. 19:3).

C. *and come down?*

D. *And the Lord spoke to Moses, Go, get down* (Ex. 32:7).

E. *Who has gathered up the wind in the hollow of his hand?*

F. This refers to Moses: *As soon as I have gone out of the city, I shall spread forth my hands to the Lord* (Ex. 9:29).

G. *Who has wrapped the waters in his garment?*

H. *With the blast of your nostrils the waters were piled up* (Ex. 15:8).

I. *Who has established all the extremities of the earth?*

J. This is Moses: Said R. Abba bar Kahana, "This refers to the standards that Moses set up: *Each man with his own standard, according to the signs* (Num. 2:2)."

K. R. Simeon in the name of R. Joshua b. Levi, "This refers to the tabernacle: *And it came to pass on the day that Moses completed setting up the tabernacle, [he anointed and consecrated it; he also anointed and consecrated its equipment, and the altar and its vessels. The chief men of Israel, heads of families, that is, the chiefs of the tribes who had assisted in preparing the detailed lists, came forward and brought their offering before the Lord]* (Num. 7:1–2)."

5. A. Our rabbis have taught: **On three things the world stands: the Torah, the Temple service [cult], and acts of loving kindness [M. Abot 1:2].**

B. And you find that twenty-six generations arose from when the world was made until the Torah was given.

C. The Holy One, blessed be he, guided them in his mercy.

D. As a counterpart to those generations, David said twenty-six times: *For his mercy endures forever* (Ps. 136).

6. A. Said R. Huna the Priest, son of Abin, in the name of R. Aha, "Moses made a veiled allusion to them at the sea: *You have led them in your mercies* (Ex. 15:13).

B. "This refers to the twenty-six generations that arose from the creation of the world until the Torah was given.

C. "*You guided them by your strength* (Ex. 15:13): this refers to the Torah, which is called strength: *The Lord will give strength to his people* (Ps. 29:11).

D. "What was the world like at that time? It was like a three-legged chair, which had only two legs and could not stand. [Thus there were the people and the Torah, but no cult.]

When the tabernacle—*to your holy habitation* (Ex. 15:13)—was set up, the universe was firmly established.

E.   "*And it came to pass on the day that Moses completed setting up the tabernacle*"

F.   "What is written is only *the* tabernacle [and the *the* adds something, namely], with the sense, setting up the world, like the creation of heaven and earth: *He who spreads them out as a tabernacle for habitation* (Is. 40:22)."

The point of No. 1 is realized at the end. Moses is the one who established the tabernacle as God's residence, as the base verse indicates. So the force of the intersecting verse is to identify Moses with the Holy One, in that Moses established the tabernacle for God *(established all the extremities of the earth)*. No. 1 then accomplishes the first of the two points, with interpolated materials, following the excellent pattern of No. 1, at Nos. 2, 3. Then No. 1 resumes at No. 4, and the point-for-point correspondence between God and Moses is worked out, reaching our climax at K. No. 5 then prepares the way for No. 6, with which it is continuous.

V:IV.   1.   A.   Another interpretation of the verse, *And it came to pass on the day that Moses completed setting up the tabernacle, [he anointed and consecrated it; he also anointed and consecrated its equipment, and the altar and its vessels. The chief men of Israel, heads of families, that is, the chiefs of the tribes who had assisted in preparing the detailed lists, came forward and brought their offering before the Lord]* (Num. 7:1–2).

B.   This is pertinent to the following verse: *Awake O north, and come O south* (Song 4:16).

C.   *Awake O north* refers to whole offerings, which are slaughtered at the north side of the altar.

2.   A.   R. Eliezer b. Pedat said, "The children of Noah offered peace offerings [and not whole offerings]."

B.   "What is the basis for that statement?

C.   "*And Abel brought of the firstlings of his flock and of their fat portions* (Gen. 4:4).

D.   "What is the sense of the phrase, *and of their fat portions* (Gen. 4:4)?

E.   "The fat of the beast was offered on the altar [and not eaten by the one who brought the beast, but the pertinent portions of the beast were eaten by the one who brought it, hence it was a peace offering that Abel brought]."

F.   And R. Yosé bar Hanina said, "They prepared them in the status of whole offerings [burning up the entire animal and not keeping any portions for the sacrificer (who does the rite) and *sacrifier* (who benefits from the rite)]."

G. How does R. Yosé bar Hanina treat this passage: *and of their fat portions* (Gen. 4:4)? He interprets it to refer to the fat animals [and not to the portions of those that were offered up, but only referring to "the best of the flock"].

H. R. Eleazar objected to R. Yosé bar Hanina, "And is it not written, *And Jethro, Moses' father-in-law, took a burnt offering and sacrifices* (Ex. 18:12)? [The reference to a burnt offering would suffice, so the inclusion of the further reference to "sacrifices" indicates that there was an offering made in a different classification, hence, peace offerings.]"

I. [How does R. Yosé bar Hanina deal with this verse?] He accords with the view of him who said that Jethro came to Moses *after* the giving of the Torah, [at which point Jethro was in the status of an Israelite. Hence the type of offering Jethro gave would indicate only what Israelites did when they made their sacrifices and would not testify to how children of Noah, prior to the giving of the Torah, in general offered up their animals.]

J. R. Yannai said, "It was after the giving of the Torah that he came."

K. R. Hiyya the Elder said, "It was prior to the giving of the Torah that he came."

L. R. Eleazar [objected to the view of R. Yosé bar Hanina], "And lo, it is written: *And he sent the young men of the children of Israel, who offered burnt offerings and sacrificed peace offerings of oxen unto the Lord* (Ex. 24:5). [This was before revelation, and hence would indicate that the children of Noah, belonging to the category of the Israelites at that time, prior to the Torah, in fact offered not only whole offerings but also peace offerings, just as Eleazar maintains.]"

M. He said to him, "Indeed, we have learned from the Torah that that was an innovation for the occasion."

N. Hezekiah b. R. Hiyya interpreted the reference to *peace offerings* to mean that they offered up the beasts with their hides, without flaying them and cutting them into pieces. [That constituted an innovation. So even though the verse refers to peace offerings, in fact the animals were offered up as whole offerings, hide and all.]

O. Said R. Joshua of Sikhnin in the name of R. Levi, "Scripture supports the view of R. Yosé b. R. Hanina."

P. R. Joshua of Sikhnin in the name of R. Levi: "Also the following verse (Lev 6:2) supports the view of R. Yosé bar

Hanina: 'When Scripture refers to the meal offering, what is stated is not, That is the meal-offering,' and when it says, *This is the Torah of the guilt offering* (Lev. 7:1), it does not say, 'That is the guilt offering.' But when Scripture comes to the matter of the whole offering, what does Scripture say? *This is the Torah governing the preparation of the whole offering, that is the whole offering [of which people 'already are informed]* (Lev. 6:2) meaning, that whole offering that the children of Noah used to offer up.

Q.   "When Scripture speaks of peace offerings, it states, *And this is the law of the sacrifice of peace offering'* (Lev. 7:11), but it is not written, '*which they offered up*,' but rather, 'which they *will* offer up' (Lev. 7:11), meaning, only in the future. [Hence peace offerings' rules, allowing the sacrificer and *sacrifier* a share in the animal that is offered up, represented an innovation, not formerly applicable, in support of the view of R. Yosé bar Hanina that such offerings' rules constituted an innovation.]"

R.   The following verse of Scripture also supports the view of R. Yosé b. Hanina: *Awake, O north wind* (Song 4:16) refers to the whole offering, which was slaughtered at the north side of the altar. What is the sense of "awake"? It speaks of something that was asleep and now wakes up.

S.   *And come, you south* (Song 4:16) speaks of peace offerings, which were slaughtered [even] at the south side of the altar. [And what is the sense of "come"? It speaks of a new and unprecedented practice. Hence the rules governing peace offerings constituted an innovation. Freedman, *Genesis Rabbah*, p. 184, n. 1: "Thus it was only now, after the giving of the Torah, that the practice of sacrificing peace-offerings was introduced."]

3.   A.   Said R. Simon in the name of R. Samuel b. R. Nahman, "Scripture says, *An altar of dirt you will make for me, and you will make an offering on it of your whole offerings and peace offerings* (Ex. 20:21)."

     B.   R. Reuben says, "In a place that is suitable for whole offerings and suitable for peace offerings [is where these offerings will be made]. From the middle of the altar and to the northern side it is suitable for whole offerings, and from the middle of the altar and southward is the area suitable for peace offerings."

4.   A.   *Blow on my garden that the spices thereof may flow out* (Song. 4:16):

    B.   This refers to the incense offering.

5. A.   *Let my beloved come into his garden* (Song 4:16):

    B.   Said R. Nehunia, "Torah teaches proper conduct. A husband should not come in until the bride gives him permission."

6. A.   *And eat his precious fruits* (Song 4:16):

    B.   This refers to the offerings.

The intersecting verse becomes relevant only at the very end, at which point we refer to the altar. No. 6 is the one point at which we regain the base verse. No. 2 raises its own question, a debate parachuted down with no bearing upon our passage at all. The reason is that our intersecting verse enters in at 2.S. Otherwise there is no point of contact. 2.T then accounts for the inclusion of No. 3, 4, and 5—that is, a hodgepodge of comments on the intersecting verse. In no way is the base verse illuminated. That is not what is at issue in the compositors' program. The model, rather, is one of a scrapbook in which one collects materials on a given topic: a file that is topical and not purposeful and composed with a proposition in mind. But in the unfolding of the whole, as we see, the composition becomes somewhat more successful.

V:V. 1. A.   *I have come into my garden, my sister, my bride* (Song 5:1):

    B.   To what is the matter compared? To the case of a king who said to the citizens of a state to build him a palace. They built it and assembled at the gate of the palace crying out, "Let the king come into the palace."

    C.   What did the king do? He went in through a side door and sent an announcement saying to them, "Do not cry out! I have already come into the palace."

    D.   So too, when the tabernacle had been erected, the Israelites said, "*Let my beloved come into his garden* (Song 4:16)."

    E.   The Holy One, blessed be he, sent to them and said, "Why are you concerned? *I have come into my garden, my sister, my bride* (Song 5:1)."

    2. A.   Another matter concerning the verse, *I have come into my garden, my sister, my bride* (Song 5:1):

    B.   Said R. Simeon bar Yosni, "What is written is not, I have come into a garden, but *I have come into my garden, [my sister, my bride]* (Song 5:1).

    C.   "What is the explanation of 'my garden'? 'I have returned to the garden from which I had departed.'

    D.   "That is in line with this verse: *The Lord God was moving about in the garden* (Gen. 3:8) [Braude, p. 102: 'The Lord God hastened and went up from the garden].'"

3. A. *I have gathered my myrrh with my spice, I have eaten my liquid honey as well as my honeycomb* (Song 5:1): this refers to the Most Holy Things and the Lesser Holy Things.

   B. *I have drunk my wine with my fat* (Song 5:1): this refers to the drink offerings and the fats.

4. A. Another interpretation of the verse *I have gathered my myrrh with my spice, I have eaten my liquid honey as well as my honeycomb, I have drunk my wine with my fat* (Song 5:1): this refers to three things that the princes did improperly, but which, nonetheless, the Holy One, blessed be he, accepted.

   B. The first is that an individual may not present as a voluntary offering an incense offering, but every prince brought an incense offering, in line with this verse of Scripture: *One golden pan of ten shekels full of incense* (Num. 7:14).

   C. An individual may not offer a sin offering unless he knows precisely what sin he has committed inadvertently: *If his sin . . . become known to him, he shall bring for his offering a goat* (Lev. 4:23), but the princes made a sin offering for a sin of which none was aware: *His offering was . . . a male of the goats for a sin offering* (Num. 7:16).

   D. An individual's offering does not override the restrictions of the Sabbath, but the offering of one prince did override the restrictions of the Sabbath: *On the seventh day . . . the prince . . . of the children of Ephraim* (Num. 7:48).

5. A. *Eat, O friends, drink, yes, drink abundantly O beloved* (Song 5:1):

   B. This refers to Israel, who are called friends: *For my brethren and friends' sakes* (Ps. 12:8).

6. A. Another interpretation of the verse *Let my beloved come into his garden* (Song 4:16):

   B. Do not read the letters for "garden" as they are given, but rather, to mean, "to the marriage canopy."

   C. When was this the case? *"And it came to pass on the day that Moses completed setting up the tabernacle"*—for the word for *"completed"* is written so that it may be read as *"nuptial"* [hence, this was the day that Israel as bride entered the marriage canopy].

Now the selection of the intersecting verse makes sense within the framework of the compositor, who wishes to dwell on the notion that the day on which the tabernacle was completed marked the marriage of Israel to God. Then the base verse, with its possibility of a play on the words for "complete" and "nuptial," has guided us to Song 4:16, 5:1, and the rest follows. But then the miscellaneous character of the rest is clear, since the treatment of Song 5:1, with its reference to liquid honey and so forth, is wholly autonomous of the purpose and direction of exegesis. So once an intersecting verse is chosen, then its interests will guide the whole, and no proposition joining each of the parts will account for the inner cogency of the composition as a whole—for there is none.

V:VI. 1. A. Another interpretation of the verse *And it came to pass on the day that Moses completed setting up the tabernacle, [he anointed and consecrated it; he also anointed and consecrated its equipment, and the altar and its vessels. The chief men of Israel, heads of families, that is, the chiefs of the tribes who had assisted in preparing the detailed lists, came forward and brought their offering before the Lord]* (Num. 7:1–2):

      B. This is relevant to the following verse: *For there is a man whose labor is with wisdom and with knowledge and with skill* (Qoh. 2:21).

      C. This refers to Bezalel, who made the tabernacle with wisdom and knowledge, in line with this verse of Scripture: *I have filled him with the spirit of God, in wisdom and understanding and knowledge* (Ex. 31:3).

      D. *Yet to a man who has not labored therein shall he leave of his portion* (Qoh. 2:21):

      E. This refers to Moses, who did not labor to create the tabernacle, yet it is called by his name, as it is said: *And it came to pass on the day that Moses completed setting up the tabernacle.*

      F. What is written is not, *And it came to pass on the day that Bezalel completed setting up the tabernacle,*

      G. but rather, *And it came to pass on the day that Moses completed setting up the tabernacle.*

      H. Thus we see the meaning of the verse: *Yet to a man who has not labored therein shall he leave of his portion.*

The focus now is upon the curious fact that Scripture assigns the making of the tabernacle to Bezalel and also credits it to Moses. The rest follows, and the intersecting verse here provides an observation upon the fact.

V:VII. 1. A. *And it came to pass on the day that Moses completed setting up the tabernacle, [he anointed and consecrated it; he also anointed and consecrated its equipment, and the altar and its vessels. The chief men of Israel, heads of families, that is, the chiefs of the tribes who had assisted in preparing the detailed lists, came forward and brought their offering before the Lord]* (Num. 7:1–2):

      B. What he said he would do, he did.

   2. A. Said R. Joshua b. Levi, "The Holy One, blessed be he, stipulated with Israel while they were yet in Egypt that he

would bring them out of Egypt only on condition that they make a tabernacle, in which he would bring his Presence to rest among them, as it is said, *And they shall know that I am the Lord their God, who has brought them forth out of the land of Egypt, that I may dwell among them* (Ex. 29:46).

B. "When the tabernacle was set up, the Presence of God descended and dwelt in it. At that moment was carried out the entire stipulation.

C. "Therefore it is said, *And it came to pass* (Num. 7:1).

D. "What he said he would do, he did."

3. A. Another matter concerning the verse: *And it came to pass* (Num. 7:1):

B. Said Rab, "[What came to pass] is something that had never been created in the world before this time.

C. "For from the time that the world was created, the Presence of God had never come to rest among the lower creatures. But once Moses had set up the tabernacle, the Presence of God came to rest among the lower creatures."

D. And R. Simeon b. Yohai says, "What is the sense of *And it came to pass* (Num. 7:1)? It had been in being and ceased and then come into being once again.

E. "For so you find that from the beginning of the creation of the world, the Presence of God was among the creatures of the lower world, in line with this verse of Scripture:

F. "*And they heard the voice of the Lord God walking in the garden* (Gen. 3:8).

G. "When the first man sinned, the Presence of God rose up to the first firmament. When Cain went and murdered his brother, the Presence of God went up to the second firmament. When the generation of Enosh went and sinned—*then the practice of calling on the name of the Lord [in vain] began* (Gen. 4:26)—it went up to the third firmament. When the generation of the Flood went and sinned, in line with this verse, *And the Lord saw that the wickedness of man was great* (Gen. 6:5), it went up to the fourth firmament. When the generation of the dispersion went and sinned—*Come, let us build a city with its top in heaven* (Gen. 11:4)—the Presence of God went up to the fifth firmament. When the people of Sodom went and sinned, it went up to the sixth: *The men of Sodom were wicked and sinners* (Gen. 13:13). When the Philistines came and sinned—*and Abimelech, king of Gerar, sent and took Sarah* (Gen. 20:2)—it went up to the seventh.

H. "Abraham came along and laid up a treasure of good deeds, and the Presence of God came down from the seventh firmament to the sixth. Isaac came along and stretched out his neck on the altar, and the Presence of God went down from the sixth to the fifth. Jacob came along and planted a tent for the Torah study, in line with this verse, *And Jacob was a perfect man, living in tents* (Gen. 25:27), and the Presence of God came down from the fifth to the fourth firmament. Levi came along and brought it down from the fourth to the third, Kohath came along and brought it from the third to the second, Amram came along and brought it from the second to the first.

I. "Fortunate are the righteous who create on earth a dwelling place for the Presence of God.

J. "For so it is written: *Truly the upright will make a dwelling place on the earth* (Prov. 2:21).

K. "Moses came along and brought the Presence down, in line with this verse: *The cloud covered the tent, and the glory of the Lord filled the tabernacle* (Ex. 40:34)."

4. A. It is written, *Behold heaven and the heaven of heavens cannot hold you* (1 Kgs. 8:27).

B. And it is written, *And the glory of the Lord filled the tabernacle* (Ex. 40:34).

C. Said R. Joshua of Sikhnin in the name of R. Levi, "To what may the matter be compared? To a cave open at the edge of the sea. The sea floods upward and fills the cave, but the sea is not diminished.

D. "So even though it is written, *And the glory of the Lord filled the tabernacle* (Ex. 40:34), nonetheless the upper worlds and the lower worlds did not lose any of the splendor of the glory of the Holy One, blessed be he, in line with this verse: *Do I not fill the heaven and the earth, says the Lord* (Jer. 23:24)."

5. A. [Resuming Simeon's statement, where 3:J left off:] "Therefore it is written here, *And it came to pass* (Num. 7:1), indicating that just as the Presence of God at the beginning of the creation of the world had been below, but had arisen upward by stages and then returned now to dwell below,

B. "so now it would remain: *And it came to pass on the day that Moses completed setting up the tabernacle*."

What is subject to interpretation is the phrase, *And it came to pass on the day that Moses completed setting up the tabernacle*. No. 1 offers a simple statement. Then No.

2 clarifies No. 1. Nos. 3, 5 work on the sense of the language *and it came to pass*, with the two positions—something new, something renewed—fully spelled out, with an interpolation at No. 4.

V:VIII.   1.   A.   Another interpretation concerning the same phrase, namely, *And it came to pass [on the day that Moses completed setting up the tabernacle, he anointed and consecrated it; he also anointed and consecrated its equipment, and the altar and its vessels. The chief men of Israel, heads of families, that is, the chiefs of the tribes who had assisted in preparing the detailed lists, came forward and brought their offering before the Lord]* (Num. 7:1–2).

B.   Said R. Hiyya b. R. Abba in the name of R. Yohanan, "The following exegetical principle we brought up from the exile of Babylonia.

C.   "Any passage in which the words, *And it came to pass* appear is a passage that relates unparalleled misfortune."

D.   Along these same lines said R. Simeon b. R. Abba in the name of R. Yohanan: "It may serve this meaning but also the opposite. Specifically, in any passage in which it says, *It came to pass in the days of*, speaks of distress without parallel, e.g.,

E.   "*And it came to pass in the days of Ahasuerus* (Est. 1:1) [cf. also: *Haman undertook to destroy, to slay, and to annihilate all the Jews, young and old, women and children, in one day* (Est. 3:13)]—can there be a greater misfortune?

F.   "*And it came to pass in the days in which the judges ruled, there was a famine in the land* (Ruth 1:1)—can there be a greater misfortune?

G.   "And any passage in which it says, *And it came to pass*, speaks of joy without parallel:

H.   "*Let there be light and there was light* (Gen. 1:3)—is there greater joy than that!

I.   "*And it came to pass on the eighth day* (Lev. 9:1)—is there greater joy than that!

J.   "So too here: *And it came to pass [on the day that Moses completed setting up the tabernacle*—is there greater joy than that!"

2.   A.   Said R. Samuel b. Nahman, "In any passage in which it is written, *And it came to pass*, there is no distress that can compare to that, and in any passage in which it is written, *And it was*, there is no greater joy than that."

B.   They said to R. Samuel b. Nahman, "Lo, it is written, *And light came to pass*. What distress came about on that occasion?"

C. He said to them, "It was that its light was destined to be
    stored away on account of the lights [of the sun and the
    moon]."

D. They said to him, "And lo, it is written, *And it came to pass
    on the eighth day* (Lev. 9:1). What distress came about on
    that occasion?"

E. He said to them, "Nadab and Abihu were going to die."

F. They said to him, "And lo, it is written, *And it came to pass
    [on the day that Moses completed setting up the tabernacle]*. What
    distress came about on that occasion?"

G. He said to them, "It is because the tabernacle was destined
    to be stored away on account of the house of the sanctuary."

H. They said to him, "And lo, it is written, *And it was when
    Jerusalem was taken* (Jer. 38:28). [What joy can be involved
    here?]"

I. He said to them, "There is no joy like it, for [had the city
    not been taken,] the prophet would not have had the right
    to say so to Israel, *The punishment of your sin has been accom-
    plished, daughter of Zion* (Lam. 5:22)."

The inquiry into the sense of *And it came to pass* unfolds at Nos. 1, 2. No. 1
deals with our passage, but No. 2 does not, which means that the composite was
complete before insertion here. Samuel b. Nahman's exercise is in any case irrelevant.

V:IX. 1. A. *And it came to pass on the day that Moses completed setting up the
                tabernacle, [he anointed and consecrated it; he also anointed and
                consecrated its equipment, and the altar and its vessels. The chief
                men of Israel, heads of families, that is, the chiefs of the tribes who
                had assisted in preparing the detailed lists, came forward and
                brought their offering before the Lord]* (Num. 7:1–2).

           B. [Since the letters of the word for and *it came to pass* may also
                be read, Woe, we ask:] who said, "Woe"?

           C. Said R. Abba, "It is as if the Holy One, blessed be he,
                said, 'Woe!'

           D. "To what may the matter be compared? To the case of a
                king who had a shrewish wife. The king said to her, 'Make
                a purple cloak for me.'

           E. "All the time that she was busy making the cloak, she kept
                her peace. But after a while she finished the cloak and gave
                it to the launderer who completed the work, and she
                brought it to the king.

           F. "When the king saw it, he began to cry, 'Woe.' She said to him, 'My lord, O King, your purple cloak is finished and you say, 'Woe'?

G. "He said to her, 'It is because I am worried that you will go back to your complaining.'

H. "So you find that the Israelites were always complaining, in line with this verse: *And the people murmured against Moses and against Aaron* (Ex. 15:24).

I. "So too: *And the whole congregation of the children of Israel murmured* (Ex. 16:23).

J. "*You have killed the people of the Lord* (Num. 17:6).

K. "The Holy One, blessed be he, asked them to make a tabernacle: *And let them make me a sanctuary* (Ex. 25:8).

L. "So you find that all the time that the Israelites were occupied with the making of the tabernacle, they did not have occasion to complain. But once they had finished the tabernacle, the Holy One, blessed be he, cried, 'Woe.'

M. "*And it came to pass on the day that Moses ended* (Num. 7:1).

N. "They said, 'Lord of the age, the tabernacle is finished, and yet you cry, 'Woe.'

O. "He said to them, 'I shall tell you why I cry, "woe!" It is because I am afraid that you are going to go and start grumbling against me as you have been in the past.'"

2. A. *And it came to pass on the day that Moses completed setting up the tabernacle, [he anointed and consecrated it; he also anointed and consecrated its equipment, and the altar and its vessels. The chief men of Israel, heads of families, that is, the chiefs of the tribes who had assisted in preparing the detailed lists, came forward and brought their offering before the Lord]* (Num. 7:1–2).

B. [Since the letters of the word for *and it came to pass* may also be read, Woe, we ask:] who said, "Woe"?

C. The firstborn said, "Woe," for the right of the priesthood was taken away from them.

D. Our rabbis have taught: **Before the tabernacle was set up, sacrifices on the high places were permitted, and the work of the sacrifice was carried on by the firstborn [M. Zeb. 14:4]**,

E. and so it is written, *Let not the priests and the people break through to come up to the Lord* (Ex. 19:24), for up to that time the Torah had not been given, and the priesthood had not been assigned to Aaron.

F. And so it is written, *Let not the priests and the people break through to come up to the Lord* (Ex. 19:24).

3. A. [As to the verse, *Let not the priests and the people break through*

to come up to the Lord (Ex. 19:24),] R. Joshua b. Qorhah and Rabbi:

B. One of them says, "The reference to the priests in fact speaks of the firstborn."

C. And his colleagues say, "The reference to the priests applies to Nadab and Abihu."

4. A. *The golden thing has ceased, the Lord has broken the staff of the wicked* (Is. 14:4–5):

B. Said R. Abba bar Mamal, "This refers to the firstborn."

5. A. Therefore when the tabernacle was set up, they cried out, "Woe."

B. *And it came to pass on the day* (Num. 7:1).

6. A. Another matter: *And it came to pass on the day that Moses completed setting up the tabernacle, [he anointed and consecrated it; he also anointed and consecrated its equipment, and the altar and its vessels. The chief men of Israel, heads of families, that is, the chiefs of the tribes who had assisted in preparing the detailed lists, came forward and brought their offering before the Lord]* (Num. 7:1–2).

B. [Since the letters of the word for *and it came to pass* may also be read, Woe, we ask:] who said, "Woe"?

C. The angels said, "Woe."

D. They said, "Now the Holy One, blessed be he, will leave the upper regions and go down and dwell in the lower regions."

E. Nonetheless, the Holy One, blessed be he, conciliated them, saying to the creatures of the upper world, "By your lives! The Principle [of God's presence] is above, in line with this verse: *His glory covers the heavens, and the earth is full of his praise* (Hab. 3:3)."

F. Said R. Simon in the name of R. Simeon in the name of R. Joshua, "The Holy One, blessed be he, in fact was joking with them when he said, 'The Principal is above,' for lo, it is written, *His glory is upon earth and heaven, for he has raised up the horn of his people* (Ps. 148:13–14). That is, first on the earth, then in heaven.

G. "Therefore they said, 'Woe.' *And it came to pass on the day that Moses completed setting up the tabernacle.*"

7. A. Another matter: *And it came to pass on the day that Moses completed setting up the tabernacle, [he anointed and consecrated it; he also anointed and consecrated its equipment, and the altar and its vessels. The chief men of Israel, heads of families, that is, the chiefs of the tribes who had assisted in preparing the detailed lists, came forward and brought their offerings before the Lord]* (Num. 7:1–2).

B. [Since the letters of the word for *and it came to pass* may also be read, Woe, we ask :] who said, "Woe"?

C. The nations of the world said, "Woe."

D. Why did they say woe? Because they said, "Before the Holy One, blessed be he, was living with them, he would watch over them and do their battles for them, and now that they have made a tabernacle for them and he dwells with them, all the more so."

E. Therefore they said, "Woe": *And it came to pass on the day that Moses completed setting up the Tabernacle.*

The exercise of interpreting the language, *And it came to pass,* leads us through a number of possibilities, all the while making a single point, which is that the Israelites' building of the tabernacle had important consequences for the entire world.

V:X. 1. A. Another matter concerning the issue at hand: *And it came to pass on the day that Moses completed setting up the tabernacle, [he anointed and consecrated it; he also anointed and consecrated its equipment, and the altar and its vessels. The chief men of Israel, heads of families, that is, the chiefs of the tribes who had assisted in preparing the detailed lists, came forward and brought their offering before the Lord]* (Num. 7:1–2).

B. What passage occurs just prior to this one? It is the blessing of the priests: *May the Lord bless you and keep you* (Num. 6:24).

C. Said R. Joshua of Sikhnin, "To what may the matter be compared? To the case of a king who betrothed his daughter and was making a banquet of betrothal for her, over which the evil eye had effect.

D. "The king went on to marry her off. What did he do [in consequence of the earlier experience]?

E. "He gave her an amulet. He said to her, 'Keep this amulet on you, so that the evil eye will not affect you anymore.'

F. "So too when the Holy One, blessed be he, came to give the Torah to Israel at Sinai, he made for them a great public celebration, in line with this verse: *And all the people perceived the thunderings* (Ex. 20:15).

G. "This event was only the betrothal, in line with the following: *Go to the people and sanctify them to me* (Ex. 19:10).

H. "But the evil eye had effect, so the tablets were broken, as it is said, *Moses broke them beneath the mountain* (Ex. 32:19).

I. "When they came some time later and made the tabernacle, the Holy One, blessed be he, first handed over to them the priestly blessings, so that the evil eye should not have effect on them.

J. "Therefore Scripture first wrote, *May the Lord bless you and keep you,* and then, *And it came to pass on the day that Moses completed setting up the tabernacle."*

2. A. Another matter concerning the issue at hand: Why does Scripture say first, *May the Lord bless you and keep you* (Num. 6:24), followed by *And it came to pass on the day that Moses completed setting up the tabernacle?*

B. Said R. Abbahu, "The traits of the Holy One, blessed be he, are not the same as the traits of mortals.

C. "When a mortal king enters a town, the townspeople praise him and exalt him and honor him, and then he carries out all of their needs. He builds them public buildings and does other deeds to please them.

D. "But the Holy One, blessed be he, is not that way. Rather, before the Israelites made the tabernacle, he gave them the blessings first, as it is written, *May the Lord bless you and keep you,* and then, *And it came to pass on the day that Moses completed setting up the tabernacle."*

3. A. Another interpretation of the verse *And it came to pass on the day that Moses completed setting up the tabernacle* [now explaining the word choice for "completed," which means also *bring to an end*]:

B. Said R. Judah b. R. Shalom in the name of R. Levi, "There is not a quarter-*qab*'s sewing space of ground in the earth which does not contain nine *qabs* of demons." [This will now be applied to the present case.]

C. Said R. Yohanan, "When the tabernacle was set up, the demons were brought to an end in the world, for it is written, *There shall no evil thing befall you, nor shall any plague come near your tent* (Ps. 91:10)—once the tabernacle was set up."

D. Said R. Simeon b. Laqish, "Why do I require proof merely from the book of Psalms? It is a matter deriving from the Torah: *May the Lord bless you and keep you*—from demons.

E. "When will this take place? *And it came to pass on the day that Moses completed setting up the tabernacle."*

F. A further statement of the same matter: *And it came to pass on the day that Moses completed setting up the tabernacle.*

G. What is written is not that "Moses set up," but Moses *completed setting up.* What then came to an end on that day were the demons, which were removed from the world.

The word "finish" bears the meaning "bring to an end," with the result that we wish to know what ended. It is the evil eye or demonic rule, which the cult counteracts. Hence when the cult was set up, demons were driven out of the world. No. 1 makes that point in terms of the misadventure involved in giving the Torah. No. 2 has its own message, not pertinent to the larger setting, and then No. 3 repeats the point of No. 1.

V:XI.   1.   A.   Another interpretation of the verse, *And it came to pass on the day that Moses completed setting up the Tabernacle, [he anointed and consecrated it; he also anointed and consecrated its equipment, and the altar and its vessels. The chief men of Israel, heads of families, that is, the chiefs of the tribes who had assisted in preparing the detailed lists, came forward and brought their offering before the Lord]* (Num. 7:1–2):

B.   One may commence discourse by citing this verse: *Go forth, you daughters of Zion, and gaze upon King Solomon* (Song 3:11).

C.   This may then be worked out as indicated in discourse on the Song of Songs.

2.   A.   Another interpretation of the verse, *And it came to pass on the day that Moses completed setting up the tabernacle, [he anointed and consecrated it; he also anointed and consecrated its equipment, and the altar and its vessels. The chief men of Israel, heads of families, that is, the chiefs of the tribes who had assisted in preparing the detailed lists, came forward and brought their offering before the Lord]* (Num. 7:1–2):

B.   One may commence discourse by citing this verse: *I shall hear what the Lord God will speak, for he will speak peace to his people and to his saints [but let them not turn back to folly]* (Ps. 85:9):

C.   You find that when the Israelites did that deed, the Holy One, blessed be he, was angry with them, in line with this verse: *I have seen this people and lo, it is a stiff-necked people* (Ex. 32:9).

D.   Moses forthwith went and sought mercy before the Holy One, blessed be he, so that he might be conciliated with Israel, as it is written, *And Moses besought the Lord his God and said, Lord, why do you get so angry? Turn from your fierce wrath and repent of this evil against your people* (Ex. 32:11).

E.   Forthwith the Holy One, blessed be he, was conciliated with them, as it is written, *And the Lord repented of the evil which he said he would do to his people* (Ex. 32:14).

F.   Moses went and [following Braude, p. 113] inclined his ear in the tabernacle, [thinking to himself,] "Is it possible that the Holy One, blessed be he, harbors a grudge against Israel?" So it is written, *I shall hear what the Lord God will speak, for he will speak peace to his people and to his saints but let them not turn back to folly* (Ps. 85:9).

G. "Is it possible that he is still bearing anger against them? But when [as in the cited verse] the name of *the Lord* appears, it is an indication that he deals mercifully with them."

H. Forthwith the Holy One, blessed be he, reassured Moses that [the Holy One] bore no grudge against Israel, in line with this verse: *And the Lord passed by before him and proclaimed, The Lord, the Lord, God, merciful and gracious* (Ex. 34:6).

I. Said R. Simon, "Why is it written in the verse *The Lord, the Lord, God* (Ex. 34:6), that is, two times?

J. "It indicates that God reassured him."

K. He said to him, "Moses, up to this time I treated them in accord with the attribute of mercy, that is, until they had done that deed. So too, even now I shall deal with them in accord with the attribute of mercy."

L. Now Moses was standing there, and the word came into his ear as through a pipe so that none of the Israelites could hear. But when Moses' face got red, the people knew that the word was with him.

3. A. Said R. Berekiah the Priest in the name of R. Judah bar R. Simon, "Said the Holy One blessed be he to him, 'Moses, in the past there was hatred between me and my children, enmity between me and my children, competition between me and my children.

B. "'But now there will be love between me and my children, fraternity between me and my children, comradeship between me and my children, in line with this verse: *I shall hear what the Lord God will speak, for he will speak peace to his people and to his saints but let them not turn back to folly* (Ps. 85:9).'"

4. A. Another interpretation of the verse *I shall hear what the Lord God will speak, for he will speak peace to his people and to his saints but let them not turn back to folly* (Ps. 85:9):

B. Said R. Joshua the Priest b. R. Nehemiah, "This is what R. Eleazar said, 'Before the tabernacle was set up, there was strife in the world, but once the tabernacle was set up, peace was made in the world.

C. "'How do we know that fact? *I shall hear what the Lord God will speak, for he will speak peace to his people and to his saints but let them not turn back to folly* (Ps. 85:9):

D. "'When is that the case? *When glory is made to dwell in our land* [because of the setting up of the tabernacle], *surely his salvation will be near those who bear him* (Ps. 85:10).'"

E.   Said R. Simeon b. Laqish, "Why do I have to draw evidence from the book of Psalms? It is a teaching of the Torah: *The Lord lift up his countenance upon you and give you peace* (Num. 6:26).

F.   "When [is this the case]? *On the day that Moses finished setting up the tabernacle.*"

5. A.   Another comment on: *On the day that Moses finished setting up the tabernacle:*

B.   Said R. Joshua b. Levi, "By a hint said the Holy One, blessed be he, to Israel, that when they should set up the tabernacle, he would bestow the blessings on them.

C.   "How do we know [that he gave such an indication in advance]? It is written, *An altar of earth you shall make for me . . . in every place where I cause my name to be mentioned I shall come to you and bless you* (Ex. 30:32).

D.   "Therefore when they made the tabernacle, the Holy One, blessed be he, bestowed the blessings upon them:

E.   "*The Lord bless you and keep you.*

F.   "When was this? *On the day that Moses finished setting up the tabernacle.*"

6. A.   Said R. Simon, "When the Holy One, blessed be he, said to Israel to put up the tabernacle, he hinted to them that when the tabernacle was set up below, a tabernacle would be set up above.

B.   "*On the day that Moses finished setting up the tabernacle:*

C.   "What is written is *the* tabernacle, bearing the sense that it was that very tabernacle that had been above."

7. A.   *On the day that Moses finished setting up the tabernacle:*

B.   Said the Holy One, blessed be he, "In this world, when the tabernacle was set up, I commanded Aaron and his sons to bless you.

C.   "But in the coming age I in my own person shall bless you, for so it is written, *The Lord bless you out of Zion, even he who made heaven and earth* (Ps. 134:3)."

No. 1 presents a note on an unrealized discourse. No. 2 introduces an intersecting verse which allows us to make the point that when the tabernacle was constructed, it represented an assurance of God's love for Israel. No. 3 makes the same point, using the same verse, but states matters more smoothly. No. 4 goes over the matter yet a third time. No. 5 then makes the same point but does so in line with the prior interest in the juxtaposition of the Priestly Blessing with the account of Moses' setting up of the tabernacle.

7.

COMPARATIVE MIDRASH: NUMBERS 7:1 IN SIFRÉ TO NUMBERS, PESIQTA DERAB KAHANA, AND PESIQTA RABBATI

Now that we have seen how Numbers 7:1 is read in three distinct documents, let us compare the Midrash compilations and their Midrash compositions. When we compare what one authorship thinks important about a verse of Scripture with what another authorship, of the same Judaism, chooses to emphasize in that same verse of Scripture, the basis of comparison and contrast is established by points in common. In this way we may see the correct mode of comparing Midrash exegeses defined by their Midrash compilations.

Two or more documents in the same canon to begin with surely bear broad affinities, having been selected by the consensus of the sages or the faithful as authoritative. They rely upon the opinion or judgment of sages of the same circle. They have been preserved and handed on by the same institutions of the faith. They presumably present basically cogent convictions about the meaning of Scripture. Accordingly, a variety of indicators justifies the judgment that the documents form a solid fit, bearing much in common. Then, it must follow, the work of comparison yields to the exercise of contrast. Being alike, the documents, in their treatment of precisely the same verse of Scripture, produce differences, and these differences make a difference. They tell us how one authorship wishes to read Scripture in one way, another in a different way. In the case at hand, however, the differences prove so profound and far-reaching that they call into question the very act of comparison.

In their shared reading of Numbers 7:1, "On the day when Moses had finished setting up the tabernacle . . . ," we have examined strikingly different topical approaches to what is important in the verse at hand. The program of Sifré to Numbers proves remarkably thin and routine; that of the first Pesiqta, rich and imaginative and—unsurprisingly—highly argumentative and cogent. The relationship of the exegetes in Pesiqta Rabbati to those in the other two documents proves equally random, though there is an affinity between the two Pesiqtas. But the three documents pursue each its own program. Quite how to sort out the amazing differences in approach, emphasis, and inquiry that separate the authorship of Sifré to Numbers from that of Pesiqta Rabbati and of Pesiqta deRab Kahana remains a puzzle. A brief reprise of the topical program of the three documents suffices to permit us to draw a simple and exemplary conclusion: the documents intersect only casually, and the later ones in no way propose simply to collect and arrange what the compilers found available. Each reading of the verse makes its own points, and each document has identified its own distinctive message. Once more we see that we can and should differentiate among documents even by their topical programs and propositions.

To show the relationships among the programs of the three compilations, I present in boldface type what is unique to a given compilation, in italics what is shared by Pesiqta Rabbati and Pesiqta deRab Kahana, and in underlining what is shared by Pesiqta deRab Kahana and Sifré to Numbers. No topic occurs in all three documents. We start with the passage just now surveyed.

PESIQTA RABBATI:

1. **The Torah's oral part is unique to Israel.**
2. **The tabernacle was credited to Moses, because he was prepared to give his life for it.**
3. *Moses is comparable to God. Cf. Pesiqta deRab Kahana No. 4.*
4. **The children of Noah offered peace offerings [and not whole offerings].**
5. **The tabernacle is comparable to the marriage canopy, in which God and Israel were united. While this theme occurs at Pesiqta deRab Kahana No. 3, the articulation of the theme is peculiar to Pesiqta Rabbati.**
6. **Bezalel made the tabernacle, but Moses got credit for it.**
7. *The tabernacle marked the reunion of God with the world, from which, in the sin of Adam, God had departed. Cf. Pesiqta deRab Kahana No. 1, 2.*
8. **Diverse meanings of the words** *And it came to pass.*
9. **The juxtaposition of the account of the tabernacle with the account of the priestly blessing is to show that the tabernacle brought a blessing.**

The authorship of Pesiqta Rabbati has learned nothing from Sifré to Numbers, but at two points has taken over materials in Pesiqta deRab Kahana. The upshot is that the bulk of the topical program of Pesiqta Rabbati on Num. 7:1 is particular to its authorship. Formally derivative, the document still finds much to say that is fresh.

SIFRÉ TO NUMBERS:

1. Moses set up the tabernacle every day and took it down every night, until he finally left it standing. Cf. Pesiqta deRab Kahana No. 5.
2. **Events on the first day of the month.**
3. As the utensils were anointed, they were not sanctified. That was a separate operation. The manner of anointing. The effect.

Some of the details of No. 3 are shared at Pesiqta deRab Kahana No. 6. But—as I shall presently emphasize—the comparison of the two compilations overall shows that the bulk of Pesiqta deRab Kahana goes its own way. The points in common are trivial in the larger composition of Pesiqta deRab Kahana.

PESIQTA DERAB KAHANA:

1. *In building the tabernacle, Moses has brought God down to earth. Cf. Pesiqta Rabbati No. 7.*
2. *The tabernacle was the place of God's presence on earth. Cf. Pesiqta Rabbati No. 7.*
3. **Exegesis of Song 3:9–11. Pesiqta Rabbati V:XI.1 alludes to the theme of this matter.**
4. *Comparison of God, Elijah, and Moses. Cf. Pesiqta Rabbati No. 3.*
5. Moses set up the tabernacle and took it down day by day, until he finally left it standing. What came to an end on the day that Moses finished setting up the tabernacle. Cf. Sifré to Numbers No. 1.
6. Anointing and consecrating the utensils. Cf. Sifré to Numbers No. 3.
7. **The meaning of the number six, as in the six covered wagons brought by the princes to the dedication of the tabernacle.**
8. **The exegesis of Num. 7:2.**

One group of exegetes exhibits little in common with the other, even though, at a few points, the exegetes of Pesiqta deRab Kahana go over ground covered by those in Sifré Numbers, and those of Pesiqta Rabbati share interests with those of Pesiqta deRab Kahana. What one set of sages wishes to know in the verse of Scripture at hand scarcely coincides with the program of the other. But the details should not obscure the character of the whole. As we read one document in its own terms, we find ourselves far from the other two. The comparison of Midrashim as exegeses of particular verses and all the more so as compilations of exegeses in this case yields a picture of differences so profound as to call into question the premise with which we started.

The upshot is that the three authorships go their respective ways, with little to say in response to one another. The compilers of these Midrash collections therefore may be characterized as different people talking about fundamentally different things—and therefore also to different people, we know not whom. The approach of each set of exegetes to the base verse derives from a clearly defined program of inquiry, one that imposes its issues on the base verse and responds to the base verse only or principally in terms of the verse's provision of exemplary *detail* for the main point already determined by the exegetes. The final Pesiqta fully realized the potentialities of propositional argument set forth by Genesis Rabbah.

The next sequence of Midrash compilations, those surrounding the Talmud of Babylonia, like their Talmud undertook to recast the exegetical medium for the purposes of propositional argument, so forming a synthesis of exegetical presentation, with points made through recurrent concrete exemplary proofs of the same abstract principle, characteristic of the earliest Midrash compilations in the tradition of the Mishnah, and the antithesis of propositional argumentation, set forth here. Working with the form of the first set of Midrash compilations and the function of the second, the final compilers recast exegesis into hermeneutics for purposes of theological expression, just as the Bavli itself did.

C

Theological Discourse: Saying One Thing Through Many Things

XVIII

Song of Songs Rabbah

1.
Identifying the Document

THE SONG OF SONGS (IN THE CHRISTIAN BIBLE, "THE SONG OF SOLOMON")—REFER-ring to the opening line, "The Song of Songs, which is Solomon's"—finds a place in the Torah because the collection of love songs in fact speaks about the relationship between God and Israel. The intent of the compilers of Song of Songs Rabbah is to justify that reading.[1] What this means is that Midrash exegesis turns to everyday experience—the love of husband and wife—for a metaphor of God's love for Israel and Israel's love for God. Then, when Solomon's song says, "O that you

---

[1] For further reading and bibliography on the topic of this chapter, see the following:

Bowker, p. 83.

Moses D. Herr, "Song of Songs Rabbah," *Encyclopaedia Judaica* 15:152–54: the name of the compilation; definition; language; sources, date: Land of Israel, middle of the sixth century.

Maccoby omits this document from his introduction.

Stemberger-Strack, pp. 342–44: text, translation.

This writer's introduction is *The Midrash Compilations of the Sixth and Seventh Centuries: An Introduction to the Rhetorical, Logical, and Topical Program.* IV. *Song of Songs Rabbah* Atlanta, 1990: Scholars Press for Brown Judaic Studies.

would kiss me with the kisses of your mouth! For your love is better than wine," (Song 1:2), sages of blessed memory think of how God kissed Israel. Reading the Song of Songs as a metaphor, the Judaic sages state in a systematic and orderly way their entire structure and system.

If, as noted in Chapter 4, the Talmud of Babylonia joined the Mishnah to Scripture in its formation of the structure of the dual Torah as one, so too, Song of Songs Rabbah joined metaphor to theology, symbol to structure, in setting forth that same whole. Standing in the same period, at the end of the canonical process, in the sixth century, its authorship accomplished in its way the same summa that the authorship of the Bavli set forth. But these writers and compilers worked with far more delicacy, dealing with not intellect but sentiment, not proposition but attitude and emotion. For the Bavli rules over the mind and tells what to think and do, while Song of Songs Rabbah tells how to think and feel, especially how to make the heart at one with God.

Mishnah tractate Yadayim 3:5 defines the setting in which sages took up the Song of Songs. The issue was which documents were regarded as holy, among the received canon of ancient Israel. The specific problem focuses upon Qohelet ("Ecclesiastes") and the Song of Songs. The terms of the issue derive from the matter of uncleanness. For our purpose, it suffices to know that if a document is holy, then it is held to be unclean, meaning, if one touches the document, he has to undergo a process of purification before he can eat food in a certain status of sanctification (the details are unimportant here) or, when the Temple stood, go to the Temple. What that meant in practice is people will be quite cautious about handling such documents, which then will be regarded as subject to special protection. So when sages declare that a parchment or hide on which certain words are written imparts uncleanness to hands, they mean to say, those words, and the object on which they are written, must be handled reverently and thoughtfully.

MISHNAH TRACTATE YADAYIM 3:5

All sacred Scriptures impart uncleanness to hands. The Song of Songs and Qohelet impart uncleanness to hands.

R. Judah says, "The Song of Songs imparts uncleanness to hands, but as to Qohelet there is dispute."

R. Yosé says, "Qohelet does not impart uncleanness to hands, but as to Song of Songs there is dispute."

Rabbi Simeon says, "Qohelet is among the lenient rulings of the House of Shammai and strict rulings of the House of Hillel."

Said R. Simeon b. Azzai, "I have a tradition from the testimony of the seventy-two elders, on the day on which they seated R. Eleazar b. Azariah in the session, that the Song of Songs and Qohelet do impart uncleanness to hands."

Said R. Aqiba, "Heaven forbid! No Israelite man ever disputed concerning Song of Songs that it imparts uncleanness to hands. For the entire age is not so worthy as the day on which the Song of Songs was given to Israel. For all the Scriptures are holy, but the Song of Songs is holiest of all. And if they disputed, they disputed only concerning Qohelet."

Said R. Yohanan b. Joshua the son of R. Aqiba's father-in-law, according to the words of Ben Azzai, "Indeed did they dispute, and indeed did they come to a decision."

Clearly, the Mishnah passage, ca. 200, records a point at which the status of the Song of Songs is in doubt. By the time of the compilation of Song of Songs Rabbah, that question had been settled. Everybody took for granted that our document is holy for the reason given.

The sages who compiled Song of Songs Rabbah read the Song of Songs as a sequence of statements of urgent love between God and Israel, the holy people. How they convey the intensity of Israel's love of God forms the point of special interest in this document. For it is not in propositions that they choose to speak, but in the medium of symbols. As we noted in Chapter 9, section 10, in our discussion of words that serve as opaque symbols in "another matter" compositions, sages here use language as a repertoire of opaque symbols in the form of words. They set forth sequences of words that connote meanings, elicit emotions, stand for events, form the verbal equivalent of pictures or music or dance or poetry. Through the repertoire of these verbal symbols and their arrangement and re-arrangement, the message the authors wish to convey emerges: not in so many words, but through words nonetheless. Sages chose for their compilation a very brief list of items among many possible candidates. They therefore determined to appeal to a highly restricted list of implicit meanings, calling upon some very few events or persons, repeatedly identifying these as the expressions of God's profound affection for Israel and Israel's deep love for God. The message of the document comes not so much from stories of what happened or did not happen, assertions of truth or denials of error, but rather from the repetitious rehearsal of sets of symbols.

2.

TRANSLATIONS INTO ENGLISH

The first translation is the excellent one of Maurice Simon, *Song of Songs,* in H. Freedman and Maurice Simon, eds., *Midrash Rabbah* (London, 1939: Soncino Press), Volume IX. The second, and first form-analytical one, is this writer's *Song of Songs Rabbah. An Analytical Translation.* Atlanta, 1990: Scholars Press for Brown

Judaic Studies. I. *Song of Songs Rabbah to Song Chapters One through Three* and II. *Song of Songs Rabbah to Song Chapters Four through Eight.*

3.

RHETORIC

The forms that govern the presentation of the document are familiar and easily cataloged:

1. INTERSECTING-VERSE/BASE-VERSE FORM: the citation of a verse other than one in the document at hand (here: Song of Songs Rabbah) followed by a protracted exposition of that cited verse, leading in the end to a clarification of the base verse of the document at hand.

2. COMMENTARY FORM: citation of a verse clause-by-clause, with attached language, brief or protracted, amplifying that clause.

3. PROPOSITIONAL FORM: citation of a verse plus the statement of a proposition, proved by appeal to diverse verses, including the one originally cited.

4. PARABLE FORM: Parables very commonly begin with attributive language; they nearly always start with, "to what is the matter to be likened?" This may be explicit or implied, e.g., simply, "to [the case of] a king who. . . ." We are supposed to know that "to what may the matter be compared?" stands prior to the initial phrase. Then the author proceeds to set forth the parable. This need not take the form of a long story. It can be a set-piece tableau, e.g., "The matter is comparable to the case of a woman of noble family who had three representatives of her family at hand." The parable always follows a proposition, and the parable may then bear in its wake an explication of its components in terms of the case at hand, again as in the cited instance. And the parable may execute its purpose through a protracted narrative. So what makes a parable unique from all other forms is not the narrative but the presence of an inaugural simile or metaphor.

5. THE DISPUTE: The dispute form here follows the model of that in the Talmud of the Land of Israel rather than the Mishnah. The formal requirements are (1) statement of a problem, e.g., a word that will be explained, (2) two or more authorities' names, followed in sequence by (3) the repetition of each name and (4) a proposition assigned to that name. The explication of the propositional language may be substantial or brief, but the formal requirements of the dispute are always simple: names, then repetition of the names followed by fairly well-balanced sentences, in which propositions held by two or more authorities on the same subject will be contrasted.

6. THE NARRATIVE IN THE FORM OF DIALOGUE: Here we have a protracted story, which unfolds through exchange of dialogue. The extrinsic narrative language is simply, "he said to him," "he said to him," and variations thereof. The

entire tale is told by means of what is said. Verses of Scripture may or may not occur; they do not define a requirement of the form.

7. THE NARRATIVE EFFECTED THROUGH DESCRIBED ACTION, THAT IS, IN THE FORM OF A STORY OF WHAT PEOPLE DO: The story here depends upon described action, rather than cited speech. In this type of narrative we have a reference to what someone did, and the dialogue is not the principal medium for conveying the action. Rather, what the actors do, not only what they say, proves integral; details extrinsic to speech, e.g., "well-balanced that man had a wife and two sons . . . ," are critical to the unfolding of the tale. The explanation of what is done then forms the burden of the spoken components. The criterion for distinguishing narrative in the form of a dialogue from narrative in the form of described action is the burden placed upon the dialogue. If it explains action, then the action is the centerpiece; if it contains and conveys the action, then the dialogue is the centerpiece.

8. NO FORMAL PATTERN TO BE DISCERNED: A small number of items do not conform to familiar patterns at all.

4.

LOGIC OF COHERENT DISCOURSE

The document holds together its individual units of thought in a variety of ways. But the means for holding together those individual units in a large-scale composition is in one logic only, and that is the logic of fixed association. So there is a mixed logic before us, one serving the compilers in their large-scale organization and composition of the whole document, the other serving the various authorships of the cogent units of sustained but completed discourse that are assembled by the ultimate compilers.

5.

TOPICAL PROGRAM

In reading the love songs of the Song of Songs as the story of the love affair of God and Israel, sages identify implicit meanings that are always few and invariably self-evident; no serious effort goes into demonstrating the fact that God speaks, or Israel speaks; the point of departure is the message and meaning the One or the other means to convey. To take one instance, time and again we shall be told that a certain expression of love in the poetry of the Song of Songs is God's speaking to Israel about (1) the sea, (2) Sinai, and (3) the world to come; or (1) the first redemption, the one from Egypt; (2) the second redemption, the one from Babylonia; and (3) the third redemption, the one at the end of days. The repertoire of symbols covers Temple and schoolhouse, personal piety and public worship, and other matched pairs and sequences of coherent matters, all of them seen as embedded within the poetry. So Israel's holy life is metaphorized through the poetry of love and beloved, Lover and Israel. Long lists of alternative meanings or interpretations end up saying just one thing, but in different ways. The implicit meanings prove very few indeed. When in Song of Songs Rabbah we have a sequence of items alleged to form a taxon, that is, a set of things that share a common taxic indicator, what we have is a list. The list presents diverse matters that all together share, and therefore also set forth, a single fact or rule or phenomenon. That is why we can list them, in all their distinctive character and specificity, in a common catalog of "other things" that pertain all together to one thing.

What do the compilers say through their readings of the metaphor of—to take one interesting example—the nut tree for Israel? First, Israel prospers when it gives scarce resources for the study of the Torah or for carrying out religious duties; second, Israel sins but atones, and Torah is the medium of atonement; third, Israel is identified through carrying out its religious duties, e.g., circumcision; fourth, Israel's leaders had best watch their step; fifth, Israel may be nothing now but will be in glory in the coming age; sixth, Israel has plenty of room for outsiders but cannot afford to lose a single member. What we have is a repertoire of fundamentals, dealing with Torah and Torah study, the moral life and atonement, Israel and its holy way of life, Israel and its coming salvation. A sustained survey of these composites shows the contradictory facts that the several composites are heterogeneous, but the components of the composites derive from a rather limited list, essentially scriptural events and personalities, on the one side, and virtues of the Torah's holy way of life, on the other. Here is a survey:

Joseph, righteous men, Moses, and Solomon;
patriarchs as against princes, offerings as against merit, and Israel as against the nations; those who love the king, proselytes, martyrs, penitents;
first, Israel at Sinai; then Israel's loss of God's presence on account of the golden calf; then God's favoring Israel by treating Israel not in accord with the requirements of justice but with mercy;
Dathan and Abiram, the spies, Jeroboam, Solomon's marriage to Pharaoh's daughter, Ahab, Jezebel, Zedekiah;
Israel is feminine, the enemy (Egypt) masculine, but God the father saves Israel the daughter;
Moses and Aaron, the Sanhedrin, the teachers of Scripture and Mishnah, the rabbis;
the disciples; the relationship among disciples, public recitation of teachings of the Torah in the right order; lections of the Torah;

the spoil at the sea = the Exodus, the Torah, the tabernacle, the ark;

the patriarchs, Abraham, Isaac, Jacob, then Israel in Egypt, Israel's atonement and God's forgiveness;

the Temple where God and Israel are joined, the Temple is God's resting place, the Temple is the source of Israel's fecundity;

Israel in Egypt, at the sea, at Sinai, and subjugated by the gentile kingdoms, and how the redemption will come;

Rebecca, those who came forth from Egypt, Israel at Sinai, acts of loving kindness, the kingdoms who well-balanced rule Israel, the coming redemption;

fire above, fire below, meaning heavenly and altar fires; Torah in writing, Torah in memory; fire of Abraham, Moriah, bush, Elijah, Hananiah, Mishael, and Azariah;

the ten commandments, show-fringes and phylacteries, recitation of the Shema and the Prayer, the tabernacle and the cloud of the Presence of God, and the mezuzah;

the timing of redemption, the moral condition of those to be redeemed, and the past religious misdeeds of those to be redeemed;

Israel at the sea, Sinai, the ten commandments; then the synagogues and schoolhouses, then the redeemer;

the Exodus, the conquest of the Land, the redemption and restoration of Israel to Zion after the destruction of the first Temple, and the final and ultimate salvation;

the Egyptians, Esau and his generals, and, finally, the four kingdoms;

Moses' redemption, which was the first, to the second redemption in the time of the Babylonians and Daniel;

the palanquin of Solomon: the priestly blessing, the priestly watches, the sanhedrin, and the Israelites coming out of Egypt;

Israel at the sea and forgiveness for sins effected through their passing through the sea; Israel at Sinai; the war with Midian; the crossing of the Jordan and entry into the Land; the house of the sanctuary; the priestly watches; the offerings in the Temple; the sanhedrin; the Day of Atonement;

God redeemed Israel without preparation; the nations of the world will be punished, after Israel is punished; the nations of the world will present Israel as gifts to the royal messiah, and here the base verse refers to Abraham, Isaac, Jacob, Sihon, Og, Canaanites;

the return to Zion in the time of Ezra, the Exodus from Egypt in the time of Moses;

the patriarchs and with Israel in Egypt, at the sea, and then before Sinai;

Abraham, Jacob, Moses;

Isaac, Jacob, Esau, Jacob, Joseph, the brothers, Jonathan, David, Saul, man, wife, paramour;

Abraham in the fiery furnace and Shadrach Meshach and Abednego, the Exile in Babylonia, well-balanced with reference to the return to Zion.

These components form not a theological system, made up of well-joined propositions and harmonious positions, nor propositions that are demonstrated syllogistically through comparison and contrast. The point is just the opposite; it is to show that many different things really do belong on the same list. That yields not a proposition that the list syllogistically demonstrates. The list yields only itself—but then the list invites our exegesis; the connections among these items require exegesis. What this adds up to, then, is not argument for proposition, hence comparison and contrast and rule-making of a philosophical order, but rather a theological structure—comprising well-defined attitudes. Because of the character of Song of Songs Rabbah, the topical program of the document is best portrayed through the actual workings of the "another matter" compositions, some of which are portrayed in the sample given below.

6.

A SAMPLE PASSAGE

SONG OF SONGS RABBAH TO SONG 1:1

I:i. 1. A. "The song of songs":

B. This is in line with that which Scripture said through Solomon: "Do you see a man who is diligent in his business? He will stand before kings, he will not stand before mean men" (Prov. 22:29).

C. "Do you see a man who is diligent in his business":

D. This refers to Joseph: "But one day, when he went into the house to do his work [and none of the men of the house was there in the house, she caught him by his garment, saying, 'Lie with me.' But he left his garment in her hand and fled and got out of the house]" (Gen. 39:10–13).

E. R. Judah and R. Nehemiah:

F. R. Judah said, "[Following Gen. R; LXXXVII:VII:] It was a festival day for the Nile. [Everybody went to see it, but he went to the household to take up his master's account books]."

G. R. Nehemiah said, "It was a day of theater. Everybody went to see it, but he went to the household to take up his master's account books."

2. A. R. Phineas says in the name of R. Samuel bar Abba, "Whoever serves his master properly goes forth to freedom.

B. "Whence do we learn that fact? From the case of Joseph.

C. "It was because he served his master properly that he went forth to freedom."

3.   A.   "He will stand before kings":

      B.   This refers to Pharaoh: "Then Pharaoh sent and called Joseph and they brought him hastily from the dungeon" (Gen. 41:14).

4.   A.   "He will not stand before mean men":

      B.   This refers to Potiphar, whose eyes the Holy One blessed be he darkened [the word for "darkened" and "mean men" share the same consonants], and whom he castrated.

5.   A.   Another interpretation of the verse, "Do you see a man who is diligent in his business" (Prov. 22:29):

      B.   This refers to our lord, Moses, in the making of the work of the tabernacle.

      C.   Therefore: "He will stand before kings."

      D.   This refers to Pharaoh: "Rise up early in the morning and stand before Pharaoh" (Ex. 8:16).

      E.   "He will not stand before mean men":

      F.   This refers to Jethro.

      G.   Said R. Nehemiah, "[In identifying the king with Pharaoh,] you have made the holy profane.

      H.   "Rather, 'He will stand before kings': this refers to the King of kings of kings, the Holy One, blessed be he: 'And he was there with the Lord forty days' (Ex. 34:28).

      I.   "'He will not stand before mean men': this refers to Pharaoh: 'And there was thick darkness' (Ex. 10:22)."

6.   A.   Another interpretation of the verse, "Do you see a man who is diligent in his business" (Prov. 22:29):

      B.   This refers to those righteous persons who are occupied with the work of the Holy One, blessed be he.

      C.   Therefore: "He will stand before kings."

      D.   This refers to "for they stand firm in the Torah": "By me kings rule" (Prov. 8:15).

      E.   "He will not stand before mean men":

      F.   This refers to the wicked: "And their works are in the dark" (Is. 29:15); "Let their way be dark and slippery" (Ps. 35:6).

7.   A.   Another interpretation of the verse, "Do you see a man who is diligent in his business" (Prov. 22:29):

      B.   This refers to R. Hanina.

8.   A.   They say:

      B.   One time he saw people of his village bringing whole offerings and peace offerings up [on a pilgrimage to the Temple].

      C.   He said, "All of them are bringing peace offerings to Jerusalem, but I am not bringing up a thing! What shall I do?"

      D.   Forthwith he went out to the open fields of his town, the unoccupied area of his town, and there he found a stone. He went and plastered it and polished it and painted it and said, "Lo, I accept upon myself the vow to bring it up to Jerusalem."

E. He sought to hire day workers, saying to them, "Will you bring this stone up to Jerusalem for me?"

F. They said to him, "Pay us our wage, a hundred gold pieces, and we'll be glad to carry your stone up to Jerusalem for you."

G. He said to them, "Where in the world will I get a hundred gold pieces, or even fifty, to give you?"

H. Since at the time he could not find the funds, they immediately went their way.

I. Immediately the Holy One, blessed be he, arranged to have fifty angels in the form of men [meet him]. They said to him, "My lord, give us five selas [a standard coin of daily use], and we shall bring your stone to Jerusalem, on condition that you help us with the work."

J. So he put his hand to the work with them, and they found themselves standing in Jerusalem. He wanted to pay them their wage, but he could not find them.

K. The case came to the Chamber of the Hewn Stone [where the high court was in session]. They said to him, "It appears that in the case of our lord, ministering angels have brought the stone up to Jerusalem."

L. Immediately he gave sages that wage for which he had hired the angels.

9. A. Another interpretation of the verse, "Do you see a man who is diligent in his business" (Prov. 22:29):

B. This refers to Solomon son of David.

C. "He will stand before kings."

D. For he was diligent in building the house of the sanctuary: "So he spent seven years in building it" (1 Kgs. 6:38).

10. A. ["So he spent seven years in building it" (1 Kgs. 6:38),] but a different verse says, "And Solomon was building his own house for thirteen years" (1 Kgs. 7:1),

B. so the building of the house of Solomon was lovelier and more elaborate than the building of the house of the sanctuary.

C. But this is what they said:

D. In the building of his house he was slothful, in the building of the house of the sanctuary he was diligent and not slothful.

11. A. Huna in the name of R. Joseph: "All help the king, all the more so do all help out on account of the glory of the King of kings of kings, the Holy One, blessed be he,

B. "even spirits, demons, ministering angels."

12. A. Isaac b. R. Judah b. Ezekiel said, "'I have surely built you a

house of habitation' (1 Kgs. 8:13): 'I have built what is already built.'"

13. A. R. Berekiah said, "'The house that they were building' is not what is said,

B. "but rather, 'the house in its being built' (1 Kgs. 6:7), which is to say, it was built of itself.

C. "'It was built of stone made ready at the quarry' (1 Kgs. 6:7):

D. "What it says is not 'built' but 'it was built,' which is to say, the stones carried themselves and set themselves on the row."

14. A. Said Rab, "Do not find this astonishing. What is written elsewhere? 'And a stone was brought and laid upon the mouth of the den' (Dan. 6:18).

B. "Now are there any stones in Babylonia? [No.] But from the land of Israel it was brought through flight, so that in a brief moment it came and rested on the mouth of the pit."

15. A. R. Huna in the name of R. Joseph said [concerning the verse, "And a stone was brought and laid upon the mouth of the den" (Dan. 6:18)], "An angel came down in the form of a lion made of stone and put itself at the mouth of the pit.

B. "That is in line with this verse: 'My God has sent his angel and has shut the lions' mouths' (Dan. 6:23).

C. "Now do not find it astonishing. If for the honor owing to that righteous man, it is written, 'a certain stone was brought' (Dan. 6:18), for the honoring of the Holy One, blessed be he, how much the more so [will stones be provided in a magical manner]."

16. A. [Resuming the discussion of 8.D:] "He will stand before kings."

B. Before the greatest authorities of the Torah he will stand.

C. "he will not stand before mean men":

D. This refers to a conspiracy of wicked men.

17. A. Said R. Joshua b. Levi, "When they took a vote and decided, **Three kings and four ordinary folk have no share in the world to come [M. San. 10:1],**

B. "they wanted to include Solomon with them.

C. "But an echo came forth and said, 'Do not lay hands on my anointed ones' (Ps. 105:15)."

D. Said R. Judah b. R. Simon, "And not only so, but he was given the place of honor at the head of three genealogical tables: 'And Rehoboam, son of Solomon, reigned in Judah' (1 Kgs. 14:21)." [Simon, p. 4: "He was placed at the head of a genealogical tree. . . ." Simon, p. 4, n. 11: "The mention of his name here being superfluous implies that he was a founder of a royal line."]

E. Said R. Yudan b. R. Simon, "Not only so, but the Holy Spirit rested on him, and he said the following three books: Proverbs, the Song of Songs, and Qohelet."

While this somewhat overburdened composition hardly conforms to the required form, its basic outlines are not difficult to discern. We have an intersecting verse, Prov. 22:29, aimed at reaching the goal of Solomon, who is author of the Song of Songs, and showing him in the context of Joseph, the righteous, and Moses, four in all. The reason in both cases is the same: each one of them "stood before kings, not before mean men." Our proposed fixed formula then involves examples of the righteous, who are judged by those worthy of judging them.

The invocation of the figure of Joseph ought to carry in its wake the contrast between the impure lust of Potiphar's wife and the pure heart of Joseph, and, by extension, Solomon in the Song. But I do not see that motif present. The form is scarcely established—clause-by-clause exegesis in light of the principal's life—before it is broken by the insertion of 1.E–G, lifted whole from Gen. R. LXXXVII:VII, where it belongs. No. 2 is then parachuted down as part of the Joseph sequence; but it does not occur in other versions of the same story. No. 3 then resumes the broken form, and No. 4 completes it. So the first statement of the formal program is not difficult to follow. The confluence of the consonants for "mean" and "dark" accounts for the sequence of applications of the third clause to the theme of darkness.

The second exercise, with Moses, is laid out with little blemish in No. 5. No. 6 goes on to the righteous, and here too the sages' passage is worked out with no interpolations. No. 7, by contrast, provides an excuse to insert No. 8. Without No. 7, No. 8 would prove incomprehensible in this context (though entirely clear standing on its own). Finally, at No. 9, we come to Solomon. Perhaps the coming theme of the magical works performed through stones, those used in the Temple, with Daniel, persuaded the person who inserted Nos. 7–8 of the relevance of those passages; but even if they prove thematically in place, the sequence is disruptive and hardly respects the formal program that clearly has guided the framer. One may theorize, to be sure, that the breakup of the initial form—three cases, disruptive insertion, then the goal and purpose of the whole—signals the advent of the central figure in the exegesis. But that would prove a viable thesis only if we should find a fair number of other instances. It is the simple fact that the Mishnah's rhetoric allows for signals of that kind, and we cannot rule out the possibility. But in the present case it seems to me we have nothing more than a rude interpolation. But that is not the only disruptive component of the passage.

No. 10 introduces the contrast of the two verses, our proof text at No. 9 plus a contradictory one. This yields a suitable harmonization, which sustains the supplements at Nos. 11, 12, and 13. Nos. 11 and 12 are simply freestanding sentences. No. 13, with Nos. 14, 15 in its wake, by contrast is a full-scale composition, again about miracles done with stones. Hanina's passage would have found a more comfortable home here (if anywhere). Only at No. 16 are we permitted to resume our progress through the established form. No. 17 is tacked on because of the reference of 16.D to a conspiracy of wicked men; the issue then is whether Solomon belongs with them, in line with 17.A-B. 17.E forms a bridge to the sustained discussion of Ps. 45:17. But since the exposition of that verse makes no reference to the foregoing, we should regard the rather run-on sequence before us as winding down at No. 17, and, despite the rhetorical joining language of "therefore," I treat the discussion of Ps. 45:17 as autonomous. It assuredly has no formal ties to the intersecting verse on which we have been working. The whole is surely coherent in that the several components complement one another.

SONG OF SONGS RABBAH TO SONG 1:2

II:I. 1. A. "O that you would kiss me with the kisses of your mouth! [For your love is better than wine]":

B. In what connection was this statement made?

C. R. Hinena b. R. Pappa said, "It was stated at the sea: '[I compare you, my love,] to a mare of Pharaoh's chariots' (Song 1:9)."

D. R. Yuda b. R. Simon said, "It was stated at Sinai: 'The song of songs' (Song 1:1)—the song that was sung by the singers: 'The singers go before, the minstrels follow after' (Ps. 68:26)."

2. A. It was taught on Tannaite authority in the name of R. Nathan, "The Holy One, blessed be he, in the glory of his greatness said it: 'The song of songs that is Solomon's' (Song 1:1),

B. "[meaning,] that belongs to the King to whom peace belongs."

3. A. Rabban Gamaliel says, "The ministering angels said it: 'the song of songs' (Song 1:1)—

B. "the song that the princes on high said."

4. A. R. Yohanan said, "It was said at Sinai: 'O that you would kiss me with the kisses of your mouth!' (Song 1:2)."

5. A. R. Meir says, "It was said in connection with the tent of meeting."

B. And he brings evidence from the following verse: "Awake, O north wind, and come, O south wind! Blow upon my garden, let its fragrance be wafted abroad. Let my beloved come to his garden, and eat its choicest fruits" (Song 4:16).

C. "Awake, O north wind": this refers to the burnt offerings, which were slaughtered at the north side of the altar.

D. "And come, O south wind": this refers to the peace offerings, which were slaughtered at the south side of the altar.

E. "Blow upon my garden": this refers to the tent of meeting.

F. "Let its fragrance be wafted abroad": this refers to the incense offering.

G. "Let my beloved come to his garden": this refers to the Presence of God.

H. "And eat its choicest fruits": this refers to the offerings.

6. A. Rabbis say, "It was said in connection with the house of the ages [the Temple itself]."

B. And they bring evidence from the same verse: "Awake, O north wind, and come, O south wind! Blow upon my garden, let its fragrance be wafted abroad. Let my beloved come to his garden, and eat its choicest fruits" (Song 4:16).

C. "Awake, O north wind": this refers to the burnt offerings, which were slaughtered at the north side of the altar.

D. "And come, O south wind": this refers to the peace offerings, which were slaughtered at the south side of the altar.

E. "Blow upon my garden": this refers to the house of the ages.

F. "Let its fragrance be wafted abroad": this refers to the incense offering.

G. "Let my beloved come to his garden": this refers to the Presence of God.

H. "And eat its choicest fruits": this refers to the offerings.

I. The rabbis furthermore maintain that all the other verses also refer to the house of the ages.

J. Said R. Aha, "The verse that refers to the Temple is the following: 'King Solomon made himself a palanquin, from the wood of Lebanon. He made its posts of silver, its back of gold, its seat of purple; it was lovingly wrought within by the daughters of Jerusalem' (Song 3:9–10)."

K. Rabbis treat these as the intersecting verses for the verse, "And it came to pass on the day that Moses had made an end of setting up the tabernacle" (Num. 7:1).

7. A. In the opinion of R. Hinena [1.C], who said that the verse was stated on the occasion of the sea, [the sense of the verse, "O that you would kiss me with the kisses of your mouth"] is, "may he bring to rest upon us the Holy Spirit, so that we may say before him many songs."

B. In the opinion of Rabban Gamaliel, who said that the verse was stated by the ministering angels, [the sense of the verse, "O that you would kiss me with the kisses of your mouth"] is, "may he give us the kisses that he gave to his sons."

C. In the opinion of R. Meir, who said that the verse was stated in connection with the tent of meeting, [the sense of the verse, "O that you would kiss me with the kisses of your mouth"] is, "May he send fire down to us and so accept the offerings that are offered to him."

D. In the opinion of R. Yohanan, who said that the verse was stated in connection with Sinai, [the sense of the verse, "O that you would kiss me with the kisses of your mouth"] is, "May he cause kisses to issue for us from his mouth.

E. "That is why it is written, 'O that you would kiss me with the kisses of your mouth.'"

Our fixed list encompasses (1) Israel at the sea; (2) the ministering angels; (3) the tent of meeting; (4) the eternal house (the Temple); (5) Sinai. This is somewhat curious, mixing as it does occasions in time, locations, the place of the cult, and the Torah. But if we hold them together, we are given the theological repertoire of suitable verbal symbols or reference points: the redemption from Egypt, the Temple and its cult, and the revealed Torah of Sinai. This composite then is not only complementary in a general sense, it also is explicit in a very particular sense, specifying as it does the range of suitable assignees for the authorship and occasion of the poem, and that range then encompasses the acceptable theological vocabulary of—shall we say, Judaism? the Torah? the Midrash exegesis of our verse? I am not sure of what, but it is clear to me that we may expect a variety of such lists, a repertoire of those topics or points that all together add up to the relationship between God and Israel that the document, the Song of Songs, portrays. Indeed, even well-balanced we may wish to propose that when we seek the theology of the Judaism of the dual Torah, we may do worse than to look at the way in which the Song of Songs is made into a metaphor for everything evocative of the relationship of God and Israel—that is to say, the subject and problematic of the theology of Judaism.

Let us attend to the specifics of the passage, if briefly. No. 7 once again shows us that our compilers are first-class editors, since they have assembled quite disparate materials and drawn them together into a cogent statement. But the subject is not our base verse, and hence the compilers cannot have had in mind the need of a commentary of a verse-by-verse principle of conglomeration and organization. The passage as a whole refers in much more general terms to the Song of Songs, and hardly to Song 1:2 in particular. That is shown by the simple fact that various opinions invoke other verses than the one to which the whole is ultimately assigned. No. 1 serves Song 1.1, and so does No. 2. Indeed, No. 2 could have been placed in the prior assembly without any damage to its use and meaning. The same is to be said for No. 3. In fact, only Yohanan requires the verse to stand where it does. No. 5 and No. 6 invoke Song 4:16 and do a fine job of reading that verse in light of the tent of meeting in the wilderness or the Temple in Jerusalem. Song 3:9–10 serves as an appropriate locus as well. Then the conclusion draws a variety of senses for Song 1:2 alone, and that conclusion points to the compilers of the whole for its authorship. This is once more highly sophisticated work of compilation, involving rich editorial intervention indeed.

SONG OF SONGS RABBAH TO SONG 1:5

V:i. 1. A. "I am very dark, but comely, [O daughters of Jerusalem, like
              the tents of Kedar, like the curtains of Solomon]" (Song 1:5):
          B. "I am dark" in my deeds.
          C. "But comely" in the deeds of my forebears.
      2. A. "I am very dark, but comely":
          B. Said the Community of Israel, "'I am dark' in my view, 'but
              comely' before my Creator."
          C. For it is written, "Are you not as the children of the Ethiopians
              to Me, O children of Israel, says the Lord" (Amos 9:7):
          D. "As the children of the Ethiopians"—in your sight.
          E. But "to Me, O children of Israel, says the Lord."
      3. A. Another interpretation of the verse, "I am very dark": in
              Egypt.
          B. "But comely": in Egypt.
          C. "I am very dark" in Egypt: "But they rebelled against me and
              would not hearken to me" (Ez. 20:8).
          D. "But comely" in Egypt: with the blood of the Passover offer-
              ing and circumcision, "And when I passed by you and saw you
              wallowing in your blood, I said to you, In your blood live"
              (Ez. 16:6)—in the blood of the Passover. [This verse is recited
              at the rite of circumcision.]
          E. "I said to you, In your blood live" (Ez. 16:6)—in the blood
              of the circumcision.
      4. A. Another interpretation of the verse, "I am very dark": at the
              sea, "They were rebellious at the sea, even the Red Sea" (Ps.
              106:7).
          B. "But comely": at the sea, "This is my God and I will be
              comely for him" (Ex. 15:2) [following Simon's rendering of
              the verse].
      5. A. "I am very dark": at Marah, "And the people murmured
              against Moses, saying, What shall we drink" (Ex. 15:24).
          B. "But comely": at Marah, "And he cried to the Lord and the
              Lord showed him a tree, and he cast it into the waters and the
              waters were made sweet" (Ex. 15:25).
      6. A. "I am very dark": at Rephidim, "And the name of the place
              was called Massah and Meribah" (Ex. 17:7).
          B. "But comely": at Rephidim, "And Moses built an altar and
              called it by the name 'the Lord is my banner'" (Ex. 17:15).
      7. A. "I am very dark": at Horeb, "And they made a calf at Horeb"
              (Ps. 106:19).
          B. "But comely": at Horeb, "And they said, All that the Lord has
              spoken we will do and obey" (Ex. 24:7).

8. A. "I am very dark": in the wilderness, "How often did they rebel against him in the wilderness" (Ps. 78:40).

B. "But comely": in the wilderness at the setting up of the tabernacle, "And on the day that the tabernacle was set up" (Num. 9:15).

9. A. "I am very dark": in the deed of the spies, "And they spread an evil report of the land" (Num. 13:32).

B. "But comely": in the deed of Joshua and Caleb, "Save for Caleb, the son of Jephunneh the Kenizzite" (Num. 32:12).

10. A. "I am very dark": at Shittim, "And Israel abode at Shittim and the people began to commit harlotry with the daughters of Moab" (Num. 25:1).

B. "But comely": at Shittim, "Then arose Phinehas and wrought judgment" (Ps. 106:30).

11. A. "I am very dark": through Achan, "But the children of Israel committed a trespass concerning the devoted thing" (Josh. 7:1).

B. "But comely": through Joshua, "And Joshua said to Achan, My son, give I pray you glory" (Josh. 7:19).

12. A. "I am very dark": through the kings of Israel.

B. "But comely": through the kings of Judah.

C. If with my dark ones that I had, it was such that "I am comely," all the more so with my prophets.

V:ii. 5. A. [As to the verse, "I am very dark, but comely,"] R. Levi b. R. Haita gave three interpretations:

B. "'I am very dark': all the days of the week.

C. "'But comely': on the Sabbath.

D. "'I am very dark': all the days of the year.

E. "'But comely': on the Day of Atonement.

F. "'I am very dark': among the Ten Tribes.

G. "'But comely': in the tribe of Judah and Benjamin.

H. "'I am very dark': in this world.

I. "'But comely': in the world to come."

The contrast of dark and comely yields a variety of applications; in all of them the same situation that is the one also is the other, and the rest follows in a wonderfully well-crafted composition. What is the repertoire of items? Dark in deeds but comely in ancestry; dark in my view but comely before God; dark when rebellious, comely when obedient, a point made at Nos. 3 for Egypt, 4 for the sea, 5 for Marah, 6 for Massah and Meribah, 7 for Horeb, 8 for the wilderness, 9 for the spies in the Land, 10 for Shittim, 11 for Achan/Joshua and the conquest of the Land, 12 for Israel and Judah. We therefore have worked through the repertoire of events that contained the mixture of rebellion and obedience; the theological substrate of this catalog is hardly difficult to articulate. At V:ii.5 we have the articulation.

XXIII:i. 1. A. "O that his left hand were under my head":
          B. This refers to the first tablets.
          C. "And that his right hand embraced me":
          D. This refers to the second tablets.

      2. A. Another interpretation of the verse, "O that his left hand were under my head":
          B. This refers to the show-fringes.
          C. "And that his right hand embraced me":
          D. This refers to the phylacteries.

      3. A. Another interpretation of the verse, "O that his left hand were under my head":
          B. This refers to the recitation of the *Shema*.
          C. "And that his right hand embraced me":
          D. This refers to the Prayer.

      4. A. Another interpretation of the verse, "O that his left hand were under my head":
          B. This refers to the tabernacle.
          C. "And that his right hand embraced me":
          D. This refers to the cloud of the Presence of God in the world to come: "The sun shall no longer be your light by day nor for brightness will the moon give light to you" (Is. 60:19). Then what gives light to you? "The Lord shall be your everlasting light" (Is. 60:20).

Now our repertoire of reference points is (1) the ten commandments; (2) the show-fringes and phylacteries; (3) the *Shema* and the Prayer; (4) the tabernacle and the cloud of the Presence of God in the world to come. Why we invoke, as our candidates for the metaphor at hand, the ten commandments, show-fringes and phylacteries, recitation of the *Shema* and the Prayer, the tabernacle and the cloud of the Presence of God, and the mezuzah, seems to me clear from the very catalog. These reach their climax in the analogy between the home and the tabernacle, the embrace of God and the Presence of God. So the whole is meant to list those things that draw the Israelite near God and make the Israelite cleave to God, as the base verse says, hence the right hand and the left stand for the most intimate components of the life of the individual and the home with God.

XXV:i. 1. A. "The voice of my beloved! Behold he comes [leaping upon the mountains, bounding over the hills]":

B.   R. Judah and R. Nehemiah and Rabbis:

C.   R. Judah says, "'The voice of my beloved! Behold he comes': this refers to Moses.

D.   "When he came and said to the Israelites, 'In this month you will be redeemed,' they said to him, 'Our lord, Moses, how are we going to be redeemed? And did not the Holy One, blessed be he, say to Abraham, "And they shall work them and torment them for four hundred years" (Gen. 15:13), and we have in hand only two hundred and ten years!'

E.   "He said to them, 'Since he wants to redeem you, he is not going to pay attention to these reckonings of yours.

F.   "'But: "leaping upon the mountains, bounding over the hills." The reference here to mountains and hills in fact alludes to calculations and specified times. "He leaps" over reckonings, calculations, and specified times.

G.   "'And in this month you are to be redeemed: "This month is the beginning of months" (Ex. 12:1).'"

2.   A.   R. Nehemiah says, "'The voice of my beloved! Behold he comes': this refers to Moses.

B.   "When he came and said to the Israelites, 'In this month you will be redeemed,' they said to him, 'Our lord, Moses, how are we going to be redeemed? We have no good deeds to our credit.'

C.   "He said to them, 'Since he wants to redeem you, he is not going to pay attention to bad deeds.'

D.   "'And to what does he pay attention? To the righteous people among you and to their deeds,

E.   "'for example, Amram and his court.

F.   "'"Leaping upon the mountains, bounding over the hills": the word "mountains" refers only to courts, in line with this usage: "I will depart and go down upon the mountains" (Judges 11:37).

G.   "'And in this month you are to be redeemed: "This month is the beginning of months" (Ex. 12:1).'"

3.   A.   Rabbis say, "'The voice of my beloved! Behold he comes': this refers to Moses.

B.   "When he came and said to the Israelites, 'In this month you will be redeemed,' they said to him, 'Our lord, Moses, how are we going to be redeemed? And the whole of Egypt is made filthy by our own worship of idols!'

C.   "He said to them, 'Since he wants to redeem you, he is not going to pay attention to your worship of idols

D.   "'Rather, "leaping upon the mountains, bounding over the hills": mountains and hills refer only to idolatry, in line with this usage: "They sacrifice on the tops of the mountains and offer upon the hills" (Hos. 4:13).

E. "'And in this month you are to be redeemed: "This month is the beginning of months" (Ex. 12:1).'"

4. A. R. Yudan and R. Hunia:

B. R. Yudan in the name of R. Eliezer son of R. Yosé the Galilean, and R. Hunia in the name of R. Eliezer b. Jacob say, "'The voice of my beloved! Behold he comes': this refers to the royal messiah.

C. "When he says to the Israelites, 'In this month you are to be redeemed,' they will say to him, 'How are we going to be redeemed? And has not the Holy One, blessed be he, taken an oath that he would subjugate us among the seventy nations.'

D. "Now he will reply to them in two ways.

E. "He will say to them, 'If one of you is taken into exile to Barbary and one to Sarmatia, it is as though all of you had gone into exile.

F. "'And not only so, but this state conscripts troops from all of the world and from every nation, so that if one Samaritan or one Barbarian comes and subjugates you, it is as though his entire nation had ruled over you and as if you were subjugated by all the seventy nations.

G. "'In this month you are to be redeemed: "This month is the beginning of months" (Ex. 12:1).'"

Nos. 1–3 form a perfectly matched set; remove one and you lose the whole. A fixed catalog emerges, which can be used in any number of ways to exploit available metaphors. The items go over the trilogy of the timing of redemption, the moral condition of those to be redeemed, and the past religious misdeeds of those to be redeemed. Against these three arguments Moses argues that God will redeem at God's own time, as an act of grace and forgiveness. The theological message emerges with enormous power through invoking the love of God for Israel, God "leaping upon the mountains." I cannot point to a better or more telling example of the rewards accruing to the framers of the document from their decision to work on just this part of Scripture. The obvious necessity of No. 4 to complete the message requires no comment. Any conception that first comes to the individual units, then the completed composition, seems to me to take second place before the notion that the plan of the whole as a theological statement came prior to the formation of the parts. Then it hardly matters whose names are tacked on to the formally matched and perfect components. The examples suffice to show what is in play in this mode of holding together a large mass of discrete and completed materials.

XIX

RUTH RABBAH

1.
IDENTIFYING THE DOCUMENT

LIKE THE OTHER MIDRASH COMPILATIONS OF ITS CLASS, RUTH RABBAH MAKES ONE paramount point through numerous exegetical details.[1] Ruth Rabbah has only one message, expressed in a variety of components but single and cogent. It concerns the outsider who becomes the principal, the Messiah out of Moab, and this miracle is accomplished through mastery of the Torah. The main points of the document are these:

---

[1] For further reading and bibliography on the topic of this chapter, see the following:

Bowker, p. 83.

Moses D. Herr, "Ruth Rabbah," *Encyclopaedia Judaica* 14:523: the name, the structure, the language, redaction, editions, the work was redacted in the Land of Israel, not prior to the sixth century.

[1] Israel's fate depends upon its proper conduct toward its leaders.

[2] The leaders must not be arrogant.

[3] The admission of the outsider depends upon the rules of the Torah. These differentiate among outsiders. Those who know the rules are able to apply them accurately and mercifully.

[4] The proselyte is accepted because the Torah makes it possible to do so, and the condition of acceptance is complete and total submission to the Torah. Boaz taught Ruth the rules of the Torah, and she obeyed them carefully.

[5] Those proselytes who are accepted are respected by God and are completely equal to all other Israelites. Those who marry them are masters of the Torah, and their descendants are masters of the Torah, typified by David. Boaz in his day and David in his day were the same in this regard.

[6] What the proselyte therefore accomplishes is to take shelter under the wings of God's presence, and the proselyte who does so stands in the royal line of David, Solomon, and the Messiah. Over and over again, we see, the point is made that Ruth the Moabitess, perceived by the ignorant as an outsider, enjoyed complete equality with all other Israelites, because she had accepted the yoke of the Torah, married a great sage, and through her descendants produced the Messiah-sage, David.

Scripture has provided everything but the main point: the Moabite Messiah. But sages impose upon the whole their distinctive message, which is the priority of the Torah, the extraordinary power of the Torah to join the opposites—Messiah, utter outsider—into a single figure, and to accomplish this union of opposites through a woman. The femininity of Ruth seems to me to be critical to the whole as the Moabite origin: the two modes of the (from the Israelite perspective) abnormal, outsider as against Israelite, woman as against man, therefore are invoked, and both for the same purpose, to show how, through the Torah, all things become one. That is the message of the document, and, seen whole, the principal message, to which all other messages prove peripheral.

We began our discussion of Midrash in Chapter 9 with the observation that through Scripture the sages accomplished their writings. It is not so much by writing fresh discourses as by compiling and arranging materials that the framers of the document accomplished that writing. It would be difficult to find a less promising mode of writing than merely collecting and arranging available compositions and turning them into a composite. But that in the aggregate is the predominant trait of this writing. That the compilers were just as interested in the exposition of the book of Ruth as in the execution of their paramount proposition through their

---

Maccoby omits this document from his introduction.

Stemberger-Strack, pp. 344–45: text, translation, bibliography.

This writer's introduction is *The Midrash Compilations of the Sixth and Seventh Centuries: An Introduction to the Rhetorical, Logical, and Topical Program*. III. *Ruth Rabbah*. Atlanta, 1990: Scholars Press for Brown Judaic Studies.

compilation is clear. A large number of entries contain no more elaborate proposition than the exposition through paraphrase of the sense of a given clause or verse.

Indeed, Ruth Rabbah proves nearly as much a commentary in the narrowest sense—verse-by-verse amplification, paraphrase, exposition—as it is a compilation in the working definition of this inquiry of mine. What holds the document together and gives it, if not coherence, then at least flow and movement, after all, are the successive passages of (mere) exposition. All the more stunning, therefore, is the simple fact that when all has been set forth and completed, there really is that simple message that the Torah (as exemplified by the sage) makes the outsider into an insider, the Moabite into an Israelite, the offspring of the outsider into the Messiah: all on the condition, the only condition, that the Torah governs. This is a document about one thing, and it makes a single statement, and that statement is coherent.

The authorship decided to compose a document concerning the book of Ruth in order to make a single point. Everything else was subordinated to that definitive intention. Once the work got under way, the task was not one of exposition so much as repetition, not unpacking and exploring a complex conception, but restating the point, on the one side, and eliciting or evoking the proper attitude that was congruent with that point, on the other. The decision, viewed after the fact, was to make one statement in an enormous number of ways. It is that the Torah dictates Israel's fate; if you want to know what that fate will be, study the Torah, and if you want to control that fate, follow the model of the sage-Messiah. As usual, therefore, what we find is a recasting of the Deuteronomic-prophetic theology.

2.

TRANSLATIONS INTO ENGLISH

The first translation into English is the excellent one of L. Rabinowitz, *Ruth,* in H. Freedman and Maurice Simon, eds., *Midrash Rabbah* (London, 1939: Soncino Press), Volume VIII. The second, and first form-analytical one, is this writer's *Ruth Rabbah. An Analytical Translation.* Atlanta, 1989: Scholars Press for Brown Judaic Studies.

3.

RHETORIC

The forms fall into the same classification as those in Song of Songs Rabbah, cata loged in Chapter 18.

4.

LOGIC OF COHERENT DISCOURSE

The logics work in the same way as those in Song of Songs Rabbah. As to the propositions, approximately 42 percent of the sequences are joined within a logic that is substantive: thematic, propositional, or teleological, and 58 percent are joined within a logic that is in no way substantive but narrowly formal: fixed associative. Long stretches of materials join together only because they refer to sequential clauses of verses or sequences of verses, some of them drawn from other books of the Hebrew Scriptures, many of them drawn from the book of Ruth. This is not a "commentary" to the book of Ruth, but the document is laid out so that it appears to be just that. For Ruth Rabbah, with 60 percent of its composites appealing to the logic of fixed association and 40 percent to propositional logic of one or the other type, we may say that the document appeals to two logics for joining compositions into composites.

So two principles of logical discourse are at play in drawing together the materials our compilers have selected or made up. For the statement of propositions, sizable arguments, and proofs, the usual philosophical logic dictates the joining of sentence to sentences and the composition of paragraphs, that is, completed thoughts. For the presentation of the whole, the other logic, the one deriving from imputed, fixed associations, external to the propositions at hand, predominates, though not decisively. The framers of Ruth Rabbah drew together the results of work that people prior to their own labors already had completed, and some of these results they formed into larger compositions—that is, propositional statements—and some into (mere) composites. And that is a mixing of logics in the work of compilation that places our document in between the highly propositional documents such as Sifra, Sifré to Deuteronomy, Leviticus Rabbah, and Pesiqta deRab Kahana, all of which form their largest units as essentially propositional statements (though utilizing the logic of fixed association in a subordinated position), and the documents assembled essentially as composites through the logic of fixed association alone, represented by the massive presence of the Bavli.

5.

TOPICAL PROGRAM

Three categories contain the topical and propositional messages of the document, as follows:

ISRAEL AND GOD: Israel's relationship with God encompasses the matter of the covenant, the Torah, and the Land of Israel, all of which bring to concrete and material expression the nature and standing of that relationship. This is a topic treated only casually by our compilers. They make a perfectly standard point. It is that Israel suffers because of sin (I:i). The famine in the time of the judges was because of Israel's rebellion: "My children are rebellious. But as to exterminating them, that is not possible, and to bring them back to Egypt is not possible, and to trade them for some other nation is something I cannot do. But this shall I do for them: lo, I shall torment them with suffering and afflict them with famine in the days when the judges judge" (III:i). This was because they got overconfident (III:ii).

Sometimes God saves Israel on account of its merit, sometimes for his own name's sake (X:i). God's punishment of Israel is always proportionate and appropriate, so LXXIV:i: "Just as in the beginning, Israel gave praise for the redemption: 'This is my God and I will glorify him' (Ex. 15:2), now it is for the substitution [of false gods for God]: 'Thus they exchanged their glory for the likeness of an ox that eats grass' (Ps. 106:20). You have nothing so repulsive and disgusting and strange as an ox when it is eating grass. In the beginning they would effect acquisition through the removal of the sandal, as it is said, 'Now this was the custom in former times in Israel concerning redeeming and exchanging: to confirm a transaction, the one drew off his sandal and gave it to the other, and this was the manner of attesting in Israel.' But now it is by means of the rite of cutting off." None of this forms a centerpiece of interest, and all of it complements the principal points of the writing.

ISRAEL AND THE NATIONS: Israel's relationship with the nations is treated with interest in Israel's history, past, present, and future, and how that cyclical pattern is to be known. This topic is not addressed at all. Only one nation figures in a consequential way, and that is Moab. Under these circumstances we can hardly generalize and say that Moab stands for everybody outside of Israel. That is precisely the opposite of the fact. Moab stands for a problem within Israel, the Messiah from the periphery; and the solution to the problem lies within Israel and not in its relationships to the nations.

ISRAEL ON ITS OWN: Israel on its own concerns the holy nation's understanding of itself: who is Israel, who is not? Within the same rubric we find consideration of Israel's capacity to naturalize the outsider, so to define itself as to extend its own limits, and other questions of self-definition. And, finally, when Israel considers itself, a principal concern is the nature of leadership, for the leader stands for and embodies the people. Therein lies the paradox of the base document and the Midrash compilation alike: how can the leader most wanted, the Messiah, come, as a matter of fact, from the excluded people and not from the holy people?

And, more to the point (for ours is not an accusatory document), how is the excluded included? And in what way do peripheral figures find their way to the center? Phrased in this way, the question yields the obvious answer: through the Torah as embodied by the sage, anybody can become Israel, and any Israelite can find his way to the center. Even more—since it is through Ruth that the Moabite becomes the Israelite, and since (for sages) the mother's status dictates the child's, we may go so far as to say that it is through the Torah that the woman may become a man (at least, in theory). But in stating matters in this way, I have gone beyond my representation of the topical and propositional program. Let us review it from the beginning to the end.

The sin of Israel, which caused the famine, was that it was judging its own judges. "He further said to the Israelites, 'So God says to Israel, I have given a share of glory to the judges and I have called them gods, and the Israelites nonetheless humiliate them. Woe to a generation that judges its judges'" (I:i). The Israelites were slothful in burying Joshua, and that showed disrespect to their leader (II:i). They were slothful about repentance in the time of the judges, and that is what caused the famine; excess of commitment to one's own affairs leads to sin. The Israelites did not honor the prophets (III:iii). The old have to bear with the young, and the young with the old, or Israel will go into exile (IV:i). The generation that judges its leadership ("judges") will be penalized (V:i). Arrogance to the authority of the Torah is penalized (V:i). Elimelech was punished because he broke the people's heart; everyone depended upon him, and he proved undependable (V:iii); so bad leadership will destroy Israel. Why was Elimelech punished? It is because he broke the Israelites' heart. When the years of drought came, his maid went out into the marketplace, with her basket in her hand. So the people of the town said, "Is this the one on whom we depended, that he can provide for the whole town with ten years of food? Lo, his maid is standing in the marketplace with her basket in her hand!" So Elimelech was one of the great men of the town and one of those who sustained the generation. But when the years of famine came, he said, "Now all the Israelites are going to come knocking on my door, each with his basket." The leadership of a community is its glory: "The great man of a town—he is its splendor, he is its glory, he is its praise. When he has turned from there, so too have turned its splendor, glory, and praise" (XI:i.1C).

A distinct but fundamental component of the theory of Israel concerns who is Israel and how one becomes a part of Israel. That theme proves fundamental to our document, so much of which is preoccupied with how Ruth can be the progenitor of the Messiah, deriving as she does not only from gentile but from Moabite stock. Israel's history follows rules that are to be learned in Scripture; nothing is random and all things are connected (IV:ii). The fact that the king of Moab honored God explains why God raised up from Moab "a son who will sit on the throne of the Lord" (VIII:i.3). The proselyte is discouraged but then accepted. Thus XVI:i.2B: "People are to turn a proselyte away. But if he is insistent beyond that point, he is accepted. A person should always push away with the left hand while offering encouragement with the right." Orpah, who left Naomi, was rewarded for the little that she did for her, but she was raped when she left her (XVIII:i.1–3). When Orpah went back to her people, she went back to her gods (XIX:i).

Ruth's intention to convert was absolutely firm, and Naomi laid out all the problems for her, but she acceded to every condition (XX:i). Thus she said, "Under all circumstances I intend to convert, but it is better that it be through your action and not through that of another." When Naomi heard her say this, she began laying out for her the laws that govern proselytes. She said to her, "My daughter, it is not the way of Israelite women to go to theaters and circuses put on by idolators." She said to her, "Where you go I will go." She said to her, "My daughter, it is not the way of Israelite women to live in a house that lacks a mezuzah." She said to her, "Where you lodge I will lodge." "Your people shall be my people": this refers to the penalties and admonitions against sinning. "And your God my God": this refers to the other religious duties. And so onward: "for where you go I will go": to the tent of meeting, Gilgal, Shiloh, Nob, Gibeon, and the eternal house. "And where you lodge I will lodge"; "I shall spend the night concerned about the offerings"; "your people shall be my people"; "so nullifying my idol"; "and your God my God"; "to pay a full recompense for my action": I find here the centerpiece of the compilation and its principal purpose. The same message is at XXI:i.1–3.

Proselytes are respected by God, so XXII:i: "And when Naomi saw that she was determined to go with her, [she said no more]": Said R. Judah b. R. Simon, "Notice how precious are proselytes before the Omnipresent. Once she had decided to convert, the Scripture treats her as equivalent to Naomi." Boaz, for his part, was equally virtuous and free of sins (XXVI:i). The law provided for the conversion of Ammonite and Moabite women, but not Ammonite and Moabite men, so the acceptance of Ruth the Moabite was fully in accord with the law, and anyone who did not know that fact was an ignoramus (XXVI:i.4, among many passages). An Israelite hero who came from Ruth and Boaz was David, who was a great master of the Torah, thus he was "skillful in playing, and a mighty man of war, prudent in affairs, good-looking, and the Lord is with him" (1 Sam. 16:18): "skillful in playing": in Scripture; "and a mighty man of valor": in Mishnah; "a man of war": who knows the give and take of the war of the Torah; "prudent in affairs": in good deeds; "good-looking": in Talmud; "prudent in affairs": able to reason deductively; "good-looking": enlightened in law; "and the Lord is with him": the law accords with his opinions.

Ruth truly accepted Judaism upon the instruction, also, of Boaz (XXXIV:i), thus: "Then Boaz said to Ruth, 'Now listen, my daughter, do not go to glean in another field." This is on the strength of the verse, "You shall have no other gods before me" (Ex. 20:3). "Or leave this one": this is on the strength of the verse, "This is my God and I will glorify him" (Ex. 15:2). "But keep close to my maidens": this speaks of the righteous, who are called maidens: "Will you play with him as with a bird, or will you bind him for your maidens" (Job 40:29). The glosses invest the statement with a vast tapestry of meaning. Boaz speaks to Ruth as a Jew by choice, and the entire exchange is now typological. Note also the typological meanings imputed at XXXV:i.1–5. Ruth had prophetic power (XXXVI:ii). Ruth was rewarded for her sincere conversion by Solomon (XXXVIII:i.1).

Taking shelter under the wings of the Presence of God, which is what the convert does, is the greatest merit accorded to all who do deeds of grace, thus: "So notice the power of the righteous and the power of righteousness are the power of those who do deeds of grace. For they take shelter not in the shadow of the dawn, nor in the shadow of the wings of the earth, nor in the shadow of the wings of the sun, nor in the shadow of the wings of the hayyot, nor in the shadow of the wings of the cherubim or the seraphim. But under whose wings do they take shelter? 'They take shelter under the shadow of the One at whose word the world was created': 'How precious is your loving kindness O God, and the children of men take refuge in the shadow of your wings' (Ps. 36:8).'"

The language that Boaz used to Ruth, "Come here," bore with it deeper reference to David, Solomon, the throne as held by the Davidic monarchy, and ultimately, the Messiah, e.g., in the following instance: "The fifth interpretation refers to the Messiah: 'come here': means, to the throne; 'and eat some bread': this is the bread of the throne; 'and dip your morsel in vinegar': this refers to suffering: 'But he was wounded because of our transgressions' (Is. 53:5); 'so she sat beside the reapers': for the throne is destined to be taken from him for a time: For I will gather all nations against Jerusalem to battle and the city shall be taken' (Zech. 14:2); 'and he passed to her parched grain': for he will be restored to the throne: 'And he shall smite the land with the rod of his mouth' (Is. 11:4)." R. Berekhiah in the name of R. Levi: "As was the first redeemer, so is the last redeemer: Just as the first redeemer was revealed and then hidden from them, so the last redeemer will be revealed to them and then hidden from them" (XL:i.1ff.).

Boaz instructed Ruth on how to be a proper Israelite woman, so LIII:i: "wash yourself": from the filth of idolatry that is yours; "and anoint yourself": this refers to the religious deeds and acts of righteousness that are required of an Israelite; "and put on your best clothes": this refers to her Sabbath clothing. So did Naomi encompass Ruth within Israel: "and go down to the threshing floor." She said to her, "My merit will go down there with you." Moab, whence Ruth came, was conceived not for the sake of fornication but for the sake of Heaven (LV:i.1B). Boaz, for his part, was a master of the Torah and when he ate and drank, that formed a typology for his study of the Torah (LVI:i). His was a life of grace, Torah study, and marriage for holy purposes. Whoever trusts in God is exalted, and that refers to Ruth and Boaz; God put it in his heart to bless her (LVII:i). David sang Psalms to thank God for his great-grandmother, Ruth, so LIX:i.5, "[At midnight I will rise to give thanks to you] because of your righteous judgments [Ps. 119:62]: [David speaks,] The acts of judgment that you brought upon the Ammonites and

Moabites. And the righteous deeds that you carried out for my great-grandfather and my great-grandmother [Boaz, Ruth, of whom David speaks here]. For had he hastily cursed her but once, where should I have come from? But you put in his heart the will to bless her: 'And he said, "May you be blessed by the Lord."'" Because of the merit of the six measures that Boaz gave Ruth, six righteous persons came forth from him, each with six virtues: David, Hezekiah, Josiah, Hananiah-Mishael-Azariah (counted as one), Daniel, and the royal Messiah.

God facilitated the union of Ruth and Boaz (LXVIII:i). Boaz's relative was ignorant for not knowing that while a male Moabite was excluded, a female one was acceptable for marriage. The blessing of Boaz was, "May all the children you have come from this righteous woman" (LXXIX:i), and that is precisely the blessing accorded to Isaac and to Elkanah. God made Ruth an ovary, which she had lacked (LXXX:i). Naomi was blessed with messianic blessings (LXXXI:i), thus: "Then the women said to Naomi, 'Blessed be the Lord, who has not left you this day without next of kin; and may his name be renowned in Israel'": just as "this day" has dominion in the firmament, so will your descendants rule and govern Israel forever. On account of the blessings of the women, the line of David was not wholly exterminated in the time of Athaliah.

David was ridiculed because he was descended from Ruth, the Moabitess, so LXXXV:i. But many other distinguished families derived from humble origins:

> Said David before the Holy One, blessed be he, "How long will they rage against me and say, 'Is his family not invalid [for marriage into Israel]? Is he not descended from Ruth the Moabitess?' 'Commune with your own heart upon your bed: [David continues,] You too have you not descended from two sisters? You look at your own origins "and shut up."' 'So Tamar who married your ancestor Judah—is she not of an invalid family? But she was only a descendant of Shem, son of Noah. So do you come from such impressive genealogy?'"

David referred to and defended his Moabite origins, so LXXXIX:i:

> Then I said, 'Lo, I have come [in the roll of the book it is written of me]' (Ps. 40:8). [David says,] Then I had to recite a song when I came, for the word "then" refers to a song, as it is said, "Then sang Moses" (Ex. 15:1).
>
> I was covered by the verse, "An Ammonite and a Moabite shall not come into the assembly of the Lord" (Dt. 23:4), but I have come "in the roll of the book it is written of me" (Ps. 40:8).
>
> "in the roll": this refers to the verse, [David continues], "concerning whom you commanded that they should not enter into your congregation" (Lam. 1:10).
>
> ""of the book it is written of me": "An Ammonite and a Moabite shall not enter into the assembly of the Lord" (Dt. 23:4).

"'It is not enough that I have come, but in the roll and the book it is written concerning me:

"'"In the roll": Perez, Hezron, Ram, Amminadab, Nahshon, Salmon, Boaz, Obed, Jesse, David.

"'"in the book": "And the Lord said, Arise, anoint him, for this is he"' (1 Sam. 16:12)." Just as David's descent from Ruth was questioned, so his descent from Judah via Tamar could be questioned too, and that would compromise the whole tribe of Judah.

6.

A SAMPLE PASSAGE

RUTH RABBAH TO RUTH 1:1

I:i.   1.   A.   ["And it came to pass in the days when the judges ruled, there was a famine in the land, and a certain man of Bethlehem in Judah went to sojourn in the country of Moab, he and his wife and his two sons. The name of the man was Elimelech, and the name of his wife Naomi, and the names of his two sons were Mahlon and Chilion; they were Ephrathites from Bethlehem in Judah. They went into the country of Moab and remained there":] "And it came to pass in the days when the judges ruled [judged]":

B.   R. Yohanan commenced discourse by citing [the following verse of Scripture]: "Hear, O my people, and I will speak; O Israel, and I will testify against you. [God, your God, I am]" (Ps. 50:7).

C.   Said R. Yohanan, "People give evidence only in the hearing [of the accused]."

2.   A.   R. Yudan b. R. Simon said, "In the past, Israel was called by a name just like every other nation, e.g., 'And Sabta and Raamah and Sabteca' (Gen. 10:7).

B.   "But from now on, 'my people,' as in the verse, 'Hear, O my people, and I will speak; O Israel, and I will testify against you.'

C.   "Whence did you gain the merit to be called 'my people'?

D.   "It is from the time that 'I will speak.'

E.   "That is, it is from what you said before me at Sinai: 'All that the Lord has spoken we will do and obey' (Ex. 24:7)."

3.   A.   Said R. Yohanan, "'Hear, O my people': concerning the past.

B.   "'and I will speak': concerning the age to come.

C.   "'Hear, O my people': in this world.

D. "'And I will speak': in the world to come.

E. "It is so that you will know what to say before the angelic princes of the nations of the world, who are destined to complain before me, saying, 'Lord of the ages, these worship idols and those worship idols, these practice fornication, and those practice fornication, these shed blood and those shed blood, these go down to the Garden of Eden, while those go down to Gehenna! [Unfair!]'

F. "At that moment the angelic defender of Israel [Michael] remains silent.

G. "That is the meaning of the verse, 'And at that time shall Michael stand up' (Dan. 12:1)."

4. A. And is there a session [of the court] that is held in heaven?

B. And did not R. Hanina say, "There is no sitting in heaven: 'I came near to one of the standing ones' (Dan. 7:16),

C. "and the meaning of the word for 'standing ones' is ones who stood by, as in this verse: 'Above him stood the seraphim' (Is. 6:2); 'And all the host of heaven standing on his right hand and on his left' (2 Chr. 18:18).

D. "And yet the verse at hand says, 'And at that time shall Michael stand up' (Dan. 12:1)!

E. "What is the meaning of 'And at that time shall Michael stand up' (Dan. 12:1)?

F. "He is silenced, as in this usage: 'And shall I wait because they speak not, because they stand still and do not answer any more' (Job 32:16)."

5. A. [Continuing 3.F:] "Said to him the Holy One, blessed be he, 'Do you stand silent and not defend my children? By your life, I shall speak in righteousness and save my children.'"

6. A. And in virtue of what righteousness?

B. R. Eleazar and R. Yohanan:

C. One said, "'In virtue of the righteousness that you did for my world by accepting my Torah. For had you not accepted my Torah, I should have turned the world back to formlessness and void.'"

D. For R. Huna in the name of R. Aha said, "'When the earth and all the inhabitants thereof are dissolved. [I myself establish the pillars of it.]' (Ps. 75:4): the world should already have been dissolved were it not for the Israelites who stood before Mount Sinai. [For had you not accepted my Torah, I should have turned the world back to formlessness and void.]"

E. "And who founded the world? 'I myself establish the pillars of it.'

F. "It is in virtue of the 'I' that 'I myself establish the pillars of it.'"

    G.   The other said, "It is in virtue of the righteousness that you did in your own behalf by accepting my Torah.

    H.   "For if you had not, I should have assimilated you among the nations."

7.   A.   "God, your God, I am":

    B.   R. Yohanan said, "'It's enough for you that I am your patron.'"

    C.   R. Simeon b. Laqish said, "'Even though I am your patron, what good does my patronage do for you in judgment?'"

8.   A.   Taught R. Simeon b. Yohanan [concerning the verse, "God, your God, I am"], "'I am God for everybody in the world, but I have assigned my name in particular only to my people, Israel.

    B.   "'I am called not "the God of all nations" but "the God of Israel."'"

9.   A.   "God, your God, I am":

    B.   R. Yudan interpreted the verse to speak of Moses: "Said the Holy One, blessed be he, to Moses, 'Even though I called you "God" as to Pharaoh, "God, your God, I am" over you.'"

10.   A.   ["God, your God, I am":]

    B.   R. Abba bar Yudan interpreted the verse to speak of Israel: "'Even though I called you "gods," as it is said, "I said, You are gods" (Ps. 82:6), nonetheless, "God, your God, I am" over you.'"

11.   A.   ["God, your God, I am":]

    B.   Rabbis interpreted the verse to speak of the judges: "'Even though I called you gods, "You shall not revile gods" [that is, judges] (Ex. 22:27), "God, your God, I am" over you.'"

    C.   "He further said to the Israelites, 'I have given a share of glory to the judges and I have called them gods, and the [Israelites] humiliate them.'"

    D.   "Woe to a generation that judges its judges."

    E.   [Supply: "And it came to pass in the days when the judges were judged."]

What joins Nos. 1, 2, 3? I see no shared proposition, but only a common reference point, which is the intersecting verse. No. 4 is interpolated to enrich 3.G, No. 5 continues No. 3, and so does No. 6. From that point on, we have a sequence of discrete compositions, none of which acknowledges the presence of anything fore or aft. So, overall, the composite is a fine example of the working of fixed-associative logic. The interest of the composition as a whole is achieved at No. 11, which (as I read it) wishes to explain why the famine came about. And the answer is that the people were judging the judges. The intersecting verse is beautifully attained in the concluding composition, therefore, and it does lead to precisely what the framer of the whole has wanted to say. But the prior twists and turns are hardly required. No. 2, for example, has no bearing upon our issue, and No. 3 scarcely is relevant. Only if we assume that the purpose of Yohanan's exposition at No. 3 is to explain how the Messiah comes about, which is at stake in the book of Ruth, can we suppose that there is any clear connection between Yohanan's exposition and the task at hand. But that is very farfetched, and, it follows, No. 3, with No. 4 tacked on, then Nos. 5–6 are simply parachuted down, serving the intersecting verse in its own terms, but the base verse in no way. Nos. 7–8 serve no more pertinently than the prior items. Nos. 9, 10, and 11 then form the bridge to our base verse, and if my interpolation of 11.E is correct, then they do make the desired point.

RUTH RABBAH TO RUTH 1:5

IX:i. 1. A. ["and both Mahlon and Chilion died, so that the woman was bereft of her two sons and her husband":] "and both Mahlon and Chilion died":

B. [Leviticus Rabbah XVII:IV.1–4:] R. Huniah in the name of R. Joshua b. R. Abin and R. Zechariah son-in-law of R. Levi in the name of R. Levi: "The merciful Lord does not do injury to human beings first. [First he exacts a penalty from property, aiming at the sinner's repentance.]

C. "From whom do you derive that lesson? From the case of Job: 'The oxen were plowing and the asses feeding beside them [and the Sabeans fell upon them and took them and slew the servants with the edge of the sword; and I alone have escaped to tell you' (Job 1:14). Afterward: 'Your sons and daughters were eating and drinking wine in their eldest brother's house, and behold, a great wind came across the wilderness and struck the four corners of the house, and it fell upon the young people, and they are dead' (Job 1:19)]."

D. Now were the oxen plowing and the asses feeding beside them? Said R. Hama b. R. Hanina, "This teaches that the Holy One, blessed be he, showed him a paradigm of the world to come.

E. "That is in line with the following verse of Scripture: 'The plowman shall overtake the reaper'" (Amos 9:13).

F. "And the Sabeans fell upon them and took them and slew the servants with the edge of the sword" (Job 1:15):

G. Said R. Abba b. R. Kahana, "They left Kefar Qurenos and went through all of the Aelin towns and came to the Tower of the Dyers and died there."

H. "Only I alone have escaped to tell you" (Job 1:15):

I. Said R. Hanina, "Whenever we find the word 'only' used, it serves to limit the sense of the passage, thus: even he survived only broken and beaten."

J.   Said R. Yudan, "From the use of the word 'alone,' we derive the fact that he meant, 'I alone have the task of telling you.' And even here, once Job had heard his bitter news, the messenger forthwith perished."

K.   "While he was yet speaking, there came another and said, 'The Chaldeans formed three companies and made a raid upon the camels and took them and slew the servants with the edge of the sword, and I alone have escaped to tell you'" (Job 1:17).

L.   R. Samuel b. R. Nahman said, "When Job heard this bitter news of his, he began to mobilize his forces for war. He thought, 'How many platoons can I enlist, how many companies can I collect?'"

M.   [Lev. R. adds:] "That is in line with the following verse of Scripture: 'Because I stood in great fear of the multitude and the contempt of families terrified me' (Job 31:34).

N.   "He said, 'This people is contemptible: "Behold the land of the Chaldeans, this people that was not" (Is. 23:13). Would that it were not! It has come only to put me in dread of it.'

O.   "When they said to him, 'A fire of God fell from heaven and burned up the sheep and the servants and consumed them, and I alone have escaped to tell you' (Job 1:16),

P.   "Job said, 'Now if this blow is from Heaven, what can I do about it?

Q.   "'A voice from heaven has fallen, and what can I do? So that I kept silence and did not go out of doors' (Job 31:34).

R.   "So he took a potsherd with which to scrape himself, in line with the verse: 'He took a potsherd with which to scrape himself and sat among the ashes' (Job 2:8)."

2. A.   So too it was in Egypt [that God punished the Egyptians' herds before he punished the people themselves: "He gave over their cattle to the hail and their flocks to thunderbolts" (Ps. 78:48).

B.   And then: "He smote their vines and fig trees and shattered the trees of their country" (Ps. 105:33).

C.   And finally: "He smote all the firstborn in their land, the first issue of all their strength" (Ps. 105:36).

3. A.   [Lev. R. XVII:IV.3 gives what is here No. 4, and then gives the following:] So when leprous plagues afflict a person, first they afflict his house. If he repents the house requires only the dismantling of the affected stones. If not, the whole house requires demolishing.

    B.   Lo, when they hid his clothing, if he repents, the clothing has only to be torn. If he did not repent, the clothing has to be burned.

    C.   Lo, if one's body is affected, if he repents, he may be purified.

    D.   If the affliction comes back, and if he does not repent, "He shall dwell alone in a habitation outside the camp."

4.   A.   So too in the case of Mahlon and Chilion:

    B.   First their horses and asses and camels died, and then Elimeleh, and finally the two sons.

5.   A.   "So that the woman was bereft of her two sons and her husband":

    B.   Said R. Hanina [son of R. Abbahu], "She was equivalent to the residue of meal offerings."

Here is a fine example of how propositional logic holds together several well-crafted compositions. The proposition is this: The merciful Lord does not do injury to human beings first. First he exacts a penalty from property, aiming at the sinner's repentance. A sequence of demonstrations on the basis of probative cases follows. I cannot imagine a better set of well-joined paragraphs. Only No. 5 breaks ranks. Nos. 1–4 are given in the version of Lev. R., as indicated. I prefer Margoliot's text of Leviticus Rabbah's version for the whole, because it is superior in clarity, but there are minor differences in Ruth Rabbah's version as now printed. No. 5 proceeds to the next clause. So Nos. 1–4 have no close relationship to this document. They serve the interests of a document that wishes to set forth proofs for various theological propositions.

RUTH RABBAH TO RUTH 1:17

XXI:i.   1.   A.   "Where you die I will die":

    B.   This refers to the four modes of inflicting the death penalty that a court uses: stoning, burning, slaying, and strangulation.

    2.   A.   "And there will I be buried":

    B.   This refers to the two burial grounds that are provided for the use of the court,

    C.   one for those who are stoned and burned, the other for the use of those who are slain or strangled.

Nos. 1, 2 fit together as readings in a common way of related components of a verse. But I see no proposition here, rather a cogent exegetical composite.

    3.   A.   "May the Lord do so to me and more also [if even death parts me from you]":

    B.   She said to her, "My daughter, whatever you can accom-

plish in the way of religious duties and acts of righteousness
in this world, accomplish.

C.   "Truly in the age to come, death parts me from you."

No. 3 may be said to relate to Nos. 1, 2 through the shared base verse, hence
via fixed associative logic. I do not see anything that joins No. 4 to No. 3 or to
No. 5.

4.   A.   This [proposition that after death one cannot repent (Rabinowitz, p. 41, n. 1)] is in line with the following verse: "The
small and great are there alike, and the servant is free from
his master" (Job 3:19).

B.   Said R. Simon, "This is one of four scriptural verses that
are alike [in presenting the same message]:

C.   "'The small and great are there alike': in this world one
who is small can become great, and one who is great can
become small, but in the world to come, one who is small
cannot become great, and one who is great cannot become small.

D.   "'And the servant is free from his master': this is one who
carries out the will of his creator and angers his evil impulse.
When he dies, he goes forth into freedom: 'and the servant
is free from his master.'"

No. 5 will now give us a story; it has no bearing on No. 4's message. The
point of No. 4 is that in the world to come there is no way of improving one's
standing, achieved in life. No. 5's story, we now see, is that people who are honored in this world are held in contempt in the world to come. But the appearance
of Ez. 21:31 in No. 5 made it logical to the compiler to add No. 6, which deals
with the same verse. How to explain the joining of two narratives that encompass
the same proof text? Clearly, the one who put them together thought that narratives on a common verse flow together, but to me the logic is still that of fixed
association, pure and simple.

5.   A.   R. Miaha son of the son of R. Joshua fell unconscious from
illness from three days, and then three days later he re-
gained consciousness.

B.   His father said to him, "What did you see?"

C.   He said to him, "In a world that was mixed up I found
myself."

D.   He said to him, "And what did you see there?"

E.   He said to him, "Many people I saw who here are held in
honor and there in contempt."

F.   When R. Yohanan and R. Simeon b. Laqish heard, they came in to visit him. The father said to them, "Did you hear what this boy said?"

G.   They said to him, "What?"

H.   He told them the incident.

I.   R. Simeon b. Laqish said, "And is this not an explicit verse of Scripture? 'Thus says the Lord God, the miter shall be removed, and the crown taken off; this shall be no more the same; that which is low shall be exalted, and that which is high abased' (Ez. 21:31)."

J.   Said R. Yohanan, "Had I come here only to hear this matter, it would have sufficed."

6. A.   R. Huna the exilarch asked R. Hisdai, "What is the meaning of this verse: 'Thus says the Lord God, the miter shall be removed, and the crown taken off; this shall be no more the same; that which is low shall be exalted, and that which is high abased' (Ez. 21:31)?"

B.   He said to him, "The miter shall be taken away from our rabbis, and the crown shall be taken away from the gentile nations."

C.   He said to him, "Your name is Hisdai [loving kindness] and what you say is full of *hesed* [grace]."

I see no way of accounting for the inclusion of the following item in just this position, that is, after Nos. 5–6. And what follows thereafter serves Qoh. 9:4, that is, Nos. 9, 10.

7. A.   It is written, "For to him who is joined to all living there is hope; for a living dog is better than a dead lion" (Qoh. 9:4):

B.   It has been taught on Tannaite authority there:

C.   One who sees an idol—what should he say? Blessed is he who is patient with those who violate his will.

D.   **[One who sees a place in which miracles were performed for Israel says, "Blessed is he who performed miracles for our fathers in this place."] One who sees a place from which idolatry has been uprooted says, "Blessed is he who uprooted idolatry from our land" [M. Ber. 9:1A–B].**

E.   "And so may it be pleasing to you, Lord our God, that you uproot it from all places and restore the heart of those who worship idolatry to worship you with a whole heart."

F.   But does he not then turn out to pray for wicked people?

G. Said R. Yohanan, "What is written [at Qoh. 9:4] is [not 'joined'] but 'chosen.'

H. "Even those who laid hands on the Temple have hope.

I. "To resurrect them is not possible, for they have indeed laid hands on the Temple.

J. "But to exterminate them is not possible, for they have already repented.

K. "To them the following verse refers: 'They shall sleep a perpetual sleep and not awake' (Jer. 51:39)."

8. A. It has been taught on Tannaite authority:

B. Gentiles who die as minors and the armies of Nebuchadnezzar are not going to be either resurrected or punished.

C. To them the following verse refers: "They shall sleep a perpetual sleep and not awake" (Jer. 51:39).

9. A. "For to him who is joined to all living there is hope; for a living dog is better than a dead lion" (Qoh. 9:4):

B. In this world one who is a dog can be made into a lion, and he who is a lion can be made into a dog.

C. But in the world to come, a lion cannot become a dog, nor a dog a lion.

10. A. Hadrian—may his bones rot!—asked R. Joshua b. Hananiah, saying to him, "I am better off than your lord, Moses."

B. He said to him, "Why?"

C. "Because I am alive and he is dead, and it is written, 'For to him who is joined to all living there is hope; for a living dog is better than a dead lion' (Qoh. 9:4)."

D. He said to him, "Can you make a decree that no one kindle a fire for three days?"

E. He said to him, "Yes."

F. At evening the two of them went up to the roof of the palace. They saw smoke ascending from a distance.

G. He said to him, "What is this?"

H. He said to him, "It is a sick noble. The physician came to him and told him he will be healed only if he drinks hot water."

I. He said to him, "May your spirit go forth [drop dead]! While you are still alive, your decree is null.

J. "But from the time that our lord, Moses, made the decree for us, 'You shall not burn a fire in your dwelling place on the Sabbath day' (Ex. 35:3), no Jew has ever kindled a flame on the Sabbath, and even to the present day, the decree has not been nullified.

K. "And you say you are better off than he is?"

Nos. 11, 12, 13, 14 to the end go over the general theme that what you do not accomplish in this world you will not get to complete in the world to come. But I see no arrangement in such a way as to demonstrate that proposition; the sequence from the viewpoint of the theme is random and repetitious, rather than pointed and syllogistic. The mode of discourse is not argumentative but illustrative. So if there is a logic that joins one composition to the next, it is a logic that makes things seem cogent merely because they are on a single topic; and that is not propositional, or narrative, or fixed associative. I would call it "agglutinative." A given topic will hold together an agglutination of topically pertinent, but individually discrete, items. We shall now see how such a logic works.

11. A.   "Tell me, O Lord, what my term is, what is the measure of my days; I would know how fleeting my life is. [You have made my life just handbreadths long; its span is as nothing in your sight; no man endures longer than a breath. Man walks about as a mere shadow; mere futility is his hustle and bustle, amassing and not knowing who will gather in]" (Ps. 39:5–7):

B.   Said David before the Holy One, blessed be he, "Lord of the world, tell me when I shall die."

C.   He said to him, "It is a secret that is not to be revealed to a mortal, and it is not possible for me to tell you."

D.   He said to him, ". . . what is the measure of my days."

E.   He said to him, "Seventy years."

F.   He said to him, "I would know how fleeting my life is. Tell me on what day I am going to die."

G.   He said to him, "On the Sabbath."

H.   He said to him, "Take off one day [not on the Sabbath, since on that day the body cannot be tended]?"

I.   He said to him, "No."

J.   He said to him, "Why?"

K.   He said to him, "More precious to me is a single prayer that you stand and recite to me than a thousand whole offerings that your son, Solomon, is going to offer before me: 'A thousand burnt offerings did Solomon offer on that altar' (1 Kgs. 3:4)."

L.   He said to him, "Add one day for me."

M.   He said to him, "No."

N.   He said to him, "Why?"

O.   He said to him, "The term of your son is at hand."

P.   For R. Simeon b. Abba said in the name of R. Yohanan, "Terms of office are defined in advance, and one does not overlap the other even to the extent of a hair's breadth."

12. A. He died on a Pentecost that coincided with the Sabbath.

   B. The sanhedrin went in to greet Solomon.

   C. He said to them, "Move him from one place to another."

   D. They said to him, "And is it not a statement of the Mishnah: **One may anoint and wash the corpse, so long as it is not moved [M. Shab. 23:5]?**"

   E. He said to them, "The dogs of father's house are hungry."

   F. They said to him, "And is it not a statement of the Mishnah: **They may cut up pumpkins on the Sabbath for an animal and a carcass for dogs [M. Shab. 24:4]?**"

   G. What did he then do?

   H. He took a spread and spread it over the body, so that the sun should not beat down on him.

   I. Some say, he called the eagles and they spread their wings over him, so that the sun should not beat down on him.

13. A. It is said, "A twisted thing cannot be made straight, a lack cannot be made good" (Qoh. 1:15):

   B. In this world one who is twisted can be straightened out, and one who is straight can become a crook.

   C. But in the world to come, one who is twisted cannot be straightened out, and one who is straight cannot become a crook.

14. A. "A lack cannot be made good" (Qoh. 1:15):

   B. There are among the wicked those who were partners with one another in this world.

   C. But one of them repented before his death and the other did not.

   D. It turns out that this one stands in the company of the righteous, while that one stands in the company of the wicked.

   E. The one sees the other and says, "Woe! Is it possible that there is favoritism in this matter? Both of us stole, both of us murdered together. Yet this one stands in the company of the righteous, while I stand in the company of the wicked."

   F. And they answer him, saying, "Fool! World-class idiot! You were despicable after you died and lay for three days, and did they not drag you to your grave with ropes? 'The maggot is spread under you, the worms cover you' (Is. 14:11).

   G. "But your partner understood this and reverted from that path, while you had the chance to repent and did not do it."

   H. He said to them, "Give me a chance to go and repent."

   I. They reply to him, saying, "World-class idiot! Don't you know that this world is like the Sabbath, while the world from which you have come is like the eve of the Sabbath? If someone does not prepare on the eve of the Sabbath, what will one eat on the Sabbath?

J.   "And furthermore, this world is like the sea, while the world from which you have come is like the dry land. If someone does not prepare on dry land, what is that person going to eat when out at sea?

K.   "And furthermore, this world is like the wilderness, while the world from which you have come is like the cultivated land. If someone does not prepare in the cultivated land, what is that person going to eat when out in the wilderness?"

L.   So what does he do?

M.   He folds his hands and chomps on his own flesh: "The fool folds his hands together and eats his own flesh" (Qoh. 4:5).

N.   And he says, "Let me at least see my partner in all his glory!"

O.   They answer and say to him, "World-class idiot! We have been commanded on the authority of the Almighty that the wicked will not stand beside the righteous, nor the righteous by the wicked, the clean with the unclean, nor the unclean with the unclean.

P.   "And on what are we commanded? Concerning this gate: 'This is the gate of the Lord. The righteous [alone] shall enter into it' (Ps. 118:20)."

15.   A.   There is the following story.

B.   On the eve of Passover (and some say it was on the eve of the Great Fast [of the day of atonement]), R. Hiyya the Elder and R. Simeon b. Halafta were in session and studying the Torah in the major schoolhouse of Tiberias.

C.   They heard the noise of the crowd murmuring.

D.   One said to the other, "As to these people, what are they doing?"

E.   He said to him, "The one who has is buying, the one who doesn't have is going to his master to make him give to him."

F.   He said to him, "If so, I too will go to my lord to make him give me."

G.   He went out and prayed in the Isis of Tiberias [Rabinowitz, p. 46, n. 1: the famous grotto], and he saw a hand holding out a pearl to him.

H.   He went and brought it to our master [Judah the patriarch], who said to him, "Where did you get it? It is priceless. Take these three denars and go and do what you have to for the honor of the day, and after the festival, we shall announce the matter in the lost and found, and whatever price we get for it you will get."

I.   He took the three denars and went and bought what he needed to buy and went home.

J.   Said his wife to him, "Simeon, have you turned into a thief? Your whole estate is not a hundred manehs, and where did you have the money for all these purchases?"

K.   He told her the story.

L.   She said to him, "What do you want? That your canopy should be lacking by one pearl less than that of your fellow in the world to come?"

M.   He said to her, "What shall we do?"

N.   She said to him, "Go and return what you have purchased to the shopkeepers and the money to its owner and the pearl to its owner."

O.   When our master heard about this, he was upset. He sent and summoned her.

P.   He said to her, "All this suffering you have brought upon this righteous man!"

Q.   She said to him, "Do you want his canopy should be lacking by one pearl less than yours in the world to come?"

R.   He said to her, "And if it does lack, can't we make it up?"

S.   She said to him, "My lord, in this world we have the merit of seeing your face. But has not R. Simeon b. Laqish said, 'Every righteous man has his own chamber'?"

T.   And he conceded her point.

U.   [Continuing S:] "'And not only so, but it is the way of the beings of the upper world to give, but it is not their way to take back.'"

V.   [Reverting to T:] [Rabinowitz: "Nevertheless the pearl was returned"] and this latter miracle was greater than the former one.

W.   When [Simeon] took it, his hand was below, but when he gave it back, his hand was on top,

X.   like a man who lends to his fellow. [Rabinowitz, p. 47, n. 1: When R. Simeon took the pearl, it was as one receiving a gift, but when he returned it, it was as one giving a gift, in that the hand which received it was below his.]

Let us now review the whole. The theme that becoming an Israelite involves special obligations and liabilities is continued at Nos. 1, 2. No. 3 completes the exposition of what is involved at 3.B. I cannot quite grasp 3.C. Rabinowitz translates, ". . . acquire in this world, for in the world to come, 'death shall part you and me.'" This seems to bear the message that whatever good one can do must be done in this world. That point is then illustrated in the series of stories from No. 4 to the end. But the stories wander far from the point at hand, in no way respond unanimously to the concerns of that point, and in fact are worked out one by one for purposes that can be discerned wholly within the limits of the successive tales. But I cannot conceive of some other document, other than a biographical one, in which stories of this kind will have served a redactional purpose we can identify with the program of the canonical redaction now in hand. These are freestanding stories; they serve indifferently in any context, but have been worked out without a documentary stimulus.

XX

LAMENTATIONS RABBATI

1.

IDENTIFYING THE DOCUMENT

THE THEME OF LAMENTATIONS RABBATI IS ISRAEL'S RELATIONSHIP WITH GOD, AND the message concerning that theme is that the stipulative covenant still and always governs that relationship.[1] Therefore everything that happens to Israel makes sense and bears meaning; and Israel is not helpless before its fate but controls its own destiny. This is the one and whole message of our compilation, and it is the only message that is repeated throughout; everything else proves secondary and deriva-

[1] For further reading and bibliography on the topic of this chapter, see the following:

Bowker, p. 84.

Moses D. Herr, "Lamentations Rabbah," *Encyclopaedia Judaica* 10:1376–78: the name (Eikhah Rabbati); the structure; language; date of redaction (at about the end of the fifth century); editions.

Maccoby omits this document from his introduction.

Stemberger-Strack, pp. 308–12: text; the name; content and redaction; the date (early origin, in Palestine); the *petihot* (proems).

This writer's introduction is *The Midrash Compilations of the Sixth and Seventh Centuries. An Introduction to the Rhetorical, Logical, and Topical Program. I. Lamentations Rabbah.* Atlanta, 1990: Scholars Press for Brown Judaic Studies. See also David Stern, *Parables in Midrash* (Cambridge, 1991: Harvard University Press), for a discussion of parables in some of the *parashiyyot*.

tive of the fundamental proposition that the destruction of the Temple in Jerusalem in 70 C.E.—as much as in 586 B.C.E.—proves the enduring validity of the covenant, its rules and its promise of redemption.

Lamentations Rabbah is a covenantal theology, in which Israel and God have mutually and reciprocally agreed to bind themselves to a common Torah; the rules of the relationship are such that an infraction triggers its penalty willy-nilly; but obedience to the Torah likewise brings its reward, in the context envisaged by our compilers, the reward of redemption. The compilation sets forth a single message, which is reworked in only a few ways: Israel suffers because of sin, God will respond to Israel's atonement, on the one side, and loyalty to the covenant in the Torah, on the other. And when Israel has attained the merit that accrues through the Torah, God will redeem Israel. That is the simple, rock-hard, and repeated message of this rather protracted reading of the book of Lamentations. Still, Lamentations Rabbah proves nearly as much a commentary in the narrowest sense— verse-by-verse amplification, paraphrase, exposition—as it is a compilation in the working definition of this inquiry of mine.

What holds the document together and gives it, if not coherence, then at least flow and movement, after all, are the successive passages of (mere) exposition. All the more stunning, therefore, is the simple fact that when all has been set forth and completed, there really is that simple message that God's unique relationship with Israel, which is unique among the nations, works itself out even now, in a time of despair and disappointment. The resentment of the present condition, recapitulating the calamity of the destruction of the Temple, finds its resolution and remission in the redemption that will follow Israel's regeneration through the Torah—that is the program, that is the proposition, and in this compilation, there is no other.

2.

TRANSLATIONS INTO ENGLISH

The first translation is A. Cohen, *Lamentations,* in H. Freedman and Maurice Simon, eds., *Midrash Rabbah* (London, 1939: Soncino Press), Volume VII. The second, and first form-analytical translation, is this writer's *Lamentations Rabbah. An Analytical Translation.* Atlanta, 1989: Scholars Press for Brown Judaic Studies.

3.

RHETORIC

The results set forth for Song of Songs Rabbah apply without variation to Lamentations Rabbati. We note that the document's opening discussion, or *petihta,* involves a base-verse/intersecting-verse construction, thus we shall see presently Petihta Twenty-Four, meaning, the twenty-fourth introductory unit.

4.
Logic of Coherent Discourse

Among the established logics, the propositions represented in this compilation are as follows:

	Number	Percent of the Whole
Propositional and philosophical discourse	21	19%
Themes worked out by teleology		
expressed in narrative	18	16%
The logic of fixed association	59	52%
The cogency of a fixed analytical method	0	0%
No clear coherence between or among		
successive units of completed discourse	8	7%
Not relevant to the issue	6	5%

If we now ask about the operative logics, that is, the first three entries, the result is as follows:

Propositional and philosophical discourse	21	21%
Themes worked out by teleology		
expressed in narrative	18	18%
The logic of fixed association	59	60%

The paramount logic of our document is that of fixed association. This is not a "commentary" to the book of Lamentations, but the document is laid out so that it appears to be just that.

5.
Topical Program

Israel's relationship with God is treated with special reference to the covenant, the Torah, and the land. By reason of the sins of the Israelites, they have gone into exile with the destruction of the Temple. The founders of the family, Abraham, Isaac, and Jacob, also went into exile. Now they cannot be accused of lacking in religious duties, attention to teachings of the Torah and of prophecy, carrying out the requirements of righteousness (philanthropy) and good deeds, and the like. The people are at fault for their own condition (I:i.1–7). Torah study defines the condition of Israel, e.g., "If you have seen [the inhabitants of] towns uprooted from their places in the land of Israel, know that it is because they did not pay the salary of scribes and teachers" (II.i).

So long as Judah and Benjamin—meaning, in this context, the surviving people, after the northern tribes were taken away by the Assyrians—were at home, God could take comfort at the loss of the ten tribes; once they went into exile, God began to mourn (II:ii). Israel (now meaning not the northern tribes, but the remaining Jews) survived Pharaoh and Sennacherib, but not God's punishment (III:i). After the disaster in Jeremiah's time, Israel emerged from Eden—but could come back (IV:i). God did not play favorites among the tribes; when any of them sinned, he punished them through exile (VI:i). Israel was punished because of the ravaging of words of Torah and prophecy, righteous men, religious duties, and good deeds (VII:i). The land of Israel, the Torah, and the Temple are ravaged, to the shame of Israel (Jer. 9:19–21) (VIII:i). The Israelites practiced idolatry, still more did the pagans; God was neglected by the people and was left solitary, so God responded to the people's actions (X:i). If you had achieved the merit (using the theological language at hand), then you would have enjoyed everything, but since you did not have the merit, you enjoyed nothing (XI:i).

The Israelites did not trust God, so they suffered disaster (XIII.i). The Israelites scorned God and brought dishonor upon God among the nations (XV:i). While God was generous with the Israelites in the wilderness, under severe conditions, he was harsh with them in civilization, under pleasant conditions, because they sinned and angered him (XVI:i). With merit one drinks good water in Jerusalem; without, bad water in the exile of Babylonia; with merit one sings songs and Psalms in Jerusalem; without, dirges and lamentations in Babylonia. At stake is people's merit, not God's grace (XIX:i). The contrast is drawn between redemption and disaster, the giving of the Torah and the destruction of the Temple (XX:i). When the Israelites went into exile among the nations of the world, not one of them could produce a word of Torah from his mouth; God punished Israel for its sins (XXI:i). Idolatry was the cause (XXII:i). The destruction of the Temple was possible only because God had already abandoned it (XXIV:ii). When the Temple was destroyed, God was answerable to the patriarchs for what he had done (XXIV:ii). The Presence of God departed from the Temple by stages (XXV:i).

The Holy One punishes Israel only after bringing testimony against it (XXVII:i). The road that led from the salvation of Hezekiah is the one that brought Israel to the disaster brought about by Nebuchadnezzar. Then the Israelite kings believed, but the pagan king did not believe; and God gave the Israelite kings a reward for their faith, through Hezekiah, and to the pagan king, without his believing and without obeying, were handed over Jerusalem and its Temple (XXX:i). Before the Israelites went into exile, the Holy One, blessed be he, called them bad. But when they had gone into exile, he began to sing their praises (XXXI:i). The Israelites were sent into exile only after they had defied the Unique One of the world, the ten commandments, circumcision, which had been given to the twentieth generation [Abraham], and the Pentateuch (XXXV:ii, iii). When the Temple was destroyed and Israel went into exile, God mourned in the manner that mortals do (XXXV:iv). The prophetic critique of Israel is mitigated by mercy. Israel stands in an ambiguous relationship with God, both divorced and not divorced (XXXV:vi, vii).

Before God penalizes, he has already prepared the healing for the penalty. As to all the harsh prophecies that Jeremiah issued against the Israelites, Isaiah first of all anticipated each and pronounced healing for it (XXXVI:ii). The Israelites err for weeping frivolously, "but in the end there will be a real weeping for good cause" (XXXVI:iv, v). The ten tribes went into exile, but the Presence of God did not go into exile. Judah and Benjamin went into exile, but the Presence of God did not go into exile. But when the children went into exile, then the Presence of God went into exile (XXXIX:iii). The great men of Israel turned their faces away when they saw people sinning, and God did the same to them (XL:ii). When the Israelites carry out the will of the Holy One, they add strength to the strength of heaven, and when they do not, they weaken the power of the One above (XL:ii). The exile and the redemption will match (XL:ii). In her affliction, Jerusalem remembered her rebellion against God (XLI:i).

When the gentile nations sin, there is no sequel in punishment, but when the Israelites sin, they also are punished (XLII:i). God considered carefully how to bring the evil upon Israel (XLVIII:i). God suffers with Israel and for Israel (L:i), a minor theme in a massive compilation of stories. By observing their religious duties the Israelites became distinguished before God (LIII:i). With everything with which the Israelites sinned, they were smitten, and with that same thing they will be comforted. When they sinned with the head, they were smitten at the head, but they were comforted through the head (LVI:i). There is an exact match between Israel's triumph and Israel's downfall. Thus: Just as these—the people of Jericho—were punished through the destruction effected by priest and prophet (the priests and Joshua at Jericho), so these—the people of Jerusalem in the time of the Babylonian conquest—were subject to priest and prophet (Jeremiah). Just as these who were punished were penalized through the ram's horn and shouting, so Israel will be saved through ram's horn and shouting (LVII:ii).

God's relationship to Israel was complicated by the relationship to Jacob, thus: "Isn't it the fact that the Israelites are angering me only because of the icon of Jacob that is engraved on my throne? Here, take it, it's thrown in your face!" (LVII:ii). God is engaged with Israel's disaster (LIX:ii). The Israelites did not fully explore the limits of the measure of justice, so the measure of justice did not go to extremes against them (LX:i, LXI:i). God's decree against Jerusalem comes from of old (LXIV:i). God forewarned Israel and showed Israel favor, but it did no good (LXIX:i). God did to Israel precisely what he had threatened long ago (LXXIII:i). But God does not rejoice in punishing Israel. The argument between God and Israel is framed in this way: the Community of Israel says that they are the only ones who accepted God; God says, I rejected everybody else for you (LXXIX:ii). Israel accepted its suffering as atonement and asked that the suffering expiate the sin (LXXV:i).

God suffers along with Israel, Israel's loyalty will be recognized and appreciated by God, and, in the meantime, the Israelites will find in the Torah the comfort that they require. The nations will be repaid for their actions toward Israel in the interval. Even though the Holy One, blessed be he, is angry with his servants, the righteous, in this world, in the world to come he goes and has mercy on them (LXXXVI:i). God is good to those that deserve it (LXXXVII:i). God mourns for Israel the way human mourners mourn (LXXXVIII:i). God will never abandon Israel (LXXXIX:i). The Holy Spirit brings about redemption (XCV:i). It is better to be punished by God than favored by a gentile king, thus: "Better was the removing of the ring by Pharaoh [for the sealing of decrees to oppress the Israelites] than the forty years during which Moses prophesied concerning them, because it was through this [oppression] that the redemption came about, while through that [prophesying] the redemption did not come about" (CXXII:i).

The upshot here is that persecution in the end is good for Israel, because it produces repentance more rapidly than prophecy ever did, with the result that the redemption is that much nearer. The enemy will also be punished for its sins, and, further, God's punishment is appropriate and well-placed. People get what they deserve, both Israel and the others. God should protect Israel and not leave them among the nations, but that is not what he has done (CXXIII:i). God blames that generation for its own fate, and the ancestors claim that the only reason the Israelites endure is because of the merit of the ancestors (CXXIX:i). The redemption of the past tells us about the redemption in the future (CXXX:i). "The earlier generations, because they smelled the stench of only part of the tribulations inflicted by the idolatrous kingdoms, became impatient. But we, who dwell in the midst of the four kingdoms, how much the more [are we impatient]!" (CXXXI:i).

God's redemption is certain, so people who are suffering should be glad, since that is a guarantee of coming redemption; thus "For if those who outrage him he treats in such a way, those who do his will all the more so!" So if the words of the prophet Uriah are carried out, the words of the prophet Zechariah will be carried out, while if the words of the prophet Uriah prove false, then the words of the prophet Zechariah will not be true either. "I was laughing with pleasure because the words of Uriah have been carried out, and that means that the words of Zechariah in the future will be carried out" (CXL:i). The Temple will be restored, and Israel will regain its place, as God's throne and consort, respectively (CXLI:i). Punishment and rejection will be followed by forgiveness and reconciliation (CXLII:i). The Jews can accomplish part of the task on their own, even though they throw themselves wholly on God's mercy. The desired age is either like that of Adam, or like that of Moses and Solomon, or like that of Noah and Abel; all three possibilities link the coming redemption to a time of perfection, Eden, or the age prior to idolatry, or the time of Moses and Solomon, the builders of the tabernacle and the Temple, respectively (CXLIII:i). If there is rejection, then there is no hope, but if there is anger, there is hope, because someone who is angry may in the end be appeased. Whenever there is an allusion to divine anger, that too is a mark of hope (CXLIV:i).

Israel's relationship with the nations is treated with interest in Israel's history, past, present, and future, and how that cyclical is to be known. But there is no theory of "the other," or the outsider here; the nations are the enemy; the compilers find nothing of merit to report about them. Israel's difference from the other, for which God is responsible, accounts for the dislike that the nations express toward Israel; Israel's present condition as minority, different and despised on account of the difference, is God's fault and choice. Israel was besieged not only by the Babylonians but also the neighbors, the Ammonites and Moabites (IX:i), and God will punish them too. The public ridicule of Jews' religious rites contrasts with the Jews' own perception of their condition. The exposition of Ps. 69:13 in terms of gentiles' ridicule of Jews' practices—the Jews' poverty, their Sabbath and Seventh Year observance—is followed by a re-exposition of the Jews' practices, now with respect to the ninth of Ab (XVII:i). Even though the nations of the world go into exile, their exile is not really an exile at all. But as for Israel, their exile really is an exile. The nations of the world, who eat the bread and drink the wine of others, do not really experience exile. But the Israelites, who do not eat the bread and drink the wine of others, really do experience exile (XXXVII:i).

The Ammonites and Moabites joined with the enemy and behaved very spitefully (XLIV:i). When the Israelites fled from the destruction of Jerusalem, the nations of the world sent word everywhere to which they fled and shut them out (LV:i). But this was to be blamed on God: "If we had intermarried with them, they would have accepted us" (LXIX:i). There are ten references to "might" of Israel; when the Israelites sinned, these forms of might were taken away from them and given to the nations of the world. The nations of the world ridicule the Jews for their religious observances (LXXXIII:i). These propositions simply expose, in their own framework, the same proposition as the ones concerning God's relationship to Israel and Israel's relationship to God. The relationship between Israel and the nations forms a subset of the relationship of Israel and God; nothing in the former relationship happens on its own, but all things express in this mundane context the rules and effects of the rules that govern in the transcendent one. All we learn about Israel and the nations is that the covenant endures, bearing its own inevitable sanctions and consequences.

Our authorship has little interest in Israel out of relationship with either God or the nations. Israel on its own forms a subordinated and trivial theme; whatever messages we do find take on meaning only in the initial framework, that defined by Israel's relationship with God. Israel is never on its own. The bitterness of the ninth of Ab is contrasted with the bitter herbs with which the first redemption is celebrated (XVIII:i). The same contrast is drawn between the giving of the Torah and the destruction of the Temple (XX:i). If Israel had found rest among the nations, she would not have returned to the holy land (XXXVII:ii). The glory of Israel lay in its relationship to God, in the sanhedrin, in the disciples of sages, in the priestly watches, in the children (XL:i). Israel first suffers, then rejoices; her unfortunate condition marks the fact that Israel stands at the center of things (LIX:iii). Israel has declined through the generations, thus: "In olden times, when people held the sanhedrin in awe, naughty words were never included in songs. But when the sanhedrin was abolished, naughty words were inserted in songs. In olden times, when troubles came upon Israel, they stopped rejoicing on that account. Now that both have come to an end [no more singing, no more banquet halls], 'the joy of our hearts has ceased; our dancing has been turned to mourning.'" (CXXXVII:i). None of this bears any interesting message.

6.

A SAMPLE PASSAGE

LAMENTATIONS RABBAH 24. PETIHTA TWENTY-FOUR

XXIV.i.   1.   A.   R. Yohanan commenced [by citing the following verse of Scripture]: "The Valley of Vision Pronouncement"—What can have happened to you that you have gone, all of you, up on the roofs, O you who were full of tumult, you clamorous town, you city so gay? Your slain are not the slain of the sword, nor the dead of battle. Your officers have all departed; they fled far away; your survivors were all taken captive, taken captive without their bows. That is why I say, "Let me be, I will weep bitterly. Press not to comfort me for the ruin of my poor people." For my Lord God of Hosts had a day of tumult and din and confusion—Kir raged in the Valley of Vision, and Shoa on the hill; while Elam bore the quiver in troops of mounted men, and Kir bared the shield—and your choicest lowlands were filled with chariots and horsemen; they stormed at Judah's gateway and pressed beyond its screen. You gave thought on that day to the arms in the Forest House, and you took note of the many breaches in the city of David. And you collected the water of the Lower Pool; and you counted the houses of Jerusalem and pulled houses down to fortify the wall; and you constructed a basin between the two walls for the water of the old pool. But you gave no thought to him who planned it, you took no note of him who designed it long before. My Lord God of Hosts summoned on that day to weeping and lamenting, to tonsuring and girding with sackcloth. Instead there was rejoicing and mer- riment, killing of cattle and slaughtering of sheep, eating of meat and drinking of wine: "Eat and drink for tomorrow we die!" Then the Lord of Hosts re- vealed himself to my ears: "This iniquity shall never be forgiven you until you die," said my Lord God of Hosts (Isaiah 22:1–14):]

	B.	"It is a valley concerning which all seers have proph- esied,
	C.	"a valley from which all seers originate."
	D.	For said R. Yohanan, "Every prophet the name of whose city of origin is not made explicit is a Jerusa- lemite."
2.	A.	"The Valley of Vision Pronouncement":
	B.	For the words of seers were thrown to the ground there.
3.	A.	"What can have happened to you that you have gone, all of you, up on the roofs":
	B.	But had they actually gone up to the roofs?
	C.	Said R. Levi, "This refers to the arrogant ones."
4.	A.	"O you who were full of tumult":
	B.	Said R. Eleazar b. Jacob, "The word for 'tumult' bears [Cohen, p. 37] three senses: troubles, disorders, and darkness.
	C.	"'Troubles': 'Neither does he hear the troubles caused by the taskmaster' (Job 39:7).
	D.	"'Disorders': 'You that are full of tumult.'
	E.	"'Darkness': 'The gloom of wasteness and desolation' (Is. 30:3)."
5.	A.	"You clamorous town":
	B.	City in an uproar.
6.	A.	"You city so gay":
	B.	City rejoicing.
7.	A.	"Your slain are not the slain of the sword nor the dead of battle":

	B.	And what are they then?
	C.	". . . the wasting of hunger and the devouring of the fiery bolt" (Dt. 32:24).
8.	A.	"Your officers have all departed, [they fled far away, your survivors were all taken captive,] taken captive without their bows":
	B.	For they loosened the strings of their bows and tied them together with them.
9.	A.	"They fled far away, your survivors were all taken captive":
	B.	They went far away from obeying the words of the Torah,
	C.	in line with this verse: "From afar the Lord appeared to me" (Jer. 31:3).
10	A.	"That is why I say, 'Let me be, I will weep bitterly. Press not to comfort me [for the ruin of my poor people]'":
	B.	Said R. Simeon b. Laqish, "On three occasions the ministering angels wanted to recite a song before the Holy One, blessed be he, but he did not allow them to do so, and these are they:
	C.	"At the generation of the flood, at the sea, and at the destruction of the house of the sanctuary.
	D.	"At the generation of the flood: 'And the Lord said, My spirit shall not abide in man for ever' (Gen. 6:3) [Cohen, p. 38, n. 2: *Yadon,* "abide," is read as *yaron,* "sing," and the word "spirit" is applied to God's messengers].
	E.	"At the sea: 'And the one came not near the other all the night' (Ex. 14:20).
	F.	"And at the destruction of the house of the sanctuary: 'That is why I say, "Let me be, I will weep bitterly. Press not to comfort me [for the ruin of my poor people]."'
	G.	"What is written is not, 'do not gather together,' but 'do not press.'
	H.	"Said the Holy One, blessed be he, to the ministering angels, 'As to these words of comfort that you recite before me, they put pressure on me.'
	I.	"Why so? 'For my Lord God of Hosts had a day of tumult and din and confusion.'
	J.	"It is a day of confusion, of plundering, of weeping."
11.	A.	"Kir raged in the Valley of Vision":
	B.	"It is a valley concerning which all seers have prophesied."

12. A.   "Kir raged [in the Valley of Vision] and Shoa on the
             hill":

     B.   They demolished the walls of their houses, made
             them into barricades, and set them upon their strong-
             holds [Cohen, p. 38].

13. A.   "While Elam bore the quiver":

     B.   Rab said, "A container for arrows."

14. A.   "In troops of mounted men, and Kir bared the
             shield":

     B.   They demolished the walls of their houses, made
             them into barricades, and set them upon their strong-
             holds [Cohen, p. 38].

15. A.   "And your choicest lowlands were filled with chariots
             and horsemen":

     B.   Rab said, "It was filled as deep as the ocean."

16. A.   "They stormed at Judah's gateway":

     B.   [Cohen, p. 38:] Troops watering their horses went,
             and troops watering their horses came, so that they
             appeared to be very numerous.

17. A.   "And pressed beyond its screen [portcullis]":

     B.   They revealed what was hidden.

18. A.   "You gave thought on that day to the arms in the
             Forest House":

     B.   Taught R. Simeon b. Yohai, "The Israelites had
             weapons at Sinai, on which the Ineffable Name of
             God was incised, but when they sinned, that name
             was removed from the weapons.

     C.   "'And the children of Israel were stripped of their
             ornament from Mount Horeb onward' (Ex. 33:6)."

     D.   How was it taken away from them?

     E.   R. Aibu and rabbis:

     F.   R. Aibu said, "It peeled off on its own."

     G.   Rabbis say, "An angel descended and peeled it off."

19. A.   "You took note of the many breaches in the city of
             David. And you collected the water of the Lower
             Pool; and you counted the houses of Jerusalem and
             pulled houses down to fortify the wall; [and you con-
             structed a basin between the two walls for the water
             of the old pool. But you gave no thought to him who
             planned it, you took no note of him who designed it
             long before]":

     B.   This teaches that they were tearing down their
             houses and adding to the wall.

	C.	But had Hezekiah not done this already?
	D.	Is it not written, "And he took courage and built up all the wall that was broken down" (2 Chr. 32:5)?
	E.	"Hezekiah trusted in the Lord, God of Israel, but you did not trust in him:
	F.	"But you gave no thought to him who planned it, you took no note of him who designed it long before."
20.	A.	"My Lord God of Hosts summoned on that day to weeping and lamenting, [to tonsuring and girding with sackcloth]":
	B.	Said the ministering angels before him, "Lord of the world, it is written, 'Honor and majesty are before him' (1 Chr. 16:27), and yet do you speak in this manner?"
	C.	He said to them, "I will teach you. This is in line with the following verse: 'Strip yourselves naked, put the cloth about your loins! [Lament upon the breasts for the pleasant fields, for the spreading grapevines, for my people's soil—it shall be overgrown with briers and thistles—yes and for all the houses of delight, for the city of mirth]' (Is. 32:11–13).
	D.	"So will you be lamenting.
	E.	"'Lament upon the breasts': for the destruction of the first Temple and for the destruction of the second.
	F.	"'For the pleasant fields': for my desirable house, which I have turned into a barren field: 'Zion shall be ploughed as a field' (Micah 3:12).
	G.	"'For the spreading grapevines': this refers to Israel: 'You did pluck up a vine out of Egypt' (Ps. 80:9)."
21.	A.	Another interpretation of the passage, "My Lord God of Hosts summoned on that day to weeping and lamenting, to tonsuring and girding with sackcloth":
	B.	This is in line with what Scripture has said through the Holy Spirit through the sons of Korah: "These things I remember and pour out my soul within me" (Ps. 42:5).
	C.	In regard to whom did the sons of Korah recite this verse? Did they not recite it with regard to the community of Israel?
	D.	For the community of Israel said before the Holy One, blessed be he, "Lord of the world, I remember full well the security and peace and prosperity in

which I dwelt, but which now are far from me, so I weep and sigh, saying, 'Would that it were like those old times, when the Temple was standing, and in it you would descend from the heavens on high and bring to dwell your presence upon me.' And the nations of the world would praise me. And when I asked mercy for my sins, you would respond to me.

E.   "But now I am shamed and humiliated."

F.   And further did the community of Israel say before him, "Lord of the world, My soul is cast down within me when I pass by your house, which is in ruins, and a still voice in it echoes, 'In the place in which the children of Abraham would offer sacrifices before you, with the priests standing on the platform, the Levites singing praises on harps, foxes now run around.

G.   "'For the mountain of Zion, which is desolate, the foxes walk upon it' (Lam. 5:18).

H.   "But what can I now do, for my sins have made this happen to me, and deceitful prophets, who were in my midst, misled me from the way of life to the way of death."

I.   That is the meaning of the verse, "These things I remember and pour out my soul within me" (Ps. 42:5).

XXIV.ii.   1.   A.   Another interpretation of the passage, "My Lord God of Hosts summoned on that day to weeping and lamenting, to tonsuring and girding with sackcloth":

B.   When the Holy One, blessed be he, considered destroying the house of the sanctuary, he said, "So long as I am within it, the nations of the world cannot lay a hand on it.

C.   "I shall close my eyes to it and take an oath that I shall not become engaged with it until the time of the end."

D.   Then the enemies came and destroyed it.

E.   Forthwith the Holy One, blessed be he, took an oath by his right hand and put it behind him: "He has drawn back his right hand from before the enemy" (Lam. 2:3).

F.   At that moment the enemies entered the sanctuary and burned it up.

G.   When it had burned, the Holy One, blessed be he, said, "I do not have any dwelling on earth anymore.

I shall take up my presence from there and go up to my earlier dwelling."

H.   That is in line with this verse: "I will go and return to my place, until they acknowledge their guilt and seek my face" (Hos. 5:15).

I.   At that moment the Holy One, blessed be he, wept, saying, "Woe is me! What have I done! I have brought my Presence to dwell below on account of the Israelites, and now that they have sinned, I have gone back to my earlier dwelling. Heaven forfend that I now become a joke to the nations and an object of ridicule among peoples."

J.   At that moment Metatron [an important angelic figure] came, prostrated himself, and said before him, "Lord of the world, let me weep, but don't you weep!"

K.   He said to him, "If you do not let me weep now, I shall retreat to a place in which you have no right to enter, and there I shall weep."

L.   That is in line with this verse: "But if you will not hear it, my soul shall weep in secret for pride" (Jer. 13:17).

2. A.   Said the Holy One, blessed be he, to the ministering angels, "Let's go and see what the enemies have done to my house."

B.   Forthwith the Holy One, blessed be he, and the ministering angels went forth, with Jeremiah before them.

C.   When the Holy One, blessed be he, saw the house of the sanctuary, he said, "This is certainly my house, and this is my resting place, and the enemies have come and done whatever they pleased with it!"

D.   At that moment the Holy One, blessed be he, wept, saying, "Woe is me for my house! O children of mine—where are you? O priests of mine—where are you? O you who love me—where are you? What shall I do for you? I warned you, but you did not repent."

E.   Said the Holy One, blessed be he, to Jeremiah, "Today I am like a man who had an only son, who made a marriage canopy for him, and the son died under his marriage canopy. Should you not feel pain for me and for my son?

F.   "Go and call Abraham, Isaac, Jacob, and Moses from their graves, for they know how to weep."

G.   [Jeremiah] said before him, "Lord of the world, I don't know where Moses is buried."

H.   The Holy One, blessed be he, said to him, "Go and stand at the bank of the Jordan and raise your voice and call him, 'Son of Amram, son of Amram, rise up and see your flock, which the enemy has swallowed up!'"

I.   Jeremiah immediately went to the cave of Machpelah and said to the founders of the world [the patriarchs and matriarchs], "Arise, for the time has come for you to be called before the Holy One, blessed be he."

J.   They said to him, "Why?"

K.   He said to them, "I don't know," because he was afraid that they would say to him, "In your time this has come upon our children!"

L.   Jeremiah left them and went to the bank of the Jordan and cried out, "Son of Amram, son of Amram, rise up, for the time has come for you to be called before the Holy One, blessed be he."

M.   Moses said to him, "What makes this day so special, that I am called before the Holy One, blessed be he?"

N.   He said to him, "I don't know."

O.   Moses left him and went to the ministering angels, for he had known them from the time of the giving of the Torah. He said to them, "You who serve on high! Do you know on what account I am summoned before the Holy One, blessed be he?"

P.   They said to him, "Son of Amram! Don't you know that the house of the sanctuary has been destroyed, and the Israelites taken away into exile?

Q.   So he cried and wept until he came to the fathers of the world. They too forthwith tore their garments and put their hands on their heads, crying and weeping, up to the gates of the house of the sanctuary.

R.   When the Holy One, blessed be he, saw them, forthwith: "My Lord God of Hosts summoned on that day to weeping and lamenting, to tonsuring and girding with sackcloth."

S.   Were it not stated explicitly in a verse of Scripture, it would not be possible to make this statement.

T.   And they went weeping from this gate to that, like a man whose deceased child lies before him,

U. and the Holy One, blessed be he, wept, lamenting, "Woe for a king who prospers in his youth and not in his old age."

3. A. Said R. Samuel bar Nahman, "When the Temple was destroyed, Abraham came before the Holy One, blessed be he, weeping, pulling at his beard and tearing his hair, striking his face, tearing his clothes, with ashes on his head, walking about the Temple, weeping and crying, saying before the Holy One, blessed be he,

B. "'How does it happen that I am treated differently from every other nation and language, that I should be brought to such humiliation and shame!'

C. "When the ministering angels saw him, they too [Cohen, p. 43:] composed lamentations, arranging themselves in rows, saying,

D. "'The highways lie waste, the wayfaring man ceases' (Is. 33:8).

E. "What is the meaning of the statement, 'the highways lie waste'?

F. "Said the ministering angels before the Holy One, blessed be he, 'The highways that you paved to Jerusalem, so that the wayfarers would not cease, how have they become a desolation?'

G. "'The wayfaring man ceases':

H. "Said the ministering angels before the Holy One, blessed be he, 'How have the ways become deserted, on which the Israelites would come and go for the pilgrim festivals?'

I. "'You have broken the covenant':

J. "Said the ministering angels before the Holy One, blessed be he, 'Lord of the world, the covenant that was made with their father, Abraham, has been broken, the one through which the world was settled and through which you were made known in the world, that you are the most high God, the one who possesses heaven and earth.'

K. "'He has despised the cities':

L. "Said the ministering angels before the Holy One, blessed be he, 'You have despised Jerusalem and Zion after you have chosen them!'

M. "Thus Scripture says, 'Have you utterly rejected Judah? Has your soul loathed Zion?' (Jer. 14:19).

N. "'He regards not Enosh':

O.	"Said the ministering angels before the Holy One, blessed be he, 'Even as much as the generation of Enosh, chief of all idol worshipers, you have not valued Israel!'

P.	"At that moment the Holy One, blessed be he, responded to the ministering angels, saying to them, 'How does it happen that you are composing lamentations, arranging yourselves in rows, on this account?'

Q.	"They said to him, 'Lord of the world! It is on account of Abraham, who loved you, who came to your house and lamented and wept. How does it happen that you didn't pay any attention to him?'

R.	"He said to them, 'From the day on which my beloved died, going off to his eternal house, he has not come to my house, and now "what is my beloved doing in my house" (Jer. 11:15)?'

S.	"Said Abraham before the Holy One, blessed be he, 'Lord of the world! How does it happen that you have sent my children into exile and handed them over to the nations? And they have killed them with all manner of disgusting forms of death! And you have destroyed the house of the sanctuary, the place on which I offered up my son Isaac as a burnt offering before you!'

T.	"Said to Abraham the Holy One, blessed be he, 'Your children sinned and violated the whole Torah, transgressing the twenty-two letters that are used to write it: "Yes, all Israel have transgressed your Torah" (Dan. 9:11).'

U.	"Said Abraham before the Holy One, blessed be he, 'Lord of the world, who will give testimony against the Israelites, that they have violated your Torah?'

V.	"He said to him, 'Let the Torah come and give testimony against the Israelites.'

W.	"Forthwith the Torah came to give testimony against them.

X.	"Said Abraham to her, 'My daughter, have you come to give testimony against the Israelites that they have violated your religious duties? and are you not ashamed on my account? Remember the day on which the Holy One, blessed be he, tried to sell you to all the nations and languages of the world, and no one wanted to accept you, until my children came to Mount Sinai and they accepted you and honored you! And now are you coming to give testimony against them on their day of disaster?'

Y.   "When the Torah heard this, she went off to one side and did not testify against them.

Z.   "Said the Holy One, blessed be he, to Abraham, 'Then let the twenty-two letters of the alphabet come and give testimony against the Israelites.'

AA. "Forthwith the twenty-two letters of the alphabet came to give testimony against them.

BB. "The *aleph* came to give testimony against the Israelites, that they had violated the Torah.

CC. "Said Abraham to her, '*Aleph,* you are the head of all of the letters of the alphabet, and have you now come to give testimony against the Israelites on the day of their disaster?

DD. "'Remember the day on which the Holy One, blessed be he, revealed himself on Mount Sinai and began his discourse with you: "I [*anokhi,* beginning with *aleph*] am the Lord your God who brought you out of the Land of Egypt, out of the house of bondage" (Ex. 20:2).

EE. "'But not a single nation or language was willing to take you on, except for my children! And are you now going to give testimony against my children?'

FF. "Forthwith the *aleph* went off to one side and did not testify against them.

GG. "The *beth* came to give testimony against the Israelites.

HH. "Said Abraham to her, 'My daughter, have you come to give testimony against my children, who are meticulous about the Five Books of the Torah, at the head of which you stand, as it is said, "In the beginning [*bereshith*] God created . . ." (Gen. 1:1)?'

II. "Forthwith the *beth* went off to one side and did not testify against them.

JJ. "The *gimel* came to give testimony against the Israelites.

KK. "Said Abraham to her, '*Gimel,* have you come to give testimony against my children, that they have violated the Torah? Is there any nation, besides my children, that carries out the religious duty of wearing show-fringes, at the head of which you stand, as it is said, "Twisted cords [*gedelim*] you shall make for yourself" (Dt. 22:12)?'

LL.   "Forthwith the *gimel* went off to one and did not testify against them.

MM.   "Now when all of the letters of the alphabet in succession then realized that Abraham had silenced them, they were ashamed and stood off and would not testify against Israel.

NN.   "Abraham forthwith commenced speaking before the Holy One, blessed be he, saying to him, 'Lord of the world, when I was a hundred years old, you gave me a son. And when he had already reached the age of volition, a boy thirty-seven years of age, you told me, "offer him up as a burnt offering before me"!

OO.   "'And I became harsh to him and had no mercy for him, but I myself tied him up. Are you not going to remember this and have mercy on my children?'

PP.   "Isaac forthwith commenced speaking before the Holy One, blessed be he, saying to him, 'Lord of the world, when Father said to me, "God will see to the lamb for the offering for himself, my son" (Gen. 22:8), I did not object to what you had said, but I was bound willingly, with all my heart, on the altar, and spread forth my neck under the knife. Are you not going to remember this and have mercy on my children!'

QQ.   "Jacob forthwith commenced speaking before the Holy One, blessed be he, saying to him, 'Lord of the world, did I not remain in the house of Laban for twenty years? And when I went forth from his house, the wicked Esau met me and wanted to kill my children, and I gave myself over to death in their behalf. Now my children are handed over to their enemies like sheep for slaughter, after I raised them like fledglings of chickens. I bore on their account the anguish of raising children, for through most of my life I was pained greatly on their account. And now are you not going to remember this and have mercy on my children!'

RR.   "Moses forthwith commenced speaking before the Holy One, blessed be he, saying to him, 'Lord of the world, was I not a faithful shepherd for the Israelites for forty years? I ran before them in the desert like a horse. And when the time came for them to enter the land, you issued a decree against me in the wilderness that there my bones would fall. And now that they have gone into exile, you have sent to me to mourn and weep for them.

SS. "'This is in line with the proverb people say: "When it's good for my master, it's not good for me, but when it's bad for him, it's bad for me!"'"

TT. "Then Moses said to Jeremiah, 'Go before me, so I may go and bring them in and see who will lay a hand on them.'

UU. "Said to him Jeremiah, 'It isn't even possible to go along the road, because of the corpses.'

VV. "He said to him, 'Nonetheless.'

WW. "Forthwith Moses went along, with Jeremiah leading the way, until they came to the waters of Babylon.

XX. "They saw Moses and said to one another, 'Here comes the son of Amram from his grave to redeem us from the hand of our oppressors.'

YY. "An echo went forth and said, 'It is a decree from before me.'

ZZ. "Then said Moses to them, 'My children, to bring you back is not possible, for the decree has already been issued. But the Omnipresent will bring you back quickly.' Then he left them.

AAA. "Then they raised up their voices in weeping until the sound rose on high: 'By the rivers of Babylon there we sat down, yes, we wept' (Ps. 137:1).

BBB. "When Moses came back to the founders of the world [the patriarchs and matriarchs], they said to him, 'What have the enemies done to our children?'

CCC. "He said to them, 'Some of them he killed, the hands of some of them he bound behind their back, some of them he put in iron chains, some of them he stripped naked, some of them died on the way, and their corpses were left for the vultures of heaven and the hyenas of the earth, some of them were left for the sun, starving and thirsting.'

DDD. "Then they began to weep and sing dirges: 'Woe for what has happened to our children! How have you become orphans without a father! How have you had to sleep in the hot sun during the summer without clothes and covers! How have you had to walk over rocks and stones without shoes and sandals! How were you burdened with a heavy bundle of sand! How were your hands bound behind your backs! How were you left unable even to swallow the spit in your mouths!'

EEE. "Moses then said, 'Cursed are you, O sun! Why did you not grow dark when the enemy went into the house of the sanctuary?'

FFF. "The sun answered him, 'By your life, Moses, faithful shepherd! They would not let me nor did they leave me alone, but beat me with sixty whips of fire, saying, "Go, pour out your light."'

GGG. "Moses then said, 'Woe for your brilliance, O Temple, how has it become darkened? Woe that its time has come to be destroyed, for the building to be reduced to ruins, for the schoolchildren to be killed, for their parents to go into captivity and exile and the sword!'

HHH. "Moses then said, 'O you who have taken the captives! I impose an oath on you by your lives! If you kill, do not kill with a cruel form of death, do not exterminate them utterly, do not kill a son before his father, a daughter before her mother, for the time will come for the Lord of heaven to exact a full reckoning from you!'

III. "The wicked Chaldeans did not do things this way, but they brought a son before his mother and said to the father, 'Go, kill him!' The mother wept, her tears flowing over him, and the father hung his head.

JJJ. "And further Moses said before him, 'Lord of the world! You have written in your Torah, "Whether it is a cow or a ewe, you shall not kill it and its young both in one day" (Lev. 22:28).

KKK. "'But have they not killed any number of children along with their mothers, and yet you remain silent!'

LLL. "Then Rachel, our mother, leapt to the fray and said to the Holy One, blessed be he, 'Lord of the world! It is perfectly self-evident to you that your servant, Jacob, loved me with a mighty love, and worked for me for Father for seven years, but when those seven years were fulfilled, and the time came for my wedding to my husband, Father planned to substitute my sister for me in the marriage to my husband. Now that matter was very hard for me, for I knew the deceit, and I told my husband and gave him a sign by which he would know the difference between me and my sister, so that my father would not be able to trade me off. But then I regretted it and I bore my passion, and I had mercy for my sister, that she should not be shamed. So in the evening for my husband they substituted my sister for me, and I gave my sister all the signs that I had given to my husband, so that he would think that she was Rachel.

MMM. "'And not only so, but I crawled under the bed on which he was lying with my sister, while she remained silent, and I made all the replies so that he would not discern the voice of my sister.

NNN. "'I paid my sister only kindness, and I was not jealous of her, and I did not allow her to be shamed, and I am a mere mortal, dust and ashes. Now I had no envy of my rival, and I did not place her at risk for shame and humiliation. But you are the King, living and enduring and merciful. How does it happen that you are jealous of idolatry, which is nothing, and so have sent my children into exile, allowed them to be killed by the sword, permitted the enemy to do whatever they wanted to them?!'

OOO. "Forthwith the mercy of the Holy One, blessed be he, welled up, and he said, 'For Rachel I am going to bring the Israelites back to their land.'

PPP. "That is in line with this verse of Scripture: 'Thus said the Lord: A cry is heard in Ramah, wailing, bitter weeping, Rachel weeping for her children. She refuses to be comforted for her children, who are gone. Thus said the Lord, Restrain your voice from weeping, your eyes from shedding tears; for there is a reward for your labor, declares the Lord; they shall return from the enemy's land, and there is hope for your future, declares the Lord: your children shall return to their country' (Jer. 31:15–17)."

This wonderful passage is made up of two completely separate entries, one following the familiar form of a clause-by-clause amplification of a verse of Scripture, the other a completely different kind of writing altogether. XXIV.i.1–21 yields a fairly well-disciplined statement on the intersecting verse cited at the head;

there is no base verse that I can identify. Perhaps at some point Lam. 5:18 was conceived to serve as the base verse, but that is hardly obvious. XXIV.ii.1 is tacked on because of the amplification of the same verse that forms the basis of the concluding unit of the foregoing. But we must regard the whole as an essentially fresh statement. I have divided the whole into three parts, since Samuel bar Nahman's massive essay clearly stands wholly on its own. It seems to me beyond reasonable doubt that the whole of XXIV.ii.3 forms a unitary and well-crafted composition, with no important interpolations or imperfections of any kind. I also see XXIV.ii.1 as essentially autonomous. But one can make the point that No. 2 continues No. 1, and I cannot make a strong case for my division. The link between No. 3 and No. 2 is via the patriarchs and Moses, and so the whole is, if divided, still quite cogent. I cannot point in Midrash compilations that reached closure prior to this one to a passage of the narrative ambition and power of Samuel bar Nahman's. We are in a completely different literary situation when we come to so long and so carefully formed a story as this one.

As to the issue before us, XXIV:i.1 is made up of a series of propositions, most of them brief and consisting only of a clause of the base or intersecting verse followed by a few words of clarification. These add up to a long sequence of propositions, e.g., Nos. 1, 2, 3, 4, 5, 6, 7, 8, 9, 10, 11, 12, 13, 14, 15, 16, 17, 19 ("this teaches that . . ."), 21. Nos. 18 and 20 fall into the category of a fairly cogent narrative. As to XXIV:ii, we have a set of beautifully crafted narratives: Nos. 1, 2, 3 (a stunning and monumental narrative, with coherence holding together a sustained and brilliant tale). But how do the stories of XXIV:ii hold together? No narrative joins the narratives, but no proposition makes them cohere. A glance at XXIV:i shows us what is the sole sustaining principle of agglutination: fixed association, with clauses or verses of the book of Lamentations—that alone.

XXI

ESTHER RABBAH PART ONE

1.

IDENTIFYING THE DOCUMENT

IN ESTHER RABBAH PART ONE (THAT IS, COVERING THE BOOK OF ESTHER'S FIRST TWO chapters), we find only one message, and it is reworked in only a few ways.[1] It is that the nations are swine, their rulers fools, and Israel is subjugated to them, though it should not be, only because of its own sins. No other explanation serves to account for the paradox and anomaly that prevail. But just as God saved Israel in the past, so the salvation that Israel can attain will recapitulate the former ones.

---

[1] For further reading and bibliography on the topic of this chapter, see the following:

    Bowker, p. 84.

    Moses D. Herr, "Esther Rabbah," *Encyclopaedia Judaica* 6:915–16: definition of the work, redacted in the Land of Israel not later than the beginning of the sixth century. Esther Rabbah II (covering Esther Chapters Three–Eight) is eleventh century.

    Maccoby omits this document from his introduction.

    Stemberger-Strack, pp. 346–47: it must be dated to 500, in Palestine.

    This writer's introduction is *The Midrash Compilations of the Sixth and Seventh Centuries: An Introduction to the Rhetorical, Logical, and Topical Program*. II. *Esther Rabbah I*. Atlanta, 1990: Scholars Press for Brown Judaic Studies.

On the stated theme, Israel among the nations, sages set forth a proposition entirely familiar from the books of Deuteronomy through Kings, on the one side, and much of prophetic literature, on the other.

The proposition is familiar, and so is the theme; but since the book of Esther can hardly be characterized as "Deuteronomic," lacking all interest in the covenant, the land, and issues of atonement (beyond the conventional sackcloth, ashes, and fasting, hardly the fodder for prophetic regeneration and renewal!), the sages' distinctive viewpoint in the document must be deemed an original and interesting contribution of their own. But the message is somewhat more complicated than merely a negative judgment against the nations. If I have to identify one recurrent motif that captures that theology, it is the critical role of Esther and Mordecai, particularly Mordecai, who, as sage, emerges in the position of Messiah. And that is a message that is particular to the exposition of the book of Esther's opening chapters.

Esther Rabbah Part One proves nearly as much a commentary in the narrowest sense—verse-by-verse amplification, paraphrase, exposition—as it is a compilation in the working definition of this inquiry of mine. What holds the document together and gives it, if not coherence, then at least flow and movement, after all, are the successive passages of (mere) exposition. All the more stunning, therefore, is the simple fact that when all has been set forth and completed, there really is that simple message that the Torah (as exemplified by the sage) makes the outsider into an insider, the woman into a heroic leader, just as, in the book of Ruth, we see how the Moabite is turned into an Israelite, the offspring of the outsider into the Messiah. These paradoxes come about on the condition, the only condition, that the Torah govern. This is a document about one thing, and it makes a single statement, and that statement is coherent, just as is the case with Ruth Rabbah, the counterpart and complement. Where we find a woman in the systemic center of a document's statement, there we uncover the document's critical message, that which can account for everything and its opposite, and for the transformation of otherwise fixed values, e.g., in this case, the exclusion of women from the center of consideration.

Gender thus defines the focus for both Esther Rabbah Part One and Ruth Rabbah, yielding the opposite of what is anticipated. Ruth Rabbah has the Messiah born of an outsider, Esther Rabbah has salvation come through a woman. For Esther and Mordecai, woman and the sage-Messiah, function in this document in much the same way that Ruth and David, woman and sage-Messiah, work in Ruth Rabbah. While the sages of Ruth Rabbah face their own, distinctive problem, the way the outsider becomes the insider, the Moabite Messiah, still, Ruth Rabbah and Esther Rabbah Part One deal with the same fundamental fact: the Messiah-sage dictates the future of Israel, because he (never she) realizes the rule of the Torah. In Esther Rabbah Part One many things say one thing: the Torah dictates Israel's fate, if you want to know what that fate will be, study the Torah, and if you want to control that fate, follow the model of the sage-Messiah.

2.

TRANSLATIONS INTO ENGLISH

The first English translation was Maurice Simon, *Esther,* in H. Freedman and Maurice Simon, eds., *Midrash Rabbah* (London, 1939: Soncino Press), Volume IX. The second, and first form-analytical one, is this writer's *Esther Rabbah Part One. An Analytical Translation.* Atlanta, 1989: Scholars Press for Brown Judaic Studies.

3.

RHETORIC

The rhetorical program is the same as that of Song of Songs Rabbah.

4.

LOGIC OF COHERENT DISCOURSE

The entire document is made up of freestanding compositions, made cogent within themselves mainly by propositions but sometimes by teleological logic, and made coherent beginning to end principally by reference to the same shared and fixed association with a common document.

	Number	*Percent of the Whole*
Propositional and philosophical discourse	12	26%
Themes worked out by teleology expressed in narrative	3	12%
The logic of fixed association	23	50%
The cogency of a fixed analytical method	0	0%
No clear coherence between or among successive units of completed discourse	7	15%
Not relevant to the issue	1	

If we now ask about the operative logics, that is, the first three entries, the result is as follows:

	Number	*Percent of the Whole*
Propositional and philosophical discourse and themes worked out by teleology expressed in narrative	15	39%
The logic of fixed association	23	61%

These results are familiar. For the statement of propositions, sizable arguments and proofs, the usual philosophical logic dictates the joining of sentence to sentences and the composition of paragraphs, that is, completed thoughts. For the presentation of the whole, the other logic, the one deriving from imputed, fixed associations, external to the propositions at hand, predominates, though not decisively.

5.

TOPICAL PROGRAM

These episodic propositions comprise the document's single message. Bad government comes about because of the sins of the people (VII:i). But that proposition is realized in discourse mainly about bad government by the nations, and, given the base document, that is hardly surprising. God was neglected by the people, so he is left solitary through his own actions, which responded to the people's actions (XVIII:iii). This serves Lamentations Rabbah as its Petihta 10; but the proposition surely is not alien to our base document. The contrast between the relative neglect of this inviting topic and the intense interest in another, the one that follows, which characterize Esther Rabbah Part One, and the opposite emphases and interests revealed in Lamentations Rabbah, is readily discerned.

Our compilation concentrates upon this one subject, and all of its important messages present the same proposition, in several parts. Israel's life among the nations is a sequence of sorrows, each worse than the preceding: "In the morning, you shall say, 'Would it were evening!' and at evening you shall say, 'Would it were morning!' In the morning, of Babylonia, you shall say, 'Would it were evening!'" But through Torah, Israel can break the cycle. Said R. Simeon b. Yohai, "You can acquire rights of ownership of members of the nations of the world, as it says, 'Moreover of the children of the strangers that sojourn among you, of them may you buy' (Lev. 25:45), but they cannot acquire rights of ownership over you. Why not? Because you acquired 'these the words of the covenant.' And the nations? They did not acquire 'these the words of the covenant' ['These are the words of the covenant']" (I:i.4–11). When Israel is subjugated by the nations, God will not spurn, abhor, destroy it or break his covenant with it—in the age of Babylonia, Media, the Greeks, and the wicked kingdom; of Vespasian, Trajan, Haman, the Romans (II:i.1). The same is repeated at III:i.1–5.

In comparing the ages through which the Jews had lived, Babylonia, Median, Greek, Roman, the same position recurs. When the righteous achieve great power, there is joy in the world, and when the wicked achieve great power, there is groaning in the world; this is so of Israelite and gentile kings (IV:i). Gentile kings may do good things or bad things (VI:i). But even the good kings are not without flaws. When a bad king rules, it is because of the sins of the people, those who will not do the will of the creator (VII:i). God worked through whomever he chose. From the beginning of the creation of the world, the Holy One blessed be he designated for everyone what was suitable: Ahasuerus the first of those who sell (people at a price), Haman the first of those who buy (people at a price) (VIII:i). There are decisions made by God that determine the life of nations and individuals; Israel's history follows rules that can be learned in Scripture; nothing is random, all things are connected, and fundamental laws of history dictate the meaning of what happens among the nations (VIII:ii).

Ultimately, God will destroy Israel's enemies (IX:i). God will save Israel when not a shred of merit will be found among the nations of the world (X:i.15). The prosperity of the nations is only for a time; then the nations will be punished and Israel redeemed (XI:i). There will be full recompense, and the contrast between Israel's subjugation and the nations' prosperity will be resolved. The principle of measure for measure governs. Pagan kings propose to do what God himself does not claim to be able to do. They cannot accomplish their goal; if God wanted to, God could do it. But in the age to come, God will accomplish the union of opposites, which in this time pagan kings claim to be able to do but cannot accomplish (XVII:i). Pagan kings rebel against not only God but also their own gods (XVIII:i). But for the slightest gesture of respect for God they are rewarded (XVIII:i).

God is in full control of everyone at all times. The salvation in the time of Ahasuerus was directly linked, detail by detail, to the punishment in the time of Nebuchadnezzar (XVIII:ii). Israel's relationship with one empire is no different from its relationship to the other. The same base verse, Ps. 10:14, accounts for both Rome and Sasanian Iran, the world empires of the day. The relationship of each to Israel is the same. Both of them call into question Israel's faith in the power of God by showing off their own power. Esau/Romulus and Remus pay back God's blessing by building temples of idolatry in Rome. Belshazzar/Vashti/Iran do the same by oppressing Israel. All intend by their power to prove that they are stronger than God. But, the premise maintains, God will show in the end who is the stronger. The upshot is to underline the irony that derives from the contrast between the empires' power and God's coming display of his power; that and one other thing: the challenge facing God in showing his power over theirs (XVIII:iv).

Israel possesses wise men, the nations' sages are fools thus: "'The impious man destroys his neighbor through speech': this refers to the seven princes of Persia and Media. 'But through their knowledge the righteous are rescued': this refers to the portion of Issachar" (XXIII:i). We have at XXIII:ii three sets of explanations for the names of various persons mentioned in the text, all of them working with the letters of the respective names and imputing to them other meanings sustained by the same consonants. The passage is worth examining in its entirety, to give the flavor of the reading:

XXIII:ii. 1. A. ["The men next to him being Carshena, Shethar, Admatha, Tarshish, Merses, Marsena, and Memucan, the seven princes of Persia and Media, who saw the king's face and sat first in the kingdom":]

B. "The men next to him":

C. They drew the punishment near to themselves.

2. A. "Being Carshena":

B. He was in charge of the vetches [*karshinim*].

3. A. "Shethar":

B. He was in charge of the wine.

4. A. "Admatha":

B. He was in charge of surveying the land [Simon: land measurements].

5. A. "Tarshish":

B. He was first in command of the household.

6. A. "Merses":

B. He would make chicken hash [Simon: he used to make a hash of (nenares) the poultry].

7. A. "Marsena":

B. He would beat the flour [with oil].

8. A. "And Memucan":

B. He was the one who provided food for all of them, for his wife would prepare for them everything they needed.

9. A. ["Carshena, Shethar, Admatha, Tarshish, Merses, Marsena, and Memucan"]:

B. Said the ministering angels before the Holy One, blessed be he, "If the counsel of that wicked man [Haman] is carried out, who will offer you offerings?" [So the names of the counselors refer to offerings in the Temple, thus]:

C. "Carshena":

D. "Who will offer you an ox of the first year [*par ben shanah*]?"

10. A. "Shethar":

B. "Who will offer you two pigeons [*shete torim*]?"

11. A. "Admatha":

B. "Who will build you an altar of earth: 'An altar of earth you shall make to me' (Ex. 20:21)?"

12. A. "Tarshish":

B. "Who will wear the priestly garments and minister before you: 'A beryl [*tarshish*] and an onyx and a jasper' (Ex. 28:20)?"

13. A. "Merses":
    B. "Who will stir [*memeres*] the blood of the birds that are sacrificed before you?"

14. A. "Marsena":
    B. "Who will mix the flour and oil before you?"

15. A. "And Memucan":
    B. "Who will set up the altar before you: 'And they set up the altar upon its bases' (Ezra 3:3)?"

16. A. Thereupon said the Holy One, blessed be he, to them, "The Israelites are my children, my companions, my nearest, my loving ones, the sons of my beloved, Abraham: 'The seed of Abraham that loved me' (Is. 41:8).
    B. "I will exalt their horn: 'And he has lifted up a horn for his people' (Ps. 148:14)."

17. A. Another explanation for the verse, "Carshena, [Shethar, Admatha, Tarshish, Merses, Marsena, and Memucan]":
    B. [As to Carshena,] said the Holy One, blessed be he, "I will scatter vetches before them and clear them out of the world [Simon, p. 58, n. 4: as one feeds an animal before killing it]."
    C. "Shethar": "I shall make them drink a cup of reeling."
    D. "Admatha, Tarshish": "I shall treat their blood as free as water."
    E. "Merses, Marsena, and Memucan": "[Simon, p. 58:] I will stir, twist, and crush [*memares, mesares, mema'ek*] their souls within their bellies."
    F. And where was the doom of all of them made ready?
    G. Said R. Josiah, "It is in line with that which Isaiah, the prophet, said, 'Prepare slaughter for his children for the iniquity of their fathers, that they may not rise up and possess the earth' (Is. 14:21)."

The first set of explanations deals with the tasks each of the princes carried out in the palace, feeding the king. The next deals with the rites of the Temple that each name stands for; here the princes are given a good task, which is to thwart the advice of Haman. But the upshot is to match feeding the wicked (or stupid) king, Ahasuerus, as against tending the King of kings of kings, God. And the third set of explanations then assigns to the seven the punishment that is owing to the wicked government that has endangered the lives of the Jews. So three distinct, and yet complementary, hermeneutical interests coincide: pagan government and the feeding of pagan kings, divine government and the counterpart, which is the Temple cult, and, finally, God's punishment for the pagan government. While, it goes without saying, each set of seven names can stand on its own, it seems to me clear that the compositor has appealed to a single cogent program in order to accomplish what I see as a beautiful piece of sustained and coherent exposition, one that makes a variety of distinct components of a single important proposition. I cannot imagine a finer execution of the exposition of details aimed at registering a major conception.

There is a correspondence between how Israel suffers and how the nations prosper, so XXVIII:i: "With the language with which the throne was taken away from her [Esther's] ancestor, when Samuel said to him, 'And he has given it to a neighbor of yours, who is better than you' (1 Sam. 15:28), with that same language, the throne was given back to him: 'let the king give her royal position to another who is better than she.'" Saul lost the throne because he did not destroy Amalek, Esther got it back because she did. Obedience to divine instructions made the difference. Persian women suffered and were humiliated because they had ridiculed Israelite women (XXXIV:i).

Those who do righteousness at all times are going to be the ones who will carry out God's salvation, thus: "When Haman wanted to exterminate Israel and weighed out ten thousand pieces of silver to those who were to do the work for Ahasuerus, it is written, 'And I will pay ten thousand talents of silver into the hands . . .' (Est. 3:9), what is then written? 'Now there was a Jew in Susa the capital whose name was Mordecai, son of Jair, son of Shimei, son of Kish, a Benjaminite.'" The point is that they who do righteousness at all times are to be remembered when God's salvation is required, and it is performed through them. Accordingly, Mordecai in his generation was equivalent to Moses in his generation: "Now the man Moses was very meek" (Num. 12:3). Just as Moses stood in the breach, "Therefore he said that he would destroy them, had not Moses, his chosen one, stood before him in the breach" (Ps. 106:23), so did Mordecai: "Seeking the good of his people and speaking peace to all his seed" (Est. 10:3). Just as Moses taught Torah to Israel, "Behold, I have taught you statutes and ordinances" (Dt. 4:5), so Mordecai did, "And he sent letters . . . with words of peace and truth" (Est. 9:30) (and truth refers to Torah): "Buy the truth and do not sell it" (Prov. 23:23).

God always responds to Israel's need. The reason this point is pertinent here is the repeated contrast also of Mordecai and Haman; the upshot is that ultimately Israel gets what it has coming just as do the nations; and when Israel gets its redemption, it is through people of a single sort: Moses, Abraham, Mordecai. The redemptions of Israel in times past then provide the model and paradigm for what is going to happen in the future. None of this has any bearing on the land and nothing invokes the covenant, which is why I see the entire matter in the present context. When God saves Israel, it is always in response to how it has been punished, thus at XXXVIII:i.9: R. Berekiah in the name of R. Levi said, "Said the Holy One, blessed be he, to the Israelites, 'You have wept, saying, "We have become orphans and fatherless" (Lam. 5:3). By your lives, I shall raise up for you in Media a savior who will have no father and no mother.' Thus: 'for she had neither father nor mother.'" If the mortal king remembers and pays back, how much the more so will God (LIV:i).

As to Israel's distinctive leadership and its life within its own boundaries, the nature of our base document, with its concern for its heroes, Mordecai and Esther, secures for this subject a more than negligible place in the propositional program of our compilation. Israel's leadership consistently follows the same norms, and what the ancestors taught, the descendants learn. Thus Esther behaved as had Rachel (LI:i), so: "Now Esther had not made known her kindred or her people, as Mordecai had charged her; [for Esther obeyed Mordecai just as when she was brought up by him]:"

> This teaches that she kept silent like Rachel, her ancestor, who kept silent. All of her great ancestors had kept silent. Rachel kept silent when she saw her wedding band on the hand of her sister but shut up about it. Benjamin, her son, kept silent. You may know that that is so, for the stone that stood for him on the high priest's breastplate was a jasper, indicating that he knew of the sale of Joseph, but he kept silent. (The word for "jasper" contains letters that stand for "there is a mouth," meaning, he could have told, but he kept silent. Saul, from whom she descended: "Concerning the matter of the kingdom he did not tell him" (1 Sam. 10:16). Esther: "Now Esther had not made known her kindred or her people, as Mordecai had charged her."

What happens now therefore has already happened, and we know how to respond and what will come in consequence of our deeds.

6.

A SAMPLE PASSAGE

ESTHER RABBAH I PETIHTA 2

II:i. 1. A. Samuel commenced by citing the following verse of Scripture: "'Yet for all that, when they are in the land of their enemies, I will not spurn them, neither will I abhor them so as to destroy them utterly and break my covenant with them, for I am the Lord their God; but I will for their sake remember the covenant with their forefathers, whom I brought forth out of the land of Egypt in the sight of the nations, that I might be their God: I am the Lord' (Lev. 26:44–45):

B.   "'I will not spurn them': in Babylonia.

C.   "'Neither will I abhor them': in Media.

D.   "'So as to destroy them utterly': under Greek rule.

E.   "'And break my covenant with them: under the wicked kingdom.

F.   "'For I am the Lord their God': in the age to come."

G.   Taught R. Hiyya, "'I will not spurn them': in the time of Vespasian.

H.   "'Neither will I abhor them': in the time of Trajan.

I.   "'So as to destroy them utterly': in the time of Haman.

J.   "'And break my covenant with them': in the time of the Romans.

K.   "'For I am the Lord their God': in the time of Gog and Magog."

The two readings are complementary, the one invoking times of trouble in ages past, the other in the perceived present. The next *petihta* moves through the same historical periods but with different texts. A good case can be made to regard this *petihta* and the next as a single sustained exercise, since the basic theme and thesis are continuous from the one to the other. What holds together the two readings, A–F, G–K (which could sustain Arabic numerals), is in form the fact that they comment on the same sequence of verses, hence the logic of fixed association. But here it seems to me that the proposition that underlies both is the same and is served by each, and hence the logic is propositional, though the form is commentary form.

ESTHER RABBAH I PETIHTA 3

III:i. 1. A.   R. Judah b. R. Simon opened by citing the following verse: "as if a man fled from a lion and a bear met him; or went into the house and leaned with his hand against the wall, and a serpent bit him" (Amos 5:19).

2. A.   R. Huna and R. Aha in the name of R. Hama bar Hanina: "'as if a man fled from a lion': this refers to Babylonia, called a lion: 'the first was like a lion' (Dan. 7:4).

B.   "'And a bear met him': this speaks of Media, called a bear: 'And behold, another beast, a second, like a bear' (Dan. 7:5)."

3. A.   R. Yohanan said, "The word for a bear is written defectively."

B.   That is consistent with the position of R. Yohanan, which is as follows: "'Therefore a lion out of the forest slays them' (Jer. 5:6): this speaks of Media.

C.   "'A leopard watches over their cities': this is Greece.

D.   "'Everyone who goes out of there is torn into pieces': this is Edom."

4. A. [Reverting to 2.B:] "'Or went into the house':

   B. "This speaks of Greece in the time of the Temple.

   C. "'And leaned with his hand against the wall, and a serpent bit him': this speaks of Edom: 'The sound thereof shall go like the serpent's' (Jer. 46:22)."

5. A. Along these same lines: "Open to me, my sister, my love, my dove, my undefiled" (Song 5:2):

   B. "Open to me, my sister": this is Babylonia.

   C. "My love": this is Media.

   D. "My dove": this is Greece.

   E. "My undefiled": this is Edom.

   F. "Dove" speaks of the age of Greece, because in the time of the rule of the Greeks the Temple was standing, and the Israelites would offer pigeons and doves on the altar.

6. A. R. Phineas and R. Levi in the name of R. Hama b. Hanina interpret the following verse of Scripture: "In my distress I called upon the Lord, and cried to my God. Out of his Temple he heard my voice, [and my cry came before him into his ears]" (Ps. 18:7).

   B. "'In my distress I called upon the Lord': in Babylonia.

   C. "'And cried to my God': in Media.

   D. "'Out of his Temple he heard my voice': in Greece."

7. A. Said R. Huna in his own name, "'Open to me, my sister, my love, my dove, my undefiled':

   B. "'My dove': this is the kingdom of Greece, because in the time of the rule of the Greeks the Temple was standing, and the Israelites would offer pigeons and doves on the altar.

   C. "Therefore: 'Out of his Temple he heard my voice.'

   D. "'And my cry came before him into his ears': this speaks of Edom."

8. A. Another interpretation of the verse, "as if a man fled from a lion and a bear met him; or went into the house and leaned with his hand against the wall, and a serpent bit him" (Amos 5:19).

   B. "As if a man fled from a lion": this speaks of Nebuchadnezzar.

   C. "And a bear met him": this is Belshazzar.

   D. "Or went into the house and leaned with his hand against the wall, and a serpent bit him": this is Haman, who hissed at people like a snake, as it is written, "Rehum the commander and Shimshai the scribe"—the latter is a son of Haman—"wrote a letter to Artaxerxes, the king, in this manner" (Ezra 4:8).

9. A. ["Rehum the commander and Shimshai the scribe wrote a letter to Artaxerxes, the king, in this manner" (Ezra 4:8).]

    B.   What was written in the letter?
    C.   "Be it known now to the king . . . that they will not pay
         minda, belo, or *halaq* and the revenue of the kings will be dam-
         aged" (Ezra 4:13).
    D.   "Minda": this is the land tax.
    E.   "Belo": this is the poll tax.
    F.   "Halaq": this is the corvée.
10. A.   "The revenue of the kings will be damaged":
    B.   R. Huna and R. Phineas: "Even the things in which the gov-
         ernment [Simon:] entertains itself such as theaters and circuses
         does [this city damage]."
    C.   When he heard this, [the king] sent word and stopped the
         building of the Temple.
11. A.   ["Now it came to pass in the days of Ahasuerus, the Ahasuerus
         who reigned from India to Ethiopia over one hundred and
         twenty-seven provinces":]
    B.   When they saw this, they all began to cry, "Woe!"
    C.   "Now it came to pass" [since the word in Hebrew for
         "now it came to pass" can yield the word "woe," hence
         the sense of the words, "Now it came to pass in the days
         of Ahasuerus" is this:] "Woe for that which was in the days
         of Ahasuerus" (Est. 1:1).

The composition is somewhat complex, because our intersecting verse, Amos 5:19, competes with Song 5:2, which serves both on its own, at No. 5, and also in conjunction with Ps. 18:7 at No. 6. No. 7 then links the two, which is an odd and rather impressive denouement. No. 8 then reverts to our opening intersecting verse. Nos. 9, 10 then appear to intend merely to gloss that composition, but, we see, 10.C forms the bridge to our conventional conclusion, No. 11. Despite the diversity of intersecting verses, the message is repeated and amazingly simple: the comparison of the several rulers under which the Jews had lived, Babylonians, Medes, Greeks, and Romans. But if we ask what holds together the several compositions bearing Arabic numerals, it is not the proposition at all. No. 1 introduces the base verse; No. 2 introduces another; No. 3 joins No. 2 because it deals with the same verse, not with a proposition. No. 4 deals with the base verse of No. 2. There is no introduction of a proposition to link No. 5's "along these same lines" to No. 4; the whole just goes over the same ground in exegetical form and we can surely not hold that a proposition shared by Nos. 4 and 5 links Nos. 4, 5. No. 6 is joined to the foregoing in no way I can see—even though it in fact covers the same ground! Nos. 7, 8, 9, 10, 11—all are freestanding entries, loosely joined in proposition, but logically linked not propositionally—they certainly do not set forth a syllogism—but solely through the logic of fixed association.

ESTHER RABBAH I
TO ESTHER 1:22

XXXI:i. 1. A. "He sent letters to all the royal provinces, to every province in its own script, and to every people in its own language, that every man be lord in his own house and speak according to the language of his people":

B. Said R. Huna, "[Simon, p. 63, n. 5: In decreeing 'that every man be lord in his own house,'] Ahasuerus had a stupid policy.

C. "Under ordinary circumstances, if someone wants to eat lentils and his wife to eat beans, can he force her? Is it not the simple fact that what she wants is what she does?"

D. Said R. Phineas, "[In decreeing 'that every man speak according to the language of his people,'] not only so, but he made himself a laughingstock in the world.

E. "Under ordinary circumstances, if a Median man marries a Persian woman, does she speak Median? If a Persian man marries a Median woman, does she speak Persian?

F. "But the Holy One, blessed be he, spoke with the Israelites in whatever language they knew: 'I am the Lord your God' (Ex. 20:1) [and the word for "I" is supposedly] the language of Egypt."

2. A. Said R. Nathan of Beth Gubrin, "There are four really beautiful languages that are used in the world:

B. "Greek for singing, Persian for lamentation, Hebrew for conversation, Latin for war."

C. Some add, "Assyrian for writing."

D. Hebrew is spoken but has no alphabet.

E. Assyrian has an alphabet but is not spoken.

F. They therefore chose Assyrian writing and Hebrew speech.

3. A. A frontier guard chose for [the Romans] Latin language out of Greek language [following Simon, p. 64, who adds, n. 6: "carved the Latin out of the Greek, so that the former is a mere dialect of the latter, as it were"].

B. R. Judah b. R. Simon said, "It is a disgrace for [Rome] that she has to sign documents in a language that is alien."

C. R. Hanina b. Adda said, "Nonetheless, 'Its nails are of brass' (Dan. 7:19)—it signs documents only in its own language."

4. A. Said R. Samuel b. R. Nahman, "From this [we learn that] one has to repeat his lessons.

    B.   "For had Moses not repeated the Torah for us, whence should we have known that the *shesuah* [an unclean animal listed at Dt. 14:6 but not at Lev. 11] [is prohibited]?

    C.   "And had Daniel not repeated what he had dreamed, how should we have known, 'Its nails were of brass'?"

No. 1 draws a further detail that shows the incompetence of Ahasuerus. He gave orders that contradicted the natural course of social life. Nos. 2, 3, and 4 are attached for their interest in languages; clearly Nos. 3 and 4, which in no way relate, were joined to No. 2 before the whole was tacked on. But since No. 2 does not refer to Egyptian, and since the reference to Persian is subordinated, the whole really cannot be said to advance the discussion, but only to fill up space. I do not see anything beyond the common theme, since No. 1 is focused upon the base verse, and No. 2 centers upon its own proposition about how different languages serve different purposes.

PART FOUR

WRITING WITHOUT AUTHORS:

The Sage in Rabbinic Literature

XXII

Rabbinic Literature and Individual Sages: Writing without Authors

1.
Why No Lives of Saints in Rabbinic Literature?

FROM THE DESCRIPTION OF THE DOCUMENTS THAT COMPRISE RABBINIC LITERA-
ture, we turn to the documents that we do not have at all or in due proportion to
the whole.[1] Specifically, we ask about documents of biography, sustained collections of sayings and stories about named sages, formed into compilations. These
are the documents we do not have in rabbinic literature, but that the other heir to

---

[1] This chapter summarizes the main points of this writer's *Why No Gospels in Talmudic Judaism* (Atlanta,
1988· Scholars Press for Brown Judaic Studies). An important discussion on the anonymity of rabbinic
documents and the role of sages in them is in Maccoby, pp. 1–2, ". . . hardly any of it is 'literary,' in
the sense of being the sustained composition of a single author, presenting an individual vision. It is
characteristic of this literature that it is presented as the work of an anonymous compiler, bringing
together the views of a large number of named rabbis, sometimes reinforcing each other, but more
often conflicting without rancour. The total impression is of a corporate literary effort, in which a
large number of experts, belonging to successive generations, is engaged in a common enterprise: the
clarification of Scripture and the application of it to everyday life. . . . The genre of the rabbinical
writings . . . is that of the compilation."

the Hebrew Scriptures of ancient Israel, Christianity, produced in abundance.[2] For, while in addition to attributed exegetical and legal sayings for Scripture and the Mishnah respectively, rabbinic literature comprises a vast volume of biographical compositions—sayings attributed to sages and stories told about them. Only two of these documents form completed compositions, and these are not devoted to individuals but to the collectivity of sages as a whole. They are Abot, the Fathers, for sayings alone, and Abot deRabbi Nathan, the Fathers According to Rabbi Nathan, for sayings and stories.

For the entire cadre of sages, we do not have a single biography devoted to an individual, or even the raw materials for a sustained and systematic biography. We do not possess a single document produced by a clearly identifiable individual author, a single coherent composite of any consequence at all that concerns itself with a named figure. The counterpart writings for Christianity, the Gospels, the letters of Paul, not to mention the huge collections of signed, personal, individual writings of church fathers, show us the documents we do not have in rabbinic literature. The theory of authorship accounts for that fact. A document to warrant recognition—thus to be accorded authority, to be written and copied, or memorized and handed on as tradition—had to attain the approval of the sages' consensus.

That meant every document in rabbinic literature emerged anonymously, under public sponsorship and authorship, stripped of all marks of individual, therefore idiosyncratic, origin. Personality and individuality stood for schism, and rabbinic literature in its very definition and character aims at the opposite, forming as it does the functional counterpart to the creeds and decisions of Church councils. Framed in mythic terms, the literature aimed to make this theological statement: sages stood in a chain of tradition from Sinai, and the price of inclusion was the

[2] I refer not to Gospels, since only concerning Jesus Christ do Christians write Gospels, and since none of "our sages of blessed memory" claimed to be the Messiah, son of David, we can hardly compare the literary genre Gospels with anything that pertains to the Judaic sages. But Christianity also produced in abundance sustained and systematic lives of saints, and at issue here is the failure of rabbinic compilers to set forth counterpart writings, even though they had in hand compositions serviceable for such documents. Hence I ask here about holy lives or biographies of sages. "Gospels" is probably to be reserved for lives of Jesus alone, contrary to the usage in my book cited just above. Whether we may ever use in a generic sense a word that comes to us from a particular theological tradition, e.g., "incarnation" for anthropomorphism, as in my *The Incarnation of God: The Character of Divinity in Formative Judaism* (Philadelphia, 1988: Fortress Press. Reprinted: Atlanta, 1992: Scholars Press for South Florida Studies in the History of Judaism), remains to be seen; some reviewers of the latter book posed that question. Since the word "Torah," meaning God's revelation, oral and written, to holy Israel, serves also with a small *t*, "torah," to mean "the governing rules," it did not seem to me that "Gospel" or "Incarnation" could be used only with capitals, meaning one specific Gospel or one specific Incarnation, the Christian one. The contrary view, however, has much to recommend it, and it is difficult to claim much is lost by moving from "Gospel" to "holy life" or "saint's biography." As is clear, the question "why no systematic biography of holy men?" can be asked with equal effect, even if we omit the more sensational formulation involving "gospel" with a small *g*. My thanks go to my editor, Professor Freedman, for raising this question in a most persuasive manner.

acceptance of the discipline of tradition—anonymous, reasoned argument to attain for a private view the public status of a consensus statement. The very definition of tradition that comes to expression in the character of rabbinic literature—God's revelation to Moses at Sinai received and handed on unimpaired and intact in a reliable process of instruction by masters to disciples—accounts for the public, anonymous character of rabbinic writing.

Not a line in the entire rabbinic literature even suggests that schismatic writing existed, even though named statements of individual authorities are preserved on every page of that literature. The point that is proven is simple. People disagreed within a permitted agendum, and the protocol of disagreement always began with the premise of concurrence on all that counted. That was, as we saw, the very goal of rabbinic dialectics: the rationality of dispute, the cogency of theology and of law as a whole. As every named saying we have examined has already shown us, dissenting views too found their properly labeled position in rabbinic literature, preserved in the name of the private person who registered dissent in accord with the rules governing the iron consensus of the collegium as a whole.

This characterization of rabbinic literature devoted to sages' sayings and exemplary deeds therefore turns first of all to the documents we do not have, that is to say, the stories that were told but never compiled into documents, or, in the comparative context, the unwritten biographies of saints of Judaism. For the compilers of the documents of rabbinic Judaism drew upon, and had in hand, a tripartite corpus of inherited materials awaiting composition into a final, closed document. First, the type of material, in various states and stages of completion, addressed the Mishnah or took up the principles of laws that the Mishnah had originally brought to articulation. These the framers of the Tosefta, the Yerushalmi, and the Bavli organized in accord with the order of those Mishnah tractates that they selected for sustained attention. Second, they had in hand received materials, again in various conditions, pertinent to Scripture, both as Scripture related to the Mishnah and also as Scripture laid forth its own narratives. These the framers of documents set forth as Scripture commentary. In this way, the penultimate and ultimate redactors of the various documents we examined in Parts Two and Three of this book laid out a systematic presentation of the two Torahs, the oral, represented by the Mishnah, and the written, represented by Scripture.

And, third, the framers of the various documents also had in hand materials focused on sages. These formed the raw material for two documents, neither of them organized around the lives and teachings of individual personalities; but the volume of such materials vastly outweighs the sole documentary loci that contain them. We shall examine such materials in two forms, first, compositions not formed into documents; second, those formed into tractate Abot and its talmud or systematic amplification, which is the Fathers According to Rabbi Nathan. The received forms of biographical sayings and stories are attested in various compilations, but, best of all, in the Bavli's pages. They were made up of compositions completed units of thought—and composites as well. Twin biographical principles define the poles around which they coalesce: either as strings of stories about great sages of the past or as collections of sayings and comments drawn together solely because the same name stands behind all the collected sayings. These can easily have been composed into biographies. In the context of Christianity and of Judaism, it is appropriate to call the biography of a holy man or woman, meant to convey the divine message, a "holy life." Hence the question raised here: why no biographies of saints in Judaism? The question is an appropriate one, because, as I shall show, there could have been. The final step—assembling available stories into a coherent narrative, with a beginning, middle, and end, for example—was not taken. And that omission forms an important fact in the characterization of rabbinic literature as a whole.

Restricting our attention to the Bavli alone suffices for the present purpose. There, we note, that document as a whole lays itself out as a commentary to the Mishnah. So the framers wished us to think that whatever they wanted to tell us would take the form of Mishnah commentary. But a second glance indicates that the Bavli is made up of enormous composites, themselves closed prior to inclusion in the Bavli. Some of these composites—around 35 percent to 40 percent of those in the Bavli—were selected and arranged along lines dictated by a logic other than that deriving from the requirements of Mishnah commentary. Accordingly, the decision that the framers of the Bavli reached was to adopt the two redactional principles inherited from the antecedent century or so and to reject the one already rejected by their predecessors, even while honoring it. They organized the Bavli around the Mishnah.

2.

COMPOSITIONS AND COMPOSITES FOCUSED UPON INDIVIDUAL SAGES

In the discourse that focuses upon the sage, e.g., a paragraph of thought, a story, things that a given authority said are strung together or tales about a given authority are told at some length. Whoever composed and preserved units of discourse on the Mishnah and on Scripture ultimately preserved in the two Talmuds did the same for the sage. What that fact means is simple. In the circles responsible for making up and writing down completed units of discourse, three distinct categories of interest defined the task: (1) exegesis of the Mishnah, (2) exegesis of Scripture, and (3) preservation and exegesis, in exactly the same reverential spirit, of the words and deeds of sages. Not only so, but the kind of analysis to which Mishnah and Scripture exegesis were subjected also applied to the exegesis of sage stories.

That fact may be shown in three ways. First, just as Scripture supplied proof texts, so deeds or statements of sages provided proof texts. Second, just as a verse of Scripture or an explicit statement of the Mishnah resolved a disputed point, so what a sage said or did might be introduced into discourse as ample proof for settling a dispute. And third, it follows that just as Scripture or the Mishnah laid down Torah, so what a sage did or said laid down Torah. In the dimensions of the applied and practical reason by which the law unfolded, the sage found a comfortable place in precisely the taxonomic categories defined, to begin with, by both the Mishnah and Scripture. Let us examine a few substantial examples of the sorts of sustained discourse in biographical materials turned out by circles of sages. What we shall see is an important fact. Just as these circles composed units of discourse about the meaning of a Mishnah passage, a larger theoretical problem of law, the sense of scriptural verse, and the sayings and doings of scriptural heroes seen as sages, so they did the same for living sages themselves.

In the simplest example we see that two discrete sayings of a sage are joined together. The principle of conglomeration, therefore, is solely the name of the sage at hand. One saying has to do with overcoming the impulse to do evil, and the other has to do with the classifications of sages' program of learning. What the two subjects have in common is slight. But to the framer of the passage, that fact meant nothing. For he thought that compositions joined by the same tradent and authority—the rabbis Levi and Simeon—should be made up.

B. BERAKHOT 4B.

XXIII.
  A. Said R. Levi bar Hama said R. Simeon b. Laqish,[3] "A person should always provoke his impulse to do good against his impulse to do evil,

  B. "as it is said, 'Provoke and do not sin' (Ps. 4:5).

  C. "If [the good impulse] wins, well and good. If not, let him take up Torah study,

  D. "as it is said, 'Commune with your own heart' (Ps. 4:5).

  E. "If [the good impulse] wins, well and good. If not, let him recite the Shema,

  F. "as it is said, 'upon your bed' (Ps. 4:5).

  G. "If [the good impulse] wins, well and good. If not, let him remember the day of death,

  H. "as it is said, 'And keep silent. Sela' (Ps. 4:5)."

  I. And R. Levi bar Hama said R. Simeon b. Laqish said, "What is the meaning of the verse of Scripture, 'And I will give you the tables of stone, the law and the commandment, which I have written, that you may teach them' (Exod. 24:12).

  J. "'The tables' [here] refers to the ten commandments.

  K. "'Torah' refers to Scripture.

---

[3] That is, the former cites the opinion of the latter, expressed in the repetition of the "said."

> L.   "'Commandment' refers to Mishnah.
>
> M.   "'Which I have written' refers to the Prophets and the Writings.
>
> N.   "'That you may teach them' refers to the Gemara.
>
> O.   "This teaches that all of them were given to Moses from Sinai."

The framer of the story at hand links A–H and I–O in a way unfamiliar to those accustomed to the principles of conglomeration in legal and biblical-exegetical compositions. In the former, a given problem or principle of law will tell us why one item is joined to some other. In the latter, a single verse of Scripture will account for the joining of two or more otherwise discrete units of thought. Here one passage, A–H, takes up Ps. 4:5; the other, I–O, Exod. 24:12. The point of the one statement hardly goes over the ground of the other. So the *sole* principle by which one item has joined the other is biographical: a record of what a sage said about topics that are, at best, contiguous, if related at all.

A second way of stringing together materials illustrative of the lives and teachings of sages is to join incidents involving a given authority or (as in the following case) two authorities believed to have stood in close relationship with one another, disciple and master, for instance. Often these stories go over the same ground in the same way. In the following, the two farewell stories make essentially the same point but in quite different language. What joins the stories is not only the shared theme but the fact that Eliezer is supposed to have studied with Yohanan b. Zakkai.

B. SANHEDRIN 68A.

> II. A.   Our rabbis have taught on Tannaite authority:
>
> B.   When R. Eliezer fell ill, his disciples came in to pay a call on him. They said to him, "Our master, teach us the ways of life, so that through them we may merit the world to come."
>
> C.   He said to them, "Be attentive to the honor owing to your fellows, keep your children from excessive reflection, and set them among the knees of disciples of sages, and when you pray, know before whom you stand, and on that account you will merit the life of the world to come."
>
> D.   And when R. Yohanan b. Zakkai fell ill, his disciples came in to pay a call on him. When he saw them, he began to cry. His disciples said to him, "Light of Israel! Pillar at the right hand! Mighty hammer! On what account are you crying?"
>
> E.   He said to them, "If I were going to be brought before a mortal king, who is here today and tomorrow gone to the grave, who, should he be angry with me, will not be angry forever, and, if he should imprison me, will not imprison me forever, and if he should put me to death, whose sentence of death is not for eternity, and whom I can appease with the right words or bribe with money, even so, I should weep.

F.   "But now that I am being brought before the King of kings of kings, the Holy One, blessed be he, who endures forever and ever, who, should he be angry with me, will be angry forever, and if he should imprison me, will imprison me forever, and if he should put me to death, whose sentence of death is for eternity, and whom I cannot appease with the right words or bribe with money,

G.   "and not only so, but before me are two paths, one to the Garden of Eden and the other to Gehenna, and I do not know by which path I shall be brought,

H.   "and should I not weep?"

I.   They said to him, "Our master, bless us."

J.   He said to them, "May it be God's will that the fear of Heaven be upon you as much as the fear of mortal man."

K.   His disciples said, "Just so much?"

L.   He said to them, "Would that it were that much. You should know that when a person commits a transgression, he says, 'I hope no man sees me.'"

M.   When he was dying, he said to them, "Clear out utensils from the house, because of the uncleanness [of the corpse, which I am about to impart when I die], and prepare a throne for Hezekiah king of Judah, who is coming."

The links between B–C and D–M are clear. First, we have stories about sages' farewells. Second, people took for granted, because of the lists of M. Abot 2:2ff., that Eliezer was a disciple of Yohanan b. Zakkai. Otherwise, it is difficult to explain the joining of the stories, since they scarcely make the same point, go over the same matters, or even share a common literary or rhetorical form or preference. But a framer of a composition of lives of saints, who is writing a tractate on how saints die, will have found this passage a powerful one indeed.

Yet another approach to the utilization of tales about sages was to join together stories on a given theme but told about different sages. A tractate or a chapter of a tractate on a given theme, for example, suffering and its reward, can have emerged from the sort of collection that follows. The importance of the next item is that the same kinds of stories about different sages are strung together to make a single point.

B. BERAKHOT 5B.

XXXI.   A.   R. Hiyya bar Abba became ill. R. Yohanan came to him. He said to him, "Are these sufferings precious to you?"

B.   He said to him, "I don't want them, I don't want their reward."

C.   He said to him, "Give me your hand."

D. He gave him his hand, and [Yohanan] raised him up [out of his sickness].

E. R. Yohanan became ill. R. Hanina came to him. He said to him, "Are these sufferings precious to you?"

F. He said to him, "I don't want them. I don't want their reward."

G. He said to him, "Give me your hand."

H. He gave him his hand and [Hanina] raised him up [out of his sickness].

I. Why so? R. Yohanan should have raised himself up?

J. They say, "A prisoner cannot get himself out of jail."

XXXII.   A. R. Eliezer became ill. R. Yohanan came to see him and found him lying in a dark room. [The dying man] uncovered his arm, and light fell [through the room]. [Yohanan] saw that R. Eliezer was weeping. He said to him, "Why are you crying? Is it because of the Torah that you did not learn sufficiently? We have learned: 'All the same are the ones who do much and do little, so long as each person will do it for the sake of heaven.'

B. "Is it because of insufficient income? Not everyone has the merit of seeing two tables [Torah and riches, as you have. You have been a master of Torah and also have enjoyed wealth].

C. "Is it because of children? Here is the bone of my tenth son [whom I buried, so it was no great loss not to have children, since you might have had to bury them]."

D. He said to him, "I am crying because of this beauty of mine which will be rotting in the ground."

E. He said to him, "For that it certainly is worth crying," and the two of them wept together.

F. He said to him, "Are these sufferings precious to you?"

G. He said to him, "I don't want them, I don't want their reward."

H. He said to him, "Give me your hand."

I. He gave him his hand, and [Yohanan] raised him up [out of his sickness].

XXXIII.   A. Four hundred barrels of wine turned sour on R. Huna. R. Judah, brother of R. Sala the Pious, and rabbis came to see him (and some say it was R. Ada bar Ahba and rabbis). They said to him, "The master should take a good look at his deeds."

B. He said to them, "And am I suspect in your eyes?"

C. They said to him, "And is the Holy One, blessed be he, suspect of inflicting a penalty without justice?"

D. He said to them, "Has anybody heard anything bad about me? Let him say it."

E. They said to him, "This is what we have heard: the master does not give to his hired hand [the latter's share of] vine twigs [which are his right]."

F. He said to them, "Does he leave me any! He steals all of them to begin with."

G. They said to him, "This is in line with what people say: 'Go steal from a thief but taste theft too!' [Simon: If you steal from a thief, you also have a taste of it.]"

H. He said to them, "I pledge that I'll give them to him."

I. Some say that the vinegar turned back into wine, and some say that the price of vinegar went up so he sold it off at the price of wine.

The foregoing composite makes the same point several times: "Not them, not their reward." Sufferings are precious, but sages are prepared to forego the benefits. The formally climactic entry at XXXIII makes the point that if bad things happen, the victim has deserved punishment. In joining these several stories about sages—two involving Yohanan, the third entirely separate—the compositor of the passage made his point by juxtaposing two like biographical snippets to a distinct one. Collections of stories about saints can have served quite naturally for this purpose when formed into tractates on pious virtues, expressing these virtues through strong and pictorial language such as is before us.

The foregoing sources have shown two important facts. First, a principle of composition in the sages' circles was derived from interest in the teachings associated with a given sage, as well as in tales and stories told about a sage or groups of sages. The first of the passages shows us the simplest composition of sayings, the latter, an equivalent conglomeration of related stories. Up to this point, therefore, the reader will readily concede that biographical materials on sages, as much as Mishnah exegesis and Scripture exegesis, came forth out of circles of sages. But I have yet to show that such materials attained sufficient volume and cogency from large-scale compilations—conglomerates so substantial as to sustain entire books.

3.

THE DOCUMENTS THAT RABBINIC LITERATURE OMITS

Had the framers of large-scale rabbinic compositions wished, they could readily have made up tractates devoted to diverse sayings of a given authority (or, tradent and authority). What follows to demonstrate the possibility are two enormous compositions, which together could have made up as much as half of a Talmud chapter in volume. If anyone had wanted to compose a chapter around rabbinical authorities' names, he is thus shown to have had the opportunity.

The first shows us a string of sayings not only in a single set of names but also on discrete subjects. We also see how such a string of sayings could form the focus of exactly the kind of critical analysis and secondary amplification to which any other talmudic passage would be subjected. So there could have been not only a Talmud based on the Mishnah and a Midrash compilation, comprising compositions based on Scripture, but also a life of a saint (a holy life?) based on a set of rabbis' sayings. Here is the talmud that could have served a collection of sayings of Yohanan in the name of Simeon b. Yohai.

B. BERAKHOT 7B-8A.

LIX. A. Said R. Yohanan in the name of R. Simeon b. Yohai, "From the day on which the Holy One, blessed be he, created the world, there was no man who called the Holy One, blessed be he, 'Lord,' until Abraham came along and called him Lord.

B. "For it is said, 'And he said, O Lord, God, whereby shall I know that I shall inherit it' (Gen. 15:8)."

C. Said Rab, "Daniel too was answered only on account of Abraham.

D. "For it is said, 'Now therefore, O our God, hearken to the prayer of your servant and to his supplications and cause your face to shine upon your sanctuary that is desolate, for the Lord's sake' (Dan. 9:17).

E. "'For your sake' is what he should have said, but the sense is, 'For the sake of Abraham, who called you Lord.'"

LX. A. And R. Yohanan said in the name of R. Simeon b. Yohai, "How do we know that people should not seek to appease someone when he is mad?

B. "As it is said, 'My face will go and then I will give you rest' (Exod. 33:14)."

LXI. A. And R. Yohanan said in the name of R. Simeon b. Yohai, "From the day on which the Holy One, blessed be he, created his world, there was no one who praised the Holy One, blessed be he, until Leah came along and praised him.

B. "For it is said, 'This time I will praise the Lord' (Gen. 29:35)."

C. As to Reuben, said R. Eleazar, "Leah said, 'See what is the difference [the name of Reuben yielding reu (see) and ben (between)] between my son and the son of my father-in-law.

D. "The son of my father-in-law, even knowingly, sold off his birth-

right, for it is written, 'And he sold his birthright to Jacob'
(Gen. 25:33).

E. "See what is written concerning him: 'And Esau hated Jacob'
(Gen. 27:41), and it is written, 'And he said, is he not rightly
named Jacob? for he has supplanted me these two times' (Gen.
27:36).

F. "My son, by contrast, even though Joseph forcibly took away
his birthright, as it is written, 'But for as much as he defiled his
father's couch, his birthright was given to the sons of Joseph'
(1 Chron. 5:1), did not become jealous of him, for it is written,
'And Reuben heard it and delivered him out of their hand'
(Gen. 37:21)."

G. As to the meaning of the name of Ruth, said R. Yohanan, "It
was because she had the merit that David would come forth
from her, who saturated (RWH) the Holy One, blessed be he,
with songs and praises."

H. How do we know that a person's name affects [his life]?

I. Said R. Eleazar, "It is in line with the verse of Scripture: 'Come,
behold the works of the Lord, who has made desolations in the
earth' (Ps. 46:9).

J. "Do not read 'desolations' but 'names' [which the same root
letters yield]." [The Hebrew letters that bear the vowels to indicate the sound for "desolations" may be given different vowels,
which yield the sound for "names."]

LXII. A. And R. Yohanan said in the name of R. Simeon b. Yohai,
"Bringing a child up badly is worse in a person's house than the
war of Gog and Magog.

B. "For it is said, 'A Psalm of David, when he fled from Absalom,
his son' (Ps. 3:1), after which it is written, 'Lord how many are
my adversaries become, many are they that rise up against me'
(Ps. 3:2).

C. "By contrast, in regard to the war of Gog and Magog it is written, 'Why are the nations in an uproar? And why do the peoples
mutter in vain?' (Ps. 2:1).

D. "But is it not written in that connection, 'How many have my
adversaries become.'

E. "'A Psalm of David, when he fled from Absalom, his son' (Ps.
3:1):

F. "'A Psalm of David'? It should be, 'A lamentation of David'!"

G. Said R. Simeon b. Abishalom, "The matter may be compared
to the case of a man against whom an outstanding bond was
issued. Before he had paid it, he was sad. After he had paid it,
he was glad.

H. "So too with David, when the Holy One had said to him, 'Behold, I will raise up evil against you out of your own house,' (2 Sam. 2:11), he was sad.

I. "He thought to himself, 'Perhaps it will be a slave or a bastard child, who will not have pity on me.'

J. "When he saw that it was Absalom, he was happy. On that account, he said a psalm."

LXIII. A. And R. Yohanan said in the name of R. Simeon b. Yohai, "It is permitted to contend with the wicked in this world,

B. "for it is said, 'Those who forsake the Torah praise the wicked, but those who keep the Torah contend with them' (Prov. 28:4)."

C. It has been taught on Tannaite authority along these same lines:

D. R. Dosetai bar Matun says, "It is permitted to contend with the wicked in this world, for it is said, 'Those who forsake the Torah praise the wicked, but those who keep the Torah contend with them' (Prov. 28:4).

E. "And if someone should whisper to you, 'But is it not written, "Do not contend with evildoers, nor be envious against those who work unrighteousness" (Ps. 37:1)?' say to him, 'Someone whose conscience bothers him thinks so.'

F. "In fact, 'Do not contend with evildoers' means, do not be like them; 'nor be envious against those who work unrighteousness' means, do not be like them.

G. "And so it is said, 'Let your heart not envy sinners, but fear the Lord all day' (Prov. 23:17)."

H. Is this the case? And lo, R. Isaac has said, "If you see a wicked person for whom the hour seems to shine, do not contend with him, for it is said, 'His ways prosper at all times' (Ps. 10:5).

I. "Not only so, but he wins in court, as it is said, 'Your judgments are far above, out of his sight' (Ps. 10:5).

J. "Not only so, but he overcomes his enemies, for it is said, 'As for all his enemies, he snorts at them' (Ps. 10:5)."

K. There is no contradiction. The one [Isaac] addresses one's own private matters [in which case one should not contend with the wicked], but the other speaks of matters having to do with heaven [in which case one should contend with them].

L. And if you wish, I shall propose that both parties speak of matters having to do with heaven. There is, nonetheless, no contradiction. The one [Isaac] speaks of a wicked person on whom the hour shines, the other of a wicked person on whom the hour does not shine.

M. And if you wish, I shall propose that both parties speak of a wicked person on whom the hour shines, and there still is no contradiction.

N. The one [Yohanan, who says the righteous may contend with the wicked] speaks of a completely righteous person, the other [Isaac] speaks of someone who is not completely righteous.

O. For R. Huna said, "What is the meaning of this verse of Scripture: 'Why do you look, when they deal treacherously, and hold your peace, when the wicked swallows up the man that is more righteous than he' (Hab. 1:13)?

P. "Now can a wicked person swallow up a righteous one?

Q. "And lo, it is written, 'The Lord will not leave him in his hand' (Ps. 37:33). And it is further written, 'No mischief shall befall the righteous' (Prov. 12:21).

R. "The fact therefore is that he may swallow up someone who is more righteous than he, but he cannot swallow up a completely righteous man."

S. And if you wish, I shall propose that when the hour shines for him, the situation is different.

LXIV. A. And R. Yohanan said in the name of R. Simeon b. Yohai, "Beneath anyone who establishes a regular place for praying do that person's enemies fall.

B. "For it is said, 'And I will appoint a place for my people Israel, and I will plant them, that they may dwell in their own place and be disquieted no more, neither shall the children of wickedness afflict them anymore as at the first' (2 Sam. 7:10)."

C. R. Huna pointed to a contradiction between two verses of Scripture: "It is written, 'To afflict them,' and elsewhere, 'To exterminate them' (1 Chron. 17:9).

D. "To begin with, merely to afflict them, but, at the end, to exterminate them."

LXV. A. And R. Yohanan said in the name of R. Simeon b. Yohai, "Greater is personal service to Torah than learning in Torah [so doing favors for a sage is of greater value than studying with him].

B. "For it is said, 'Here is Elisha, the son of Shaphat, who poured water on the hands of Elijah' (2 Kings 3:11).

C. "It is not said, 'who learned' but 'who poured water.'

D. "This teaches that greater is service to Torah than learning in Torah."

It is not difficult to pick up the main beams of the foregoing construction, since they are signified by Yohanan-Simeon sayings, LIX.A, LX.A, LXI.A, LXII.A, LXIII.A, LXIV.A, LXV.A—seven entries in line. The common theme is not prayer; no other topic is treated in a cogent way either. The sort of inner coherence to which any student of the Bavli is accustomed does not pass before us. Rather we have a collection of wise thoughts on diverse topics, more in the manner of

Proverbs than in the style of the great intellects behind the sustained reasoning in passages of the Bavli and much of the Yerushalmi as well. What is interesting is that at a later stage other pertinent materials have been inserted, for example, Rab's at LIX.C–E, and so on down. There is no reason to imagine that these sayings were made up in response to Yohanan-Simeon's statement. Quite to the contrary, framed in their own terms, the sayings were presumably tacked on at a point at which the large-scale construction of Yohanan-Simeon was worked over for a purpose beyond the one intended by the original compositor. For what he wanted to do he did, which is, compose a collection of Yohanan-Simeon sayings. If he hoped that his original collection would form part of a larger composition on Yohanan, he surely was disappointed. But even if he imagined that he would make up material for compositions of lives and sayings of saints, he could not have expected his little collection to end up where and how it did, as part of a quite different corpus of writing from one in which a given authority had his say or in which stories were told in some sort of sensible sequence about a particular sage. The type of large-scale composition, for which our imagined compositor did his work, in the end never came into being in the rabbinic canon.

In the following, still longer example I begin with the passage to which the entire composition, organized in the name of a tradent and a sage, is attached. At B. Berakhot 6B/1:1.XLI, we have a statement that a synagogue should have a regular quorum. Then the next passage, 1:1.XLII, makes the secondary point that a person should pray in a regular place—a reasonable amplification of the foregoing. That is, just as there should be a quorum routinely organized in a given location, so should an individual routinely attach himself to a given quorum. This statement is given by Helbo in Huna's name. What follows is a sizable set of sayings by Helbo in Huna's name, all of them on the general theme of prayer but none of them on the specific point at hand. Still more interesting, just as in the foregoing, the passage as a whole was composed so that the Helbo-Huna materials themselves are expanded and enriched with secondary accretions. For instance, at XLIII the base materials are given glosses of a variety of types. All in all, we see what we may call a little tractate in the making. But, as we shall hardly have to repeat, no one in the end created a genre of rabbinic literature to accommodate the vast collections of available compositions on sages' sayings and doings.

B. BERAKHOT 6B.

XLI.   A.   Said R. Yohanan, "When the Holy One, blessed be he, comes to a synagogue and does not find ten present, he forthwith becomes angry.

       B.   "For it is said, 'Why when I came was there no one there? When I called, there was no answer' (Isa. 50:2)."

XLII. A.   Said R. Helbo said R. Huna, "For whoever arranges a regular place for praying, the God of Abraham is a help, and when he dies, they say for him, 'Woe for the humble man, woe for the pious man, one of the disciples of Abraham, our father.'

B. "And how do we know in the case of Abraham, our father, that he arranged a regular place for praying?

C. "For it is written, 'And Abraham got up early in the morning in the place where he had stood' (Gen. 19:27).

D. "'Standing' refers only to praying, for it is said, 'Then Phinehas stood up and prayed' (Ps. 106:30)."

E. Said R. Helbo said R. Huna, "He who leaves the synagogue should not take large steps."

F. Said Abayye, "That statement applies only when one leaves, but when he enters, it is a religious duty to run [to the synagogue].

G. "For it is said, 'Let us run to know the Lord' (Hos. 6:3)."

H. Said R. Zira, "When in the beginning I saw rabbis running to the lesson on the Sabbath, I thought that the rabbis were profaning the Sabbath. But now that I have heard what R. Tanhum said R. Joshua b. Levi said,

I. "namely, 'A person should always run to take up a matter of law, and even on the Sabbath, as it is said, "They shall walk after the Lord who shall roar like a lion [for he shall roar, and the children shall come hurrying]" (Hos. 11:10),'

J. "I too run."

XLIII. A. Said R. Zira, "The reward for attending the lesson is on account of running [to hear the lesson, not necessarily on account of what one has learned.]"

B. Said Abayye, "The reward for attending the periodic public assembly [of rabbis] is on account of the crowding together."

C. Said Raba [to the contrary], "The reward for repeating what one has heard is in reasoning about it."

D. Said R. Papa, "The reward for attending a house of mourning is on account of one's preserving silence there."

E. Said Mar Zutra, "The reward for observing a fast day lies in the acts of charity one performs on that day."

F. Said R. Sheshet, "The reward for delivering a eulogy lies in raising the voice."

G. Said R. Ashi, "The reward for attending a wedding lies in the words [of compliment paid to the bride and groom]."

XLIV. A. Said R. Huna, "Whoever prays behind the synagogue is called wicked,

B. "as it is said, 'The wicked walk round about' (Ps. 12:9)."

C. Said Abayye, "That statement applies only in the case of one who does not turn his face toward the synagogue, but if he turns his face toward the synagogue, we have no objection."

D. There was a certain man who would say his prayers behind the synagogue and did not turn his face toward the synagogue. Elijah came by and saw him. He appeared to him in the guise of a Tai Arab.

E. He said to him, "Are you now standing with your back toward your master?" He drew his sword and killed him.

F. One of the rabbis asked R. Bibi bar Abayye, and some say, R. Bibi asked R. Nahman bar Isaac, "What is the meaning of the verse, 'When vileness is exalted among the sons of men' (Ps. 12:9)?"

G. He said to him, "This refers to matters that are exalted, which people treat with contempt."

H. R. Yohanan and R. Eleazar both say, "When a person falls into need of the help of other people, his face changes color like the kerum-bird, for it is said, 'As the kerum was to be reviled among the sons of men' (Ps. 12:9)."

I. What is the meaning of "kerum-bird"?

J. When R. Dimi came, he said, "There is a certain bird among the coast towns, called the kerum. When the sun shines, it turns many colors."

K. R. Ammi and R. Assi both say, "[When a person turns to others for support], it is as if he is judged to suffer the penalties of both fire and water.

L. "For it is said, 'When you caused men to ride over our heads, we went through fire and through water' (Ps. 66:12)."

XLV. A. And R. Helbo said R. Huna said, "A person should always be attentive at the afternoon prayer.

B. "For lo, Elijah was answered only at the afternoon prayer.

C. "For it is said, 'And it came to pass at the time of the offering of the late afternoon offering, that Elijah the prophet came near and said, "Hear me, O Lord, hear me"' (1 Kings 18:36–37)."

D. "Hear me" so fire will come down from heaven.

E. "Hear me" that people not say it is merely witchcraft.

F. R. Yohanan said, "[A person should also be attentive about] the evening prayer.

G. "For it is said, 'Let my prayer be set forth as incense before you, the lifting up of my hands as the evening sacrifice' (Ps. 141:2)."

H. R. Nahman bar Isaac said, "[A person should also be attentive about] the morning prayer.

I.   "For it is said, 'O Lord, in the morning you shall hear my voice, in the morning I shall order my prayer to you, and will look forward' (Ps. 5:4)."

XLVI.   A.   And R. Helbo said R. Huna said, "Whoever enjoys a marriage banquet and does not felicitate the bridal couple violates five 'voices.'

B.   "For it is said, 'The voice of joy and the voice of gladness, the voice of the bridegroom and the voice of the bride, the voice of those who say, "Give thanks to the Lord of hosts"' (Jer. 33:11)."

C.   And if he does felicitate the couple, what reward does he get?

D.   Said R. Joshua b. Levi, "He acquires the merit of the Torah, which was handed down with five voices.

E.   "For it is said, 'And it came to pass on the third day, when it was morning, that there were voices [thus two], and lightnings, and a thick cloud upon the mount, and the voice of a horn, and when the voice of the horn waxed louder, Moses spoke and God answered him by a voice' (Exod. 19:16, 19) [thus five voices in all]."

F.   Is it so [that there were only five voices]?

G.   And lo, it is written, "And all the people saw the voices" (Exod. 20:15). [So this would make seven voices.]

H.   These voices came before the giving of the Torah [and do not count].

I.   R. Abbahu said, "It is as if the one [who felicitated the bridal couple] offered a thanksgiving offering.

J.   "For it is said, 'Even of them that bring thanksgiving offerings into the house of the Lord' (Jer. 33:11)."

K.   R. Nahman bar Isaac said, "It is as if he rebuilt one of the ruins of Jerusalem.

L.   "That is because it is said, 'For I will cause the captivity of the land to return as at the first, says the Lord' (Jer. 33:11)."

XLVII.   A.   And R. Helbo said R. Huna said, "The words of any person in whom is fear of heaven are heard.

B.   "For it is said, 'The end of the matter, all having been heard: fear God and keep his commandments, since this is the whole man' (Qoh. 12:13)."

C.   What is the meaning of the phrase, "For this is the whole man" (Qoh. 12:13)?

D.   Said R. Eleazar, "Said the Holy One, blessed be he, 'The entire world has been created only on account of this one.'"

E.   R. Abba bar Kahana said, "This one is worth the whole world."

F.   Simeon b. Zoma says, "The entire world was created only to accompany this one."

XLVIII.   A.   And R. Helbo said R. Huna said, "Whoever knows that his fellow regularly greets him should greet the other first.

B.   "For it is said, 'Seek peace and pursue it' (Ps. 34:15).

C.   "If he greeted him and the other did not reply, the latter is called a thief.

D.   "For it is said, 'It is you who have eaten up the vineyard, the spoil of the poor is in your houses' (Isa. 3:14)."

What we noted in connection with the Yohanan-Simeon collection needs no re-statement here. The scope and dimensions of the passage prove impressive. Again we must wonder for what sort of composition the framer of the Helbo-Huna collection planned his writing. Whatever it was, it hardly fit the ultimate destination of his work.

4.

THE SAGE AND THE TORAH
IN RABBINIC LITERATURE

One reason for not forming biographies of saints could have been that the sage did not stand at the level of the Torah, while the Mishnah and Scripture constituted the Torah. Hence forming documents around the lives of the sage, as much as around the amplification of Scripture and the Mishnah, could have made no sense. But the opposite is the fact. The sage stood at the same level of authority as did the Torah, on the one side, and the Mishnah, on the other. Therefore the failure to compose biographies of saints alongside Midrash compilations and Mishnah exegesis is not to be explained away as a by-product of the conception of revelation through words but not through persons that is imputed to the Judaism of the dual Torah. Quite to the contrary, God reveals the Torah not only through words handed down from Sinai in the form of the Torah, written and oral, but also through the lives and deeds of saints, that is, sages. Reference to the discussion of the Torah in Chapter 2 will suffice to make the simple point that the same modes of exegetical inquiry pertaining to the Mishnah and Scripture apply without variation to statements made by rabbis of the contemporary period themselves.

We turn to the way in which the rabbis of the Yerushalmi proposed to resolve differences of opinion. Precisely in the same way in which talmudic rabbis settled disputes in the Mishnah and so attained a consensus about the law of the Mishnah, they handled disputes among themselves. The importance of that fact for our argument again is simple. The rabbis represented in the Yerushalmi treated their own contemporaries exactly as they treated the then-ancient authorities of the Mishnah. In their minds the status accorded to the Mishnah, as a derivative of the Torah, applied equally to sages' teachings. In the following instance we see how the same discourse attached to (1) a Mishnah rule is assigned as well to one in (2) the Tosefta and, at the end, to differences among (3) the Yerushalmi's authorities.

YERUSHALMI KETUBOT (MISHNAH TRACTATE KETUBOT AS SET FORTH BY THE TALMUD OF THE LAND OF ISRAEL) 5

1.VI. A. R. Jacob bar Aha, R. Alexa in the name of Hezekiah: "The law accords with the view of R. Eleazar b. Azariah, who stated, If she was widowed or divorced at the stage of betrothal, the virgin collects only two hundred zuz and the widow, a maneh. If she was widowed or divorced at the stage of a consummated marriage, she collects the full amount [M. Ket. 5:1E,D]."

   B. R. Hananiah said, "The law accords with the view of R. Eleazar b. Azariah."

   C. Said Abayye, "They said to R. Hananiah, 'Go and shout [outside whatever opinion you like.' But] R. Jonah, R. Zeira in the name of R. Jonathan said, 'The law accords with the view of R. Eleazar b. Azariah.' [Yet] R. Yosa bar Zeira in the name of R. Jonathan said, 'The law does not accord with the view of R. Eleazar b. Azariah.' [So we do not in fact know the decision.]"

   D. Said R. Yosé, "We had a mnemonic: Hezekiah and R. Jonathan both say one thing."

   E. For it has been taught:

   F. He whose son went abroad, and whom they told, "Your son has died,"

   G. and who went and wrote over all his property to someone else as a gift,

   H. and whom they afterward informed that his son was yet alive—

   I. his deed of gift remains valid.

   J. R. Simeon b. Menassia says, "His deed of gift is not valid, for if he had known that his son was alive, he would never have made such a gift" [T. Ket. 4:14E–H].

   K. Now R. Jacob bar Aha said, "The law is in accord with the view of R. Eleazar b. Azariah, and the opinion of R. Eleazar b. Azariah is the same in essence as that of R. Simeon b. Menassia."

   L. Now R. Yannai said to R. Hananiah, "Go and shout [outside whatever you want].

   M. "But, said R. Yosé bar Zeira in the name of R. Jonathan, 'The law is not in accord with R. Eleazar b. Azariah.'"

> N.   But in fact the case was to be decided in accord with the view of
>   R. Eleazar b. Azariah.

What is important here is that the Talmud makes no distinction whatever when
deciding the law of disputes (1) in the Mishnah, (2) in the Tosefta, and (3) among
talmudic rabbis. The same already-formed colloquy applied at the outset to the
Mishnah's dispute is then held equally applicable to the Tosefta's. The process of
thought is the main thing, without regard to the document to which the process
applies. Scripture, the Mishnah, the sage—the three spoke with equal authority.
True, one had to come into alignment with the other, the Mishnah with Scripture,
the sage with the Mishnah. But it was not the case that one component of the
Torah, of God's word to Israel, stood within the sacred circle, another beyond.
Interpretation and what was interpreted, exegesis and text, belonged together. The
sage, or rabbi, constitutes the third component in a tripartite canon of the Torah,
because, while Scripture and the Mishnah govern what the sage knows, in the
Yerushalmi as in the Bavli it is the sage who authoritatively speaks about them.
What sages were willing to do to the Mishnah in the Yerushalmi and Bavli is
precisely what they were prepared to do to Scripture—impose upon it their own
judgment of its meaning.

The sage speaks with authority about the Mishnah and the Scripture. As much
as those documents of the Torah, the sage too, therefore, has authority deriving
from revelation. He himself may participate in the process of revelation. There is
no material difference. Since that is so, the sage's book, whether the Yerushalmi
or the Bavli to the Mishnah or Midrash to Scripture, belongs to the Torah, that is,
is revealed by God. It also forms part of the Torah, a fully canonical document.
The reason, then, is that the sage is like Moses, "our rabbi," who received torah
and wrote the Torah. So while the canon of the Torah was in three parts, two
verbal, one incarnate—Scripture, Mishnah, sage—the sage, in saying what the
other parts meant and in embodying that meaning in his life and thought, took
primacy of place. If no document organized itself around sayings and stories of
sages, it was because that was superfluous. Why so? Because all documents, equally,
whether Scripture, whether Mishnah, whether Yerushalmi, gave full and complete
expression of deeds and deliberations of sages, beginning, after all, with Moses,
our rabbi.

5.

INDIVIDUALITY AND CONSENSUS:
NAMED AUTHORS VS. AUTHORSHIPS

No document in rabbinic literature is signed by a named author or is so labeled
(except in a few instances long after the fact, e.g., Judah the Patriarch wrote the

Mishnah) as to represent the opinion of a lone individual. In their intrinsic traits of uniform discourse all documents speak out of the single, undifferentiated voice of Sinai, and each makes a statement of the Torah of Sinai and within that Torah. That anonymity, indicative for theological reasons, comes to expression in the highly formalized rhetoric of the canonical writings, which denies the possibility of the individuation not only of the writings themselves, but also of the sayings attributed to authorities in those writings.

Books such as the Mishnah, Sifré to Deuteronomy, Genesis Rabbah, or the Bavli, which after formulation were accepted as part of the canon of Judaism, that is, of "the one whole Torah of Moses our rabbi revealed by God at Sinai," do not contain answers to questions of definition that commonly receive answers within the pages of a given book. Such authors as (the school of) Matthew or Luke, Josephus, even the writers of Ezra-Nehemiah, will have found such a policy surprising. And while Socrates did not write, Plato and Aristotle did—and they signed their own names (or did the equivalent in context). In antiquity books or other important writings, e.g., letters and treatises, ordinarily, though not always, bore the name of the author or at least an attribution, e.g., Aristotle's or Paul's name, or the attribution to Enoch or Baruch or Luke. For no document in the canon of Judaism produced in late antiquity, by contrast, is there a named author internal to the document. No document in that canon contains within itself a statement of a clear-cut date of composition, a defined place or circumstance in which a book is written. There is none of the usual indicators by which we define the authorship, therefore the context and the circumstance, of a book.

The purpose of the sages who in the aggregate created the canonical writings of the Judaism of the dual Torah is served by not specifying differentiating traits such as time, place, and identity of the author or the authorship. The Judaic equivalent of the Biblical canon ("the Old Testament and the New Testament") is "the one whole Torah of Moses, our rabbi," and that "one, whole Torah" presents single books as undifferentiated episodes in a timeless, ahistorical setting: Torah revealed to Moses by God at Mount Sinai, but written down long afterward. Received in a canonical process of transmission under the auspices of a religious system, any canonical writing, by definition, enjoys authority and status within that canon and system. Hence it is deemed to speak for a community and to represent, and contribute to, the consensus of that community. Without a named author, a canonical writing may be represented, on the surface, as the statement of a consensus. That consensus derives not from an identifiable writer or even school but from the anonymous authorities behind the document as we have it.

How do we know that a document has been so composed as to speak not for an author but for a consensus or authorship? We have to ask whether this writing exhibits a cogent character and shows conformity to laws and regularities, and therefore derives from a considered set of decisions of a rhetorical, logical, and topical order. If it does, then, as a matter of definition, it derives from an authorship, a collectivity that stands behind the exhibited consensus in this particular writing. Accordingly, if we can find regularities of rhetoric, logic, and topical program, we may fairly claim to discern the consequences of rules people—an author-ship—have made, decisions they have reached, concerning the character of this writing of theirs: its structure, organization, proposition, cogent statement. If we find no regularities and indications of an orderly program, then this writing is different from one that speaks in behalf of people who have made rules or adopted them for the inclusion of fresh ideas of their own. It belongs in a classification not of a composition but of a scrapbook, not of a collage, which uses fixed materials in a fresh way, let alone of a sustained statement of a single system, but of a mish-mash of this and that that fell together we know not how.

A consensus of an entire community, the community of Judaism, reaches its full human realization in the sage. In that context, for reasons that await analysis, writing down of that consensus will not permit individual traits of rhetoric to differentiate writer from writer or writing from writing. The individual obliterates the marks of individuality in serving the holy people by writing a work that will become part of the Torah, and stories about individuals will serve, in that context, only so far as they exemplify and realize traits characteristic of all Torah-sages. That is why Christianity produced Gospels about a unique individual, and lives of saints later on, and that also explains why the Gospels have named authors. It also ac-counts for why the Judaism of the dual Torah, while valuing exemplary stories about sages, did not make provision for the counterpart, about Aqiba, of Mishnah (and therefore also Yerushalmi or Bavli) tractates, or, about Eliezer, of Midrash compilations either. While the raw materials in hand, inclusive of stories about wonder-working by sages and also stories about incidents in the lives of sages, could have generated biographies of saints or lives of saints, no one compiled the stories into biographies. It was a literary category that was excluded by the funda-mental and indicative traits of the system as a whole.

XXIII

TRACTATE ABOT (THE FATHERS)

1.

IDENTIFYING THE DOCUMENT

TRACTATE ABOT IS MADE UP OF FIVE CHAPTERS OF WISDOM-SAYINGS, NEITHER LEGAL nor exegetical in character, but mainly a handbook of wise sayings for disciples of sages, especially those involved in administration of the law.[1] These sayings, miscellaneous in character, are assigned to named authorities. The rhetoric of the Fathers is dictated by aphoristic style, producing wise sayings presented as a list.

[1] For further reading and bibliography on the topic of this chapter, see the following:

Bowker, pp. 87f.

Judah Goldin, "Avot," *Encyclopaedia Judaica* 3:983–84: unique among Mishnah treatises, lacking law; provides credentials of sages in chain of tradition; sages are given sayings: "these sayings reveal the convictions which shaped the Pharisaic and the early dominant tannaitic schools." The fifth chapter may have been part of the original core. The work is recited in the synagogue.

M. Bialik Lerner, "The Tractate Avot" (name, contents and structure; literary characteristics; Perek Kinyan Tora, the textual criticism of tractate Avot [by S. Sharvit]), in Safrai, *Literature of the Sages*, pp. 263–82.

Maccoby, pp. 31, 39, 40, 125 (Abot restricts itself to ethic surrounding the rabbinic emphasis on the religious duty of study and education; Abot is unique in that it is a treatise on education

The topic, above all, derives from the realm of wisdom: right conduct with God, society, self. The logic of cogent discourse derives from the notion that a list of sages constitutes a principle of coherent composition, and the diverse sayings fit together within the sustaining logic of a list of authorities of a given classification. The list holds together because everything on it is part of a chain of formulation and transmission—tradition—beginning with Moses on Sinai. So one sentence joins the next because all the sentences enjoy the same status, that imparted by the Torah. That logic deriving from authority makes it possible for the audience of the document to see relationships of order, proportion, and sustained discourse, where we see merely a sequence of essentially discrete sayings. The rhetorical device rests upon the same principle of cogent discourse: listing authorities suffices as a principle of rhetorical composition—and persuasion. The topical program—with its recurrent emphasis on Torah study and the social and intellectual and personal virtues required for Torah study—is equally cogent with the logical and rhetorical decisions made by the authorship of the whole.

Always published along with the Mishnah but autonomous of that document in all differentiating formal and programmatic attributes, the compilation cites authorities of the generation generally assumed to have flourished after the closure of the Mishnah and hence may be situated at ca. 250 C.E.—a mere guess. The Mishnah's rhetorical program exercised no influence whatsoever on the formulation of tractate Abot. The mnemonic patterns characteristic of the Mishnah are not to be found. The topical division and organization of the Mishnah tractates one by one and as a set play no role. Tractate Abot therefore bears no formal, or substantive, relationship to the Mishnah. Its rhetoric, logic of coherent discourse, and topic mark the document as utterly anomalous in rabbinic literature; it has no parallel.

But its proposition and message form the keystone and centerpiece of that literature, which explains the inclusion, in this chapter, of the entire text of the tractate. The document serves as the Mishnah's first and most important documentary apologetic, stating in abstract and general terms the ideals for the virtuous life that are set forth by the Mishnah's sages and animate its laws. Its presentation of sayings of sages extending from Sinai to figures named in the Mishnah itself links the Mishnah to Sinai. The link consists of the chain of tradition handed on through the chain of sages itself. It follows that because of the authorities cited in

---

which not only enjoins study and teaching as a feature of the religious life, but seeks to isolate the moral and spiritual characteristics necessary for good teaching and good studying. Selections: pp. 124–26.

Stemberger-Strack, pp. 120–21, 137 (bibliography).

This writer's commentary is *Torah from Our Sages: Pirke Avot. A New American Translation and Explanation.* Chappaqua, NY, 1983: Rossel/Behrman House. Note also the importance of tractate Abot in defining the conception of the Torah, spelled out in *The Foundations of Judaism. Method, Teleology, Doctrine.* Philadelphia, 1983–85: Fortress Press. I–III. III. *Torah: From Scroll to Symbol in Formative Judaism.* Second printing: Atlanta, 1988: Scholars Press for Brown Judaic Studies.

its pages, the Mishnah constitutes part of the Torah of Sinai, for by the evidence of the chain of tradition, the Mishnah too forms a statement of revelation, that is, "Torah revealed to Moses at Sinai." This is expressed in the opening sentence of tractate Abot:

> 1:1. Moses received the Torah at Sinai and handed it on to Joshua, Joshua to elders, and elders to prophets. And prophets handed it on to the men of the great assembly. They said three things: Be prudent in judgment. Raise up many disciples. Make a fence for the Torah.

The verbs "receive" and "hand on" in Hebrew yield the words *qabbalah,* "tradition," and *masoret,* also "tradition."

The theological proposition that validates the Mishnah is that the Torah is a matter of tradition. The tradition goes from master to disciple, Moses to Joshua. And, further, those listed later on the same list include authorities of the Mishnah itself. That fact forms an implicit claim that (1) part of the Torah was, and is, orally formulated and orally transmitted, and (2) the Mishnah's authorities stand in the tradition of Sinai, so that (3) the Mishnah too forms part of the Torah of Sinai.

This position is different from that taken by pseudepigraphic writers, who imitate the style of Scripture or who claim to speak within the same gift of revelation as Moses. It is one thing to say one's holy book is Scripture because it is like Scripture, or to claim that the author of the holy book has a revelation independent of that of Moses. These two positions concede to the Torah of Moses priority over their own holy books. The Mishnah's first apologists make no such concession when they allege that the Mishnah is part of the Torah of Moses. They appeal to the highest possible authority in the Israelite framework, claiming the most one can claim in behalf of the book which, in fact, contains the names of men who lived fifty years before the apologists themselves. The sages' apologia for the Mishnah, therefore, rests upon the persons of the sages themselves: incarnations of the Torah of Sinai in the here-and-now.

2.

TRANSLATIONS INTO ENGLISH

Among the innumerable translations into English are the following: C. Taylor, *Sayings of the Jewish Fathers* (Cambridge, 1877) and J. Goldin, *The Living Talmud. The Wisdom of the Fathers* (New York, 1957). This writer's translation is *Torah from Our Sages: Pirke Avot. A New American Translation and Explanation.* Chappaqua, NY, 1983: Rossel/Behrman House.

3.

RHETORIC

A catalog of the forms of the Fathers produces only two forms, name + attributive ("says") + apophthegm; and the list. The document as a whole is formally simple and repetitive, which is one striking way of producing a uniform and cogent message. There is only a single form: a list of names, made up of attributions (named authority) + the attributive "says" + a wise saying that is attributed. While the authorship of the Fathers sometimes amplifies a saying, e.g., with a secondary expansion, on the one side, or a scriptural proof text, on the other, in the main it shows a clear preference for an unadorned presentation of wise sayings joined to named authorities by the connective *says*. A random sample of three items makes this point clear:

> 1:1.   Moses received the Torah at Sinai and handed it on to Joshua, Joshua to elders, and elders to prophets. And prophets handed it on to the men of the great assembly. They said three things: Be prudent in judgment. Raise up many disciples. Make a fence for the Torah.
> 3:1A.   Aqabiah b. Mehallalel says, "Reflect upon three things and you will not fall into the clutches of transgression: Know (1) from whence you come, (2) whither you are going, and (3) before whom you are going to have to give a full account of yourself.
> 3:1B.   "From whence do you come? From a putrid drop. Whither are you going? To a place of dust, worms, and maggots.
> 3:1C.   "And before whom are you going to give a full account of yourself? Before the King of kings of kings, the Holy One, blessed be he."
> 4:4B.   R. Yohanan b. Beroqa says, "Whoever secretly treats the Name of Heaven as profane publicly pays the price. All the same are the one who does so inadvertently and the one who does so deliberately, when it comes to treating the name of Heaven as profane."
> 4:5A.   R. Ishmael, his son, says, "He who learns so as to teach—they give him a chance to learn and to teach. He who learns so as to carry out his teachings—they give him a chance to learn, to teach, to keep, and to do."

We see a single pattern. The opening defines the paradigm for the whole. Once we pass the introductory remark, we have *they said* plus *three things*. That pattern then governs Chapter One of the tractate; the pattern of Chapter Two is somewhat varied, since it provides names + connective + a sizable catalog of "things." Chapter Two (not cited) has a secondary colloquy, in which a master tells the disciples to go out and find the answer to a riddle, which they do, in a highly formalized construction. But the colloquy in no way corresponds to a narrative; there is scarcely a narrative component in all of the Fathers. Chapter Three presents us with a fine, if not common, instance of a secondary expansion, with 3:1A worked out by 3:1B–C. But most of the sayings are deprived even of that much amplification. The naked form is at 4:4B, and so on.

The only trait that intersects with the rhetorical protocol of the Mishnah comes in Chapter Five, which consists of a list of items of a single classification, e.g.,

> 5:5.   Ten wonders were done for our fathers in the Temple: (1) A woman never miscarried on account of the stench of the meat of Holy Things. (2) And the meat of the Holy Things never turned rotten. (3) A fly never made an appearance in the slaughterhouse. (4) A high priest never suffered a nocturnal emission on the eve of the Day of Atonement.

The list, which proceeds through ten items and is given in full below, collects information of a single classification. I see no point that the collection, on its own, proposes to establish. There is no hierarchization, for example, nor do the diverse items on the list make a point all together that none makes by itself. The list of Chapter Five accords with a different principle of conglomeration and composition. The point of difference is only that what is listed in the earlier chapters is names of authorities; these by themselves make no point, beyond Chapter One's chain of tradition. To the names, then, as a secondary matter, wise sayings are affixed, but these in the aggregate make no further point beyond themselves any more than do the collected items in the list of Chapter Five. What is listed in the final chapter is a set of items—that is, we move from the list of attributions, which makes no point through the list itself, to the list of items that bear a trait in common.

4.
LOGIC OF COHERENT DISCOURSE

The document in the main is just a collection of sayings. Chapters Three to Five form a mere scrapbook, since the names of the sages are random, and what is attributed, freestanding. So we cannot claim that those chapters reveal a logic of coherent discourse at all. Chapters One and Two do form coherent fixed associative lists. The other three chapters are arranged in accord with no discernible pattern.

5.
TOPICAL PROGRAM

Unlike Mishnah tractates, tractate Abot deals with no single topic, and, it follows, the document also contains no proposition that is argued in detail. But the first chapter does set forth a proposition, which is to be discerned not from what is said but from the chain of names that is set out in that chapter. Specifically, the list of names and the way in which they are arranged contains the claim that the two great pillars of the Mishnah—the patriarch of the Jewish community in the Land of Israel, that is, Judah the Patriarch (Hebrew: *nasi*), sponsor of the document and recognized by the Roman government as ruler of the Jewish ethnic group in the country, and the sages, who studied and where relevant applied the laws of the Mishnah—stand equally in the chain of tradition backward to Sinai. This union of the patriarch and the sages forms the document's proposition concerning the sponsorship of the Mishnah and the divine authority that is accorded to its sages.

In Chapter One's list of names there is a clear logic of fixed association in play. The names of the listed sages form a coherent pattern. What is attributed to the sages exhibits a certain topical coherence but in substance is random and episodic. Major authorities of the Mishnah stand in a chain of tradition to Sinai; hence, the Mishnah contains the Torah of Sinai. The order of the names is therefore deliberate and unites what is attributed, though the sentences themselves bear slight connections among themselves:

1:2.   Simeon the Righteous was one of the last survivors of the great assembly. He would say: "On three things does the world stand: On the Torah, and on the Temple service, and on deeds of loving-kindness."

1:3.   Antigonus of Sokho received [the Torah] from Simeon the Righteous. He would say: "Do not be like servants who serve the master on condition of receiving a reward, but [be] like servants who serve the master not on condition of receiving a reward. And let the fear of Heaven be upon you."

1:4.   Yosé ben Yoezer of Zeredah and Yosé ben Yohanan of Jerusalem received [the Torah] from them. Yosé ben Yoezer says: "Let your house be a gathering place for sages. And wallow in the dust of their feet, and drink in their words with gusto."

1:5.   Yosé ben Yohanan of Jerusalem says: "Let your house be open wide. And seat the poor at your table ["make the poor members of your household"]. And don't talk too much with women." (He referred to a man's wife, all the more so is the rule to be applied to the wife of one's fellow. In this regard did sages say: "So long as a man talks too much with a woman, he brings trouble on himself, wastes time better spent on studying the Torah, and ends up an heir of Gehenna.")

1:6.   Joshua ben Perahyah and Nittai the Arbelite received [the Torah] from them. Joshua ben Perahyah says: "Set up a master for yourself. And get yourself a companion-disciple. And give everybody the benefit of the doubt."

1:7.   Nittai the Arbelite says: "Keep away from a bad neighbor. And don't get involved with a bad person. And don't give up hope of retribution."

1:8A.   Judah ben Tabbai and Simeon ben Shetah received [the Torah] from them.

1:8B.   Judah ben Tabbai says: "Don't make yourself like one of those who advocate before judges [while you yourself are judging a case]. And when the litigants stand before you, regard them as guilty. But when they leave you, regard them as acquitted (when they have accepted your judgment)."

1:9.   Simeon ben Shetah says: "Examine the witnesses with great care. And watch what you say, lest they learn from what you say how to lie."

1:10.   Shemaiah and Avtalyon received [the Torah] from them. Shemaiah says: "Love work. Hate authority. Don't get friendly with the government."

1:11.   Avtalyon says: "Sages, watch what you say, lest you become liable to the punishment of exile, and go into exile to a place of bad water, and disciples who follow you drink bad water and die, and the name of Heaven be thereby profaned."

1:12.   Hillel and Shammai received [the Torah] from them. Hillel says: "Be disciples of Aaron, loving peace and pursuing grace, loving people and drawing them near to the Torah."

1:13A.   He would say [in Aramaic]: "A name made great is a name destroyed, and one who does not add, subtracts."

1:13B.   And who does not learn is liable to death. And the one who uses the crown, passes away.

1:14.   He would say: "If I am not for myself, who is for me? And when I am for myself, what am I? And if not now, when?"

1:15.   Shammai says: "Make your learning of the Torah a fixed obligation. Say little and do much. Greet everybody cheerfully."

1:16.   Rabban Gamaliel says: "Set up a master for yourself. Avoid doubt. Don't tithe by too much guesswork."

1:17.   Simeon his son says: "All my life I grew up among the sages, and I found nothing better for a person [the body] than silence. And the learning is not the thing, but the doing. And whoever talks too much causes sin."

1:18.   Rabban Simeon ben Gamaliel says: "On three things does the world stand: on justice, on truth, and on peace. As it is said, Execute the judgment of truth and peace in your gates (Zech 8:16)."

The intent of the list is not only to establish the link to Sinai; the fixed-associative list bears a second polemic, which emerges in the pairs of names and how they are arranged:

Moses
Joshua
Elders
Prophets
Men of the Great Assembly
Simeon the Righteous
Antigonus of Sokho

1.	Yosé ben Yoezer		Yosé b. Yohanan
2.	Joshua b. Perahyah		Nittai the Arbelite
3.	Judah b. Tabbai		Simeon b. Shetah
	4.	Shemaiah	Avtalyon
	5.	Hillel	Shammai

Gamaliel

Simeon his son [that is, Simeon b. Gamaliel]

Rabban Simeon b. Gamaliel

Once the pairs end, we find Gamaliel, who is (later on) represented as the son of Hillel, and then Gamaliel and Simeon, his son, Hillel's grandson.

The cogency of the list emerges when we realize that the names Gamaliel, then Simeon, continued through this same family of primary authorities through Gamaliel II, ruler of the Jewish community after the destruction of the second Temple in 70 and into the second century; then his son, Simeon b. Gamaliel, ruler of the Jewish community after the defeat of Bar Kokhba in 135—and also, as it happens, the father of Judah the Patriarch, this same Judah the Patriarch who sponsored the Mishnah. Judah the Patriarch stands in the chain of tradition to Sinai. So not only the teachings of the sages of the Mishnah, but also the political sponsor of the document, who also was numbered among the sages, formed part of this same tradition. The list itself bears the message that the patriarch and sages employed by him carry forward the tradition of Sinai.

This same point of equivalence emerges in Chapter Two, which is as follows:

2:1.   Rabbi says: "What is the straight path which a person should choose for himself? Whatever is an ornament to the one who follows it, and an ornament in the view of others. Be meticulous in a small religious duty as in a large one, for you do not know what sort of reward is coming for any of the various religious duties. And reckon with the loss [required] in carrying out a religious duty against the reward for doing it; and the reward for committing a transgression against the loss for doing it. And keep your eye on three things, so you will not come into the clutches of transgression. Know what is above you. An eye which sees, and an ear which hears, and all your actions are written down in a book."

2:2.   Rabban Gamaliel, a son of Rabbi Judah the Patriarch, says: "Fitting is learning in the Torah along with a craft, for the labor put into the two of them makes one forget sin. And all learning of the Torah which is not joined with labor is destined to be null and causes sin. And all who work with the community—let them work with them [the community] for the sake of Heaven. For the merit of the fathers strengthens them, and the righteousness which they do stands forever. And, as for you, I credit you with a great reward, as if you had done [all the work required by the community]."

2:3.   Be wary of the government, for they get friendly with a person only for their own convenience. They look like friends when it is to their benefit, but they do not stand by a person when he is in need.

2:4.   He [the sage noted just above] would say: "Make His wishes into your own wishes, so that He will make your wishes into His wishes. Put aside your wishes on account of His wishes, so that He will put aside the wishes of other people in favor of your wishes."

Hillel says: "Do not walk out on the community. And do not have confidence in yourself until the day you die. And do not judge your companion until you are in his place. And do not say anything which cannot be heard, for in the end it will be heard. And do not say: When I have time, I shall study, for you may never have time."

2:5.   He would say: "A coarse person will never fear sin, nor will an unlettered person ever be pious, nor will a shy person learn, nor will an ignorant person teach, nor will anyone too occupied in business get wise. In a place where there are no individuals, try to be an individual."

2:6.   Also, he saw a skull floating on the water and said to it [in Aramaic]: "Because you drowned others, they drowned you, and in the end those who drowned you will be drowned."

2:7.   He would say: "Lots of meat, lots of worms; lots of property, lots of worries; lots of women, lots of witchcraft; lots of slave girls, lots of lust; lots of slave boys, lots of robbery. Lots of the Torah, lots of life; lots of discipleship, lots of wisdom; lots of counsel, lots of understanding; lots of righteousness, lots of peace. [If] one has gotten a good name, he has gotten it for himself. [If] he has gotten teachings of the Torah, he has gotten himself life eternal."

2:8A.   Rabban Yohanan ben Zakkai received [the Torah] from Hillel and Shammai. He would say: "If you have learned much Torah, do not puff yourself up on that account, for it was for that purpose that you were created." He had five disciples, and these are they: Rabbi Eliezer ben Hyrcanus, Rabbi Joshua ben Hananiah, Rabbi Yosé the Priest, Rabbi Simeon ben Nethanel, and Rabbi Eleazar ben Arakh.

2:8B.   He would list their good qualities: Rabbi Eliezer ben Hyrcanus—a plastered well, which does not lose a drop of water. Rabbi Joshua—happy is the one who gave birth to him. Rabbi Yosé—a pious man. Rabbi Simeon ben Nethanel—a man who fears sin, and Rabbi Eleazar ben Arakh—a surging spring.

2:8C.   He would say: "If all the sages of Israel were on one side of the scale, and Rabbi Eliezer ben Hyrcanus were on the other, he would outweigh all of them."

2:8D.   Abba Saul says in his name: "If all of the sages of Israel were on one side of the scale, and Rabbi Eliezer ben Hyrcanus was also with them, and Rabbi Eleazar [ben Arakh] were on the other side, he would outweigh all of them."

2:9A.   He said to them: "Go and see what is the straight path to which someone should stick."

2:9B.   Rabbi Eliezer says: "A generous spirit." Rabbi Joshua says: "A good friend." Rabbi Yosé says: "A good neighbor." Rabbi Simeon says: "Foresight." Rabbi Eleazar says: "Goodwill."

2:9C.   He said to them: "I prefer the opinion of Rabbi Eleazar ben Arakh, because in what he says is included everything you say."

2:9D.   He said to them: "Go out and see what is the bad road, which someone should avoid." Rabbi Eliezer says: "Envy." Rabbi Joshua says: "A bad friend." Rabbi Yosé says: "A bad neighbor." Rabbi Simeon says: "A loan (All the same is a loan owed to a human being and a loan owed to the Omnipresent, the blessed, as it is said, The wicked borrows and does not pay back, but the righteous person deals graciously and hands over [what is owed]) (Ps. 37:21)."

2:9E.   Rabbi Eleazar says: "Ill will."

2:9F.   He said to them: "I prefer the opinion of Rabbi Eleazar ben Arakh, because in what he says is included everything you say."

2:10A.   They [each] said three things.

2:10B.   Rabbi Eliezer says: "Let the respect owing to your companion be as precious to you as the respect owing to yourself. And don't be easy to anger. And repent one day before you die. And warm yourself by the fire of the sages, but be careful of their coals, so you don't get burned—for their bite is the bite of a fox, and their sting is the sting of a scorpion, and their hiss is like the hiss of a snake, and everything they say is like fiery coals."

2:11.   Rabbi Joshua says: "Envy, desire of bad things, and hatred for people push a person out of the world."

2:12.   Rabbi Yosé says: "Let your companion's money be as precious to you as your own. And get yourself ready to learn the Torah, for it does not come as an inheritance to you. And may everything you do be for the sake of heaven."

2:13.   Rabbi Simeon says: "Be meticulous about the recitation of the Shema and the Prayer. And when you pray, don't treat your praying as a matter of routine; but let it be a [plea for] mercy and supplication before the Omnipresent, the blessed, as it is said, For He is gracious and full of compassion, slow to anger and full of mercy, and repents of the evil (Joel 2:13). And never be evil in your own eyes."

2:14.   Rabbi Eleazar says: "Be constant in learning of the Torah; And know what to reply to an Epicurean. And know before whom you work, for your employer can be depended upon to pay your wages for what you do."

2:15.   Rabbi Tarfon says: "The day is short, the work formidable, the workers lazy, the wages high, the employer impatient."

2:16.   He would say: "It's not your job to finish the work, but you are not free to walk away from it. If you have learned much Torah, they will give you a good reward. And your employer can be depended upon to pay your wages for what you do. And know what sort of reward is going to be given to the righteous in the coming time."

The chapter is in two parts, and the joining of the parts bears the same message as the list of names in Chapter One. "Rabbi"—that is, Judah the Patriarch, the rabbi par excellence, often referred to only by the title "Rabbi," without the name following—and his successors and sons, Gamaliel and Hillel, in fact carry forward Chapter One's list, which (ignoring the chapter break, which is hardly intrinsic to the chapter) is then: Shammai, then Hillel-Gamaliel-Simeon-Judah the Patriarch-Gamaliel-Hillel. The continuity from Hillel, however, also is through Yohanan ben Zakkai and his disciples, so there is a separate list: Shammai, then Hillel-Yohanan ben Zakkai-Joshua-Eliezer and the others, with Tarfon tacked on. Here again, the chain of tradition from Sinai is passed on through two figures: the patriarch and the sage.

6.
TRACTATE ABOT
CHAPTERS THREE THROUGH FIVE

Because of the importance of tractate Abot in rabbinic literature, we examine the remainder of the document.

TRACTATE ABOT

Chapter Three

3:1A.   Aqabiah b. Mehallalel says, "Reflect upon three things and you will not fall into the clutches of transgression: Know (1) from whence you come, (2) whither you are going, and (3) before whom you are going to have to give a full account of yourself.

3:1B.   "From whence do you come? From a putrid drop. Whither are you going? To a place of dust, worms, and maggots.

3:1C.   "And before whom are you going to give a full account of yourself? Before the King of kings of kings, the Holy One, blessed be he."

3:2A.   R. Hananiah, Prefect of the Priests, says, "Pray for the welfare of the government. For if it were not for fear of it, one man would swallow his fellow alive."

3:2B.   R. Hananiah b. Teradion says, "[If] two sit together and between them do not pass teachings of the Torah, lo, this is a seat of the scornful, as it is said, Nor sits in the seat of the scornful (Ps. 1:1). But two who are sitting, and words of the Torah do pass between them—the Presence is with them, as it is said, Then they that feared the Lord spoke with one another, and the Lord hearkened and heard, and a book of remembrance was written before him, for them that feared the Lord and gave thought to his name (Mal 3:16). I know that this applies to two. How do I know that even if a single person sits and works on the Torah, the Holy One, blessed be He, set aside a reward for him? As it is said, Let him sit alone and keep silent, because he has laid it upon him (Lam. 3:28)."

3:3.   R. Simeon says, "Three who ate at a single table and did not talk about teachings of the Torah while at that table are as though they ate from dead sacrifices (Ps. 106:28), as it is said, For all tables are full of vomit and filthiness [if they are] without God (Ps. 106:28). But three who ate at a single table and did talk about teachings of the Torah while at that table are as if they ate at the table of the Omnipresent, blessed is he, as it is said, And he said to me, This is the table that is before the Lord (Ez. 41:22)."

3:4.   R. Hananiah b. Hakhinai says, "(1) He who gets up at night, and (2) he who walks around by himself, and (3) he who turns his desire to emptiness—lo, this person is liable for his life."

3:5.   R. Nehunia b. Haqqaneh says, "From whoever accepts upon himself the yoke of the Torah do they remove the yoke of the state and the yoke of hard labor. And upon whoever removes from himself the yoke of the Torah do they lay the yoke of the state and the yoke of hard labor."

3:6.   R. Halafta of Kefar Hananiah says, "Among ten who sit and work hard on the Torah the Presence comes to rest, as it is said, God stands in the congregation of God (Ps. 82:1). And how do we know that the same is so even of five? For it is said, And he has founded his group upon the earth (Am. 9:6). And how do we know that this is so even of three? Since it is said, And he judges among the judges (Ps. 82:1). And how do we know that this is so even of two? Because it is said, Then they that feared the Lord spoke with one another, and the Lord hearkened and heard (Mal. 3:16). And how do we know that this is so even of one? Since it is said, In every place where I record my name I will come to you and I will bless you (Ex. 20:24)."

3:7A.   R. Eleazar of Bartota says, "Give him what is his, for you and yours are his. For so does it say about David, For all things come of you, and of your own have we given you (I Chron. 29:14)."

3:7B.   R. Simeon says, "He who is going along the way and repeating [his Torah tradition] but interrupts his repetition and says, How beautiful is that tree! How beautiful is that plowed field!—Scripture reckons it to him as if he has become liable for his life."

3:8.   R. Dosetai b. R. Yannai in the name of R. Meir says, "Whoever forgets a single thing from what he has learned—Scripture reckons it to him as if he has become liable for his life, as it is said, Only take heed to yourself and keep your soul diligently, lest you forget the words which your eyes saw (Deut. 4:9). Is it possible that this is so even if his learning became too much for him? Scripture says, Lest they depart from your heart all the days of your life. Thus he becomes liable for his life only when he will sit down and actually remove [his learning] from his own heart."

3:9A.   R. Haninah b. Dosa says, "For anyone whose fear of sin takes precedence over his wisdom, his wisdom will endure. And for anyone whose wisdom takes precedence over his fear of sin, his wisdom will not endure."

3:9B.   He would say, "Anyone whose deeds are more than his wisdom—his wisdom will endure. And anyone whose wisdom is more than his deeds—his wisdom will not endure."

3:10A.   He would say, "Anyone from whom people take pleasure—the Omnipresent takes pleasure. And anyone from whom people do not take pleasure, the Omnipresent does not take pleasure."

3:10B.   R. Dosa b. Harkinas says, "(1) Sleeping late in the morning, (2) drinking wine at noon, (3) chatting with children, and (4) attending the synagogues of the ignorant drive a man out of the world."

3:11.   R. Eleazar the Modite says, "(1) He who treats Holy Things as secular, and (2) he who despises the appointed times, (3) he who humiliates his fellow in public, (4) he who removes the signs of the covenant of Abraham, our father (may he rest in peace), and (5) he who exposes aspects of the Torah not in accord with the law, even though he has in hand learning in the Torah and good deeds, will have no share in the world to come."

3:12.   R. Ishmael says, "(1) Be quick [in service] to a superior, (2) efficient in service [to the state], and (3) receive everybody with joy."

3:13.   R. Aqiba says, "(1) Laughter and lightheadedness turn lewdness into a habit. (2) Tradition is a fence for the Torah. (3) Tithes are a fence for wealth. (4) Vows are a fence for abstinence. (5) A fence for wisdom is silence."

3:14A.   He would say, "Precious is the human being, who was created in the image [of God]. It was an act of still greater love that it was made known to him that he was created in the image [of God]. As it is said, For in the image of God he made man (Gen. 9:6).

3:14B.   "Precious are Israelites, who are called children of the Omnipresent. It was an act of still greater love that it was made known to them that they were called children of the Omnipresent, as it is said, You are the children of the Lord your God (Deut. 14:1).

3:14C.   "Precious are Israelites, to whom was given the precious thing. It was an act of still greater love that it was made known to them that to them was given that precious thing with which the world was made, as it is said, For I give you a good doctrine. Do not forsake my Torah (Prov. 4:2).

3:15.   "Everything is foreseen, and free choice is given. In goodness the world is judged. And all is in accord with the abundance of deed[s]."

3:16A.   He would say, "(1) All is handed over as a pledge. (2) And a net is cast over all the living. (3) The store is open, (4) the storekeeper gives credit, (5) the account book is open, and (6) the hand is writing.

3:16B.   "(1) Whoever wants to borrow may come and borrow. (2) The charity collectors go around every day and collect from man whether he knows it or not. (3) And they have grounds for what they do. (4) And the judgment is a true judgment. (5) And everything is ready for the meal."

3:17A.   R. Eleazar b. Azariah says, "If there is no learning of the Torah, there is no proper conduct. If there is no proper conduct, there is no learning in the Torah. If there is no wisdom, there is no reverence. If there is no reverence, there is no wisdom. If there is no understanding, there is no knowledge. If there is no knowledge, there is no understanding. If there is no sustenance, there is no Torah learning. If there is no Torah learning, there is no sustenance."

3:17B.   He would say, "Anyone whose wisdom is greater than his deeds—to what is he to be likened? To a tree with abundant foliage, but few roots. When the winds come, they will uproot it and blow it down. As it is said, He shall be like a tamarisk in the desert and shall not see when good comes, but shall inhabit the parched places in the wilderness (Jer. 17:6). But anyone whose deeds are greater than his wisdom—to what is he to be likened? To a tree with little foliage but abundant roots. For even if all the winds in the world were to come and blast at it, they will not move it from its place, as it is said, He shall be as a tree planted by the waters, and that spreads out its roots by the river, and shall not fear when heat comes, and his leaf shall be green, and it shall not be careful in the year of drought, neither he shall cease from yielding fruit (Jer. 17:8)."

3:18.   R. Eleazar Hisma says, "The laws of bird offerings and of the beginning of the menstrual period—they are indeed the essentials of the Torah. Calculation of the equinoxes and reckoning the numerical value of letters are the savories of wisdom."

Chapter Four

4:1.   Ben Zoma says, "Who is a sage? He who learns from everybody, as it is said, From all my teachers I have gotten understanding (Ps. 119:99). Who is strong? He who overcomes his desire, as it is said, He who is slow to anger is better than the mighty, and he who rules his spirit than he who takes a city (Prov. 16:32). Who is rich? He who is happy in what he has, as it is said, When you eat the labor of your hands, happy will you be, and it will go well with you (Ps. 128:2). ["Happy will you be—in this world, and it will go well with you—in the world to come."] Who is honored? He who honors everybody, as it is said, For those who honor me I shall honor, and they who despise me will be treated as of no account (I Sam. 2:30)."

4:2.   Ben Azzai says, "Run after the most minor religious duty as after the most important, and flee from transgression. For doing one religious duty draws in its wake doing yet another, and doing one transgression draws in its wake doing yet another. For the reward of doing a religious duty is a religious duty, and the reward of doing a transgression is a transgression."

4:3. He would say, "Do not despise anybody and do not treat anything as unlikely. For you have no one who does not have his time, and you have nothing which does not have its place."

4:4A. R. Levitas of Yavneh says, "Be exceedingly humble, for the future of humanity is the worm."

4:4B. R. Yohanan b. Beroqa says, "Whoever secretly treats the Name of Heaven as profane publicly pays the price. All the same are the one who does so inadvertently and the one who does so deliberately, when it comes to treating the Name of Heaven as profane."

4:5A. R. Ishmael, his son, says, "He who learns so as to teach—they give him a chance to learn and to teach. He who learns so as to carry out his teachings—they give him a chance to learn, to teach, to keep, and to do."

4:5B. R. Sadoq says, "Do not make [Torah teachings] a crown in which to glorify yourself or a spade with which to dig. So did Hillel say, 'He who uses the crown perishes.' Thus have you learned: Whoever derives worldly benefit from teachings of the Torah takes his life out of this world."

4:6. R. Yosé says, "Whoever honors the Torah himself is honored by people. And whoever disgraces the Torah himself is disgraced by people."

4:7. R. Ishmael, his son, says, "He who avoids serving as a judge avoids the power of enmity, robbery, and false swearing. And he who is arrogant about making decisions is a fool, evil, and prideful."

4:8. He would say, "Do not serve as a judge by yourself, for there is only One who serves as a judge all alone. And do not say, 'Accept my opinion.' For they have the choice in the matter, not you."

4:9. R. Jonathan says, "Whoever keeps the Torah when poor will in the end keep it in wealth. And whoever treats the Torah as nothing when he is wealthy in the end will treat it as nothing in poverty."

4:10. R. Meir says, "Keep your business to a minimum and make your business the Torah. And be humble before everybody. And if you treat the Torah as nothing, you will have many treating you as nothing. And if you have labored in the Torah, [the Torah] has a great reward to give you."

4:11A. R. Eleazar b. Jacob says, "He who does even a single religious duty gets himself a good advocate. He who does even a single transgression gets himself a powerful prosecutor. Penitence and good deeds are like a shield against punishment."

4:11B. R. Yohanan Hassandelar says, "Any gathering which is for the sake of heaven is going to endure. And any that is not for the sake of heaven is not going to endure."

4:12. R. Eleazar b. Shammua says, "The honor owing to your disciple should be as precious to you as yours. And the honor owing to your fellow should be like the reverence owing to your master. And the reverence owing to your master should be like the awe owing to heaven."

4:13A.   R. Judah says, "Be meticulous about learning, for error in learning leads to deliberate [violation of the Torah]."

4:13B.   R. Simeon says, "There are three crowns: the crown of the Torah, the crown of priesthood, and the crown of sovereignty. But the crown of a good name is best of them all."

4:14.   R. Nehorai says, "Go into exile to a place of the Torah, and do not suppose that it will come to you. For your fellow disciples will make it solid in your hand. And on your own understanding do not rely."

4:15A.   R. Yannai says, "We do not have in hand [an explanation] either for the prosperity of the wicked or for the suffering of the righteous."

4:15B.   R. Matya b. Harash says, "Greet everybody first, and be a tail to lions. But do not be a head of foxes."

4:16.   R. Jacob says, "This world is like an antechamber before the world to come. Get ready in the antechamber, so you can go into the great hall."

4:17.   He would say, "Better is a single moment spent in penitence and good deeds in this world than the whole of the world to come. And better is a single moment of inner peace in the world to come than the whole of a lifetime spent in this world."

4:18.   R. Simeon b. Eleazar says, "(1) Do not try to make amends with your fellow when he is angry, or (2) comfort him when the corpse of his beloved is lying before him, or (3) seek to find absolution for him at the moment at which he takes a vow, or (4) attempt to see him when he is humiliated."

4:19.   Samuel the Small says, "Rejoice not when your enemy falls, and let not your heart be glad when he is overthrown, lest the Lord see it and it displease him, and he turn away his wrath from him (Prov. 24:17)."

4:20.   Elisha b. Abuyah says, "He who learns when a child—what is he like? Ink put down on a clean piece of paper. And he who learns when an old man—what is he like? Ink put down on a paper full of erasures."

4:21A.   R. Yosé b. R. Judah of Kefar Habbabli says, "He who learns from children—what is he like? One who eats sour grapes and drinks fresh wine. And he who learns from old men—what is he like? He who eats ripe grapes and drinks vintage wine."

4:21B.   Rabbi says, "Do not look at the bottle but at what is in it. You can have a new bottle of old wine, and an old bottle which has not got even new wine."

4:22A.   R. Eleazar Haqqappar says, "Jealousy, lust, and ambition drive a person out of this world."

4:22B.   He would say, "Those who are born are [destined] to die, and those who die are [destined] for resurrection. And the living are [destined] to be judged—so as to know, to make known, and to confirm that (1) he is God, (2) he is the one who forms, (3) he is the one who creates, (4) he is the one who understands, (5) he is the one who judges, (6) he is the one who gives evidence, (7) he is the one who brings suit, (8) and he is the one who is going to make the ultimate judgment.

4:22C.   "Blessed be he, for before him are no (1) guile, (2) forgetfulness, (3) respect for persons, or (4) bribe-taking, for everything is his. And know that everything is subject to reckoning. And do not let your evil impulse persuade you that Sheol is a place of refuge for you. For (1) despite your wishes, were you formed, (2) despite your wishes, were you born, (3) despite your wishes, do you live, (4) despite your wishes, do you die, and (5) despite your wishes, are you going to give a full accounting before the King of kings of kings, the Holy One blessed be he."

Chapter Five

5:1.   By ten acts of speech was the world made. And what does Scripture mean [by having God say ten times]? But it is to exact punishment from the wicked, who destroy a world that was created through ten acts of speech, and to secure a good reward for the righteous, who sustain a world that was created through ten acts of speech.

5:2.   There are ten generations from Adam to Noah, to show you how long-suffering is [God]. For all those generations went along spiting him until he brought the water of the flood upon them. There are ten generations from Noah to Abraham, to show you how long-suffering is [God]. For all those generations went along spiting him, until Abraham came along and took the reward which had been meant for all of them.

5:3.   Ten trials were inflicted upon Abraham, our father, may he rest in peace, and he withstood all of them, to show you how great is His love for Abraham, our father, may he rest in peace.

5:4.   Ten wonders were done for our fathers in Egypt, and ten at the sea. Ten blows did the Holy One, blessed be he, bring upon the Egyptians in Egypt, and ten at the sea. Ten trials did our fathers inflict upon the Omnipresent, blessed be he, in the Wilderness, as it is said, Yet they have tempted me these ten times and have not listened to my voice (Num. 14:22).

5:5.   Ten wonders were done for our fathers in the Temple: (1) A woman never miscarried on account of the stench of the meat of Holy Things. (2) And the meat of the Holy Things never turned rotten. (3) A fly never made an appearance in the slaughterhouse. (4) A high priest never suffered a nocturnal emission on the eve of the Day of Atonement. (5) The rain never quenched the fire on the altar. (6) No wind ever blew away the pillar of smoke. (7) An invalidating factor never affected the 'omer, the Two Loaves, or the show bread. (8) When the people are standing, they are jammed together. When they go down and prostrate themselves, they have plenty of room. (9) A snake and a scorpion never bit anybody in Jerusalem. (10) And no one ever said to his fellow, "The place is too crowded for me (Is. 49:20) to stay in Jerusalem."

5.6A.   Ten things were created on the eve of the Sabbath [Friday] at twilight, and these are they: (1) the mouth of the earth [Num. 16:32]; (2) the mouth of the well [Num. 21:16–18]; (3) the mouth of the ass [Num. 22:38]; (4) the rainbow [Gen. 9:13]; (5) the manna [Ex. 16:15]; (6) the rod [Ex. 4:17]; (7) the Shamir; (8) letters, (9) writing, (10) and the tables of stone [of the ten commandments, Ex. 32:15f.].

5:6B.   And some say, "Also the destroyers, the grave of Moses, and the tamarisk of Abraham, our father."

5:6C.   And some say, "Also: the tongs made with tongs [with which the first tongs were made]."

5:7.   There are seven traits to an unformed clod, and seven to a sage. (1) A sage does not speak before someone greater than he in wisdom. (2) And he does not interrupt his fellow. (3) And he is not at a loss for an answer. (4) He asks a relevant question and answers properly. (5) And he addresses each matter in its proper sequence, first, then second. (6) And concerning something he has not heard, he says, "I have not heard the answer." (7) And he concedes the truth [when the other party demonstrates it]. And the opposite of these traits apply to a clod.

5:8.   There are seven forms of punishment which come upon the world for seven kinds of transgression. (1) [If] some people give tithes and some people do not give tithes, there is a famine from drought. So some people are hungry and some have enough. (2) [If] everyone decided not to tithe, there is famine of unrest and drought. (3) [If all decided] not to remove dough offering, there is a famine of totality. (4) Pestilence comes to the world on account of the death penalties which are listed in the Torah but which are not in the hands of the court [to inflict]; and because of the produce of the Seventh Year [which people buy and sell]. (5) A sword comes into the world because of the delaying of justice and perversion of justice, and because of those who teach the Torah not in accord with the law.

5:9A.   (6) A plague of wild animals comes into the world because of vain oaths and desecration of the Divine Name. (7) Exile comes into the world because of those who worship idols, because of fornication, and because of bloodshed, and because of the neglect of the release of the Land [in the year of release].

5:9B.   At four turnings in the year pestilence increases: in the fourth year, in the seventh year, in the year after the seventh year, and at the end of the Festival [of Tabernacles] every year: (1) in the fourth year, because of the poor man's tithe of the third year [which people have neglected to hand over to the poor]: (2) in the seventh year, because of the poor man's tithe of the sixth year; (3) in the year after the seventh year, because of the dealing in produce of the seventh year; and (4) at the end of the Festival every year, because of the thievery of the dues [gleanings and the like] owing to the poor [nor left for them in the antecedent harvest].

5:10.   There are four sorts of people. (1) He who says, "What's mine is mine and what's yours is yours"—this is the average sort. (And some say, "This is the sort of Sodom.") (2) "What's mine is yours and what's yours is mine"—

this is a boor. (3) "What's mine is yours and what's yours is yours"—this is a truly pious man. (4) "What's mine is mine and what's yours is mine"—this is a truly wicked man.

5:11. There are four sorts of personality: (1) easily angered, easily calmed—he loses what he gains; (2) hard to anger, hard to calm—what he loses he gains; (3) hard to anger and easy to calm—a truly pious man; (4) easy to anger and hard to calm—a truly wicked man.

5:12. There are four types of disciples: (1) quick to grasp, quick to forget—he loses what he gains; (2) slow to grasp, slow to forget—what he loses he gains; (3) quick to grasp, slow to forget—a sage; (4) slow to grasp, quick to forget—a bad lot indeed.

5:13. There are four traits among people who give charity: (1) he who wants to give, but does not want others to give—he begrudges what belongs to others; (2) he wants others to give, but he does not want to give—he begrudges what belongs to himself; (3) he will give and he wants others to give—he is truly pious; (4) he will not give and he does not want others to give—he is truly wicked.

5:14. There are four sorts among those who go to the study house: (1) he who goes but does not carry out [what he learns]—he has at least the reward for the going; (2) he who practices but does not go [to study]—he has at least the reward for the doing; (3) he who both goes and practices—he is truly pious; (4) he who neither goes nor practices—he is truly wicked.

5:15. There are four traits among those who sit before the sages: a sponge, a funnel, a strainer, and a sifter. (1) A sponge—because he sponges everything up; (2) a funnel—because he takes in on one side and lets out on the other; (3) a strainer—for he lets out the wine and keeps in the lees; (4) and a sifter—for he lets out the coarse flour and keeps in the finest flour.

5:16. [In] any loving relationship that depends upon something, [when] that thing is gone, the love is gone. But any that does not depend upon something will never come to an end. What is a loving relationship that depends upon something? That is the love of Amnon and Tamar [II Sam. 13:15]. And one that does not depend upon something: That is the love of David and Jonathan.

5:17. Any dispute that is for the sake of heaven will in the end yield results, and any that is not for the sake of heaven will in the end not yield results. What is a dispute for the sake of heaven? This is the sort of dispute between Hillel and Shammai. And what is one that is not for the sake of heaven? It is the dispute of Korah and all his party.

5:18. He who brings merit to the community never causes sin. And he who causes the community to sin—they never give him a sufficient chance to attain penitence. Moses attained merit and bestowed merit on the community. So the merit of the community is assigned to his [credit], as it is said, He executed the justice of the Lord and his judgments with Israel (Deut. 33:21).

Jeroboam sinned and caused the community of the Israelites to sin. So the sin of the community is assigned to his [debit], as it is said, For the sins of Jeroboam that he committed and wherewith he made Israel to sin (I Kings 15:30).

5:19.   Anyone in whom are these three traits is one of the disciples of Abraham, our father; but [if he bears] three other traits, he is one of the disciples of Balaam, the wicked: (1) a generous spirit, (2) a modest demeanor, and (3) a humble soul—he is one of the disciples of Abraham, our father. He who exhibits (1) a grudging spirit, (2) an arrogant mien, and (3) a proud soul—he is one of the disciples of Balaam, the wicked. What is the difference between the disciples of Abraham our father and the disciples of Balaam the wicked? The disciples of Abraham our father enjoy the benefit [of their learning] in this world and yet inherit the world to come, as it is said, That I may cause those who love me to inherit substance, and so that I may fill their treasures (Prov. 8:21). The disciples of Balaam the wicked inherit Gehenna and go down to the Pit of Destruction, as it is said, But you, O God, shall bring them down into the pit of destruction; bloodthirsty and deceitful men shall not live out half their days (Ps. 55:24).

5:20A.   Judah b. Tema says, "Be strong as a leopard, fast as an eagle, fleet as a gazelle, and grave as a lion, to carry out the will of your Father who is in heaven."

5:20B.   He would say, "The shameless go to Gehenna, and the diffident to the garden of Eden.

5:20C.   "May it be found pleasing before you, O Lord our God, that you rebuild your city quickly in our day and set our portion in your Torah."

5:21.   He would say, "(1) At five to Scripture, (2) ten to Mishnah, (3) thirteen to religious duties, (4) fifteen to Talmud, (5) eighteen to the wedding canopy, (6) twenty to responsibility for providing for a family, (7) thirty to fullness of strength, (8) forty to understanding, (9) fifty to counsel, (10) sixty to old age, (11) seventy to ripe old age, (12) eighty to remarkable strength, (13) ninety to a bowed back, and (14) at a hundred—he is like a corpse who has already passed and gone from this world."

5:22.   Ben Bag Bag says [in Aramaic], "Turn it over and over because everything is in it. And reflect upon it; now grow old and worn in it and do not leave it, [in Hebrew] for you have no better lot than that."

5:23.   Ben He He says, "In accord with the effort is the reward."

XXIV

ABOT deRABBI NATHAN (THE FATHERS ACCORDING TO RABBI NATHAN)

1.
IDENTIFYING THE DOCUMENT

IN 250 MISHNAH TRACTATE ABOT, THE FATHERS, DELIVERED ITS MESSAGE THROUGH aphorisms assigned to named sages. A few centuries later—the date is indeterminate but it is possibly ca. 500—the Fathers According to Rabbi Nathan, a vast secondary expansion of that same tractate, endowed those anonymous names with flesh-and-blood form, recasting the tractate by adding a sizable number of narratives.[1] The authorship of the Mishnah tractate the Fathers, ca. 250, presented its

---

[1] For further reading and bibliography on the topic of this chapter, see the following:

    Bowker, pp. 87–88.

    Judah Goldin, "Avot de-Rabbi Nathan," *Encyclopaedia Judaica* 3:984–86: description of the document; its two versions; no certain date, "in language and in content and style there is virtually nothing to compel a late dating. No amoraim are quoted . . . the flavor of the work is tannaitic."

    M. Bialik Lerner, "The External Tractates," in Safrai, *Literature of the Sages,* pp. 369–79 on Abot deR. Natan: name and character; structure and contents; versions A and B; date of redaction of versions A and B; bibliography.

    Maccoby, pp. 39, 128 (ARN is to Abot as Tosetta is to the Mishnah).

    Saldarini, A. J., *The Fathers According to Rabbi Nathan (Abot de Rabbi Nathan) Version B: A Translation*

teachings in the form of aphorisms, rarely finding it necessary to supply those aphorisms with a narrative setting, and never resorting to narrative for presentation of its propositions. The testamentary authorship, the Fathers According to Rabbi Nathan, provided an amplification and supplement to the Fathers and introduced into its treatment of the received tractate a vast corpus of narratives of various sorts. In this way, the later authorship indicated that it found in narrative in general, and stories about sages in particular, modes of discourse for presenting its message that the earlier authorship did not utilize. And the choice of the medium bore implicit meanings, also, for the message that would emerge in the later restatement of the received tractate.

To call the Fathers According to Rabbi Nathan the talmud (or the tosefta) of the Fathers leads to the false expectation that the successor document subjects the principal one to sustained analytical reading. But the character of the Fathers does not sustain analysis, since the compilation presents no theses for argumentation, only wise sayings. The work of the Fathers according to Rabbi Nathan was defined by the fact that the authorship of the Fathers presented the message of sages solely in aphoristic form. Apophthegms bore the entire weight of that authorship's propositions, and—quite consistently—what made one saying cogent with others fore and aft was solely the location of the authority behind that saying: here, not there. The framers of the successor writing vastly augmented the Fathers by recasting aphorisms in narrative form, and, more important, by according to the names of sages listed in the prior writing the rudiments of biography.

Among the four types of narrative (in a moment defined in detail in our treatment of the teleological logic of coherent discourse that prevails) we find in the Fathers According to Rabbi Nathan, precedent, precipitant, parable, and story (whether an expansion of one that was scriptural or one that concerned sages), three have no counterpart in the Fathers, and therein lies the definition, as a talmud, of the Fathers According to Rabbi Nathan. The authorship of the Fathers completely neglected three. The authorship of the Fathers fully acknowledged the

---

and Commentary (Leiden, 1975: E. J. Brill). Studies in Judaism in Late Antiquity, ed. Jacob Neusner, Volume XIII.

Stemberger-Strack, pp. 245–47: bibliography; text; translations; "the use of a version of Abot which diverges from the Mishnah's suggests that the core of ARN is to be dated no later than the early third century . . . the widely accepted dating of the final version between the seventh and ninth centuries is essentially based on the fact that ARN is regarded as one of the minor tractates. However, the language, substance, and the cited rabbis do not justify such a late date."

This writer's translation of the document is The Fathers According to Rabbi Nathan. An Analytical Translation and Explanation. Atlanta, 1986: Scholars Press for Brown Judaic Studies. His systematic introduction to, and analysis of, the document, both in relationship to tractate Abot and also in its own terms, is Judaism and Story: The Evidence of The Fathers According to Rabbi Nathan. Chicago, 1992: University of Chicago Press. Further studies relevant to the same problem are in Form-Analytical Comparison in Rabbinic Judaism. Structure and Form in The Fathers and The Fathers According to Rabbi Nathan. Atlanta, 1992: Scholars Press for South Florida Studies in the History of Judaism.

importance of the past, referring to historical events of Scripture. But they did not retell and include in their composition the scriptural stories of what had happened long ago. They understood that their predecessors lived exemplary lives. But they did not narrate stories about sages. They had every reason to appreciate the power of parable. But they did not think it necessary to harness that power for delivering their particular message, or even for stating in colorful ways the propositions they wished to impart. The framers of the Fathers resorted to narrative, but only to serve as a precipitant, with great economy, to describe the setting in which a stunning saying was set forth. They did not cite narratives in the form of precedents.

Given a saying of an apophthegmatic character, whether or not that saying is drawn from the Fathers, the authorship of the Fathers According to Rabbi Nathan will do one of the following:

[1] give a secondary expansion, including an exemplification, of the wise saying at hand;

[2] cite a proof text of Scripture in that same connection;

[3] provide a parable to illustrate the wise saying (as often as not instead of the proof text).

These three exercises in the structuring of their document—selecting materials and organizing them in a systematic way—the authors of the Fathers According to Rabbi Nathan learned from the framers of the Fathers. In addition they contributed two further principles of structuring their document:

[1] adding a sizable composition of materials that intersect with the foregoing, either by amplifying the proof text without regard to the wise saying served by the proof text, or by enriching discourse on a topic introduced in connection with the base saying;

[2] tacking on a protracted story of a sage and what he said and did, which story may or may not exemplify the teaching of the apophthegm at hand.

The Fathers According to Rabbi Nathan presents two types of materials and sets them forth in a fixed order. The document contains (1) amplifications of sayings in the Fathers as well as (2) materials not related to anything in the original document. The order in which the Fathers According to Rabbi Nathan arranges its types of material becomes immediately clear. First that authorhip presents amplifications of the prior document, and only second does it tack on its own message. The Fathers According to Rabbi Nathan first of all presents itself as continuous with the prior document, and then shows itself to be connected to it. That is the strategy of both Talmuds in connecting with the Mishnah. And where the authorship gives us compositions that are essentially new in rhetoric, logic, and topic, it is in that second set of materials that we find what is fresh. Let me spell out matters as they will soon become clear. Where the authorship of the later document has chosen (1) to cite and amplify sayings in the earlier one, that exercise comes first. There may be additional amplification, and what appears to augment often turns out to be quite new and to enter the second of our two categories, in the form of (i) proof texts drawn from Scripture, (ii) parables, (iii) other sorts of stories, sometimes involving named sages, that illustrate the same point, or (iv) sequences of unadorned sayings, not in the Fathers, that make the same point. These come later in a sequence of discourses in the Fathers According to Rabbi Nathan. Where an appendix of secondary materials on a theme introduced in the primary discourse occurs, it will be inserted directly after the point at which said theme is located in the counterpart, in the later document, to that passage in the earlier one, and only afterward will the exposition of the saying in the Fathers proceed to a further point. This general order predominates throughout.

The authorship of the Fathers According to Rabbi Nathan clearly found inadequate the mode of intelligible discourse and the medium of expression selected by the framers of the document they chose to extend. The later writers possessed a message they deemed integral to that unfolding Torah of Moses at Sinai. They resorted to a mode of intelligible discourse, narrative, that conveyed propositions with great clarity, deeming the medium—again, narrative—a vehicle for conveying propositions from heart to heart. Not only so, but among the narratives utilized in their composition, they selected one for closest attention and narrative development. The sage story took pride of place in the Fathers According to Rabbi Nathan, and that same subclassification of narrative bore messages conveyed, in the document before us, in no other medium. The framers made ample use of formerly neglected matters of intellect, aesthetics, and theology, specifically, to compose their ideas through a mode of thought and cogent thought, so as to construct intelligible discourse through a medium meant to speak with immediacy and power to convey a message of critical urgency.

Accordingly, they found place for all four types of narrative, and, of greatest interest, they made use of the sage story to convey powerful propositions lacking all precedent in the Fathers and, in context, therefore of an utterly fresh order. That they made the shift from a document that articulated propositions principally through aphorisms to one that made points through narrative and particularly through sage stories is entirely clear. Three traits define the sage story in this document.

[1] The story about a sage has a beginning, middle, and end, and the story about a sage also rests not only on verbal exchanges ("he said to him . . . , he said to him . . ."), but on (described) action.

[2] The story about a sage unfolds from a point of tension and conflict to a clear resolution and remission of the conflict.

[3] The story about a sage rarely invokes a verse of Scripture and never serves to prove a proposition concerning the meaning of a verse of Scripture.

What about Scripture stories? The traits of stories about scriptural figures and themes prove opposite:

[1] In the story about a scriptural hero there is no beginning, middle, and end, and little action. The burden of the narrative is carried by "he said to him . . . , he said to him . . ." Described action is rare and plays a slight role in the unfolding of the narrative. Often the narrative consists of little more than a setting for a saying,

and the point of the narrative is conveyed not through what is told but through the cited saying.

[2] The story about a scriptural hero is worked out as a tableau, with description of the components of the stationary tableau placed at the center. There is little movement, no point of tension that is resolved.

[3] The story about a scriptural hero always invokes verses from Scripture and makes the imputation of meaning to those verses the center of interest.

So the Fathers According to Rabbi Nathan systematically enriches the Fathers with a variety of narratives, each with its own conventions. When the narrators wish to talk about sages, they invoked one set of narrative conventions, deemed appropriate to that topic, and when they turned to make up stories about scriptural heroes and topics, they appealed to quite different narrative conventions.

2.

TRANSLATIONS INTO ENGLISH

This document exists in two versions. One is printed in the standard editions of the Talmud and consists of forty-one chapters; the other was first published in full in 1887 by Solomon Schechter and comprises forty-eight chapters. Schechter called the Talmud's version A, and the one he published in addition to it, B. The differences between the two versions involve readings, substance, arrangement, and extent. Judah Goldin states, "A comparative study of the two versions reveals that though in essence, both have the same purpose—to interpret Avot—each version favors [a] particular emphasis of its own. What contributes to the special interest of ARN [the standard version] is that it has preserved a number of old more or less conservative views, unacceptable to later normative tannaitic teaching."[2] The discussion here is based on the standard version printed in the Talmud.

The first translation into English of Version A is Judah Goldin, *The Fathers According to Rabbi Nathan* (New Haven, 1955: Yale University Press). The second, and the first form-analytical translation of the same version, is this writer's *The Fathers According to Rabbi Nathan. An Analytical Translation and Explanation*. Atlanta, 1986: Scholars Press for Brown Judaic Studies. The only translation of Version B is A. J. Saldarini, *The Fathers According to Rabbi Nathan (Abot deRabbi Nathan) Version B: A Translation and Commentary* (Leiden, 1975: E. J. Brill).

[2] Judah Goldin, "Avot de-Rabbi Nathan," *Encyclopaedia Judaica* 3:985.

3.
RHETORIC

The forms of the Fathers are three: the list of names + attribution + wise sayings; secondary amplifications of sayings, and the list of items of a single classification. The forms of the Fathers According to Rabbi Nathan differ only in one way: the appendix, with the subdivision the genre of biographical tale, following diverse formal patterns or no clear pattern at all. This may include a parable, a secondary restatement as a proposition of a lesson that is originally conveyed as a story. The appendix is not a form, but appendices are highly formalized. Ordinarily they are made up of the familiar form: citation of a verse of Scripture, followed by secondary expansion of the cited verse. That is to say, the form that follows the pattern of citing a statement of the Fathers and then saying, *how so?* or *this teaches that . . . ,* finds its counterpart in the entirely familiar formal pattern of citation and gloss of Scripture. Indeed, we may say that the Fathers According to Rabbi Nathan serves the Fathers much as the two Talmuds serve the Mishnah and the several compilations of scriptural exegeses serve Scripture. So what makes the appendix different in its formal traits is solely the subdivision of *the story*—and that does not constitute a difference in form at all.

4.
LOGIC OF COHERENT DISCOURSE

The medium and the message of the Fathers According to Rabbi Nathan appeal to a mode of thought different from the logic that dominates in the Fathers. What holds together those many units of discourse, which constitute more than sequences of unrelated declarative sentences, is the teleological logic of narrative. Narrative may encompass one of four modes of the concrete portrayal of a message, noted at the beginning of this chapter: (1) the parable, (2) the precipitant: the narrative setting for, or formal precipitant of, a saying, (3) the (ordinarily legal, but sometimes moral) precedent, and (4) the story. The story furthermore is divided into two subspecies: (4A) scriptural or Scripture story, (4B) sagacious or sage story.

THE PARABLE: A parable unfolds through resort to narrative. There was a king who had such and so, who said such and such, who did so and so—with the result that such and such happened. The parable is a narrative in that the appeal for cogency is to teleology, and the proposition of the parable emerges (whether made explicit or not) as a self-evident exemplification of the teleology at hand. So the explanation, the principle of cogency, derives from the order of events: do this with that result, say this with that consequence.

THE PRECIPITANT: THE NARRATIVE SETTING FOR A SAYING:

What I call formal setting, or "precipitant," for a saying merely portrays a situation to which a setting pertains, e.g., "He saw a skull and said." That hardly adds up to a substantial narrative, let alone a sustained story, since nothing happens to draw out the significance of the event, *he saw*, but it does demand classification as a narrative, because something has happened, not merely been said. Such a formal setting for a saying may prove substantial, but it will not constitute a narrative in the way that a parable or a sage story or other kind of story does, because not the action but the saying forms the focus of interest, and the potentialities of tension and resolution constituted by the precipitating action ("*one day he saw a skull and said . . .*") are never explored.

A PRECEDENT OR ILLUSTRATION OF A LAW:

A precedent narrates a case, often enough in the form of a tale of something done, not merely said. The setting is always discourse on the law, but what marks the narrative as precedent as different from the narrative as story is not its setting but the definitive narrative convention that pertains in the precedent but not in the story (sage, scriptural, or other). Specifically, the precedent will portray a tableau *of completed action*, in which the tension is established not by the action but by the (sage's) ruling, and in which the resolution of the tension is accomplished solely by the same component, the decision of the sage. In line with this convention that nothing really happen, in the precedent we rarely find a beginning, middle, and end, such as we always find in a parable and a story. The precedent or illustration is concrete and specific, in the way a story is, but not to a distinctive named person and time and place, in the way a story is. The precedent, unlike a story, is paradigmatic and makes a general point, rather than historical and peculiar to a distinctive situation. A precedent or illustration of the law is like a parable in that it presents no concrete details that allow us to identify a particular place or actor.

THE STORY (SCRIPTURAL OR SAGE):

Among narratives, we may always distinguish a story from any other type of narrative in one fundamental and definitive way. Its importance requires emphasis: while meaning to provide a good example of how one should behave, the teller of a story always deals with a concrete person and a particular incident. The person is concrete in that he (in our document there is not a single story about a woman) is always specified by name. It concerns a particular incident in that the viewpoint of the narrator makes clear the one-timeness and specificity of the event that is reported. The story always happens in historical time, and the point it wishes to make is subordinate to the description of action, the development of a point of tension, at which the story commences, and its resolution, at which the story concludes: beginning, middle, and end.

5.

TOPICAL PROGRAM

The topical program of the Fathers According to Rabbi Nathan in particular emerges only in identifying topics treated in the successor compilations but not in the principal one. Points of emphasis in the Fathers lacking all counterpart in restatement and development in the Fathers According to Rabbi Nathan are three. First, the study of the Torah alone does not suffice. One has also to make an honest living through work. In what is peculiar to the Fathers According to Rabbi Nathan we find not that point but its opposite: one should study the Torah and other things will take care of themselves—a claim of a more supernatural character than the one in the Fathers. A second point of clear interest in the earlier document to which, in the later one, we find no response tells sages to accommodate their wishes to those of the community at large, to accept the importance of the government, to work in community, to practice self-abnegation and restraint in favor of the wishes of others. The sage here is less a supernatural figure than a political leader, eager to conciliate and reconcile others. The third and most important, indicative shift in the later document imparts to the teleological question an eschatological answer altogether lacking in the earlier one.

If we were to ask the authorship of Abot to spell out their teleology, they would draw our attention to the numerous sayings about this life's being a time of preparation for the life of the world to come, on the one side, and to judgment and eternal life, on the other. The focus is on the individual and how he or she lives in this world and prepares for the next. The category is the individual, and, commonly in the two documents before us when we speak of the individual, we also tend to find the language of "this world" and "the world to come," *olam hazzeh, olam habba*. The sequence of sayings about this world and the next form a stunning contrast to the ones about this *age* and the next age, *olam hazzeh, le'atid labo*. In general, though not invariably, the shift in language draws in its wake a shift in social category, from individual to social entity of group, nation, or people. The word *olam* bears two meanings, "world," and "age." In context, when we find the word bearing the sense of "world," the category under discussion is the private person, and where the required sense, in English, is "age," then—as a rough rule of thumb—what is promised is for the nation.

We can tell that the definitive category is social, therefore national, when at stake is the fate not of the private person but of holy Israel. The concern then is what will happen to the nation in the time to come, meaning the coming age, not the coming life of the resurrection. The systemic teleology shifts its focus to the holy people, and, alongside, to the national history of the holy people—now and in the age to come. So in the movement from "this world" and "the world to come," to "this age" and "the age to come," often expressed as "the coming future," *le'atid labo*, we note an accompanying categorical shift in the definitive context: from individual and private life of home and family, to society and historical, public life. That shift then characterizes the teleological movement, as much as the categorical change. And, as we see, it is contained both in general and in detail in the differences we have noticed between the Fathers and the Fathers According to Rabbi Nathan.

The national-eschatological interest of the later document, with its focus on living only in the Land of Israel, on the one side, and its contrast between this age, possessed by the gentiles, and the age to come, in which redeemed Israel will enjoy a paramount position, which has no counterpart in the earlier composition, emerges not only in sayings but also in stories about the critical issue, the destruction of Jerusalem and the loss of the Temple, along with the concomitant matter, associated with the stories about repentance and how it is achieved at this time.

Yet a further point of development lies in the notion that study of the Torah combined with various virtues, e.g., good deeds, fear of sin, suffices, with a concomitant assurance that making a living no longer matters. Here too the new medium of the later document—the stories about sages—bears the new message. For that conviction emerges not only explicitly, e.g., in the sayings of Hananiah about the power of Torah study to take away many sources of suffering, Judah b. Ilai's that one should treat words of the Torah as the principal, earning a living as trivial, and so on, but also in the detail that both Aqiba and Eliezer began poor but through their mastery of Torah ended rich.

The Fathers According to Rabbi Nathan differs from the Fathers in one aspect so fundamental as to change the face of the base document completely. While the earlier authorship took slight interest in lives and deeds of sages, the later one contributed in a systematic and orderly manner the color and life of biography to the named but faceless sages of the Fathers. The stories about sages make points that correspond to positions taken in statements of viewpoints peculiar to the Fathers According to Rabbi Nathan. The Fathers presents an ideal of the sage as model for the everyday life of the individual, who must study the Torah and also work, and through the good life prepare now for life after death, while the Fathers According to Rabbi Nathan has a different conception of the sage, of the value and meaning of the study of the Torah, and of the center of interest—and also has selected a new medium for the expression of its distinctive conception. To spell this out:

[1] The sage is now—in the Fathers According to Rabbi Nathan—not a judge and teacher alone but also a supernatural figure.

[2] Study of the Torah in preference to making a living promises freedom from the conditions of natural life.

[3] Israel as the holy people seen as a supernatural social entity takes center stage. And these innovative points are conveyed not only in sayings but in stories about sages.

What follows is that the medium not only carries a new message but also forms a component of that new message. The sage as a supernatural figure now presents Torah teachings through what he does, not only through what he says. Therefore telling stories about what sages did and the circumstances in which they made their sayings forms part of the Torah, in a way in which, in the earlier document, it clearly did not. The interest in stories about sages proves therefore not merely literary or formal; it is more than a new way of conveying an old message. Stories about the sages are told because sages stand for a message that can emerge only in stories and not in sayings alone. So we turn to a close reading of the stories themselves to review that message and find out why through stories in particular the message now emerges. For what we see is nothing short of a new mode of revelation, that is, of conveying and imparting God's will in the Torah.

People told stories because they wanted to think about history, and, in their setting, history emerged in an account of what happened, with an implicit message of the meaning of events conveyed in the story as well. They further conceived of the social entity, Israel, as an extended family, children of a single progenitor, Abraham, with his son and grandson, Isaac and Jacob. Consequently, when they told stories, they centered on family history. That accounts in general for the details of what the authorship of the Fathers According to Rabbi Nathan have chosen to add to the topical program of the Fathers. The sage in the system of the Fathers According to Rabbi Nathan constituted the supernatural father, who replaced the natural one; events in the life of the sage constituted happenings in the history of the family-nation, Israel. So history blended with family, and family with Torah study. The national, salvific history of the nation-family, Israel, took place in such events as the origins of the sage, i.e., his beginnings in Torah study; the sagacity of the sage, the counterpart to what we should call social history; the doings of the sage in great turnings in the family's history, including, especially, the destruction of the Temple, now perceived as final and decisive; and the death of the sage, while engaged in Torah study. And these form the four classifications of story in this document.

6.

A SAMPLE PASSAGE

Of interest to readers of this Introduction will be the contrast between sage story and Gospel story. That is readily drawn when we compare Matthew's story of the birth of Jesus with the stories about the origins of Aqiba and Eliezer in the Fathers According to Rabbi Nathan. The interest of the former is well-known. "Now the birth of Jesus Christ took place in this way" (Mt. 2:18): the birth of the child was announced to the virgin mother, Mary. Herod was told that the king of the Jews had been born. The Magi worshiped the infant. Herod killed the newborn babes; Joseph and Mary fled to Egypt. When Herod died, Joseph and Mary returned. And so on. The well-known story covers a variety of details. Stories about sages present us with a counterpart to not a single detail of Matthew's story; there is no birth legend comparable, for example, to the birth of Samuel or Joseph either. The counterpart is structural: telling the tale of the starting point.

The Fathers According to Rabbi Nathan contains stories not of the birth but of "the origins" as masters of the Torah of two sages, Aqiba and Eliezer. By "origins," the storytellers mean the beginnings of the Torah study of a famed authority. Life begins at birth, but when we wish to tell sage stories, beginnings are measured differently. The sage begins life when he begins Torah study. And the sages whose origins are found noteworthy both began in mature years, not in childhood (despite the repeated emphasis of the Fathers upon the unique value of beginning Torah study in childhood). The proposition implicit in origins stories then is that any male may start his Torah study at any point in life and hope for true distinction in the Torah community. But that does not account for the germ of the story, the critical tension that creates an event worthy of narrative, that poses a question demanding an answer, a problem requiring a solution through a tale with a beginning, middle, and end.

While told each in its own terms and subject to differentiation from the other, the stories make essentially the same point, which is that one can begin Torah study in mature years and progress to the top. When one does so, one also goes from poverty to wealth through public recognition of one's mastery of the Torah, and a range of parallel propositions along the same lines. The supernatural relationship, which has superseded the natural ones to wife and father, generates glory and honor, riches and fame, for the sage, and, through reflection, for the natural family as well. That is the point of the stories of the origins of sages, which take up what is clearly a pressing question and answer it in a powerful way. (I give in boldface type citations of language in the Fathers.)

> VI:IV. 1. A. Another comment on the statement, **And wallow in the dust of their feet:**
> B. This refers to R. Eliezer.
> C. . . . **and drink in their words with gusto:**
> D. This refers to R. Aqiba.

This pericope serves as a prologue to the vast stories to follow, first on Aqiba, then on Eliezer.

> VI:V. 1. A. How did R. Aqiba begin [his Torah study]?
> B. They say: He was forty years old and had never repeated a tradition [that is to say, he was completely illiterate and had

never studied the Torah or learned its traditions.] One time
he was standing at the mouth of a well. He thought to himself, "Who carved out this stone?"

C.   They told him, "It is the water that is perpetually falling on
it every day."

D.   They said to him, "Aqiba, do you not read Scripture? *The
water wears away stones* (Job. 4:19)?"

E.   On the spot R. Aqiba constructed in his own regard an argument *a fortiori*: now if something soft can [Goldin:] wear
down something hard, words of Torah, which are as hard as
iron, how much the more so should wear down my heart,
which is made of flesh and blood.

F.   On the spot he repented [and undertook] to study the
Torah.

G.   He and his son went into study session before a children's
teacher, saying to him, "My lord, teach us Torah."

H.   R. Aqiba took hold of one end of the tablet, and his son
took hold of the other end. The teacher wrote out for him
Alef Bet and he learned it, *Alef Tav* and he learned it, *the
Torah of the Priests* [the books of Leviticus and Numbers] and
he learned it. He went on learning until he had learned the
entire Torah.

I.   He went and entered study sessions before R. Eliezer and
before R. Joshua. He said to them, "My lords, open up for
me the reasoning of the Mishnah."

J.   When they had stated one passage of law, he went and sat
by himself and said, "Why is this *alef* written? Why is this
bet written? Why is this statement made?" He went and
asked them and, in point of fact, [Goldin:] reduced them
to silence.

Clearly, our opening component in the *magnalia Aqibae* is a narrative. The tone
and program establish the mood of narrative: he was . . . he had . . . he did. . . . But
how shall we classify the narrative, and by what criteria? One important criterion is
whether the narrative describes a situation or tells about something that happened,
with a beginning, middle, and end. The one is at rest, the other in movement.
These constitute questions with objective answers. Do we have a tableau or a story,
or, for that matter, a parable, or any of those other types of narratives we have
already classified? By the simple criterion that a story has a beginning, middle, end,
which dictate points of narrative tension, and a clearly delineated program of action, we have a story. The components do more than merely set up pieces in
a static tableau. They flow from one to the next and yield movement—hence
narrative action.

What about the Scripture story? The blatant differences require slight amplification. We note that verses of Scripture scarcely intervene, and there is no focus on the exegesis of a verse of Scripture. At D, Aqiba and his interlocutors do not interpret the verse but simply draw upon its statement of fact. A sage story, as I said, following the pattern determined by Aristotle has a beginning, middle, and end: movement from tension to resolution. In the present story there is a beginning: he had not studied; a middle, he went and studied; and an end, following Goldin's persuasive rendering, "he reduced them to silence." True, the action takes place mainly in what Aqiba thought, rather than in what he did. But in the nature of things, the action of going to study the Torah forms the one genuinely dramatic deed that is possible with the present subject matter. The beginning then works its way out at B–F. The middle is at G–H: Aqiba was so humble as to study with his own son. Then at I–J we have a climax and conclusion: Aqiba proved so profound in his question-asking that he reduced the great authorities to silence. That conclusion hardly flows from A–H, but it is absolutely necessary to make the entire sequence into a cogent story. Otherwise we have merely bits and pieces of an uncompleted narrative.

Let us proceed to what follows in the context of the telling of the story of Aqiba's origins. Here we shall see most strikingly how, given the opportunity for a sustained narrative of the life of a man, the framers of the Fathers According to Rabbi Nathan do not exploit the occasion. Rather than dealing with other tales about the man, they focus upon the theme which he has served to realize in his own life, Torah study.

VI:V.　2.　A.　R. Simeon b. Eleazar says, "I shall make a parable for you. To what is the matter comparable? To a stonecutter who was cutting stone in a quarry. One time he took his chisel and went and sat down on the mountain and started to chip away little sherds from it. People came by and said to him, 'What are you doing?'

B.　"He said to them, 'Lo, I am going to uproot the mountain and move it into the Jordan River.'

C.　"They said to him, 'You will never be able to uproot the entire mountain.'

D.　"He continued chipping away at the mountain until he came to a huge boulder. He quarried underneath it and unearthed it and uprooted it and tossed it into the Jordan.

E.　"He said to the boulder, 'This is not your place, but that is your place.'

F.　"Likewise this is what R. Aqiba did to R. Eliezer and to R. Joshua."

The parable without F simply says that with patience one may move mountains. The parable by itself—not applied—amplifies or at least continues VI:V.1.E, the power of words of Torah to wear down the hard heart of a human being. But the parable proves peculiar to the preceding story, since the add-on, E–F, applies the parable to VI:V.1.J, the humiliation of Joshua and Eliezer. We may wonder whether, without the announcement at A that we have a parable, the parabolic character of the tale would have impressed us. The answer is that the general traits of a parable—an anonymous illustration in concrete and everyday terms of an abstract proposition—do occur in A–D, at which point the parable worked out its proposition: "he continued chipping away. . . ." Even E, without F, can remain within the limits of the announced proposition of the parable, that is, the power of patience and persistence. So only F is jarring. It clearly serves the redactor's purpose. It does not transform the parable into a story (!), since it does not impose upon the prior narrative that particularity and concrete one-time-ness that form the indicative traits of the story alone. In all, we may dismiss from the evidence of the story the present complement to the foregoing.

> VI:V. 3. A. Said R. Tarfon to him, "Aqiba, in your regard Scripture says, *He stops up streams so that they do not trickle, and what is hidden he brings into the light* (Job 28:11).
>
> B. "Things that are kept as mysteries from ordinary people has R. Aqiba brought to light."

"He said to him" does not make a story, and what is said does not bear the marks of a story, as a whole or in part.

> VI:V. 4. A. Every day he would bring a bundle of twigs [Goldin: straw], half of which he would sell in exchange for food, and half of which he would use for a garment.
>
> B. His neighbors said to him, "Aqiba, you are killing us with the smoke. Sell them to us, buy oil with the money, and by the light of a lamp do your studying."
>
> C. He said to them, "I fill many needs with that bundle, first, I repeat traditions [by the light of the fire I kindle with] them, second, I warm myself with them, third, I sleep on them."
>
> VI:V. 5. A. In time to come R. Aqiba is going to impose guilt [for failing to study] on the poor [who use their poverty as an excuse not to study].
>
> B. For if they say to them, "Why did you not study the Torah," and they reply, "Because we were poor," they will say to them, "But was not R. Aqiba poorer and more poverty-stricken?"
>
> C. If they say, "Because of our children [whom we had to work to support]," they will say to them, "Did not R. Aqiba have sons and daughters?"

D. So they will say to them, "Because Rachel, his wife, had the merit [of making it possible for him to study, and we have no equivalent helpmates; our wives do not have equivalent merit at their disposal]."

It is hard to classify VI:V.4 as other than a narrative setting for a conversation. But the conversation makes no point by itself. In fact the whole forms a prologue to VI:V.6, which does make a powerful point.

VI:V. 6. A. It was at the age of forty that he went to study the Torah. Thirteen years later he taught the Torah in public.
B. They say that he did not leave this world before there were silver and golden tables in his possession,
C. and before he went up onto his bed on golden ladders.
D. His wife went about in golden sandals and wore a golden tiara of the silhouette of the city [Jerusalem].
E. His disciples said to him, "My lord, you have shamed us by what you have done for her [since we cannot do the same for our wives]."
F. He said to them, "She bore a great deal of pain on my account for [the study of] the Torah."

This item completes the foregoing, the narrative of how Rachel's devotion to Aqiba's study of the Torah produced a rich reward. The "they said to him . . . he said to them" sequences do not comprise a story or even establish much of a narrative framework. The upshot is that for Aqiba we have a sequence of narratives but only one story, that at the beginning. The composite does not hang together very well, but it does make a few important points.

This brings us to the story of the origins, in the Torah, of Eliezer. Let us turn directly to the account:

VI:VI. 1. A. How did R. Eliezer ben Hyrcanus begin [his Torah study]?
B. He had reached the age of twenty-two years and had not yet studied the Torah. One time he said, "I shall go and study the Torah before Rabban Yohanan ben Zakkai."
C. His father, Hyrcanus, said to him, "You are not going to taste a bit of food until you have plowed the entire furrow."
D. He got up in the morning and plowed the entire furrow.
E. They say that that day was Friday. He went and took a meal with his father-in-law.
F. And some say that he tasted nothing from the sixth hour on Friday until the sixth hour on Sunday.

The narrative is rather strange, since none of the actions is given a motivation. That immediately evident difference between Eliezer's and Aqiba's story will later on prove still more striking than it does now. But it suffices to note the points on which the two stories diverge in narrative technique. While in the case of Aqiba, we know why the great master originally determined to study the Torah, in the instance of Eliezer we do not. All we know is that at the mature age of twenty-two, he determined to study in the session of Yohanan ben Zakkai. My judgment is that the storyteller has in mind the task of explaining Eliezer's origins as Yohanan's disciple, not working out the inner motivation of the disciple. That accounts, also, for the random details, none of which fits together with the next. I see only a sequence of unintegrated details: he was twenty-two and decided to study the Torah. His father said, "Do not eat until you plow the furrow." He plowed the furrow. Then he went and ate with his father-in-law. Some say he did not eat until Sunday. These details, scarcely connected, produce no effect either of narrative or of a propositional character.

VI:VI. 2. A. On the way he saw a rock. He picked it up and took it and put it into his mouth.

B. And some say that what he picked up was cattle dung.

C. He went and spent the night at his hostel.

Even if we read VI:VI.2 as part of VI:VI.1, all we have is more unintegrated details. Nothing in VI:VI.1–2 points to a cogent narrative, let alone a story. All we have are odd bits of information about what someone "said." The whole conglomerate does serve, however, to set the stage for VI:VI.3. The details necessary to understand what is coming have now made their appearance, and the climax is before us: he went and studied, and, because he had not eaten, produced bad breath. Yohanan recognized the bad breath and said, "Just as you suffered, so you will enjoy a reward."

VI:VI. 3. A. He went and entered study session before Rabban Yohanan ben Zakkai in Jerusalem.

B. Since a bad odor came out of his mouth, Rabban Yohanan ben Zakkai said to him, "Eliezer my son, have you taken a meal today?"

C. He shut up.

D. He asked him again, and he shut up again.

E. He sent word and inquired at his hostel, and asked, "Has Eliezer eaten anything with you?"

F. They sent word to him, "We thought that he might be eating with my lord."

G. He said, "For my part, I thought that he might be eating

with you. Between me and you, we should have lost R. Eliezer in the middle."

H.   He said to him, "Just as the odor of your mouth has gone forth, so will a good name in the Torah go forth for you."

VI:VI. 4. A.   Hyrcanus, his father, heard that he was studying the Torah with Rabban Yohanan ben Zakkai. He decided, "I shall go and impose on Eliezer my son a vow not to derive benefit from my property."

B.   They say that that day Rabban Yohanan ben Zakkai was in session and expounding [the Torah] in Jerusalem, and all the great men of Israel were in session before him. [Eliezer] heard that [his father] was coming. He set up guards, saying to them, "If he comes to take a seat, do not let him."

C.   He came to take a seat and they did not let him.

D.   He kept stepping over people and moving forward until he came to Ben Sisit Hakkeset and Naqdimon b. Gurion and Ben Kalba Sabua. He sat among them, trembling.

E.   They say, On that day Rabban Yohanan ben Zakkai looked at R. Eliezer, indicating to him, "Cite an appropriate passage and give an exposition."

F.   He said to him, "I cannot cite an appropriate passage."

G.   He urged him, and the other disciples urged him.

H.   He went and cited an opening passage and expounded matters the like of which no ear had ever heard.

I.   And at every word that he said, Rabban Yohanan ben Zakkai arose and kissed him on his head and said, "My lord, Eliezer, my lord, you have taught us truth."

J.   As the time came to break up, Hyrcanus his father stood up and said, "My lords, I came here only to impose a vow on my son, Eliezer, not to derive benefit from my possession. Now all of my possessions are given over to Eliezer my son, and all my other sons are disinherited and will have no share in them."

We have a beginning: Hyrcanus plans to go and place Eliezer under vow that would ban the son from all contact with, or benefit from, his family; he would say something like "Qorban [as a Temple offering], all my possessions are forbidden to you as though they were holy, an offering to the Lord in the Temple." That would then prevent Eliezer from deriving any benefit from his father's estate and would cut him off from his family. That is a considerable and weighty act, as we can well imagine. So the stated plan of disinheritance through a ferocious vow not only begins the story, but it also creates an enormous tension. A dramatic setting is then portrayed: do not let the father sit down at the back, so that the father will sit among the greatest men of Jerusalem (B–D). Yohanan then calls upon Eliezer to speak, and, after appropriate urging, he does. The tension is resolved at the climax, which also is the conclusion. I cannot think of a more perfect story, since every detail contributes to the whole, and the storyteller's intent—to underline the reward coming to the disciple, even though his family originally opposes his joining the sage—is fully realized. We note, therefore, that the conglomerate of narratives involving both Aqiba and Eliezer in fact rests in each case on a single story, and that story forms the redactional focus, permitting the aggregation of further materials, not all of them of a finished character, and some of them not stories at all.

Let us now stand back and review the whole composite involving both Aqiba and Eliezer, which, in the aggregate, makes the point that one can start Torah study in mature years. VI:IV.1 serves only as a preface to the autonomous materials collected on the theme of how two famous masters began their studies late in life, having had no prior education. Both figures, moreover, started off poor but got rich when they became famous. These are Eliezer and Aqiba. There is no clear connection between the materials and the original saying. Perhaps the reference to wallowing in the dust of their feet in connection with Eliezer is meant to link up to the detail that he put a piece of dirt or cow dung in his mouth, but that seems to me farfetched. We refer first to Eliezer, then to Aqiba, but tell the stories in reverse order.

The diverse stories on Aqiba are hardly harmonious, since one set knows nothing of his wife, while the other introduces her as the main figure. I also find puzzling the failure of the storyteller to take an interest in the source of Aqiba's great wealth. The sequence on Eliezer goes over a recurrent theme, but is as incoherent as the foregoing. No. 1 presents a number of problems of continuity, since 1.1A–D are simply gibberish, there being no clear relationship between C and B. How 1.E–F fit in I cannot say. One may make a good case for treating VI:VI.1 and VI:VI.2 as continuous. But because of the detail on the way he saw a rock, it seems to me that we are on good ground in treating the latter as a fragment of yet another story, rather than as a bridge. VI:VI.3 is on its own coherent and complete, a cogent and readily comprehended statement on its own. VI:VI.4 also works well, beginning to end.

PART FIVE

THE TARGUMIM

XXV

The Targumim in the Context

of Rabbinic Literature

Paul V. McCracken Flesher

THE HEBREW NOUN *TARGUM* AND ITS VERBAL FORMS ORIGINALLY HAD THE SAME range of meanings as the English word "translation." It referred to—and still refers to—both the act of translating from one language into another and the resulting written text. But during the rabbinic period, the word *targum* developed a more specific meaning—that of translation into Aramaic, used most often of written translations. Indeed the rabbinic period saw the composition of a number of *targumim* (targums). To judge by the targums we now possess, the Pentateuch received the most interest, but the prophetic books were all translated into Aramaic, as were most of the books of the Writings.

The targums have long been the poor cousins of rabbinic literature. In the scholarly hierarchy, the Babylonian Talmud has had pride of place, followed by other legal literature, and then the Midrashim. If rabbinic scholars had any time left over after studying these texts (which few have had), they then turned to the targumim. This hierarchy matches the historical emphasis of Judaism on the halakhic approach to life; scholars studied the Talmud and its associated legal writings for guidance on how to properly lead a Jewish life. The targumim were irrelevant because they contained little useful or authoritative material. Over the past few decades, however, a second, historical goal of study has gained importance— particularly in the universities—that of understanding how Jews in the past lived, what they believed, and how they organized their religion. This emphasis provides the study of targums with a larger role to play.

This chapter aims to place the targumim within the broader scheme of rabbinic Judaism. Indeed, the key to the targums' usefulness to modern scholarship lies in understanding where and when different targums were composed, and in how they functioned in the rabbinic world. This essay draws a schematic picture of how different targums were created and used in the rabbinic period; it does not provide a "state of the field," or a history of scholarship.[1] Like any scheme, it will be overly simple, with the bumps and kinks glossed over. But my goal is to provide the reader with a working foundation for understanding the targums' place in rabbinic Judaism, a foundation that can be built upon as the reader acquires more detailed knowledge.[2]

1.

IDENTIFYING THE DOCUMENTS

A. *The Pentateuchal Targum*   Two sets of targums to the Pentateuch appeared during the rabbinic period: the Palestinian Targums—which include Targum Neofiti, Targum Pseudo-Jonathan, the Fragmentary Targums, the targum fragments from the Cairo Geniza, and the targumic *toseftot*—and the sole Babylonian targum, Targum Onqelos.[3] While the Palestinian Targums and Targum Onqelos use different styles, different approaches to translation, and different dialects, they nonetheless have influenced each other over the centuries. This influence

---

[1] For other introductions that provide this type of information, see: Philip S. Alexander, "Jewish Aramaic Translations of Hebrew Scriptures," *Mikra*, ed. Martin Jan Mulder and Harry Sysling (Minneapolis, MN: Fortress Press, 1990) 217–54; idem, "Targum, Targumim," *The Anchor Bible Dictionary*, (New York: Doubleday, 1992) 6:320–31; Roger Le Déaut, "The Targumim," *The Cambridge History of Judaism*, ed. W. D. Davies and Louis Finkelstein (Cambridge: Cambridge University Press, 1989) 2:563–90; and E. Schürer, *The History of the Jewish People in the Age of Jesus Christ*, ed. G. Vermes and F. Millar (Edinburgh: T&T Clark, 1973) 1:99–114. For more comprehensive bibliography, see: B. Grossfeld, *A Bibliography of Targum Literature* (New York: Sefer Hermon Press, 1972–90), and *The Newsletter for Targumic and Cognate Studies*, begun in 1974 and presently edited by E. G. Clarke of the University of Toronto. For collections of the most recent studies, see *Targum Studies*, vol. 1, ed. Paul V. M. Flesher (Atlanta: Scholars Press, 1992); *Textus* vol. 16. M. McNamara and D.R.G. Beattie are currently editing the proceedings of the 1992 conference, "The Aramaic Bible: Targums in Their Historical Context," held at the Irish National Academy for Sheffield Academic Press (hereinafter, McNamara and Beattie, forthcoming).

[2] This chapter draws on the research of many scholars over many decades. But due to the synthetic nature of its discussion, it cannot cite them all. Please refer to the works in the opening footnote for fuller bibliographic details.

[3] The Neofiti manuscript also contains marginal and interlinear glosses. Many of these belong to the Palestinian Targum tradition, while others derive from Targum Onqelos.

moved in both directions, from the Palestinian Targums to Onqelos the Babylonian Targum, and later back again. To explain this interaction, I shall describe these targums by focusing on the three stages in which they were composed.

The earliest rabbinic targums for which we possess texts are Targum Neofiti and the targum fragments found in the Cairo Geniza. Targum Neofiti was discovered in 1956 by A. Díez Macho in the Vatican Library, where it had lain miscataloged since the nineteenth century. The manuscript comprises a sixteenth-century copy of a targum originally composed sometime between the mid-second and the early fourth centuries C.E. (Unless otherwise specified, all dates refer to the Common Era.) It was written in Jewish-Palestinian Aramaic and covers every verse of the five pentateuchal books, except for those missing due to copyist errors or erasures by a censor.

Neofiti's text combines literal translation with a significant amount of additional material. The translation is word-for-word, often representing not just every Hebrew word, but every particle, prefix, and suffix as well. Within this literal rendering, the targumist has inserted nontranslation material. These additions, or expansions, are sometimes only a word or two long, other times a paragraph or two. Neofiti's targumist has woven most of the expansions into the translation so that they fit without interruption or break. This approach essentially allows the additions to masquerade as translation, disguising them from all but the most learned. The hidden character of the additional material, in turn, enables the targumist to add details, change the meaning, and even to rewrite a story—all without the audience or readers being aware. At times the expansions appear by themselves, adding a single, exegetical point or recasting a law to match current halakhic understandings. Other times, several expansions work together to recast a single story, such as that of Adam and Eve in Gen. 2–3, or to predict the future, as in Moses' blessings in Deut. 33.

The Cairo Geniza targum fragments were originally found by S. Schechter who, at the turn of the century, discovered that the Ben Ezra Synagogue in Cairo had been depositing in an attic storeroom its worn-out religious texts as well as other documents that contained the divine name. This room—a *geniza*—had served the Jewish community for over a millennium. Schechter obtained permission to ship its contents to the Cambridge Library. Schechter never fully knew the wide variety of material he had discovered. Despite the acquisition of this material nearly a century ago, scholars are still sifting through the fragments and discovering new documents, including targum fragments.

The fragments of the continuous, non-Onqelos targums from the Cairo Geniza fall into the rubric of the Palestinian Targums. Fragments from seven different targums have been found. Like Neofiti, they are written in Jewish Palestinian Aramaic. The copies date from the ninth to the fourteenth centuries, but they copy Palestinian targums written before the fourth century. Unfortunately, the fragments are few; none of the manuscripts comprise even half of Genesis—the book most frequently represented—let alone the whole Pentateuch. Nevertheless, enough fragments remain from the different targums to reveal that they were composed in the same manner as Neofiti; they combine a word-for-word translation with interwoven expansions. Furthermore, wherever extant, the Cairo Geniza fragments include the same expansions as Targum Neofiti. With few exceptions, we can say that where Neofiti has an expansion, so do any extant Geniza fragments, and where Neofiti just translates, so do the existing Geniza fragments.

Targum Neofiti and the Cairo Geniza fragments contain the same expansions because they acquired those expansions from the same source. This source, called Proto-PT, supplies the sizable expansions—those more than just a few words—to every targum classed as a Palestinian Targum to the Pentateuch.[4] It may supply many of the smaller units of additional material and the translation as well, but at this stage of scholarly research, this remains unclear.

The Proto-PT source may also provide the link between the Palestinian Targums and Targum Onqelos, but to understand the link, we must first describe Onqelos' character. There is no doubt that Targum Onqelos as we know it derives from Babylonia. To begin with, it constituted the official targum for the Babylonian rabbinic scholars. In the Babylonian Talmud, the Babylonian rabbis refer to it as "our targum" (BT Qid. 49a). Whenever an Aramaic translation of a pentateuchal passage appears in the Talmud, the quote matches that of Targum Onqelos. Its exegesis is valid even for deciding questions of halakhah (i.e., law). In addition, Targum Onqelos' Aramaic contains eastern grammatical forms and vocabulary, which indicate that it derived from the Babylonian region.

In contrast to this purely eastern characterization, Targum Onqelos contains other features that link it to the west and specifically to the Palestinian Targums. First, Onqelos contains many elements that link it to Palestinian dialects of Aramaic, in particular, that evidenced by the Aramaic texts from Qumran. Second, despite its usually word-for-word approach to translation, Targum Onqelos occasionally adds a few words to its translation or renders a verse in an interpretive form rather than in a literal or even paraphrastic manner. These deviances from literal translation usually occur at places where the Palestinian Targums contain additional material. Indeed, to the extent permitted by the insertion's brevity, Onqelos' additional words or interpretive rendering often echo or allude to the larger Palestinian expansions found at those verses.

To explain the evidence for both western and eastern features, scholars think that Targum Onqelos originated in Palestine and then was thoroughly revised in Babylonia. The first version of what became Targum Onqelos was probably written in Palestine prior to 135 C.E. This accounts for the Qumran-like aspects of its Aramaic. The exact nature of this text, sometimes designated Proto-Onqelos, is unclear. But its links with the expansive material of the Palestinian Targums suggest

---

[4]For a fuller discussion of the sources underlying the Palestinian Targums to the Pentateuch, see Paul V. M. Flesher, "Exploring the Sources of the Synoptic Targums to the Pentateuch," in *Targum Studies*, pp. 101–34.

that Proto-Onqelos might have been Proto-PT or a Palestinian Targum based upon it. The second stage of Targum Onqelos came about when this text was brought to Babylonia. There, sometime prior to the end of the fourth century, it was revised, with the targumist taking out much of the nontranslation material and recasting the language into a more eastern dialect. This revised version became authoritative among Babylonian Jewry and became the text we know today as Targum Onqelos. The importance of Targum Onqelos led to the Babylonian scholars devising a *masorah* for it to ensure accurate copying of the text. This gave Targum Onqelos a much more stable textual tradition than the Palestinian Targums.

But the story of the interrelationships between the Palestinian Targums and Targum Onqelos does not stop there. After its acceptance among Babylonian Jewry, Targum Onqelos moved back west into the eastern Mediterranean region (e.g., Syria, Palestine, and Egypt), perhaps accompanying the migration of the Babylonian Talmud. Here, Targum Onqelos established itself as the predominant targum to the Pentateuch and gradually supplanted the Palestinian Targums. This movement began sometime after the fourth century and before the seventh century, and probably was largely complete by the ninth century.

Among Jews in the eastern Mediterranean region, there were several different reactions to the rising ascendancy of Targum Onqelos. These reactions can be seen by the different Palestinian Targums that developed. First, a version of the Palestinian Targums was developed that could be used alongside Onqelos, without competing with it, namely, the so-called Fragmentary Targums. These targums are not continuous, but appear to contain "extracts" from one. These extracts are arranged consecutively in the pentateuchal order—sometimes including words or phrases from a few verses in a chapter, other times skipping several chapters at once.[5] The most obvious type of extract is the additional material based on Proto-PT, but others often contain just a few words which update technical terms, define *hapax legomena*, or correct "errors." Although most of the literal translation has been left out, a few extracts contain just a translation of a verse. Like Neofiti, the two main recensions of the Fragmentary Targums—represented by manuscripts in the Paris and Vatican libraries—are written in Jewish-Palestinian Aramaic. They constitute a reaction to Targum Onqelos' importance—presenting material not found in it. Thus, with Onqelos supplying the literal translation and the Fragmentary Targum supplying the interpretive material, the two targums could be used together without competition.

In addition to Fragmentary Targums which contain extracts arranged consecutively through the Pentateuch, there are also collections of Proto-PT expansions organized according to a liturgical order. These are called Festival Collections, some of which were found in the Cairo Geniza. They bring together expansions

---

[5] These should not be confused with the Cairo Geniza targum fragments, which are remains of once complete texts.

of the Proto-PT type that would have been read on specific holidays. Thus, one collection (Klein, MS J) contains readings for Shavuot, Purim, and the Seventh Day of Passover, while another (Klein, MS Y) has readings for Shavuot, Passover, and Rosh HaShanah. These collections apparently comprise the forerunners of the medieval Maḥzorim—prayer books for the holidays, some of which contain targums to the biblical readings. Maḥzor Vitry even translates the readings for the Passover liturgy (Ex. 13:17–15:26 and Ex. 19:1–20:26) by interweaving the literal translation of Onqelos with the Proto-PT expansions as found in the Paris Fragmentary Targum. The Festival Collections were probably organized sometime after the seventh century.

The second reaction to the new importance of Targum Onqelos in the west appears in Targum Pseudo-Jonathan. It attempts to combine Targum Onqelos' translation with the Proto-PT additions and with other interpretive material. This results in a second complete targum to the Pentateuch, but one with significantly more expansive material than Targum Neofiti. The new additions are often gleaned from known rabbinic writings, such as Sifra and the Babylonian Talmud, but some are unparalleled. Usually this material is simply added into the targum, but Pseudo-Jonathan's targumist sometimes uses it to recast the Proto-PT material. The combination of these sources results in a targum written in three different types of Aramaic: the Eastern dialect of Onqelos, the Palestinian dialect of Proto-PT, with most of the newer additions written in Late Jewish Literary Aramaic—a dialect similar to Syriac. The exact date of this targum is unclear, with scholars arguing for dates ranging from the mid-fourth up to the late eighth century.[6]

The third reaction to Onqelos' ascendency appears in the Tosefta targums, or targumic *toseftot*. These are individual Proto-PT expansions—usually fairly large—that have been recast into an Onqelos-like dialect. They appear in manuscripts of Targum Onqelos—either in the text, written into the margins, or placed at the end. Some have been brought together into independent collections. The dating for this material is uncertain; apart from the suggestion that they were created in the medieval period, there is little else to say.

B. *Targums to the Prophets*

Two targums to the Prophets existed in the rabbinic period. Among Babylonian Jewry, Targum Jonathan dominated, while among Palestinian Jewry, the Palestinian Targum to the Prophets seems to have been used.

The description of Targum Jonathan to the Prophets—apocryphally attributed to Jonathan b. Uziel (BT Meg. 3a)—is quite similar to that of Targum Onqelos.

---

[6] For a discussion of the dating of Pseudo-Jonathan, see S. A. Kaufman, "Dating the Language of the Palestinian Targums and Their use in the Study of First Century CE Texts," in McNamara and Beattie, forthcoming. The author would like to thank Professor Kaufman for his helpful answers to inquiries concerning linguistic matters. For a contrary view, see Robert Hayward, "Red Heifer and Golden Calf: Dating Targum Pseudo-Jonathan," in *Targum Studies*, pp. 9–32.

Targum Jonathan's translation tends to be literal, but it contains somewhat more expansive material than Onqelos. In addition, like Onqelos' rendition of the Pentateuch, Targum Jonathan became for the Babylonian rabbis the authoritative targum to the prophetic books, both the Former and the Latter Prophets. In several passages in the Babylonian Talmud, a verse from Targum Jonathan is cited as giving the correct rendering of a biblical passage. Indeed, in BT Moed Qatan 28b, Targum Jonathan's rendering provides the correct interpretation of Zech. 12:11, which R. Joseph claims would be unknown without the targum.

But the similarities between the two targums come out most strongly when we realize that Targum Jonathan migrated across the Middle East with Targum Onqelos. Like Onqelos, Jonathan was composed in two stages. The first took place in Palestine about the same time as Proto-Onqelos, probably between 70 and 135. In the second stage, this early Jonathan was taken to Babylonia, where in the third or fourth century it was extensively revised. These revisions enabled it to become the authoritative translation of the Prophets among Babylonian Jewry. When Targum Onqelos was taken west, Targum Jonathan accompanied it, likewise rising to importance among the Jews in the eastern Mediterranean region. It eventually supplanted the Palestinian Targum to the Prophets to become the sole prophetic targum.

The evidence for the two-stage development of Targum Jonathan is twofold. First, the targum contains two types of Aramaic: a Palestinian form close to that found in the Qumran Aramaic texts and the Bar Kochba letters, and a Babylonian form. This dialectical mix directly parallels that of Targum Onqelos, which underwent the same two-part process.[7] Second, Bruce Chilton's study of key theological terms in the Targum to Isaiah reveals that the targum was composed in two stages. The first stage was done in Palestine between 70 and 135, and the second in Babylonia during the amoraic period (third through fifth centuries).[8] The convergence of these two types of evidence supports the conclusion that Targum Jonathan took shape in two stages and in different geographical locations.

The movement of Targum Jonathan westward to become the dominant prophetic targum among eastern Mediterranean Jewry affected the Palestinian Targum to the Prophets then in use. More successful than Onqelos, Jonathan essentially eliminated the Palestinian Targum. Just one set of evidence remains to indicate that such a targum ever existed, namely, the targumic *toseftot* of the Prophets found in Targum Jonathan manuscripts. Just as the Palestinian Targum to the Pentateuch provided nontranslation material that was transformed into targumic *toseftot*, so the

[7] For an alternate and intriguing interpretation of the linguistic conundrum, see E. M. Cook, "A New Perspective on the Language of Onqelos and Jonathan" in McNamara and Beattie, forthcoming.
[8] B. D. Chilton, *The Glory of Israel* (Sheffield: JSOT Press, 1983). Chilton does not emphasize the geographical provenance of his comparative material. But even a cursory reading shows that the early texts he uses are mostly Palestinian and that among the later ones, the Babylonian Talmud figures most prominently. In the Introduction to his translation of Targum to Isaiah in *The Aramaic Bible* series, published in 1987, Chilton expands the early period from 70–135 to the tannaitic period (70–200).

Palestinian Targum to the Prophets provided material that was likewise trans-
formed. Some eighty of these *toseftot*—labeled as "Targum Yerushalmi" or "An-
other Targum"—appear in Codex Reuchlinianus' text of Targum Jonathan.[9]
Other *toseftot* appear in other manuscripts. Like the pentateuchal *toseftot*, these are
Palestinian expansions that have been recast into a dialect matching that of Targums
Onqelos and Jonathan.

C. The Targums to the Writings   Nearly every book of the Writings has a
targum; only Ezra, Nehemiah, and Daniel do not. Each book has its own, individual targum; no single targum covers all the Writings as does Targum Onqelos for
the Pentateuch and Targum Jonathan for the Prophets. In general, most of the
targums to the Writings are late, probably composed between the sixth and the
ninth centuries. Most contain additional material borrowed from the Babylonian
Talmud and other rabbinic texts. In fact, whereas the Talmud speaks of the targums
to the Pentateuch and the Prophets, it states that there is no targum to the Writings
(BT Meg. 3a). Furthermore, many of the Writings Targums have been influenced
by both the Palestinian Targums to the Pentateuch and Targum Onqelos, and occasionally even Targum Jonathan to the Prophets. Finally, the Writings Targums
blend characteristics from both eastern and western dialects of Aramaic. Most frequently these features derive from the dialects of the Palestinian Targums to the
Pentateuch (western) and Targum Onqelos (eastern), but they often include aspects
found in the Aramaic of the Babylonian Talmud. All these factors point to the
conclusion that the different Writings Targums were composed in the eastern
Mediterranean region after the Babylonian Talmud and the Babylonian targums
of Onqelos and Jonathan came west—that is, during the seventh century or
later.[10]

We can divide the targums to the Writings into three general categories: (1)
the Five Megillot, (2) Job and Psalms, and (3) Proverbs and Chronicles.[11]

The Five Megillot—Qohelet, Song of Songs, Lamentations, Ruth, and Esther—all have targums. Esther, in fact, has two.[12] These targums are quite expansive. Each targum contains two or three times the amount of material in the Hebrew book they translate. They possess identifiable additions borrowed from the

---

[9] Codex Reuchlinianus has been dated to 1105 and is housed in the Badische Landesbibliothek in
Karlsruhe.

[10] There is also a targum to Tobit, which is based on the Greek text. It has no similarities with the
Qumran Aramaic fragments of Tobit being edited by J. Fitzmyer. He argues in his forthcoming analysis
that the fragments constitute remains of the original form of Tobit, not translations.

[11] These groupings should not be taken to imply common authorship. They merely indicate shared
characteristics.

[12] Some scholars have argued that there are three targums to Esther. But recent studies have shown that
the third is a Renaissance reworking of the first. See R. Le Déaut and B. Grossfeld, "The Origin and
Nature of the Esther Targum in the Antwerp Polyglot: Exit Targum Esther III?" *Textus* 16 (1991):
95–115.

Babylonian Talmud and other rabbinic texts. Most of them also share material with the Midrash Rabbah to their book (Targum to Qohelet with Qohelet Rabbah, Targum to Ruth with Ruth Rabbah, and so on). While showing Palestinian features in their language, they also contain elements of eastern dialects—elements found in Targum Onqelos or the Babylonian Talmud.

The targums to Job and Psalms mix literal translation with expansive material, somewhat like the Palestinian pentateuchal targums.[13] But they also show the influence of rabbinic midrashim in a style not found in other targums. In a number of verses, these targums have two or more different translations and/or interpretations. Each one is marked by the words "another targum," or "another wording [literally "language"]." This echoes the Midrashic term for introducing multiple Midrashic interpretations, namely, "another matter." These are the only targums to interrupt the text's narrative flow and introduce to the reader an awareness that there is no single translation. In other words, instead of hiding the additions by interweaving them with the translation, these targums identify the different translations and interpretations. Finally, the targums are written in the dialect of Late Jewish Literary Aramaic, which is also found in Targum Pseudo-Jonathan.

The targums to Proverbs and Chronicles fit together because both show evidence of links to the Peshitta versions of these books (Christian translations into the Aramaic dialect of Syriac). This is most pronounced in the Proverbs Targum, where nearly a third of the verses are word-for-word identical to the Peshitta. It has no rabbinic exegesis at all, not even any material identifying wisdom as Torah—a theme prevalent in rabbinic literature and emphasized in the Qohelet Targum. The Targum to Chronicles also shows signs of links with the Peshitta, but these are not as extensive as those in the Targum to Proverbs. While consisting of a literal translation, the Targum to Chronicles occasionally incorporates expansive material, often borrowed from the Babylonian Talmud. Furthermore, wherever Chronicles shares material with the books of Samuel and Kings, the base translation of the Chronicles Targum often seems to have copied from their targums. The Chronicles Targum also has borrowed some material from a Palestinian Targum to the Pentateuch, probably Pseudo-Jonathan.

In conclusion, the targums to all three divisions of the Hebrew Bible fit into the three-stage scheme we outlined for the pentateuchal targums. Stage one comprises the early Palestinian Targums represented by Targum Neofiti and the Cairo Geniza fragments, as well as the Palestinian Targum to the Prophets. Stage two, in Babylonia, consists of Targum Onqelos and Targum Jonathan to the Prophets. Stage three includes the later Palestinian Pentateuchal Targums—Pseudo-Jonathan, the Fragmentary Targums, and the targumic *toseftot*—and most of the Writings Targums.

---

[13] The rabbinic targum to Job bears no relationship to the Job targum found at Qumran, 11QTgJob. The Qumran targum is highly literal, with practically no additional material; it was composed prior to the rabbinic period in an earlier form of Aramaic. (See below.)

2.
TRANSLATIONS INTO ENGLISH

The rabbinic targums are being translated into English in *The Aramaic Bible* series, under the editorship of Martin McNamara. Initially, Michael Glazier Press of Wilmington, Delaware, published the volumes. But this imprint has been acquired by the Liturgical Press of Collegeville, Minnesota. Translations of most of the targums have already appeared: Targum Onqelos, Targum Jonathan to the Prophets, Job, Proverbs, Qohelet, Esther, Chronicles, and Ruth. The Genesis volumes of Targums Neofiti and Pseudo-Jonathan have also been published. Each volume contains introductory essays and select bibliography.

Critical editions to each of the Palestinian Targums to the Pentateuch have been published separately. The discoverer of Targum Neofiti, Alexandro Díez Macho, published the targum in six volumes as *Neophyti I. Targum Palestinense Ms de la Biblioteca Vaticana* (Barcelona-Madrid: Consejo Superior de Investigaciones Científicas, 1968–79). These volumes include translations into English, Spanish, and French. There are several editions of the sole manuscript of Pseudo-Jonathan; the best is by E. G. Clarke, W. E. Aufrecht et al., *Targum Pseudo-Jonathan of the Pentateuch* (Hoboken, N.J.: Ktav, 1984). It includes a concordance. An earlier edition of Pseudo-Jonathan still being widely used is D. Rieder, *Pseudo-Jonathan: Targum Jonathan ben Uziel on the Pentateuch Copied from the London MS . . .* (Jerusalem: Salomon's Printing Press, 1972). The Fragmentary Targums have been edited and translated by Michael L. Klein as *The Fragment-Targums of the Pentateuch: According to Their Extant Sources* (Rome: Biblical Institute Press, 1980). Klein has also edited and translated all the Palestinian Targum fragments from the Cairo Geniza, including festival collections and *toseftot*, in his *Genizah Manuscripts of Palestinian Targum to the Pentateuch* (Cincinnati: Hebrew Union College Press, 1986). Finally, A. Díez Macho has brought together, in a synoptic format, Targums Neofiti and Pseudo-Jonathan, the Paris and Vatican Fragmentary Targums, and some of the Geniza fragments in his *Biblia Polyglotta Matritensia* (Madrid: Consejo Superior de Investigaciones Científicas, 1977–80). Only Díez Macho's polyglot edition of Pseudo-Jonathan notes the difference between the manuscript and the edition printed in early rabbinic Bibles.

Critical editions of most of the targums not belonging to the Palestinian Targums to the Pentateuch have been published by Alexander Sperber in his series *The Bible in Aramaic* (Leiden: Brill, 1959–73). The volumes include Targum Onqelos (with some *toseftot*), Targum Jonathan to the Prophets, and most of the Writings Targums. Sperber includes the targums to Qohelet, Chronicles, Ruth, Song of Songs, and Lamentations and one targum to Esther, but leaves out the second Esther targum as well as the targums to Psalms, Proverbs, and Job. No critical editions have been published for these last targums. (Several doctoral dissertations have produced critical texts of the targums to Psalms, Job, Qohelet; see Grossfeld's bibliography, vol. 3.) Finally, L. Díez Merino is currently preparing an edition of the prophetic targumic *toseftot* found in Codex Reuchlinianus.

3.
SAMPLE PASSAGES

A brief look at a few sample passages will illustrate the nature of the different targums described above. We shall begin with the pentateuchal targums.

The first stage of the Palestinian Targums for which we have evidence consists of Targum Neofiti and the Cairo Geniza fragments. I present in parallel columns Gen. 29:20–23 from the Hebrew Text, Targum Neofiti, and MS E of the Cairo Geniza targum fragments. The roman typeface indicates the literal translation of the Hebrew, while the italics indicates additions or changes.

Gen. 29:20–23[14]

Hebrew Text	Targum Neofiti	Cairo Geniza MS E
(20) And Jacob served for Rachel seven years, and they were in his eyes as but a few days because of his love of her.	(20) And Jacob served for Rachel seven years, and they were in his *face* as but a few days because of the love *with which he loved her.*	(20) And Jacob served for Rachel seven years *of days*, and they were in his *face* as but a few days because *of the extent that* he loved her.
(21) And Jacob said to Laban: "Give [me] my wife because the days are completed and I will go in to her."	(21) And Jacob said to Laban: "Give me my wife because the days *of my service* are completed and I will go in to her."	(21) And Jacob said to Laban: "Give me my wife because the days *of my service* are completed and I will *be joined with* her."
(22) And Laban gathered together all the people of the place and made a feast.	(22) And Laban gathered together all the people of the place and made a feast.	(22) And Laban gathered together all the people of the place and made a feast.

[14] The Hebrew translation is my own. The translations of Neofiti and the Cairo Geniza are from McNamara's translation in *The Aramaic Bible* series.

Gen. 29:20–23

Hebrew Text	Targum Neofiti	Cairo Geniza MS E
	Laban spoke up and said to them: "Behold, this pious man has dwelt among us seven years.	*Laban spoke up and said to the people of the place: "Behold this man has dwelt among us seven years of days;*
	Our wells have not diminished; our watering troughs have multiplied and now, what counsel do you give me that we may make him dwell amongst us here seven more years?"	*our springs have been blessed and our flocks of sheep have multiplied; and, now, give me counsel as to what we should do for him so that he dwell beside us seven further years."*
	And they gave him	*And the people of the place stood up and gave him*
	deceptive counsel: to marry him to Leah instead of Rachel	*deceptive counsel and they married him to Leah instead of Rachel*
(23) And it came to pass in the evening and he took Leah his daughter and brought her to him; and he went in to her.	(23) And it came to pass that in the evening and he took Leah his daughter and brought her to him; and he went in to her.	(23) And it came to pass that in the evening and he took Leah his daughter and brought her to him; and he was joined with her.

Except for the large addition in v. 22, both Neofiti and Cairo Geniza MS E are quite literal; they reproduce nearly every word in the Hebrew Text. Occasionally, they add a word or two, but these are woven into the translation in a manner that makes them part of the translation. Even v. 22's addition fits into the narrative, adding a conversation at the party in such a way that no one who did not have the Hebrew text memorized would suspect it was not part of the translation. The important point to note is that the large additions in Neofiti and Geniza MS E are essentially the same, differing occasionally in wording, but not in structure or rhetoric. This is a Proto-PT expansion, part of the shared source among the Palestinian Targums to the Pentateuch.

The Proto-PT expansion in Gen. 29:22 occurs in the later targums of stage two as well. The Fragmentary Targums and Targum Pseudo-Jonathan contain the expansion, although no targumic tosefta exists.

Both the main Fragmentary Targums—Paris and Vatican—contain the expansion of Gen. 29:22, but they lack the adjacent verses. The wording of Paris' addition is close to that of Geniza MS E, while that of the Vatican more closely parallels Neofiti's wording. While neither are exact copies of the earlier targums, they are close enough that their links stand out.

Targum Pseudo-Jonathan's version of Gen. 29:22's expansion follows Targum Neofiti's, but adds a twist. Instead of just seeking advice, Laban implores his audience to give deceitful advice.

I aban gathered all the men of the place and made *them* a feast. *He spoke up and said to them, "Behold, it is seven years since Jacob came among us; our wells have not failed, and our watering troughs have multiplied. So now, come, let us plan a plan of deceit so that he may remain among us." And they gave him a counsel of deceit, to marry I eah to him instead of Rachel.*[15]

The wording of Pseudo-Jonathan's expansion is similar to that of Targum Neofiti's, and its structure and rhetoric are nearly identical. Only Laban's request for "deceitful" advice provides a noticeable change in any meaning.

If we look at Targum Onqelos' version of the Genesis 29:20–23, its literal character clearly stands out.

Gen. 29:20–23[16]

Hebrew Text	*Targum Onqelos*
(20) And Jacob served for Rachel seven years, and they were in his eyes as but a few days because of his love of her.	(20) And Jacob served for Rachel seven years, and they were in his eyes as but a few days because of his love of her.
(21) And Jacob said to Laban: "Give [me] my wife because the days are completed and I will go in to her."	(21) And Jacob said to Laban: "Give [me] my wife because the days *of my service* are completed and I will go in to her."
(22) And Laban gathered together all the people of the place and made a feast.	(22) And Laban gathered together all the people of the place and made a feast.
(23) And it came to pass in the evening and he took Leah his daughter and brought her to him; and he went in to her.	(23) And it came to pass in the evening and he took Leah his daughter and brought her to him; and he went in to her.

[15] The translation is from Michael Maher's translation of Pseudo-Jonathan in *The Aramaic Bible* series.
[16] The Hebrew translation is my own, as is that of Targum Onqelos.

In these four verses, TO is completely literal except for "of my service" in verse 21. This single Aramaic word actually copies a word that appears in all the Palestinian Targums, as can be seen in TN and CG above.

We now turn to Targum Jonathan to the Prophets. Usually the Targum to the Prophets, like Onqelos, is quite literal. For example, the following quote shows how closely the targum follows the Hebrew text. Of the few words that are not exact translations (indicated by italics), half are simply changes in prepositions.

Targum Jonathan to Jeremiah 11:1–3[17]
(1) The word of *prophecy* which was *with* Jeremiah from *before* the Lord, saying,
(2) "*Heed* the words of this covenant. So you shall speak *with* the men of Judah, and concerning the inhabitants of Jerusalem.
(3) "And you shall say to them, Thus says the Lord, the God of Israel, Cursed be the man who does not *heed* the words of this covenant."

Sometimes, however, the Targum to the Prophets gives an interpretive translation, which although it builds on the Hebrew, expands far beyond it. The following comparison between the Hebrew and targum texts of Jer. 2:1–3 reveals how extensive this can be.

Jeremiah 2:1–3[18]

Hebrew Text	Targum Jonathan
(1) The word of the Lord came to me, saying:	(1) And a word of *prophecy from before* the Lord was *with* me, saying:
(2) Go and proclaim in the hearing of Jerusalem, Thus says the Lord:	(2) "Go, and *prophesy before the people who are in* Jerusalem, saying: Thus says the Lord,
I remember the devotion of your youth,	I remember in your favour the *good things of the days of old*,
Your love as a bride,	the love *of your fathers who believed in my Memra*
how you followed me in the wilderness, in a land not sown.	and followed *my two messengers, Moses and Aaron*, in the wilderness *for forty years without provisions* in a land not sown.

---

[17] Robert Hayward, *The Targum of Jeremiah* (Wilmington, Del.: Michael Glazier, 1987), pp. 81.
[18] The translation of the Hebrew text is from the New Revised Standard Version, that of Targum Jonathan is from Hayward, pp. 48–49.

Jeremiah 2:1–3

Hebrew Text	Targum Jonathan
(3) Israel was holy to the Lord,	(3) *The house of* Israel are holy *before* the Lord—*in respect of those who plunder them*—
the first fruits of his harvest. All who ate of it were held guilty;	like *fruits of heave-offering of harvest*, of which whoever eats is guilty *of death; and like firstlings of harvest, the sheaf of the heave-offering, of which every one who eats, before the priests the sons of Aaron offer it as a sacrifice upon the altar*, is guilty. *Even so are all those who plunder the house of Israel guilty:*
disaster came upon them, says the Lord.	evil shall come upon them, says the Lord."

It is harder to give a passage from the Writings Targums that represents all the targums, since they were composed individually. But let me give an example of how expansive these later targums can be. Lamentations 1:1 is typical of the size of the expansions in some of the Writings Targums, especially those of the Megillot. While the Targum to Lamentations in some places provides literal translations, most verses of the first two chapters are expanded similarly to the first verse.

Lamentations 1:1[19]
Hebrew Text: How lonely sits the city that once was full of people! How like a widow she has become, she that was great among the nations! She that was a princess among the provinces has become a vassal.

Targum (parallels to the Hebrew text marked in italics): Jeremiah, the Prophet and High Priest, told how it was decreed against Jerusalem and against her people: that they would be punished by banishments, and that eulogy would be made over them by Lamentations. Just as Adam and Eve, who were punished, banished from the garden of Eden, and over whom the Lord of the Universe eulogized with Lamentations. The Attribute of Justice reported her great sinfulness, and she was evicted. Because of her many sins within her, *she will dwell alone*, as a man whose body is stricken with leprosy dwells alone. And the city that teemed with populaces and large throngs has been emptied of them, and *has become like a widow*. She who was exalted *among the nations* and reigning over

---

[19] The Hebrew translation is from the New Revised Standard Version and the targum translation is from E. Levine, *The Aramaic Version of Lamentations* (New York: Sefer Hermon, 1976), p. 63.

provinces that paid her tribute has been reduced to lowliness, and paying them head tax thereafter.

The expansion, as you can see, dwarfs the translation of the Hebrew text. While most of its meaning appears in the Aramaic, its form has been lost in the vastly larger addition. A person moderately familiar with the opening of the book of Lamentations would know that the targum contains much additional material.

4.
THE PLACE OF THE TARGUMIM
IN RABBINIC LITERATURE

The discovery of a targum to Job at Qumran shows that the rabbis were not the only ones translating the Hebrew Bible into Aramaic and raises the possibility that other people were writing targums as well.[20] The targums we have been discussing, however, were all composed by members of the rabbinic movement—not by people outside of and unfamiliar with the rabbinic world. The Palestinian Targums to the Pentateuch and the Writings Targums contain numerous additions—many of which parallel narrative or legal passages in other rabbinic texts. Both Targum Onqelos and Targum Jonathan, by contrast, originated in Palestine, but were re-edited and reshaped in Babylonia to follow more closely the Hebrew text. This cutting back of a longer translation indicates a rabbinic desire to produce a translation designed to accurately reflect the Hebrew text in accord with the legal and nonlegal beliefs of the targumists. The heavy editing did not completely eliminate aspects of Babylonian halakhic and interpretive views.

As rabbinic literature, the targums stand out from the other texts. They comprise continuous renditions of Scripture which attempt to weave additional and interpretive material into the translation in an inconspicuous manner. All other rabbinic texts consist of series of discrete, identifiable units which display interpretation, and even assemble multiple interpretations of the same passage. Indeed, the Midrashim and the talmudic literature emphasize rabbinic authority by identifying the (supposed) individuals responsible for specific interpretations and legal rulings.

---

[20] For a discussion of the Job targum, see Stephen A. Kaufman, "The Job Targum from Qumran," *JAOS* 93 (1973): 317–27. On the possibility of a Leviticus targum at Qumran, see J. A. Fitzmyer, "The Targum of Leviticus from Qumran Cave 4," *Maarav* 1 (1978): 5–23. While a number of fragments of other Aramaic texts were discoverd at Qumran, most have yet to be published. The most extensive of the published material is the so-called Genesis Apocryphon, of which we have fragments concerning Noah and Abraham. It seems to combine extensive rewriting with targumlike combinations of literal translation and additional material. Editions of the published texts, including the Job targum, can be found in J. A. Fitzmyer and D. J. Harrington, *A Manual of Palestinian Aramaic Texts* (Rome: 1978).

The targums, by contrast, erase individuals and even the knowledge that interpretations derive from human beings.

The key difference is this: the targums present themselves as Scripture, as divine revelation, while the rest of rabbinic literature promotes human authority. This makes the targums ideal tools for promoting ideas, for the views incorporated into targums are presented as divine revelation, not as human understanding. Thus targums become the perfect vehicle for propagating the rabbinic worldview not only to adherents of the rabbinic movement, but more important, to Jews who do not participate in the rabbinic movement. It can promulgate the rabbinic worldview to people who do not know about, do not understand, or are hostile to the rabbinic movement. It can do this because the beliefs and legal rulings contained in the targums are not associated with the rabbis; understanding them does not even require education.

Before we explore further the concept of targums as means for propagating views, we need to perform a reality check. Were targums used in ways that would publicize their contents to a broad audience? The answer is yes, to the best of our knowledge. While most of our evidence comes from remarks in rabbinic texts, many of the remarks suffer from the problem of definition mentioned in this chapter's opening paragraph, namely, does the term "targum" refer to general activities of translating or specifically to Aramaic translations? While the former does not necessarily exclude written targums, neither does it provide specific evidence of them.

According to different rabbinic texts, the general practice of translation occurs in three places, each of which provides an opportunity for the use of written targums: synagogue worship, education in the schools, and private study. The Mishnah (M. Meg. 4:4–6) states that in synagogue worship the weekly readings of the Torah and the *haftarah* should be read in Hebrew and then translated into Aramaic. Later, the Talmud of the Land of Palestine (Y. Meg. 4:1, 74d) forbids the use of written texts in the service (although this does not prevent their use by the translator in preparation). Sifré Deuteronomy 161 reveals that although education begins with Torah, it is followed by translation (*targum*). It is not clear whether translation in this passage means the practice of translating or the study of a written translation. The Babylonian Talmud (B. Ber. 8a–b) reveals that individuals are expected to study the weekly Scripture portion—twice in Hebrew and once in translation (*targum*). Again, it is not clear whether translation means a written text or the act of translating.

Although we cannot definitively determine whether any of the above situations involved written targumim, there is evidence to suggest that written targumim were being used by Jews in the rabbinic period. The Tosefta provides the earliest rabbinic evidence of the existence of written targums in Aramaic, although it does not reveal how they were used (Tos. Shab. 13:2–3). Furthermore, it approves of the use of Scripture translations into any language: permitting people who know no Hebrew to read Esther in their own language on Purim (Tos. Meg. 2:6) and to read most of the weekly Torah portion in their own language (Tos. Meg. 3:13). The similarity between the synagogue worship here and that discussed in the previous paragraph suggests that until the time of the Palestinian Talmud, written Aramaic targums may have been used in synagogue worship. Even more significantly, the Babylonian Talmud mentions the use of written targums in halakhic discussions—acknowledging their authority and adhering to their interpretations (e.g., B. Nazir 39a and B. San. 94b). So in the Palestinian texts, we see evidence of both translating and translations being used in synagogue worship, while in the Babylonian documents, we find that targums are valid even for establishing halakhah.

Now that we have established that targums were used in several situations and could be used in others, we return to the observation that targums were used to disseminate rabbinic viewpoints. The question is, what views did the targums portray? The answer depends on which targum we analyze, for different rabbinic groups seem to have had different concepts about the nature of Scripture and its translation. These differences in turn resulted in those groups treating the targum differently and inserting material on different subjects as well as different views on the same subjects. These differences generally correspond with the three stages of targum development previously set out.

The first stage consists of Palestine from roughly the second to the fourth centuries; it includes Targum Neofiti and the targums that remain only in the Cairo Geniza fragments. The scribes responsible for writing these targums had a clear attitude toward Scripture and its translation. While the translation should adhere to the form of the Hebrew text, the Scripture translation constituted a vehicle for its own interpretation. Thus the translation could carry with it the material that makes it understandable to its users. This attitude allowed the targumists to combine their word-for-word translation with additional material that brought the meaning of Scripture into line with their understanding. Thus when the targums' users—readers and listeners—approached it, they found a Scripture that reflected the view of the rabbinic movement. A story like that of Adam and Eve became a lesson about rabbinic values: the study, knowledge and practice of Torah, the righteous and the wicked, reward and punishment, Eden and Gehenna, this world and the world to come, and even the messiah. The targums explained obscure terms, updated geographical and historical items, shaped the theology of the text, presented the appropriate manner of talking about God, and even wrote halakhic rulings into the scriptural text.

In the second stage, Targums Onqelos and Jonathan to the Prophets were recast and rewritten. This happened in Babylonia prior to the composition of the Babylonian Talmud. These targums are thus the only texts written before the Talmud dominated the religious life of Babylonian Jewry. That these texts were cut down from more expansive targums shows that the composers felt that the form of Scripture alone was important—a dictum from which they deviated only when they could not reproduce that form, such as in poetic passages. Thus the targum became a model of Scripture—an imitation—which served to reinforce Scripture's own importance. The targum's readers, according to the Talmud, saw a translation which was authoritative, which could substitute for the Hebrew text. Even rabbis relied on it for interpretation and for guidance in deciding matters of halakhah. Thus, these targums—because of their close adherence to the biblical text—could replace that scriptural text in an official capacity. Targums Onqelos and Jonathan meant what Scripture meant, even when the meaning of Scripture was not known (e.g., BT Nazir 39a and Ber. 28b).

The targums at stage three, composed by Jews in the eastern Mediterranean region, represent a continuation of the Palestinian targums of stage one. These targums—primarily Pseudo-Jonathan and most of the Writings Targums—continue and indeed increase the tendency of the Palestinian targums to insert expansions and other additional material into the targum's translation.[21] These targums also continue the attitudes toward Scripture and its translations of the stage-one targums. The main difference is that the newer targums incorporate new material—namely, material from the Babylonian Talmud. They are influenced by both the Talmud's dialect and by those of the Targums Onqelos and Jonathan. Thus, these later targums provide some of the best evidence concerning the reception of Babylonian Judaism—including the Talmud and the Babylonian Targums—among eastern Mediterranean Jewry. We can study not only what topics, rulings, and interpretations were received but how (positively or negatively) they were received. Pseudo-Jonathan's use of talmudic materials often reveals differing halakhic positions, suggesting that the adoption was not smooth.

In conclusion, by showing the place of different targumim within rabbinic literature, we have indicated the context within which each targum developed. This in turn reveals the starting point for further investigation into each targum. Even within the limits of this chapter, we have shown that the targums are integrally linked with rabbinic Judaism in its growth.

---

[21] The Fragmentary Targums are just excerpts of earlier targums, without much change. The highly literal Targum to Proverbs also does not fit this description. Some of the targumic *toseftot* may match some of these characteristics.

PART SIX

CONCLUSION

XXVI

RABBINIC LITERATURE AND THE

FORMATION OF JUDAISM

WHAT THE PORTRAYAL OF THE RABBINIC LITERATURE GIVEN IN THE PRECEDING chapters makes possible is the documentary history of the formation of Judaism, a chapter in what is called "the documentary history of ideas."[1] The documentary history of the ideas of a religious system is a mode of relating writing to religion through history through close attention to the circumstance in which writing reached closure. It is accomplished, specifically, by assessing shifts exhibited by a sequence of documents and appealing to the generally accepted dates assigned to writings in explaining those shifts. In this way we may confront questions of cultural order, social system, and political structure, to which the texts respond explicitly and constantly. For in rabbinic literature we deal with writings that set forth an account of how the Jews are to constitute the Israel of which Scripture speaks, forming a kingdom of priests and a holy people. In that context, confronting writings of a religious character, we err by asking questions of a narrowly historical character: what did X really say on a particular occasion, and why. These questions not only are not answerable on the basis of the evidence in hand. They also are trivial, irrelevant to the character of the evidence. Even if we were to concede the

---

[1] This chapter adumbrates the account of the history of Judaism in the formative age that I present in my forthcoming *Rabbinic Judaism. A Historical Introduction* (New York, 1995: Anchor Bible Reference Library).

historical accuracy and veracity of all the many allegations of the scholars we have surveyed, how little we should know—but how much we should have *missed*—if that set of questions and answers were to encompass the whole of our inquiry.

If we are to trace the unfolding, in the sources of formative Judaism, of a given theme or ideas about a given problem, the order in which we approach the several books, that is, components of the entire canon, gives us the sole guidance on sequence, order, and context that we are apt to find. We have no way of demonstrating that authorities to whom, in a given composition, ideas are attributed really said what is assigned to them. Assuming without corroboration that we have *ipsissima verba* merely because a saying is attached to a name simply contradicts the basic premises of all contemporary historical scholarship.

What we cannot show we do not know. Lacking firm evidence, for example, in a sage's own, clearly assigned writings, or even in writings redacted by a sage's own disciples and handed on among them in the discipline of their own community, we have for chronology only a single fact. It is that a document, reaching closure at a given time, contains the allegation that Rabbi X said statement Y. So we know that people at the time that the document reached closure took the view that Rabbi X said statement Y. We may then assign to statement Y a position, in the order of the sequence of sayings, defined by the location of the document in the order of the sequence of documents. The several documents' dates, as is clear, all constitute guesses. But the sequence explained in the Introduction, Mishnah, Tosefta, Yerushalmi, Bavli, for the exegetical writings on the Mishnah is absolutely firm and beyond doubt. The sequence for the exegetical collections on Scripture, Sifra, the Sifrés, Genesis Rabbah, Leviticus Rabbah, the Pesiqtas, and beyond, is not entirely sure. Still, the position of the Sifra and the two Sifrés at the head, followed by Genesis Rabbah, then Leviticus Rabbah, then Pesiqta deRab Kahana and Lamentations Rabbati and some related collections, seems likely.

What are the canonical mainbeams that sustain the history of ideas? Three principal periods, spelled out in the preceding chapters, presently delineate the canonical sequence: the Mishnah's, in the first two centuries; the Yerushalmi's, in the next, ca. 200–400; and the Bavli's, in the third, ca. 400–600. The formative age of Judaism is the period marked at the outset by the Mishnah, taking shape from sometime before the Common Era and reaching closure at ca. 200 C.E., and at the end by the Talmud of Babylonia, ca. 600 C.E. In between these dates, two streams of writings developed, one legal, explaining the meaning of the Mishnah, the other theological and exegetical, interpreting the sense of Scripture. The high points of the former come with tractate Abot: which is the Mishnah's first apologetic; the Tosefta, a collection of supplements ca. 300 C.E.; the Talmud of the Land of Israel ca. 400 C.E.; followed by the Babylonian Talmud. The latter set of writings comprises compositions on Exodus, in Mekilta Attributed to R. Ishmael and of indeterminate date; Sifra on Leviticus; Sifre on Numbers; and another Sifre, on Deuteronomy, at a guess to be dated at ca. 300 C.E.; then Genesis Rabbah ca. 400 C.E.; Leviticus Rabbah ca. 425 C.E.; and at the end, Pesiqta deRab Kahana,

Lamentations Rabbati, and some other treatments of biblical books, all of them in the fifth or sixth centuries. The so-called Tannaitic Midrashim, Mekhilta, Sifra, and the two Sifrés, form transitional documents between the Mishnah and the Yerushalmi and its Midrash companions, Genesis Rabbah, Leviticus Rabbah, and Pesiqta deRab Kahana. Alongside the Bavli are its Midrash associates, Lamentations Rabbah, Song of Songs Rabbah, Esther Rabbah I, and Ruth Rabbah. These books and some minor related items together form the canon of Judaism as it had reached its definitive shape by the end of late antiquity.

If we lay out these writings in the approximate sequence in which—according to the prevailing consensus—they reached closure beginning with the Mishnah, the Tosefta, then Sifra and its associated compositions, followed by the Talmud of the Land of Israel, and alongside Genesis Rabbah and Leviticus Rabbah, then Pesiqta deRab Kahana and its companions, and finally the Talmud of Babylonia, we gain "canonical history." This is, specifically, the order of the appearance of ideas when the documents, read in the outlined sequence, address a given idea or topic. The consequent history consists of the sequence in which a given statement on the topic at hand was made (early, middle, or late) in the unfolding of the canonical writings. To illustrate the process, what does the authorship of the Mishnah have to say on the theme? Then how does the compositor of Abot deal with it? Then the Tosefta's compositor's record comes into view, followed by the materials assembled in the Talmud of the Land of Israel, alongside those now found in the earlier and middle ranges of compilations of scriptural exegeses, and as always, the Talmud of Babylonia at the end. In the illustrative exercise that follows we shall read the sources in exactly the order outlined here. I produce a picture of how these sources treat an important principle of the Judaism of the dual Torah. We shall see important shifts and changes in the unfolding of ideas about the symbol under study.

So, in sum, this story of continuity and change rests upon the notion that we can present the history of the treatment of a topical program in the canonical writings of that Judaism. I do not claim that the documents examined in this book represent the state of popular or synagogue opinion. I do not know whether the history of the idea in the unfolding official texts corresponds to the history of the idea among the people who stand behind those documents. Even less do I claim to speak about the history of the topic or idea at hand outside of rabbinical circles, among the Jewish nation at large. All these larger dimensions of the matter lie wholly beyond the perspective of this book. The reason is that the evidence at hand is of a particular sort and hence permits us to investigate one category of questions and not another. The category is defined by established and universally held conventions about the order in which the canonical writings reached completion. Therefore we trace the way in which matters emerge in the sequence of writings followed here.

We trace the way in which ideas were taken up and spelled out in these successive stages in the formation of the canon. Let the purpose of the exercise be emphasized. *When we follow this procedure, we discover how, within the formation of the rabbinical canon of writings, the idea at hand came to literary expression and how it was then shaped to serve the larger purposes of the nascent canonical system as a whole.* By knowing the place and uses of the topic under study within the literary evidences of the rabbinical system, we gain a better understanding of the formative history of that system. What do we not learn? Neither the condition of the people at large nor the full range and power of the rabbinical thinkers' imagination come to the fore. About other larger historical and intellectual matters we have no direct knowledge at all. Consequently we claim to report only what we learn about the canonical literature of a system evidenced by a limited factual base. No one who wants to know the history of a given idea in all the diverse Judaisms of late antiquity, or the role of that idea in the history of all the Jews in all parts of the world in the first seven centuries of the Common Era, will find it here.

In order to understand the documentary method we must again underline the social and political character of the documentary evidence presented. These are public statements, preserved and handed on because people have adopted them as authoritative. The sources constitute a collective, and therefore official, literature. All of the documents took shape and attained a place in the canon of the rabbinical movement as a whole. None was written by an individual in such a way as to testify to personal choice or decision. Accordingly, we cannot provide an account of the theory of a given individual at a particular time and place. We have numerous references to what a given individual said about the topic at hand. But these references do not reach us in the authorship of that person, or even in his language. They come to us only in the setting of a *collection* of sayings and statements, some associated with names, others unattributed and anonymous. The collections by definition were composed under the auspices of rabbinical authority—a school or a circle. They tell us what a group of people wished to preserve and hand on as authoritative doctrine about the meaning of the Mishnah and Scripture. The compositions reach us because the larger rabbinical estate chose to copy and hand them on. Accordingly, we know the state of doctrine at the stages marked by the formation and closure of the several documents. That is what permits us to speak of "Judaism."

We follow the references that we find to a topic in accord with the order of documents just now spelled out. In this study we learn the order in which ideas came to expression in the canon. We begin any survey with the Mishnah, the starting point of the canon. We proceed systematically to work our way through tractate Abot, the Mishnah's first apologetic, then the Tosefta, the Yerushalmi, and the Bavli at the end. In a single encompassing sweep, we finally deal with the entirety of the compilations of the exegeses of Scripture, arranged, to be sure, in that order that I have now explained. Let me expand on the matter of my heavy emphasis on the order of the components of the canon. The reason for that stress is simple. We have to ask not only what documents viewed whole and all at once ("Judaism") tell us about our theme. In tracing the order in which ideas make their appearance, we ask about the components in sequence ("history of Judaism") so far as we can trace the sequence. Then and only then shall we have access to issues of *history*, that is, of change and development. If our theme makes its appearance early on in one form, so one set of ideas predominates in a document that reached closure in the beginnings of the canon and then that theme drops out of public discourse or undergoes radical revision in writings in later stages of the canon, that fact may make a considerable difference. Specifically, we may find it possible to speculate on where and why a given approach proved urgent, and also on the reasons that that same approach receded from the center of interest.

What do I conceive to be at stake in the documentary history of Judaism? It is to set forth the history of the formation of Judaism, as the canonical writings of late antiquity allow us to trace that history. The ultimate system of Judaism itself formed during those seven centuries in three distinct stages, marked in each case by the distinctive traits of the literature that reached closure at the end of each successive stage, as I shall explain. More to the point, each stage produced a Judaic system. Formed in the first two hundred years and represented by the Mishnah and its associated writings, the first is utterly freestanding. The second, taking shape from 200 to 400 and represented by the Talmud of the Land of Israel and its companions, is connected to the first but essentially distinct from it. The third, expressed in documents that reached closure between 400 and 600 within and around the Talmud of Babylonia, is connected to the second but in important traits distinct from it as well.

These three systems, autonomous when viewed synchronically but connected when seen diachronically, ultimately, at the end of their formative age, formed a single, wholly and utterly continuous structure, that one we call Judaism. But in their successive stages of autonomy, then autonomy and connection, the three distinct systems may be classified, respectively, as philosophical, religious, and theological. Judaism then took shape in a passage from a philosophical, to a religious, and finally to a theological system, each one taking over and revising the definitive categories of the former and framing its own fresh, generative categories as well. The formative history of Judaism then is the story of the presentations and re-presentations of categorical structures. In method it is the exegesis of taxonomy and taxic systems.

To begin with, then, the classification of types of systems—philosophical, religious, theological—requires explanation.

A philosophical system forms its learning inductively and syllogistically by appeal to the neutral evidence of the rules shown by the observation of the order of universally accessible nature and society.

A religious system frames its propositions deductively and exegetically by appeal to the privileged evidence of a corpus of writing deemed revealed by God.

A theological system imposes upon a religious one systematic modes of thought of philosophy, so in its message regularizing and ordering in a cogent and intellectually rigorous way the materials received from a religious system. The movement from the religious to the theological will involve the systematization and harmonization of the religious categories, their reformation into a single tight and cogent statement. It is an initiative as radical, in its way, as the passage from the philosophical to religious formation is in its way. For the modes of thought, media of expression, and, as a matter of fact, categorical structure and system are reworked in the enterprise of turning a merely imputed order, imputed within the single heart of the faith, into a wholly public order, subject to sustained and cogent representation and expression, each component in its place and proper sequence, beginning, middle, and end. Religious conviction differs from theological proposition as do bricks and mortar from a building.

Religious and theological systems work over the same issues in ways that are common to themselves and that also distinguish them jointly from philosophical ones. But the rigorous task of forming, out of religious attitudes and convictions, a cogent composition, a system and not merely a structure of beliefs, imposes on systems of the theological sort disciplines of mind and perception, modes of thought and media of expression, quite different from those that characterize the work of making a religious system. The connection is intimate, for a theological system succeeding and reshaping a religious one appeals to the same sources of truth in setting forth (often identical) answers to (ordinarily) the same urgent questions. But the theological type of system is different from the religious type in fundamental ways as well, for while there can be a religious system without theological order, there can be no theological system without a religious core. So much for the distinctions among types of systems.

The documents we have examined, read in the rough sequence in which they took shape and came to closure, therefore produce a documentary history of the formation of Judaism. Let me now specify the shape and structure of that documentary history.

The history of the formation of Judaism tells the story of how (1) philosophy became (2) religion, which was then re-presented as (3) theology. The medium of theological re-presentation was hermeneutics, so that when we know how the Torah is properly read, we discern the theology of Judaism. Before proceeding, I hasten to give a simple definition of hermeneutics, that of Wilhelm Dilthey, since the rest of this book depends upon my claim that in its hermeneutics, the Talmud re-presents the Torah: "The methodological understanding of permanently fixed life-expressions we call explication . . . explication culminates in the interpretation of the written records of human existence. . . . The science of this art is hermeneutics."[2] When we know the rules of explication that instruct us on how to interpret the Torah, we gain access to the theology that governs the presentation of the religion Judaism.

The priority of hermeneutics in the theological venture is not difficult to explain. We deal with a Judaism that affords religious experience—knowledge of God, meeting with God—in particular in books. While that same Judaism, like

[2] Cited by K. M. Newton, *Interpreting the Text,* p. 42.

any other religious system, also meets God in prayer, obedience to the covenant, and right conduct, and expresses the sense of the knowledge of God in music and in art, in pilgrimage and in dance, in rite and in cult, and in most of the ways that religions in general celebrate God, what makes this Judaic system distinctive is its insistence that God is made manifest in, and therefore known through, documents, which preserve and contain the encounter with God that in secular language we call "religious experience." Just as, if the principal medium for meeting God were theater or music, we should search for theology in aesthetics, so since the principal meeting or encounter with God is the Torah, and the Torah is given in writing and oral formulation as well, this Judaism promises knowledge of God through the documents of the Torah, and its theological medium will be hermeneutics (as much as philosophy).

The character of the evidence therefore governs. Because the formation of (this particular) Judaism as a religious system is fully exposed in its successive documents, the history of that Judaism's formative age—the first six centuries of the Common Era—comes to us in the right reading of the Torah. In this Judaism, the Torah comprises the holy documents and persons—written and oral documents, and the person of "our sages of blessed memory"; the deeds and teachings of sages take the form of stories and statements preserved in the same documents. Not only so, but because the medium for theology in this Judaism was a fully exposed hermeneutics, the message was conveyed through unarticulated but ubiquitous initiatives of a hermeneutical character. Then theological method consisted in constantly and ubiquitously showing the same few things through that hermeneutics, worked out in the Talmuds for the oral Torah and in the Midrash compilations for the written Torah. But, as we shall see, matters ended up in hardly so simple a way, for the profound hermeneutical problem will emerge only at the end, in the documentary re-presentation of the Torah accomplished by the Talmud of Babylonia, and its hermeneutics is not one of words, phrases, or sentences, but connections and continuities: identifying the questions. The answers flow, once we know what to ask.

Stated in documentary terms, the formative history of Judaism tells a story in three stages. It shows, first, how the Judaic system emerged in the Mishnah, ca. 200 C.E., and its associated Midrash compilations, ca. 200–300 C.E., as (1) a philosophical structure comprising a politics, philosophy, economics. These categories were defined as philosophers in general understood them: a theory of legitimate violence, an account of knowledge gained through the methods of natural history, and a theory of the rational disposition (and increase) of scarce resources.

This philosophical system then was turned by the Talmud of the Land of Israel and related Midrash compilations, ca. 400–500 C.E., into (2) a religious system. The system was effected through the formation of counterpart categories: an anti-politics of weakness, an anti-economics of the rational utilization of an infinitely renewable resource, a philosophy of truth revealed rather than rules discovered.[3]

---

[3] The characterization of the first two stages in the formation of Judaism is contained within these books of mine: *The Economics of the Mishnah*. Chicago, 1989: University of Chicago Press; *Rabbinic Political*

Then, finally, the religious system was restated by the Talmud of Babylonia and its companions of Midrash collection, ca. 500–600 C.E. In those writings it was given (3) theological re-presentation through the recovery of philosophical method for the formulation of religious conceptions. In the great tradition, we may say, the formation of Judaism took place through (3) the final synthesis of (1) the initial thesis and (2) the consequent antithesis. That Hegelian pattern helps make sense of the history of religious expression and ideas that the canonical books of Judaism expose.

Theology is the science of the reasoned knowledge of God, in the case of a Judaism made possible by God's self-manifestation in the Torah. Seen in its whole re-presentation in the Talmud of Babylonia, the theology of Judaism sets forth knowledge of God. This is in two ways. The first (as I just said) is to know God through God's self-revelation in the Torah. This requires that we know what the Torah is, or what torah is (in a generic sense, which can pertain to either message or media or modes of thought). Then knowing how to define and understand the Torah affords access to God's self-revelation. The second is to know through that same self-revelation what God wants of Israel and how God responds to Israel and humanity at large.[4] That specific, propositional knowledge comes through reasoned reading of the Torah, oral and written, the Mishnah and Scripture, represented by the Talmuds and Midrash compilations, respectively.[5] The hermeneutics governing these documents encapsulate that knowledge of reasoned explication.

The schematic classifications of the successive, related Judaic systems as philosophical, religious, and theological therefore derive from the character of the successive documents, the Mishnah, Yerushalmi, and Bavli.[6] What makes all the difference in the second Talmud's re-presentation of the Judaic religious system therefore is the character of that Talmud itself. Through analysis of the hermeneutics that conveys the intellectual program of that medium, a religion rich in miscel-

---

Theory: Religion and Politics in the Mishnah. Chicago, 1991: University of Chicago Press; *Judaism as Philosophy. The Method and Message of the Mishnah.* Columbia, 1991: University of South Carolina Press; and *The Transformation of Judaism. From Philosophy to Religion.* Champaign, 1992: University of Illinois Press.
[4] I paraphrase Ingolf Dalferth, "The Stuff of Revelation: Austin Farrer's Doctrine of Inspired Images," in Ann Loades and Michael McLain, eds., *Hermeneutics, the Bible and Literary Criticism* (London, 1992: MacMillan), p. 71. Dalferth was my colleague when I was Buber Professor of Judaic Studies at the University of Frankfurt, and it was in reading his writing that I began to think along the lines that come to fruition in this theory. Other definitions and premises will yield other ways of reading the theology of the Judaism of the dual Torah.
[5] And that explains why we still will have to undertake a separate account of the theology yielded by the hermeneutics of the Midrash compilations (not only, or mainly, specific words or phrases or sentences found hither and yon in "the Midrash," as the ignorant conduct the inquiry). The characterization of the hermeneutics of Midrash compilations, early, middle, and late, will stand side-by-side with the theory set forth here.
[6] That is within the qualification that the Yerushalmi did part of the work of theologizing the Mishnah, the work of showing its proportion, composition, harmony, and coherence. The second Talmud did this work, but it also accomplished the far more sophisticated intellectual tasks.

laneous but generally congruent norms of behavior and endowed with a vast store of varied and episodic but occasionally contradictory ideas was turned into a proportioned and harmonious theology.[7]

Having laid heavy emphasis on the priority of the Bavli, I hasten to qualify matters. As a matter of fact, the process of theological re-presentation went forward in two stages. In the first, in the Talmud of the Land of Israel, the philosophical document that stated that system gained a vast amplification, in which the categories and methods of the original statement were amplified and instantiated, but also in which took place a remarkable reformulation in counterpart categories. Of the three traits of "tradition," e.g., as defined in the tractate Abot in its apologia for the Mishnah—harmony, linearity, and unity—the first of the two Talmuds systematically demonstrated the presence of two: harmony and linearity. The second undertook to demonstrate all three, all together and all at once and everywhere, that is to say, the law behind the laws, meaning, the unity, the integrity of truth. That shown, we know the mind of God, the character of truth.

Viewed as a whole, the result is then to be classified as not philosophical but religious in character and theological in re-presentation. Alongside, earlier Midrash compilations undertook the task of showing the relationship between the two media of the Torah, the oral and the written, by insisting that the Mishnah rested on Scripture. The goal was to show linearity and harmony. They furthermore began the definition of the Torah—in our terms, the reading of Scripture—by systematizing and generalizing the episodic cases of Scripture. The goal was to demonstrate the comprehensiveness of the Torah: its cases were meant to yield governing rules. The later Midrash compilations continued that reading of Scripture by formulating syllogistic propositions out of the occasional data of Scripture.

The religious writings that formed the second stage in the unfolding of Judaism—Talmud of the Land of Israel, Sifra and the two Sifrés somewhat before, Genesis Rabbah and Leviticus Rabbah somewhat afterward—finally were succeeded—and replaced—by the Talmud of Babylonia and related Midrash compilations, particularly Song of Songs Rabbah, Lamentations Rabbah, and Ruth Rabbah. These were documents that restated in rigorous, theological ways the same religious convictions, so providing that Judaism or Judaic system with its theological statement. In these writings, the religious system was restated in a rigorous and philosophical way. The associated Midrash compilations succeeded in making a single, encompassing statement out of the data of the several books of Scripture they presented.

The re-presentation of the religious system in the disciplined thought of theology took the form of rules of reading the Torah—oral and written—and through those rules exposing the character of the intellectual activity of thinking like God,

---

[7] But I maintain that an important part of the theological work was undertaken by the first of the two Talmuds, which means the differentiation between the two Talmuds provides the key, in literary analysis, to the hermeneutical priority of the second of the two.

that is, thinking about the world in the way God thinks. The theology of Judaism—reasoned knowledge of God[8] and God's will afforded by God's self-manifestation in the Torah[9]—affords access in particular to the mind of God, revealed in God's words and wording of the Torah. Through the Torah, oral and written, we work our way back to the intellect of God who gives the Torah. Thus through learning in the Torah in accord with the lessons of the Talmuds and associated Midrash compilations, humanity knows what God personally has made manifest about mind, that intellect in particular in which "in our image, after our likeness" we too are made. That defines the theology of the Judaism of the dual Torah and in particular forms the upshot of the Talmud's re-presentation of that theology.

Reading the Mishnah together with one or the other of its Talmudic amplifications, the Talmud of the Land of Israel or the Talmud of Babylonia, or Scripture together with any of the Midrash compilations, on the surface does not convey such an account. The canonical writings—the Mishnah and Talmud of the Land of Israel or the Mishnah and Talmud of Babylonia and their associated Midrash collections—portray not successive stages of the formation of a system but rather a single, continuous Judaism, which everywhere is read as unitary and uniform. Not only so, but in the persons and teachings of sages that same Torah makes part of its statement. But, when examined as single documents, one by one, in the sequence of their closure, to the contrary, matters look otherwise. Each writing then may be characterized on its own, rather than in the continuous context defined by the canon of which it forms a principal part.

The formation of Judaism, correctly described, may be stated in a single sentence. (1) The Mishnah, then (2) the first Talmud, then (3) the second Talmud, together with their respective sets of associated Midrash compilations, yield the history of a three-stage formation.

The first tells how the document that set forth the first Judaic system formed a philosophy, utilizing philosophical categories and philosophical modes of thought (philosophy, politics, economics, for categories, Aristotelian methods of hierarchical classification).

The second explains how the categorical formation was recast into religious classifications, from philosophy to Torah, from a politics of legitimate power to an anti-politics of weakness, from an economics of scarce resources to an anti-politics of the abundant resource of Torah learning.

The third then spells out how the received categorical system and structure were restated in their main points in such a way as to hold together the philosophical method and the religious message through a hermeneutical medium. Here I specify the character of that medium and its content. As I have already indicated,

[8] That is a standard definition of theology.
[9] That is my restatement of a standard definition of theology to state what I mean by, the theology of Judaism.

I once more stress, lest I be misunderstood, that this division between the second and the third should be shaded somewhat, since, as I shall show, by the operative definition of theology here, part of the theological work was carried on in the second—the Yerushalmi's—stage, part in the third. But, withal, the Bavli formed the summa, holding the whole together and making its own supreme and unique statement.

I have used the terms "philosophy" and "religion" and suggested they be treated as distinct categories of thought. Let me now spell out what I mean by "philosophy" and "religion." By "philosophy" I refer to the category formation, inclusive of categorical definitions, put forth by philosophy in ancient times. By "religion" I refer to the category formation put forth on a wholly-other-than philosophical basis in that same period. The one is secular and worldly in its data, utilizing the methods of natural history for its analytical work; the other is transcendental, finding its data in revelation, utilizing the methods of the exegesis of revelation for its systematic work. Both are exercises of sustained rationality, in the case of this Judaism, of applied reason and practical logic.

But the one begins in this world and its facts, which are analyzed and categorized through the traits inherent in them, and the other commences in the world above and its truths, which are analyzed and categorized by the categories of revelation. The one yields philosophy of religion, the other, religious statements, attitudes, convictions, rules of life; the one represents one way of knowing God, specifically, the way through the data of this world, the other, a different way to God altogether, the way opened by God's revelation and self-manifestation, whether through nature or beyond. Let me now spell out this distinction with reference to the systemic results of a reading of the Mishnah and the Yerushalmi.

The Mishnah set forth in the form of a law code a highly philosophical account of the world ("worldview"), a pattern for everyday and material activities and relationships ("way of life"), and a definition of the social entity ("nation," "people," "us" as against "outsiders," "Israel") that realized that way of life and explained it by appeal to that worldview. We have no difficulty in calling this account of a way of life an economics, because the account of material reality provided by the Mishnah corresponds, point for point, with that given in Aristotle's counterpart. The Mishnah moreover sets forth a politics by dealing with the same questions, about the permanent and legitimate institutions that inflict sanctions, that occupy Greek and Roman political thinkers. There is no economics of another-than-this-worldly character, no politics of an inner "kingdom of God." All is straightforward, worldly, material, and consequential for the everyday world. Then the successor documents, closed roughly two centuries later, addressed the Mishnah's system and recast its categories into a connected, but also quite revised, one. The character of their reception of the received categories and of their own category formation, emerging in the contrast between one set of documents and another, justifies invoking the term "transformation," that is, of one thing into something else. That something else was a religious, as distinct from a philosophical, category formation.

The first Talmud and associated Midrash compilations attest to a system that did more than merely extend and recast the categorical structure of the system for which the Mishnah stands. They took over the way of life, worldview, and social entity defined in the Mishnah's system. And while they rather systematically amplified details, framing a program of exegesis around the requirements of clerks engaged in enforcing the rules of the Mishnah, they built their own system. For at the same time they formed categories corresponding to those of the Mishnah, a politics, a philosophy, an economics. But these categories proved so utterly contrary in their structure and definition to those of the Mishnah that they presented mirror-images of the received categories.

The politics, economics, and philosophy of the Mishnah were joined by the Yerushalmi to an anti-politics, an anti-economics, and an utterly transformed mode of learning. In the hands of the later sages, the new mode of Torah study—the definition of what was at stake in studying the Torah—redefined altogether the issues of the intellect. Natural history as the method of classification gave way to a different mode of thought altogether. As a matter of fact, the successor system recast not the issues so much as the very stakes of philosophy or science. The reception of the Mishnah's category formations and their transformation therefore stands for the movement from a philosophical to a religious mode of thinking. For the system to which the Mishnah as a document attests is essentially philosophical in its rhetorical, logical, and topical program; the successor system is fundamentally religious in these same principal and indicative traits of the media of intellect and mentality.

Given the definitions with which I began, how do I know whether a system is philosophical or religious? The answer is not subjective, nor the criteria private or idiosyncratic. The indicative traits in both instances, to begin with, derive from and are displayed by documents, for—I take it as axiomatic—the mode of the writing down of any system attests to both the method and the message that sustain that system. From how people express themselves, we work our way backward to their modes of thought: the classification of perceived data, the making of connections between fact and fact, the drawing of conclusions from those connections, and, finally, the representation of conclusions in cogent compositions. All of these traits of mind are to be discerned in the character of those compositions, in the rhetoric that conveys messages in proportion and appropriate aesthetics, in the logic that imparts self-evidence to the making of connections, the drawing of conclusions, and in the representation of sets of conclusions as cogent and intelligible, characteristic of writing and expressed in writing.

In the Yerushalmi (and the Bavli later on) scarce resources, so far as these are of a material order of being, e.g., wealth as defined by the Mishnah and Aristotle, are systemically neutral. A definition of scarce resources emerges that explicitly involves a symbolic transformation, with the material definition of scarce resources set into contradiction with an other-than-material one. So we find side by side clarification of the details of the received category and adumbration of a symbolic revision and hence a categorical transformation in the successor writings. The representation of the political structure of the Mishnah undergoes clarification, but alongside, a quite separate and very different structure also is portrayed. The received structure presents three political classes, ordered in a hierarchy; the successor structure, a single political class, corresponding on earth to a counterpart in heaven. Here too a symbolic transaction has taken place, in which one set of symbols is replicated but also reversed, and a second set of symbols given instead.

The Mishnah's structure comprising a hierarchical composition of foci of power in the Yerushalmi gives way to a structure centered upon a single focus of power. That single focus, moreover, now draws boundaries between legitimate and illegitimate violence, boundaries not conceived in the initial system. So in all three components of the account of the social order the philosophical system gives way to another. The worldview comes to expression in modes of thought and expression—the logic of making connections and drawing conclusions—that are different from the philosophical ones of the Mishnah. The way of life appeals to value expressed in other symbols than those of economics in the philosophical mode. The theory of the social entity comes to concrete expression in sanctions legitimately administered by a single class of persons (institution), rather than by a proportionate and balanced set of classes of persons in hierarchical order, and, moreover, that same theory recognizes and defines both legitimate and also illegitimate violence, something beyond the ken of the initial system. So, it is clear, another system is adumbrated and attested in the successor writings.

The categorical transformation that was under way in the Yerushalmi, signaling the movement from philosophy to religion, comes to the surface when we ask a simple question. Precisely what do the authorships of the successor documents, speaking not about the Mishnah but on their own account, mean by economics, politics, and philosophy? That is to say, to what kinds of data do they refer when they speak of scarce resources and legitimate violence, and exactly how—as to the received philosophical method—do they define correct modes of thought and expression, logic and rhetoric, and even the topical program worthy of sustained inquiry? The components of the initial formation of categories were examined thoughtfully and carefully, paraphrased and augmented and clarified. But the received categories were not continued, not expanded, and not renewed. Preserved merely intact, as they had been handed on, the received categories hardly serve to encompass all of the points of emphasis and sustained development that characterize the successor documents—or, as a matter of fact, any of them. On the contrary, when the framers of the Yerushalmi, for one example, moved out from the exegesis of Mishnah passages, they also left behind the topics of paramount interest in the Mishnah and developed other categories altogether. Here the framers of the successor system defined their own counterparts.

These counterpart categories, moreover, redefined matters, following the main outlines of the structure of the social order manifest in the initial system. The counterpart categories set forth an account of the social order just as did the ones of the Mishnah's framers. But they defined the social order in very different terms altogether. In that redefinition we discern the transformation of the received system, and the traits of the new one fall into the classification of not philosophy but religion. For what the successor thinkers did was not continue and expand the categorical repertoire but set forth a categorically fresh vision of the social order— a way of life, worldview, and definition of the social entity—with appropriate counterpart categories. And what is decisive is that these served as did the initial categories within the generative categorical structure definitive for all Judaic systems. So there was a category corresponding to the generative component of worldview, but it was not philosophical; another corresponding to the required component setting forth a way of life, but in the conventional and accepted definition of economics it was not an economics; and, finally, a category to define the social entity, "Israel," that any Judaic system must explain, but in the accepted sense of a politics it was not politics.

What is the difference between the philosophical and the religious systems? What philosophy kept distinct, religion joined together: that defines the transformation of Judaism from philosophy to religion. The received system was a religious system of a philosophical character; this-worldly data are classified according to rules that apply consistently throughout, so that we may always predict with a fair degree of accuracy what will happen and why. And a philosophical system of religion then systematically demonstrates out of the data of the world order of nature and society the governance of God in nature and supernature: this world's data pointing toward God above and beyond. The God of the philosophical Judaism then sat enthroned at the apex of all things, all being hierarchically classified. Just as philosophy seeks the explanation of things, so a philosophy of religion (in the context at hand) will propose orderly explanations in accord with prevailing and cogent rules. The profoundly philosophical character of the Mishnah has already provided ample evidence of the shape, structure, and character of that philosophical system in the Judaic context. The rule-seeking character of Mishnaic discourse marks it as a philosophical system of religion. But, we shall now see, the successor system saw the world differently. It follows that a philosophical system forms its learning inductively and syllogistically, by appeal to the neutral evidence of the rules shown to apply to all things by the observation of the order of universally accessible nature and society.

A religious system frames its propositions deductively and exegetically by appeal to the privileged evidence of a corpus of truths deemed revealed by God. The difference pertains not to detail but to the fundamental facts deemed to matter. Some of those facts lie at the very surface, in the nature of the writings that express the system. These writings were not freestanding but contingent, and that in two ways. First, they served as commentaries to prior documents, to the Mishnah and Scripture, by the Talmud and Midrash compilations respectively. Second, and more consequential, the authorships insisted upon citing Scripture passages or Mishnah sentences as the centerpiece of proof, on the one side, and program of discourse, on the other. But the differences that prove indicative are not merely formal. More to the point, while the Mishnah's system is steady-state and ahistorical, admitting no movement or change, the successor system of the Yerushalmi and Midrash com pilations tells tales, speaks of change, accommodates and responds to historical moments. It formulates a theory of continuity within change, of the moral con nections between generations, of the way in which one's deeds shape one's des tiny—and that of the future as well. If what the framers of the Mishnah want more than anything else is to explain the order and structure of being, then their succes sors have rejected their generative concern. For what they, for their part, intensely desire to sort out are the currents and streams of time and change, as these flow toward an unknown ocean.

The shift from the philosophical to the religious modes of thought and media of expression—logical and rhetorical indicators, respectively—came to realization in the recasting of the generative categories of the system as well. These categories were transformed, and the transformation proved so thoroughgoing as to validate the characterization of the product of the change as "counterpart categories." The result of the formation of such counterpart categories in the aggregate was to en compass not only the natural but also the supernatural realms of the social order. That is how philosophical thinking gave way to religious thinking. The religious system of the Yerushalmi and associated documents sets forth the category forma tion that produced in place of an economics based on prime value assigned to real wealth one that now encompassed wealth of an intangible, impalpable, and supernatural order, but a valued resource nonetheless. It points toward the replace ment of a politics formerly serving to legitimate and hierarchize power and differ entiate among sanctions by appeal to fixed principles by one that now introduced the variable of God's valuation of the victim and the anti-political conception of the illegitimacy of worldly power.

This counterpart politics then formed the opposite of the Mishnah's this-worldly political system altogether. In all three ways—economics, politics, and philosophy—the upshot is the same: the social system, in the theory of its framers, now extends its boundaries upward to heaven, drawing into a whole the formerly distinct, if counterpoised, realms of Israel on earth and the heavenly court above. So if I had to specify the fundamental difference between the philosophical and the religious versions of the social order, it would fall, quite specifically—to state with emphasis—*upon the broadening of the systemic boundaries to encompass heaven.* The formation of counterpart categories therefore signals not a reformation of the re ceived system but the formation of an essentially new one.

The first fundamental point of reversal, uniting what had been divided, is the joining of economics and politics into a political economy, through the conception of *zekhut,* a term to be defined presently. The other point at which what the one system treated as distinct, the next and connected system chose to address as one and whole is less easily discerned, since to do so we have to ask a question the framers of the Mishnah did not raise in the Mishnah at all. That concerns the character and source of virtue, specifically, the effect, upon the individual, of knowledge, specifically, knowledge of the Torah or Torah study. To frame the question very simply, if we ask ourselves, what happens to me if I study the Torah, the answer, for the Mishnah, predictably is, my standing and status change. Torah study and its effects form a principal systemic indicator in matters of hierarchical classification, joining the *mamzer*-disciple of sages in a mixture of opposites, for one example. That is, the *mamzer* is the child of parents who can never legally wed; he himself is an outcast in an exact sense, being permitted to marry another *mamzer* or equivalent. And yet if he is also a disciple of sages, he is deemed to stand at the apex of society, above the priesthood, a truly systemic reversal.

But am I changed within? In vain we look in the hundreds of chapters of the Mishnah for an answer to that question. Virtue and learning form distinct categories; I am not changed as to my virtue, my character and conscience, by my mastery of the Torah. And still more strikingly, if we ask, does my Torah study affect my fate in this world and in the life to come, the Mishnah's authorship is strikingly silent about that matter too. Specifically, we find in the pages of that document no claim that studying the Torah either changes me or assures my salvation. But the separation of knowledge and the human condition is set aside, and studying the Torah is deemed the source of salvation, in the successor system. The philosophical system, with its interest in *homo hierarchicus*, proved remarkably silent about the effect of the Torah upon the inner man. The upshot is at the critical points of bonding, the received system proved flawed, in its separation of learning from virtue and legitimate power from valued resources. Why virtue joins knowledge (I call this "the gnostic Torah"), politics links to economics, in the religious system but not in the philosophical one is obvious. Philosophy differentiates, seeking the rules that join diverse data; religion integrates, proposing to see the whole all together and all at once, thus (for anthropology, for example) seeing humanity whole: "in our image, after our likeness." Religion by its nature asks the questions of integration, intended to hold together within a single boundary earth and heaven, this world and the other.

The second systemic innovation is the formation of an integrated category of political economy, framed in such a way that at stake in politics and economics alike were value and resource in no way subject to order and rule, but in all ways formed out of the unpredictable resource of *zekhut*, sometimes translated as "merit," but which, being a matter of not obligation but supererogatory free will, should be portrayed, I think, as "the heritage of virtue and its consequent entitlements." Between those two conceptions—the Torah as a medium of transformation, the heritage of virtue and its consequent entitlements, which can be gained for oneself and also received from one's ancestors—the received system's this-worldly boundaries were transcended, and the new system encompassed within its framework a supernatural life on earth. And appealing to these two statements of worldview, way of life, and social entity, we may as a matter of fact compose a complete description of the definitive traits and indicative systemic concerns of the successor Judaism. It remains to observe very simply: the Bavli in no way innovated in the category formation set forth by the Yerushalmi, and, it follows, no important component of the Bavli's theological statement will have surprised the framers of the Yerushalmi's compositions and compilers of its composites.

My account of the formation of Judaism therefore may be stated in these simple stages, involving method, message, and medium:

[1] THE METHOD OF PHILOSOPHY: The initial statement of the Judaism of the dual Torah took the form of a philosophical law code and set forth a philosophical system of monotheism, providing an economics, politics, and philosophy that philosophers in the Aristotelian and Middle- or Neo-Platonic traditions could have understood as philosophical (if they grasped the idiom in which the philosophical system was expressed). That is the point of my *The Economics of the Mishnah;*[10] *Rabbinic Political Theory: Religion and Politics in the Mishnah;*[11] and *Judaism as Philosophy. The Method and Message of the Mishnah.*[12]

[2] THE MESSAGE OF RELIGION: Through the formation of counterpart categories to economics, politics, and philosophy, the successor system, which came to expression in the Talmud of the Land of Israel and associated Midrash compilations, set forth a religious system and statement of the same Judaism of the dual Torah. That is the point of my *The Transformation of Judaism. From Philosophy to Religion.*[13]

[3] THE MEDIUM OF THEOLOGY, MELDING METHOD AND MESSAGE: Taking over that system and reviewing its main points, the final Talmud then restated the received body of religion as theology. That then is the point of this book, which explains how Judaism came to completion in its definitive statement when (1) the disciplines of philosophy were used to set forth the message of (2) religion so that Judaism stated (3) its theology. That Talmud re-presented the Judaism of the dual Torah by joining the method of philosophy to the message of religion. In the context of the historical formation of its principal ideas, that accounts for the formation of normative Judaism.

---

[10] Chicago, 1989: University of Chicago Press.
[11] Chicago, 1991: University of Chicago Press.
[12] Columbia, 1991: University of South Carolina Press. See also *The Making of the Mind of Judaism.* Atlanta, 1987: Scholars Press for Brown Judaic Studies, and also The *Formation of the Jewish Intellect. Making Connections and Drawing Conclusions in the Traditional System of Judaism.* Atlanta, 1988: Scholars Press for Brown Judaic Studies; and *The Philosophical Mishnah.* Atlanta, 1989: Scholars Press for Brown Judaic Studies. Volume I. *The Initial Probe;* Volume II. *The Tractates' Agenda. From Abodah Zarah to Moed Qatan;* Volume III. *The Tractates' Agenda. From Nazir to Zebahim;* and Volume IV. *The Repertoire.*
[13] Champaign-Urbana, 1992: University of Illinois Press.

APPENDIX

TWO OPEN QUESTIONS IN THE STUDY

OF RABBINIC LITERATURE

THIS INTRODUCTION TO RABBINIC LITERATURE HAS SUMMARIZED WHAT I THINK WE know about the various documents of the Judaic canon in its formative age. Here we turn to two fundamental questions to which, to date, I have found no answers at all. These questions complement each other. The first concerns dating documents, the second, using attributions of sayings to named authorities. We cannot now assign determinate dates to a single document of rabbinic literaure; unless we simply determine to accept at face value all of the attributions of sayings to named authorities and the historicity of all stories told about them, we also do not know what to make of the persistent and ubiquitous practice of assigning sayings to specific ages. In both instances I propose to define what we do not now know and how we should pursue future inquiries by asking well-crafted and appropriate questions in place of the presently regnant formulations of the issues.

1.

DATING DOCUMENTS

The questions before us, as yet left unresolved by contemporary learning, are these: "On dating documents, are there any absolute dates? What are the main criteria for relative dating?" To answer this question directly: there are no absolute dates. The criteria for relative dating—one document is prior to another in time because the (theoretically) later document can be shown to cite the (theoretically) earlier one—serve where they serve, which is to say, episodically. Let me spell out these two points and then reformulate the question in a much different way.

We have no basis on which to assign a firm, specific, determinate date to any document of the Judaism of the dual Torah, not the Mishnah, not Tosefta or Sifra, not the Talmud of the Land of Israel or the one of Babylonia, not Genesis Rabbah or Leviticus Rabbah or the Fathers According to Rabbi Nathan—not to a single compilation of any kind. We have reasonable grounds on which to place some of the documents into relationship with one another. Specifically, when a composition is primary to one document but secondary to another, then the document to which the composition is secondary may be assumed to have reached closure later than the document to which said composition is primary. Determinations of what is primary or secondary rest on quite formal, therefore objective, criteria. If the formal traits of a composition shared between two compilations are definitive in the one but found in the other only in items shared with the one, then the composition is primary to the one to the definitive traits of which it conforms, and secondary to the other.

A concrete example comes to us from the Mishnah, which occurs also in the two Talmuds, Tosefta, and Sifra. That the Mishnah is prior to Sifra is shown very simply. The Mishnah is cited verbatim in Tosefta and Sifra. The formal traits dominant in Sifra involve citation of a verse of Scripture followed by a few words of paraphrase or extension, often with some secondary development; the formal traits dominant in the Mishnah involve simple declarative sentences, disputes, and other freestanding formulations, rarely including citation and paraphrase of a verse of Scripture. Where we find in Sifra freestanding propositional compositions, they ordinarily are shared with the Mishnah; materials particular to Sifra do not exhibit the formal traits of said compositions. So, it follows, the materials common to the Mishnah and Sifra are primary to the Mishnah and secondary to Sifra, which cites them for its own purposes; and, it further follows, Sifra is later than the Mishnah, which it cites. The same argument of course applies to the Tosefta and two Talmuds. But this mode of placing into an order of temporal priority a sequence of documents serves only where it serves, and the conception that Genesis Rabbah and Leviticus Rabbah are fifty years later than the Talmud of the Land of Israel rests on nothing so tangible as the type of evidence I have just now set forth.

My documentary history of ideas rests on the order of documents, in some instances, demonstrable, as just noted; in others, a matter of conventional opinion at this time. People generally suppose that we have a reasonably reliable order of writings, the Mishnah standing at the head of the line, the Talmud of Babylonia at the end, between 200 and 600. Histories of ideas formed on documentary lines then tell us what came first and what happened then, as the sequence of documents permits us to trace the unfolding or the sequential treatments of a given idea. Still, we have no clear knowledge of when the "first" or the "then" took place. When a well-grounded consensus on what we mean by a date for a document, as well as how we may determine the date of the document's contents, has taken shape, all historical work, including the histories of ideas that provide such academic history of the formation of Judaism as we now have, will be redone, and, I think, even redefined. But the documentary history of ideas and the history of ideas obviously stand at some distance from one another. The one is relative to the order of writings, but does not permit us to localize a particular idea within a particular historical context or circumstance, let alone to relate such an idea to the events of a specific time and place.

Now to generalize: with documents such as those of rabbinic Judaism, bearing no named author, coming to us in an indeterminate and sparse textual tradition, we have yet to formulate a valid means for dating, or even a clear definition of what we might mean by assigning a date to a document. It is easier to explain what we do not now know than to define what we should want to find out. This minimalist position of course contradicts the maximalist one that reigns in the standard accounts of rabbinic documents and their dates.

That position assigns very specific dates to the various rabbinic documents; these assignments take for granted a position rejected by nearly the entire academic world, which is, believe everything unless you find reason to doubt something, the formulation regnant at last glance in the Jerusalem school, the Jewish seminaries of the United States, and other centers of the study of Judaism other than academic ones. Since all documents present numerous attributed statements, we date the various documents in accord with the assumed dates of the authorities that are cited in them. Now this conception, gullible and primitive and nearly universally rejected, yields groupings of documents, e.g., before 200 are "Tannaite" in that all the authorities in said compilations are assumed to have flourished in the first and second centuries. Not only so, but attributions date sayings within documents, so the date of 200 signifies not only closure at that time but also the latest date for whatever is unattributed in the document; much that is in the document, in accord with this theory, is much earlier.

Most talmudic historians, and all of them in the State of Israel, accept as fact all attributions of sayings and therefore assume that if a document's authorship presents a saying in a given sage's name, that sage really made such a statement, which therefore tells us what he, and perhaps others, were thinking in the time and place in which he lived. A corollary to this position is that a saying that bears no attribution is "earlier than" a saying that has one. Hence what is anonymous is older than what is assigned (how much older depends on the requirement of the person who assumes that fact). If, for instance, we have a named saying and, in context, an anonymous one that bears a contrary view, the anonymous saying is not deemed contemporary with the named saying on the same topic but earlier than the assigned one. It goes without saying that much energy goes into restating these propositions, but not much has been invested in demonstrating them. That is because they lie far beyond the limits of the evidence. Still, these two complementary positions presuppose a literary process in which sayings circulated independently of the documents in which they (later on) are written down and took shape within the circle of the disciples of a master to whom they are attributed. The position on the literary process that yields the documents that now contain these sayings has not yet been squared with the literary traits of those same documents, and analysis of those traits scarcely sustains the hypothesis of inerrant attribution and its corollary. These results of course also dictate the dates of documents. Tannaite documents contain only authorities who occur in the Mishnah, so they all are supposed to originate before ca. 200, even though, as a matter of fact, they ordinarily cite the Mishnah and therefore ought to be dated later than the Mishnah, after 200, and I think, much later.

I do not exaggerate. Consult any encyclopedia, and you will find that the Mishnah was redacted in 200, the Talmud of Babylonia in 500, and so on and so forth. One consideration makes improbable the certainty that presently prevails. The established protocol for dating a document rests on the premise that statements attributed to a given rabbi really were said by a historical figure, at a determinate time, and so permit us to date the document at the time of, or just after, that figure; if all the rabbis of a document occur in the Mishnah as well, then that document is assigned to the period of the Mishnah and given a date of ca. 200. If the last-named rabbi of a document is assumed to have lived in ca. 500, then the document gets the date of 501. In general, documents presently are dated by reference to the names of the authorities who occur in them, e.g., if the last-named authority is a rabbi who flourished in the Mishnah's period, the document as a whole is assigned to "Tannaitic times," that is, the first and second centuries, when, it is generally supposed, the Mishnah came to closure. But that date then presupposes the reliability of attributions and does not take account of pseudepigraphy in the rabbinic manner. The same sayings may be assigned to two or more authorities; the Talmud of Babylonia, moreover, presents ample evidence that people played fast and loose with attributions, changing by reason of the requirements of logic what a given authority is alleged to have said, for instance. Since we have ample evidence that in later times people made up sayings and put them into the mouths of earlier authorities (the Zohar is only the best-known example!), we have no reason to assign a document solely by reference to the names of the authorities found therein.

But no other basis for dating documents than gullibility about their contents has yet been devised, and since language usages are dated (in the Judaic and Jewish institutions) in accord with the dates of sages to whom sayings are attributed, dates that derive from Gaonic historians who flourished half a millennium after the times of those to whom they assign precise dates, philology provides no help whatsoever. Not only so, but the so-called philological dating, based on language usages, rests on precisely the same premise. If a saying is attributed to Aqiba, that means the usage of language in that saying attests to first- or early-second-century conventions, and, consequently, other such usages also place the documents that contain them in the first or early second century. What we have therefore is simply an extension, to the dating of documents and of their contents, of the familiar gullibility and credulity of talmudic studies: our holy rabbis really made these statements, so the rest follows.

The problem of dating documents proves still more complicated by two further considerations. First, precisely what we date in dating a document proves less clear than once was supposed. Studies of the enormous variation in the formulation of writings given the same title, e.g., some of the so-called mystical texts, make us wonder what, exactly, we date when we assign a date to a writing. Is it every word in the writing? Then what are we to make of the uncertain text tradition of every rabbinic compilation, beginning, after all, with the Mishnah itself? But if the date does not situate at a determinate time (and place) the entirety of the document, then what in fact is alleged?

Second, if a document is assigned, for convenience' sake, to ca. 400 or ca. 600, people take for granted that the document accurately portrays the state of opinion not only at that specific time but for any time prior, the attributions of sayings to earlier authorities being taken at face value. It is commonly argued that merely because a saying occurs in a writing assigned the date of 200, that does not mean that the writing conveys no accurate information on opinions held prior to 200. If that view prevails, then we have to ask what else we know if we are supposed to know that the document was redacted (or reached closure) in 200. New Testament scholarship places a heavy burden on rabbinic literature to portray the Judaism of the first century, the Judaism that Jesus and Paul knew. But nearly all New Testament scholars today rightly dismiss as uncritical the promiscuous citation, for that purpose, of rabbinic writings dated many centuries after the first. Clearly, we have reached a negative consensus; it is time to frame a positive one, beginning with a clear formulation of what "dating a document" requires—and explains.

Any account of dating documents, moreover, must take account of a very broadly held method of assigning dates to the contents of documents. By "assigning dates to the contents," I refer to the composites—the completed, self-contained stories or propositional statements—that are held together in large-scale composites, e.g., complete chapters of a Midrash compilation or of one of the Talmuds. That the method I shall set forth still serves will surprise colleagues who work in the more sophisticated fields of ancient studies, such as critical study of biblical history, for example, but in work in the Hebrew language that is set forth as exemplary, that of Gedaliahu Alon, reprinted only a few years ago by Harvard University Press without a line to suggest the forty-year-old work had been criticized and in fact superseded, this mode of analysis is routine. I therefore do not exaggerate the primitive state of thought on dating documents when I call attention to the method of dating documents by appeal to their contents. Specifically, a fixed trait of mind characteristic of the received, and uncritical, tradition in the use of talmudic tales for historical purposes instructs us to "date" stories by their contents. This works two ways, one positive, the other negative. If a story refers to the destruction of the Temple, for example, then that story was made up after

A.D. 70, a reasonable, if trivial, supposition. That positive evidence is uncommon and therefore solves few problems. The negative side tells us that if a story does not "know" about a certain important event or fact, then said story was made up or reflects conditions prior to that event. The possibility that the storyteller may have chosen not to refer to that important event is not considered, and other explanations for the allegedly indicative negative trait of the story are not proposed.

Not only so, but in a given document, stories and sayings are treated as individual and autonomous units, without relationship to the larger document in which they are found. Consequently, if a given story or saying in a document omits reference to what is regarded as an emblematic event, then without any reference to the literary setting in which the saying occurs, that saying, raised up out of its context, is assigned to a provenience prior to the event at hand. In these two ways stories are not only dated through their silences, but they also are represented out of all relationship to the documents that now preserve said stories. There is yet a third trait of mind. If we have two or more versions of a given story, then both of them refer to things that really happened—but different events. Consequently, if a given story comes to us in diverse documents, and each document tells the tale in its own way, we may be asked to believe that each story describes its own event. These three principles of historical explanation derive from ancient times but go forward into the twenty-first century. And that is why it is important to review them, first, in their realization in the classical texts of Judaism. Only then shall we understand how, in the hands of contemporary, younger scholars, they live on.

Sages of ancient times recognized that sayings and stories appeared in diverse versions. They too proposed explanations of how a given saying or story could come down in more than a single statement. The principal approach to the question posited that each detail represented a different stage in the history of the story, or of the life of its hero in particular, with one version characteristic of one such stage, and another version attesting to a different, and later one. So the successive versions of a saying or story supply a kind of incremental history. How so? Each version tells something about concrete events and real lives (biographies) that earlier versions did not reveal. The classic talmudic expression of the incremental theory takes up a passage of the Mishnah in which Rabban Yohanan ben Zakkai is called merely "Ben Zakkai":

> The precedent is as follows:
> Ben Zakkai examined a witness as to the character of the stalks of figs [under which an incident now subject to court procedure was alleged to have taken place] [Mishnah Sanhedrin 5:2B].

Exactly the same story is reported at Babylonian Talmud Sanhedrin 47A, on Tannaite authority. Now *Rabban Yohanan* ben Zakkai is alleged to have made exactly the same ruling, in exactly the same case. The item is worded in the same way except for the more fitting title. Then, at P–Q, the two versions are readily explained as facts of history. The one of Ben Zakkai was framed when he was a mere disciple. When, later on, he had become a recognized sage, the story was told to take account of that fact. So the theory I call "incremental history" is simple: each story related to, because it derives from, historical moments in a linear progression. The talmudic passage, which appears at Babylonian Talmud Sanhedrin 41a–b, is as follows:

IX. A. Who is this "Ben Zakkai"?

B. If we should propose that it is R. Yohanan ben Zakkai, did he ever sit in a sanhedrin [that tried a murder case]?

C. And has it not been taught on Tannaite authority:

D. The lifetime of R. Yohanan ben Zakkai was a hundred and twenty years. For forty years he engaged in trade, for forty years he studied [Torah], and for forty years he taught.

E. And it has been taught on Tannaite authority: Forty years before the destruction of the Temple the sanhedrin went into exile and conducted its sessions in Hanut.

F. And said R. Isaac bar Abodimi, "That is to say that the sanhedrin did not judge cases involving penalties."

G. Do you think it was cases involving penalties? [Such cases were not limited to the sanhedrin but could be tried anywhere in the Land of Israel!]

H. Rather, the sanhedrin did not try capital cases.

I. And we have learned in the Mishnah:

J. After the destruction of the house of the sanctuary, Rabban Yohanan b. Zakkai ordained . . . [M. R.H. 4:1]. [So the final forty years encompassed the period after the destruction of the Temple, and Yohanan could not, therefore, have served on a sanhedrin that tried capital cases.]

K. Accordingly, at hand is some other Ben Zakkai [than Yohanan b. Zakkai].

L. That conclusion, moreover, is reasonable, for if you think that it is Rabban Yohanan ben Zakkai, would Rabbi [in the Mishnah passage] have called him merely, "Ben Zakkai"? [Not very likely.]

M. And lo, it has been taught on Tannaite authority:

N. There is the precedent that Rabban Yohanan ben Zakkai conducted an interrogation about the stalks on the figs [so surely this is the same figure as at M. 5:2B].

The key language is as follows, given in italics:

O. *But [at the time at which the incident took place, capital cases were tried by the sanhedrin and] he was a disciple in session before his master. He said*

> *something, and the others found his reasoning persuasive, [41B] so they*
> *adopted [the ruling] in his name.*
>
> P.   *When he was studying Torah, therefore, he was called Ben Zakkai, as a*
>   *disciple in session before his master, but when he [later on] taught, he was*
>   *called Rabban Yohanan ben Zakkai.*
>
> Q.   *When, therefore, he is referred to as Ben Zakkai, it is on account of his being*
>   *a beginning [student] and when he is called Rabban Yohanan b. Zakkai, it*
>   *is on account of his status later on.*

On the basis of this analysis, scholars of the life of Yohanan ben Zakkai present the two versions as formulations of his opinion at different stages in his career. We have here the model, out of antiquity, for modes of thought characteristic of contemporary scholarship of an order I regard as primitive and uncritical.

So much for the problem and the received solutions. Let me now frame the problem in my own way. I state at the outset I do not know how to date documents. But I can make a contribution to the formulation of the question. For that purpose we turn to the elementary issue, precisely what do we date when we date documents? My answer is, two distinct issues require attention. First, we have to define the document as a whole and propose a point at which that document came to closure, if it did come to closure. Second, we have to identify the several components of the document, and identify a point at which we think these reached the form in which we have them (controlling for variations in wording and phrasing, which may continue to evolve for many centuries after closure). Closure therefore stands for two distinct entities, the one, the document as a whole, the other, the document's principal parts.

By "the document as a whole," I mean, the document as we know it, defined by its governing traits of program and proposition, form and rhetoric, cogent argument and coherent, intelligent re-presentation of thought. Each of the score of documents that make up the canon of Judaism in late antiquity exhibits distinctive traits in logic, rhetoric, and topic, so that we may identify the purposes and traits of form and intellect of the authorship of that document. It follows that documents possess integrity and are not merely scrapbooks, compilations made with no clear purpose or aesthetic plan. When we date a document as a whole, we assign a determinate point in time at which, in our judgment, the definitive traits of the writing coalesced to govern whatever would enter that writing or to dictate the reshaping of candidates for inclusion. Now, that point could have arrived earlier or later in the process of accumulation. That is to say, a document may reach its definitive form but continue to admit new materials, indeed, may make provision for their inclusion. The Siddur (Daily Prayer Book) and the Mahzor (Prayerbook for the Days of Awe, the New Year and the Day of Atonement) represent likely candidates; the form of prayer was well established early on, but the documents kept expanding and contracting for many centuries to come. But, as a matter of theory (for reasons I shall suggest), other writings too could without losing this distinctive character have taken into their composites new compositions, aggregations of materials originally written for some other purpose altogether. Later writers imitate earlier ones; heirs of a document may expand its limits while adhering to its protocol. It follows that a document reaches definition well before it comes to definitive closure, and we have to take account of that possibility. But that simple fact also calls into question what we mean by "redaction," "closure," and dating.

If, as a matter of fact, we mean the point at which the writing ceased to accommodate new candidates for admission, so that closure is definitive, then we have to rely upon manuscript evidence to show us the point at which the writing simply had jelled, with variations now limited to words and phrases. That is to say, we may know for certain that a document has come to closure—"redaction" in the conventional sense—when a population of manuscripts shows us pretty much the same version of the same writing: contents, character, wording. So too, when external witnesses tell us that various people have access to a uniform version of the document, with variations only as to wording, a few lines here, a few lines there, we may say that at that point, the writing had come to closure. For rabbinic compilations, to be sure, manuscript evidence is so late that such definitive evidence proves difficult to amass. But when we speak of "redaction" meaning "closure," that is the sort of evidence required to validate our language.

And this brings me to a much more important question, which is, how do we date not only the compilation of a document but the compositions of which it is made up? For we may demonstrate, for most, though not all, rabbinic compilations that a long process of writing produced some of the compositions collected in a given compilation, and that that process of writing produced completed compositions long before said compositions were selected for inclusion in the documents that now preserve them. I realize that in making that statement, I shall be understood to be saying pretty much what those I criticize allege about the writing: the compositions reach us through a long process of tradition, so that we cannot assign to everything in a document the final date of the document overall. We have, rather—so it is claimed—to date each sentence, each paragraph, each completed unit of thought, in its own terms. And that leads directly to reliance upon attributions, on the one side, and to appeal to the very allegations or contents of the writing, on the other, that I insist we must set aside as not demonstrated. I have broadly argued, what we cannot show, we do not know. How then do I propose to show that not everything in a given document must be dated to the point at which the document as a whole is assigned?

Absent attributions, on the one side, and allegations as to facts, on the other, where do we turn? The answer requires that I specify material and concrete facts, facts that compel assent and that do not consist of unprovable allegations that Rabbi X said such and so. I have, also, to appeal to the possibility of others' reaching the same conclusions that I present, which is to say, I have to show how to conduct experiments through which others can test and replicate my results. In other words, for once, objective evidence must intervene, and the subjective pronouncements of "great authorities" must be dismissed as merely someone's opinion, buttressed by politics, not by well-crafted propositions, arguments, and evidence, such as, in ordinary, secular fields of learning, we expect to be given.

I have already adumbrated the main lines of my theory on how to identify components of a document that come prior to the compilation of the document as a whole. It rests on the allegation that a document exhibits definitive traits of rhetoric, logic of coherent discourse, and topical program, even proposition. Let me now spell this out and explain the consequences for the analysis of a piece of writing and the dating of its contents.

I identify—and I maintain anyone examining the same evidence also will discern—three stages in the formation of writing. Moving from the latest to the earliest, one stage is marked by the definition of a document, its topical program, its rhetorical medium, its logical message. The document as we know it in its basic structure and main lines therefore comes at the end. It follows that writings that clearly serve the program of that document and carry out the purposes of its authorship were made up in connection with the formation of *that* document. Another, and I think, prior stage is marked by the preparation of writings that do not serve the needs of a particular document now in our hands, but could have carried out the purposes of an authorship working on a document of a *type* we now have. The existing documents then form a model for defining other kinds of writings worked out to meet the program of a documentary authorship.

But there are other types of writings that in no way serve the needs or plans of any document we now have, and that, furthermore, also cannot find a place in any document of a type that we now have. These writings, as a matter of fact, very commonly prove peripatetic, traveling from one writing to another, equally at home in, or alien to, the program of the documents in which they end up. These writings therefore were carried out without regard to a documentary program of any kind exemplified by the canonical books of the Judaism of the dual Torah. They form what I conceive to be the earliest in the three stages of the writing of the units of completed thought that in the aggregate form the canonical literature of the Judaism of the dual Torah of late antiquity.

As a matter of fact, therefore, a given canonical document of the Judaism of the dual Torah draws upon three classes of materials, and these—I propose as a mere hypothesis—were framed in temporal order. Last comes the final class, the one that the redactors themselves defined and wrote; prior is the penultimate class that could have served other redactors but did not serve these in particular; and earliest of all in the order of composition (at least, from the perspective of the ultimate redaction of the documents we now have) is the writing that circulated autonomously and served no redactional purpose we can now identify within the canonical documents.

We start from the whole, therefore, and work our way back toward the identification of the parts. In beginning the inquiry with the traits of documents seen whole, I reject the assumption that the building block of documents is the smallest whole unit of thought, the lemma, nor can we proceed on the premise that a lemma traverses the boundaries of various documents and is unaffected by the journey. The opposite premise is that we start our work with the traits of documents as a whole, rather than with the traits of the lemmas of which documents are (supposedly) composed. Having demonstrated beyond any doubt that a rabbinic text is a document, that is to say, a well-crafted text and not merely a compilation of this and that, and further specified in acute detail precisely the aesthetic, formal, and logical program followed by each of those texts, accordingly, I am able to move to the logical next step. That is to show that in the background of the documents that we have is writing that is *not* shaped by documentary requirements, writing that is not shaped by the documentary requirements of the compilations we now have, and also writing that is entirely formed within the rules of the documents that now present that writing. These then are the three kinds of writing that form, also, the three stages in the formation of the classics of Judaism.

My example of a document that is written down essentially in its penultimate and ultimate stages, that is, a document that takes shape within the redactional process and principally there, is the Mishnah. In that writing, the patterns of language, e.g., syntactic structures, of the apodosis and protasis of the Mishnah's smallest whole units of discourse are framed in formal, mnemonic patterns. They follow a few simple rules. These rules, once known, apply nearly everywhere and form stunning evidence for the document's cogency. They permit anyone to reconstruct, out of a few key phrases, an entire cognitive unit, and even complete intermediate units of discourse. Working downward from the surface, therefore, anyone can penetrate into the deeper layers of meaning of the Mishnah. Then at the same time, while discovering the principle behind the cases, one can easily memorize the whole by mastering the recurrent rhetorical pattern dictating the expression of the cogent set of cases. For it is easy to note the shift from one rhetorical pattern to another and to follow the repeated cases articulated in the new pattern downward to its logical substrate. So syllogistic propositions, in the Mishnah's authors' hands, come to full expression not only in *what* people wish to state but also in *how* they choose to say it. The limits of rhetoric define the arena of topical articulation.

Now to state my main point with heavy emphasis: *the Mishnah's formal traits of rhetoric indicate that the document has been formulated all at once, and not in an incremental, linear process extending into a remote (mythic) past (e.g., to Sinai).* These traits, common to a series of distinct cognitive units, are redactional, because they are imposed at that point at which someone intended to join together discrete (finished) units on a given theme. The varieties of traits particular to the discrete units and the diversity of authorities cited therein, including masters of two or three or even four strata from the turn of the first century to the end of the second, make it highly improbable that the several units were formulated in a common pattern and then preserved until later on, still further units, on the same theme and in the same pattern, were worked out and added. The entire indifference, moreover, to historical order of authorities and the concentration on the logical unfolding of a given theme or problem without reference to the sequence of authorities confirm the supposition that the work of formulation and that of redaction went forward together.

The principal framework of formulation and formalization in the Mishnah is the intermediate division rather than the cognitive unit. The least formalized formulary pattern, the simple declarative sentence, turns out to yield many examples of acute formalization, in which a single distinctive pattern is imposed upon two or more (very commonly, groups of three or groups of five) cognitive units. While an intermediate division of a tractate may be composed of several such conglomerates of cognitive units, it is rare indeed for cognitive units formally to stand wholly by themselves. Normally, cognitive units share formal or formulary traits with others to which they are juxtaposed and the theme which they share. It follows that the principal unit of formulary formalization is the intermediate division and not the cognitive unit. And what that means for our inquiry is simple: we can tell when it is that the ultimate or penultimate redactors of a document do the writing.

Can I point to a kind of writing that in no way defines a document now in our hands or even a type of document we can now imagine, that is, one that in its particulars we do not have but that conforms in its definitive traits to those that we do have? Indeed I can, and it is the writing of stories about sages and other exemplary figures. To show what might have been, I point to the simple fact that the final organizers of the Bavli, the Talmud of Babylonia, had in hand a tripartite corpus of inherited materials awaiting composition into a final, closed document. The first type of material, in various states and stages of completion, addressed the Mishnah or took up the principles of laws that the Mishnah had originally brought to articulation. This the framers of the Bavli organized in accord with the order of those Mishnah tractates that they selected for sustained attention. Second, they had in hand received materials, again in various conditions, pertinent to Scripture, both as Scripture related to the Mishnah and also as Scripture laid forth its own narratives. These they set forth as Scripture commentary. In this way, the penultimate and ultimate redactors of the Bavli laid out a systematic presentation of the two Torahs, the oral, represented by the Mishnah, and the written, represented by Scripture.

And, third, the framers of the Bavli also had in hand materials focused on sages. These in the received form, attested in the Bavli's pages, were framed around twin biographical principles, either as strings of stories about great sages of the past or as collections of sayings and comments drawn together solely because the same name stands behind all the collected sayings. These could easily have been composed into biographies. In the context of Christianity and of Judaism, it is appropriate to call the biography of a holy man or woman, meant to convey the divine message, a holy life. This is writing that is utterly outside of the documentary framework in which it is now preserved; nearly all narratives in the rabbinic literature, not only the biographical ones, indeed prove remote from any documentary program exhibited by the canonical documents in which they now occur.

The Bavli as a whole lays itself out as a commentary to the Mishnah. So the framers wished us to think that whatever they wanted to tell us would take the form of Mishnah commentary. But a second glance indicates that the Bavli is made up of enormous composites, themselves closed prior to inclusion in the Bavli. Some of these composites—around 35 percent to 40 percent of the Bavli, if my sample is indicative—were selected and arranged along lines dictated by a logic other than that deriving from the requirements of Mishnah commentary. The components of the canon of the Judaism of the dual Torah prior to the Bavli had encompassed amplifications of the Mishnah, in the Tosefta and in the Yerushalmi, as well as the same for Scripture, in such documents as Sifra to Leviticus, Sifré to Numbers, another Sifré, to Deuteronomy, Genesis Rabbah, Leviticus Rabbah, and the like. But there was no entire document, now extant, organized around the life and teachings of a particular sage. Even the Fathers According to Rabbi Nathan, which contains a good sample of stories about sages, is not so organized as to yield a life of a sage, or even a systematic biography of any kind. Where events in the lives of sages do occur, they are thematic and not biographical in organization, e.g., stories about the origins, as to Torah study, of diverse sages; death scenes of various sages. The sage as such, whether Aqiba or Yohanan ben Zakkai or Eliezer b. Hyrcanus, never in that document defines the appropriate organizing principle for sequences of stories or sayings. And there is no other in which the sage forms an organizing category for any material purpose.

Accordingly, the decision that the framers of the Bavli reached was to adopt the two redactional principles inherited from the antecedent century or so and to reject the one already rejected by their predecessors, even while honoring it. (1) They organized the Bavli around the Mishnah. But (2) they adapted and included vast tracts of antecedent materials organized as scriptural commentary. These they inserted whole and complete, not at all in response to the Mishnah's program. But, finally, (3) while making provision for small-scale compositions built upon biographical principles, preserving both strings of sayings from a given master (and often a given tradent of a given master) as well as tales about authorities of the preceding half millennium, they *never* created redactional compositions, of a sizable order, that focused upon given authorities. But sufficient materials certainly lay at hand to allow doing so.

We have now seen that some writings carry out a redactional purpose. The Mishnah was our prime example. Some writings ignore all redactional considerations we can identify. The stories about sages in the Fathers According to Rabbi Nathan, for instance, show us kinds of writing that are wholly out of phase with the program of the document that collects and compiles them. We may therefore turn to Midrash compilations and find the traits of writing that clearly are imposed by the requirements of compilation. We further identify writings that clearly respond to a redactional program, but not the program of any compilation we now have in hand. There is little speculation about the identification of such writings. They will conform to the redactional patterns we discern in the known compilations, but presuppose a collection other than one now known to us. Finally, we turn to pieces of writing that respond to no redactional program known to us or that are not susceptible to invention in accord with the principles of defining compilation known to us.

My analytical taxonomy of the writings now collected in various Midrash compilations points to three stages in the formation of the classics of Judaism. It also suggests that writing went on outside of the framework of the editing of documents, and also within the limits of the formation and framing of documents. Writing independent of documents such as we now have then constituted a kind of literary work to which redactional planning proved irrelevant. Other sorts of writing did respond to redactional considerations—for instance, commentary on Scripture or the Mishnah. So in the end we shall wish to distinguish between writing intended for the making of books—compositions of the first three kinds listed just now—and writing not in response to the requirements of the making of compilations.

The distinctions upon which these analytical taxonomies rest are objective and in no way subjective, since they depend upon the fixed and factual relationship between a piece of writing and a larger redactional context:

[1] We know the requirements of redactors of the several documents of the rabbinic canon, because I have already shown what they are in the case of a large variety of documents. When, therefore, we judge a piece of writing to serve the program of the document in which that writing occurs, it is not because of a personal impulse or a private and incommunicable insight, but because the traits of that writing self-evidently respond to the documentary program of the book in which the writing is located.

[2] When, further, we conclude that a piece of writing belongs in some other document than the one in which it is found, that too forms a factual judgment.

A piece of writing that serves nowhere we now know may nonetheless conform to the rules of writing that we can readily imagine and describe in theory. For instance, a propositional composition, which runs through a wide variety of texts to make a point autonomous of all of the texts that are invoked, clearly is intended for a propositional document, one that (like the Mishnah) makes points autonomous of a given prior writing, e.g., a biblical book, but that makes points that for one reason or another cohere quite nicely on their own. Authors of propositional compilations self-evidently can imagine that kind of redaction. We have their writings, but not the books that they intended to be made up of those writings. In all instances, the reason that we can readily imagine a compilation will prove self-evident: we have compilations of such a type, if not specific compilations called for by a given composition.

[3] Some writings stand autonomous of any redactional program we have in an existing compilation or of any we can even imagine on the foundations of said writings. Compositions of this kind, as a matter of hypothesis, are to be assigned to a stage in the formation of classics prior to the framing of all available documents. For, as a matter of fact, all of our now extant writings adhere to a single

program of conglomeration and agglutination, and all are served by composites of one sort, rather than some other. Hence we may suppose that at some point prior to the decision to make writings in the model that we now have but in some other model people also made up completed units of thought to serve these other kinds of writings. These persist, now, in documents that they do not serve at all well. And we can fairly easily identify the kinds of documents that they could and should have served quite nicely indeed. These then are the three stages of literary formation in the making of the classics of Judaism.

This set of definitions returns us to the matter of dating documents, a problem I have now reformulated into its components: closure of the whole, definition of the protocol governing the parts, and formulation of the individual compositions that are collected into composites and ultimately included in the compilation as a whole.

Of the relative temporal or ordinal position of writings that stand autonomous of any redactional program we have in an existing compilation or of any we can even imagine on the foundations of said writings we can say nothing. These writings prove episodic; they are commonly singletons. They serve equally well everywhere, because they demand no traits of form and redaction in order to endow them with sense and meaning. Why not? Because they are essentially freestanding and episodic, not referential and allusive. They are stories that contain their own point and do not invoke, in the making of that point, a given verse of Scripture. They are sayings that are utterly ad hoc. A variety of materials fall into this—from a redactional perspective—unassigned, and unassignable, type of writing. They do not belong in books at all. By that I mean, whoever made up these pieces of writing did not imagine that what he was forming required a setting beyond the limits of his own piece of writing; the story is not only complete in itself but could stand entirely on its own; the saying spoke for itself and required no nurturing context; the proposition and its associated proofs in no way was meant to draw nourishment from roots penetrating nutriments outside of its own literary limits.

Where we have utterly hermetic writing, able to define its own limits and sustain its point without regard to anything outside itself, we know that here we are in the presence of authorships that had no larger redactional plan in mind, no intent on the making of books out of their little pieces of writing. We may note that among the "unimaginable" compilations is not a collection of parables, since parables rarely stand free and never are inserted for their own sake. Whenever in the rabbinic canon we find a parable, it is meant to serve the purpose of an authorship engaged in making its own point; and the point of a parable is rarely, if ever, left unarticulated. Normally it is put into words, but occasionally the point is made simply by redactional setting. It must follow that in this canon, the parable could not have constituted the generative or agglutinative principle of a large-scale compilation. It further follows, so it seems to me, that the parable always takes shape within the framework of a work of composition for the purpose of either a large scale exposition or, more commonly still, of compilation of a set of expositions into what we should now call the chapter of a book; that is to say, parables link to purposes that transcend the tale that they tell (or even the point that the tale makes).

Once we recognize those sizable selections of materials that circulated from one document to another, we are able to ask, can we date them to a time prior to the definition of a document's protocol and also the writings that were formulated in close adherence to, in accord with, that protocol? I think we can, and let me explain why I tend to think they were formed earlier than the writings particular to documents. The documentary hypothesis affects our reading of the itinerant compositions, for it identifies what writings are extra-documentary and non-documentary and imposes upon the hermeneutics and history of these writings a set of distinctive considerations. The reason is that these writings serve the purposes not of compilers (or authors or authorships) of distinct compilations, but the interests of another type of authorship entirely: one that thought making up stories (whether or not for collections) itself an important activity; or making up exercises on Mishnah-Scripture relationships; or other such writings as lie beyond the imagination of the compilers of the score of documents that comprise the canon. When writings work well for two or more documents therefore they must be assumed to have a literary history different from those that serve only one writing or one type of writing and, also, demand a different hermeneutic.

My "three stages" in ordinal sequence correspond, as a matter of fact, to a taxic structure, that is, three types of writing. The first—and last in assumed temporal order—is writing carried out in the context of the making, or compilation, of a classic. That writing responds to the redactional program and plan of the authorship of a classic. The second, penultimate in order, is writing that can appear in a given document but better serves a document other than the one in which it (singularly) occurs. This kind of writing seems to me not to fall within the same period of redaction as the first. For while it is a type of writing under the identical conditions, it also is writing that presupposes redactional programs in no way in play in the ultimate, and definitive, period of the formation of the canon: when people did things this way, and not in some other. That is why I think it is a kind of writing that was done prior to the period in which people limited their redactional work and associated labor of composition to the program that yielded the books we now have.

The upshot is simple: whether the classification of writing be given a temporal or merely taxonomic valence, the issue is the same: have these writers done their work with documentary considerations in mind? I believe I have shown that they have not. Then where did they expect their work to make its way? Anywhere it might, because, so they assumed, fitting in nowhere in particular, it found a suitable locus everywhere it turned up. But I think temporal, not merely taxonomic, considerations pertain.

The third kind of writing seems to me to originate in a period prior to the other two. It is carried on in a manner independent of all redactional considerations such as are known to us. Then it should derive from a time when redactional considerations played no paramount role in the making of compositions. A brief essay, rather than a sustained composition, was then the dominant mode of writing. My hypothesis is that people could have written both long and short compositions—compositions and composites, in my language—at one and the same time. But writing that does not presuppose a secondary labor of redaction, e.g., in a composite, probably originated when authors or authorships did not anticipate any fate for their writing beyond their labor of composition itself.

Along these same lines of argument, this writing may or may not travel from one document to another. What that means is that the author or authorship does not imagine a future for his writing. What fits anywhere is composed to go nowhere in particular. Accordingly, what matters is not whether a writing fits one document or another, but whether, as the author or authorship has composed a piece of writing, that writing meets the requirements of any document we now have or can even imagine. If it does not, then we deal with a literary period in which the main kind of writing was ad hoc and episodic, not sustained and documentary.

Now extra- and non-documentary kinds of writing seem to me to derive from either (1) a period prior to the work of the making of Midrash compilations and the two Talmuds alike; or (2) a labor of composition not subject to the rules and considerations that operated in the work of the making of Midrash compilations and the two Talmuds. As a matter of hypothesis, I should guess that non-documentary writing comes prior to making any kind of documents of consequence, and extra-documentary writing comes prior to the period in which the specificities of the documents we now have were defined. That is to say, writing that can fit anywhere or nowhere is prior to writing that can fit somewhere but does not fit anywhere now accessible to us, and both kinds of writing are prior to the kind that fits only in those documents in which it is now located.

And given the documentary propositions and theses that we can locate in all of our compilations, we can only assume that the non-documentary writings enjoyed, and were assumed to enjoy, ecumenical acceptance. That means, very simply, when we wish to know the consensus of the entire textual (or canonical) community—I mean simply the people, anywhere and any time, responsible for everything we now have—we turn not to the distinctive perspective of documents, but the (apparently universally acceptable) perspective of the extra-documentary compositions. That is the point at which we should look for the propositions everywhere accepted but nowhere advanced in a distinctive way, the "Judaism beyond the texts"—or behind them.

I am inclined to suppose that non-documentary compositions took shape not only separated from, but in time before, the documentary ones did. My reason for thinking so is worth rehearsing, even though it is not yet compelling. The kinds of non-documentary writing I have identified in general focus on matters of very general interest. These matters may be assembled under two very large rubrics: virtue, on the one side, reason, on the other. Stories about sages fall into the former category; all of them set forth in concrete form the right living that sages exemplify. Essays on right thinking, the role of reason, the taxonomic priority of Scripture, the power of analogy, the exemplary character of cases and precedents in the expression of general and encompassing rules—all of these intellectually coercive writings set forth rules of thought as universally applicable, in their way, as are the rules of conduct contained in stories about sages, in theirs. A great labor of generalization is contained in both kinds of non-documentary and extra-documentary writing. And the results of that labor are then given concrete expression in the documentary writings in hand; for these, after all, do say in the setting of specific passages or problems precisely what, in a highly general way, emerges from the writing that moves hither and yon, never with a home, always finding a suitable resting place.

Now, admittedly, that rather general characterization of the non-documentary writing is subject to considerable qualification and clarification. But it does provide a reason to assign temporal priority, not solely taxonomic distinction, to the non-documentary compositions. We could have had commentaries of a sustained and systematic sort on chronicles of saints' lives, on one side, treatises on virtue, on the second, holy lives or miracle stories, on the third—to complete the triangle. But we do not have these kinds of books. We have what we have, and those are the writings we have to date. In specifying the complexity of the problem of dating—once we abandon reliance upon attributions and allegations as to facts—I mean to suggest paths for further inquiry. The road from here to reliable conclusions on when a document reached ultimate closure, when the materials collected in the document were formulated on their own and reformulated in accord with the protocol governing their ultimate, documentary destination—that road is a very long one indeed. In the interim, we have to formulate our work of history and history of ideas with careful attention to what, out of the mass of things we do not know, we actually can say for certain. We have, in other words, to formulate our questions and our problems in response to the character of not only the evidence, but the things that the evidence as we now grasp it permits us to investigate. Future research will commence when we have asked a well-crafted question. These remarks outline only some of the problems that await attention when we want to know about dating documents—and their contents. Since, however the question is framed, attributions of sayings to named authorities will play a considerable role in future study of the dates of documents, we turn to the correlative question of what, if anything, assigning a name to a saying, or telling a story about a specific, distinct person, is supposed in the rabbinic literature to mean.

2.

THE MEANING OF ATTRIBUTIONS

The second question awaiting systematic study concerns the meaning of a simple fact: throughout rabbinic literature, numerous sayings are assigned to named masters. To understand the issue at hand we have to take account of two contradictory facts. First, all rabbinic documents are anonymous, and all of them include vast numbers of compositions bearing no assignments, none of the compositions of which a document is comprised is assigned to a named author; no document bears a dependable attribution to a specific person. But, by way of contradiction to these facts, every one of the documents of the Judaism of the dual Torah produced in the formative age is characterized by numerous attributions of statements to specific figures. So individuals at the same time play no role and also dominate the representation of discourse. The literary situation is characterized by William Green in the following way:

> Most rabbinic documents are unattributed works; all in fact are anonymous. . . . Rabbinic literature has no authors. No document claims to be the writing of an individual rabbi in his own words; and all contain the ostensible sayings of, and stories about, many rabbis, usually of several generations. Selected to suit the purposes of compilers and redactors, the documents' components are not pristine and natural. They have been revised and reformulated in the processes of transmission and redaction, with the consequence that the ipsissima verba of any rabbis are beyond recovery. Rabbinic literature is severely edited, anonymous, and collective.[1]

These contradictory traits—exclusion of distinctive, personal traits of style, absolute refusal to recognize an individual in his own setting, e.g., by preserving a book written by, or about, a named authority, and, at the same time, ubiquitous and persistent inclusion of names along with sayings—provoke the question at hand. If the literature were anonymous as well as collective, or if it exhibited the marks of individuality along with its constant references to named figures, we should not find puzzling the definitive trait before us. So to the work at hand.

The question is addressed to me, Why is the rabbinic literature so interested in coupling utterances and decisions with names? The question finds a facile answer for those who take for granted that issues of history govern in the formulation of the Judaism of the dual Torah. If the primary interest lies in what really happened, so that events of a specific, one-time character bear incontrovertible and compelling truth, then names are attached to sayings to indicate who actually said them; then the word "really" carries the meaning, which particular authority stands behind a given statement? That premise, at the same time historical and biographical, certainly has much to recommend it, since in our culture, with its two-century-old stress on the authority of demonstrable, historical fact, if we can show that something really happened or was truly said by the person to whom it is attributed, then much else follows. But for our sages of blessed memory,

---

[1] William Scott Green, "Storytelling and Holy Men," in J. Neusner, ed., *Take Judaism, For Example. Studies toward the Comparison of Religions* (Atlanta, 1992: Scholars Press for South Florida Studies in the History of Judaism), p. 30.

particularly in the two Talmuds, that premise will have presented considerable difficulty.

For we look in vain in the analytical documents for evidence to sustain the stated premise that people really concerned themselves with the issue of who really said what. That is to say, while sayings are attributed, the purpose of the attribution—what is at stake in it, what else we know because we know it—requires analysis on its own terms. Since, as a matter of fact, a saying assigned to one authority in document A will circulate in the name of another in document B, the one-time, determinate assignment of said saying to authority X rather than authority Y cannot be accorded enormous consequence. If the documents were broadly circulated and known, then people ought to have observed that a given saying is assigned to more than a single authority and ought also to have asked why that was the fact. But discussion on that question nowhere takes a central position in the literature. It is no more troublesome than the fact that a given authority will be assigned a given saying in two or more contexts; then, as with the Sermon on the Mount and the Sermon on the Plain, people will simply maintain (as do the true believers in the historicity of everything in the rabbinic literature who dominate scholarly discourse in the Israeli universities and the Western yeshivot and seminaries), "He would often say . . . ," or, "Many times he said. . . ."

Where, when, and why, then, do the names of authorities play a consequential role in the unfolding of discourse? What role is assigned to them, and what premises seem to underpin the constant citation of sayings in the names of particular masters? To answer these questions, it will hardly suffice to speculate. Our task is to turn to the documents themselves and to ask the broad question, what role do named sages play in these compilations, and on what account do specific names joined with particular statements come under discussion? That question forms a particular detail of a broader issue, which is, how come specific sages play so critical a role in the rabbinic literature?

When we consider counterpart writings in Christian circles, by contrast, we find a very different kind of writing. There, very commonly, a named figure, whether Matthew or Paul, presents a piece of writing, and he bears responsibility for everything in that document, either as an account of what he has seen and heard, as in the case of Matthew's Gospel, or as an account of his own systematic views, as in the case of Paul's letters. True, we find anonymous writings; but such documents as Hebrews, which bears no named author (though it probably belongs to Paul), also contain no sayings assigned to specific authorities, in the way in which the rabbinic writings contain attributions not only to Scripture but to living or recently deceased holy men. A counterpart would have been a citation in Hebrews of a statement of Matthew or Mark, Paul or Peter. But that insistence on citing current authorities, a paramount trait of rabbinic literature, start to finish, has no parallel in Christian literature. The much later Zoroastrian law codes, which intersect in contents and at some points even in form with the Judaic ones, assign a given code to a named authority. So we should regard as emblematic and enormously consequential the constant intrusion of the names of authorities in the rabbinic writings, from beginning to end, from the Mishnah through the Bavli.

Rather than address the question in general terms, let us first ask about the role of attributions in some few specific documents: how seriously are they taken, and for what purpose? The first document is the Mishnah. There we find a principal and constitutive form, the dispute, built around the names of opposing authorities, e.g., the Houses of Shammai and Hillel, or Aqiba and Tarfon, or Meir and Judah, and the like. We also find in some few passages clear evidence of the collection of statements about a given, cogent problem in the name of a specific authority, e.g., Mishnah tractate Kelim Chapter Twenty-Four is a statement of Judah's views. But, overall, the Mishnah must be described as an entirely anonymous document, which at the same time contains extensive citations of named figures. The same names occur throughout; we cannot demonstrate that a given authority was viewed as particularly knowledgeable in a specific area of law, most of the sages being treated as generalists. At the same time that names predominate everywhere, sixty-two of the sixty-three tractates are organized around not named figures but topics, and, as indicated, perhaps 98 percent of the chapters of which those tractates are made up likewise focus on subjects, not named authorities. Only tractate Eduyyot as a whole is set up around names.

If we turn to that tractate devoted not to a particular subject or problem but rather the collection of attributed sayings and stories told about authorities, what do we find? The answer is, collections of rules on diverse topics, united by the names of authorities cited therein, either disputes, e.g., between Shammai and Hillel and their houses, or sets of rulings representative of a single authority. A single representative passage shows how the document does its work:

> 1:2.II. A. Shammai says, "[Dough which is made] from a qab [of flour is liable] to a dough offering [Num. 15:20]."
>
> B. And Hillel says, "[Dough made] from two qabs."
>
> C. And sages say, "It is not in accord with the opinion of this party or in accord with the opinion of that party,
>
> D. "But: [dough made] from a qab and a half of flour is liable to the dough offering."

Now what is interesting here—and not characteristic of the document through-out—is the inclusion of a final ruling on the dispute, which is different from the rulings of the houses' founders. That pattern being repeated and so shown to be definitive of the redactor's subtext, the question is raised: why record not only the official rule, but the opinion of a named, therefore schismatic figure as well? And that of course forms the heart of the matter and tells us the document's answer to our question. First let us consider the source, then draw the conclusion it makes possible:

1:5.   A.   And why do they record the opinion of an individual along with that of the majority, since the law follows the opinion of the majority?

        B.   So that, if a court should prefer the opinion of the individual, it may decide to rely upon it.

        C.   For a court does not have the power to nullify the opinion of another court unless it is greater than it in wisdom and in numbers.

        D.   [If] it was greater than the other in wisdom but not in numbers,

        E.   in numbers but not in wisdom,

        F.   it has not got the power to nullify its opinion—

        G.   unless it is greater than it in both wisdom and numbers.

1:6.   A.   Said R. Judah, "If so, why do they record the opinion of an individual against that of a majority to no purpose?

        B.   "So that if a person should say, 'Thus have I received the tradition,' one may say to him, 'You have heard the tradition in accord with the opinion of Mr. So-and-so [against that of the majority].'"

The premise of this passage is simple. The law follows the position of the anonymously formulated rule. Then why attribute a rule to a named figure? It is to identify the opinion that is not authoritative, but, nonetheless, subject to consideration. Then it follows, the purpose of citing sayings in the names of authorities is to mark those positions as schismatic and not authoritative—not to validate, but to invalidate.

To test this surmise, we turn to the Tosefta's commentary on the passage of Mishnah tractate Eduyyot that is before us. Here we find explicitly articulated the premise I identified:

1:4.   A.   Under all circumstances the law follows the majority, and the opinion of the individual is recorded along with that of the majority only so as to nullify it.

        B.   R. Judah says, "The opinion of an individual is recorded along with that of the majority only so that, if the times necessitate it, they may rely upon [the opinion of the individual]" [cf. M. Ed. 1:5B].

        C.   And sages say, "The opinion of the individual is recorded along with that of the majority only so that, if later on, this one says, 'Unclean,' and that one says, 'Clean,' one may respond that the one who says it is unclean is in accord with the opinion of R. Eliezer [and the law must follow the majority, which opposed his opinion], so they say to him, 'You have heard this opinion in accord with the ruling of R. Eliezer.'"

Judah's theory of matters—that of the minority—is that the minority opinion registers, so that, under duress, it may serve as precedent; sages take the view that the very opposite consideration pertains; once an opinion is given to an individual, that opinion is to be dismissed as schismatic wherever it occurs—even when not in the name of the individual. So we find here confirmation of the surmise that at stake in assigning opinions to names is the formulation of the legal process in such a way as to permit reliable decisions to be made.

But there is a second consideration important to the Mishnah, and that emerges in another passage in the same tractate:

5:6.   A.   Aqabia b. Mahalalel gave testimony in four matters.
       B.   They said to him, "Aqabia, retract the four rulings which you laid down, and we shall make you patriarch of the court of Israel."
       C.   He said to them, "It is better for me to be called a fool my whole life but not be deemed a wicked person before the Omnipresent for even one minute,
       D.   "so that people should not say, 'Because he craved after high office, he retracted.'"

The passage proceeds to specify the disputes, and then the narrative continues, reporting that because he refused to retract, sages excommunicated him:

       M.   They excommunicated him, and he died while he was subject to the excommunication, so the court stoned his bier. . . .
5:7.   A.   When he was dying, he said to his son, "My son, retract the four rulings which I had laid down."
       B.   He said to him, "And why do you retract now?"
       C.   He said to him, "I heard the rulings in the name of the majority, and they heard them in the name of the majority, so I stood my ground on the tradition which I had heard, and they stood their ground on the tradition they had heard.
       D.   "But you have heard the matter both in the name of an individual and in the name of the majority.
       E.   "It is better to abandon the opinion of the individual and to hold with the opinion of the majority."
       F.   He said to him, "Father, give instructions concerning me to your colleagues."
       G.   He said to him, "I will give no instructions."
       H.   He said to him, "Is it possible that you have found some fault with me?"
       I.   He said to him, "No. It is your deeds which will bring you near, or your deeds which will put you off [from the others]."

The crux of the matter then comes at 5:7C: Aqabia has received rulings in the name of the majority and therefore regards them as valid. So the purpose of assigning names to sayings once more is to label the unreliable ones: those in the names of individuals. And at stake, underneath, is of course the shape and structure of the tradition, which is once more stated explicitly: "I stood my ground on the tradition that I had heard. . . ." What comes down anonymously is tradition—from Sinai, obviously—and what bears a name is other than tradition. But matters, we see, also prove subject to negotiation. Sages bear the obligation to remember what they heard in the name of the majority but also in the name of individuals. So the inclusion of names forms part of a larger theory of tradition and how to be guided by tradition, and the Mishnah's account of itself makes that point in so many words.

We hardly need to find that fact surprising, since the Mishnah's first apologetic, tractate Abot, the sayings of the fathers, points to Sinai as the origin of the Mishnah's tradition when it formulates its opening chapter. Tractate Abot in its opening chapter responds to the question: what is the Mishnah? Why should we obey its rules? How does it relate to the Torah, which, we all know, God gave to Israel through Moses at Sinai? The answer is contained in the opening sentence:

THE SAYINGS OF THE FATHERS CHAPTER ONE

1:1.   Moses received the Torah at Sinai and handed it on to Joshua, Joshua to elders, and elders to prophets. And prophets handed it on to the men of the great assembly. They said three things: Be prudent in judgment. Raise up many disciples. Make a fence for the Torah.

What is important here is three facts. First, the verbs "receive" and "hand on" in Hebrew yield the words *qabbalah*, "tradition," and *masoret*, also "tradition." There is no more lucid or powerful way of making the statement than that: the Torah is a matter of tradition. Second, the tradition goes from master to disciple, Moses to Joshua. So the tradition is not something written down, it is something that lives. Third, we know that the tradition is distinct from the written Torah, because what is attributed to "the men of the great assembly" (and we have no interest in who these might be assumed to have been) are three statements that do not occur in Scripture. In fact, among all of the sayings in the entire tractate, only very rarely is there attributed to a sage who stands in this chain of tradition a verse of Scripture. So the essence of "the tradition" is not what is said, e.g., citing a verse of Scripture and expanding on it, but that a saying is said and who does the saying: a master to a disciple, forward through all time, backward to Sinai. Torah—revelation—stands for a process of transmitting God's will. That process is open-ended but it also is highly disciplined.

How is the question of the origin and authority of the Mishnah answered? The chain of tradition from Sinai ends up with names that are prominent in the Mishnah itself, for example, Shammai and Hillel, and their disciples, the House of Shammai and the House of Hillel. So the message is blatant: major authorities of the Mishnah stand in a chain of tradition to Sinai; hence, the Mishnah contains the Torah of Sinai. It is that straightforward: through discipleship, we reach backward; through the teaching of the sage, we reach forward; the great tradition endures in the learning of the ages. It follows that when sayings are assigned to sages, a quite separate issue is in play. I cite only a small sample of the opening chapter of Abot, which suffices to make my point, since in the body of this book, we have already considered the matter in detail:

> 1:2. Simeon the Righteous was one of the last survivors of the great assembly. He would say: On three things does the world stand: On the Torah, and on the Temple service, and on deeds of loving-kindness.
>
> 1:3. Antigonus of Sokho received [the Torah] from Simeon the Righteous. He would say: Do not be like servants who serve the master on condition of receiving a reward, but [be] like servants who serve the master not on condition of receiving a reward. And let the fear of heaven be upon you.

Now the key point comes with the beginning of the Mishnah sages themselves, and that is with the pairs, five sets, with named authorities who carry us deep into the pages of the Mishnah itself. But there is another point not to be missed. As we saw in Chapter Twenty-three, once the pairs end, whom do we find? Gamaliel, who is (later on) represented as the son of Hillel, and then Gamaliel and Simeon, his son, Hillel's grandson.

What the sages say in these sayings in no way contradicts anything we find in Scripture. But most of what is before us also does not intersect with much that we find in Scripture. We see, then, two distinct but closely related considerations that operate in the persistent interest in assigning sayings to named authorities. Identifying an authority serves as a taxic indicator of the standing of a saying—classified as not authoritative; but identifying an authority bears the—both correlative and also contradictory—indication that the authority had a tradition. Enough has been said even in these simple observations to point to a broader conclusion. If we wish to ask why names are included, we have to examine the various writings that contain assigned sayings, looking for the importance accorded to attributions by the authors of the compositions and redactors of the composites of each such compilation. It suffices to note that in the later documents, a variety of positions emerges. One of the most weighty is also most surprising. In the Tosefta, we find that what is attributed in the Mishnah to a given authority will be rewritten, so that the cited sage will say something different from what he is supposed in the Mishnah to have said. Nothing in the Mishnah's statements' theory of matters prepares us for the way in which the Tosefta's authorities treat attributions. So far as they are concerned, I shall now show, while attributions set forth fixed positions on a disputed point, precisely what was subject to dispute was itself a contentious matter.

Attributions in the Tosefta bear a task quite distinct from that of those in the Mishnah. A set of names signifies two persistent positions, principles guiding the solution to any given problem. We find in the Tosefta two or more positions assigned to the same named authority, and these positions contradict one another. It follows that attributions bear a quite distinct sense. What they stand for, as we shall see now, is a fixed difference. Party A and Party B will differ in the same way on a variety of issues, and if we know the issues, we also know the positions to be taken by the two parties. Then all consideration of tradition is set aside; all we have in the attribution is the signification of a fixed difference, a predictable position on an unpredictable agenda of issues. A fair analogy, I think, will be the fixed difference between political conservatives and political liberals; whatever the issue, the positions are predictable. Then in place of the House of Shammai and the House of Hillel, X and Y or black and white or pigeon and turtledove would serve equally well. Neither history, nor tradition, nor designation of the accepted and the schismatic position, comes into play, when all that is at stake is the matter of invoking fixed and conventional positions. Then the attributive serves as a formal protocol, nothing more.

What we shall see in the following is that the Mishnah presents a picture of a dispute and the opinions of cited authorities, and the Tosefta provides a quite different account of what was said. The Tosefta has opinions attributed to Judah and Yosé and "others say," and at stake are three distinct positions on the law. So the framers of the Tosefta's composition exhibit access to no single tradition at all; and subject to dispute is not the outcome of a case, but the formulation of the case itself.

BESAH CHAPTER ONE

A. The House of Shammai say, "They do not bring dough offering and priestly gifts to the priest on the festival day,

B. "whether they were raised up the preceding day or on that same day."

C. And the House of Hillel permit.

D. The House of Shammai said to them, "It is an argument by way of analogy.

E. "The dough-offering and the priestly gifts [Deut. 18:3] are a gift to the priest, and heave offering is a gift to the priest.

F. "Just as [on the festival day] they do not bring heave offering [to a priest], so they do not bring these other gifts [to a priest]."

G. Said to them the House of Hillel, "No. If you have stated that rule in the case of heave offering, which one [on the festival] may not designate to begin with, will you apply that same rule concerning the priestly gifts, which [on the festival] one may designate to begin with?"

M. 1:6

The Hillelites allow designating and delivering the priestly gifts owing to the priests from animals slaughtered on the festival day. The House of Shammai do not allow doing so, since the restrictions of the festival day come to bear. We shall now see a completely different picture of matters; I underline the points at which the dispute is reformulated:

A. Said R. Judah, "The House of Shammai and the House of Hillel concur that they bring [to the priest] gifts which were taken up on the day before the festival along with gifts which were taken on the festival [vs. M. 1:5A–C].

B. "Concerning what did they differ?

C. "Concerning [bringing to the priest on the festival] gifts which were taken up on the day before the festival by themselves.

D. "For the House of Shammai prohibit.

E. "And the House of Hillel permit.

F. *"The House of Shammai said, 'It is an argument by way of analogy. The dough offering and the priestly gifts are a gift to the priest, and heave offering is a gift to the priest. Just as they do not bring heave offering [to a priest on the festival day], so they do not bring these other gifts [to a priest on the festival day]'* [M. 1:6D–F].

G. *"Said to them the House of Hillel, 'No. If you have stated that rule in the case of heave offering, which one may not designate to begin with, will you apply that same rule concerning the priestly gifts, which one may designate to begin with?'"* [M. 1:6G].

H. R. Yosé says, "The House of Shammai and the House of Hillel concur that they do bring the priestly gifts to the priest on the festival day.

I. "Concerning what do they differ?

J. "Concerning heave offering.

K. "For the House of Shammai prohibit [bringing heave offering to the priest on the festival day].

L. "And the House of Hillel permit."

T 1:12 L p. 283, ls. 46–54

A. *"Said the House of Hillel, 'It is an argument by way of analogy. Dough offering and priestly gifts are a gift to the priest, and heave offering is a gift to the priest. Just* as they do bring the priestly gifts to the priest on the festival day, so they should bring heave offering to the priest on the festival day.'

B. "Said the House of Shammai to them, 'No. If you have stated the rule in the case of the priestly gifts, which is permitted to be designated [on the festival], will you state that rule concerning heave offering, which may not be designated [on the festival day]?'"

C. Others say, "The House of Shammai and the House of Hillel concur that they do not bring heave-offering on a festival.

D.   "Concerning what did they differ?
E.   "Concerning priestly gifts.
F.   "For the House of Shammai prohibit [bringing them to the priest on
     the festival].
G.   "And the House of Hillel permit" [= M. 1:6A–C]

                                        T. 1:13 L pp. 283–284, ls. 54–60

What we see is three distinct positions on what is at stake in the dispute of the
Houses of Shammai and Hillel, and, a bit of study would show us, these positions
express three distinct principles concerning what is at stake. The second-century
authorities are alleged to have three distinct "traditions" on what is at issue between the houses; each then assigns to the houses the same language in the same
words, along with the same secondary arguments for its distinctive viewpoint. All
that varies is the definition of that about which the houses to begin with are conducting their dispute—no small thing!

Now that we have seen ample evidence that attributions serve, even in the
Mishnah and the Tosefta, to carry out three quite distinct functions—distinguishing regnant from schismatic opinion, identifying the traditionality of a saying, and
marking off fixed points of difference concerning a variable agendum of issues—
a measure of humility guides us as we revert to our original question, "Why is the
rabbinic literature so interested in coupling utterances and decisions with names?"
The question has received only a preliminary answer, but the method before us is
clear: we have to ask, document by document, what function is served by attributions, what importance is assigned to them, what difference the presence of an
attribution makes in one context or another, and, finally, what conclusions, if any,
are drawn from attributions.

Certainly a survey of the two Talmuds, with their intense interest in the consistency of positions assigned to principal authorities, alongside their quite facile practice of following the dictates of logic, not tradition at all, in switching about among
various names the opinions assigned to one or another of them, will yield puzzling
evidence. But the outlines of the answer are clear. We may reject as simply irrelevant to the character of the evidence any interest in preserving historical information concerning named figures, e.g., for the purpose of biography. The sages of
rabbinic documents have opinions, but no biography; many individuals play critical roles in the formation of the several documentary statements, but no individual
is accorded a fully articulated individuality, either as to his life or as to his philosophy or theology.

What conclusions may we draw from this inquiry into the uses of attributions
in the earliest of the rabbinic compilations? Let us note, first, what we do not have.
For the entire cadre of sages, we do not have a single biography devoted to an
individual, or even the raw materials for a sustained and systematic biography; we
do not possess a single document produced by a clearly identifiable individual au-

thor, a single coherent composite of any consequence at all that concerns itself with a named figure. The counterpart writings for Christianity, the lives of saints and holy men and women, the letters of Paul, not to mention the huge collections of signed, personal, individual writings of church fathers, show us the documents we do not have in rabbinic literature. The theory of authorship accounts for that fact. A document to warrant recognition—thus to be accorded authority, to be written and copied, or memorized and handed on as tradition—had to attain the approval of the sages' consensus.

That meant, every document in rabbinic literature emerged anonymously, under public sponsorship and authorship, stripped of all marks of individual, therefore idiosyncratic, origin. Personality and individuality stood for schism, and rabbinic literature in its very definition and character aims at the opposite, forming as it does the functional counterpart to the creeds and decisions of church councils. Framed in mythic terms, the literature aimed to make this theological statement: sages stood in a chain of tradition from Sinai, and the price of inclusion was the acceptance of the discipline of tradition—anonymous, reasoned argument to attain for a private view the public status of a consensus statement. The very definition of tradition that comes to expression in the character of rabbinic literature—God's revelation to Moses at Sinai received and handed on unimpaired and intact in a reliable process of instruction by masters to disciples—accounts for the public, anonymous character of rabbinic writing.

Not a line in the entire rabbinic literature even suggests that schismatic writing existed, even though named statements of individual authorities are preserved on every page of that literature. The point that is proven is simple. People disagreed within a permitted agendum, and the protocol of disagreement always began with the premise of concurrence on all that counted. That was, as we saw, the very goal of rabbinic dialectics: the rationality of dispute, the cogency of theology and of law as a whole. As every named saying we have examined has already shown us, dissenting views too found their properly labeled position in rabbinic literature, preserved in the name of the private person who registered dissent in accord with the rules governing the iron consensus of the collegium as a whole.

The final question raised by the ubiquity of attributions to named authorities is, what then is the standing of the named sage? We have seen that the sage is subordinate to tradition, on the one side, and the consensus of sages, on the other. That means the individual as such bore only instrumental importance; he mattered because, and only when, he served as a good example. Or his value derived from the traditions he had in hand from prior authorities. But that fact accords to the individual very high standing indeed—when the individual exemplifies the Torah, attests to tradition, or through wit in sound reasoning demonstrates the validity of a position and compels the consensus to favor his view. So attributions fulfill contradictory tasks. They both call into question the validity of what is attributed and also validate the sage as exemplar of the Torah.

GENERAL INDEX

INDEX TO TEXTS

PALESTINIAN TALMUD